MEXICO SINCE INDEPENDENCE

The following titles drawn from
The Cambridge History of Latin America edited by Leslie Bethell
are available in hardcover and paperback:

Colonial Spanish America

Colonial Brazil

The Independence of Latin America

Spanish America after Independence, *c.* 1820 – *c.* 1870

Brazil: Empire and Republic, 1822–1930

Latin America: Economy and Society, 1870–1930

Mexico since Independence

Central America since Independence

MEXICO
SINCE
INDEPENDENCE

edited by
LESLIE BETHELL
Professor of Latin American History
University of London

Published by the Press Syndicate of the University of Cambridge
The Pitt Building, Trumpington Street, Cambridge CB2 1RP
40 West 20th Street, New York, NY 10011-4211, USA
10 Stamford Road, Oakleigh, Melbourne 3166, Australia

This contents of this bookwere previously published as parts of
volumes III, V, and VII of *The Cambridge History of Latin America*,
copyright © Cambridge University Press 1985, 1986, 1990

First published 1991
Reprinted 1992, 1994

Printed in the United States of America

Library of Congress Cataloging-in-Publication Data is available

A catalogue record for this book is available from the British Library

ISBN 0-521-41306-0 hardback
ISBN 0-521-42372-4 paperback

CONTENTS

MAPS

PREFACE

The Cambridge History of Latin America is a large scale, collaborative, multi-volume history of Latin America during the five centuries from the first contacts between Europeans and the native peoples of the Americas in the late fifteenth and early sixteenth centuries to the present.

Mexico since Independence brings together chapters from Volumes III, V, and VII of *The Cambridge History* to provide in a single volume an economic, social, and political history of Mexico since its independence from Spain in 1821. This, it is hoped, will be useful for both teachers and students of Latin American history and of contemporary Latin America. Each chapter is accompanied by a bibliographical essay.

1

FROM INDEPENDENCE TO THE LIBERAL REPUBLIC, 1821–1867

The royalist brigadier, Agustín de Iturbide, proclaimed the independence of Mexico on 24 February 1821 at Iguala, a small town in the heart of the southern, tropical *tierra caliente* or 'hot country'. In his manifesto, the Plan of Iguala, Iturbide called for independence, the union of Mexicans and Spaniards and respect for the Roman Catholic Church. The form of government was to be a constitutional monarchy in which the emperor would be chosen from a European, preferably Spanish, dynasty 'so as to give us a monarch already made and save us from fatal acts of ambition', and the national constitution was to be drawn up by a congress. With this the first of his so-called 'three guarantees', Iturbide won the support of the old guerrilla fighters for independence, particularly General Vicente Guerrero who at this time was operating not far from Iguala. The second guarantee offered security to Spanish-born residents of Mexico, and with the third he sought to attract the clerical establishment by promising to preserve ecclesiastical privileges, recently under attack in Spain by the liberal, revolutionary regime. The army would take upon itself the task of 'protecting' the guarantees.

Iturbide's appeal proved remarkably successful. In less than six months, he was master of the country, except for the capital city and the ports of Acapulco and Veracruz. It was at Veracruz that the newly appointed Spanish captain-general, Juan O'Donojú, disembarked on 30 July. He had been instructed to introduce liberal reforms in New Spain but at the same time to ensure that the colony remained within the Spanish empire. His instructions, however, were based on information received in Madrid about events which had taken place in the colony some four or five months previously, and he at once recognized that the

[1] The Author and the Editor wish to acknowledge the help of Professor Michael P. Costeloe, University of Bristol, in the final preparation of this chapter.

I

situation had changed significantly since then. Mexican independence appeared to him already a fact and, wanting to depart as quickly as possible from the yellow fever infested port, he decided to seek a meeting with Iturbide. They met on 24 August in Córdoba, at the foot of the snow-capped Citlaltepetl volcano, and they signed a treaty which recognized 'The Mexican Empire' as a sovereign and independent nation. The treaty paraphrased the Iguala manifesto, but there were several modifications. According to the manifesto, the throne was to be offered to Ferdinand VII, or, in case of his refusal, to a prince of a reigning dynasty. It was assumed that there would be at least one prince willing to accept. The text signed in Córdoba, however, named four specific candidates, all of the Spanish dynasty, and no reference was made to other European royal families. If the four Spaniards were to refuse the throne, the future emperor was to be selected by the Mexican congress. This change is unlikely to have been fortuitous, and it was to have important consequences, especially in the career of the ambitious Iturbide. As the meeting at Córdoba lasted only a few hours, it seems certain that Iturbide had already carefully prepared the long text in advance and was well aware of the implications of the changes made to the original Iguala declaration. O'Donojú, on the other hand, who must have been tired following his long journey from Spain and was possibly ill, overlooked the modification. He signed the document with his constitutional title of Captain General and Superior Political Chief, although to the present day he remains known in Mexico as the last Spanish viceroy. Brigadier Iturbide signed as First Chief of the Imperial Army. Within a few months he was to be Generalísimo.

The acceptance of independence by O'Donojú facilitated the transfer of power in the capital. Having delayed his entrance so that it coincided with his thirty-eighth birthday, Iturbide rode into Mexico City on 27 September. On the next morning, he chose the thirty-eight members of the governing junta stipulated in both the Iguala manifesto and the treaty of Córdoba. In a formal act, this junta then declared the independence of Mexico. With Iturbide acting as its president, the junta consisted of well-known ecclesiastics, lawyers, judges, members of the Mexican nobility and a few army officers, among them Colonel Anastasio Bustamante who, like Iturbide, was a former royalist officer. Old fighters for independence such as Nicolás Bravo, Guadalupe Victoria and Guerrero were not members, but O'Donojú was included in accordance with the agreement reached at Córdoba. It was expected that he would give

Iturbide a helping hand in the transition between the viceroyalty and a future empire under a Spanish prince. In fact, O'Donojú fell ill and died ten days later before being able to appoint the commissioners who were to have gone to Madrid to negotiate a settlement, again as envisaged in the Córdoba agreement. As president of the junta and regent of the empire, Generalísimo Iturbide could still have sent envoys to Madrid but he did not do so.

Not surprisingly, the Spanish attitude towards Mexican independence was hostile from the beginning. Although the greater part of the Spanish army stationed in Mexico swore allegiance to the new nation, a group of royalist diehards withdrew to San Juan de Ulúa, an island fortress in front of Veracruz harbour, and waited there for reinforcements with which to reconquer the country. They were not disavowed by the Madrid government and on 13 February 1822 the Spanish Cortes rejected the Córdoba treaty. The news of this refusal by the mother country to accept Mexico's independence reached Mexico City several months later.

Independence in 1821 did not bring any immediate revolutionary change in the social or economic structure of the country. The first and principal effect was that the political power formerly exercised by the royal bureaucracy was transferred to the army, that is to say, to a coalition of Iturbide's royalist and Guerrero's republican armies.

The second pillar of the new nation was the Roman Catholic Church. Like all the established colonial institutions, it had suffered significant losses in its manpower and material possessions during the decade of war. By 1822 there were ten dioceses but only four had bishops, and from a total of 4,229 in 1810 the secular clergy had decreased to 3,487. The male regulars had decreased from 3,112 in 1810 to approximately 2,000 by the end of 1821 and the number of monasteries from 208 to 153. In sum, the total number of clergy fell from 9,439 to 7,500 and the number of parishes also declined. Church revenues, particularly from tithes, showed a substantial fall. In the archbishopric of Mexico, the tithe income was reduced from 510,081 pesos in 1810 to 232,948 pesos in 1821 and in the dioceses of Michoacán, from 500,000 pesos to 200,000 pesos by 1826.

The tithe figures reflect the general economic decline which had taken place. The statistics provided by the amount of coinage minted indicate that mining decreased by more than a half from a yearly average of $22\frac{1}{2}$ million pesos in 1800–9 to approximately 10 million pesos in 1820 and 1822. (In 1821 only about 6 million pesos were minted.) There is no reliable information available on agriculture and manufacturing. Cereal production may have recovered by 1820, but sugar cane and other farming sectors remained depressed. Manufacturing output may have declined by as much as a half and public finances were reduced by a similar proportion. Government revenues in 1822 amounted to over 9 million pesos but expenditure rose to 13 million pesos, leaving a deficit of 4 million pesos. The public or national debt had shown a marked increase from 20 million pesos in 1808 to 35 million pesos in 1814 and 45 million pesos by 1822.

It was against this background of economic recession and budget deficit that the constitutional congress assembled in the capital on 24 February 1822. To Iturbide's unpleasant surprise, most of the deputies were either 'bourbonists', that is, pro-Spanish monarchists, or republicans. They were in dispute with him over several matters from the very first day and it was against a background of rapidly deteriorating relations between Iturbide and the deputies that the Spanish rejection of the Córdoba agreement became known. Until that moment, Spain, the mother country with which the bonds of kinship and religion remained strong, had still been venerated by almost everyone. Now Spain denied freedom to her daughter country. The ensuing resentment and disappointment quickly gave rise to the feeling that there was no reason why Mexico should not have a monarch of its own choosing. Spain, by its refusal to accept the reality of independence and its rejection of the opportunity to keep Mexico within the Bourbon dynasty, played into the hands of Iturbide. On the night of 18 May 1822, the local army garrison proclaimed him Emperor Agustín I and on the next morning, under considerable military and popular pressure, congress accepted the situation and acknowledged its new monarch. Since Spain had rejected the Córdoba treaty, said deputy Valentín Gómez Farías, a physician and future liberal leader, Mexico was free to determine its own destiny. In the absence of the archbishop who declined to anoint the new ruler, Iturbide was crowned by the president of the congress on 21 July in the capital's magnificent cathedral.

Iturbide's empire was not to last. From the outset, there were basic obstacles to its survival. The Mexican nobility yearned for a European prince and looked with disdain on Iturbide, the son of a merchant; *hacendados* and traders, most of whom were Spanish born, hoped for a European prince to deliver them from forced loans and other fiscal burdens; and finally there was a strong body of republicans which included some prominent journalists, lawyers and progressive clergy. One such cleric was Servando Teresa de Mier who, after an adventurous life in Europe and the United States, had been imprisoned in the dungeons of the San Juan de Ulúa fortress. Its shrewd Spanish commander released him at the end of May and Servando soon occupied a seat in congress. Both within that assembly and in the public arena outside, he was to propagate his republican ideas with great vigour.

It is not surprising, therefore, that Iturbide's fall was even faster than his elevation. The bourbonists charged him with having violated his promise to offer the throne to a European prince. Iturbide's own arbitrary acts encouraged the spread of republican ideas which until then had by and large been restricted to intellectuals. Ambitious army officers were also discontented; while a foreign prince might be tolerable, they found it difficult to accept one of their own kind; if an imported prince was not to be had, then the solution was a republic, which was at least a system in which they could become presidents. Opposition to Iturbide grew and in an atmosphere of restricted freedom of expression, conspiracies mushroomed. By 26 August, just five weeks after his coronation, Iturbide had already imprisoned nineteen members of congress and several army officers. On 31 October, he dissolved the troublesome congress altogether. He weakened his position even further by a series of confiscatory fiscal measures and the merchants who suffered, for the most part Spanish, turned to the bourbonists for support.

The port of Veracruz was especially important to Iturbide's security. It was situated opposite the island fortress of San Juan de Ulúa which remained in Spanish hands.[2] A rebellion might be started there, with Spanish acquiescence if not support, and in the event of failure, rebel leaders could take refuge in the fortress. Distrusting the ambitious young military commander of Veracruz, a twenty-eight-year old colonel, Antonio López de Santa Anna, Iturbide summoned him to Jalapa, a town in the mountains over a hundred kilometres from the port, where he relieved him of his command and ordered him to report to Mexico City. Santa Anna had not the slightest intention of obeying the emperor. After galloping all night, he returned to his barracks the following morning and, before news of his removal reached Veracruz, on the afternoon of the same day, 2 December 1822, he publicly accused Iturbide of tyranny. He proclaimed a republic, calling for the reinstallation of congress and

---

[2] The Spaniards in San Juan de Ulúa did not capitulate until 1825.

the formation of a constitution based on 'Religion, Independence and Union', that is, the same three guarantees of the Iguala manifesto which he claimed had been infringed by the emperor. He also made a bid for the support of influential local Spanish merchants at Veracruz by calling for peace and commerce with the mother country.[3]

Within a few days, however, Santa Anna had changed his mind about his hasty profession of republican faith. In 1822, Mexican republicans did not often use the term 'republic' in their propaganda; instead, they spoke of Liberty, Nation and the Sovereignty of Congress. A decade previously, Hidalgo had not formally proclaimed independence and it had taken several years for the idea of a Mexico not subject to the king of Spain to take root. Now, similarly, the word republic also sounded too revolutionary. Hence Santa Anna revised his position and, four days later, he issued a more moderate and detailed manifesto. This document was probably drawn up by the former minister of the newly independent republic of Colombia to Mexico, Miguel Santa María (a native of Veracruz), who had been expelled by Iturbide for participating in a republican conspiracy and was at that time in Veracruz awaiting a ship to take him home. Without mentioning a republic, the manifesto called for the removal of the emperor. 'The true liberty of the fatherland' meant a republic to the republicans and a constitutional monarchy to bourbonists and Spaniards. Thus both factions were urged to unite against Iturbide. The insistence on the Iguala guarantees had the same purpose: 'independence' was essential to Mexicans, 'union' to Spaniards, and 'religion' to both. It is not known whether Santa Anna was sincere about the republic or whether he had imperial ambitions of his own.

A fortuitous circumstance helped Santa Anna: the inveterate guerrilla fighter, Guadalupe Victoria, who had recently escaped from prison, chanced to be in Veracruz and he signed Santa Anna's manifesto of 6 December 1822. Thus Santa Anna, who had been a royalist officer during the war of independence and until now a supporter of Iturbide, secured the aid of a famous insurgent general who was already suspected of republican inclinations. A few weeks later, Generals Bravo and Guerrero, former comrades-in-arms of Morelos, escaped from Mexico City and once back in their own region of the *tierra caliente*, they declared their support for the Veracruz uprising. 'We are not against the established system of government', they declared: 'we do not intend to

---

[3] The proclamation is reproduced in C. M. Bustamante, *Diario Histórico de México*, I, *1822–1823* (Zacatecas, 1896), 16–17.

become republicans; far from that, we only seek our liberty.' Such denials, however, seem to confirm the impression that they were indeed republicans, but their own support was among Indian peasants who were held to be not only religious but also monarchist. Finally, the majority of the army in which the officers – many of them Spaniards by birth – had been royalists and later supporters of Iturbide succumbed to the influence of two former Mexican liberal deputies to the Spanish Cortes, the priest Miguel Ramos Arizpe and José Mariano Michelena. The army 'pronounced' itself against Iturbide. The emperor abdicated on 19 March 1823, and the reassembled congress promptly appointed a provisional triumvirate consisting of Generals Victoria, Bravo and Negrete, the first two of whom were generally thought to be republicans. On 8 April, congress nullified the Iguala manifesto as well as the Córdoba treaty and decreed that Mexico was henceforth free to adopt whatever constitutional system it wished. The republic was a fact.

Thus Santa Anna had unleashed a movement which brought down Iturbide's empire and ended with the establishment of a republic. Even if the new political system was conceived by intellectuals, it was the army which had converted it into reality and at the same time become its master. The speed with which it succeeded pointed the way to future uprisings by dissatisfied military officers.

Bearing in mind Iturbide's past services to the nation's independence, congress did not at first deal with him harshly. He was offered a generous allowance provided that he resided in Italy. But the former emperor was not happy in exile. Misled by rumours of support, he returned in July 1824, landing near Tampico on the Gulf Coast, and unaware that, during his absence, congress had declared him a traitor. He was arrested and executed within a few days of his arrival.

Iturbide's inability to introduce some measure of order into the Treasury had been an important cause of his downfall. The triumvirate applied itself at once to the task of restoring public confidence and the improved atmosphere made it possible to obtain two loans on the London market: 16 million pesos were borrowed at the beginning of 1824 with Goldschmitt and Company and a similar amount with Barclay and Company a few months later.[4] Mexico thereby assumed a burden of 32 million pesos in foreign debt, but because of a low contract price and bankers' deductions, only about 10 million pesos was in fact received.

---

[4] Throughout the period examined in this chapter one peso equalled one U.S. dollar.

The government originally expected to use this money for long-term improvements, but when it finally arrived it was quickly absorbed by current expenses such as salaries of public employees, notably the military. Nevertheless, the proceeds of these loans seem to have been a stabilizing factor in the first years of the republic and in 1823–4 the foreign debt which they entailed did not seem excessive.[5] With British interest in the mineral resources of the country very evident, Mexico was optimistic about its future. During the years 1823 to 1827 the British invested more than 12 million pesos in Mexican mining ventures, especially silver-mining companies. Thus a total of well over 20 million pesos were injected into the ailing economy.

The person who was most instrumental in bringing British capital to Mexico was Lucas Alamán, who from April 1823 was Minister of the Interior and of Foreign Affairs (one of four Cabinet members). The brilliant son of a Mexican mining family which had acquired a Spanish title of nobility, Alamán had returned from a prolonged stay in Europe shortly after Iturbide's fall from power. As Marquis of San Clemente, he had perhaps dreamt of becoming a minister in the court of a Mexican Bourbon monarch, but the end of Iturbide's empire was not followed by any renewal of attempts to offer the throne to a European prince. On the contrary, it meant the end of serious monarchist plans for many years to come. Alamán entered, therefore, into the service of a republican government.

With the republic now taken for granted and monarchism being viewed almost as treason, new labels began to be adopted. Former supporters of a Mexican empire with a European prince at its head became centralist republicans, advocating a strong, centralized régime, reminiscent of the viceroyalty. Most of the republican opponents of Iturbide became federalists, supporting a federation of states on the United States model. The old destructive struggle between royalists and independents, who had in 1821 become bourbonists and republicans respectively and then temporary allies against Iturbide, re-emerged in 1823 under different slogans. After Iturbide's abdication power fell briefly into the hands of the bourbonist faction, but then a perhaps unexpected turn of events had helped the republican cause. Blaming the bourbonists for having overthrown Iturbide, the former emperor's supporters now joined the republicans and the elections for the new constitutional congress produced a majority for the federalists.

[5] There was at this time an internal public debt of 45 million pesos.

The constitutional congress met in November 1823 and almost a year later adopted a federal constitution which closely resembled that of the United States. The Mexican constitution of 1824 divided the country into nineteen states which were to elect their own governors and legislatures, and four territories which were to be under the jurisdiction of the national congress. The usual division of powers – executive, legislative and judicial – was retained but in one important respect the Mexican constitution differed from its northern model: it solemnly proclaimed that: 'The religion of the Mexican nation is and shall be perpetually the Catholic, Apostolic, Roman religion. The nation protects it with wise and just laws and prohibits the exercise of any other.'[6] Of the three guarantees in the Iguala manifesto only two remained; independence and religion. The third, union with Spaniards which implied a monarchy with a European prince, had been replaced by the federal republic.

In contrast to the insurgent constitution of Apatzingán in 1814 which specified that the law should be the same for everyone, the 1824 charter did not mention equality before the law. This omission was certainly not intended to safeguard the interests of the small, if not insignificant, Mexican nobility which only comprised a few dozen families. Its significance was much greater because it permitted the continuation of the *fueros* or legal immunities and exemptions from civil courts enjoyed by the clergy and the military. These privileges had, of course, existed before independence but then both the Church and the army had been subject to royal authority on which civil obedience to laws depended and which had not been seriously questioned for three centuries. With the supreme regal authority gone, and in the absence of a strong nobility or bourgeoisie, the vacuum was at once filled by the popular heroes of the victorious army. Freed of royal restraint, the army became the arbiter of power in the new nation. Federalist or centralist, a general was to be president of the republic.

Mexico also adopted the United States practice of electing a president and a vice-president. The two leading executives could be men of different or opposing political parties with the obvious danger of rivalry continuing between them while in office. Indeed, the first president was a liberal federalist, General Guadalupe Victoria, a man of obscure origins, and the vice-president a conservative centralist, General Nicolás Bravo, a wealthy landowner. Both men had been

---

[6] Felipe Tena Ramírez, *Leyes fundamentales de México, 1808–1973* (Mexico, 1973), 168.

guerrilla fighters for independence but by 1824 they belonged to two hostile factions. Political parties were as yet unknown but the two groups used the masonic movement as a focal point for their activities and propaganda. The centralists tended to become masons of the Scottish Rite while the federalists, with the help of the United States minister to the new republic, Joel R. Poinsett, became members of the York Rite. The lodges provided the base from which the conservative and liberal parties would arise almost a quarter of a century later.

President Victoria sought to maintain in his cabinet a balance between the centralists and the federalists in the hope of keeping some semblance of unity in the national government. Nevertheless, the most able of the pro-centralist ministers, Lucas Alamán, was, as early as 1825, quickly forced out of office by federalist attacks. In the following year, after a long and bitterly fought electoral campaign, the federalists gained a significant majority in Congress, particularly in the chamber of deputies. Tension increased in January 1827 with the discovery of a conspiracy to restore Spanish rule. Spain was the only important country not to have recognized Mexican independence and with many wealthy Spanish merchants still resident in the new republic, as well as others who retained their posts in the government bureaucracy, it was not difficult to incite popular hatred against everything Spanish. Mexican nationalism became a convenient and effective weapon used by the federalists to attack the centralists who were widely believed to favour Spain. Fighting on the defensive and using religion as a counter to nationalism, the centralists took revenge for Alamán's dismissal in a campaign against the American minister Poinsett who was a Protestant. As the well-intentional but ineffectual President Victoria was unable to control the ever more aggressive federalists, the centralist leader and vice-president, Bravo, finally resorted to rebellion against the government. Bravo was promptly defeated by his former comrade-in-arms, General Guerrero, and sent into exile. Both had fought the Spaniards side by side under the command of Morelos, but Guerrero had chosen the federalist cause which allowed him to keep control of his native *tierra caliente*.

The main political issue was the forthcoming presidential election, scheduled for 1828. Bravo's revolt spoiled the chances of the centralists who were unable even to present a candidate. Then the federalists split into moderates and radicals. The centralists or conservatives chose to rally behind the moderate candidate, General Manuel Gómez Pedraza, the Minister of War in Victoria's cabinet and a former royalist officer and then supporter of Iturbide. His opponent was General Guerrero, nominally the leader of the federalists but believed by many to be little more than a figurehead controlled by the liberal journalist and former senator for Yucatán, Lorenzo Zavala. Gómez Pedraza was elected president and General Anastasio Bustamante vice-president, but Guerrero refused to recognize the result and, on his behalf, Zavala organized a successful revolution in the capital in December 1828. Mere formalities followed. Guerrero was duly 'elected' in January 1829 and received the office from Victoria on 1 April. Constitutional order had collapsed after only four years.

Guerrero, a popular hero of the war against Spain, was a symbol of Mexican resistance to everything Spanish. The expulsion of Spaniards still living in the republic was quickly decreed[7] and preparations to resist a long-expected Spanish invasion force were begun. Guerrero's minister of finance, Zavala, found the Treasury almost empty and set about raising revenue. Obtaining some funds by selling Church property nationalized by the colonial authorities, he also decreed a progressive income tax, a unique attempt of its kind in this period of Mexico's history. His moves against ecclesiastical property and his well-known friendship with Poinsett made him unpopular with the Church and his attempts at social reform and at seeking support among the lower classes made him hated by all the propertied groups.

The long-awaited invasion by Spanish troops came at the end of July 1829, and it served to cause a temporary lull in the factional political conflict as the nation rallied to the call for unity. General Santa Anna hurried from his Veracruz headquarters to Tampico where the invading force had landed, and he promptly defeated it. He became an instant war hero and the country enjoyed the exhilaration of victory. But the euphoria was brief and with the external threat overcome, the Catholic and conservative faction soon renewed their campaign against the Guerrero administration. It did not yet dare to touch the president, still the hero of independence and now the saviour of the nation from Spanish aggression. Instead, the targets became the Protestant Poinsett and the democrat Zavala. The attacks on them became so fierce that Zavala was obliged to resign on 2 November and Poinsett, an easy, expendable scapegoat, left Mexico soon afterwards.

Deprived of the support of Zavala and Poinsett, Guerrero lost his

---

[7] The expulsion of certain groups of Spaniards had already been decreed in 1827.

office the following month when Vice-president Bustamante led a revolt with the support of General Bravo, already returned from his recent exile. Guerrero retired, unmolested, to his hacienda in the south, far from the central government's control. On 1 January 1830, Bustamante, acting as president, formed his cabinet. In contrast with the governments of 1823–7, which had tried to keep an uneasy balance of federalists and centralists, and with the populist inclined Guerrero régime, the new administration was openly conservative. The leading cabinet member was Alamán, once again occupying the key post of Minister of Internal and Foreign Affairs. He began to implement his political programme at once: opposition was suppressed after years of complete freedom; for the first time since Iturbide's fall, the central government sought to curb the states in several of which new, liberal ideas were rampant; property rights which in the last analysis could be traced to the Spanish conquest were safeguarded, and the Church's privileges were reaffirmed. Alamán evidently had in mind a settlement with Spain and with the Holy See.

Some of these and other developments were not to Guerrero's liking and he again revolted in the south at the head of a band of guerrilla fighters. General Bravo chose to remain loyal to Bustamante and Alamán, and he was appointed to lead the army against Guerrero who was captured in January 1831 and executed by order of the central government a few weeks later.

The cruel treatment of Guerrero requires an explanation. Bravo had been defeated in 1827 but was merely exiled and there were other similar cases. It is reasonable to ask, therefore, why in the case of Guerrero the government resorted to the ultimate penalty. The clue is provided by Zavala who, writing several years later, noted that Guerrero was of mixed blood and that the opposition to his presidency came from the great landowners, generals, clerics and Spaniards resident in Mexico. These people could not forget the war of independence with its threat of social and racial subversion. Despite his revolutionary past, the wealthy creole Bravo belonged to this 'gentleman's club', as did the cultured creole, Zavala, even with his radicalism. Hence Guerrero's execution was perhaps a warning to men considered as socially and ethnically inferior not to dare to dream of becoming president.

The conservative government of Bustamante was not negative and reactionary in everything it did. The country's economy and finances were improved as a result of a variety of measures. Since the end of 1827 when the civil conflict had begun to emerge Mexico had been unable to pay interest on the two foreign loans contracted in London. Now it was agreed with bondholders that the debt arrears, amounting to more than 4 million pesos, should be capitalized. Confidence was thus restored at the price of increasing the capital debt, but there was probably no other solution. Silver-mining remained in a depressed condition as a result of the overexpansion of previous years, and of military and civil disturbances. There was not much that could be done at the time to revive the industry and Alamán turned his attention to other spheres of economic activity. For example, he established a government bank which was to finance the introduction of cotton spinning and weaving machines and he prohibited the import of English cottons. The bank's funds were to come from high protectionist tariffs. Money was lent to Mexican and foreign merchants and financiers interested in becoming manufacturers. Machines were ordered in the United States and the first cotton-spinning mills began to operate in 1833. By this time, the Bustamante–Alamán government was no longer in power, but Alamán had laid the foundations of a revolution in the textile industry which, once started, continued to grow while the governments around it changed. As a result of his initiatives, a decade later Mexico had some fifty factories which could reasonably supply the mass of the population with cheap cotton cloth. The industry was especially prominent in the traditional textile city of Puebla and in the cotton-growing state of Veracruz where water power was abundant. The rate of growth can be seen in the following figures: in 1838, the factories spun 63,000 lb of yarn and in 1844 over 10,000,000 lb: in 1837 they wove 45,000 bolts of cloth and in 1845, 656,500. Thereafter the growth was slow. Alamán did not restrict his attention to textiles but he failed to accomplish any such spectacular results in, for example, agriculture which, although a devout Roman Catholic himself, he had to acknowledge was severely hampered by the ecclesiastical tithe.

Bustamante was not strong enough to impose a permanent centralized republic and rival political groups soon emerged. Francisco García, governor of the silver-mining state of Zacatecas, had carefully developed a powerful civilian militia, and he decided to challenge the pro-clerical regime in the capital. His friend, the senator and former supporter of Iturbide, Valentín Gómez Farías, suggested that the state sponsor an essay competition on the respective rights of Church and State in relation to property. The winning entry, submitted in December 1831 by an impecunious professor of theology, José María Luis Mora, justified the disentailment of ecclesiastical property and thus provided a theoretical basis for an anti-clerical, liberal ideology and movement. The timing was propitious. With the defeat of Guerrero and Zavala, the rights of private property had been definitively safeguarded. Hence there was no real danger that an attack on Church property might develop into a radical assault on property in general. The essence of liberalism lay precisely in the destruction of Church property combined with a strengthening of private property.

Mora was a theoretician rather than a man of action and it fell to Gómez Farías to organize the opposition against Bustamante. Since the Zacatecas militia of volunteers was merely a local force, he needed an ally in the professional army. General Santa Anna had been in revolt against Bustamante since January 1832. His personal ideology was obscure, but in the public mind he was widely associated with Guerrero whom he had consistently supported. Here, therefore, was an opportunity for him to benefit from the unpopularity of Guerrero's execution. Furthermore, as he was still a national hero, having reaped the glory from the defeat of the Spanish invasion of 1829, he could seek to take Guerrero's place as the popular favourite. The combination of Gómez Farías's liberal campaign and Santa Anna's military revolt forced Bustamante to dismiss Alamán and his Minister of War, José Antonio Facio, the two men who were widely held to have been responsible for Guerrero's death. Such cabinet changes were not sufficient and by the end of 1832, Bustamante was obliged to admit defeat. As the new Minister of Finance in the interim administration, Gómez Farías took control of the government in the capital. Zavala, who had returned to Mexico after more than two years in the United States, was not offered a cabinet post; his brand of populism was now replaced by a middle class anti-clericalism and he had to be satisfied with the governorship of the state of Mexico. In March 1833, Santa Anna was elected president and Gómez Farías, vice-president, with their term of office beginning formally on 1 April. Gómez Farías was eager to introduce liberal reforms and Santa Anna, for the time being, preferred to leave the exercise of power to his vice-president while remaining on his Veracruz estate and awaiting the reaction of public opinion.

Freed of presidential restraint, Gómez Farías initiated a broad reform programme, particularly in respect of the Church. The obligation under civil law to pay tithes was removed and payment became entirely voluntary. Then civil enforcement of monastic vows was removed and friars and nuns were permitted to leave the monastery or nunnery at their convenience. All transfers of property belonging to the regular orders since independence were also declared null and void. While the first law affected mainly the bishops and canons, whose income came mostly from the tithe revenues, the last two decrees were intended to bring about the eventual disappearance of the regular orders. The disposal of monastic real estate was already under discussion in congress and the sale of such property was declared illegal to prevent the Church from selling to trusted persons and thus evade the disentailment. Even so, the liberals were not to see the disentailment implemented for many years to come.

Gómez Farías, his cabinet and the liberal congress also attempted to reduce the size of the army and it was not long before senior military officers and the higher clergy were imploring Santa Anna to intervene. At last, when several army officers and their troops revolted in May 1834 and when the rebellion spread, he chose to leave his hacienda and assume his presidential authority in the capital. The consequences were soon apparent. The reforms were repealed and, in January 1835, Gómez Farías was stripped of his vice-presidential office. Two months later, a new congress approved a motion to amend the 1824 constitution with a view to introducing a centralist republic. Well aware that the bastion of federalism was Zacatecas, Santa Anna invaded the state, defeated its militia and deposed Governor García. On 23 October 1835 Congress delivered a provisional centralist constitution which replaced the states by departments, the governors of which would henceforth be appointed by the president of the republic.

Santa Anna was not, however, to complete the establishment of a strong, centralized régime. Not long after the defeat of Zacatecas, an unforeseen and, for Mexico as well as for Santa Anna, a most unwelcome complication arose in the north. The province of Texas resisted the move towards centralism and finally resorted to arms. After colonists had driven out the northern Mexican forces Santa Anna decided to lead in person what he regarded as a mere punitive expedition. Before leaving Mexico City, he told the French and British ministers that if he found that the United States government was aiding the rebels, 'he could continue the march of his army to Washington and place upon its Capitol the Mexican flag'.[8] Santa Anna succeeded in capturing San Antonio at the beginning of March 1836, but was decisively defeated and taken prisoner

[8] W. H. Callcott, *Santa Anna, the story of an enigma who once was Mexico* (Hamden, Conn., 1964), 126.

the following month. By this time, the Texans had already declared their independence. The vice-president of the new Texan republic was none other than the liberal from Yucatán, Lorenzo Zavala, but he died six months later. In the hands of the Texans as a prisoner of war, Santa Anna signed a treaty granting Texas its independence and recognizing the Rio Grande as the boundary between the two countries. He was subsequently released and in February 1837 he returned to Mexico in disgrace, for the Mexican government had meanwhile repudiated the treaty and refused to relinquish its claim to the former province.

To some extent, Mexico managed to balance its defeat in the north with a success on the European diplomatic front: Spain and the Holy See finally recognized the nation's independence at the end of 1836. At about the same time, Congress approved a detailed centralist constitution. In the hope of giving the country much needed stability, this increased the presidential term from four to eight years, and it seemed for a time that a period of peace could be anticipated. The hopes were premature. Bustamante was returned to office as the new president, but those conservatives who remembered his strong régime of 1830–2 were disappointed. The two leading centralists, Santa Anna and Alamán, had been discredited, and without their support or pressure Bustamante showed an increasing inclination to lean towards the federalists who agitated for the return of the 1824 constitution. A conservative politician warned the president that the clergy and the wealthy classes might feel compelled to 'deliver themselves into the hands of General Santa Anna'.

It was a French invasion of Veracruz in 1838, undertaken to exact compensation for damages to French-owned property, which gave Santa Anna the opportunity to regain popular esteem. He marched to Veracruz and his brave conduct once again made him a national hero. The following year, he was appointed interim president while Bustamante left the capital to fight federalist rebels. A few months later, however, he returned the office to its legitimate holder and retired to his rural retreat to wait for favourable developments. He did not have long to wait. Bustamante's popular support was dwindling, and in July 1840 he was captured by federalist army units. They summoned Gómez Farías – who on his return from exile had been in and out of prison – and proclaimed a federal republic. The uprising was suppressed after several days' street fighting and Bustamante was released. In a reaction against the growing chaos, the writer José María Gutiérrez Estrada advocated a monarchy with a European prince as the solution for the ills of Mexico. Gutiérrez Estrada, like Zavala, was a native of Yucatán, although he took the opposite road. While Yucatán, encouraged by the success of Texas, was fighting its own battle against Mexican centralism, he concluded that the centralist republic was too weak to impose order. Although few shared Gutiérrez Estrada's monarchist opinions, Bustamante had clearly lost the support of both radical federalists and extreme conservatives. Santa Anna was also unhappy with the 1836 constitution which had introduced a curious 'supreme conservative power' as a restraint on the power of the president. Finally, Yucatán declared its independence and Bustamante proved unable to bring it back into the republic, either by negotiation or by force of arms. An increase in taxes, tariffs and prices served only to spread the mood of discontent even wider. The country was ripe for another revolution.

Thus, in August 1841, General Mariano Paredes Arrillaga, commander of Guadalajara, called for the removal of Bustamante and amendments to the 1836 constitution to be enacted by a new constitutional congress. He was promptly supported by the army, and Santa Anna stepped in as an intermediary, becoming provisional president in October 1841. Another former royalist officer, General Paredes was known as a conservative and the new situation constituted, in effect, a centralist revolt against centralism. Santa Anna was, however, too shrewd to let himself be tied to any one party. He needed funds for the reconquest of Texas and Yucatán, as well as for his own ostentatious behaviour, and only the Church could provide them. As a way of putting pressure on the clergy, he offered the portfolio of finance to Francisco García, the former liberal governor of Zacatecas whom he himself had deposed in 1835. The elections to the new congress were sufficiently free to produce a majority of federalist or liberal deputies many of whom were young and were to achieve prominence years later. In 1842 they were obliged to labour on the new constitution in the shadow of Santa Anna's presidency. Nevertheless they managed to produce two drafts. Both still recognized the Roman Catholic faith as the only permitted religion and, in order not to annoy Santa Anna, they spoke of departments rather than states. The distinctive feature of the second draft, however, was the inclusion of a declaration of human rights, or 'guarantees'; in particular, it specified that the law should be the same for all and that no special law courts should exist. In other words, immunities from civil law should be abolished and all government monopolies were to end. Moreover, education was to be free.

In December 1842 the army disbanded Congress while it was discussing the constitutional reforms and, in the absence of Santa Anna, acting

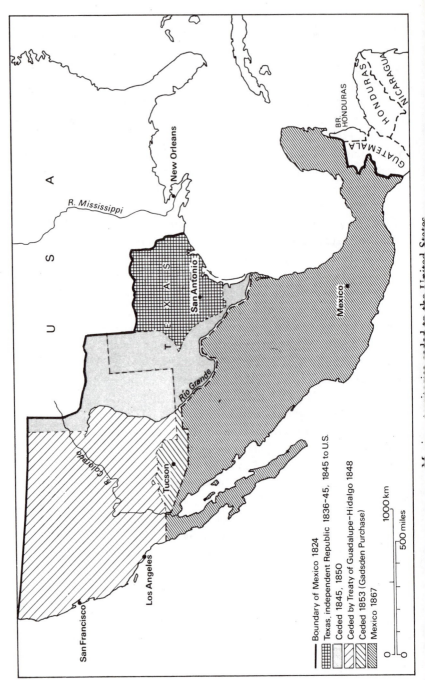

Mexican territories ceded to the United States

Boundary of Mexico 1824
Texas, independent Republic 1836–45, 1845 to U.S.
Ceded 1845, 1850
Ceded by Treaty of Guadalupe–Hidalgo 1848
Ceded 1853 (Gadsden Purchase)
Mexico 1867

President Bravo appointed a committee of leading conservative land-owners, clerics, army officers and lawyers which a few months later had devised a constitution acceptable to Santa Anna. The document was centralist and conservative, and human rights, especially equality, were not mentioned. Presidential powers, however, were enhanced by the omission of the 'supreme conservative power' introduced in the 1836 constitution. The president's power was not to be absolute, for although the authors of the new charter wanted a strong head of state, they did not want a despot.

The new Congress proved little more tractable than the disbanded one and when Santa Anna's fiscal extortions became unbearable, General Paredes, known for his honesty in financial matters, rebelled in Guadalajara. The Chamber of Deputies in the capital showed sympathy with his movement and other army units soon declared their support. Santa Anna was overthrown at the end of 1844, imprisoned and then exiled for life. Congress elected General José Joaquín Herrera, reputed to be a moderate, to the presidency.

This latest round of political upheavals in the capital had taken place against the background of deteriorating relations between Mexico and the United States. In 1843 Great Britain and France had arranged a truce between Mexico and Texas, but the truce did not lead to recognition of Texan independence by the Mexicans. On the contrary, insisting that Texas was still part of Mexico, Santa Anna announced that its annexation by the United States, which was favoured by many Americans, would be tantamount to a declaration of war.

Annexation was in fact approved by the United States Congress in February 1845, and thereafter the pace of events quickened. Mexican public opinion, both conservative and liberal, was inflamed against the aggressive politicians in Washington, but the new president, General Herrera, soon found that the financial and military state of the country made resistance hopeless and that help from Europe would not be forthcoming. Hence he attempted to negotiate a settlement. In the atmosphere of the time such a move was seen as treasonable by the Mexican people. In December 1845 General Paredes rebelled again on the pretext that 'territory of the Republic was to be alienated, staining forever national honour with an everlasting infamy in consenting to deal with the perfidious cabinet of the United States'.[9] He demanded the

[9] T. E. Cotner, *The military and political career of José Joaquín Herrera, 1792–1854* (Austin, Texas, 1949), 146.

removal of Herrera and another extraordinary congress to produce a new constitution. The army units in the capital obeyed the call, Herrera resigned and Paredes became president at the beginning of January 1846. At that time, the 1843 conservative constitution was in force and in seeking to change it, Paredes, a Catholic conservative, was clearly not looking towards a liberal republic. He gave an inkling of his views when he proclaimed: 'We seek a strong, stable power which can protect society; but to govern that society, we do not want either the despotic dictatorship of a soldier or the degrading yoke of the orator.'[10] It soon became apparent that he meant monarchy and, under his protection, Lucas Alamán publicly revived the central idea of Iturbide's Plan of Iguala, that of setting up a Mexican monarchy with a European prince on the throne. Given the international situation, such a monarchy could have been a bulwark against United States expansion, but it should by then have been clear to every educated Mexican that a monarchy had to stand on the shoulders of a strong and numerous nobility. A member of one of the few Mexican noble families, Alamán had overlooked this pre-condition of a monarchy, although it is possible that he expected it to be supported by European armies. He also seemed to have ignored the fact that the ruling group in Mexico, the army, was republican.

In any event, there was simply no time to import a European prince and thus obtain help against the United States. Hostilities broke out in April 1846 and in two or three months the United States army had defeated the Mexican forces and occupied parts of northern Mexico. Paredes' inability to defend the country and his monarchist sympathies swayed public opinion to the other extreme; perhaps, it was thought, the old federalist Gómez Farías and the once-national-hero Santa Anna, both known to hate the United States, might be more effective. Santa Anna, in his Cuban exile, had foreseen this possible reaction as early as April when he wrote to Gómez Farías, then in exile in New Orleans. As if nothing had happened between them, Santa Anna suggested in his customary verbose style that they should work together; that the army and the people should unite; and that he now accepted the principles of freedom. Possibly thinking that the army needed Santa Anna and that he could get rid of him later, Gómez Farías agreed. It was tacitly understood that Santa Anna would again become president and Gómez Farías vice-president.

[10] J. F. Ramírez, *Mexico during the war with the United States*, ed., W. V. Scholes, trans., E. B. Scherr (Columbia, Missouri, 1950), 38.

Gómez Farías departed for Mexico and at the beginning of August, aided by army units headed by General José Mariano Salas, the capital was taken and the constitution of 1824 restored. The United States government then permitted Santa Anna to pass through the blockade and land at Veracruz – in the belief, perhaps, that with the fall of the extreme anti-American Paredes the war might be stopped or that Santa Anna would make peace on terms favourable to the United States, or that he would simply bring more chaos into the already chaotic Mexico. On 16 September 1846, the two contrasting heroes, Santa Anna and Gómez Farías, rode together through the capital in an open carriage, and their relationship was formalized in December when congress appointed Santa Anna president and Gómez Farías, vice-president.

Santa Anna soon left to lead the army, and Gómez Farías, to satisfy the pressing needs of the army, nationalized ecclesiastical properties to the value of 15 million pesos, approximately one-tenth of the Church's total wealth. As there was no time for their valuation, he then ordered the immediate confiscation and sale of Church assets estimated at 10 million pesos. The Church, of course, protested and a reactionary military revolt began in the capital towards the end of February 1847. Santa Anna returned on 21 March and a week later he repealed both confiscatory decrees but not without first receiving a promise from the Church authorities that they would guarantee a loan of a million and a half pesos. Santa Anna had evidently learned to use the liberals to blackmail the Church. The clergy complied, knowing that the loan would probably never be repaid. They did not have the ready cash, however, and the money was raised by the government selling short-term bonds at a discount to financiers with the guarantee that the Church would redeem them. As Gómez Farías resisted dismissal the vice-presidency was abolished on 1 April. This second partnership of the two leading politicians of the period was to be their last.

On 9 March, while the capital city was the theatre of civil war, the United States forces, under the command of General Winfield Scott, landed near Veracruz, and the port surrendered on 29 March. The invading forces took Puebla in May, and despite many acts of heroism by the city's inhabitants, the capital was occupied on 15 September. The following day, Santa Anna resigned as president (but not as commander-in-chief) and eventually left the country. Mexican resistance ended and the United States army did not proceed further inland. It set up a municipal council in the capital, consisting of prominent liberals, among them Miguel Lerdo who would achieve fame some years later, while it awaited the emergence of a Mexican government with which the peace negotiations could begin. With General Herrera holding together the remnants of the army, a new government was formed in non-occupied Toluca and later Querétaro under the presidency of Manuel de la Peña y Peña, the non-political chief justice of the Supreme Court. Anti-American liberals like Gómez Farías and, among the rising new generation, Melchor Ocampo, also to become famous in later years, would have no part in the new administration. Defeat was generally attributed to the incompetence and treason of Santa Anna. Some Mexicans blamed the 'colossus of the north'. Fifteen prominent men wrote thus in 1848: 'The Mexican Republic, to whom nature has been prodigal, and full of those elements which make a great and happy nation, had among other misfortunes of less account, the great one of being in the vicinity of a strong and energetic people.'[11] Not everybody looked for a scapegoat. One writer complained of 'the iniquitous and shameful rule the Americans have imposed on us', but he added, 'the sad thing about it is that the punishment has been deserved.'[12]

The United States army did its best to shorten the suffering and the humiliation of the Mexican people. The new government was contacted and a peace treaty negotiated and finally signed on 2 February 1848. Mexico forfeited what was already in fact lost: Texas, New Mexico and California. The Mexican negotiators, however, did obtain the return of much that the United States believed it had occupied on a permanent basis, like, for example, Lower California. Even so, the lost provinces amounted to about half of Mexico's territory, although they only contained between one and two per cent of its total population and had then few known natural resources. Hence their loss did not disrupt the Mexican economy, and Mexico was to receive an indemnity of 15 million dollars. Understandably, sections of Mexican society viewed the treaty as ignominious and its signatories as traitors, and some wished to wage a guerrilla war against the invaders. But reason prevailed. A reluctant congress finally ratified the treaty on 30 May and the occupation forces left shortly afterwards, to the mixed joy of the Mexican landed class which was by this time threatened by a social revolution.

[11] Ramón Alcaráz *et al.*, *Apuntes para la historia de la guerra entre México y los Estados Unidos* (Mexico, .848); Eng. trans., *The other side: or notes for the history of the war between Mexico and the United States* (New York, 1850), 1.
[12] Ramírez, *Mexico during the war*, 161.

In 1829, the United States' diplomat, Poinsett, had summed up the situation in the Mexican countryside with the following words:

Here therefore is wanting that portion of a community which forms the strength of every nation, a free peasantry. The Indians cannot as yet be regarded in that light. They are laborious, patient and submissive, but are lamentably ignorant. They are emerging slowly from the wretched state to which they had been reduced . . . At present seven-eighths of the population live in wretched hovels destitute of the most ordinary conveniences. Their only furniture a few coarse mats to sit and sleep on, their food Indian corn, pepper and pulse, and their clothing miserably coarse and scanty. It is not that the low price of labour prevents them from earning a more comfortable subsistence in spite of the numerous festivals in each year but they either gamble away their money or employ it in pageants of the Catholic Church . . . All these evils would be greatly mitigated by education.[13]

The condition of Indian peasants in Mexico remained the same in 1847. The rural areas consisted of haciendas, which may be described as large farming enterprises, settlements or estates, and Indian villages with communal lands. On the hacienda labourers were often bound to the estate by peonage or debt-servitude – a legacy of the colonial period. The peon in debt was not permitted to leave until he had paid it, or unless another *hacendado* paid it for him. In other words, rural labourers were bought and sold for the price of their debt. If a peon in debt fled, he could be hunted down, brought back and punished. This *de facto* peonage was typical of central Mexico. In the isolated Yucatán peninsula and in the thinly populated north legalized servitude still existed.

Melchor Ocampo was the first liberal *hacendado* to write on the sensitive subject of the Mexican rural labour system. In a short article published in 1844, he condemned peonage not only as immoral but as not conducive to progress. Ocampo wrote that he had cancelled the full debt of all his peons four times. If one of his labourers in debt fled from his farm, perhaps to find work with another *hacendado* offering higher wages, he claimed him only if he was guilty of a criminal offence. He ended by exhorting peons not to borrow money and employers to lend only in cases of emergency.

Recent research has shown that not all rural labourers owed money to their employers. On some haciendas, at least, a considerable number of workers owed nothing and there were even some to whom the hacienda owed money. The peons would usually withdraw this from what

[13] *Diplomatic correspondence of the United States concerning the Independence of the Latin-American Nations*, William R. Manning (ed.) (New York, 1925), III, 1673–6; reproduced in Lewis Hanke (ed.), *History of Latin American civilization*, II *The modern age* (London, 1967), 22–6.

amounted to a savings account to make purchases at the hacienda store. Finally, some *hacendados* either did not bother to denounce indebted fugitives to the authorities or were not successful in bringing them back.[14] Even if they owed nothing, the peons were not entirely free to leave their employment at will. Vagrancy laws, also inherited from the colonial period, made it difficult for landless peons to wander around the country looking for another or better job. It was safer to attach oneself to a hacienda and stay there permanently. Curiously, it was to the peon's advantage to borrow as much and work as little as possible because then he could never be dismissed. This was another feature of the system specifically criticized by Ocampo.

Indians in the villages were better off because they could work as seasonal labourers on the neighbouring hacienda. This was a convenient arrangement because few peasants had enough land to support themselves throughout the year. They were free men, but, on the other hand, if their harvest failed they starved. One advantage of peonage was that the peons could always borrow maize from the *hacendado*.

There were several other rural groups who must be distinguished from peons and village peasants. These were squatters, renters, tenants, or sharecroppers who lived within the bounds of the hacienda, usually in small settlements. Rarely able to pay rent in cash, they were often forced to pay with their own or their sons' labour, and, if they resisted, their animals, perhaps a few head of cattle, might be confiscated. They could also, of course, be evicted although this was probably rare because it was to the landowner's convenience to have them there as potential peons. The *hacendado* was obviously a lord on his territory. The social and ethnic inequalities were accepted by all and peons, peasants and tenants do not seem to have resented their inferior status. Their protests were restricted to the abuses of the powerful against which it was difficult, if not impossible, to find redress through normal channels.

Special conditions prevailed in Yucatán. The local *hacendados* were successfully growing *henequén* – sisal, a fibre-producing agave – for export and had few ties with central Mexico.[15] Quite naturally, Yucatán

---

[14] See J. Bazant, *Cinco haciendas mexicanas. Tres siglos de vida rural en San Luis Potosí, 1600–1910* (Mexico, 1975), 103–8; *idem, A concise history of Mexico from Hidalgo to Cárdenas 1801–1940* (Cambridge, 1977), 64–6, 88–9; *idem*, 'Landlord, labourer and tenant in San Luis Potosí, northern Mexico, 1822–1910', in *Land and labour in Latin America*, Kenneth Duncan and Ian Rutledge (eds.) (Cambridge, 1977), 59–82.

[15] Howard Cline, 'The henequén episode in Yucatán', *Interamerican Economic Affairs*, 2/2 (1948), 30–51.

embraced federalism and in 1839 rebelled against Mexico with the help of Mayan soldiers, becoming for all practical purposes an independent state. In 1840, the American traveller, John L. Stephens, found the Indian peons submissive and humble. Two years later, after his second visit, he warned:

What the consequences may be of finding themselves, after ages of servitude, once more in the possession of arms and in increasing knowledge of their physical strength is a question of momentous import to the people of that country, the solution of which no man can foretell.[16]

Stephen's forebodings were borne out five years later. In return for the service of Indian peasants as soldiers, the whites had promised to abolish or at least reduce parochial fees, to abolish the capitation tax payable by all Indian adults, and to give them free use of public and communal lands. None of these promises were fulfilled and the Mayas rebelled in the summer of 1847 with the aim of exterminating or at least expelling the white population. The revolt soon developed into full-scale war, known ever since as the War of the Castes. Mexico had just been defeated by the United States and, even had it wished to do so, was unable to send an army to Yucatán to suppress the revolt. In the cruel war which followed, the Indians almost succeeded in driving their enemies into the sea. In their despair, the whites went as far as to offer Yucatán to Great Britain, the United States, or, indeed, any country willing to protect them.

While Yucatán was in the throes of this race war, Indian tribes, forced southward by the expansion of the United States, invaded the sparsely populated regions of northern Mexico, burning haciendas, villages and mining settlements, and indiscriminately killing their inhabitants. Again, the Mexican government was too weak to prevent these incursions.

Social and ethnic revolt took a different form in central Mexico. Here the Indians did not form a compact, linguistic group and nor were they in a clear majority, as were the Mayas in Yucatán. However, deserters from the army, fugitives from justice, vagrants and similar elements, taking advantage of Mexico's military defeat and the chaos which followed, formed armed bands which began to terrorize the countryside. In at least one district, in the mountains of the states of Guanajuato, Querétaro and San Luis Potosí, a revolutionary agrarian movement developed. This so-called Sierra Gorda rebellion sought to give free land to hacienda tenants and peons, but the rebels were not strong enough to attack cities, and

---

[16] John Lloyd Stephens, *Incidents of travel in Yucatán* (Norman, Oklahoma, 1962), II, 214.

they had to be satisfied with the burning of haciendas. The Mexican ruling class, demoralized, embittered and divided, watched helplessly as the remnants of their once great country were beginning to fall apart.

But then the situation began slowly to improve. The United States military historian, R. S. Ripley, commented in 1849:

The effect of the war upon Mexico has been and will continue to be greatly beneficial. The first great apparent good is that the prestige of the army . . . has been entirely swept away. That this has been the case is demonstrated by the comparative quietude which has existed in Mexico since the conclusion of peace, and the at least apparent stability of a government administered upon republican principles.[17]

The main explanation for the improvement, however, was the war indemnity. President Herrera's government of moderate liberals had no revenues and no doubt would have collapsed had it not received at the outset 3 million pesos of the indemnity on account. With this money it was able to purchase surplus military equipment from the United States army, re-establish social order in central Mexico and send reinforcements to the north and to Yucatán. After several years of fighting in Yucatán, in which the local landowners had enlisted the support of their peons and also hired United States mercenaries, the insurrection of the Mayan Indians was gradually quelled. The Yucatán creoles saved their skins and their property, but lost forever their hope of becoming independent of Mexico. Moreover, the population of Yucatán had been reduced by almost half.[18]

Payments on account of the indemnity continued, and Mexico was able to put its public finances in order. In 1846, the principal of the foreign public debt was fixed, after protracted negotiations in London, at 51 million pesos. Then the war intervened, and interest on the new principal was not paid, but in a friendly gesture towards Mexico, the London committee of bondholders sacrificed the arrears and agreed to a reduction of the annual interest rate from 5 per cent to 3 per cent. Thereafter, the fairly reasonable payments were met until 1854. The economy as a whole also seems to have improved. On the evidence of coinage figures, silver and gold-mining, the most important industry, showed some recovery. From a yearly average production of over 20 million pesos before the war of independence which fell to 10 million

---

[17] R. S. Ripley, *The war with Mexico* (1849; New York, 1970), II, 645.
[18] The population in 1837 was 582,173; in 1862, 320,212.

pesos in 1822, there was a gradual increase thereafter, reaching almost 20 million pesos a year again in 1848–50, the three years in which the indemnity payments were available. This was followed by a decline to 16 million pesos in 1854 and a rise in the decade 1858–67 to 17,800,000 pesos.

The final months of 1850 saw presidential elections once more in Mexico. Herrera's favourite was his own minister of war, General Mariano Arista, a moderate liberal. Other groups backed their own candidates and although Arista did not receive an absolute majority, he secured a commanding lead. Early in January 1851, the Chamber of Deputies elected him president with the delegations of eight states voting for him as against five who preferred General Bravo. This was the first time since independence that a president had been able not only to complete his term, although not a full one, but also to hand over office to a legally elected successor. The constitutional process was, however, soon to break down once again.

As long as social subversion threatened the established order, liberals and conservatives were willing to unite in mutual self-defence. The conservative, anti-American Alamán had even deplored the withdrawal of the hated Protestant army of occupation which had protected his and everybody else's property against bandits and rebels. The liberal oracle, Mora, had written from Europe to his friends in Mexico that Indian rebellions should be rigorously suppressed. But once the immediate danger was swept away, conservative opposition to the moderate liberal regime had intensified once more. More than one-third of the votes in the elections at the beginning of 1851 went to the conservative Bravo. Moreover, the financial outlook for the new government was far from promising; the funds of the United States indemnity were almost exhausted; government revenues had fallen because of increased contraband made easier by the closer proximity of the United States border; the size of the army had been reduced, but military expenditure was still enormous because of renewed Indian invasions of northern Mexico (and dismissed officers joined the ranks of the opposition). The budget deficit exceeded 13 million pesos in 1851.[19] The government of General Arista soon came under attack from conservatives, radical liberals and supporters of Santa Anna. It did not matter that some leading conservatives were tarnished by their past monarchist views, some radical liberals by their

[19] In the period 1821–67 government expenditure averaged $17.5 million, revenue only $10 million a year.

collaboration with the occupation authorities and, of course, Santa Anna by his ineptitude bordering on treason. The tide was moving against the moderate liberals who, in the popular mind, had betrayed the nation by signing the peace treaty and by 'selling' one-half of its territory; they were responsible for the present disaster.

In July 1852, in Guadalajara, José M. Blancarte, a former colonel in the national guard, deposed the state governor, Jesús López Portillo, a moderate liberal, and yet another military revolt spread to other states. It was not immediately clear who was in revolt, whether conservatives or liberals, or both, nor for what purpose. When the dust settled a few months later, it appeared that everybody wanted the return of Santa Anna. Arista resigned and the generals, believing themselves unable to rule, agreed to summon the former dictator, then living in Colombia. On 17 March 1853, Congress duly elected Santa Anna to be president and the government sent for him to return.

In a letter to Santa Anna Alamán explained the conservative programme: full support for the Church; a strong army; the abolition of federalism; and a strong executive subject to certain principles and responsibilities. He did not make clear, however, who was to watch over Santa Anna. Perhaps he viewed Santa Anna's next presidency as a stepping stone to a Bourbon monarchy. The conservatives were not alone in their renewed activity. When Santa Anna landed at Veracruz, he was greeted by Miguel Lerdo de Tejada, who had been sent there as a representative of the radical liberals. As early as 1848, Lerdo had accused the army and the Church of being the cause of Mexico's ruin. Santa Anna asked him to submit his ideas in writing and Lerdo complied with a long letter in which he reiterated his earlier criticisms and ended by proposing various material improvements which the republic badly needed.

Santa Anna took possession of the presidency on 20 April 1853. On this occasion his support was broader than it had been in 1846 when the radical liberals alone of organized political groups had called for his return. Now both conservatives and liberals were bowing to his leadership, each convinced that they could bring him to their side. He formed a mixed cabinet with the conservative Alamán in the Ministry of Internal and Foreign Affairs and the independent liberal, Antonio de Haro y Tamariz, as Minister of Finance. The latter was a particularly important appointment in view of Santa Anna's previous use of liberals to blackmail the Church. Lerdo de Tejada became Under-Secretary of the new Ministry of Development and did much to promote the building of telegraph lines, essential for progress in the mountainous terrain of

Mexico. The 1824 constitution was suspended but nothing was proclaimed in its place. Santa Anna could have reinstated the 1843 centralist constitution but, conservative though it was, it did put severe limits on the power of the president. Among other things, for example, it prohibited the president from selling, giving away, exchanging, or mortgaging any part of the national territory. For reasons known at the time only to himself, such restrictions were not to his liking. He governed, therefore, without a constitution.

During the first months of his government, Santa Anna lost his two most able Ministers: Alamán died in June and Haro resigned in August, after failing in his attempt to cover the budget deficit of 17 million pesos with the issue of bonds guaranteed by Church property. The clergy had protested vehemently against Haro's policy and Santa Anna had to devise another means of finding the money. In March, just a few weeks before he became president, the United States had seized what is now part of southern Arizona. Mexico was powerless to expel the invaders and was strongly invited to sell it to the United States. An agreement was reached towards the end of 1853. From the sale price of 10 million pesos, Mexico was to receive immediately 7 million pesos.[20]

Santa Anna's regime became increasingly reactionary and autocratic. He loved the pageantry and pomp of office but despised the daily work of administration. During his several earlier periods as head of state, he had resolved the problem by leaving the presidential work to a civilian vice-president while reserving affairs of the army and the glory to himself. In 1853, with the country split into two hostile parties and on the brink once more of disintegration, he found that he had to accept the full burden of the presidency. He embellished it, however, with such a variety of titles and prerogatives that he became a monarch in all but name. Iturbide's execution meant that he could never assume the title of emperor but instead he acquired more real power than Iturbide had even imagined. In December 1853, he was granted the right to name his successor and when the sealed envelope was later opened, it was found to contain the name of Iturbide's son. To bolster his authority and prestige, and perhaps also to ease his conscience, Santa Anna did everything he could to appear as heir of the man to whose downfall he had so much contributed. For example, in November 1853 he announced the posthumous award to Iturbide of the title of liberator and had his portrait placed in government buildings.

---

[20] The territory in question is called, in Mexico, La Mesilla; in the United States, the transaction is known as the Gadsden purchase.

In accordance with his reactionary posture, he also granted many concessions to the Church, allowing the reinstatement of the Jesuits and repealing the 1833 law which had removed the civil enforcement of monastic vows. He restricted the press and sent many liberals to gaol and exile. Eventually he went too far. In February 1854, several army officers in the south, led by Colonel F. Villareal, rose in arms and on 1 March, at Ayutla, the revolution was provided with a programme, which was amended ten days later at Acapulco. Its main points were as follows: the removal of Santa Anna; the election of a provisional president by representatives appointed by the commander-in-chief of the revolutionary army; and, finally, a demand for an extraordinary congress to produce a new constitution. Similar appeals had been proclaimed earlier and elsewhere but with little impact. This Ayutla–Acapulco manifesto made no mention of the well-known liberal demands and nobody could have suspected that out of this army uprising with limited objectives liberal Mexico would be born. In Acapulco, the obscure colonel who had launched the revolt at Ayutla was replaced by a retired colonel, Ignacio Comonfort, a wealthy merchant and landowner and a friend of General Juan Alvarez, the *cacique* of the ever rebellious south.

Alvarez had inherited control of the *tierra caliente* from Guerrero who had himself inherited the prestige of Morelos. They had all fought together in the War of Independence. The power of Alvarez, himself a *hacendado*, was based on the support of Indian peasants whose lands he protected. His army was drawn from the Indians and their support was sufficient to keep him in power on the Pacific coast for more than a generation. Eventually, the area under his control was separated from the state of Mexico to form the new state of Guerrero. He had no higher ambition and as long as central governments, liberal or conservative, did not meddle in his domain, his relations with them were good. Certainly, Santa Anna had displeased him when he appointed Alamán to the cabinet because Alamán was widely regarded as the author of Guerrero's execution, but, as the able conservative minister died soon after being appointed, relations between Santa Anna and Alvarez improved.

Then the ageing dictator made a mistake. Perhaps he no longer trusted Alvarez or perhaps he simply wished to pursue his plan to centralize the administration. Whatever the case, he removed some army officers and government officials on the Pacific coast, whereupon they flocked to Alvarez. It was on his hacienda that the revolution was planned. The strategy was to unite the nation against Santa Anna and hence the programme was restricted to generalities. The only indication that the revolution might be liberal in character was the presence of Comonfort, a moderate liberal. Alvarez assumed the leadership but, as had been the case with Guerrero, his views on basic national issues were unknown. The revolt spread irresistibly and in August 1855 Santa Anna relinquished the presidency and sailed into exile. The revolutionary government confiscated his property which had once been worth the enormous sum of one million pesos.[21] Soon a forgotten man, he was not permitted to re-enter the country until 1874 when the then president, Sebastián Lerdo, allowed him to return to Mexico City where he died two years later.

As the capital was in the hands of Alvarez's Indian soldiers it was not surprising that he was elected president by the representatives he had chosen from among the leaders of the revolt and the liberal intellectuals returned from prison and exile. Bravo had recently died leaving him as the sole surviving hero of the War of Independence, and his election thus symbolized the revolutionary tradition of Hidalgo, Morelos and Guerrero. Yet Alvarez had not sought the presidency – he was sixty-five years old – and he did not feel at home in the capital. He must also have resented the way in which he and his Indians were treated by both conservatives and moderate liberals who feared a renewal of race and class war. Instinctively perhaps, they recalled the democratic undercurrent in Morelos's rebellion and Guerrero's association with the radical Zavala. Alvarez now had the opportunity to punish the ruling groups and avenge Guerrero's death but his objective may have been limited to strengthening his hold on the south by enlarging the state of Guerrero and moving its boundaries closer to the capital. Whatever his aims, he ignored Comonfort's advice and, with one exception, appointed to the cabinet radical liberals, or *puros* as they were known. Leaving the Ministry of War to Comonfort himself who, as a moderate, could be expected to hold the army together, Alvarez entrusted the portfolio of Foreign Affairs to Melchor Ocampo and appointed Benito Juárez to the Ministry of Justice, Guillermo Prieto to the Treasury, Miguel Lerdo de Tejada to the Ministry of Development and Ponciano Arriaga to the Ministry of the Interior.

These five ministers belonged to a new generation, untainted by the failures of previous liberal governments. All except one had been born

---

[21] Robert A. Potash; 'Testamentos de Santa Anna', *Historia Mexicana*, 13/3 (1964), 428–40.

during the War of Independence and they only remembered an independent Mexico with its perpetual disorders. Although they dreamed of an orderly regime based on the rule of law, none of them was a systematic thinker or theoretician. This was not perhaps a serious weakness, for Mora had worked out the liberal programme many years before. Apart from Lerdo, they shared one other thing in common; they had all been persecuted by Santa Anna.

Ocampo and Lerdo have already been mentioned above. Both as governor of the state of Michoacán and as a private citizen, Ocampo had acquired a reputation for his attacks on high parochial fees which were one of the main causes of the indebtedness of hacienda peons. Because both birthrate and infant mortality were high, hacienda labourers spent a great deal of their money on baptisms and funerals. In most cases, it was the *hacendado* who paid the actual fees and then charged them to their peons' accounts. Marriage fees were also so high that many couples did not marry. In striking at the root of the problem Ocampo inevitably attracted the hatred of thousands of parish priests whose livelihood depended on the fees, in contrast to the higher clergy, bishops and canons, who lived mainly from the tithe revenues (the payment of which had been voluntary since 1833). Not surprisingly, Ocampo had been exiled from Mexico soon after Santa Anna's rise to his last presidency. In New Orleans, where the liberal exiles gathered, Ocampo befriended the former governor of the state of Oaxaca, Benito Juárez, the only Indian in the group, who had been exiled by Santa Anna for having opposed him in the Mexican–American war. Under Ocampo's influence, Juárez became a radical liberal.

In November 1855 Juárez, the Minister of Justice, produced a law which abolished clerical immunities by restricting the jurisdiction of ecclesiastical courts to ecclesiastical cases. It also proposed to divest the army of some of its privileges. Perhaps thinking that he had done enough to create irreversible changes, or perhaps compelled by the storm of protest raised by the so-called 'Juárez Law', Alvarez appointed Comonfort as substitute president at the beginning of December and resigned a few days later. Short as his presidency had been – only two months – it was decisive for the future of the country.

Comonfort appointed a cabinet of moderate liberals, but it was already too late. In several parts of the country, groups of laymen, army officers and priests had rebelled with the cry of *religión y fueros* (religion and immunities). One armed band called for the repeal of the Juárez Law, the removal of Comonfort and the return to the 1843 conservative constitution. In January 1856, it managed to seize the city of Puebla and establish a government there. Moderate though he was, Comonfort had to suppress the uprising and he forced the surrender of Puebla at the end of March. The local bishop, Labastida, took pains to disassociate himself from the rebels, but Comonfort put the blame on the Church and decreed the attachment of ecclesiastical property in the diocese until the cost of his campaign had been covered. Feeling that the Church should not be blamed for the insurrection, Labastida refused to pay the indemnity with the result that the government expelled him and confiscated the clerical property. In one way or another, Church property was being used to finance rebellion against the government and the answer seemed to be confiscation. But in view of the violent reaction unleashed by the Puebla confiscatory decree, it seemed prudent to try a different, indirect approach which would appear less anti-clerical. This was probably the reasoning behind the disentailment law enacted at the end of June 1856 by Lerdo de Tejada, now Minister of Finance.

Lerdo de Tejada has already been mentioned as the radical liberal who had 'collaborated' with the United States' occupation army in the municipal council of the capital and then with the reactionary Santa Anna in the Ministry of Development. He had been pessimistic about Mexico's ability to carry out a liberal revolution; he believed it would have to be imposed from above or from abroad. But finally, in 1856, he had the opportunity to carry out a programme of radical anti-clericalism. The main feature of the so-called 'Lerdo Law' was that the Church must sell all its urban and rural real estate to the respective tenants and lessees at a discount which would make the transaction attractive to buyers. Should buyers refuse to purchase, the property would be sold by government officials at public auction. The ecclesiastical corporations most affected by the law were the regular orders. The monasteries owned large country estates as well as town houses and the convents possessed the best real estate in the cities. The higher clergy were not to suffer much because its wealth was of a different kind and parish priests were not affected directly because parishes did not generally own any property except the parish house itself.[22] In the villages, however, there were brotherhoods or confraternities devoted to religious purposes, and many of them owned land or property which was now to be disentailed, much to the

---

[22] Parish priests might, of course, have property of their own; but that would not be affected by the law.

grief of villagers and priests alike. At first sight, the law did not look confiscatory: the Church was to be paid either in instalments equal to former rents or in a lump sum equal to the capitalized rent. But there was a loophole. According to the law, the Church in the future would not be able to acquire or own properties. The Church would therefore have no safeguards and hence would face a gradual despoilment. Consequently, the Church authorities protested and refused to comply.

As believers in private property, the liberals also sought the liquidation of the property of civil corporations. This affected in particular the Indian villages, most of which were still large landholders. These villages possessed various types of property including communal pastures, or *ejidos*, which were exempted from disentailment because Lerdo considered them essential for the village. Nevertheless, in actual practice, parts of the *ejidos* began to be sold, despite protests by the peasants.

The Lerdo Law was put into effect at once. As the Church in most cases refused to sell, government officials signed the deeds of sale to the former tenants or lessees and now house or landowners. Many pious tenants refrained from claiming the property which was then purchased by wealthy speculators, some of whom were well-known financiers who specialized in loans to the government and had thus become important holders of government bonds. Whereas they might have been previously connected with conservative regimes, their investments in the disentailed clerical properties tended to make them allies of the liberals. Tenants loyal to the Church ignored the new landlords, continuing to pay their rent to the former ecclesiastical owner, awaiting the day when the house would be returned to the Church. This confused and complex situation regarding the disentailed properties was evident within a few months of the law's implementation and it was clear that it could not be permitted to last indefinitely.

While Lerdo was dealing with Church property, his colleague, José María Iglesias, the new Minister of Justice, was working on a law to limit parochial fees. In general, the 'Iglesias Law' of 11 April 1857 declared as valid the fees charged in the colonial period or at the beginning of independent Mexico and which were evidently low. It then prohibited the collection of parochial fees from the poor who were defined as persons earning the minimum amount necessary for survival. As most parishioners were poor, this meant the end of wealthy curates. The law prescribed severe penalties for those priests who charged the poor for their services or refused to baptize, marry or bury them free of charge.

Again, the Church condemned the law as illegal and immoral, and refused to comply.

In the meantime, approximately 150 deputies in congress, most of whom were young liberals drawn from the professional classes – lawyers, government officials or journalists – were debating the new constitution. Among the older generation there was Valentín Gómez Farías, after Mora's death in Paris in 1850 the patriarch of Mexican liberalism and now seventy-five years old. The issues and problems in 1856 were different from those which Ocampo had faced in 1842 and even more so than those confronting Gómez Farías in 1833. The war with the United States had inevitably left a mark on the mind of most liberals. For example, in 1848 Ocampo described the struggle between the states and the central, federal government, as 'systematic anarchy'.[23] He came to the conclusion that federation, as it had existed in Mexico since the adoption of the 1824 constitution, had made easier the separation of Texas and the temporary secession of Yucatán, and had subsequently been a cause of the defeat and dismemberment of the country. He must have recalled Servando Teresa de Mier's opinion that Mexico needed a strong central government in the first phase of its independence. Perhaps centralism was the right course after all, though not if it meant the domination of the army and the Church. Now that the government was a liberal one, it was advisable to strengthen it, especially since the proximity of the American border weakened the hold of central Mexico on the states to the north, making a further dismemberment of the country possible in the future. Liberals, therefore, became just as centralist as their conservative rivals, although they continued to pay lip service to the federalism with which liberalism had been identified for so many years. The new constitution, approved on 5 February 1857 following almost a year of discussion, kept the federal structure but, characteristically, while the official title of the 1824 document had been the Federal Constitution of the United Mexican States, the new charter was named the Political Constitution of the Mexican Republic.

Now that federalism had lost its meaning, the Church took its place as the main issue between liberals and conservatives. In a radical departure from the 1842 constitutional projects, and even more from the 1824 constitution, the liberals in 1856 wished to introduce full freedom of worship for all religions; in other words, religious toleration. The

---

[23] Moisés González Navarro, *Anatomía del poder en México (1848–1853)* (Mexico, 1977), 378.

proposal turned out to be too advanced. Mexico's population consisted mostly of peasants loyal to their Church, and although the educated classes may have been as liberal as their European counterparts, they could not antagonize the mass of villagers, already stirred by their priests. The Minister of the Interior warned Congress: 'the Indians are excited and for this reason it is very dangerous to introduce a new element which will be exaggerated by the enemies of progress in order to drown us in a truly frightening anarchy'.[24] The proposal was dropped, but, at the same time, the traditional assertion that Mexico was a Roman Catholic nation was also omitted, thus leaving a curious gap in the constitution. Not daring to touch the image, sacred to the common people, of a Catholic Mexico, the delegates nevertheless included in the constitution all the other anti-clerical demands, especially the basic concepts of the 'Juárez Law' (1855) and the 'Lerdo Law'(1856).

The liberals were as anti-militaristic as they were anti-clerical. In this respect, however, they realized that they had to tread carefully because General Comonfort, president and commander-in-chief of the army, was already showing signs of impatience with Congress. Hence the liberal deputies restricted themselves to the abolition of the judicial privileges of the army, thereby confirming what had already been enacted in the Juárez Law.

Finally, the new constitution affirmed complete freedom for all citizens. For the first time since the 1814 Apatzingán constitution, every Mexican, however poor (but excluding vagrants and criminals), was given the right to vote and to be elected, and a declaration of human rights, including the inviolability of private property, was also specified. With its ban on the corporate ownership of real estate, the constitution was more sweeping than the Lerdo Law. Lerdo had exempted village *ejidos* or communal pastures, but the constitution did not mention them, the implication being that they could be disentailed. Their disentailment was, in fact, attempted on the basis of the new constitution, but it had to be halted because of Indian opposition. The liberals could not afford to wage war on two fronts, against the Church and against the Indian peasants. As far as the Church was concerned, they sought to isolate it by gaining allies among all social strata. They succeeded in doing so in urban centres where the middle and some of the upper classes profited by the disentailment of corporate property. In the rural areas where the Church was traditionally strong, they were unable to isolate it, but they

[24] Francisco Zarco, *Historia del Congreso Constituyente (1856–1857)* (2nd edn, Mexico, 1956), 630.

did drive a wedge into the hitherto solidly conservative countryside by letting large landowners purchase former ecclesiastical haciendas. Ironically, it was the rural rich, not the rural poor, who tended to support the liberals.

Most liberals saw in the adoption of the constitution of 1857 a realization of their life-long dreams. They were now able to assume a more conciliatory attitude in some respects. For example, a subtle change in public opinion caused the government to reopen the Franciscan monastery in the capital which had been closed some months previously because an alleged conspiracy had taken place within its walls. Moreover, with the resignation of Lerdo at the beginning of the year, the disentailment of property slowed down. The government was ready to negotiate and on 1 May 1857, Comonfort sent his Minister of Justice to Rome. The Holy See appeared ready to accept the disentailment transactions so far implemented, but it demanded that the legal right to acquire and own property should be restored to the Church. Even the conservative Mexican press suggested in August that the disentailment should be legalized through an agreement with Rome.

It seemed obvious that a compromise with both the Church and the conservatives would require the repeal of the more extreme articles of the constitution. Comonfort, elected constitutional president in September with only reluctant support from the radicals who preferred Lerdo, was believed to favour such a course as the only way of avoiding civil war. But compromise was not to prevail. The liberals saw in Comonfort a conservative and the conservatives a liberal, and he was left without support. In the civil war which followed it was the conservatives who took the initiative. Reactionary army units in the capital, led by General Félix Zuloaga, rebelled in December 1857 with the avowed aim of annulling the constitution. While upholding Comonfort's authority, the army took control of the city, dissolved Congress and arrested, among others, the new president of the Supreme Court, Benito Juárez. After some hesitation, Comonfort approved Zuloaga's programme. A month later, Zuloaga took the second step: he removed Comonfort and assumed the presidency himself. Perhaps out of revenge against ungrateful conservatives, Comonfort, in the final moments of his power, managed to release Juárez from prison before leaving the country, unmolested by conservatives and ignored by liberals. Yet his decision to free Juárez rendered an immense service to the liberal cause, as future events were to show.

Juárez fled to Querétaro. From there, he proceeded to Guanajuato and, arguing that the constitutional order had been destroyed, he proclaimed himself president of the republic and appointed a cabinet with Ocampo as its most distinguished member. As head of the Supreme Court – the office of vice-president not having been adopted by the 1857 constitution – he had the constitutional right to the presidential succession in the absence of the legally elected president. Shortly after his arrival at Guanajuato, a resident wrote to a friend in Mexico City: 'An Indian by the name of Juárez, who calls himself president of the republic, has arrived in this city.'[25]

Thus, with a conservative president in Mexico City and a liberal president in Guanajuato, the Three Years War began. In earlier decades, when faced by a counter-revolution, the liberals had submitted to the army virtually without resistance. Now, they still did not have an army of consequence, but they had mass support in cities and parts of the rural areas which made it possible for them gradually to create a new army with former liberal lawyers and journalists as officers. In contrast, since Alamán's death, there had been a curious lack of educated civilians among the conservatives. Events were to reveal that the regular army and the Church were not by themselves strong enough to resist the liberal movement. This was not to be a walkover, as Santa Anna's counter-revolutionary coups had once been.

Following Zuloaga's second coup, some state governors acknowledged him as president, others declared their opposition and some reversed their original stance. Amidst this confusion, Juárez was able to escape to Veracruz, the governor of which had invited him to establish his administration in the port. The country as a whole soon divided into two sections of approximately equal strength. The states bordering on the Gulf of Mexico were under liberal control, with the exception of the exhausted Yucatán which chose to remain neutral. The far northern states were also liberal. The central core of the country was conservative, except for the states of Michoacán and Zacatecas.

From the start, both factions had to find ways of financing their war efforts. Zuloaga, fulfilling a promise to the Church, declared the Lerdo Law null and void: the Church was to regain ownership of its disentailed property. In exchange for this, the metropolitan chapter was obliged to promise him a loan of one and a half million pesos, but as the ecclesiastical corporations had little ready cash, nine-tenths of the amount was paid in

[25] Ralph Roeder, *Juárez and his Mexico* (2 vols., New York, 1947), I, 161.

bills guaranteed by clerical property. The conservative government sold these bills at a discount to financiers who in due course acquired the clerical real estate because the Church was unable to redeem them. A discount was necessary because the liberal government had declared illegal all acts and transactions of the conservative regime. Hence the price was lowered in proportion to the risk. Other similar loans followed, including one granted by the House of Rothschild. In this way, moneylenders financed Zuloaga at the expense of the Church which was obliged to watch its wealth dispersed. Arguing that the Church was voluntarily financing Zuloaga, liberal governors and military commanders of relatively isolated areas such as Michoacán and the north decreed forced loans on the clergy which for all practical purposes amounted to confiscation of Church property. At Veracruz, the conditions were rather different. Soon after Juárez's arrival in May 1858, a shipload of rifles, consigned to a French captain, José Yves Limantour, reached the port. Of course, the constitutional government promptly requisitioned the weapons. As it could not pay for them with the limited amount of Church property left in the Gulf states, and as it had no cash available, payment was made in the form of clerical real estate in Mexico City. With the capital held by Zuloaga, all the liberal regime could do was to promise to hand over the property in the event of a liberal victory. Again, the price set for the weapons was proportional to the risk of this credit arrangement and thus Limantour, and other foreign importers, were to acquire urban property in Mexico City at a fraction of its real value.

Juárez faced a critical situation in February–March 1859 when the new conservative president and military commander, Miguel Miramón, attempted to capture Veracruz. The attempt failed, but, at almost the same time, the liberal commander of western Mexico, Santos Degollado, also failed in his attempt to seize Mexico City. After Degollado's defeat, more than a dozen liberal officers, including seven army surgeons, were taken prisoner and executed in a suburb of the capital. The conflict was becoming increasingly cruel and destructive with almost the entire country now a theatre of war. No end was in sight. The nation was divided into irreconcilable camps.

The moment had arrived for the liberals to put their aims before the nation. Thus, the constitutional government in Veracruz issued a manifesto on 7 July 1859. The document, signed by President Juárez and the two most prominent cabinet members, Ocampo and Lerdo, put all the blame for the war on the Church and a series of reforms was announced:

the confiscation of all Church wealth, both real estate and capital; the voluntary payments of parochial fees; the complete separation of Church and State; the suppression of all monasteries and abolition of novitiates in nunneries. Full freedom of worship was not proclaimed. The manifesto also recognized the need for a division of landed property, but it added that such a redistribution would take place in the future as a natural consequence of economic progress. For the moment, it promised only a law which would remove legal obstacles to the voluntary division of rural estates.

The specific laws to enact these reforms were issued during the following four weeks. The confiscated, 'nationalized' wealth, both real estate and mortgages, were to be sold to buyers of clerical properties under the Lerdo Law. Lerdo, who as Minister of Finance in the Veracruz government had drafted the confiscatory law, insisted on the continuity between the earlier disentailment and the present nationalization. The buyers who had returned the properties to the Church in areas occupied by the conservatives would, in the event of a liberal victory, recover them and then pay the government for them either in instalments extending for long periods of time or in cash at a fraction of their value. The measure was bound to attract both former and potential buyers to the liberal cause, particularly in conservative occupied central Mexico where the most valuable clerical properties were concentrated. In the areas under liberal control, most of the Church property had already been disposed of and in some states, like Veracruz, the Church had always been poor. Hence the liberal government itself obtained only a small immediate revenue from the sale of the confiscated wealth.

But the die had been cast. Now it was a life-and-death struggle of the Church and the old army against the middle class professionals, of the old world against the new. The revolutionary 'reform' laws of July 1859 drove political passions to their highest pitch, fighting increased and the demands of the Treasury became ever greater. In desperation, the constitutional government granted the United States, in exchange for 2 million dollars, transits and right of way across the Isthmus of Tehuantepec and from the Rio Grande and Arizona to the Gulf of California, as well as the right to employ its own military forces for the protection of persons and property passing through these areas. This so-called McLane–Ocampo treaty was negotiated by Melchor Ocampo who was certainly no friend of the United States, and it was signed on 14 December 1859. A liberal newspaper commented: 'Does not Señor

Juárez know that the liberal party prefers to fall anew under the double despotism of the army and the clergy before committing itself to a foreign yoke?'[26] We do not know if the liberal government was sincere in its proposed treaty or whether it was playing for time. Whatever the case, the United States Senate repudiated the treaty a few months later, thus freeing the liberals from the embarrassing position into which their extreme penury had placed them. In fact, the 2 million dollars were not needed. The war of propaganda was bearing fruit, and after the failure of Miramón's second attempt to capture Veracruz in the spring of 1860, the fortunes of the conservative armies began to decline. They began to retreat towards the capital where Miramón was trying to raise money. He now did, with the archbishop's permission, what the liberals had done against the will of the Church; in August he confiscated wrought silver from churches for coinage as well as gold and other jewels which were pawned to moneylenders. Then, in November, without either credit or funds, he confiscated 660,000 pesos which had been entrusted to the British legation on behalf of English bondholders who were going to receive part of the interest due to them for the first time since 1854. It was too late: the liberal armies were closing in on the capital.

Early in December 1860, victory was so certain that the liberal government at Veracruz finally decreed complete religious toleration. It no longer mattered what priest-led Indians might think. The liberals had won the war. On 22 December, the liberal commander, General Jesús González Ortega, a former journalist from Zacatecas, defeated Miramón in the battle for possession of Mexico City and he occupied it three days later, on Christmas day. President Juárez arrived from Veracruz three weeks later. With the cities taken by the liberals and the conservative armies scattered into rural guerrilla groups, Mexico was free to enjoy a political campaign, and the presidential contest began almost with the arrival of the president and his cabinet.

Among the liberal leaders there were four possible presidents: Melchor Ocampo, Miguel Lerdo, Benito Juárez and González Ortega. Ocampo did not seek the presidency. Considered as heir to Mora, he was satisfied with being the prophet of liberalism and hence he helped his protégé, Juárez, against Lerdo in whom he sensed a rival. Juárez may have needed such help for, even though president, he was viewed by many as second rate in comparison with Ocampo and Lerdo. Reserved and

[26] Walter V. Scholes, *Mexican politics during the Juárez regime, 1855–1872* (2nd edn, Columbia, Missouri, 1969), 36.

unassuming, he was described later as 'not a leader who conceived and gave impulse to programmes, reforms, or ideas. That task reverted to the men who surrounded him, and he acquiesced in or rejected their leadership'.[27] As author of the revolutionary laws affecting Church wealth, Lerdo had prestige and authority, and he was popular with radical liberals. González Ortega in turn was a national hero – the man who had defeated the conservative army. These three man – Juárez, Lerdo and González Ortega – were candidates for the highest office.

At the end of January 1861, it seemed that six states favoured Juárez, six were for Lerdo and five for González Ortega; there was no information about the remaining seven states. Lerdo won in the capital and two states, only to die on 22 March. The protracted system of indirect elections had to continue with the two remaining candidates, Juárez against González Ortega, and in the final count, Juárez obtained 57 per cent of the vote, Lerdo almost 22 per cent and González Ortega over 20 per cent. It would seem that in the districts where after Lerdo's death the elections were still in progress, his supporters had given their votes to Juárez. One obvious explanation was liberal mistrust of the military. The most distinguished liberal politicians had been civilians: Zavala, Mora, Gómez Farías, Ocampo, Lerdo, Otero and de la Rosa. None of them had become president. The army, by nature conservative, was unwilling to share power with them. Excepting the transitional presidency of de la Peña, there had been no civilian head of state before Juárez. Although González Ortega was a good liberal, he was a general and therefore not to be trusted.

In June 1861, Congress declared Juárez to be president of Mexico. He was to bear the whole burden of office alone, for Ocampo had recently been captured and executed by conservative guerrillas, thus surviving his rival, Lerdo, by just over two months. Nor would Juárez ever get rid of the shadow of the army, even though it was a liberal, revolutionary force. While González Ortega was in the field fighting the conservatives, he was elected by Congress (unconstitutionally, since he should have been directly elected) president of the Supreme Court and thus next in line for the presidency. The anti-Juárez faction felt that as the president of the republic was a presumably weak civilian, some provision should be made for any possible emergency. To González Ortega's credit, it must be said that he did not attempt a military takeover

The problems facing Juárez were staggering. The sale of confiscated

27 Frank Averill Knapp, Jr., *The life of Sebastián de Tejada, 1823–1889* (Austin, Texas, 1951), 157.

Church wealth valued at around 150 million pesos – perhaps one-fifth of the total national wealth – had begun in January 1861. To attract Mexican buyers who, as good Roman Catholics, were opposed to the confiscation, and to create a broad social base for itself, the liberal government had been accepting all kinds of paper, credits, promissory notes and depreciated internal debt bonds in payment for, or at least in part payment for, the clerical properties. Consequently, from the sale in 1861 of confiscated properties in the Federal District, worth 16 million pesos which was already a depreciated value, the government received only one million pesos in actual cash. Moreover, Veracruz financiers, like Limantour and others, had already paid for their properties in kind or cash. Finally, the government recognized as valid the purchases of ecclesiastical properties made by the powerful House of Rothschild during the conservative regime. The fact that the properties had been purchased at a fraction of their value and that many had been paid for in advance explains the extremely low revenue from the confiscation in 1861. The English bondholders, who expected some of their arrears of interest from the proceeds of the sale, received nothing. Similarly, France was pressing her claims for the Jecker bonds issued by the conservative government and recently acquired by influential politicians in France. There were all sorts of other claims for damages allegedly or actually suffered during the civil war by foreign nationals. Juárez, however, refused to accept responsibility for the acts of the conservative regime: he simply had no money. His government was obliged to suspend all payments in July. European creditors felt cheated and pressed their governments to obtain redress. On 31 October 1861, France, Great Britain and Spain signed in London a Tripartite Convention in favour of military intervention in Mexico. Their troops landed at Veracruz shortly afterwards. It soon became clear, however, that Napoleon III had ulterior motives and designs for Mexico. Hence Britain and Spain withdrew their forces, leaving the enterprise to the French.

These developments provided Mexican monarchists living in Europe, like Gutiérrez Estrada, for example, with the opportunity they had been looking for. A French occupation of Mexico would make it possible to realize their life-long dream of establishing a Mexican empire under European – this time, French – protection. And a suitable candidate for the monarchy was found in the person of the Austrian Archduke Maximilian.

Meanwhile, the French armies were advancing in Mexico. The invasion aroused genuine patriotic feelings in the country, not only among the liberals. It was not known at this point whether France was seeking to help conservatives against liberals, or in fact trying to subjugate the country. The two former conservative presidents, Zuloaga and Miramón, hesitated. As generals and former presidents, they were not enthusiastic about an empire with a foreign prince. Furthermore, they distrusted France and were devoted to their country's independence. Miramón finally offered his sword to Juárez. The issue was not liberalism against conservatism, as it had been in 1858–60, but Mexican independence against conquest by a foreign power. Certainly, in their hatred of Juárez most conservatives did accept the French as liberators from the liberal yoke, but some also found their way into the army which was fighting the invaders. For example, Manuel González (future president of Mexico 1880–4), who had been an officer in the conservative army in 1858–60, volunteered and was accepted to fight the French. Comonfort was also accepted by Juárez and he was to die on the battlefield in 1863

Temporarily repulsed by General Zaragoza in the battle of Puebla in May 1862, the French forces were reorganized and, under Marshall Forey, they embarked on a more powerful campaign. Zaragoza died and Juárez had to appoint González Ortega, whom he had kept without military assignment, to the command of the eastern armies. He surrendered in Puebla in May 1863, after a two months' siege of the city. The French were free to take the capital and from there extended their domination to other parts of the country. Aiming to continue the fight from the north, Juárez left Mexico City on 31 May, and ten days later he established his government in San Luis Potosí. He was joined by González Ortega who had managed to escape from the French while being taken to Veracruz.

The conservatives in the capital, especially the former bishop of Puebla and now archbishop of Mexico, Labastida, expected the French to do as Zuloaga had done in 1858, that is, repeal all the confiscatory laws and return the nationalized wealth to the Church. Napoleon, however, had decided to adopt the liberal programme and to the dismay of Church dignitaries, Marshal Forey recognized the validity of the nationalization and sale of ecclesiastical property. On accepting the crown of Mexico at Miramar, his castle near Trieste, on 10 April 1864, Maximilian, whose liberal background was well known, had undertaken to follow French policy in respect of the Church and the nationalization of its property. On his arrival in Mexico City in June, he found the republican government of Juárez still in control of northern Mexico and the republican guerrillas fighting the occupation forces. He attempted to bring Juárez to his side and to persuade him to submit to his empire but, of course, he failed. Nevertheless, he did succeed in winning over some of those liberals who had chosen to remain in the capital under the French occupation. He rejected the support of the conservatives and sent their best-known leader, General Miramón, abroad. Thus, he was able to form a cabinet consisting almost entirely of liberals, among them two former deputies to the constituent congress of 1856–7, Pedro Escudero y Echánove and José M. Cortés y Esparza. Escudero became Minister of Justice and Ecclesiastical Affairs and Cortés, Minister of the Interior. Foreign Affairs, Development and the new Ministry of Public Education were also in the hands of liberals. The Treasury was managed directly by the French.

Maximilian even went so far as to draft a liberal constitution. Known as the Provisional Statute of the Mexican Empire, it was signed by the emperor on the first anniversary of his acceptance of the Mexican crown. Together with a 'moderate hereditary monarchy with a Catholic prince', it proclaimed freedom of worship as one of the rights of men. As the first and foremost of these rights, 'the Government of the Emperor' guaranteed equality under the law 'to all inhabitants of the Empire',[28] a right which had only been implied in the 1857 constitution. Freedom of labour was also established. While the liberal regime had never enacted a law expressly prohibiting debt peonage, Maximilian did so on 1 November 1865. Labourers were granted the right to leave their employment at will, independently of whether or not they were in debt to their employer: all debts over ten pesos were cancelled; hours of work and child labour were restricted; corporal punishment of labourers was forbidden; and to allow competition with hacienda stores, peddlers were permitted to enter haciendas and offer their wares to peons. Finally, in a departure from the 1857 constitution, Maximilian restored to Indian villages the right to own property and granted communal lands to those villages which did not have them.

It is possible that Maximilian was seeking support among the Mexican poor – the overwhelming majority of the nation – because his authority depended so far entirely on the strength of a foreign army of occupation. But this in the eyes of most Mexicans was more important than the question of his liberal or conservative convictions. In 1858–60 the

[28] Ramírez, *Leyes fundamentales de México*, 670–80

struggle had been between Mexican liberals and Mexican conservatives. Now the issue was between Mexico and France, between the Mexican republic and a foreign monarchy. The liberal government of Juárez came to represent Mexico and the empire was seen as an instrument of a foreign power.

The conquest and the empire almost succeeded. In the final months of 1865, the advancing French armies pushed Juárez to Paso del Norte, a town on the Rio Grande across the United States border. At the same time, Juárez faced a serious internal crisis. His four-year term as president was due to expire on 1 December 1865 and it was impossible to hold elections with the French occupying most of the country. Basing himself on the extraordinary powers previously granted to him by Congress, Juárez extended his own term of office until such time as new elections again became possible. This action was no doubt unconstitutional and General González Ortega, the (also) unconstitutional president of the Supreme Court, claimed the presidency of the republic. It seemed that the days of Juárez, and even the republic, were numbered, but the general had neither the nerve nor the strength to attempt a military takeover. Juárez arrested and imprisoned him. For the moment, he weathered the storm.

In 1866 the military situation turned against the empire as a result of Napoleon's decision to withdraw his troops. They began to leave, exposing the weakness of Maximilian's position. For two years he had tried to lure the liberals into his camp and many of them had become imperial civil servants, but with the French expeditionary force about to depart he had to replace it with a Mexican army. Unable to find liberals willing to fight and, if necessary, die for his empire, he turned to the conservatives. After the departure of the French, it would once again be a war of Mexican conservatives against Mexican liberals. Maximilian appointed a conservative cabinet and welcomed the best conservative commander, Miramón, back to Mexico. Without knowing it, the conservatives and the Austrian archduke had sealed a death pact.

Republican armies closed the circle around the tottering empire which retained control of central Mexico. The eastern army moved against Puebla, and the northern army against Querétaro and it was there that Maximilian decided to make what was to be his last stand. He was defeated and became a prisoner of war, together with Generals Miramón and Mejía, the latter a conservative of Indian origins. Executions of military and civilian prisoners had been common both in the civil war of

1858–60 and during the French invasion of 1862–6. If Ocampo had been shot, why should Maximilian be spared? His royal blood made no difference. He had to come to the same end as Iturbide. Juárez intended to warn the world that an attempted conquest of Mexico, for whatever aim, did not pay. The execution of Maximilian, Miramón and Mejía was, therefore, a foregone conclusion. They were court-martialled, convicted of war crimes and faced the firing squad on 19 June 1867. After an absence of more than four years, President Juárez returned to his capital city on 15 July 1867.

In retrospect, the second Mexican empire appears to have been a tragi-comedy of errors. The conservatives had picked the wrong man. They needed a strong, conservative monarch to bolster their cause, not someone who put only obstacles in their way. They might have done better had they obtained an ultra Catholic Spanish prince. As it was, Maximilian's attempt to graft a liberal, European monarchy on a Church-dominated Latin American republic was a forlorn enterprise. He quarrelled with Miramón without winning over Juárez. His social reforms brought him into conflict with the ruling classes, particularly the large landowners. His reforms came too late to earn him popularity with the poor. In the end, he was in a country which did not want him, especially not as a gift from an invading army. In sum, the emperor who had sought to bring together liberals and conservatives, rich and poor, Mexicans and Europeans, ended by being repudiated and abandoned by almost all.

And yet, at the beginning, in 1863–4, some Mexicans did see in an empire an answer to their problems and a reasonable, even desirable alternative to the almost fifty years of anarchy and civil war that had gone before. They had lost faith in the ability of their nation to govern itself. Only a European of royal blood could command the respect of all, restrain individual ambition and be an impartial judge of their disputes. Did not the empire fulfil the Plan of Iguala of 1821 which had insisted on a European prince as the only force capable of holding the nation together? The answer, of course, is that it did, but it had come too late. Had it come immediately after independence, it might have given some stability to the new country. But now Mexico had a group of men capable of ruling, as they were soon to show, and it was these men who fought and defeated the empire.

Restored by Juárez in 1867, the liberal republic lasted until 1876 when General Porfirio Díaz, a hero of the patriotic war against the French, overthrew the civilian president, Sebastián Lerdo, a younger brother of

Miguel Lerdo and successor to Juárez after his death in 1872. Using parts of his predecessor's political machine, Díaz built one of his own which helped him to retain power for thirty-five years. He was to bring considerable stability to Mexico, making possible unprecedented economic development, but his absolute control of political offices and what to most younger contemporaries appeared to be the regime's mounting tyranny finally brought his downfall in 1911 in the first stage of the Mexican Revolution.

2

THE LIBERAL REPUBLIC AND THE
PORFIRIATO, 1867-1910

The aftermath of war

The Liberals who came to power in 1855, 34 years after Mexico's independence from Spain, had hoped to give Mexico the productivity and stability of its northern neighbour, the United States. Having seen their country lose almost half of its territory to the United States in the recent Mexican–American War (1846–8), they feared that without a measure of both economic growth and political stability the very existence of Mexico as an independent nation–state would be in jeopardy. Their programme envisaged the replacement of what they considered the unsteady pillars of the old order – the church, the army, the regional caciques, the communal villages – with a 'modern foundation'. True to their programme they proceeded first in a series of reform laws and then in the constitution of 1857 to weaken the position of the church. Catholicism ceased to be the official religion of the state. Ecclesiastic courts lost much of their jurisdiction. Marriages could be effected through a civil ceremony. The clergy could now be tried in civil courts. Church lands were put up for sale. The army too was stripped of many of its former prerogatives. Like the church, it lost its judicial privileges. Officers could now be tried in civil courts. For the first time in Mexico's history its head of state and cabinet were, by and large, civilians. In addition many of the once omnipotent caciques, the mainstay of the ousted Conservative regime, who for so long had ruled their local strongholds with virtually complete autonomy, were forced to yield power to new Liberal appointees. With the adoption of the Ley Lerdo in 1856 the Liberals had launched an all out assault not only on the church but also on the communal villages. The new law prohibited ecclesiastical institutions from owning or administering property not directly used for religious purposes and extended the prohibition on corporate property to civil institutions, thus effectively abolishing communal land tenure. Communal land holdings had to be sold. Only individual farmers or private partnerships and companies could henceforth own land.

By declaring that Catholicism was no longer the official religion of Mexico, diminishing the political role of the church and destroying the economic basis of its political power, the Liberals hoped that Mexico, like the United States, would attract European immigrants of all religions. As in the United States, these immigrants would constitute an agrarian middle class which would ensure rapid economic growth, political stability and the development of democratic institutions. At the same time the Liberals expected that the constitutional provisions prohibiting the church and the Indian communities from owning lands would have similar effects. Both institutions were to be replaced by a large class of small landowners who would, some Liberal leaders hoped, like the immigrants become the sinews for modernization, stability and democracy in Mexico. At the very worst, if such development did not come about, many liberals expected that if the land passed from the 'dead hand' of the church into the 'living hand' of capitalist-orientated landowners, a significant economic boom and increasing stability would ensue. These landowners might not be interested in political democracy, but like their counterparts in Argentina, Brazil and Chile they would require political stability as a means of ensuring the success of their newly developed commercial properties. At the same time, the destruction of the old army, dominated by Conservative officers, would put an end to military uprisings and coups. A new army organized by the Liberals would constitute a basically different formation.[1]

When the Liberal president, Benito Juárez, returned to Mexico City in July 1867 after the war against the French, which had followed three years of civil war between the Liberals and the Conservatives, the flush of military triumph could only briefly disguise the extent to which the Liberals had thus far fallen short of many of the goals they had set themselves twelve years earlier. The execution of Maximilian and so the defeat of Napoleon III had indeed removed the threat of European intervention for a long time, and Mexico's survival as an independent nation seemed assured. The church had lost most of its economic and

---

[1] For a detailed discussion of Mexican politics in the period 1855–67, see Chapter 1.

political hold on the country; church-inspired coups were a thing of the past. The old Conservative army, so prone to indiscipline and revolt, had been dissolved for good. Regional government was firmly in Liberal hands. Communal land holdings had been greatly reduced in number. But these developments did not bring the hoped for results. The expropriation of church land did not give rise to a class of small farmers – since the land was auctioned off to the highest bidder, rich local landowners acquired most of it. It thus only added to the economic strength and political cohesiveness of an already dominant class of wealthy hacendados, much to the chagrin of the more radical of Liberals. The new Liberal army was no greater guarantor of stability than the old Conservative one. It consisted of a loose conglomeration of troops – both regular army corps and guerillas – each headed by a different local commander with varying degrees of loyalty to the central government. It was much too large for peace-time needs; yet simply sending the veterans of two wars home without adequate reward for their long service threatened to trigger off new revolts. Despite the new sense of nationalism awakened by the victory against the French and the emergence of Juárez as a genuinely popular national leader, the country was further away from integration than ever before. During the years of war different provinces had come to lead a nearly autonomous existence, deeply isolated in their social, economic, and political life from the rest of Mexico. The parcelling out of communal lands had swelled only slightly the ranks of the middle class. Some of the best lands had been lost to wealthy hacendados. The few peasants who did acquire a plot of their own came to be known among their less fortunate brethren as *los riquitos*. They were evolving into a group very much like the Russian *kulaks* or French *coqs du village*.

These structural problems were compounded by those the civil war and the war against the French had created. Ten years of warfare had left Mexico's economy in chaos. The church wealth on which the Liberals had counted to pay for some of their more ambitious projects had been consumed by the war effort. Mines and fields lay in ruin. The federal tax base had shrunk to vanishing point. During the larger part of Juárez's presidency, as Juárez's last finance minister Francisco Mejía noted in his memoirs, there was literally not a penny in the treasury. The frosty relations with Europe in the aftermath of Maximilian's execution and Juárez's refusal to honour Maximilian's debts did not help matters. The United States, on which Mexico became increasingly dependent as a consequence, could not make up for the loss of European markets and investment capital.

The Mexican state consisted on the one hand of an overdeveloped army, most of whose contingents were only loosely controlled by the central administration, and on the other the enormously weakened remaining branches of the government. After the initial defeat of the Liberals in 1863, most of the bureaucracy had abandoned the Juárez government and joined Maximilian's administration. Even if the bureaucrats had remained loyal to Juárez, they could have done very little for many years as the Liberals' administration only ruled over a small fraction of the country. The state's weakness and the lack of control of the government over the army would have been less severe if its social and political base had been a united and coherent force. Its constituency was the Liberal movement, and the Liberal movement was badly splintered. In name, programme, and terminology Mexico's Liberal party resembled those of Europe, but not in social composition. Only a fraction of its support came from the Mexican bourgeoisie. To begin with, that group was small, consisting chiefly of textile manufacturers and the so-called *agiotistas*, merchants who speculated in loans to the government. The rest of the bourgeoisie was by and large not indigenous but foreign. After Mexico achieved independence, British merchants replaced the formerly dominant Spaniards. By the 1840s and 1850s, the Germans had begun to take over from them. They, in turn, were driven out of many commercial enterprises by French traders, mainly known as Barcelonettes for the town in southern France from which the majority came.

The Liberal movement drew more substantial support from large landowners. Some joined the Liberals because, like the German barons of the fifteenth and sixteenth century, they hoped to succeed to the large land holdings of the church. Others objected to the Conservatives' attempt to impose centralized control over them. Luis Terrazas is typical of this group, except for the fact that he was not born into wealth, but, having started out as a butcher, married into it. Terrazas's grievances against the Conservative regime were manifold. He was contemptuous of its inability to protect his home state of Chihuahua against marauding Indians. He was resentful of its refusal to admit him into its closely knit oligarchy. And he was covetous of the public lands controlled by the central government. Once he became Liberal governor of his native state he utilized his power both to enrich himself by acquiring huge tracts of public lands (and some church properties) and to carry out a popular policy of resisting, with far more energy than his predecessors, the increasingly ferocious attacks on the population of Chihuahua by Apache marauders.

Landowners, like Terrazas, viewed with keen suspicion another group from which the Liberals drew support, the middle class: local merchants, small entrepreneurs, *rancheros*, low-level government employees, and some radical intellectuals. The middle class had come to view the power held by the landowners as a major impediment to its own advancement. They encouraged the central government to tighten the reins on its regional barons by, for instance, exacting a fairer portion of its tax revenues from large estates.

Both wings of the party managed to maintain an uneasy truce and to co-operate in periods of war, but as soon as war subsided profound quarrels and conflicts broke out between them. Nevertheless, landowners and middle class were united in their opposition to the demands of a third group, the 'popular sector'. Its composition, still only incompletely known, was diffuse. It encompassed some peasants and an inchoate proletariat of textile workers, blacksmiths, shop clerks, and the like. Its aims were radical redistribution of property on a large scale. The Liberals had been very reluctant to mobilize this group in the course of the civil war. They remembered well what an uncontrollable force the peasants had become when Father Hidalgo in 1810, and one of the warring factions within the state's oligarchy during the caste wars in Yucatán in the late 1840s, had called on them to join ranks. In the war against the French, however, Juárez had thrown caution to the wind, and issued a general call to arms against the foreign invaders. And again, once organized, the popular movements did not show signs of subsiding quickly.

Juárez's political strategy

In the face of these deep rifts it seems at first surprising that Juárez managed to retain his leadership of the Mexican Liberal movement for more than five years. But in fact it was the divided nature of the Liberal movement that helped Juárez to survive. The two mainsprings of the movement – hacendados and middle classes – alternately attacked him for not being sufficiently responsive to its interests, but neither tried to unseat him because it knew that as long as he remained in power the other side would not prevail. Neither did the popular sector seek to overthrow him. Although acutely discontented with the Ley Lerdo which Juárez continued to implement, they venerated him as one of their own, a once poor Indian who had risen to govern his country and had never ceased proudly to acknowledge his origins.

Shortly after achieving victory over the French and the Conservatives, Juárez reacted to the increasing divisions and impotence of the Liberal movement by attempting to set up a strong centralized state which would have immeasurably increased his independence from his increasingly divided social and political constituency. His prestige then at its peak, he issued a call for new elections and, simultaneously, a referendum on a series of proposed amendments to the constitution. The first added a Senate to the already existing Chamber of Deputies and was intended to divide and dilute the power of Congress. The second gave the president the right to veto any bill subject to the ability of a two-thirds majority in Congress to override it. A third permitted members of his cabinet to answer congressional enquiries in writing rather than in person. A fourth deprived the permanent commission of parliament, a body that continued in session while parliament was in recess, of the right to call for a session of the full Congress at any time. The referendum was not, strictly speaking, over the adoption of these proposals but over the right of Congress to adopt them by simple majority vote rather than having to submit them for special approval by each of the state legislatures. For a brief period, the two main antagonistic wings of the Liberal party united in opposition to Juárez's measures, and as pressure against them mounted, the Mexican president was forced to withdraw the proposed amendments.

To remain in power Juárez now had to resort to greater concessions to the two social groups that had thwarted him. He gave Liberal hacendados virtually unbridled authority over their local strongholds. To win the support of the middle class Juárez expanded the size of the state bureaucracy, one of the favourite sources of employment of the middle class, and directed federal expenditures into areas of particular interest to it, such as improvement of public education, especially in the cities. In 1857 there were 2,424 public primary and secondary schools in Mexico. In 1874, two years after Juárez's death, a government census revealed that their number had increased to 8,103. Perhaps even more important for the middle classes was the fact that Juárez maintained (he probably had little choice in the matter) some democratic institutions. While the government did intervene in elections, these were more honest than they had previously been. Parliament, no longer an impotent body, housed a vocal opposition. The freedom of the press to criticize was nearly complete. Some of the country's best known intellectuals – Manuel de Zamacona, Ignacio Altamirano, Francisco Zarco – became increasingly outspoken in their attacks on the mistakes made by the Juárez government.

One segment of the Liberal middle class whose influence was on the rise in the latter years of the Juárez presidency were those Liberal army officers who continued in active service. There was a certain contradiction in this since both Juárez and the main ideologues of the Liberal party considered militarism one of the principal banes of Mexico. In the constitution of 1857 they had abrogated the judicial privileges of the military, and after the victory over Maximilian large parts of the Mexican army had been demobilized. Nevertheless, as the contradictions within Mexican society mounted and revolts were on the increase, the dependence of the government upon the army grew more and more, and officers were again able to exercise political, social and economic influence in the Mexican countryside.

In order to broaden support for his regime, Juárez also attempted to reach a compromise with some of his old antagonists. The ostensible losers in the ten years of war which had racked Mexico between 1857 and 1867 came off better than they or many contemporaries had expected. This was especially true of the Conservative politicians, landowners and bureaucrats. In 1870, three years after his victory, Juárez issued a broad amnesty for all those who had co-operated with Maximilian. Lands were returned to the landowners and Conservative bureaucrats could once again apply for positions in the government. The church on the whole fared worse than its allies. It never regained the lands and properties it lost and its economic supremacy as Mexico's most important source of credit ceased. It could no longer legally impose taxes on the population. The legal privileges of the clergy, the official supremacy of Catholicism, and the influence of the church in educational matters were never restored to their pre-1857 status. The reform laws continued to be the laws of the land. Nevertheless, in practical terms, the church began to recuperate rapidly from its losses. Contributions from wealthy church members flowed into its coffers and were surreptitiously invested once again in urban property. Juárez made no effort to curtail this renewed accumulation of wealth by the clergy, and the latter gave up its former intransigence towards the Liberals. This attitude may have been inspired by the overwhelming victory of the Liberals after many years of civil war, but it was also the realization of some church leaders that the loss of its lands had actually strengthened its position in the countryside by reducing the potential for conflict between the church and large segments of the rural population. Many peasants now saw the Liberal landowners as their enemy rather than the church. This attitude grew even stronger as church officials became more responsive than in previous years to peasants' complaints and demands.

Juárez had hoped that these conciliatory measures towards Mexico's upper and middle classes as well as towards segments of the army would prevent him from being toppled by a coup and would allow him to pacify the country. The Mexican president's hopes proved to be correct on the first count. Juárez remained in office until he died of natural causes in 1872. His hopes on the second count, however, proved to be illusory. In order to conciliate the country's elite, Juárez had sacrificed the interests of the peasantry. As a result, social unrest in the countryside reached unprecedented proportions during the period of the Restored Republic. The government was too weak to suppress this unrest, and the unrest weakened the Juárez administration even further. This encouraged other forces, ranging from nomadic tribes on the frontier to middle- and upper-class opponents of the regime, to take up arms and challenge the government. As a result the government was even less able to suppress unrest in the countryside. It was a vicious circle.

The causes of peasant unrest ranged from frustrated expectations to a real deterioration in peasant living conditions. The liberal government did nothing to meet the expectations of the peasants or even to protect the peasantry from a further erosion of its economic and social position. The end of the war sent droves of landless and unemployed war veterans into Mexico's countryside, adding to the already overflowing pool of landless and unemployed. The Ley Lerdo had ousted many from the communal lands they had once farmed, then distributed the property, usually unequally, amongst them, if it was not appropriated outright by hacendados or speculators.

The Liberal administration could not have prevented, even had it wanted to, the transfer of church lands from the clergy to large landowners instead of to the peasants. It only controlled a fraction of Mexico during the long years of war against the Conservatives and the French, and its armies needed revenues from the sale of church lands to finance the war. After victory the Liberals could have used both the estates of the defeated Conservatives and the vast and frequently empty public lands to set up a programme of land distribution and to create a class of Mexican farmers. Except for granting some public lands to a limited number of war veterans, however, the Juárez administration never seriously considered implementing such an option. Lands of Conservative hacendados were either returned to their former owners or at best given or sold to Liberal landowners. The Mexican government never attempted to do what the United States government did after the American civil war: diffuse the social tensions brought about by the war with a Homestead Act granting free public lands to settlers. Some of the government lands began to be granted or sold to Mexican hacendados while others were kept in reserve for a vast expected wave of foreign peasant immigrants who never arrived.

Nor did Juárez address another major source of peasant discontent, the unequal burden of taxation. The *alcabala*, internal customs, and the personal contribution – the equivalent of six to twelve days' wages for the typical hacienda labourer – exacted a disproportionately higher toll from the poor than the rich. A hacendado owning land worth 20,000 pesos paid the government the same tax as his employee who had no assets to speak of. The Liberals had originally advocated the elimination of the *alcabala*, not so much because of its disproportionate impact on the poor but because of its interference with free trade. The empty coffers of the treasury kept them from following this through. The hacendados, of course, would not hear of readjusting the tax burden. The only measure finally taken to afford relief to the most hard pressed of taxpayers was to waive the personal contribution for anyone earning less than 26 centavos a day.

Nor did Juárez make more than a feeble effort to relieve the worst excesses of debt peonage and, closely linked to it, the arbitrary power of the hacendado over his peons. In 1868 a Liberal congressman, Julio Zarate, asked that landowners be prohibited from setting up private jails, administering corporal punishment, or visiting the debts of parents on their children. Congress rejected the proposal, claiming that it lacked jurisdiction over the matter and that this was a matter exclusively for the local judiciary. Juárez favoured Zarate's proposal and tried to intervene, but the limited measures which he decreed restricting debt peonage were never implemented.

Peasant uprisings in the Juárez era

During the colonial era armed conflict in the countryside had been of three types, each specific to a certain region. First, there were local rebellions, generally confined to a single village and aimed chiefly at eliminating particular grievances with the colonial administration, rather than seeking to overthrow the colonial system *in toto*. This type of unrest was concentrated in the core regions of the country in central Mexico. Second, there were large-scale uprisings against the colonial system as a whole by groups which had only superficially assimilated Spanish civilization and the Christian religion, and which sought to restore what they considered to be the pre-hispanic social, economic, and religious order. These tended to occur mainly in southern Mexico. Finally, there were the resistance movements of as yet unconquered peoples to Spanish attempts to colonize them. These were confined almost exclusively to the northern frontier.

During the period of the Restored Republic revolts broke out in all three of these regions, but they tended to be more radical in character, larger in scope, longer in duration, and more violent than during the colonial period. One of the most radical eruptions to occur in central Mexico took place in 1868 close to the capital itself. The rebels were denounced as 'rabid socialists' in the Mexico City press, and they seem to have viewed themselves that way. They were strongly influenced by the socialist Plotino Rhodakanati, who saw in Jesus Christ the 'divine socialist of humanity' and 'saviour of the freedom of the world'. He set up a school in Chalco where his theories were propagated by two of his disciples. Their teachings in turn inspired one of their pupils, a peasant named Julio López, to issue a proclamation calling on the peasants of Chalco, Texcoco and other neighbouring towns to rise against local landowners. 'We want socialism', he wrote, 'we want to destroy the present vicious state of exploitation . . . We want land of our own to till in peace.'[2] López's men in fact succeeded in seizing some land around the towns of Chalco and Texcoco and immediately set upon dividing it up amongst themselves. Five months later federal troops routed the rebels: López was arrested and shot.

Socialist influence also manifested itself in states more remote from the capital, like Hidalgo. Two peasants, Francisco Islas and Manuel

---

[2] Quoted in Gaston García Cantu, *El socialismo en México* (Mexico, 1969), 173.

Domínguez, leading a contingent of several thousand men, managed to occupy the town of Tezontepec and the mining centre of Mineral del Monte. Their chief objective was the restoration of land they believed to have been misappropriated by local hacendados. 'Violence is our means of righting the wrongs done us', wrote Francisco Islas in a letter to the newspaper *La Libertad*. 'The government stands behind the hacendados, "society" stands behind them as well, and so do the journalists who are not ashamed to sell their conscience to the highest bidder. What else is there for us to do but fight?'[3] The rebels held out for two months, December 1869 and January 1870. When federal troops finally retook the cities many of them, including Islas and Domínguez themselves, made a getaway into the mountains of Hidalgo, and survived to lead another rebellion against the government several years later.

Peasant movements in southern Mexico continued to be what they had been throughout the colonial period, intensely messianic, intertwining social and religious ideas in one single millenarian vision. The most notable example is a story of a peasant girl, Augustina Gómez Chechep, who lived in the village of Tzarjalhemel among the Chamula Indians. She became the patron of a new religious cult which soon turned into a vehicle of social protest – against white domination. The Chamula uprising (12 June 1869 – 20 October 1870) was eventually quelled by federal troops with the minimum of bloodshed.

The Mayas were more successful. Following the caste wars of 1847–55 they managed to set up an independent state in southern Yucatán and until 1901 resisted numerous attempts by federal troops to re-establish Mexican sovereignty. Moreover, armed with weapons they purchased in neighbouring British Honduras, they frequently ventured out to raid adjacent Mexican territories with relative impunity.

Mexico's northern frontier continued to elude federal control, as it had during the colonial era. The Apache wars, which had gone on unabated since 1831, were reaching a new climax. Pushed further and further west by an onslaught of American settlers, the Indians preyed with increasing frequency on the more vulnerable Mexican frontier. Under the leadership of the legendary Cochise and his successors Victorio and Ju, they all but paralysed frontier life for a time. 'The land cannot be tilled because anyone working it would be murdered by the Apaches. There is no work in the cities because there is scarcity, everything is in decline and no one

---

[3] *Ibid.*, 60, 76.

invests', an editorial in a Sonoran paper stated as late as 1879.[4] Within the span of a few years Cochise's bands caused the death of 15,000 people. The weak and underpaid soldiers sent to fight on the northern frontier were no match for the Apaches.

Only gradually toward the end of Juárez's presidency did Mexico summon the strength to withstand the raiders. The hacendados began to arm and train their peons and to organize them into private militias. The government began to offer generous land grants to anyone willing to defend his property with his life. As a result, existing military colonies were strengthened and new ones were set up. Thus, while the independent peasantry was being decimated in the central and southern regions of the country, it was being strengthened and reinforced in the north. A new alliance between the northern hacendados and the peasants, directed against the Apaches, was developing; in the peasants' eyes, the hacendados acquired legitimacy by organizing the wars against the raiders. In Chihuahua, the leader of the militia who fought the Apache was Joaquín Terrazas, cousin of governor Luis Terrazas who himself helped to organize and finance the Indian wars. In spite of these peasant militias, however, the governments of the Restored Republic proved as incapable of controlling the northern frontier as they were of curbing other types of rebellion.

Organized social protest was only part of the social unrest that characterized the closing years of Juárez's reign. Banditry was rampant. Fugitive peons, dissatisfied peasants, demobilized soldiers scoured the countryside robbing stagecoaches, attacking large estates, and plundering convoys from mines loaded with gold and silver. By the end of 1868 the number of bandits operating on the outskirts of just one city, Guadalajara, in the state of Jalisco, was thought to number around a thousand. Juárez's newly organized police force, the Rurales, made only minimal headway against this most ubiquitous of hazards plaguing the Mexican countryside.

The first Díaz uprising

Juárez's declining popular support was a constant invitation to rivals to unseat him. Some of these men were former conservative *caudillos* whom Juárez had ousted from state government and had replaced with his own

---

[4] Quoted in Luís González y González, 'Los campesinos', in Daniel Cosío Villegas (ed.), *Historia moderna de México: La República Restaurada. Vida social* (Mexico, 1956), 186.

men. Some were former Liberal generals who felt that Juárez had not given them their due. They would issue a proclamation in the local newspaper they controlled, promising 'higher wages', 'juster laws', and a 'more democratic government', assemble a ragtag army of peons working on their haciendas and diverse malcontents, and seize control of a small city or municipality in the vicinity. They rarely got much further before federal troops dispersed them.

There was one exception. Perhaps the most popular figure to emerge from the war against the French was Juárez's erstwhile subordinate, General Porfirio Díaz. Díaz was born in 1830 in the state of Oaxaca, also Juárez's birthplace. He received his schooling in the same Catholic seminary as Juárez. At the age of seventeen, he enlisted in the army to fight the invading American forces. He came too late to see much fighting, but he more than made up for it in the war against the French. He advanced quickly to the position of brigadier general, and in 1862 for the first time gained renown when he was one of the Mexican commanders whose troops inflicted on the French their most humiliating defeat at the first battle of Puebla. Shortly thereafter he was captured by the French but managed to escape. Sometime later he presided over another major military victory at the battle of La Carbonera. He was 37 when the war ended and considered himself Juárez's equal. In 1867 he was a candidate for the presidency against Juárez. He ran again in 1871, and again lost. In 1871, in the Plan of La Noria, named after Díaz's hacienda, he declared that the elections had been fraudulent and called on the people to revolt. Although the plan also contained some vague allusions to the need for social reform it really had only one specific plank: that the presidency should be limited to a single term. To make the programme seem less self-serving than it was, Díaz promised not to run in the next election.

Díaz's call to arms met with some success, provoking an uprising that was more than local in nature. Díaz's brother, Félix, mobilized a formidable strike force in his home state of Oaxaca, consisting of state militia and even some federal troops stationed in the vicinity, and captured the state capital. A number of northern generals, foremost among them the governor of Nuevo León, Gerónimo Treviño, assembled an army of several thousand men and seized large parts of Nuevo León, Durango, Sinaloa, and Zacatecas. Porfirio Díaz himself headed a contingent of one thousand troops with which he aimed to take control of Mexico City. He reached the city's outskirts at Chalco and

Texcoco and reiterated his call for a general uprising, but it was not answered. Juárez sent troops of his own to deal with the rebels and Díaz withdrew precipitously. Meanwhile Félix Díaz's troops in Oaxaca fell into disarray when their leader was murdered by an unknown assassin, and shortly thereafter were routed by federal troops. Treviño's forces did not hold out much longer. Juárez had weathered the most serious uprising he faced since the defeat of Maximilian. But he did not live long to savour it.

The Juárez succession

On 17 July 1872 Juárez suffered a heart attack, and he died the following day. His successor under the constitution was the Chief Justice of the Supreme Court, Sebastián Lerdo de Tejada. Unlike Juárez, Lerdo was not of Indian descent but was Creole; his father was a Spanish merchant. Like Juárez he began his schooling in a Catholic seminary; he went as far in preparing for the priesthood as to take his minor vows. He then turned his back on the priesthood and began to study law. While still a law student he involved himself in Liberal politics and caught the eye of one of the leaders of the Liberal movement, Ignacio Comonfort. Through Comonfort's patronage he was appointed to the Supreme Court when he was only 27 years old. When Comonfort was deposed, Lerdo resigned his seat in the court and became rector of his alma mater, the Colegio de San Ildefonso in Mexico City. Comonfort's successor, Juárez, summoned Lerdo to join his cabinet, first as minister of justice, later as secretary of state. Lerdo became one of the major voices for an independent Mexico during the French invasion. After the war, Lerdo returned to the Supreme Court as its chief justice. In 1871, he challenged Juárez for the presidency, but lost. Unlike Díaz, he did not rebel but resumed his post on the Supreme Court. Although entitled to assume the presidency on Juárez's death by virtue of his position, Lerdo immediately called for new elections which took place in October 1872. This time he won.

The backbone of Juárez's rule during his waning years was the coalition of Liberal intellectuals, whose social liberalism was being replaced more and more by economic liberalism, and the Liberal landowners whose single claim to political or social liberalism – their opposition to the economic and political power of the church – had disappeared once the church lost its preeminence, together with the army, whose influence increased steadily. They now gave their support to Lerdo. In their eyes he seemed to possess the virtues but not the faults of Juárez. Like Juárez in his last years, Lerdo was a conservative on social issues. Unlike Juárez, however, he came from the Creole upper class and lacked his predecessor's occasional bursts of sympathy for the plight of the poorest segments of society.

In many respects Lerdo, implementing similar policies, was far more successful than Juárez had been in his last years. He was able to strengthen the role of the state considerably. In the first days of his presidency the Chamber of Deputies was more responsive to his desires than it had ever been to Juárez's. Moreover, Lerdo was allowed the creation of a Senate thus diluting considerably the power of the Chamber and enhancing correspondingly the pivotal role of the executive.

Lerdo also had, at first, greater success than his predecessor in pacifying the country. The roots of this pacification had been established under Juárez. Lerdo reaped the benefits of his predecessor's recent military victory over Porfirio Díaz. Díaz having been crushed, Lerdo was able to convey an impression of magnanimity by offering an amnesty to Díaz and his men. Díaz was in no position to refuse, however humiliating he found its terms. He was stripped of his military role and permanently exiled to his hacienda, La Noria. Díaz's defeat served to discourage would-be revolutionaries for a time and the first three and a half years of Lerdo's rule were significantly more peaceful than the years of Juárez's presidency.

Lerdo succeeded in extending the power of the federal government to regions that had eluded Juárez's control. He was able to destroy the one regional *caudillo* who had established a kind of peasant republic in Mexico: Manuel Lozada in the territory of Tepic. Lozada, referred to in the Mexican press as the 'Tiger of Arica' (Arica was the mountain range where he frequently had his headquarters), was in some ways characteristic of many *caudillos* who ruled their regions with an iron fist in nineteenth-century Mexico. The term tiger referred to his ferocity in crushing opponents. He was willing to make alliances with anyone who would recognize his power and had thrown his support to both Maximilian and Juárez. For a time he maintained close relationships with the trading house of Barron and Forbes, who in return for supporting Lozada wanted large-scale concessions in Tepic. In other respects, however, Lozada was atypical in comparison with most other *caudillos*.

The basis of his power was the Indian villages to whom he had returned the land that the haciendas had taken from them. Village representatives assumed increasing power within his movement which as a result was increasingly feared and resented by hacendados both in Tepic and in neighbouring states. In return for nominal subordination to his government, Juárez had allowed Lozada widespread control of his region. Lerdo, by contrast, sent federal troops to crush him. In 1873 Lozada was captured and shot, his Indians defeated and many of their lands granted to hacendados.

Mexico's economy developed more rapidly than in previous years, thus increasing Lerdo's prestige. This was due to the greater pacification of the country and to the fact that Lerdo was able to reap the fruits of several economic initiatives taken by his predecessor. In particular, he was able in 1873 to inaugurate Mexico's first important railway line connecting Mexico City to the port town of Veracruz, which greatly hastened Mexico's economic development.

In view of these successes it seems at first surprising that Lerdo was not able to repeat what his predecessor had done: continue in office for more than one term. In 1876 Díaz's attempt to topple Lerdo was far more successful than his previous attempt to topple Juárez. In part this was due to the fact that Lerdo lacked the prestige that the years of leadership during the war against the French had conferred upon Juárez. He was also unsuccessful in maintaining the upper-class consensus in his favour which he enjoyed when he assumed the presidency. Lerdo's standing with these forces had been undercut by a policy of proceeding with far more energy against the church than Juárez had during the years of the Restored Republic. After his victory over church-led forces in Mexico, his expropriation of church properties, and having implemented the reform laws, Juárez had tried to avoid any confrontation with the church and had turned a blind eye on violations by the clergy of some reform laws such as a new accumulation of wealth. Lerdo, by contrast, expropriated church properties, banished foreign-born Jesuits from Mexico and as a symbolic gesture had the reform laws newly incorporated into the constitution.

Lerdo's support among Mexico's upper classes was also undermined by his contradictory policies towards the building of railways. While the Mexican president had enthusiastically supported the construction of the Mexico–Veracruz railway and was just as enthusiastic in advocating an east–west connection between both coasts of Mexico, he was far more reticent about constructing a railway line linking Mexico to the United States. 'Between weakness and strength the desert', he is reported to have said. When pressure mounted on him to accede to the construction of a north–south railway, he tried to get a Mexican company to undertake the bulk of construction. When this company failed to obtain sufficient capital Lerdo finally granted a concession for building the major part of a trunk line to the United States to an American railway promoter, Edward Lee Plumb. As a result of these policies he alienated both the supporters and opponents of the construction of the Mexican–American railway line. Its supporters felt he had waited too long to grant an effective concession for the construction of this line, while its opponents feared that as the result of closer economic and communications links with the United States the latter would control and absorb Mexico. These opponents joined the traditional 'outs' who felt that the fall of an existing administration would give them access to power and government positions. In 1876 they joined Lerdo's strongest opponent, Porfirio Díaz.

THE FIRST DÍAZ ADMINISTRATION, 1876–80

The rising of Tuxtepec

After his forcible retirement to La Noria, Díaz appeared a crushed man, his daily activities ostensibly limited to planting crops and manufacturing chairs. In fact he remained active, soliciting the support of former military cronies for another assault on the presidency. Lerdo's political fortunes having sufficiently soured, Díaz struck in January 1876. At Díaz's request, the military commander of Oaxaca issued a proclamation, the Plan of Tuxtepec, calling for armed revolt against Lerdo and for Díaz's election to the presidency. Like the Plan of La Noria, it embraced the principle of non-re-election. But unlike the Plan of La Noria it extended the principle to the municipal level. The insistence upon municipal democracy was a very popular cause with both the middle and the lower classes of society, as well as with some hacendados whose power was being constantly eroded by the increasing authority of the governors, who were frequently also the state's most important landowners. It had a special appeal for the middle class, who had exercised a large measure of control not only in towns, where they were strongly represented, but even in many villages, which frequently chose as mayors and village administrators people who could read and write and were better off economically than most peasants. The demand for municipal autonomy seemed to have led some members of the peasantry to support Porfirio Díaz, although there is no evidence that he showed any strong interest in gaining their adherence.

At first Díaz's second revolt seemed to peter out even more quickly than his first. Lerdo's troops handily routed Oaxaca's makeshift militia. At Icamole, Lerdo's army defeated troops led by Díaz himself. Lerdo felt he was in a strong enough position to call for new elections, and he was re-elected. But Díaz's dissent was infectious. The new Chief Justice of the Supreme Court, José María Iglesias, constitutionally the next in line for the presidency, charged Lerdo with election fraud and refused to recognize the results. Instead he tried to assume the presidency himself. He gained the support of several governors, senators and deputies who had felt left out by the Lerdo administration. This division within the government infused Díaz's rebellion with new vitality. His troops engaged Lerdo's at Tecoac and inflicted a painful defeat. Under the combined pressure of Iglesias and Díaz, Lerdo resigned and fled the country. Díaz offered to recognize Iglesias as provisional president if he, in turn, would recognize him as the head of the new revolutionary army and promise to hold a new round of elections quickly. Iglesias, overestimating his strength, refused. When Díaz marched against him, Iglesias's troops simply disintegrated. In the spring of 1877, elections were held and Díaz became the new president.

The regime of Porfirio Díaz at first represented much less of a discontinuity with his predecessors than has frequently been assumed. It was a more militarily orientated regime than those of either Juárez or Lerdo, in the sense that a far greater part of the budget was allocated to the military. In order to maintain the loyalty of the army, Díaz placed his own troops as well as those who had fought for Lerdo and Iglesias on the payroll. Nevertheless, Díaz obviously felt that the army was too weak, too divided and too unreliable, to constitute the only or even the main power basis of his regime. He attempted to restore and even strengthen the upper- and middle-class coalition that had constituted the social and political basis of his predecessors' power. With respect to the upper classes, Díaz practised a policy of 'divide and rule'. He removed from power local caciques, loyal to his predecessors, such as Chihuahua governor Luis Terrazas, and put rivals of similar social origins in their place. Nevertheless, as long as they did not resist him, he allowed the men he had so removed to keep their property and to expand their economic influence. For many hacendados, loss of political power was more than offset by Díaz's policy of selling public lands, which gave them great opportunities for enrichment.

At first glance it would seem to have been more difficult for Díaz to gain middle-class support since the economic resources at his disposal had been drastically curtailed by the large amounts of money he had to pour into the reconstituted army. Since at this stage he was incapable of offering large economic rewards to the middle class, Díaz's most important option was to make political concessions. He had the newly elected Congress proclaim the principle of no re-election not only of the president but of the governors as well, which meant that the many 'outs' among the middle classes would have a better chance of gaining power once the terms of office of existing officials had run out. By strengthening municipal autonomy, Díaz gained some support among regional middle classes who had been largely ignored by both Juárez and Lerdo.

Díaz carried out no massive repression, imprisonment, or execution of his enemies. The existing civilian political groups were not banned but continued to exist and to participate in political life. National, regional and local elections continued to be held, and they were no more nor less honest than the ones which his predecessors had organized. The press continued to have a wide margin of freedom. The fact that the opposition to Díaz did not utilize their legal opportunities to combat him in the same way that the opponents of Juárez and Lerdo had done was largely due to the emergence of the first external threat to Mexico's sovereignty since Maximilian's defeat.

For ten years, from 1867 to 1877, Mexico had known a kind of respite from outside intervention which it had rarely experienced before and was rarely to have again. France's fatal experience had killed whatever colonial hopes Europe once nurtured for Mexico. Diplomatic relations with the one-time aggressors, France, Great Britain, and Spain, were not restored but none of these countries was inclined to risk another direct intervention in Mexico. Germany established diplomatic relations, and German merchants assumed some key positions in Mexico's foreign trade, but Germany at this time had no political ambitions in Mexico either.

Relations with the United States had been friendly during the time of the French intervention. Between 1867 and 1877 they began to cool considerably, setting the stage for the confrontations that followed. The sources of conflict were several. As American settlers continued their westward push, Indian tribes and cattle thieves often used the less densely settled and less well defended Mexican border as a sanctuary from which to launch raids into the United States. As a result authorities on both sides of the border were incessantly levelling accusations at each other for not proceeding with sufficient energy against the marauders. There was also the fact that the Mexican government, in order to attract settlers to this dangerous and poverty-stricken region, had established a ten-mile duty-free zone along the American border. Goods sold in the zone were cheaper than those in the adjacent Mexican or American territories. This led to widespread smuggling activities and caused acute discontent among American merchants. Finally, there was Díaz's stated opposition to the generous concessions Lerdo had finally granted American railway promoters. Díaz had publicly given expression to the fears, which he probably did not really share, of Mexican nationalists that the penetration of American railways into Mexico would be but a prelude to the country's wholesale annexation.

In general, during the nineteenth century, both the United States and the European countries recognized 'revolutionary' governments in Latin America once they proved themselves in control and able to stand by their international obligations. In the case of Mexico, the United States abandoned this principle. The Grant administration, in power when Díaz triumphed, refused to recognize Díaz unless he favourably resolved at least some of the controversies between the two countries. Díaz showed himself very amenable. One of his first administrative measures on entering the City of Mexico was to gather together a large number of bankers and merchants in the Mexican capital to raise money for the first instalment on payments which the Lerdo administration had promised to the United States as compensation for damages suffered by Americans in Mexico. The Hayes administration, which succeeded that of Grant, accepted the payment of $300,000, and Díaz took this to imply recognition. He was wrong: Hayes had no intention of recognizing Díaz. Hayes wanted more than such piecemeal concessions, he wanted a piece of Mexico.

One of Hayes's first acts in office was to grant General C. Ord, commander of the military districts along the Mexican border, permission to pursue marauders, Indian raiders, cattle rustlers, and whoever he felt had violated United States law, across the Mexican border without first seeking the Mexican government's consent. Díaz could not brook such a measure without seriously impairing Mexico's sovereignty and opening himself up to charges of having 'sold out' to the Americans. As soon as he was apprised of the Ord instructions, Díaz positioned along the border a large contingent of troops, led by Gerónimo Treviño, and gave orders to resist any American advance into Mexico with every means at their disposal. War between both countries seemed all but inevitable when suddenly both the Americans and the Mexicans began to show extreme circumspection. American troops crossed into Mexico only when they had made relatively sure that Mexican troops were not in the vicinity. Conversely, Mexican troops tried to avoid any meeting with American military units which would have forced them into a conflict. Instead of war there was merely an impasse.

What ultimately defused the crisis was Díaz's persistent wooing of American investors. Díaz sent one of his most capable and trusted advisers, Manuel de Zamacona, to the United States in order to interest American businessmen in Mexican investments. Zamacona enlisted the help of Matías Romero, for many years Juárez's ambassador to the United States, who edited a series of books and pamphlets describing the allegedly boundless opportunities which Mexico offered American investors. At the same time Díaz welcomed to Mexico vocal and influential groups of American promoters, such as Ulysses S. Grant, the former president, granted them valuable railway concessions, and promised them further subsidies. As a result, American investors, only a short time after clamouring vociferously for intervention, became enthusiastic adherents of the Díaz regime and began to pressure the Hayes administration to recognize his government. Moreover, as the prospect of another war, scarcely more than ten years after the last one, became a real possibility, domestic opposition to Hayes's policies mounted. Finally, in 1878 Hayes gave in and recognized Díaz, and in 1880 he withdrew the Ord instruction as well.

Elaboration of the Porfirian strategy

It is not easy to assess what influence Díaz's conflicts with the Americans in 1877 and 1878 had in shaping his regime. They seem to have strongly inspired the three major policies followed by Díaz after 1878, by his temporary successor Manuel González (1880–4) and by Díaz again after 1884. First, Americans as well as other foreign investors and promoters were granted concessions of every kind on extremely generous terms.

Secondly, the Mexican government also attempted to do everything in its power to renew and then to strengthen its links to Europe to balance American influence. Thirdly, political stability was to be maintained at any price. Until about 1900, the application of these policies strengthened the Mexican state. From 1900 to 1910 they laid the basis for one of the most profound social upheavals to take place in twentieth-century Latin America: the Mexican Revolution.

During what remained of his first term in office, internal stability was Díaz's first priority. In order to achieve it, Díaz carried out a complex policy of concessions and repression. During his first term, apart from maintaining many of the political liberties that had existed under Juárez, Díaz made another important political concession: the decision to keep his word and not to run for a second term. This satisfied the 'outs' within both the elite and the middle classes, who now felt that they had a chance of participating in the next administration and thus saw no need to stage the 'traditional' revolution. Where necessary Díaz was of course ready and willing to use brute force to keep dissenters in check. When the governor of Veracruz, Mier y Terán, reported that a number of prominent citizens were plotting against him, Díaz responded with a laconic telegram: *Mátalos en caliente* – kill them in cold blood. He was no less ruthless in dealing with peasants in Hidalgo, Puebla and San Luis Potosí who occupied some neighbouring haciendas thinking that Díaz would support them in their revolutionary endeavour. Díaz in fact opened negotiations with several such groups, and promised to examine their grievances, if they would lay down their arms. Once disarmed, he ordered them shot.

Díaz's domestic policies, which held out the promise of internal stability as well as extremely generous government subsidies, led American promoters to sign contracts for the building of two major railway lines linking the United States to Mexico. Mexico's political elite came to view railway construction as the only means of safeguarding the country's political independence from possible United States military aggression. Díaz clearly hoped that American promoters as well as financiers and politicians would have too much at stake to run the risk of another Mexican–American war, which might finally ruin Mexico. His opponents, however, insisted that massive foreign investments in the long run increased rather than decreased the risks of foreign intervention. If the Mexican government proved incapable of maintaining the type of stability these investors wanted, they would then constitute an extremely powerful lobby in favour of intervention in Mexico.

Díaz also succeeded in the last years of his first term in re-establishing diplomatic relations with France. Such a step was anything but easy, in view of Napoleon's intervention in Mexico. There were strong pressures in Mexico demanding that, in order for relations to be resumed between the two countries, the French should not only give up all claims against Mexico but pay a large indemnity as well. At the same time the Mexican government had repeatedly stated that relations with France could only be re-established if the initiative came from the French. The fall of Napoleon in 1870 and the proclamation of the French Republic had created a new and far more favourable situation. It nevertheless took ten years for both countries officially to exchange ambassadors. This finally happened in 1880 when the French renounced all claims against Mexico and the Mexican government gave up the idea of obtaining reparations from France. By re-establishing relations with France, Díaz sought to create an economic counterweight both to the United States and to other European powers. French capital and French bankers played a decisive role in the establishment of the Mexican National Bank and in later years France became one of the main sources of loans to Mexico.

During and after the Porfirian era, France was to become more than just 'another' European country in the eyes of Mexico's elite. French fashion, culture and architecture were models they sought to imitate. August Comte's positivism strongly influenced the ideology of the regime though it was combined with Herbert Spencer's social Darwinism which soon overshadowed it. Absentee landlords spent part of their time in Paris, and members of the elite sent their children to French schools. Mexico's army was supplied with French artillery, and some of its most distinguished officers studied French military techniques. When Díaz was finally driven from power in 1911, it was to France that he retired.

THE GONZÁLEZ INTERREGNUM, 1880–4

In keeping with his promise, Díaz was not a candidate in the 1880 presidential election; instead, his hand-picked successor, General Manuel González, ran in his place. Many a cynic marvelled at the ingenuity of Díaz's choice. González was widely regarded as the most corrupt and least able of Díaz's protégés. He was likely to be a weak rival should Díaz decide to run for another term in 1884.

González distinguished himself by his corruption, although rumours that he removed all the furniture from the National Palace when he left office turned out to have been exaggerated. González was far less inept than he was frequently made out to be and he appointed an able cabinet of Porfiristas, but he was no Porfirio Díaz. During his term of office, he attempted to implement his predecessors' three basic policies: concessions to foreign and especially US interests, rapprochment with Europe, and maintenance of internal stability at any price. On the whole, however, he was far less able than Díaz had been to prevent profound contradictions from emerging as a result of his efforts to apply all three of these strategies simultaneously.

Seeking to maintain and heighten the interest of foreign investors, especially American railway companies in Mexico, González bolstered the special concessions which Díaz had granted to them with new ones. At González's behest, the Mexican Congress passed a new law to encourage further the transfer of public lands to private hands. The law allowed González to entrust private companies with the task of surveying the public lands and to compensate them with one-third of the land they determined to be 'public'. Not surprisingly the companies rode roughshod over the rights of small landowners, many of whom had farmed these lands for generations but who were unable to produce formal titles. The benefits to both foreign and domestic bidders were several. Much public land could now be acquired that had not been for sale before. Much private land, reclassified as 'public', could now be acquired in one large bid rather than through piecemeal negotiations with a multitude of small plot owners.

An even greater concession to foreign investors was the Mexican government's decision to revoke the old Spanish mining code which had stipulated that a landowner did not also own the minerals beneath his property. This had meant that mining rights had to be acquired separately from surface land so that the state was in possession of a far greater amount of the country's wealth. The new law of 1884 put an end to this principle and proved to be a bonanza both to Mexican landowners and to foreign investors.

But the most powerful of the foreign investment lobbies in Mexico, the American, wanted still more. González's problem was that catering to American demands meant risking a deterioration of his newly restored relations with Europe. In 1882 the United States government proposed to Mexico a special reciprocity arrangement whereby import tariffs on certain goods from each of the two countries would be lifted. The United States hinted that further railway construction in Mexico would be unprofitable and would stop unless such a treaty were signed. González was less than enthusiastic. The treaty not only would fly in the face of the sought-after rapprochment with Europe, but would deprive an already pinched treasury of much-needed tax revenues. Yielding to American pressure, the Mexican Congress in 1883 nevertheless approved the treaty. But several months later it turned around and approved another treaty granting Germany most-favoured-nation status, in effect bestowing the same tariff reductions on Germany and voiding many of the unilateral advantages the United States had gained through its treaty. The United States ambassador protested vehemently. The German minister in Mexico bluntly warned González that not standing by its treaty with Germany would jeopardize Mexico's relations with all of Europe. González narrowly escaped a final showdown: American farmers, fearful of Mexican competition in agricultural goods, pressured the United States Senate into rejecting the treaty.

On other occasions the pursuit of better relations with Europe came into conflict with the need for internal stability. After long and complicated negotiations, González was able to persuade Great Britain to reopen diplomatic relations with Mexico. In return González recognized a debt of £15.4 million to British bondholders contracted by preceding Conservative governments. This agreement was announced in 1884, in the midst of an acute financial crisis. It was denounced in Congress. Rioters took to the streets and peace was reached only after some resounding sabre rattling and several pounds of lead had been fired into densely packed crowds.

The González administration has gone down in history as one of Mexico's most corrupt governments. Its reputation is probably deserved, although in the public eye González's negative image was in part the result of the economic crisis that gripped Mexico in 1884 and a conscious effort on the part of Porfirio Díaz to discredit his successor. As a result of this image, attention has been deflected from the profound transformation that occurred in Mexico between 1880 and 1884. The legal changes that have been outlined above only constitute part of the picture. The first railway line between Mexico and the United States was inaugurated in 1884. US investments in Mexico were increasing at a breathtaking pace. For the first time since Maximilian's defeat Mexico had diplomatic relations with all major European countries. Railway construction and the final defeat of the Apaches, which occurred in the years between 1880 and 1884, opened up vast new expanses of Mexico's northern frontier, much of which had been hitherto inaccessible. Then under Porfirio Díaz, who was elected president again in 1884 and remained president until 1911, Mexico underwent its most profound economic, political and social transformation since the advent of independence in 1821.

THE DÍAZ REGIME, 1884–1900

Between 1877 and 1900 Mexico's population increased from nearly ten million to more than fifteen million. No recent war had checked the increase. A modest improvement in the standard of living had helped it along. The periodic droughts and famines that once penetrated the economic life of many regions ceased to have the devastating impact they once did: now there were railways to bring food to starving villagers and to carry the excess labour force to regions where there was greater demand for it. Medical care by contrast improved only marginally. Although the number of doctors rose from 2,282 in 1895 to 3,021 in 1900, they were concentrated in the cities. Life expectancy in Mexico continued to lag far behind Western Europe and the United States.

The population expansion was quite uneven. Previously sparsely populated frontier states as well as urban areas gained most heavily. Between 1877 and 1910 the population of the border states of Sonora, Chihuahua, Coahuila, Nuevo León and Tamaulipas rose by 227 per cent. Mexico City, Guadalajara, Monterrey and Torreón grew even more markedly. These trends were essentially due to an increase of the native population. In spite of the efforts and hopes of the Díaz administration, immigration continued to be minimal and consisted mainly of upper- and middle-class merchants, investors and technicians. Salaries in industry were far too low to attract European workers except for a few skilled mechanics who were paid very high wages. European farm workers would not accept the low wages paid by Mexican hacendados and as long as the United States was still open to immigration they saw no reason to go south of the border.

Economic development under Díaz

Between 1884 and 1900 Mexico experienced rapid economic growth. The flood of foreign investments – almost $1,200 million worth – helped gross national product to rise at an annual rate of 8 per cent. It was a rate of growth unprecedented in Mexico's history as an independent state. It also produced unprecedented disparities: between agricultural enterprises outfitted with the most modern technology and others where work was often carried out in the most primitive ways; between the development of light and heavy industry; between foreign and domestic control of the economy; and between the evolution of different regions.

Economic progress was most pronounced in the export-orientated sectors of the economy. Mining registered the most rapid growth. Until the railways were built mining in Mexico had been confined to precious metals, mainly silver and some gold. Transportation by mule was too expensive for anything else. Virtually non-existent when Díaz first came to power, the railway system comprised 14,000 kilometres of track by the turn of the century, and as a result the extraction of copper, zinc and lead as well as silver became profitable. Silver production rose from 607,037 kilograms in 1877–8 to 1,816,605 kilos in 1900–1 (and 2,305,094 kilos in 1910–11). The production of lead began with 38,860 tons in 1891–2 and rose to 79,011 tons in 1900–1 (and 120,525 tons in 1910–11). The production of copper increased from 6,483 tons in 1891–2 to 28,208 tons in 1900–1 (and 52,116 tons in 1910–11). The cultivation of agricultural cash crops also grew by leaps and bounds. The most spectacular example was henequén (sisal), the production of which rose from 11,383 tons in 1877 to 78,787 tons in 1900 (and to 128,849 tons by 1910). The output of rubber, guayule (a rubber substitute), coffee, and cochineal also increased dramatically. Some export-orientated industry also began to gain a foothold in Mexico. In 1891 the United States passed the McKinley tariff which imposed high customs fees on imported unprocessed ores. Tariffs for processed ores were much lower and as a result the largest United States companies, above all the Guggenheim-controlled American Smelting and Refining Company, set up ore smelters in Mexico.

Economic progress was rapid until the turn of the century for domestically orientated light industry. Textile manufacturing flourished. When the value of silver, on which Mexican currency was based, began to fall in the 1880s, textile imports became too expensive, and the French merchants who had carried on that trade switched to manufacturing textiles in Mexico itself. Huge plants, like that of Río Blanco, sprang up in the regions of Orizaba and Puebla. Light industrial plants for the production of paper, glass, shoes, beer and food processing were also erected. Heavy industry lagged far behind and only emerged after the turn of the century. In 1902 the Compañía Fundidora de Fierro y Acero built a steel plant in Monterrey which by 1910 was turning out 72,000 tons annually.

After 1900 industrial development greatly slowed down. In part this was due to a fall in the living standard after the turn of the century so that the market for industrial goods expanded in a much more limited way than before. Industrial growth was also limited as a result of government policies. The Díaz administration did not go out of its way to lend a helping hand to struggling domestic producers. The New Industries Act of 1881 granted some generous tax exemptions to budding local industries, and accorded some selective tariff protection to certain local industries such as textiles. But it never afforded heavy industries the kind of special protection common in European countries, such as forcing American railway promoters to buy the material they used from Mexican producers. Nor was heavy industry accorded preferential access to credit.

Unlike railways, industry never received subsidies. The Díaz government had no plans for developing particular industries, no programme to stimulate the import of technology, no policies for protecting infant industries. Above all its investments in what could be called human capital were extremely limited. While expenditures for education did increase during the Porfiriato the results were very limited in scope. Between 1895 and 1910 the percentage of the population which could read and write increased from 14.39 to 19.79 per cent. Public vocational education destined to train skilled workers was insignificant. From 1900 to 1907 enrolment in vocational schools increased from 720 to 1,062.

During the Porfiriato, significant discrepancies emerged in the agricultural sector, not so much in the production of goods (both export crops and food staples production increased, though at different rates) as in the level of technical modernization. While a kind of technological revolution took place on plantations producing such cash crops as henequén and sugar, wheat- and corn-producing haciendas were still utilizing old and very traditional techniques. The failure of these landowners to modernize has often been attributed to psychological rather than economic causes. Landowners, it is asserted, had an essentially feudal mentality, valuing land as a status symbol, not an economic resource. They were too preoccupied hobnobbing with the *haute couture* of Paris, visiting the spas of Gstaad (and Garmisch Partenkirchen), and gambling in Monte Carlo to give serious attention to the affairs of their estates. But that does not explain why the people to whom they had entrusted their estates in the meantime would not themselves undertake whatever seemed most likely to return a profit.

Technological advances that resulted in modernizing and cheapening agricultural production in the United States remained unimportant in a country with as cheap a labour supply as Mexico's. In 1911 one of Mexico's leading agricultural experts, Lauro Viadas, compared the cost of an American farmer using modern agricultural implements and a Mexican hacendado working with more primitive technology but employing cheap labour. Production of a similar amount of wheat cost the American farmer 4.95 pesos and the Mexican hacendado 4.50 pesos.

Apart from the disparity between export and domestically orientated production, another significant disparity emerged as a result of Mexico's rapid economic growth: the disparity between foreign and domestic control of the economy. With the exception of agriculture, the most significant branches of the economy were in the hands of foreign capital. Until the end of the nineteenth century, the Díaz government made no effort whatsoever to encourage either Mexican control of some branches of the economy or even to further Mexican participation.

While the Díaz administration was relatively indifferent to Mexican ownership and participation in the new enterprises springing up in the country, the same cannot be said with regard to its attitude towards American versus European control of important segments of the economy. The Díaz government did everything in its power to further European investments without restricting those of the United States. Until the end of the nineteenth century, loans were placed only in Europe and banking concessions were granted exclusively to European bankers. Public works projects, such as port installations in Veracruz or drainage works in the valley of Mexico, were entrusted to British enterprises, above all those owned and controlled by a young but highly experienced British promoter and politician, Sir Weetman Pearson.

On the whole, however, these policies of the Mexican government, while substantially contributing to European economic penetration into Mexico, did not lead to any significant amount of competition or conflict between the Europeans and the United States until the end of the nineteenth century. The United States was still mainly a debtor and not a creditor nation and the largest American banks were still primarily interested in investments within the United States, so that they did not resent European investment in Mexico or the European inroads into the

Mexican financial system. Even in those fields where Europeans (especially the British) and Americans shared similar interests (railways and mines), a kind of division of labour between them had developed, with the British concentrating essentially on central and southern Mexico while American investments tended to be directed above all into the north of the country.

The sharpest and most conflictive rivalry for economic influence in Mexico until the end of the nineteenth century involved not the United States and Britain but two other powers, France and Germany, whose interests in Mexico were on the whole far smaller. The first area of conflict between them was that of Mexico's foreign trade which, until the 1870s, had to a large extent been controlled by German merchants from the Hanseatic cities of Hamburg, Bremen, and Lübeck. By the 1870s French merchants from Barcelonette (the main street of the town is still called Avenue Porfirio Díaz today) displaced their German rivals. This proved to be just the first battle in a long and intense Franco-German struggle in Mexico. A few years later, Franco-German competition emerged at a higher level. In 1888 the Mexican government signed its first important loan agreement with a foreign bank since the fall of Maximilian's government. It negotiated with the German banking house of Bleichroeder, which also handled the personal finances of German Chancellor Bismarck. The Germans not only secured extremely advantageous interest rates, but also forced the Mexican government to sign a secret treaty practically granting the firm a monopoly over the country's external finances. The Mexican government would not have the right to take out any loans without making a prior offer to the house of Bleichroeder. Mexico accepted the onerous German terms, but only six years later, with French help, managed to break Bleichroeder's contract and his hold over Mexican finances.

In yet another field the French won even more significant victories over their German rivals. In all of Latin America, German and French arms manufacturers were vying for the lucrative Latin American arms market. The most important German company in this field was the house of Krupp. While in most of Latin America Krupp was extremely successful, in Mexico, in spite of intense efforts to sell artillery to the country's army, he lost out to his French rivals from Saint Chamond.

Until the end of the nineteenth century, these conflicts were not critical for the Mexican government. It was only in the twentieth century that another type of conflict emerged involving the two major powers interested in Mexico, the United States and Great Britain, which in contrast with the Franco-German rivalry was to have important and lasting consequences for Mexico.

Regional disparities in Mexico's development

Another deep-seated discrepancy that Porfirian development produced was an increasing regional disparity in Mexico between the centre, the south and the north of the country. This disparity was not new. In fact, it went back all the way to the origins of civilization in that region. Long before the European conquest, intensive agriculture, large cities, a highly stratified society, and a complex culture had developed in the central and southern part of present-day Mexico, while the northern region had been inhabited by nomadic hunters and gatherers and some primitive agriculturalists. The coming of the Spaniards brought new differences to these regions. The south-east to a very large degree became marginal in the colonial economy of New Spain, because no mines were found there. The north on the other hand became an essential part of colonial New Spain. It was there that some of the richest mines were discovered after the conquest of Mexico. Unfortunately for the Spaniards, they were not capable of populating this region and constant and relentless attacks by nomadic Indians, above all by the Apaches in the eighteenth century, which continued into the period of Independence, seriously inhibited the economic development of this area. During the Porfirian era, both the north and the south-east of Mexico underwent a tremendous economic boom and both were absorbed into the world market.

Mexico's south-east began to assume traits that were characteristic of much of central America and the Caribbean. The economies of most south-eastern states were geared to one or two export crops with very little agricultural diversification and even less industry. The Peninsula of Yucatán is perhaps the most outstanding example of such a development. Sisal, or henequén as it was called in Mexico, had always been an important crop in Yucatán. As long as it was used mainly for making rope and cordage, its use and thus its market were limited. Demand for henequén rose dramatically when it began to be used by the McCormick reaper in the 1880s and an export boom took place in Yucatán. The haciendas where henequén was produced, as well as the railway system that transported it from Yucatán's interior to the coast, were in the hands of Mexican owners. The buyers and users of the fibre, the largest of which was the American Peabody Company, competed for henequén, but by the end of the century most of these companies had been fused into one large conglomerate: the Chicago-based International Harvester Corporation. It soon came to dominate the market and in co-operation with local merchant firms attempted to manipulate the price of henequén to its advantage.

In contrast to the Yucatán situation, where practically all the estates were Mexican-owned, conditions in other south-eastern states, especially in Chiapas and Tabasco, were somewhat different. Such staples as rubber and to a lesser degree coffee were produced directly by foreign investors. What these states had in common with Yucatán was their one- or two-crop economies and their complete dependence upon world market conditions.

Like the south-eastern periphery, the northern periphery of Mexico also underwent an extremely rapid economic development, and it too was largely orientated towards the world market. Nevertheless, the resemblance between the two regions stops at this point. In contrast to the south-east, the north had a much more diversified economy. It exported a large variety of minerals; copper, tin, and silver as well as commodities such as chick peas, cattle and lumber. A much more important segment of the northern economy, in contrast to that of the south-east, was geared toward production for the domestic market. This was above all the case for new large and highly productive irrigated cotton fields in the Laguna region in the states of Coahuila and Durango. In relation to the rest of the economy, industrial development was more important in the north than in most other parts of Mexico. A steel industry developed in the city of Monterrey and smelters for minerals, both Mexican and American owned, were constructed in the north. On a number of large estates, food-processing industries had sprung up, so that in many respects the northern economy was the most balanced in the country. Foreign investment, however, was far more important and preponderant there than in the south-east. Nevertheless, this was also one of the regions of the country where Mexican capital played an important, though generally subordinate, role in the development of the new industries (except mining) and cash crops during the Porfirian period.

It was in large parts of central Mexico where, in overall terms, the economy underwent the least changes. This was above all the case for the large corn- and wheat-producing estates. This very slow development constituted a stark contrast to a very rapid industrial expansion in the valley of Mexico and its surroundings as well as to new industrial centres in the states of Puebla and Veracruz.

In the eyes of most Porfirian intellectuals, these profound transformations of the economy created the basis for the evolution of Mexico into a modern, independent state on the model of Western Europe or the United States. What really emerged, however, was a country that depended to an unprecedented degree on foreign interests. This dependence took two different but complementary forms. On the one hand, its clearest manifestation was foreign predominance or ownership of important, non-agricultural sectors of the Mexican economy: banking, mining, industry and transportation. On the other hand, Mexico had become a classic example of an underdeveloped country producing raw materials that depended on markets in the industrialized north Atlantic.

The political transformation of Mexico

In the years after 1884 the Díaz regime became the first effective and long-lasting dictatorship to emerge in Mexico since the advent of Independence. During his second term in office Díaz effectively prevented the election of any opponent to the Mexican Congress. By 1888 it had for all practical purposes become a rubber stamp institution. Every candidate had to receive the prior approval of Díaz to be either elected or re-elected. The now subservient Congress approved amendments to the constitution which made it possible for Díaz to 'accede' to the wishes of the population and have himself re-elected in 1888, 1892 (in that year the constitution was changed so as to extend the presidential terms to six years), 1898, 1904 and 1910. Mexico's previously combative opposition press, where criticism of the government was frequently combined with literary brilliance, was largely muzzled and brought under control although opposition at times flared up in small newspapers.

The consolidation of the dictatorship was closely tied to two processes: the achievement of internal stability (the Pax Porfiriana) and the emergence of an effective and powerful Mexican state. These developments in turn were inextricably linked to the economic development of the country.

The 'pacification' of the country was a multi-faceted and complex process which until 1900 was largely (though not entirely) successful and constituted the proudest of achievements for Porfirian ideologists. The conflicts which had constantly erupted in Mexico before the Díaz period had many layers: military coups, *caudillo* uprisings, banditry in the countryside, attacks by nomadic Indians and revolts by peasants and frontier Indian tribes. By the end of the nineteenth century, only two forms of violence were still endemic in Mexico: revolts by frontier Indian groups, and revolts by scattered peasant communities, mainly in the north. All other types of violence had either completely disappeared or had greatly subsided.

This reduction in the level of violence was closely linked to the formation of the Mexican state. And the precondition for the development of the Porfirian state was a constant increase of its revenues. Díaz did not want to use the means by which previous governments had attempted to increase their income (forced loans or higher taxes) since such methods contributed to driving away foreign investors and antagonizing the country's domestic oligarchy. Mexico's revenues under Díaz mainly came from the limited taxes that foreign enterprises paid, the relatively large customs duties levied on goods entering the country, and taxes on precious metals. All of these revenues depended on increasing the level of foreign investments and on improving Mexico's international credit rating which would allow it to secure more loans on better terms. Apart from luring foreign investors into the country, Díaz's main means of increasing revenue was to streamline the financial administration of the country and to modernize it. This process had begun under Juárez but the most effective modernizer proved to be one of the country's most capable financiers, José Yves Limantour, whom Díaz appointed as finance minister in May 1893. By 1896, for the first time in Mexican history, Limantour had balanced the budget. This, in turn, tremendously increased Mexico's credit rating and international loans were not only easier to come by but could now be secured by the Díaz regime at much more advantageous interest rates than ever before.

With such solid financial backing Díaz was in a good position to tighten the reins on the more mutinous and independent-minded groups within the country. One group were the regional caciques who ruled their provinces like feudal fiefdoms. Díaz's first move was to replace many of the most powerful men left over from another era, like Luis Terrazas in Chihuahua, and Ignacio Pesqueira in Sonora, with men loyal to him. There was nothing very novel in this strategy. Virtually all of Díaz's predecessors had done the same when they could. Unfortunately for the government, this had in the past often proved a very temporary remedy. Once firmly in power, the newly installed caciques tended to seek for themselves the same kind of autonomy their predecessors had enjoyed. Moreover, their demoted predecessors usually lingered on in the background, waiting for an opportunity to overthrow the regime that had unseated them. As a result political stability remained precarious and fighting between rival caciques or even conflict between the newly appointed *caudillos* and the federal government were frequent. Under Díaz, the remedy worked much better. The newly constructed railways gave Díaz's army ready access to the provinces and helped to keep potential rebels in check.

Perhaps more important than this was the fact that Díaz encouraged or at least allowed both the caciques in power and those who had been removed from their positions to enrich themselves by acting as intermediaries for foreign investors who wished to settle in these regions or to acquire property there. In this way Díaz gave the members of the local oligarchy, both the 'ins' and the 'outs', a powerful stake in the stability of their region. Any uprising, any local turbulence, might easily frighten potential investors and thus close an important avenue of revenue to the members of the local oligarchy.

There were two other ways in which Díaz attempted to counteract possible uprisings by local strong men. One was to appoint military commanders without any roots in the region they commanded to oversee the local civilian officials. The other was to upgrade the office of *jefe político*, the district administrators, who before the Díaz regime had been officials with limited power. They now commanded the police and auxiliary armed forces in their districts, named district and municipal officials, paved the way for foreign investors and frequently owed their primary loyalty not to the governors to whom they were directly subordinated but to the central government.

Díaz applied a similar tactic of repression combined with co-option and other inducements to a second group which for a long time had opposed a strong central government. This was the traditional middle-class opposition, which operated mainly in the capital city of Mexico. Traditionally, these groups played an important role in the Mexican Congress and edited the most important opposition newspapers. Díaz prevented the election of opponents to the Mexican Congress and continued a policy implemented during the González administration of outlawing all opposition newspapers. The opposition of the middle classes to these repressive measures, however, was muted, because at the same time Díaz was giving thousands of their members new opportunities for economic and social advancement. The number of positions in the state bureaucracy between 1884 and 1900 greatly increased. At the same time, in those states where Díaz had dismissed the local caciques, new positions opened up for ambitious men. The dismissal of local strong men rarely meant their complete elimination in political terms. Luis Terrazas, the strong man of Chihuahua, remained a potent force in local politics and set up a powerful political organization, which Díaz was forced to tolerate and which opposed the existing structure of political power in the state. As a result, a kind of two-party system emerged in Chihuahua and a number of other states at a time when in Mexico City the remnants of democracy were being more and more eroded. This system in turn gave the regional middle classes increased political leverage as both parties competed for their support.

These 'parties' were only regional in nature and far more similar to extended family groups or patron–client coalitions than to the political parties which were developing in Europe during this period. Not only did Díaz never allow real opposition parties to be formed, he was also just as opposed to a government political party. In 1891 some of his principal intellectual and upper-class supporters attempted to cement the Porfirian regime by calling for the formation of a Liberal party based on the 'scientific' principles of positivism. (As a result these men came to be known in Mexico as *científicos*.) The aims of this proposal were at one and the same time to broaden the basis of the regime in order to strengthen it and to impose some kind of restraint upon Díaz himself. At the same time the creation of a party would ensure some kind of orderly succession and prevent what a large part of the Mexican elite most feared: the resurgence of turmoil and conflict in the country were Díaz to die or be incapable of completing his term in office.

Díaz, however, rejected the formation of a political party; he preferred to continue a tactic he had successfully begun to apply after assuming office in 1876, which was to play off different cliques within Mexico's elite against each other. One of these cliques was led by Manuel Romero Rubio, who had been a minister in the government of Lerdo and who later joined Díaz and became his minister of the interior in 1884. Romero Rubio was in many respects the architect of the Porfirian state. He it was who transformed the institution of the *jefe político* and who controlled and manipulated the country's governors. His clique consisted mainly of civilians: financiers, landowners, technocrats, bureaucrats, and so on. After his death in 1895 his most successful and intelligent pupil José Yves Limantour, finance minister from 1893, became the acknowledged leader of this clique. Its main competitor was another clique led by military men. Former president Manuel González was its main spokesman in the first years after Díaz reassumed power, while one of Díaz's closest confidants, Bernardo Reyes, assumed this function in later years. It was composed of military cronies of Díaz, traditional regional strong men and some bureaucrats, and was sharply critical of the increasing power and influence of the *científicos*.

Díaz applied methods of repression combined with inducements similar to those he utilized to pacify regional strong men towards a third force, which throughout the nineteenth century had been a constant threat to any central government in the country: the army. On the one hand, Díaz augmented the military budget (in absolute though not in relative terms) and bought modern arms in Europe, installed many army leaders in important political offices, and allowed them to pad the payroll. He also set up a modern military academy where he attempted to form an elite officers' corps. At the same time, however, Díaz weakened the influence of the army by establishing other para-military forces which were frequently of a better calibre than the army. Much of the internal repression was carried out by auxiliary troops not directly subordinated to the army. One of the most important such forces were the national Rurales, a professional police corps which had existed before Díaz but whose influence and size Díaz greatly reinforced. The soldiers in the army were forcibly inducted into the military and badly paid, so they frequently had only a limited sense of loyalty to their institution. The Rurales, on the other hand, were better paid and better treated. To a lesser degree the same was true of the state Rurales, armed units directly subordinated to the individual state administrations, but with ultimate authority over them retained by the federal government. At the same time, Díaz enlisted into police units some of the most notable bandits, thus turning their energy and talents to his advantage. But it was not Díaz and the central state alone which played a decisive role in putting an end to banditry. Local strong men who had frequently been in league with the outlaws, or at least had turned a blind eye to their depredations as long as their own property was not affected, now discovered that these same bandits might stop the flow of foreign investments into their districts and thus kill the goose that laid the golden egg. Their active help to the government was frequently of decisive importance.

Díaz's policy of repression, conciliation and co-option of all the upper- and middle-class forces which had been the source of uprisings and instability in the early nineteenth century extended to yet another force which for a time had constituted one of the main threats to every liberal government: the Catholic church. Díaz did not pursue Lerdo's anti-clerical policies. While the Díaz government never abolished the legal restrictions which the reform laws placed on the church and did not restore its former properties, in practice a policy reversal was taking place. In many surreptitious ways, which nevertheless were not difficult to detect, the church was accumulating new wealth from investments and from the donations of the faithful. The government made no attempt to restrict this process. It allowed more than twenty-three newspapers which were closely linked to the church to be published, and church-inspired and organized schools multiplied all over Mexico. Díaz's marriage to Carmen Romero Rubio, a devout Catholic who was on the best of terms with the church hierarchy, further underlined the church-state reconciliation, as did the cordial relations of such bishops as Monsignor Gillow of Oaxaca with high administration officials.

In this period the main threat to the church came not from the state but from Protestant missionaries and from dissident movements in the countryside. As American investments and immigration into Mexico increased, so did American missionaries, who were especially active in the northern part of the country. In Chihuahua, Methodist missionaries penetrated even into remote villages and were highly successful in influencing the peasants. As a result many church officials became increasingly nationalistic and increasingly anti-American.

Perhaps an even greater danger to the church were dissident movements among the peasantry. Such movements had always existed but as long as Catholicism was the official religion of the country the church always had the means to repress these movements. Now its possibilities of fighting back were sharply curtailed as 'saints' and 'holy' men and women strongly opposed to the church emerged in different parts of the country. In the state of Sonora thousands of people venerated a young sixteen-year-old girl, Teresita, known as the Saint of Cabora, who healed the sick and was said to perform miracles; in Cohuilimpo, the Indian villagers believed that one of their number whom they called San Juan was a saint. All over central Mexico pre-Columbian idols were hidden and worshipped in caves.

The state only persecuted these cults if they advocated social or political changes. US-based Protestant missionaries were tolerated and at times even supported by Porfirian authorities. Bereft of state aid, the church had to find new ways to counter its religious foes. For priests to preach against idolatry was not enough, since many of these saints and rebels were not just religious but social dissidents as well. The need to pre-empt these social movements and the thirteenth encyclical, Rerum Novarum, of Pope Leo XIII calling for church involvement in social problems led to social activism by segments of the Catholic church. The main proponent of this new trend was the Bishop of Tulancingo. With his help several Catholic congresses to discuss the problems of the peasantry took place during the latter years of the Porfirian era. At a Catholic conference held in 1903 in the city of Tulancingo, Catholic laymen called on hacendados to abolish peonage and to give more instruction and schooling to the peasants. At the same time they appealed to the peasants to accept the God-given order of things and not to rise against their superiors. Church-inspired newspapers frequently protested against expropriations of village lands. The church's new policy was doubtless facilitated by the fact that it had lost its lands and thus was not as involved as it had been in the early nineteenth century in peonage and other forms of peasant servitude.

While the church finally failed to stabilize the situation in the countryside, it was eminently successful in other respects. With Díaz's support it made a political and economic comeback and managed at the same time to increase its support among the peasantry. This support clearly manifested itself during the Revolution when the most radical agrarian revolutionaries (above all the Zapatistas in Morelos) carried out no anti-clerical policies.

On the whole the strengthening of the Porfirian state cost large segments of both the traditional upper and middle classes much of the political power they had hitherto exercised. In return they partook of the fruits of Mexico's rapid economic growth. The same cannot be said of the peasantry which during the Díaz period lost its traditional political rights at the same time that it suffered profound economic losses. It has been frequently stated that Díaz's abolition of existing democratic structures in Mexico scarcely affected the peasants. Most of them were illiterate and could not read the opposition newspapers even when they reached their remote villages, which seldom occurred. They were neither interested in nor did they participate in national elections.

This was probably true, but there was one aspect of democracy in

Mexico which was of decisive importance for a large segment of the peasantry: local autonomy. Most villagers traditionally elected their councils and mayors whose power was not only political but also economic. These officials allocated access to community lands, water and pastures, frequently resolved conflicts within the villages and at times determined who would join the army and who would be exempted from military service. The origins of this village autonomy can frequently be traced back to the pre-Columbian period when the villages in southern and central Mexico enjoyed a large measure of self-sufficiency and political rights. It did not end with the Spanish conquest. Spain allowed many Indian communities to retain lands and communal institutions and granted them a certain measure of autonomy, albeit under the close supervision of state and church officials. Many communities in the northern frontier areas were granted a new and greater degree of freedom from state control as an incentive to settle in this dangerous region and to fight against Indian marauders. On the whole the power and autonomy of village communities tended to increase after Independence. The federal government was far too weak to impinge upon their traditional rights. The only authority powerful enough to seriously challenge village councils and mayors were local and regional caciques. Many of them utilized their new-found power (unlike the colonial state, the weak national state of the nineteenth century could not impose effective restraints upon them) to force their rule upon the villages. Many others, however, were hesitant to attack vested peasant rights. The local caciques were often involved in Mexico's endless civil wars and in critical times they entered into alliances with the villages in order to maintain themselves against rivals or against a hostile federal government. Thus they tended to blend a certain measure of repression and control with attempts to gain the loyalty and support of many of the villages they controlled. This situation changed radically in the last years of the Porfiriato.

The domestication of the northern frontier

During the last quarter of the nineteenth century the Mexican state began to assert its dominion over Mexico's northern frontier: Sonora, Chihuahua, Nuevo León and Durango. The subjugation of the Apaches and the construction of the railways set the stage for a mass immigration from both the United States and the Mexican south. More than 15,000

Americans came to settle there. They were similar in some respects to the Americans who streamed into the rest of Mexico during this period. Like their counterparts in southern and central Mexico many of them were wealthy investors or executives of large corporations. Numerous technicians had been brought in by the American Smelting and Refining Company, owner of most of the mines and smelters of northern Mexico, and similar outfits. Many administrators had been brought in by men like William Randolph Hearst, who needed them to oversee his vast landholdings in the region, and William C. Greene, who needed them to operate his cattle and lumber empire. Numerous other Americans who came into the north, however, belonged to social groups scarcely represented in the rest of Mexico. American railway men occupied all the higher positions not only in the administration, but in the operations division of most Mexican railways, above all in the north, while American miners constituted an important segment of the labour force in mining, especially in one of Mexico's largest mining centres, Cananea in the state of Sonora. In the United States their status would have been no different from that of other workers, but in Mexico they constituted a privileged minority, better paid and better treated than their Mexican counterparts.

The 300,000 or so Mexicans who settled in northern Mexico between 1877 and 1910 bore a somewhat different social character. The mass of migrants were displaced peasants, ruined artisans, or adventurers hoping for better opportunities. Their impact on the region's demographic make-up was enormous: they helped to swell the population of Monterrey from 14,000 in 1877 to 78,528 in 1910 and to transform the obscure village of Torreón, which in the 1870s had numbered a few hundred, into Mexico's most modern and fastest growing city with a population of 23,000 by 1900 and 43,000 by 1910.

The newcomers to the north did not displace the region's elite. The north's great families had indeed relinquished some of their political power in favour of the central government and shared economic power with foreign entrepreneurs, but on the whole they emerged immensely strengthened by the transformations taking place in the border region. The Terrazas–Creel clan in Chihuahua, the Maderos in Coahuila, the steel mill owners of Monterrey constituted the Mexican equivalent of the Rockefellers and Guggenheims in the United States.

In both economic and social terms, the north was one of the most 'modern' regions of Mexico by the turn of the century. Not only was its economy the most diversified in the country, the percentage of rural population was lower than in the rest of Mexico. The literacy rate in the north was the highest in the country. Modern capitalist relations had largely replaced traditional forms of social relations in the countryside. Until the 1890s, peons on large estates had often been paid not in cash but with tokens only redeemable at the estate store. Many peons were bound by debt to the big estates and, even when this was not the case, the insecurity of the countryside, bad communications and Apache raids had made it extremely difficult and dangerous for them to leave their place of residence.

The end of the Apache wars, the newly established communications with the United States, the possibilities many Mexican agricultural workers and especially cowboys had to find work across the border in the United States, and the unwillingness of either the US authorities, American entrepreneurs or, for that matter, Mexican industrial entrepreneurs to return fugitive peons to their haciendas made the system of debt peonage more and more expensive and unprofitable. As a result, Mexican estate owners were forced to find other methods to keep cowboys and agricultural workers on their haciendas. Some of them, such as the cotton producers of the newly irrigated Laguna cotton fields, paid the highest agricultural wages in Mexico. Others granted sharecropping and tenancy arrangements on far more favourable terms than in the rest of the country. While in central Mexico arrangements predominated whereby tenants or sharecroppers received at the most 50 per cent of what they harvested, in the north they usually obtained two-thirds. Many northern cowboys were allowed to have cattle of their own and to graze them on hacienda lands. If they stayed long enough in the same job, they could easily become foremen and earn double what they had obtained before. Some especially progressive landowners such as Francisco Madero in the state of Coahuila set up schools and clinics on their estates, and in times of hunger and bad harvests fed the population of the surrounding villages.

Until the end of the nineteenth century, the economic and social changes produced by the political and economic absorption of the north by both central Mexico and the United States led to substantial improvements for important segments of not only the upper but also the middle and lower classes of society. Nevertheless, the north was also the region that witnessed the most social and political violence during the Porfirian period. In some respects, until the end of the nineteenth century, these conflicts took place between what could be designated as the modern sector of society on the one hand and the 'traditional' elements of northern society on the other. However, the only segment of northern society that completely rejected practically every characteristic of modern industrial society were some of the approximately 50,000 Tarahumara Indians who were concentrated mainly in the state of Chihuahua, many of them in the mountain fastnesses of the Sierra Madre, and who were only marginally involved in the social conflicts which gripped northern Mexico during the Porfiriato and the Revolution of 1910–20.

The Yaqui Indians of Sonora and the former military colonists of Chihuahua, who offered the greatest resistance to Porfirian modernization and who repeatedly staged armed uprisings against the authorities, constituted a traditional sector in the sense that they clung to their established rights and lands. They were not 'traditional' if the term implies opposition to modern technology, industry or production for the market. Under the aegis of Jesuit missionaries during the colonial period, the Yaquis had assimilated sophisticated techniques of intensive agriculture which they successfully applied to the fertile soil of the Yaqui river valley. Many of their products were sold in the markets of the mining regions. At the same time, many Yaqui Indians went to work far away from their native region in mines and haciendas and were considered by their employers to be among their most reliable and expert labourers.

During both the colonial period and the nineteenth century, the former military colonists, who settled mainly in the state of Chihuahua, constituted one of the mainstays of what could best be considered an agrarian middle class. Not only did they own far more land than the average peasant in central or southern Mexico, but they were economically independent. Not only did they have sufficient lands and cattle to subsist on their own, but even if they had wanted to work for neighbouring haciendas the dangerous state of communications during the Apache wars would have made such an option extremely unattractive. Unlike the peasants of southern and central Mexico, whose lands were communally owned until the reform law of 1856 and who thus were not allowed to sell their land, land was a commodity in northern villages that could be freely bought and sold.

The reason that both the Yaqui Indians and many of the former military colonists in the north staged a series of uprisings against the Díaz regime was not that they were opposed to a 'modern' capitalist economy but that they resented the fact that this economy was developing at their expense. The Yaqui Indians staged several bloody uprisings against the Mexican authorities when the latter attempted to confiscate large amounts of their fertile lands for the benefit of the American Richardson Company. For the military colonists in Chihuahua, who in 1891–3 rose in arms against both the state government and the Díaz regime, the land problem was closely intertwined with a tradition of municipal autonomy. The municipal authorities, freely elected by them, had been their main instruments in warding off all kinds of outside attacks both on their lands and on their social and economic status. In 1891 a new law was drafted by the state government which allowed the *jefe políticos* to name the mayors of larger towns. Many of the villages in Chihuahua rose to arms to prevent the authorities from applying the law. These villagers had one thing in common with the Yaquis: an uncommon fighting ability, nurtured through more than one-and-a-half centuries of fighting the Apaches, and the possession of arms. There was one significant difference, however, between the two groups. The Yaquis in Sonora stood alone, isolated by ethnic and social differences from the rest of the population of the state. The military colonists, on the other hand, had powerful though secret allies: some of the largest landowners in the state, former *caudillos* such as Luis Terrazas, attempted to utilize these peasants to exert pressure on the government.

These differences induced the Díaz government to apply very different tactics in the two cases. After years of unsuccessful attempts to convince the Yaquis to accept the loss of most of their lands or to subdue them by increasing intensive military campaigns, the government resorted to new and unprecedented methods of repression. Between 1903 and 1907 it launched a full-scale campaign against the Yaqui Indians and deported a mass of them, whether they resisted the government or not, to the henequén plantations of Yucatán. This tactic not only decimated the Yaquis, it was profitable as well. Colonel Francisco B. Cruz who in the course of three years deported 15,700 Yaquis to Yucatán received 65 pesos per head (man, woman or child) from the hacendados; 10 pesos was paid to him personally and 55 to the war ministry.

The government, however, showed itself far more inclined to carry out a policy of compromise with the rebellious military colonists in Chihuahua, although the compromises were arranged with their elite manipulators rather than with the peasants themselves. As a result of a series of rural uprisings in Chihuahua backed by Terrazas from 1891 to 1893, the latter's rival, Lauro Carrillo, was removed from the governorship of Chihuahua and a man far closer to Terrazas assumed control of the state government. The peasants themselves, except for being granted amnesty, were given far smaller concessions – a slowing down of the land expropriations and the maintenance of some elements of municipal autonomy. In most cases this strategy was successful, but in one case, the most famous of all, it was not. This concerned the small and obscure village of Tomochi in the mountain fastness of western Chihuahua. The Tomochi rebellion of November 1891 was at first no different from that of dozens of other villages in the north. It began as a revolt against the newly installed mayor, a nephew of the district *jefe político*, who grazed his sheep on the villagers' pastures and forced them to work at reduced wages on his own land or on the estates of the finance minister, José Yves Limantour, which were located near the village. When some of Tomochi's inhabitants protested against these exactions the mayor subjected them to the *leva*, the much-feared recruitment into the army. Tomochi's inhabitants protested against these exactions the mayor messianic visions. The leaders of the village, Cruz and Manuel Chávez, were adherents of the cult of the young sixteen-year-old girl, Teresita, the Saint of Cabora. The inhabitants of Tomochi felt that with God on their side they would not have to fear a head-on collision with government troops. After the 80 or so men of the village had twice defeated more than 500 soldiers sent to fight them, a concentrated federal attack by 1,200 troops finally reduced the village to rubble. The leader of the uprising, Cruz Chávez, together with all remaining male inhabitants of Tomochi, were shot. For its part the government had suffered nearly 500 casualties. In all of Chihuahua popular legends soon sprang up about the Tomochi uprising.

In view of the odds on both sides it was a victory that had far more the hallmark of a defeat. The government was forced to carry out a tacit retreat from previous policies by slowing down still further, for a time at least, both the pace of land expropriations and its attacks on village autonomy. As a result, peasant uprisings in Chihuahua began to subside. By the end of the nineteenth century the Díaz government felt that it had the situation in the north well in hand. Except in the Yaqui region, the level of violence subsided and the *caudillos* seemed to have given their unreserved support to the government. Nevertheless, this was only a respite. In the early twentieth century, the conflicts between the modern and the traditional sector flared up once again, this time complicated by new and profound tensions arising within the modern sector itself. Rebellious elements from both groups would in the final account bring down the Díaz regime and overrun all of Mexico in the years between 1910 and 1920.

The expropriation of the peasantry in central and southern Mexico

Even in the Juárez era serious inroads had been made into the lands of the communal villages. But during the Díaz era what had once been mere encroachments turned into a veritable onslaught. When Mexico gained its independence from Spain in the early nineteenth century, it is estimated that approximately 40 per cent of all land suited for agriculture in the central and southern parts of the country belonged to communal villages. When Díaz fell in 1911, only 5 per cent remained in their hands. Over 90 per cent of Mexico's peasants became landless. While there exist no exact yearly statistics on this process, it is generally thought that the wave of expropriations reached a high point under Díaz.

There were more incentives for this kind of expropriation than ever before. As new foreign and domestic markets emerged for the products of Mexican agriculture, the hacendados sought to augment their landholdings in order to maximize output. Some of the most notable cases in which massive increases in market production were coupled with the economic destruction of village communities were caused by the sugar plantations of Morelos and the henequén haciendas of Yucatán.

The emergence of new markets, however, did not constitute the only incentive for land expropriation. Speculation was an equally potent motive. Once a railway was being built, or even if such a line was only in a planning stage, land values along it would soar and speculators of all shapes would pounce upon the land. Acquiring new holdings without having to pay for them was also one way of increasing production without carrying out large-scale investments. For many hacendados this might have been the easiest way to maximize production without any substantial costs.

A more controversial hypothesis is that the hacendados destroyed the villages in order to undermine their economic independence and thus force the inhabitants to work hacienda lands. While this factor did motivate some land expropriation, its importance has been exaggerated.

Only three families of Tarascan Indians of the village of Naranja whose lands had been expropriated from the community by the hacienda of Cantabria worked on that estate. All the others were employed by other haciendas which had no connection with the expropriation. There is strong evidence to indicate that most estates could find sufficient labourers without having to destroy the economic base of surrounding villages. One of the reasons for this increasing availability of labour was the demographic increase of the population of the free villages, which had made it imperative for an increasing number of peasants to find supplementary work on haciendas. There is also some evidence to indicate that when an hacienda expropriated a neighbouring village, the bitterness and resentment this caused among the peasants was so great that most of them worked on other estates rather than the one that had destroyed their community.

Not only were the incentives for expropriating the lands of village communities greater than ever before, but during the Díaz period they found new legal underpinnings. To the Ley Lerdo (see above), which constituted the legal basis for such actions during the Restored Republic, new laws had been added during the administration of Manuel González which allowed private companies to survey public lands, and to keep one-third of what they found for themselves. More important than these new legal underpinnings was the fact that only during the Porfirian era was the Mexican government strong enough to enforce a mass attack on the village communities. The newly built railways gave both the army and the newly strengthened Rurales greater possibilities than ever before of crushing peasant resistance.

There are no exact statistics to establish with any degree of certainty when the process of land expropriation took place and when it reached a high point. Nor is there sufficient explanation for the frequent and at times great disparity in regional developments. Why were so many Indian villages expropriated in Yucatán while in Oaxaca, with perhaps the highest percentage of Indians in Mexico, the villages managed to retain most of their lands and many of their traditional rights? Was this due to the fact that export production was far more important in Yucatán than in Oaxaca? What role did other factors, such as the greater cohesion of communities in Oaxaca, the traditional weakness of the hacienda in that state, the existence of an Indian middle class, and Díaz's personal links to Oaxaca, play? These are questions for which no definite answer exists as yet.

An even more complex problem is who the beneficiaries of these expropriations were. For a long time, too simple a picture of the results of expropriations has been drawn; it was assumed that as a result of Porfirian changes, only two social classes, in the final account, peopled the countryside: an increasingly wealthy group of hacendados and an impoverished group of landless peons.

In reality, however, a growing agrarian middle class, whose existence is not always easy to document, seems to have played an ever-increasing role in the social processes taking place in the countryside. In many villages, groups of wealthy peasants, village usurers and local strong men who were not hacendados profited as much as the latter and at times more from the expropriations of peasant lands. Many of them emerged long before the Porfirian period. The increase of Mexico's population had led to strong differentiations within the villages, and the richer inhabitants became partners of both the landlords and the Porfirian authorities in the expropriation of village lands. Some of them acquired middle-sized properties (*ranchos*), and thus are included in the census data in 1895 and 1900, in which 32,000 '*ranchos*' are counted (not all *ranchos* were independent units as some constituted parts of haciendas). Others, however, invested their wealth in ways which are more difficult to document statistically. Some became wealthy tenants, others rented out cattle to sharecroppers and poorer tenants. The 1900 census names about 400,000 *agricultores*, and while the basis for that category is not well established, it probably embraced most of this agricultural middle class which constituted a substantial segment of the rural population in Mexico's countryside. Their relationships to the villagers were extremely varied. Some of them became usurers, agents of the state or of the hacendados, while others became popular leaders. Many changed in time from one category into the other.

In the village of Anenecuilco in the state of Morelos, the villagers in the late summer of 1909 elected a relatively well-to-do peasant, Emiliano Zapata, to represent them in their attempts to regain the lands which the neighbouring Hacienda del Hospital had taken from them. Hundreds of miles to the north in the frontier village of Cuchillo Parado the villagers also elected a leader, Ezequiel Montes, to help them ward off the attempt of one of Chihuahua's wealthiest hacendados, Muñoz, to seize their land. Both Zapata and Montes enjoyed a higher social status than most other villagers. Zapata came from a well-known family and was relatively well off since he owned land, horses and mules. Ezequiel Montes had no such family credentials. In the 1880s he came to Cuchillo Parado as a landless labourer, bringing with him nothing but his guitar, as a village chronicler disrespectfully wrote. But Montes obviously had more gifts than the ability to sing. He could speak very well, could read and write, knew the surrounding world, and soon gained the confidence of the villagers. In 1903 they elected him to the leadership of the Junta de Vecinos of Cuchillo Parado which was set up to fight Muñoz. Montes was at first far more successful than Zapata. While the Hacienda del Hospital retained the lands it had seized, Muñoz abandoned his attack on Cuchillo Parado.

The two leaders utilized the power and prestige they had acquired by leading their villages' attempts to secure their rights in extremely divergent ways. Zapata led the men of Anenecuilco and finally of all of Morelos into the Mexican Revolution. Montes was appointed mayor of Cuchillo Parado by the state authorities, became the village usurer and was ultimately expelled from the village on the day the Revolution broke out.

It is possible that the rise of this agrarian middle class provides one of the best explanations, though not the only one, for a fact that has puzzled historians for a long time: the relative lack of resistance of peasants in central and southern Mexico to the widespread expropriation of their land. There is little doubt that the weakening of peasant resistance in the 1880s and 1890s as compared to the period between 1876 and 1880 was also linked to the increasing power of the state, the strengthening of the army and its increased mobility with the railways, and the creation of new police units. Repression alone, however, does not offer a sufficient explanation. In addition to the increasing support that the government gained among the emerging middle class, two other phenomena probably contributed to diffusing peasant resistance. One was the dismantling of their main organs of resistance, the village communal administration. With the end of village autonomy, the peasants no longer could count on the traditional organization which had led them in former times in resisting encroachments by landowners or by the state. Another factor, perhaps even more important, was the transformation of the traditional patron–client relationship, which for a long time had dominated life in the Mexican countryside. During the colonial period the patron was the Spanish state, which frequently tried to protect the peasants from the encroachments of landowners in order to prevent the latter from becoming too powerful. Early in the nineteenth century, regional *caudillos*, dependent on peasant support to wage their frequent civil wars with rivals in other regions, had assumed this function. When some hacendados in the state of Guerrero attempted to expropriate lands belonging to free villages, the peasants called on Juan Alvarez, the wealthiest hacendado and most powerful liberal *caudillo* of the region, for redress. Alvarez could and did help. In return thousands of peasants joined his army in 1855 when he overthrew the conservative government of Santa Anna. Alvarez was not unique. Other *caudillos*, such as Conservative Manuel Lozada in Tepic, also heeded calls for help from peasants. Many traditional protectors were absorbed by the Porfirian state and later turned against their former protégés. Having lost their traditional patrons many peasants felt leaderless and abandoned. Porfirio Díaz's personal prestige as well as some limited steps to help a few villages may also have prevented peasant resistance from emerging. There are indications that Díaz at times attempted to assume the traditional mantle of the Spanish colonial state as protector and patron of Indian villages. Repeatedly Díaz wrote to governors and local officials asking them to respect Indians' property rights when the latter could show titles to them, or even to respect *de facto* property rights of Indians. Thus, in 1897 villagers of Tamazunchale asked him for help in preventing expropriation of their land. Díaz sent them to search in the National Archives for the title to their land, and then wrote to the governor of the state of San Luis Potosí:

With reference to the Indians of San Francisco, Matlapa and the rest, there can be no doubt that they are the owners by viceregal grants in long ago times, even though their titles suffer somewhat from defects and irregularities; but even supposing that their titles were irregular or void, they have been considered the owners of the lands which now an outsider is trying to buy because the Indians lack the means to pay for them. The practical result would be an expropriation and the substitution of those villages of Indians by outsiders who would come to inhabit the places they left, but probably after many bloody scenes which the Indians would consider their just vengeance, fanatically convinced with the certain or erroneous consciousness of their rights.[5]

These principles nevertheless conflicted with other more profound tenets of the Porfirian administration: the desire to attract foreign capital and the wish to conciliate the hacendados. Díaz was either unwilling or unable to implement these policies of restraint beyond intervening in a

[5] Quoted in Donald Fithian Stevens, 'Agrarian policy and instability in Porfirian Mexico', *The Americas*, 39 (October 1982), 161.

few cases. Until the last years of his regime Díaz took no steps which could have effectively restrained the loss of land or autonomy of the villagers.

In 1910 Díaz took the one measure on a national scale which, had it been taken years before, might have effectively restricted village expropriations. He decreed that no more sales of public lands should take place. By then some of the richest of these lands had already been adjudicated and sold and the measure was of little consequence. It was only in the twentieth century, when for reasons that are described below new patrons were to emerge who called on the peasants to revolt, that they would respond and finally constitute a decisive force in the revolutionary storm that erupted in Mexico after 1910.

The evolution of peonage into slavery or freedom

On many haciendas in central and southern Mexico the status of labourers, generally known as peons, was subject to changes no less drastic than those in the free villages which had been expropriated. As the production of cash crops became more and more profitable, many hacendados began to cut down on tenancy arrangements, preferring instead to employ labourers who tilled the land of the estates for the owners. Tenancy was by no means abolished, but the tenants were more and more pushed on to marginal lands where they were far more subject than ever before to fluctuations of weather. In other cases, sharecropping arrangements even more unfavourable to the peasants replaced existing tenancy conditions. The way the haciendas accomplished this is most clearly illustrated by the evolution of sharecropping patterns on a hacienda near Celaya in the state of Guanajuato. Up to the latter part of the nineteenth century there had been two types of sharecroppers on this hacienda: the *medieros al rajar* and the *medieros al quinto*. The *medieros al rajar* furnished their own agricultural implements and oxen and received 50 per cent of the harvest. The *medieros al quinto* borrowed farm machinery and animals from the hacienda and in return had to pay the usual 50 per cent of their crops, plus one-fifth of the remaining harvest as payment for the use of machinery and animals. This left them with at most 40 per cent of the harvest. By the end of the nineteenth century this hacienda began to cut down on the number of *medieros al rajar* simply by not allowing the sharecroppers to use hacienda grazing lands to tend their cattle. By the beginning of the twentieth century only a few privileged retainers still worked their lands on a half-share basis. All others had become *medieros al quinto*.

A further differentiation took place in the type of labourer that the hacendados employed. In both the southern and northern peripheries of the country, far more sparsely settled than central Mexico, the hacendados frequently faced drastic labour shortages. They reacted to them in very different ways. While in the north peonage tended to disappear, in the southern parts of the country, especially in the henequén plantations of Yucatán, the tobacco-producing Valle Nacional in Oaxaca and the coffee plantations in Chiapas, labourers were bound to the estates by conditions of debt peonage frequently akin to slavery. They were not allowed to leave their estates until their debts had been repaid, and the hacendado made sure by fraud, by overcharging in the company store, and by forcing peasants to accept credits that they frequently did not need that these debts could not be repaid. In Yucatán debt peonage became institutionalized to a far greater degree than in any other part of Mexico. In 1901 an observer reported that:

the legal means to bind *criados* to hacienda consists in an advance payment which in this state means that a worker who leaves can be returned by force by the police to the hacienda. These advance payments are generally made when a young man born on the hacienda reaches the age of 18 or 20 and marries. His master then gives him a hundred to a hundred and fifty, sometimes two hundred pesos, to set up a household and both parties silently agree that this sum as well as other sums which might be advanced at a later date in case of accident or illnesses would never be repaid. They are the price for which the young Yucateco sells his freedom.[6]

In cases where such institutionalization was fragile, brute force was applied.

In 1914 Woodrow Wilson's special representative in Mexico, John Lind, together with the commander of the American fleet in Veracruz, Admiral Fletcher, was invited to visit a Veracruz sugar plantation owned by an American, Sloane Emery, which depended entirely on contract workers. 'They were contract laborers', John Lind later reported:

who were virtually prisoners and had been sent there by the government. Admiral Fletcher and I saw this remarkable situation in the twentieth century of men being scattered through the corn fields in little groups of eight or ten accompanied by a driver, a cacique, an Indian from the coast, a great big burly fellow, with a couple of revolvers strapped to a belt, and a black snake that

[6] Karl Kaerger, 'Landwirtschaft und Kolonisation', in *Spanisches Südamerika* (2 vols., Leipzig, 1901–2), II, 637.

would measure eight or ten feet, right after the group that were digging, and then at the farther end of the road a man with a sawed-off shotgun. These men were put out in the morning, were worked under these overseers in that manner, and locked up at night in a large shed to all intents and purposes. Both Admiral Fletcher and I marveled that such conditions could exist, but they did exist.[7]

The isolation of many southern regions, the lack of an industry which would have competed with the estate owners for scarce labourers, the strengthening of both hacienda police forces and the organs of the state made it extremely difficult for the peons to circumvent their owners. These repressive measures were strengthened by a process of divide and rule: rebellious Yaquis from the state of Sonora, vagrants from central Mexico, Chinese and Korean coolies were all brought into the southern regions where the hacendados made use of their antagonisms towards each other and towards the native Maya population of the region to prevent any kind of resistance from emerging. On the whole, the land owners were successful in the economic as well as the social and political fields. Production soared, resistance was extremely limited, and the ensuing stability attracted new capital and investment.

The contradictory tendencies in the countryside – more economic incentives and freedom, versus repression and semi-enslavement – that manifested themselves in the northern and southern peripheries of the country, also appeared in central Mexico. The reason for this was that factors producing labour shortage and others leading to a labour surplus affected central Mexico at the same time, though obviously not always in the same regions. The expropriation of village lands as well as the demographic increase created large segments of unemployed labourers, which in many regions were more than sufficient to meet the needs of the haciendas. In such cases some hacendados discovered the advantages of free over servile labour.

In 1906 Manuel Brassetti, the administrator of the hacienda of Tochatlaco, reported that

on this estate the predominant labour system was based on peons paid by the year (this meant that they received a small advance and purchased all their needs on credit from the *tienda de raya*, settling accounts once a year). They had all contracted large debts with the estate, were lazy, drunk and on the whole bad and rebellious workers; after carefully studying the problem I decided to forgo the 3,000 pesos they owed me and for two years now they are paid by the week

---

[7] United States Senate Documents, Foreign Relations Committee, Investigation of Mexican Affairs, Report and Hearings 66th Congress, 2nd Session, Senate Document No. 285 (2 vols., Washington, 1920), II, 2326.

. . . When they were in debt they did not work on the Saturday before Holy Week, they became drunk all of Holy Week and it was extremely difficult to get them to work on Easter Tuesday. Since they are paid by the week they work Holy Monday and Tuesday and they are at work on Easter Monday.[8]

According to Manuel Brassetti, the peons were now far happier than before, telling indebted peons on other estates 'you are in bondage, we are free'. In other parts of central Mexico, however, the competition of newly created industries, railway construction, and hacendados in need of more labourers to till their cash crops produced the reverse effect and brought about a shortage of labourers. These real or, at times, perceived shortages led many hacendados to maintain conditions of debt peonage even when they were sometimes economically counterproductive and probably not necessary.

The emergence of a national ruling class

At the other end of the social scale there was also a significant transformation taking place during the Díaz period: the creation of what might be called a national ruling class. Except for the church, which was always national in character, the Mexican economic elite in the early part of the nineteenth century had been essentially local or regional. Some of its members were landowners whose wealth was generally concentrated in one or two states, while those among the elite who lived in Mexico City were essentially merchants and *agiotistas*, speculators whose main income came from granting loans to the government and speculating in government finances. There were few industrialists, none of whom controlled major industries, while most miners and merchants were foreigners.

Some members of the emerging national ruling class of the Porfiriato were regional landowners, but regional landowners who had begun to extend their activities into other branches of the economy and into other regions of the country. The Terrazas–Creel group, probably the wealthiest and most powerful family clan in Porfirian Mexico, is the most notable example. Luis Terrazas was one of the most prominent hacendados in the state of Chihuahua and his son-in-law, Enrique Creel, was a well-to-do landowner and middle-sized financier there. By the turn of the century the two men had combined their activities and

---

[8] Biblioteca del Boletín de La Sociedad Agrícola Mexicana; Segundo Congreso Agrícola de Tulancingo, Mexico, 1906, 144–5.

tremendously expanded their scale of operations. They owned food-processing plants throughout Chihuahua, and controlled Chihuahua's largest bank. They also owned a bank in the newly developed Laguna region of Coahuila. Creel sat on the Board of Directors of two of Mexico City's largest banks, the Banco de Londres y México and Banco Nacional de México. The two men acted as intermediaries for numerous foreign corporations wishing to do business in Mexico, and Creel was chairman of the board of one of the largest and most powerful of these, the Mexican Eagle Oil Company, owned by Sir Weetman Pearson (later Lord Cowdray). Similarly, finance minister José Yves Limantour, the son of a prosperous French merchant, branched out into enterprises in many different states. He acquired large tracts of land in Chihuahua, and, like Creel and Terrazas, sat on the boards of many of the large foreign and Mexican companies doing business in the country.

The wealth of Mexico's new ruling class, other than its land, was above all due to its role as intermediaries for foreign companies. Any large company wishing to do business in Mexico soon learned that retaining these men as lawyers or, better yet, as members of its board of directors was the best way of cutting red tape and surmounting any other kind of economic or political obstacle to their penetration of the Mexican economy. The most powerful, and articulate, segment of this new ruling class was the group of men known as the *científicos*, the group of financiers, technocrats and intellectuals brought together by Manuel Romero Rubio, Díaz's minister of the interior (and his father-in-law) and after the death of Romero Rubio in 1895 led by the finance minister Limantour (see above).

One of the most characteristic traits of the Mexican ruling class was their pro-European orientation. This was very lucidly defined by the German minister in Mexico when he wrote:

In their view, the political future of the country depends entirely on the development of the economy. To realize this, however, the country needs help from abroad, including the United States. Mexico is thus increasingly destined to become an area of activity for capitalist firms from all countries. The cosmopolitans, however, paradoxical as this may sound, see precisely in economic dependency the guarantee of political independence, in so far as they assume that the large European interests that have investments here constitute a counter-weight to American annexationist appetites and that they will pave the way for the complete internationalization and neutralization of Mexico. Behind the scenes, but at the head of the cosmopolitan group, stands the finance minister, Señor Limantour. His allies are *haute finance*, as well as the top-level civil servants with interests in the domestic and foreign companies, senators and deputies, and, finally, the local representatives of European capital invested in Mexico.⁹

These views cannot simply be explained by the fact that the *científicos* represented European interests, while other members of Mexico's oligarchy represented the Americans. The *científicos* in fact were intermediaries for both European and American companies. The reason that they nevertheless preferred the Europeans to the Americans was due precisely to the fact that they had become a national ruling class, whose viewpoints transcended regional limits and assumed national proportions. European support, they felt, was crucial to the maintenance of Mexico's independence. On the other hand, there is little doubt that their intermediary function for European interests was quite different from the role they played with respect to the Americans. Because of their relative weakness in Mexico, the Europeans were far more willing than the Americans to make real concessions to their Mexican intermediaries. It is significant, for instance, that the largest British oil company in Mexico, the Mexican Eagle, took on members of Mexico's elite as partners, though only in a junior capacity. The largest US oil companies in Mexico, Doheny's Mexican Petroleum Company and the Waters Pierce Oil Company, the second of which had links to Standard Oil, never entered into this kind of partnership with members of Mexico's oligarchy.

The European sympathies of Mexico's ruling class were reinforced by an alliance with another group of European origin, which until the late nineteenth century had rarely entered into partnership arrangements with Mexicans. These were the merchants of European origin, essentially French, and to a lesser degree German, who had begun to set up industries in Mexico as imports from Europe became too expensive because of the fall in the price of silver. They requested and obtained substantial capital investment from Mexico's elite, and above all the *científicos*, in their plants.

As a result of these manifold activities, the attitude of the new ruling class seemed schizophrenic to many observers. On some issues they would be completely subservient to foreign interests, while on others they would manifest unexpected surges of nationalism. This national ruling class and the predominant role of the *científicos* within it led to

⁹ German Foreign Office papers, Archives of the German Foreign Office in Bonn, Mexico, vol. 17, Wangenheim to Bülow, 7 January 1907.

strong divisions among Mexico's elite. Regional elites frequently opposed their pre-eminence and were supported in their attitude by the one other group which considered itself to be 'national' in character, the army. It was certainly no coincidence that Bernardo Reyes, who led upper-class opposition to the *científicos*, was an army general and one of the most powerful military men in Mexico.

On the whole the changes and transformations that the Díaz regime wrought in Mexico's upper class may have increased the tensions and conflicts among them. Until the turn of the century, however, the Díaz regime succeeded in preventing any of these groups from attempting to further their interests by armed revolt. His regime granted them so many opportunities for accumulating wealth that they simply had too much to lose to wish for an armed uprising.

The emergence of an industrial proletariat

Porfirian modernization greatly increased the size of Mexico's working class, altered its status and its living conditions and profoundly transformed its consciousness. Rapid economic growth led to an increase in the number of industrial workers. Between 1895 and 1900 their number grew from 692,697 to 803,294 (excluding those employed in transportation and the public sector). They were mainly concentrated in the capital and in the states of Mexico, Puebla, Jalisco, Guanajuato and Veracruz and the northern border states.

The conditions under which they lived varied greatly. In the oil region the companies provided housing, built some schools and even established a rudimentary medical service. In return they asked unquestioning obedience. The mayors of the oil company towns were in the pockets of the companies, who also established and controlled the police forces. Unions and strikes were prohibited. In textile factories conditions could be much harsher. In the textile mill of Santa Teresa y Contreras in the capital the workers were not paid in cash but in tokens redeemable only at the company store. Workers complained bitterly that a surcharge of 18 per cent was imposed on all products sold at that store. At the Hercules Textile factory in Querétaro, workers voiced similar complaints, but complained above all about the arbitrary system of punishment established by the company: anyone arriving even a minute later than 5 a.m. when work started could be immediately dismissed. There were no provisions for medical, accident or disability insurance.

Nevertheless until the turn of the century strikes and other protest movements by industrial workers were rare. Not only were living standards rising but, difficult as conditions were, they were still better than those on the haciendas from which so many workers came, or in villages where so many former peasants had lost their lands. In addition the Díaz regime was actively attempting to control industrial workers by encouraging labour organizations like the Congreso Obrero and the Convención Radical which maintained close links with the government. These organizations disseminated propaganda in favour of Díaz and against radical ideologies. They edited two newspapers which preached that 'the respect of a people for the police is the thermometer which marks its civilization'.[10] In 1891 the Congreso Obrero prevented the workers from observing the May Day celebration.

At the same time, these organizations attempted to mediate in some disputes between workers and industrialists and helped to set up mutualist societies. The latter were self-help organizations of workers, exclusively financed by worker contributions which provided minimum benefits in cases of accidents, disability or death.

By the end of the nineteenth century the attitudes of Mexico's emerging working class towards the state as well as towards their employers gradually began to change. One element that greatly shaped and influenced their way of thinking was increasing contact with foreigners. Most factories, especially the large ones, were foreign-owned and even in Mexican-owned enterprises foreigners were frequently taken on as managers. A sense of nationalism gradually developed among Mexican workers which became even stronger when they were confronted with foreign workers in the same enterprises earning several times their own salaries. This was especially the case on the railways where American employees were granted preferential status both in access to jobs and in terms of the salary they earned.

There was yet another way in which Mexican workers came into contact with foreigners. This was through migration to the United States. Thousands of Mexican labourers, especially from northern states, began crossing the border either permanently or for long periods to work in American mines and industries as well as on ranches. The discrimination to which they were frequently subjected provoked strong feelings of nationalism in many of them. In others, however, this

[10] David Walker, 'Porfirian labor politics: working class organizations in Mexico City and Porfirio Díaz, 1876–1902', *The Americas* 37 (January 1981), 268, 272.

nationalism was linked to a burgeoning class consciousness as they came into contact with American trade unions, especially with the radical Industrial Workers of the World (IWW).

One of the great differences between the Mexican industrial working class and their counterparts in more developed industrialized countries was the relative weakness of the privileged upper segment of skilled workers. This was on the one hand due to the predominance of extractive and light industries in Mexico which required a lesser number of skilled workers than other industries, but it was also due to the large number of foreigners among the skilled workers.

The taming of the middle class

One of the Porfirio Díaz's greatest successes was his regime's ability to tame Mexico's traditionally rebellious and mutinous middle classes, comprising government bureaucrats, merchants, intellectuals, white-collar employees, artisans and the like. Until the turn of the century this was accomplished with a limited degree of violence and repression.

After returning to office in 1884 Díaz gradually suppressed the rights he had allowed the middle classes to retain during his first term in office. Autonomous political parties all but disappeared, parliamentary elections scarcely existed, and Congress became practically powerless. The press, once the domain of liberal intellectuals, was more and more government controlled. Large segments of the middle classes accepted these restrictions on their power and freedom without manifesting any substantial resistance to the regime. The Porfiriato offered unprecedented opportunities of advancement in economic terms. In many states, where Díaz replaced *caudillos* whom he did not trust by officials loyal to his regime, new opportunities for sharing local and regional power arose for many of the 'outs' among the middle classes.

Many members of Mexico's middle classes were consciously willing to pay a price for Porfirian peace and economic development. Others were simply co-opted by the regime. Those who did not enter government service profited from the general upsurge of the economy. Nevertheless, the number of opponents of the regime gradually began to increase. In contrast to the beneficiaries of the Díaz regime, substantial groups among the middle classes had either not profited or begun to suffer economic losses by the turn of the century.

The greatest losers were muleteers and local transporters who were displaced by the newly constructed railways, and artisans who could not compete with the newly emerging textile industry. The main middle-class opponents of the regime were dissatisfied intellectuals. Some were independent newspapermen such as Filomeno Mata in Mexico City or Silvestre Terrazas in Chihuahua. Even mild criticism of the regime led to newspaper closings and the jailing of dissident editors (Filomeno Mata was jailed 34 times).

Teachers, whose number rose from 12,748 in 1895 to 21,017 in 1910, were especially vocal in their opposition to the regime. While the increase in their number attests to some development of education in Mexico in the Díaz era, a large number of teachers believed that the government was doing far too little to educate the people. The percentage of illiterates scarcely decreased during the Porfiriato in spite of the fact that new schools were built, especially in the large cities. Higher education remained underdeveloped and the relative number of students in the country scarcely increased. The educational politics of the Porfiriato and the underpaid status of many teachers do not constitute the sole explanation for their opposition to the regime, however; the close contact many teachers maintained with the rural population, their strong sense of nationalism and their resentment at the preference given to foreign cultures were no less important.

While the opposition of intellectuals to a dictatorship was an almost natural phenomenon, the same cannot be said of the massive opposition of merchants to the Díaz regime. Merchants do not generally constitute a radical segment of society. Nevertheless in assessing the causes of the Mexican Revolution of 1910, Pablo Martínez del Río, scion of one of the Porfiriato's leading families, attributed the revolutionary upheavals largely to dissatisfied merchants. The roots of this dissatisfaction lay in the fact that in many towns Mexican merchants either had to compete with foreigners or with clients of the oligarchy who secured concessions from foreign companies for running company stores. Small entrepreneurs who attempted to set up factories or small businesses depended on credit from banks which either belonged to foreigners or to members of the oligarchy. All other things being equal these banks gave preferential treatment to well-connected debtors.

THE CRISIS OF THE PORFIRIATO, 1900–10

In spite of the profound social and economic changes that Díaz brought about and the antagonisms that they engendered, the Mexican president was astonishingly successful until the turn of the century in preventing significant forces of opposition to his regime from emerging. Uprisings had been mainly limited to the periphery of the country and they affected either Indian tribes or only a limited number of villages. Industrial labourers, on the whole, tended to be docile and no significant strikes took place. No opposition political groups on a national scale or even on a regional scale emerged. As a result, not only members of Mexico's elite but foreign statesmen as well heaped sycophantic praise on Díaz. In the short span of ten years, from 1900 to 1910, this situation changed dramatically. Regional opposition movements developed. Strikes affecting thousands of workers took place. Three national opposition movements emerged, two of which called for the violent overthrow of the regime.

The Pax Porfiriana had been based on the fact that Díaz had either won over or neutralized groups and classes which had traditionally led revolutionary and armed movements in Mexico: the army, the upper class, and the middle class. Without them, those lower-class rebellions which did break out in spite of the repressive machinery of the Díaz state were easily crushed and never transcended the local level. The profound change in the situation in the first decade of the twentieth century occurred when the Díaz regime proved less and less capable of maintaining this upper- and middle-class consensus. A major split within these two classes took place at a time of increasing lower-class discontent as well as US dissatisfaction with the regime. When members of all these different groups and classes joined forces, the Mexican Revolution broke out and the Díaz regime fell.

There was no single cause for this dramatic turn of events. An economic depression of unprecedented proportions, political changes at both the regional and national level, increasing and more visible government repression, a struggle over the succession of the ageing president, a new surge of nationalism, and Mexico's emergence as a centre of European–American rivalry were all factors which helped to destroy first the Pax Porfiriana and then the regime.

Between 1900 and 1910 the flow of foreign investments into Mexico assumed torrential proportions. It amounted to nearly three billion dollars, three times as much as in the first twenty-four years of Porfirian rule. This new wave of investments led to a sharp rise in prices, which was further accentuated by the decision of the Mexican government to give up silver and adopt the gold standard. The result of these developments was a sharp fall in real wages in many parts of Mexico. This tendency was accentuated when the boom gave way to one of the greatest economic crises that Porfirian Mexico had ever faced. In 1907–8, a cyclical downturn in the United States extended into Mexico, leading to massive lay-offs and reductions in wages. Domestic unemployment was reinforced by the return of thousands of labourers who had migrated to the United States and who had been the first to be dismissed when the recession affected the economy of Mexico's northern neighbour. The economic downturn was compounded by a simultaneously occurring agricultural crisis. Bad harvests, partly due to drought and partly to floods, decimated Mexico's food production and led to sharp price increases at a time when not only real wages but even nominal wages in industry were being reduced.

At this point the full consequences of the Porfirian road to modernization made themselves felt. The Porfirian regime was neither willing nor able to grant relief to important segments of the upper classes, most of the middle classes and the poorest segments of society. It did not provide any tax relief to middle-sized enterprises profoundly affected by the crisis. On the contrary, with full government approval the oligarchy attempted to shift the burden of the crisis not only on to the shoulders of the poorest segments of society but also to the middle classes and to those members of the upper classes who were not closely linked to the *científicos*. During the boom period both foreign entrepreneurs and members of Mexico's new national ruling class were granted significant tax exemptions. When government revenue began to drop sharply as a result of decreased economic activity, the *científicos* attempted to increase taxes paid by Mexico's middle classes. At the same time banks which both foreigners and the oligarchy controlled not only reduced the amount of credit they granted and increased the price of loans, they also began to collect outstanding debts at an accelerating pace.

The government made no attempt to relieve the credit squeeze in any way. While Díaz's administration lowered some tariffs in order to encourage the importation of basic foodstuffs, it did nothing more. The result was ruin or at least great economic difficulties for many of Mexico's middle-class entrepreneurs and a catastrophic reduction in living standards of large segments of the country's population. This policy was partly due to the *laissez-faire* ideology of the Porfirian oligarchy, but even if the Díaz administration had been willing to do more to relieve the effects of the crisis, its capacity to do so was extremely limited. Government revenues at all levels – federal, state, and municipal – accounted for only 8 per cent of the gross national product.[11] This economic crisis, severe as it was, was not the only immediate cause which provoked Mexico's social explosion in the years 1910–20. The internal contradictions that finally produced the Mexican Revolution were deeper and far more complex than the dislocation the crisis of 1907 produced, although this crisis accentuated the already existing contradictions within Mexican society.

One important factor that contributed to the destabilization of the Díaz regime in its last years was the emergence of a strong working-class opposition. Its main manifestations were strikes, unprecedented in their scope and in the official repression they brought forth, and the emergence of a national opposition political party with strong anarcho-syndicalist leanings. The roots of this working-class opposition were multiple. A new generation of workers had emerged who were not former peasants and who did not compare their present situation with even worse conditions on haciendas or villages. An increasing number of workers had at one time or another gone north of the border to work in the United States. There they had been influenced both by the example of higher living standards and union rights and by the anarcho-syndicalist ideology of the IWW. Nationalism played an increasing role in workers' consciousness as they were pitted not only against foreign investors and managers but foreign workers as well.

The most immediate cause of worker dissatisfaction was the sharp decline in living standards between 1900 and 1910. Even in the boom period up to 1907 real wages were eroded by inflation. Between 1907 and 1910 conditions deteriorated drastically, above all in northern Mexico. In Chihuahua the German consul estimated in 1909 that prices of essential foods and products had risen by 80 per cent while nominal wages had fallen by 20 per cent. The result was a catastrophic drop in real wages for those who still had work. For thousands of others who had been laid off in the course of the recession, conditions were obviously even worse. Interestingly enough, however, the most important social movements of Mexican workers which occurred between 1900 and 1910 did not take place during the economic downturn but during the preceding boom. Of the three major labour conflicts that received national attention in those

[11] John Coatsworth, 'The state and the external sector in Mexico 1800–1900' (unpublished essay). Estimates of GDP based on Leopoldo Solís, 'La evolución económica de México a partir de la Revolución de 1910', *Demografía y Economía*, 3/1 (1969), 4.

years – a strike in the textile factory of Río Blanco in the state of Veracruz in June 1906; a miners' strike in Cananea in the state of Sonora in January 1907; and a railway workers' movement in Chihuahua in 1908 – purely economic issues were preponderant only in the Río Blanco strike. Even there labour conditions were at least as important. In the other two cases, nationalism was intrinsically linked to the demands that the workers made. The Mexican miners of Cananea resented the fact that American miners brought in from across the border were paid more than double for doing exactly the same work they did. Similar resentments were at the core of a strike staged by Mexican railway men in Chihuahua, who complained that all the best positions in Mexico's railway system were reserved for American workers and employees. In the railway strike a limited compromise was reached, but the other two strikes were suppressed with a ruthless brutality that surpassed anything that had occurred in the early years of the Díaz regime. 'Thank God I can still kill', Díaz is said to have exclaimed, and ordered the ruthless execution of dozens of textile workers in Río Blanco who had called on the Mexican president as arbitrator in their dispute with the company. By this time another blood bath, though of smaller proportions, had taken place in Cananea, where the flames of resentment were fanned by the arrival of hundreds of armed Americans from across the border to put down the miners' movement.

This kind of massive and highly visible repression had constituted the exception rather than the rule during the preceding years of the regime. Díaz preferred to make deals rather than to repress and when he did use repressive means he attempted to keep them as secret as possible. Both the scope and the unprecedented character of the massacres as well as the existence of a labour-orientated national opposition party made Río Blanco and Cananea household words for hundreds of thousands of Mexicans. It led thousands to sympathize with the first and most radical opposition movement on a national scale to emerge during the Porfiriato. This was the Partido Liberal Mexicano (PLM), founded by a number of provincial intellectuals at the beginning of the century. It called for a return to the principles of the radical factions of the liberal movement under Juárez. Increasing repression by the government contributed to a rapid swing to the left, and the party soon assumed anarcho-syndicalist traits and pronouncements. Its most outstanding leaders were two brothers, Enrique and Ricardo Flores Magón, who led their party from exile in St Louis. The newspaper they issued,

Regeneración, was banned in Mexico and had to be brought in illegally from the United States. Nevertheless, it apparently sold over 25,000 copies per issue in Mexico and played a role in inspiring the great strikes which broke out in the country.

The PLM was not only influential among industrial workers but among parts of Mexico's middle classes as well. For them the conflict with the Díaz administration was in part a class conflict and to a very large degree a generational struggle. In the eyes of many of the young, the Díaz regime was a closed dictatorial society subservient to foreign and above all US interests which many of the young felt threatened the integrity and independence of Mexico. Their opportunities for social mobility, they felt, were far smaller than those of the generation of their fathers. The older generation still filled the positions in the federal bureaucracy and Díaz gave no indication that he planned any kind of a turnover. A deeply worried French minister reported to his government in 1900:

in spite of the peace which now reigns in the country there is a real dissatisfaction . . . the basis of this dissatisfaction is a party of the young which under the disguise of adherence to principles hides a lust for power and wishes to take part in the perquisites and privileges of power. Lawyers, judges, engineers, writers and journalists constitute the majority of this party. It pretends to speak in the name of the whole of civilian society and declares that the present military regime should be replaced by a regime of parliamentarianism and free discussion.[12]

The large foreign enterprises that were entering Mexico provided no avenue of escape, no new opportunities for the young educated Mexicans who found no possibility of entering the federal or local bureaucracy. The foreigners preferred to choose middle- and upper-level managers from among their own. Their Mexican employees at higher levels tended to be either friends, family members or clients of their Mexican partners who generally were also members of the oligarchy.

The frustration of the young, educated members of Mexico's middle class did not only have economic roots. Many resented what they considered to be the Porfirian elite's blind acceptance of foreign values and foreign culture. For many, 'dollar diplomacy', the rising emigration of Americans to northern Mexico, and the increasing US investment in that region revived fears of a new US annexation. These fears were

---

[12] French Foreign Ministry Archives, Paris, CC, Mexique, Bd 17, Blondel to Delcassé, 3 December 1900.

strengthened by repeated calls in the American press for the annexation of Mexico.

The PLM was successful in inspiring or strengthening large-scale opposition to the Díaz regime. Its call for a national revolution, however, went unheeded. A series of local revolts did break out, most of them in northern Mexico, under the leadership of returning exiles who brought arms and propaganda with them. They failed not only because they were frequently unco-ordinated, but because the groups that led them were often infiltrated by government agents. A very different kind of opposition ranging all the way from dissident hacendados to militant peasants was to force Porfirio Díaz from power. Its emergence was closely linked to political and social changes which emerged at both the national level and at the regional level in the northern border states of Sonora, Coahuila and Chihuahua and in the central state of Morelos.

At the turn of the century a profound political change took place in Mexico. During the last ten years of his administration, Díaz greatly weakened one of his basic policies, the application of a strategy of divide and rule that had so greatly strengthened his regime in its first years. Until the turn of the century at both the national and regional level Díaz had set up a complex system of checks and balances that prevented any one group or clique from achieving too much power. At the national level Díaz allowed and at times encouraged the growth of cliques rivaling the *científicos*. Their most influential rivals consisted of a loose alliance of northern landowners and businessmen as well as military men whose leader, Bernardo Reyes, was one of Díaz's most powerful generals, and who for many years had been military commander and later governor of Nuevo León and from 1900 to 1904 secretary of war. At the local level traditional *caudillos* who generally held the reins of political and economic power had been replaced by men who owed their ascent to Porfirio Díaz. Some of them were officials sent in from other parts of the country with very few local roots, others were less powerful members of the local elite. They frequently had to compete with their predecessors and there were constant conflicts between elite cliques and groups. Díaz was the great arbitrator who maintained a precarious balance between them. At the turn of the century it became increasingly clear that Díaz was either less willing or less able to apply this increasingly complex strategy with the same vigour that he had in his first years in office.

At the national level the *científicos* were pressuring Díaz to grant them increasing power, but above all they wanted the Mexican president, who was now over 70 years of age, to indicate very clearly that in case of his death a member of their group would succeed him. The increasing economic power of this group and its success in managing the economy of the country by augmenting Mexico's revenues and enhancing its credit rating abroad certainly played a major role in influencing Díaz. At least as important may have been the fact that the foreign interests who were investing more and more in Mexico wanted some kind of guarantee from the Mexican president that in case of his death the policies he had carried out would continue. In their eyes the best guarantee that Díaz could give them was an indication that the *científicos* with whom they were intimately linked would continue in power. In 1903 Díaz felt that the time had come to make a decisive gesture to reassure both the *científicos* and the foreign investors and financiers. He agreed to Ramón Corral, a member of the *científico* group from the north-western state of Sonora, becoming his vice president and thus indicated that Corral would succeed him should he die during his term of office. Corral was elected vice president in 1904. It was a major victory for the *científicos* that Díaz underlined when he removed their most powerful enemy, Bernardo Reyes, from his post as secretary of war. At the same time the *científicos* set out to undermine both the economic and political power of elite members opposed to them. In Sonora itself the state government, closely linked to Corral, rode roughshod over the opposition of many landowners, including one of the state's wealthiest hacendados, José María Maytorena. In Coahuila, Díaz forced Governor Miguel Cárdenas, who enjoyed the support of large groups of hacendados, to resign and prevented the election of another landowner, Venustiano Carranza, who was backed by most of the state's upper class. Díaz's opposition to important sections of the north-eastern elite as well as the latter's mounting bitterness towards him may have been compounded by their increasing conflicts with foreign interests. The best-known, but by no means unique, conflict of this kind concerned the Madero clan, the wealthiest and most powerful family in the Laguna, if not Coahuila, which had never supported Reyes, although one of its most prominent members, Francisco Madero, had for some years attempted to set up political opposition to the Díaz administration. In contrast to the Torres and Terrazas families, the Maderos had never co-operated harmoniously with the US companies and had become notorious among these companies for their ill-concealed confrontation tactics. At the turn of the twentieth century, Francisco Madero had formed and led a coalition of hacendados in the Laguna region to oppose attempts by the Anglo-American Tlahualilo Company to monopolize the water rights of that irrigation-dependent area. When the Maderos cultivated the rubber substitute, guayule, they had clashed with the Continental Rubber Company. Another conflict developed because prior to 1910 the Maderos owned the only smelting oven in northern Mexico that was independent of the American Smelting and Refining Company.

In Chihuahua the *científico* offensive was not directed against dissident hacendados who scarcely existed but against the peasants and important segments of the middle classes. It was here that the *científicos* scored one of their greatest successes by obtaining full control of the state for one of their most powerful associates, Luis Terrazas and his family clan. In 1903 they effected a reconciliation between the Chihuahuan *caudillo* and Díaz who had fought on opposite sides when Díaz revolted in 1871 and 1876. With Díaz's backing, Terrazas again became governor of his native state in 1903. Chihuahua was now converted into a family undertaking. It was alternately ruled by Luis Terrazas, his son-in-law, Enrique Creel, Luis's son Alberto, and in between by candidates appointed by them. Their power now exceeded the wildest dreams of their predecessors in the pre-Díaz era. Anyone wishing to hold a government post, whether at the local or state level, had to go through the new power brokers. Anyone going to court had to appeal to judges appointed by them. Anyone needing credit had to turn to banks controlled by them. Anyone seeking employment with a foreign company probably had to depend on their mediation. Anyone losing his land to a surveying company or to a hacendado could blame them. The new local oligarchy had not only gained unprecedented power, it also threw off the constraints and obligations its predecessors had borne. It did not respect municipal autonomy, nor did it have to provide protection against the assaults of the Apaches or the federal government. The result was a growing polarization of forces and increasing middle-class bitterness.

The state's free peasants and especially the former military colonists suffered even more as a result of Terrazas' return to power. A new railway line, the Kansas Pacific Railroad, was being built through the mountain region of western Chihuahua where a large part of the former military colonies were located. Land values rose accordingly. Since the government did not need the fighting power of these colonists any more, a full-scale offensive to deprive them of their lands was undertaken by Enrique Creel. A new agrarian law was drafted for the state. It specified that municipal lands could now be sold to the highest bidder. As a result the last holdings of the military colonies began to be expropriated. 'If you do not grant us your protection we will lose our lands for which our ancestors have fought against the barbarians', the inhabitants of one of the state's oldest and most prestigious military colonies, Namiquipa, wrote to Porfirio Díaz.[13] In dozens of the state's villages, such as San Andrés, Cuchillo Parado, and Bocoyna, villagers vainly protested to the central government against the expropriation of their lands. Previous expropriations had impoverished the peasants. Creel's new law threatened their very existence.

The *científico* offensive and the economic crisis of 1907 created an unprecedented and unique situation in the northern triangle of Sonora, Chihuahua and Coahuila. What was unique to this region was that substantial portions from all classes of society ranging from hacendados and the middle classes to industrial workers to the dispossessed former military colonists were united in their opposition to the Díaz regime.

A dissatisfied middle class which resented the fact that it was excluded from political power, that it seemed to garner only the crumbs of Mexico's economic boom, and that foreigners were playing an increasingly important role in the country's economic and social structure existed in most parts of Mexico. Nowhere, however, had it grown as rapidly as in the north, and nowhere had it suffered such losses in so short a span of time. Not only was the northern middle class profoundly affected by the crisis of 1907 which hit the north far more than any other part of Mexico, but as Díaz gave political control of their states to the oligarchy and put an end to the two-party system it also suffered greater political losses.

The same crisis affected the north's industrial working classes to a degree unprecedented in their experience and unparalleled in the rest of Mexico. With the possible exception of Mexico City it was in the north of the country that the greatest number of unemployed workers could be found on the eve of the Revolution. Hacendados who were dissatisfied with some of the policies of the Díaz regime (and especially with the way the *científicos* attempted to shift the burden of the 1907 crisis to other sectors of society) could be found in many parts of Mexico. Most of them were far too afraid of the peasants, from whose expropriation so many of them had benefited, to challenge the Díaz regime. A number of dissident

[13] Departamento Agrário, Dirección de Terrenos Nacionales, Diversos, Chihuahua, Exp. 178, Letter of the inhabitants of Namiquipa to President Porfirio Díaz, 20 July 1908.

hacendados in northern Mexico, especially in Sonora and Coahuila, however, entertained no such fears. In Coahuila most of the dissident hacendados were located in the Laguna area. The Laguna had been an unpopulated wasteland before the hacendados reclaimed it. They did not have to confront a mass of peasants whom they had expropriated. The fact that the peons on their estates received the highest wages and enjoyed the greatest freedom found anywhere in the Mexican countryside had created a new kind of paternalistic relation between these landowners and their peons. The hacendados attempted to strengthen this relationship by providing schools and medical care to their workers. Some enlightened landowners, such as Francisco Madero, even extended many of these services to non-resident peons, thus earning their loyalty. In Sonora José María Maytorena protected his Yaqui labourers from deportation by the federal authorities and they regarded him as their patron. The three northern states which had been the main objects of the *científico* offensive constituted the most powerful basis of the opposition movements which emerged in Mexico between 1907 and 1910.

In the state of Morelos the *científico* offensive had equally deep repercussions, but it affected mainly one class of society: the peasantry. The state's governor, Manuel Alarcón, a traditional *caudillo*, not unfriendly to the planters but still considered by a large part of the state's population to have been his own man with whom they could at least deal in times of crisis and who was not a part of the local oligarchy, had died in 1908. He was replaced by Pablo Escandón, who belonged to the landed oligarchy of the state and had close links to the *científicos*. As in Chihuahua power now fell completely into the hands of the local oligarchy. For the state's free villages, Escandón's rule was an unmitigated disaster. As demand for sugar rose, the sugar planters began to expropriate the remaining lands from the hundred or so of free villages which dotted the state of Morelos. The peasants now felt completely abandoned by the Mexican state. Many of them had for a long time considered the central government to be a kind of neutral power to which they could appeal. Now that the myth of a benevolent government in Mexico City, which would act in favour of the peasants if only it knew what really happened, was removed by the appointment of a planter as governor of the state, their readiness to revolt mounted. Like the three northern states of Sonora, Chihuahua and Coahuila, Morelos was to become one of the main centres of the 1910 Revolution.

As a new presidential election approached in 1910 a new struggle for the succession broke out. Dissident members of Mexico's upper and middle classes again sought to limit *científico* influence and to persuade Díaz to choose a non-*científico* as his vice-presidential nominee. Their candidate was Bernardo Reyes and their political organization called itself the Democratic party. Its influence and vigour was greatly increased as the result of a significant tactical error that Díaz committed in 1908. In an interview with an American newspaper correspondent, James Creelman, Díaz seemed to invite candidates to present themselves at the polls. In this interview the Mexican dictator declared that he felt that Mexico was now ripe for democracy, that he would not be a candidate in the next presidential elections and that he welcomed the formation of opposition political groups. It is not clear why Díaz made verbal commitments he did not seriously mean, but their consequences were very definite.

Opponents of the regime felt that Díaz had given his official blessing to an opposition party and that they would suffer no reprisal if they joined such a group. The authorities became disorientated, and for a time allowed such movements a far greater degree of freedom than they had ever enjoyed before. As thousands of people, mainly of middle-class origin, began rallying behind Reyes, Díaz openly told Reyes that he would never accept him as vice-presidential candidate and sent him on a military mission to Europe. Facing the choice of either rebelling or accepting the president's decision, Reyes bowed out of the presidential race.

With the exile of Reyes his upper-class supporters faced an agonizing decision. They had hoped to pressure Díaz and perhaps even remove him from power with the help of a coalition similar to the one that had brought Díaz to power more than 30 years before: an alliance of dissident members of the upper and middle classes with potential rebels within the army. The link to whatever dissidents existed within the army was Reyes. Once he submitted to Díaz this link was broken and the military option ceased to exist. Any serious attempt to pressure Díaz or to overthrow him would have to be based on an entirely different strategy: an alliance with the lower classes of society, including the peasantry. For many of Reyes's supporters, especially in central Mexico, this was an unacceptable option since they feared that once mobilized the peasants would move against them as well and become an uncontrollable force; they therefore withdrew from any active opposition to Díaz.

The dissident hacendados of northern Mexico, especially in Sonora and Coahuila, as we have seen, had no such fears of the peasants. The former Reyes supporters there threw their support behind another national opposition party that was emerging: the Anti-Reelectionist party led by Francisco I. Madero, a wealthy hacendado from Coahuila. Madero became a national figure in 1908 when he published a book on the presidential succession. In it, he characterized Mexico's fundamental problem as that of absolutism and the unlimited power of one man. Only the introduction of parliamentary democracy, a system of free elections, and the independence of the press and of the courts could transform Mexico into a modern, democratic state. The book was very cautiously written. While harshly criticizing the Díaz system, it praised the dictator's personal qualities. It came out, however, against excessive concessions to foreigners and reproached Díaz for being too soft towards the United States. Social questions were scarcely mentioned.

Some post-revolutionary historians, as well as Porfirio Díaz himself, considered Madero a naive dreamer for taking Díaz's promise to hold democratic elections in Mexico seriously. Madero saw himself in a somewhat different light. In an interview he gave in 1911 he said:

At the beginning of the political campaign the majority of our nation's inhabitants believed in the absolute effectiveness of the public vote as a means of fighting against General Díaz. Nevertheless, I understood that General Díaz could only have been toppled by armed force. But in order to carry out the revolution the democratic campaign was indispensable because it would prepare public opinion and justify an armed uprising. We carried out the democratic campaign as if we had no intention of resorting to an armed uprising. We used all legal means and when it became clear that General Díaz would not respect the national will . . . we carried out an armed uprising . . . [Díaz] respected me because since I was not a military man he never believed that I was capable of taking up arms against him. I understood that this was my only defense and without resorting to hypocrisy I succeeded in strengthening this concept in his mind.[14]

When Madero formed his party Díaz did not take it seriously. Moreover, he felt that it might divide and weaken the one opposition group he really feared – Reyes's Democratic party. As a result, in 1908 and part of 1909 Madero was relatively free in his presidential campaign. The philanthropically minded hacendado succeeded in doing what the PLM had conspicuously failed to do. He aroused and mobilized

---

[14] These remarks were part of an interview that Madero gave to the Hearst Press in 1911. They are quoted in Jerry W. Knudson, 'When did Francisco I. Madero decide on Revolution?', *The Americas*, 30 (April 1974), 532–4.

important sectors of the Mexican peasantry, although his agrarian programme was very diffuse and never called for the kind of land reform that the liberals advocated. When disillusioned supporters of Reyes joined the party, the *anti-reeleccionistas* became the only group in Mexico which embraced members of all classes of society, from wealthy hacendados to lowly peons on large estates. This heterogeneous and unexpected coalition led by a man with no military experience succeeded in overthrowing the Díaz regime in 1910–11.

There are indications, although no absolute proof, that when the Revolution broke out some US corporations (above all, oil interests) actively supported it while the Taft administration showed a degree of 'tolerance' toward Madero's activities which profoundly worried the Díaz government. While US links to the 1910–11 revolutionaries are still the subject of much debate, there is little doubt that relations between the Díaz administration and the US government as well as some American corporations had become more and more strained between 1900 and 1910.

Both the Mexican government and the *científicos* deeply resented the rising tide of US interventionism in Central America and the Caribbean after the Spanish–American War. They were greatly worried by the fact that by the turn of the century, larger and more powerful US corporations were replacing the middle-sized American companies which predominated among US investors in the early years of the Porfiriato. 'The Mexican government has now formally taken a position against the trusts formed with American capital', the Austrian minister to Mexico reported as early as 1902. 'A series of articles appeared in semi-official newspapers pointing to the growing dangers that the intensive activities of the trusts are presenting to the Mexican producers. The latter will soon be slaves of the North American money market.'[15] Díaz refused to heed the calls for more nationalistic policies which emanated above all from Mexico's middle classes, but he did attempt to counteract US influence by encouraging a stronger European presence in Mexico.

These efforts by the Mexican president and the *científicos* elicited strong support in Great Britain. One of the country's most important financiers, Sir Weetman Pearson (Lord Cowdray), who had been active in Mexican public works projects for many years, became the country's most important oil producer in the early twentieth century, challenging

---

[15] Haus-, Hof- und Staatsarchiv Wien, Politisches Archiv, Mexico Reports, 1902, Auersthal to Goluchowsky, 24 November 1902.

the supremacy which US oilmen had until then exercised in Mexico. The British government showed a strong interest in Mexican oil which was increasingly important to its efforts to have the British navy fuelled by oil instead of coal. For its part the Mexican government went out of its way to help British oil interests by granting them leases on government land and exclusive contracts to supply the government controlled railways (in the process cancelling another contract for oil supplies which a preceding administration had signed with the US-owned Mexican Petroleum Company).

This was the strongest anti-American measure the Mexican government took. But it was not the only one. The US government greatly resented the support Díaz had granted Nicaraguan President Zelaya, whom they were attempting to oust, as well as Mexico's cancellation of a concession for a coaling station which it had previously accorded to the US Navy in Baja California. This cancellation was widely considered in the USA as a Mexican effort to woo Japan. On the whole, the Díaz government's anti-American gestures remained limited in scope and Díaz did his best never to publicize them. As a result, by 1910 his administration was in a paradoxical situation. While the Mexican president's policies were increasingly resented by some US corporations and the Washington administration, Mexico's opposition considered him a satellite of the United States. In the final account, this paradox would contribute greatly to his fall.

The end of the Porfiriato

On 16 September 1910 the Díaz regime seemed to have reached the apex of its power. On that day special ambassadors from all countries in the world participated in lavish ceremonies to commemorate the one hundredth anniversary of the day on which Father Miguel Hidalgo proclaimed the independence of Mexico in the small village of Dolores. Díaz seemed to have resolved most of the difficulties that had plagued him in the two preceding years. Not only had Reyes gone into exile but Francisco Madero, at least in the eyes of the Porfirian authorities, had been eliminated as a serious political force. On 5 June 1910, shortly before the elections, he had been arrested on a charge of sedition. On 21 June the elections took place amid massive charges of fraud by the Anti-Reelectionist party. The government declared that the Díaz–Corral ticket had been re-elected, and that not a single opposition candidate had received sufficient votes to become a member of the new Congress. A few sporadic local uprisings in Valladolid in Yucatán and in Veracruz were put down, and the government was convinced that it was now in full control of the situation. It felt so secure that on 22 July it agreed to release Madero on bail. 'I consider general revolution to be out of the question as does public opinion and the press', the German envoy to Mexico, Karl Bünz, optimistically wrote to his government on 4 December 1910.[16]

On 6 October, Madero had escaped from the city of San Luis Potosí where he had been free on bail awaiting his trial. From San Antonio, Texas, he issued his programme, the Plan of San Luis Potosí. Accusing Díaz of having carried out fraudulent elections, Madero assumed the office of provisional president and called for the people to revolt on 20 November 1910. While the plan was essentially political in character, Madero included a clause in which he promised to return lands unjustly confiscated from village communities to their rightful owners.

The revolt in Madero's native state of Coahuila for which the revolutionary president had hoped did not materialize. An attempt at revolt by Aquiles Serdan, the head of the Anti-Reelectionist party in Puebla, was crushed by the Porfirian authorities. But to the surprise of both Díaz, who was inaugurated on 1 December, and Madero, a popular uprising broke out in the mountains of western Chihuahua. Led by Pascual Orozco and Pancho Villa the revolutionaries soon controlled a large part of the state.

On 14 February 1911 Madero crossed the border from the United States into Mexico and assumed the leadership of the Chihuahuan revolutionaries. In February and March local revolts began to break out all over Mexico. Emiliano Zapata led a peasant uprising in the state of Morelos, while Jesús Agustín Castro, Orestes Pereira and Calixto Contreras revolted in the Laguna region of Coahuila. Smaller revolts broke out in the rest of the country and by April 1911 most of the Mexican countryside was in the hands of revolutionaries. In May the rebels captured their first large city, the border town of Ciudad Juárez. In March the Díaz administration had suffered an enormous blow to its prestige when President Taft mobilized 20,000 men along the US–Mexican border and sent American warships to Mexican ports. While the US government officially stated that the mobilization was intended to

---

[16] GFO Bonn, Mexico 1, vol. 25, Bünz to Bethmann-Hollweg, 4 December 1910.

facilitate enforcement of the neutrality laws, it was not a neutral move. It generated fears in Mexico that the US was prepared to intervene and increased pressure on Díaz, even from his closest supporters, to resign and find a compromise with the revolutionaries. On 21 May 1911 the Treaty of Ciudad Juárez was signed between Madero and the federal government. It provided for the resignation of Díaz and Corral from office by the end of May and their replacement by Francisco León de la Barra, who had not participated in the Revolution, as provisional president. The provisional government was to carry out elections in October 1911. In the meantime, the revolutionary army would be disbanded. Feeling that an imminent victory had been taken away from them, large segments of Madero's supporters strongly objected to the treaty. Madero nevertheless accepted its provisions and in the ensuing months co-operated with the provisional government in attempting to implement it, above all by doing everything in his power to assist in the dissolution of the revolutionary army that had brought about his victory. After some hesitation he even threw his support behind the provisional government's efforts to disarm by force the revolutionaries of the state of Morelos led by Emiliano Zapata. In many parts of the country the revolutionaries did lay down their arms peacefully, convinced that once Madero was elected, the social changes for which so many of them had fought would finally be implemented. On 15 October 1911 Madero was elected president by an overwhelming majority in what was probably the most honest election the country had ever had. He was sworn into office on 6 November 1911, firmly convinced that the Mexican Revolution had ended, its objectives, as he saw them, having been achieved.

3

THE MEXICAN REVOLUTION,
1910—1920

Three theoretical assumptions in liberal sociology long ruled historical study of the Mexican Revolution: mass action is consensual, intentional, and redistributive; collective violence measures structural transformation; and nationalism aggregates interests in a limited division of labour. In plain words, movement of 'the people' is movement by 'the people' for 'the people'; the bloodier the struggle, the deeper the difference between ways of life before and after the struggle; and familiarity breeds solidarity. The most influential scholars of the subject also made two radical suppositions about Mexico in particular. First, the most significant fact in the country in 1910 was the struggle between the upper and lower classes. Second, the conflict was about to explode. And on these premises respectable research and analysis framed a pro-revolutionary story of the rise of the downtrodden: the Revolution began over a political issue, the succession to Porfirio Díaz, but masses of people in all regions quickly involved themselves in a struggle beyond politics for sweeping economic and social reforms. Enormous material destruction throughout the country, the ruination of business, and total defiance of the United States were necessary for the popular struggle to triumph, as it did. And through the struggle the champions of 'the people' became the revolutionary leaders. Economic and social conditions improved in accordance with revolutionary policies, so that the new society took shape within a framework of official revolutionary institutions. The struggle ended in 1917, the year of the revolutionary constitution. The new revolutionary state enjoyed as much legitimacy and strength as its spokesmen said it did.

Hence the professional historical judgement, widely accepted until the 1970s, that the Mexican Revolution had been a 'social' revolution. The movements from 1910 to 1917 were represented as a massive,

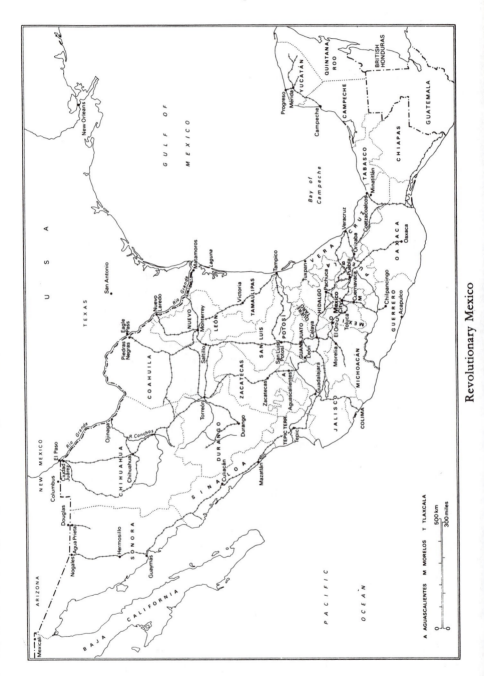

Revolutionary Mexico

extremely violent and intensely nationalist uprising, in which 'the people' destroyed the old regime, peasants reclaimed their lands, workers organized unions, and the revolutionary government started the development of the country's wealth for the national welfare, opening a new epoch in Mexican history. In some versions the Mexican Revolution appeared as 'the first social revolution of the twentieth century', for better or worse comparable to the Russian and Chinese Revolutions.

There were problems in this interpretation. From the beginning critics insisted that 'the people' had been used by deceitful leaders for a false cause and dragged into worse conditions. But almost all scholars dismissed such versions as counter-revolutionary propaganda. More troublesome to interpret was a challenge to revolutionary legitimacy by tens of thousands of 'the people' in a Catholic rebellion in the 1920s. The problem that professional historians could not ignore was a sense spreading after 1940 that Mexico was developing along the lines more of the old regime than of the supposed Revolution. Although revolutionary institutions remained formally intact and revolutionary rhetoric continued to flow, peasants and workers benefited less than before, while businesses, above all American companies, multiplied, grew, and made their profits the register of national welfare. If Mexico had had a social revolution in the decade after 1910, what explained the recurrence of old practices in up-to-date patterns 30 years later? Historians who admitted the question gave various answers: the Revolution had died, been betrayed, passed into a new stage. None was convincing. In 1968 the Mexican government bloodily repressed a popular movement for civil rights. The standard interpretation of the Revolution, according to which the people's will had been institutionalized in the government, made historical explanation of the repression impossible. For some young scholars the most tempting explanation was to argue, as the critics always had, that the Revolution had been a trick on 'the people'.

Scholarly debate on the Revolution increased substantially in the 1960s and 1970s. Implicit in the most thoughtful new studies was an impartial mistrust of the old assumptions, a sophisticated use of the old criticisms. 'The people' may move on their own or be moved by others to fight among themselves, and by itself the distinction between autonomous and manipulated movements predicts nothing about differences between their consequences. Bloody struggles may deeply change a society, but not in the ways initially proposed, or they may change it only on the surface. And familiarity often breeds contempt.

Guided by conceptualization more objective than before, new research and analysis have significantly modified the old story and warranted a new interpretation. The struggle that began in 1910 featured not so much the lower versus the upper class as frustrated elements of the upper and middle classes versus favoured elements of the same classes. In this struggle masses of people were involved, but intermittently, differently from region to region, and mostly under middle-class direction, less in economic and social causes than in a bourgeois civil war. In some places destruction was terrible, in others scant and passing or nil. On the whole, business adjusted and continued. Over the long run it increased. From beginning to end foreign activities figured crucially in the Revolution's course, not simple antagonism from the US government, but complicated Euro-American imperialist rivalries, extremely intricate during the first world war. What really happened was a struggle for power, in which different revolutionary factions contended not only against the old regime and foreign concerns, but also, often more so, against each other, over matters as deep as class and as shallow as envy: the victorious faction managed to dominate peasant movements and labour unions for the promotion of selected American and native businesses. Economic and social conditions changed a little according to policy, but largely according to shifts in international markets, the contingencies of war, and the factional and personal interests of temporarily ascendant regional and local leaders, so that relations at all levels were much more complex and fluctuating than official institutions indicated. The state constituted in 1917 was not broadly or deeply popular, and under pressure from the United States and domestic rivals it barely survived until the faction supporting it split, yielding a new faction sufficiently coherent to negotiate its consolidation. Hence several new periodizations, the most plausible running from 1910 to 1920, the year of the last successful factional revolt.

A few old theses are not in dispute. During the Revolution, Mexican society did undergo extraordinary crises and serious changes. Peasant movements and labour unions became important forces. And the constitution represented a new respect for claims to egalitarian and fraternal justice. But from the revisions it now seems clear that basically there was continuity in Mexico between 1910 and 1920. The crises did not go nearly deep enough to break capitalist domination of production. The great issues were issues of state. The most significant development was the improvised organization of new bourgeois forces able to deal with the United States, cope with peasants and workers, and build a new regime and put it into operation. In practice the economic and social reforms were not very different from those accomplished in the same years, without civil war, in Peru, Chile, and Argentina. For all the violence this is the main historical meaning of the Mexican Revolution: capitalist tenacity in the economy and bourgeois reform of the state, which helps to explain the country's stability through the struggles of the 1920s and 1930s and its booming, discordant growth after 1940.

The subject is therefore no longer so much social revolution as political management. And the interpretation here is primarily a political history. It is short on social movements, because however important their emergence, their defeat or subordination mattered more. It is long on the politics that created the new state, because where *fortuna* and *virtú* do their damnedest, only the details reveal the reason for the result.

OCTOBER 1910 – FEBRUARY 1913

The spectre haunting Mexico in 1910 was the spectre of political reform. The country's politics had to change soon, because its central political institution, President Porfirio Díaz, was mortal and 80. And the change would go deep, because after 30 years of vigorous capitalist development and shrewd personal dictatorship, politics meant business. In maze upon maze of graft and collusion between politicians and businessmen, reform meant renegotiation of a myriad of shady deals.

Of the country's several important kinds of conflict, the two most pressing were about business. One was the rivalry between twenty or so big British, American, French, German, Canadian and Mexican banks and companies, for bonds, concessions, and national markets. Treated in the highest and tightest financial and political circles, it remained orderly. The other kind was the conflict between the major firms and hundreds of small Mexican enterprises over local opportunities for profit. These struggles were almost always disturbing, because they threatened established deals. If entrepreneurs big or small pursued a new venture, they risked subverting a local hierarchy of interests and authority; vice versa, subversion could open a new field of transactions. Since the crash of 1907, disappointments in politics and business had so angered some entrepreneurs that they considered a revolution necessary to promote their deals. After the electoral fraud and repression in the summer of 1910, many *anti-reeleccionistas* considered a revolution their duty.

The Porfiriato was a formidable regime to overthrow. Its obvious strengths in a country with a population of 15 million included international respect worth 450 million pesos in loans from European and American bondholders, the treasury running a ten million peso surplus, the Federal Army of 30,000 men, at least another 30,000 men in the Federal Auxiliaries and Irregulars and National Guard, 12,000 miles of railway for troop movements, and 2,500 Rurales. But the entire regime was not in question among the new subversives. For them the removal of the aged dictator and his closest associates would open the country's affairs sufficiently for their purposes.

In October 1910 plans for this revolution matured in San Antonio, Texas. There, having escaped from Mexico, Francisco I. Madero conferred with leading *anti-reeleccionistas* and the most enterprising members of his big, rich family. In early November he published his programme, the Plan de San Luis Potosí. Denouncing the recent presidential, congressional, and judicial elections as fraudulent, he declared himself provisional president, announced a national insurrection on 20 November, and promised 'democratic' elections for a new government. 'Democratic' or not, the prospect of a new government interested financially straitened and politically angry landlords in the northern states, and excited small farmers and merchants throughout the country. A minor clause in the San Luis plan, a promise to review villages' complaints about the loss of their lands, attracted peasants' attention, particularly in Chihuahua and Morelos.[1]

The private Madero strategy for revolution was tidier. Francisco's brother Gustavo – a German diplomat later called him the family's main *Geschäftemacher* – hired a Washington lawyer, Sherburne G. Hopkins, as the movement's legal counsel in the United States. The world's best rigger of Latin American revolutions, in close contact with Standard Oil, Hopkins was to stir up American sympathy for a short uprising of 'the Mexican people'. On 20 November Francisco would lead the capture of a Coahuila border town, Piedras Negras (then called Ciudad Porfirio Díaz), where he would set up a provisional government; and *anti-reeleccionista* agents would raise revolts in Mexico City, Puebla City, and

---

[1] Isidro and Josefina E. de Fabela (eds.), *Documentos históricos de la revolución mexicana* (27 vols., Mexico, 1960–76), v, 69–76.

Pachuca and in rural districts in Chihuahua and Guerrero. Propaganda would focus on Díaz's connection with the *científicos*, to gratify the Reyistas, the bellwethers of the army. Without much of a fight, Díaz would resign in a couple of months. And the 'democratic' election would go to Francisco Madero.

Parts of this strategy proved successful. Standard Oil negotiated encouragingly with Gustavo Madero. US officials bent neutrality laws for the revolutionaries. And General Reyes, who might have taken the initiative from the Maderos, remained in exile in Europe. But the revolution went haywire.

The government broke the major plots for 20 November. Francisco Madero retreated to Texas, and on 1 December Díaz was reinaugurated. But by January 1911 Maderistas in the Chihuahua mountains had raised some 2,000 guerillas. The Magonista anarchists, resurfacing in Baja California, captured the border town of Mexicali. In February Francisco Madero joined the Maderistas in Chihuahua, where instead of reliable *anti-reeleccionista* agents he found unfamiliar and unruly chiefs, foremost a local haulier, Pascual Orozco, who counted among his lieutenants a notable bandit, Francisco Villa. And the guerillas were not docile peons, but peasants from old military colonies counting on recovery of lost lands.

The army and the Rurales maintained regular order in almost all sizeable towns and along the railways. But on 6 March the United States took crucial action: President Taft ordered the mobilization of US forces on the border. In effect this was an intervention in Mexican politics, and to Mexicans it meant the United States had condemned Díaz. In New York, finance minister Limantour negotiated with Francisco's father, brother Gustavo, and the *anti-reeleccionista* vice-presidential candidate, Francisco Vázquez Gómez. In Mexico, businessmen and politicians hurried to rearrange their deals. Díaz exiled Vice President Ramón Corral to Europe, which opened the possibility of negotiations to replace him.

But revolutionaries multiplied in the northern states. In mid-April Sonora Maderistas occupied the border town of Agua Prieta. South of Mexico City several new bands revolted, most significantly village peasants in Morelos, determined to reclaim from the haciendas the lands their ancestors had farmed. The Maderos then tried to wind down the uprising in new negotiations. But on 10 May, against orders, Pascual Orozco captured Juárez, the most important town on the northern border. New Maderista bands sprang up in every state. Altogether maybe 25,000 revolutionaries were in the field, capturing sizeable towns, threatening state capitals, fighting for office, deals, loot, revenge, and, most alarmingly, land. The national insurrection for which Francisco Madero had called but made no provisions had materialized, with the obvious danger of uncontrollable peasant movements.

The Maderos seized on Orozco's victory to negotiate again. Francisco Madero set up his provisional government in Juárez, and on 21 May signed with Díaz's envoys a treaty ending the hostilities. In effect he repudiated the San Luis plan for a connection with the *científicos*. Under the treaty Díaz resigned on 25 May; he sailed for France a week later. Constitutionally replacing him was his foreign minister, Francisco León de la Barra, until a special election in October. All the Porfirian governors resigned, and several of them and Díaz's closest associates, including Limantour, went into exile too. But replacing Limantour was a banker and businessman whom the *científicos* counted virtually as their own, Francisco's uncle Ernesto Madero. And almost all congressmen, judges, and the federal bureaucracy stayed in place. So did the entire Federal Army and the Rurales, guaranteeing stability. The revolutionary forces were to be disarmed and discharged.

León de la Barra took office, recognized by the US and European governments. With all the regime's formidable resources, he had four months to liquidate the revolution and lubricate the transition to a Madero–*científico* government. Francisco Madero arrived in Mexico City on 7 June, a popular idol, 'the apostle of democracy'. He and his brother Gustavo had four months to transform popularity into votes.

Their campaign suffered no antagonism from the United States, which co-operated with the Federal Army to disperse the anarchists in Baja California. And it suffered no extraordinary difficulties from the economy. The recent fighting had done only slight damage to centres of production and railways. Both the US-owned Mexican Petroleum and Lord Cowdray's Águila Oil had just made major discoveries in the Gulf fields. The Fundidora steel plant in Monterrey was well on its way to a splendid year in output and sales. (For statistics on some important lines of production, see table 1.) And the summer rains were good, promising full harvests in the autumn.

Even so *maderismo* lost political ground. It had no direct support from banks and big companies, which backed the *científicos*. The *científicos* accepted 'the apostle' only to foil Reyes, in case he returned; many of

Table 1. *Production in the Mexican economy, selected commodities, 1910–20*

(metric tons, except oil in barrels)

Year	Barley	Corn	Cotton	Henequén	Sugar	Wheat	Copper	Gold	Monterrey iron/steel	Oil	Silver
1910	131,700	—	42,776	94,790	159,049	320,785	48,160	41.420	165,373	3,634,080	2,416.669
1911	139,264	—	34,203	116,547	152,551	320,54C	56,072	37.120	217,999	12,552,798	2,518.202
1912	120,128	2,062,971	51,222	139,902	146,323	320,849	57,245	32.431	155,247	16,558,215	2,526.715
1913	211,308	—	43,830	145,280	125,922	286,549[a]	52,592	25.810	46,321	25,692,291	1,725.861
1914	232,271	1,961,073	—	169,286	108,262	214,288	26,621	8.635	5	26,235,403	810.647
1915	214,260	—	20,336	162,744	88,480	207,144	206	7.358	8,741	32,910,508	712.599
1916	211,308	—	18,109	201,990	49,210	286,549[a]	28,411	11.748	37,513	40,545,712	925.993
1917	—	—	13,582	127,092	65,396	—	50,946	23.542	49,536	55,292,770	1,306.988
1918	379,525	1,899,625	78,040	140,001	68,894	280,441	70,200	25.313	68,710	63,828,326	1,944.542
1919	—	—	—	113,870	90,546	381,599	52,272	23.586	90,020	87,072,954	2,049.898
1920	—	—	—	160,759	113,183	400,469	49,192	22.864	76,000	157,068,678	2,068.938

Note: [a] Incomplete data

Sources: Institut International d'Agriculture, Service de la statistique générale, *Annuaire international de statistique agricole, 1909 à 1921* (Rome, 1922), tables 7, 13, 19, 33, 56; Enrique Aznar Mendoza, 'Historia de la industria henequenera desde 1919 hasta nuestros días', in *Enciclopedia Yucatanense* (8 vols, Mexico, 1947), III, 779; Frédéric Mauro, 'Le développement économique de Monterrey (1890–1960)', *Caravelle*, 2 (1964), tables 21, 22, 24; Lorenzo Meyer, *México y los Estados Unidos en el conflicto petrolero* (1917–1942) (Mexico, 1968), table 1; and G. A. Roush and Allison Butts (eds.), *The mineral industry, its statistics, technology and trade during 1921* (New York, 1922), 845. The annual average production of corn, 1906–10, was 3,219,624 metric tons. Robert G. Cleland (ed.), *The Mexican year book* (Los Angeles, 1924), 240.

them joined a new and suddenly strong Partido Nacional Católico, which promoted a Madero–León de la Barra slate. General Reyes did return and accepted his presidential candidacy. The Maderistas themselves divided. In Sonora and Coahuila local *anti-reeleccionistas* whom the Maderos trusted, landlords in their own image, emerged in firm control. But in Chihuahua, where the family sponsored *anti-reeleccionista* Abrahám González for governor, it bitterly disappointed revolutionary hero Orozco; he did not rest content as commander of his old force, saved from discharge by conversion into state militia. In Morelos, Francisco Madero infuriated revolutionary leaders by advising them that village claims against haciendas had to await 'study' of 'the agrarian question'. To provoke a scandal favouring Reyes, federal forces under General Victoriano Huerta occupied Morelos. Madero's attempts to mediate failed, and outraged villagers fought back under a chief from a village near Cuautla, Emiliano Zapata. Resentful over the Madero–*científico* coalition, Francisco Vázquez Gómez and his brother Emilio connected with other local chiefs determined to keep their forces in arms as local militia. Gustavo Madero responded by reorganizing the Anti-Reelectionist party into the Partido Progresista Constitucional, which nominated a Yucatán lawyer, José María Pino Suárez, as its vice-presidential candidate. This prompted severe political feuding in half a dozen important states.

On 1 October, in probably the freest election in Mexico's history, Francisco Madero's personal popularity and Gustavo's *progresista* machine carried the day. The Madero–Pino Suárez slate won 53 per cent of the vote; four other slates shared the remainder. On 6 November 1911, recognized by the US and European governments, Madero took office to serve a five-year term. Ernesto Madero remained finance minister.

President Madero stood above all for political freedom. He was no doubt sincere, but in fact he had no choice. He had effective power only over his Cabinet. And in memorable contrast to Díaz's dictatorship a lively public politics did develop, most surprising for its serious political parties. The Partido Progresista and the Partido Católico organized energetically and extensively for the congressional elections in mid 1912.

As long as Madero's government lasted, it enjoyed a growing economy. With rising world mineral prices, mining production increased. The big American Smelting and Refining Company (ASARCO) reported larger smelting profits than ever before; oil production boomed; good rains again in 1912 yielded bigger harvests for domestic

Table 2. *Value of Mexican exports and imports, 1910–20*
(dollars)

	Total exports	Exports to US	Total imports	Imports from US
1910	138,006,937	61,092,502	99,864,422	63,858,939
1911	147,462,298	57,311,622	96,823,317	53,454,407
1912	149,119,955	76,767,931	93,438,730	56,079,150
1913	154,392,312	81,735,434	90,610,659	48,052,137
1914	92,285,415	86,280,966	52,391,919	33,215,561
1915	125,199,568	83,551,993	26,331,123[a]	41,066,775
1916	242,688,153	105,065,780	42,214,449[a]	54,270,283
1917	152,872,380	130,370,565	94,915,092[a]	111,124,355
1918	182,199,284	158,643,427	137,666,784	97,788,736
1919	196,264,936	148,926,376	118,139,912[a]	131,455,101
1920	426,178,872	179,331,755	197,706,190[a]	207,858,497

[a] Incomplete data.
Sources: Columns 1 and 3 are derived from Banco Nacional de Comercio Exterior, *México exportador* (Mexico, 1939), 11–12. The first five rows in these columns were recalculated from years ending in 30 June to calendar years. Columns 2 and 4 are from US Department of Commerce, *Statistical abstracts of the United States, 1919* and *1920*, table 283, p. 399, and table 288, p. 407, respectively.

consumption and export. (For statistics on exports and imports, see table 2.)

But better business did not restore the old order. Since political controls had slackened, the economy's growth made the conflict among the big companies worse, rocking the new government hard. The most troublesome conflict was over oil, with Standard and Mexican Petroleum demanding concessions like Águila's, Águila defending its privileges. ASARCO and its American, British, German, French and Mexican rivals and customers lobbied almost as roughly against each other.

Without tight political control economic growth also brought out vigorous organizing among workers. The Mexican Union of Mechanics (UMM, founded in 1900), the Mexican Railway Alliance (AFM, 1907), the Mutualist Society of Dispatchers and Telegraphers (SMDT, 1909), and most powerfully the Union of Conductors, Engineers, Brakemen, and Firemen (UCMGF, 1910) established wide authority in the railway companies. Encouraged by strikes, the new Mexican Mining Union multiplied its branches in the north-east, and the Veracruz and Tampico port workers unionized. Strikes swept the textile mills and urban trades too. Although no textile unions emerged, printers and other trades-men unionized almost evangelically, some with anarchist leaders.

In addition, Madero faced violent opposition. On 25 November, disgusted with the government's academic attitude towards 'the agrarian question', the Morelos peasant chiefs under Zapata formally denounced Madero, proclaiming in their Plan de Ayala a national campaign to return land from haciendas to villages. This was a deeply disturbing movement, a serious threat of social revolution, at least in the south. Federal troops spent the dry season burning Morelos villages, but could not stop Zapatista guerillas – nor could any other force for the next nine years. In December a very different avenger, General Reyes, revolted in the north-east. From El Paso Emilio Vázquez Gómez urged revolt in Chihuahua.

For a few months the government performed successfully. Most important, it managed Standard's and Mexican Petroleum's contention with Águila so as to preserve Madero's measure of *científico* support. Reyes's revolt fizzled out, ending with Mexico's most prestigious soldier interned in the Mexico City military prison and three anti-Reyista generals promoted to divisional general, the army's highest rank. On Pino Suárez's encouragement, Yucatán set up a Comisión Reguladora del Mercado de Henequén, a valorizing agency that stood against International Harvester and captured the henequén planters' loyalty. In January 1912, a Labour Department opened in the public works ministry. It scarcely interfered with the railway or port unions; they were too powerful. It had no part in resolving a conflict on the National Railways in April, when a strike by American crews brought the entire system to a halt, and the UCMGF replaced them. But it restored order in the mining districts and persuaded Congress to legislate new safety regulations for miners. And it calmed the textile industry by sponsoring grievance committees for workers and conventions for companies to co-ordinate prices and wages.

The government passed a major test in the spring of 1912, a revolt in the state of Chihuahua. On 4 February, after a Vazquista uprising in Juárez, President Taft had ordered US forces to prepare for field service on the border. Although he intended – in a year of US presidential elections – to discourage another Mexican revolution, to Mexicans the order had meant United States condemnation of Madero. Chihuahua's big American mining companies and the Terrazas family whose taxes Governor Abrahám González had raised, quietly connected with the em-bittered Orozco. On 3 March Orozco and his militia revolted, many of his men again counting on securing land when they won. On 23 March 8,000 Orozquistas destroyed a federal expedition along the railway in southern Chihuahua, where they then posed a threat to Torreón, the strategic point between Juárez and the Bajío. Orozquistas not only dominated Chihuahua but soon operated in Sonora and Coahuila too. Already, however, Taft had corrected his error; on 14 March he had placed an embargo on arms and ammunition shipments from the United States to Mexico, except to the government. On 1 April Madero commissioned General Victoriano Huerta to take a new federal expedition north, where on 23 May Huerta defeated the Orozquistas in southern Chihuahua. Meanwhile Sonora and Coahuila recruited state militia for local defence and duty in the war zone, and the UCMGF, the UMM, and the Mining Union raised volunteer corps. On 7 July Huerta entered Chihuahua City.

But this particular success came dear. It cost so much money that the government could not pay interest on the foreign debt. On 7 June Madero contracted with James Speyer and Company, the *científicos'* favourite New York bank, for a one-year $10 million loan to meet the payments immediately due. But to restore financial respectability he would need a much longer and bigger loan within a year, which Congress would have to authorize. The repression also left Madero with a heavy political debt to the army, which increased its share of the budget from 20 to 25 per cent and doubled in size to 60,000 men, with five more divisional generals, pre-eminent among them Huerta.

During the summer of 1912 foreign conditions for the government's stability began to fail. Crucially, Mexican oil became an issue in the American presidential campaigns. On 3 June, in order to increase revenue to warrant a big loan in the coming year, Madero decreed Mexico's first tax on oil production – 20 centavos a ton, about $0.015 a barrel. American oil companies condemned the tax as 'confiscation'.[2] And they carried much weight both in the Republican party, which on 22 June nominated Taft, and in the Democratic party, which on 2 July nominated Woodrow Wilson. (In August the Progressive party nominated Theodore Roosevelt, the universal jingoist.) The US Senate Foreign Relations Committee named a subcommittee to investigate Taft's policy towards Mexico. Taft sent warships to visit Mexico's Gulf and Pacific coasts, and in September the State Department demanded that the Mexican government secure law and order in its territory or the

2 Lorenzo Meyer, *Mexico and the United States in the oil controversy, 1917–1942* (Austin, Texas, 1977), 31.

United States would 'consider what measures it should adopt to meet the requirements of the situation'.[3]

Meanwhile Gustavo Madero boldly prepared to free the government from dependence on the *científicos*. He had only a part of the base he needed, for in the congressional elections on 30 June, while his Partido Progresista won a majority in the Chamber of Deputies and a majority of the contestable half of the Senate's seats, the Partido Católico took a large minority in the Chamber and enough seats in the Senate, including one for León de la Barra, to make a majority with the remaining *científicos* and Reyistas there. But he would not wait for a better chance later. In July Ernesto Madero, the finance minister, started secret negotiations outside *científico* banking circles to borrow £20 million (nearly 200 million pesos) in France. If the Maderos succeeded at this financial coup, a purely Maderista government could comfortably hold power until 1916 when Gustavo himself might well be elected president.

The direct road to Maderista ruin opened with the 26th Congress on 14 September. While the government continued secret financial negotiations, Gustavo had his *progresistas* – led by Deputy Luis Cabrera – rant like Jacobins. Styling themselves *renovadores*, they urged a 'renovation' of the country even beyond the San Luis plan's 'democratic' promises, including agrarian reform for the villages.[4] The *católicos* and *científicos*, led by León de la Barra, made the Senate into a bulwark of opposition. By then *científico* exiles in Paris had wind of the government's financial scheme, and they advised their friends in Mexico to subvert it, even in co-operation with the Reyistas.

The first attempt to depose Madero by a military coup failed. In mid October, hurrying to get in before the American elections in November, a group of *científicos* organized a revolt around General Félix Díaz, Porfirio Díaz's nephew. With US warships waiting offshore, Díaz seized the port of Veracruz and called on the army to take command of the country. Not a single general responded. Within the week the army reoccupied the port, and a court-martial soon locked Díaz into a Veracruz dungeon. But Madero's debt to the military mounted.

On 5 November Wilson won the US presidential election, and his party won both Houses of Congress. High Maderista officials made contact once more with Sherburne Hopkins, who restored friendly

---

[3] P. Edward Haley, *Revolution and intervention. The diplomacy of Taft and Wilson with Mexico, 1910–1917* (Cambridge, 1970), 48.

[4] Luis Cabrera, *La revolución es la revolución. Documentos* (Guanajuato, 1977), 137–45.

relations with Standard Oil. Mexican politicians deduced that under the Democrats, US pressure on the Madero government would ease. But Taft had four more months in the presidency, until March 1913, and in radical distrust of Wilson and Madero he apparently decided that before he left office a president beholden to the United States and the Republican party should rule Mexico. The US ambassador to Mexico scarcely disguised his new mission. This gave the *católico–científico–Reyista* opposition new courage and a deadline. In December the Mexican government formally requested that Congress authorize the borrowing of £20,000,000 'in Europe'. This gave the opposition a major public issue. On 13 January the bill for the authorization passed the Chamber. But the opposition in the Senate picked it to pieces.

There was trouble too from organized labour. On 26 December, demanding an eight-hour day, the UMM called a strike on the National Railways and snarled up transportation throughout the country. The labour department tried to mediate, in vain. Not until 11 January, thanks to UCMGF intervention, did the UMM accept a ten-hour day and a 10 per cent pay rise. Then, independently, an anarchist centre, the Casa del Obrero, founded in September for unions in Mexico City, encouraged strikes there for shorter hours and higher pay. Anarchist-led unions in Veracruz called a convention of working-class organizations to meet in the port on 1 May and form a national confederation to struggle for the eight-hour day.

The second attempt at a military coup also failed. Better organized than the first, it revolved around General Manuel Mondragón, a *científico* favourite who was supposed to suborn elite units in Mexico City, seize the National Palace, liberate Reyes and Díaz (the latter recently transferred to the capital), instal Reyes as provisional president, and after a decent interval have Díaz elected president. On 9 February Mondragón's units freed Reyes and Díaz. But in the fighting to enter the palace, Reyes was killed. Mondragón, Díaz, and the surviving rebels barely escaped into an armory across town, the Ciudadela. That same day Madero appointed Huerta, who had crushed the Orozquistas, to wipe out the new rebellion. On 11 February Huerta began attacks supposedly against the Ciudadela. The battle, however, soon spread and became more generalized, with artillery daily killing many civilians and destroying much property. Mondragón and Díaz kept demanding Madero's and Pino Suárez's resignation and urging other generals to overthrow the government. Privately the US ambassador and León de la Barra, directing the *católico–*

científico–Reyista alliance, plotted for the same cause. Most assiduously the rebels and conspirators sought to win over Huerta, in vain. Of the army's 100 or so generals, all but the two in the Ciudadela remained loyal. But now Madero depended totally on his generals.

The third attempt succeeded. On 18 February, advised that the now desperate rebels would try to break out of the Ciudadela, Huerta ordered a cease-fire, managed the arrest of the president, vice president, Cabinet members, Gustavo Madero, and the general closest to the Maderos, Felipe Ángeles, and declared himself in charge of the country. Some of the other generals at once recognized his authority. That evening at the US ambassador's invitation Huerta and Díaz met at the embassy and signed a pact: Huerta would become provisional president, appoint a cabinet of *católicos, científicos,* and Reyistas, and – most important to the ambassador – honour Díaz's campaign in 'the coming election' for the regular presidency.[5] That night Gustavo Madero was murdered. On 19 February Francisco Madero and Pino Suárez submitted their resignations, and the *progresista*-dominated Chamber overwhelmingly accepted them. The foreign minister, now provisional president, immediately appointed Huerta as minister of the interior and resigned himself, and Huerta became provisional president. The new Cabinet included León de la Barra as minister of foreign relations, Mondragón as minister of war, and Reyes's son Rodolfo as minister of justice. Almost all the generals who had not yet recognized Huerta's authority now did so; a few retired, none resisted. On 21 February the Supreme Court congratulated the new president. Privately Huerta indicated that he would allow Madero and Pino Suárez to go into exile, but on the night of 22 February, under military guard, the two prisoners were murdered.

FEBRUARY 1913 – AUGUST 1914

The new government lacked support from important quarters. Crucially, it did not satisfy the United States. Since 1910 the rivalry between the United States and Great Britain in Mexico had become more tense, largely because of oil, and to the new administration in Washington the coup looked like a *científico* counter-revolution to favour British interests, namely Águila. The Foreign Office reasoned that when Wilson settled into his presidency, he would recognize Huerta anyway in

[5] Luis Liceaga, *Félix Díaz* (Mexico, 1958), 216.

order to reassert American influence over him. In anticipation Britain, therefore, extended recognition on 31 March 1913, and other European governments soon followed suit. Wilson consequently refused recognition, supposing that he could soon evoke a government more reassuring to Americans. This confusion worried bankers and big businessmen, dubious whether without US blessing the new government could clear the foreign debt payments due in early June.

Besides, extraordinary difficulties soon arose in the economy. Although the oil companies boomed, a decline in the world price of silver during the spring of 1913 increased the flow of precious metals out of the country, depressed the mining industry, and in the northern border states where mining mattered most caused a broad slump in business. Organized labour remained combative. The anarchist unions in Veracruz did not hold their convention for a national confederation, but the Casa del Obrero in Mexico City, in a new organizing drive, staged the country's first public celebration of 1 May. The main railway and port unions together formed the Confederación de Gremios Mexicanos. Representing most of the country's transport workers, the CGM suddenly loomed as a national power.

Moreover the new government soon faced extensive armed resistance. Like the army, Congress, and the Supreme Court, all but a few governors accepted Huerta's authority. But the resurgence of the *científicos* aggravated conflicts, old and new. And revolts against 'usurpation' soon broke out in several states, most dangerously along the nothern border in Sonora, Chihuahua and Coahuila. There, despite the US embargo on arms and ammunition exports to rebels, local leaders mobilized not only the state militias still standing from the campaign against Orozco, but also new recruits from the increasing numbers of unemployed. Sonora's governor had fled into Arizona in late February, but his militia officers had the legislature appoint an acting governor, declare the state's independence from the federal government, and collect federal customs and taxes. A regular state army took shape under the command of a young farmer-politician, Álvaro Obregón. By late March it numbered 8,000 and had isolated the main federal force in Guaymas. In Chihuahua, where Governor González had been murdered in early March, the revolt began disjointedly. But by late March several militia units and many new rebels hoping again to make a claim on land operated together under Francisco Villa. Their revolt encouraged others in Durango and Zacatecas.

In Coahuila, Governor Venustiano Carranza led the resistance. A 53-year-old veteran of Porfirian provincial politics, a landlord related by blood and law to several big north-eastern families (but not to the Maderos), he tried first to rally other governors in defiance of Huerta's coup, but in vain. On 26 March 1913 he had his local subordinates proclaim the Plan de Guadalupe. Denouncing Huerta, Congress, and the Supreme Court for treason, and announcing the organization of the Constitutionalist Army, the Coahuilans named Carranza its First Chief, eventually to assume interim national executive authority and convoke elections for the return to constitutional rule. The Guadalupe plan contained not a word on economic or social reform. And the Constitutionalist Army was small, its highest ranking officer a refugee militia general from Veracruz, Cándido Aguilar, its forces only a few local militia under Carranza's brother Jesús and his cousin Pablo González. But on 1 April Constitutionalist agents hired Hopkins for counsel in Washington. On 18 April envoys from the Sonora and Chihuahua revolutions signed the Guadalupe plan, and on 26 April, to avoid forced domestic loans or dependence on foreign creditors, Carranza authorized the printing of five million paper pesos to pay for the Constitutionalist campaigns.

Elsewhere the main resistance came from the Zapatistas in Morelos. A few chiefs, who had come to regard Madero as the worst enemy, quit the field. But under the Plan de Ayala the others followed Zapata in an independent guerilla war to regain land for their villages. Their very disdain of changes that were only political strengthened their commitment to a national peasant cause and broadened the horizons of their strategy. Zapata found an excellent administrative secretary to manage his headquarters, a one-time engineering student and former accountant, Manuel Palafox. In mid-April 1913 he launched a serious offensive in eastern Morelos. By May the Zapatista movement had the determination and the organization to win at least a regional social revolution.

But the new government survived its debut. As it took shape, it revealed its difference from the previous government as merely factional and personal: its ministers pursued practically the same policies as before on business, labour, and 'the agrarian question'. Most surprisingly and significantly, not Félix Díaz but Huerta emerged as dominant. In March and April 1913 Felicistas organized themselves throughout the country to promote a Díaz–León de la Barra slate in 'the coming election'. But the provisional president raised the army's pay, rigged the appointment of

Table 3. *Value of the paper peso in dollars, 1913–16*

Month	1913	1914	1915	1916
January	0.4955	0.3699	0.1431	0.0440
February	0.4873	0.3478	0.1314	0.0407
March	0.4830	0.3138	0.1190	0.0285
April	0.4592	0.3001	0.0923	0.0343
May	0.4702	0.3360	0.0863	0.0229
June	0.4761	0.3313	0.0926	0.0970
July	0.4306	0.3146	0.0739	0.0970
August	0.3936	0.2629	0.0676	0.0380
September	0.3649	0.2108	0.0659	0.0311
October	0.3607	0.2055	0.0714	0.0232
November	0.3580	0.1986	0.0716	0.0099
December	0.3594	0.1870	0.0590	0.0046

Source: Edwin W. Kemmerer, *Inflation and revolution: Mexico's experience of 1912–1917* (Princeton, 1940), 14, 45, 46, 101.

several personally loyal generals as provisional governors, and made peace and a political alliance with Orozco. On 23 April he got a *progresista* majority in the Chamber to set the date for the presidential election six months away on 26 October. Díaz and León de la Barra resigned their candidacies, to embarrass him; some of their underlings plotted to kill him. But unembarrassed and unafraid, Huerta pressed for new negotiations in *científico* circles for the £20 million loan. On 30 May Congress authorized the debt, and on 8 June, just in time to clear the payments due, a consortium led by the Banque de Paris et des Pays-Bas underwrote a ten-year £6 million loan and took six-month options on another £10 million.

The loan could not help the economy. At mid-year ASARCO anu other big mining companies reported sharply reduced income; some of them sharply reduced production. Small businesses in the north failed so fast that the state banks pushed their Mexico City clearing house into the red. The rains that summer were poor, leading to higher grain prices and a wider depression. From June to September the peso dropped from $0.48 to $0.36 (for the value of the peso in this period, see table 3).

But politically the new credit amounted to a Huertista coup. Flouting the pact with Díaz, Huerta purged his cabinet of Felicistas, most importantly the war minister Mondragón, who went into exile, followed by León de la Barra. Policies on business, labour and 'the agrarian question' remained the same, but Huerta now had his own men administering them. In mid-July he exiled Díaz as 'special ambassador' to Japan and released Ángeles for exile in France.[6] Britain, approving the changes, announced the appointment of a new minister to Mexico who boasted of his friendship with Lord Cowdray, owner of Águila Oil.

In full control of the army, Huerta increased its share of the budget to 30 per cent and its size to 85,000, reorganized its commands, promoted 50 or so officers to general, appointed several new divisional generals, enlarged the arsenals, and expanded the Rurales to 10,000. Through the summer he threw his forces against the revolutionaries. And under serious federal attacks the Constitutionalist Army fell apart. In Sonora, which remained a Constitutionalist powerhouse, the federals still could not move out of Guaymas. But in the north, reinforced by Orozco and his militia, they regained command over the main towns and railways. In late July they dispelled a Constitutionalist attack on Torreón so thoroughly that Carranza almost lost his First Chieftainship. In the north-east in August they wrecked González's forces and recovered command everywhere but Piedras Negras and Matamoros. In Morelos, where they drove villagers into concentration camps, they scattered the Zapatista guerillas into the surrounding states.

As Huerto grew stronger, the United States went increasingly sour on him. American oil companies and Wilson saw not just a military man but British capital building power in Mexico. In July the United States recalled its ambassador. Thanks to Hopkins, its border officials winked at Constitutionalist smuggling of war material into Sonora and Tamaulipas. In August, before the new British minister had left for Mexico, Wilson sent a special agent to demand that Huerta declare an immediate cease-fire and hold 'an early and free election'.[7] The United States would help to impose the armistice, recognize the new government, and sponsor a new loan. If Huerta refused, the United States would not 'stand inactively by'.[8] Huerta refused. On 27 August Wilson announced his policy of 'watchful waiting' and an embargo without exceptions on shipments of arms and ammunition to Mexico. But Huerta soon placed new orders for arms in Europe and Japan.

By September 1913 Huerta had consolidated his power. He could count not only on the army but also – in a depressed economy – on army-contract suppliers, who had become his fiercely loyal supporters. Playing

[6] *Ibid.*, 302–3.   [7] Haley, *Revolution and intervention*, 98.
[8] Arthur S. Link, *Wilson: the new freedom* (Princeton, 1956), 357–8, 361.

on resentment of the United States, he had developed a programme of military training for civilians that attracted wide subscription by patriotic bureaucrats and clerks. When Congress reconvened, it displayed such disarray among *progresistas, católicos, científicos*, and Reyistas that Huerta took more liberties. He dictated to the Partido Católico its presidential and vice-presidential candidates for the 26 October election, and on 30 September he won from Mexico City banks a three-month loan of 18 million pesos.

The Huertista government then faced three severe tests. The first came from every opposition camp – an attempt to discredit the election of 26 October. During September the Constitutionalist bands in Chihuahua, Durango and Zacatecas had combined under Villa as the Division of the North. On 1 October, in the first major Constitutionalist victory, they captured Torreón and a large military booty. Also during September the Sonora Constitutionalists had welcomed Carranza into their state. There the First Chief took new political positions. He declared that after constitutional restoration 'the social struggle, the class struggle in all its power and grandeur, must begin'.[9] He reordered the Constitutionalist Army, commissioning Álvaro Obregón commander of the North-west Army Corps and Pablo González commander of the North-east. On 17 October he announced the formation of a provisional government, including in his cabinet General Felipe Ángeles, back from France, as undersecretary of war. And on 21 October he affirmed that on the Constitutionalist triumph he would dissolve the Federal Army. On 23 October González's North-east Corps attacked Monterrey. Meanwhile the Zapatistas co-ordinated attacks around Mexico City. And Félix Díaz disembarked in Veracruz to stand in the election.

Huerta reacted shrewdly and boldly. On 10 October, having waited for the new British minister to arrive in Mexico City, he dissolved Congress and convoked elections for the Chamber and Senate coincidentally with the presidential election. The next day the British minister presented his credentials to the provisional president, virtually blessing his latest coup. The Constitutionalist attack on Monterrey failed. On 24 October Huerta decreed the expansion of the army to 150,000. At the polls on 26 October a militarily rigged majority gave Huerta the presidency, his war minister the vice-presidency, and the *católicos* most of Congress, but as Huerta and his war minister were ineligible for elective

[9] Jesús Carranza Castro, *Origen, destino y legado de Carranza* (Mexico, 1977), 199.

office, the executive election was invalid – Huerta remained provisional president. On 27 October Díaz escaped from Veracruz in an American warship.

The second test was another Constitutionalist offensive. From Sonora Obregón co-ordinated with forces in Sinaloa, and on 14 November captured Culiacán. González captured Victoria on 18 November, installed his main Tamaulipas subordinate, Luis Caballero, as provisional governor, and drove on towards Tampico. Villa's Division of the North – now 10,000 men with artillery and trains – pinned down the Chihuahua City garrison, captured Juárez and more military supplies on 15 November, crushed Orozco's militia, compelled the evacuation of the state capital, and occupied it on 7 December. The army reacted competently. In the north-west the federal artillery and gunboats in Guaymas and Mazatlán, targeted on the railways that passed nearby, blocked Obregón from substantial troop or supply movements south. González's drive towards Tampico broke down before federal defences. Throughout the central states federal generals managed a massive conscription, and on 9 December a fresh federal force recaptured Torreón, throwing Villa back into Chihuahua. To consolidate his base there, Villa took a giant step towards economic and social reform, decreeing on 21 December the confiscation without compensation of the vast haciendas in the state, for revenue immediately and allotment to his troops at the war's end. But on 28 December, keenly vexed at Villa for starting 'the social struggle' too soon, Carranza in effect admitted that the government still held the strategic upper hand by authorizing his treasury to issue 15 million more paper pesos to pay for the long campaigns still to come.

The third test was further antagonism from the United States. When Huerta dissolved Congress with the British minister's blessing, President Wilson's opposition became implacable. On 13 October he warned that the United States would not recognize the results of the elections of 26 October. On 1 November he threatened Huerta: resign, or – for the first time – the United States would support the Constitutionalists. On 7 November the State Department announced that Wilson would 'require Huerta's retirement'; the United States would then mediate in the formation of a new provisional government to hold the 'free election' to restore constitutional order.[10] On 12 November a US special agent met

---

[10] Kenneth J. Grieb, *The United States and Huerta* (Lincoln, 1969), 115–16.

Carranza in Nogales. Under this pressure Great Britain instructed it. minister to abandon Huerta, and the French finance ministry notified the Mexican government that French banks would not underwrite the £10 million loan.

But the government reacted stubbornly and resourcefully. On 15 November the *católico*-dominated Congress opened. On 15 December it confirmed Huerta as provisional president and scheduled another presidential election on 5 July. As a reward Huerta purged the *católico* leadership but let the church dedicate Mexico to the Sacred Heart of Jesus and stage grand public ceremonies in honour of Christ the King – most impressively in Guadalajara – on 11 January 1914. He also tolerated a new church organization increasingly active in civic affairs, the Catholic Association of Mexican Youth (ACJM). Compensating for the failure of credit abroad, he more than tripled the oil tax, got Congress to authorize a new 100 million peso internal debt, imposed heavy forced loans on business, decreed a tax on bank deposits, and monetized bank notes. On 23 December, after another slip in the price of silver triggered a run on the Banco de Londres, he declared a banking moratorium. On 7 January he lowered reserve requirements from 50 to $33\frac{1}{3}$ per cent, then suspended interest payments on the national debt until the banks lent the newly creatable money to the government. American, British, and French banks protested, but Huerta knew that he could count on private support from the British minister and Lord Cowdray. And his military programme for civilians enrolled many new patriots.

In short, by early 1914 the Huertista government had proved itself the paramount power in Mexico. Although it had lost valuable ground, it ruled the two-thirds of the country where probably four-fifths of the population lived. It still controlled all the sea ports. It held hostage the interests of bishops, businessmen, and bankers. And in the central cities, because of its anti-Americanism and pro-clericalism, it enjoyed considerable popular allegiance. This moved the United States to boost the Constitutionalists outright. On 29 January 1914 Wilson advised Great Britain that he now saw peace in Mexico as coming not from mediation but from the military victory of the strongest. On 3 February he revoked the arms embargo, allowing legal exports of war material from the United States indiscriminately into Mexico. Arms and ammunition flooded into Sonora, Chihuahua and Tamaulipas. The British minister was soon recalled to London.

So favoured, on 12 February Carranza authorized the printing of another ten million pesos, and on 3 March dispatched the Constitutionalist marching orders. González's North-east Corps, which by then boasted several notable subordinate chiefs – Luis Caballero, Jesús Carranza, Cesáreo Castro, Francisco Coss, Francisco Murguía, and Antonio I. Villarreal – was to capture Monterrey, Tampico and Saltillo. Obregón's North-west Corps – with Salvador Alvarado, Lucio Blanco, Plutarco Elías Calles, Manuel Diéguez, and Benjamín Hill its principal chiefs – was to conquer the west coast and capture Guadalajara. Villa's Division of the North, which Ángeles joined to command the artillery, was to recapture Torreón for the strategic campaign down the railway towards the centre of the country. Carranza moved his government to Chihuahua to supervise Villa and the drive south.

Huerta again expanded the army, to 200,000 in February and 250,000 in March, with another massive conscription in the central states. He promoted some 250 officers to general, commissioned several new divisional generals, and named Orozco to command a new offensive in the north. He appointed a *católico*-nominated in-law of Limantour's, Eduardo Iturbide, as governor of the Federal District. And on 31 March, having with Lord Cowdray's help exacted from Mexican banks a 45 million peso loan, he announced resumption of payments on the national debt on 15 April.

But the Constitutionalist campaigns developed momentum. On 26 March González had Caballero lay siege to Tampico, and on 8 April, while Jesús Carranza, Coss and Murguía harassed the federal troops elsewhere in the north-east, he, Castro and Villarreal attacked Monterrey. Obregón, having left Calles in command of Sonora and Alvarado besieging Guaymas, took Blanco, Diéguez and Hill to prepare forces in southern Sinaloa and Tepic for movement into Jalisco. On 23 March Villa and Ángeles led 15,000 men against 10,000 federal troops in Torreón, on 2 April took the town and on 14 April destroyed 12,000 federal reinforcements. As Constitutionalist generals conquered new territory, they opened a new and characteristic agency, the Oficina de Bienes Intervenidos, to manage the attachment of private property for military housing and supplies. Meanwhile the Zapatistas had coordinated their guerillas into a regular Army of the South and commenced an offensive in Guerrero. By early April they controlled most of the state and its silver mines.

These advances moved the United States to resume attempts at mediation, this time by force. On 10 April Wilson seized upon an arrest of

American sailors in Tampico to demand that the Mexican government salute the American flag, or face 'the gravest consequences'.[11] Huerta refused. On 14 April Wilson ordered the Atlantic Fleet to Tampico and Veracruz. Four days later the State Department received word that a German ship with arms and ammunition for the Federal Army would dock at Veracruz on 21 April. On 20 April, assured that federal garrisons in the ports would not resist American landings, Wilson decided to occupy Veracruz and Tampico. If Huerta still did not resign, Wilson had plans to run an expedition of marines by rail from Veracruz into Mexico City to overthrow him. The United States could then supervise negotiations between his replacement and the Constitutionalists for a new provisional government, a 'free election', and constitutional restoration. On 21 April 1,200 marines and bluejackets landed in Veracruz.

The intervention failed. The Veracruz garrison resisted, and the Tampico landing never started, because the force had to be diverted to help in Veracruz. By 22 April 6,000 US troops held the port. But instead of resigning, Huerta obtained from Congress dictatorial powers in war, finance, and communications, named railway union leaders to manage the National Railways, mobilized patriotic demonstrations into his programme for militarizing civilians, and urged all rebels to join the federal troops against a Yankee invasion. The *católicos*, the ACJM, and the bishops publicly supported his appeals for national unity against Protestant defilement of the fatherland. On 22 April Carranza denounced the US intervention as a violation of sovereignty. On the advice of private counsel in Washington, to avoid disastrous hostilities along the border, he did not call it an act of war, but he did demand immediate US withdrawal and vowed to fight American intrusions into Constitutionalist territory, including by then the environs of Tampico. Zapata also vowed to fight American forces that moved into his territory. Europeans scoffed at the intervention. South Americans lamented it. Even the American public tended to oppose it.

Accordingly Wilson confined it to Veracruz. On 25 April, to save the shreds of his plan for mediation, he accepted an offer by Argentina, Brazil and Chile to hold a conference to mediate 'between the United States and Mexico'.[12] On 27 April he reimposed a full arms embargo, but it did not stop Constitutionalist border smuggling.

[11] Link, *Wilson: the new freedom*, 396.   [12] *Ibid.*, 407.

Huerta accepted the 'ABC' countries' offer of mediation, planning to use it against the Constitutionalists. But deprived of Veracruz customs revenue and military supplies, the government floundered. It could no longer clear the interest on the foreign debt; the peso fell to $0.30 (see table 3). The army pushed conscription and militarization of civilians too far, into the ranks of organized labour, and anarchists in Mexico City resisted. On 27 May the government closed the Casa del Obrero.

Superficially, Constitutionalism gained strength. The First Chief accepted 'ABC' mediation only 'in principle', assuming it would treat only the Tampico incident and the Veracruz intervention, and declared defiantly that his government would continue its war to restore the constitution.[13] But below the surface, because of his displays of independence from the United States, his forces began to divide. North-eastern generals, in whose region the major sources of revenue were American mining and oil companies, welcomed their First Chief's declaration of national authority: it would encourage the companies to pay Constitutionalist taxes. Northern generals, who had their major sources of revenue in expropriated Mexican cattle ranches in Chihuahua and British cotton plantations around Torreón, but had to sell the cattle and cotton to Americans, resented Carranza's defiance of Washington: it might provoke retaliation at El Paso customs. The angriest was Villa, who publicly professed his friendship for the United States.

This division brought out old jealousies. For three months, since Wilson had backed Constitutionalism, the Madero elders in exile in the United States had been manoeuvring to define constitutional restoration narrowly as Maderista restoration. They had considerable allies in Sonora, where the Maderista governor who had fled in 1913 sought to reinstate himself, and in Chihuahua, where the family's old friend Ángeles had much influence with Villa. By May, Villa was convinced that Carranza intended to sabotage him. Constitutionalist chiefs anxious about a Madero revival began pushing Carranza to restrain Villa.

The Constitutionalists continued to move militarily. Already during the Veracruz crisis González, Castro and Villarreal had captured Monterrey, where Villarreal became provisional governor of Nuevo León. On 14 May González, Caballero and Castro took Tampico and began collecting the oil taxes. On 18 May Cándido Aguilar took Tuxpan, where he became provisional governor of Veracruz. On 21 May Villa

---

[13] *Ibid.*, 408–9.

took Saltillo, delivered it to González, and returned to Torreón. In the west, Obregón, Blanco, Diéguez, and Hill captured Tepic on 16 May and started the campaign toward Guadalajara. Everywhere in Constitutionalist territory more *oficinas de bienes intervenidos* opened, in which some generals discovered irresistible opportunities for private deals. The conquering forces also vented passions for revenge. In rancour against the church – an old northern Liberal anti-clerical anger whetted by the collaboration of the *católicos*, the bishops and the ACJM with Huerta – some generals exercised a particular fury on churches and priests. From Guerrero the independent Zapatista Army of the South recovered all of Morelos but Cuernavaca, and moved strongly into Mexico State and Puebla. In the territory it now controlled villagers were already recovering the land for the sowing season.

But the pressures for division increased. The United States deliberately brought them to bear through the ABC Conference, which opened on 20 May 1914 at Niagara Falls, Ontario. In the following weeks the State Department eliminated Huerta's last private British support by recognizing extant British oil and mining concessions. In addition, under American direction the conference did not limit itself to mediating 'between the United States and Mexico' to resolve the Tampico incident and the Veracruz intervention, but kept proposing to mediate between the United States, Huerta and the Constitutionalists to form a new provisional government. A recurrent plan featured Ángeles as president.

Constitutionalism entered a crisis in early June. Carranza moved his government from Chihuahua to Saltillo, ordered that the estates confiscated by Villa be redesignated as merely attached (for eventual return to their owners), stopped Coahuila coal shipments to Villa's railways, and on 11 June had local Zacatecas–Durango forces attack Zacatecas City, to try to build a Central Division to block the Northerners from moving south. On 13 June Villa resigned his command, but on 14 June his generals put him back in charge and against Carranza's orders moved down the railway to attack Zacatecas. On 19 June Carranza dismissed Ángeles from the war ministry. On 23 June the Northerners destroyed a federal force of 12,000 at Zacatecas, delivered the city to local chiefs, and returned to Torreón. On 29 June Carranza appointed González and Obregón as the Constitutionalist Army's first divisional generals, leaving Villa in military limbo.

In this crisis the Constitutionalists held together. On 4 July González had Caballero, Castro and Villarreal meet with Villa's delegates in Torreón to negotiate reunification. The delegates all agreed that Carranza would remain First Chief, and Villa commander of the Division of the North. But they also agreed on radical changes in the Guadalupe plan for reconstituting a regular government. On the triumph of the revolution the Constitutionalist Army would dissolve the Federal Army, take its place, and instate Carranza as provisional president, thereby making him ineligible to stand for regular office. His only function would be to convoke a junta of Constitutionalist chiefs, who would name delegates to a convention. The convention would frame a programme of reforms – to punish the church for its collaboration with Huerta, provide for 'the welfare of the workers', and 'emancipate the peasants economically' – and then oversee the election of a regular government to carry out the reforms.[14] Signed on 8 July, the Pact of Torreón received no approval from Carranza, but no challenge either.

On 13 July the ABC Conference closed with the United States still in Veracruz and committed to recognizing a provisional government negotiated between Huerta and the Constitutionalists. But on 7 July, in the North-west Corps's first major battle, Obregón, Blanco, Diéguez, Hill and a force of 15,000 destroyed a federal force of 12,000 at the railhead west of Guadalajara, and on 8 July occupied the city. There Obregón immediately inflicted shocking anti-clerical punishments on the church.

The day that Guadalajara fell Huerta named Francisco C. Carbajal as foreign minister. Carbajal had represented the Díaz government in the negotiations which led to the Juárez treaty in 1911, and might again preserve the Federal Army and bureaucracy. On 15 July Huerta resigned, and Carbajal became provisional president. On 20 July, aboard a German ship, Huerta sailed from Coatzacoalcos (then called Puerto México) into exile.

Jesús Carranza had already occupied San Luis Potosí, opening the North-east Corps's way straight into the Bajío. Carbajal requested a cease-fire for negotiations. The First Chief refused. On 23 July Wilson warned him that the United States might not recognize his government if it disregarded foreign interests or allowed reprisals against its opponents, and on 31 July he reminded him that without US recognition a

---

[14] Jesús Silva Herzog, *Breve historia de la revolución mexicana* (2 vols., Mexico, 1960), II, 144–60.

Constitutionalist government 'could obtain no loans and must speedily break down'.[15] Carranza replied that the Constitutionalists would offer the same guarantees as always to foreigners and justice according to 'our national interests' to Mexicans.[16]

For the last campaign, to take Mexico City itself, the First Chief revised his strategy. Although the main Constitutionalist force was the Division of the North, by then 30,000 strong, he would not risk letting Villa and Ángeles participate in the final victory. To hold them in Torreón, he had González and Murguía bring 22,000 North-easterners through San Luis Potosí into the Bajío. He ordered Obregón to advance from the west and compel the Federal Army to surrender unconditionally. On 26 July Obregón left Diéguez in Guadalajara as provisional governor of Jalisco and took Blanco, Hill and a force of 18,000 into the Bajío. On 9 August, waiting twenty miles north of Mexico City, he received word that the federal commanders would surrender.

On 12 August Carbajal and most of his Cabinet left for Veracruz and exile. The governor of the Federal District, Iturbide, and Carranza's lately appointed agent in Mexico City, Alfredo Robles Domínguez, assumed responsibility for transitional order in the capital. On 13 August Obregón and Blanco, without González (to his resentment), signed a treaty with representatives of the Federal Army and Navy formally ending the war. The federal troops and Rurales in the capital were evacuated along the railway to Puebla, where Castro and Coss were to manage their disarmament and discharge. Carranza ordered his provisional governors and state commanders to muster out the defeated forces elsewhere. In particular he appointed his brother Jesús to take command of the entire quarter of the country from Oaxaca, where all the federal forces in the west and south were to assemble for discharge, to Yucatán, where there were no local revolutionaries. The most hated federal officers fled into exile, among them Orozco; a few die-hards went into hiding in the Puebla–Oaxaca mountains.

On 15 August Obregón led 6,000 men of the North-west Corps into the capital, posting Blanco with 10,000 more in the southern suburbs to prevent the Zapatistas from entering too. On 20 August Carranza paraded into the city. The next day he established his government in the National Palace and commenced a purge of the bureaucracy. Although

---

[15] Haley, *Revolution and intervention*, 149–50.
[16] United States Department of State, *Papers relating to the foreign relations of the United States, 1914* (Washington, DC, 1922), 575.

the war had ended, many more *oficinas de bienes intervenidos* opened, old and new offices increasingly serving private interests.

AUGUST 1914 – OCTOBER 1915

The struggle within the Mexican regime to restore its constitutionality had resulted in its destruction – the collapse of all the labyrinthine national, regional and local political and business deals developed over the previous 30 years, the loss of all the powers of international credit, the exhaustion of an overflowing treasury, and the dissolution of the Federal Army and the Rurales. Worse, the ruins remained to encumber the construction of a new regime. The foreign debt had piled up to 675 million pesos, with no prospect of payments on it while the United States held Veracruz; heavy foreign claims for death and destruction of property had also accumulated. The banking system verged on bankruptcy. Against metallic reserves of 90,000 pesos, bank notes and other obligations ran to 340 million pesos, and purely by fiat various Constitutionalist currencies circulated for 60 million pesos more, at an exchange value of only $0.25. Damage to railways and the disruption of mines, mills and factories had aggravated the country's economic depression. Monterrey's Fundidora had almost suspended operations. And as if the war had undone the weather too, for the second summer in a row the rains were poor, which meant either famine or food imports in 1915.

Moreover the victorious forces were at odds over the kind of new regime to construct. Their conflict went deeper than personal rivalry. Because the big revolutionary armies had developed in materially and socially different regions, north-east, north-west, north, and south, each represented a particular array of social forces. Three of the four armies had developed so differently that the struggle to build the new regime would begin as a struggle, however obscured, over the social relations of production. And having developed so separately, the different forces had no party in which to mediate the conflict.

The North-east and North-west Corps were similar. Built around the nuclei of Coahuila and Sonora militia, they had grown into professional armies, the troops fighting for pay, together now 60,000 strong. In reality both consisted of several professional units, belonging to the several generals who had raised them, guaranteed their wages, and (except for Jesús Carranza and a couple of others) obeyed the First Chief and co-operated with each other only for Machiavellian reasons. In both the north-east and the north-west these revolutionary chiefs typically had been enterprising young provincial merchants, farmers, and ranchers around the turn of the century. Frustrated as they matured – some of them Magonistas in 1906, most of them *anti-reeleccionistas* in 1910, almost all of them Maderistas in 1911, all of them municipal or state officials in 1912, and Constitutionalists to save their careers in 1913 – they took the national collapse of old deals as an opportunity to remake them with new partners. In the territories they dominated, thriving inside and outside the *oficinas de bienes intervenidos*, they were reassigning local corners to themselves, their kin, friends, and staffs. And they were asserting their patronage of organized labour. Immediately on the occupation of Mexico City they reformed the National Railways management, threatened the UCMGF and UMM leaderships with punishment for *huertismo*, and cancelled the port unions' contracts; the CGM dissolved. They declared themselves custodians of the already depressed Mining Union and the textile mill committees. On 21 August, on a subsidy from Obregón's headquarters, they re-opened Mexico City's Casa del Obrero. Regarding 'the agrarian question', they saw only the peon and only the symptoms of his plight – his old debts, which they cancelled, and his low wages, which they decreed should increase. Except for a quixotic two or three, they had no interest in redistributing land to peasants.

Pancho Villa's Division of the North was also a professional army, 30,000 regularly paid soldiers, the strongest military body in the country. But formed through a history more complicated than that in the north-east or north-west, it was a more heterogeneous force. Its original units had included militia and contingents of peasants fighting for land. But as the army grew, it had incorporated many new elements, unemployed miners, cowboys, railway trackmen and bandits, who fought for pay, promotion and the main chance. It had the most diverse collection of chiefs. Some had been young sharecropper spokesmen around the turn of the century, humiliated as they matured, often in trouble with the Rurales, Maderistas in 1910, captains of militia against Orozco in 1912, Constitutionalists to save their lives and their men in 1913. Many more had come virtually from nowhere, having distinguished themselves only since 1913, when their nerve, bloodthirstiness and luck had lifted them into high command. In the territory they ruled, they were grabbing everything they could, old and new. The contradictions in the Northern force emerged most clearly in the disposition of the confiscated haciendas. Villa intended to satisfy the peasants who had fought under him to reclaim lost lands, and to grant 'colonies' to the rest of his soldiers.[17] But he could not proceed as long as he might need an army to operate outside his region, because once his men had farms they would not easily go to fight far away. His agency for confiscated properties managed the haciendas like a trust, leasing them to tenants, spending the revenue on military supplies and wages, pensions for Division widows and orphans, and state administration, postponing redistribution of the land until the army could safely disband. But some Division chiefs held large estates which they ran like baronies.

Compounding these complications, Villa had saddled himself with the Maderista politicians resurgent in Sonora and Chihuahua. No more than the North-eastern or North-western generals did these revolutionary leaders have use for projects of allotting land to the troops. Their goal was to have the Division of the North make Ángeles president, so as to pick up the pieces of February 1913 and remake them into a new regime fit for enterprising landlords.

Of all the revolutionary armies, the Zapatista Army of the South was the simplest. It was not professional; its now 15,000 regulars and 10,000 guerillas drew no pay. The Southern Army belonged not to Zapata or to him and all his chiefs, but to the villages that had reared and raised both them and their troops and given the support necessary for a war for land. Rooted, trusted, and trusting in their villages, the Southern chiefs were therefore the most determined of all the revolutionaries to make serious economic and social changes. Neighbourhood heroes at the turn of the century, matured in local struggles to reclaim ancient rights to particular fields, woods, and streams, always in trouble with the police, village leaders by 1910, almost all of them Maderistas in 1911, all Zapatistas by 1912, and Zapatistas since, they had fought longest against the old deals, and now they moved, ignorant of theory but nevertheless compelled, towards the construction of an agrarian anarcho-communism. It helped their cause substantially that with Guerrero's silver they enjoyed the soundest currency in the country. It helped no less that administration of the headquarters remained the charge of Manuel Palafox, who had proved himself an honest, responsible, shrewd, decisive, fearless and

---

[17] Friedrich Katz, 'Agrarian changes in northern Mexico in the period of Villista rule, 1913–1915', in *Contemporary Mexico: Papers of the IV International Congress of Mexican History* (Los Angeles, 1976), 261, 272.

visionary executor of agrarian reform. In their territory, having shattered the old local monopolies, the Southern chiefs were rearranging trade to furnish local needs. And having expropriated the haciendas, they had Palafox authorizing villages to reoccupy their old lands, administering the rest for army revenue, pensions, and local subsidies, and preparing to grant farms to settlements that had never had them. Another Southern peculiarity was that the headquarters harboured refugee anarchist intellectuals from the Casa del Obrero. The anarchists did not figure in Zapatista decisions on strategy or policy. But they did publicize *zapatismo* as the source of bourgeois civilization.

These conditions alone invited foreign arbitration. Much more importantly, war had just exploded in Europe, which magnified the imperialist responsibilities of the neutral United States. In particular, it confirmed the Monroe Doctrine as a mandate for American hegemony in the western hemisphere. And because it threw world shipping into turmoil, it slowed Mexico's production for export (especially of oil), stunted the country's material capacities for order, and practically dictated American attempts to manage Mexican affairs. Since Carranza had installed himself in the National Palace without US mediation, Wilson refrained from recognizing his government. The United States therefore involved itself directly with Mexico's major social forces. Washington's goals – reconciliation of the remnants of the old regime with at least some champions of the new for a conservative but reputably popular constitutional restoration, an American loan to reform the foreign debt and fund a claims commission, and American financial supervision of Mexico's economic development – tallied well enough with the interests of the twenty or so large foreign and domestic companies. Because of the havoc in Europe, companies that had traded there would have to trade more in American markets now, anyway. But big business had no party or army.

As the best of a bad lot the United States put their money on Villa to build the new regime. Apparently the most pro-American of the Constitutionalist generals, apparently under the renewed Maderista conservative sway, Villa held firm command of the country's strongest fighting machine. If Washington supported him, enough of the North-eastern and North-western generals should flock into his camp to intimidate most of the others into joining him too. A formula for unification was already at hand in the Torreón pact, the convention of

Constitutionalist delegates. By late August 1914 the State Department agent at the Division of the North headquarters had Villa and Obregón negotiating the preparations for the convention. On 1 September, having spied the drift, Hopkins resigned as Carranza's counsel.

So disfavoured, the First Chief became more flexible. On 5 September he called the convention for 1 October in Mexico City. To keep the prospects in his own camp interesting, he decreed the replacement of previously issued Constitutionalist currency by a new issue of 130 million paper pesos. And he manoeuvred to split his opposition. When the Convention opened, its presiding officer was a lawyer who had become one of Carranza's closest advisers, Gustavo Madero's old whip and the 26th Congress's leading *renovador*, Luis Cabrera. There were no Northern or Southern delegates.

The shift toward Villa nevertheless occurred. On 5 October, following Obregón's arguments, the Convention voted to move north to Aguascalientes, in neutral territory, but near Villa's base at Torreón, and to exclude civilians (in particular Cabrera). On 15 October in Aguascalientes it invited Zapata to send delegates, and, once they arrived, approved 'in principle' the Ayala programme for redistributing land to peasants.[18] On 30 October it voted to depose the First Chief, and on 1 November it elected a provisional president, Eulalio Gutiérrez, a San Luis Potosí general. The next day it accepted Villa's occupation of Aguascalientes. On 6 November Gutiérrez was sworn into office. On 10 November, Carranza having refused to retire, the Convention declared him in rebellion, and Gutiérrez appointed Villa commander of the Convention's armies. Already the First Chief had moved his government from Mexico City to Orizaba. By then the value of his peso had fallen to $0.20 (see table 3). Washington judged the trend so satisfactory that on 13 November Wilson ordered the evacuation of the port of Veracruz in ten days' time.

But Carranza had prepared a surprisingly broad resistance. From the first he had the loyalty of Aguilar in Veracruz, González, who headed back north-east, and Jesús Carranza, who had remained in Coatzacoalcos, for the revenue from the Minatitlán oil fields. Once the sudden expansion of Northern control over the Convention alarmed other North-eastern and North-western generals, he had deftly played on

---

[18] John Womack, Jr., *Zapata and the Mexican Revolution* (New York, 1968), 217–18.

their jealousies. Within a week of the Convention declaring the First Chief in rebellion, almost all the important North-eastern and North-western subordinates – Alvarado, Caballero, Calles, Castro, Coss, Diéguez, Hill, Murguía, Villarreal – declared themselves to be Carran-cistas. Obregón too then joined the First Chief in Orizaba. Of all the important subordinates, only Blanco stuck with the Convention. When the United States evacuated Veracruz on 23 November, Aguilar occupied it. On 26 November Carranza established his government in the port, where he had revenue from customs and an outlet for exports to gain dollars to import contraband arms and ammunition.

Not all revolutionaries took one side or another. In many isolated districts local chiefs set themselves up as petty warlords. The most notable, Manuel Peláez, appeared in the northern Veracruz mountains. In November he began selling the oil companies protection for their operations in the nearby lowlands, between Tampico and Tuxpan.

Late in November 1914 Villista and Zapatista forces together occupied Mexico City. In early December Gutiérrez announced his cabinet, including a subordinate of Villa's as undersecretary of war and Manuel Palafox as minister of agriculture. Big businesses in the city received the new government without serious complaint. So did the unions. In almost explicit support, the Mexico Power and Light workers organized the Mexican Electrical Workers' Union (SME), assuring a friendly control of energy not only for the city's factories and trolleys but also for the big mines in Hidalgo and Mexico State.

From Chihuahua into the Bajío, Villista generals recruited thousands of new troops for immediate action. By mid-December their forces had captured Guadalajara and launched offensives against Carrancista garrisons from Sonora to Tamaulipas; and Zapatistas had captured Puebla City. On 4 January in Mexico City Villa incorporated some 1,500 ex-Federal Army officers (including seven divisional generals) for new commands and staff in his expanded armies.

But the Carrancista forces had also gained strength. On 4 December, anticipating a return to the offensive, Carranza decreed the attachment of almost all the country's railways. And wherever Carrancista generals held control, they opened a characteristically Carrancista agency, a local Comisión Reguladora del Comercio, to control the distribution of local supplies and encourage enlistment in their ranks. From Coatza-coalcos, Jesús Carranza crossed the Isthmus of Tehuantepec, sailed up the west coast rallying loyal chiefs as far as Sinaloa, and returned to raise an army in Oaxaca for a southern–western campaign. Diéguez in Jalisco connected with Murguía in Michoacán, where the Villista occupation of Mexico City had accidentally stranded him, and together they harrassed Villista communications through the Bajío. By late December Villarreal held Monterrey, and González held Tampico and its revenue. While the Villistas scoured the depressed north for hard money to import arms and ammunition to maintain their broad offensives, and while the Zapatistas hoarded their silver and redistributed land, the Carrancistas pumped the Gulf's richest companies for taxes and loans to build a new Army of Operations. Under Obregón, with Castro and Coss as his main subordinates, the new corps quickly formed into a skilled and well-supplied force of 12,000. On 15 January 1915 it easily recaptured Puebla, and prepared to move on Mexico City.

Politically too the Carrancistas reorganized. To justify their defiance of the Convention, the generals persuaded the First Chief to publish a programme of reforms. On 12 December 1914 Carranza declared not only that his Constitutionalist movement would continue, but also that in respect for the nation's urgent needs he would issue provisional decrees to guarantee political freedoms, return land to the dispossessed, tax the rich, improve the condition of 'the proletarian classes', purify the courts, re-expel the church from politics, reassert the national interest in natural resources, and facilitate divorce.[19] On 14 December he reformed his Cabinet, with Luis Cabrera as finance minister and other *renovadores* in most of the other ministries. On 6 January he authorized agrarian commissions to hear complaints of dispossession and consider expropriation for grants to landless villages. On 7 January 1915 he ordered oil companies to obtain new licences from his government for all their operations.

The United States upped its bet on Villa. On 8–9 January the US Army chief of staff and the State Department agent in the north met publicly with him in Juárez and El Paso. In the north-east, Ángeles beat Villarreal, taking Monterrey on 10 January. In Oaxaca, for local reasons but with nevertheless important national consequences, a local chief had Jesús Carranza murdered.

To Washington's dismay the Convention collapsed. On 16 January, exposed in correspondence with Carrancistas, provisional president Gutiérrez fled Mexico City for San Luis Potosí and obscurity. His

---

[19] Fabela and Fabela, *Documentos históricos*, IV, 107–12.

replacement, the Villista Roque González Garza, could preside only over the city's accumulating woes, including food shortages and a typhoid epidemic. Diéguez and Murguía recaptured Guadalajara. And as Obregón's Army of Operations approached Mexico City, the Villista–Zapatista garrison evacuated it, and the Convention retreated into Morelos. On 28 January Obregón occupied the city.

Villa organized his own government in the north, and in mid-February recaptured Guadalajara. His inclination then was to destroy Diéguez and Murguía, to clear his right flank for an attack on Obregón. But Ángeles insisted on heavy reinforcements in Monterrey for a campaign on Tampico. Deferring to him, Villa shifted the bulk of his forces back through Torreón to the north-east. This move alone so demoralized Villarreal that he retired into exile in Texas. And Villa gained a new kind of support in Yucatán, where ex-federal troops revolted in his name.

Meanwhile, as world shipping adjusted to the war in Europe, the oil companies in Mexico resumed booming production for export to the United States. They did not relicence their operations as Carranza had ordered, but Carrancista oil revenue soared. With this and the customs at Veracruz, Carranza sent Alvarado to fight for Yucatán, its Henequén Commission, and more revenue. In Mexico City, in a Jacobin burst of anti-clericalism and anti-mercantilism, Obregón forced loans from the church, levied special taxes on big commercial houses, jailed recalcitrant clergy and merchants, bought the support of the Casa del Obrero, and through it recruited some 5,000 workers to form 'Red Battalions'.

After three months of Carrancista resistance, Wilson tried a more threatening course. On 6 March the United States informed Obregón and Carranza that it would hold them 'personally accountable . . . for suffering caused American lives or property' in Mexico City.[20] For a response Carranza had the benefit of advice from his new legal counsel in the United States, Charles A. Douglas. Another Washington lawyer, long a confidant of the Secretary of State and legal agent in the United States also for the Cuban, Nicaraguan, and Panamanian governments, Douglas was at the time in Veracruz. After consultation with him the First Chief retreated. On 10 March he had Obregón evacuate the famished and fever-ridden capital, which the Zapatistas and the Convention reoccupied. But the Carrancistas gained more valuable ground when on 19 March Alvarado occupied Mérida and the next day Progreso.

[20] Haley, *Revolution and intervention*, 155.

By March 1915 the war involved some 160,000 men – 80,000 Carrancistas, 50,000 Villistas, 20,000 Zapatistas, and 10,000 others. The beginning of its end occurred during the next month. In late March Villa launched his campaign toward Tampico. Undistracted, he probably would have crushed the defences mounted there by a newly notable Carrancista subordinate, Jacinto Treviño, González himself having rejoined Carranza in Veracruz. But Diéguez and Murguía threatened Guadalajara again. And Obregón, having left Mexico City, moved with Castro and Hill north into the Bajío, counting on Carrancista chiefs in Hidalgo and Puebla to protect the railway that kept him supplied from Veracruz. On 4 April he fortified the Bajío's key junction, Celaya, with 11,000 men, artillery and machine guns. Villa rushed 12,000 men and artillery to attack the town. The Villistas almost won on 6–7 April, but Obregón's forces held firm. Both sides reinforced, Obregón's to 15,000, with a heavy shipment of ammunition from Veracruz, Villa's to 20,000. The second battle of Celaya began on 13 April. It ended on 15 April with the Villistas retreating north. On 18 April Diéguez and Murguía took Guadalajara.

In Washington in the spring of 1915 the news about German submarines in the North Atlantic shipping lanes buried the news from Celaya. But because the war in Europe had begun to limit American freedom of action abroad, Washington needed political order in Mexico soon. Already it suffered the threat of new trouble: since January Orozco, Felicistas, and Huertistas in the United States had made contact with rebellious Mexican–Americans in South Texas, American Catholic bishops, and Wall Street lawyers, and on 12 April Huerta himself arrived in New York with German funds for a counter-revolution. On 23 April Carranza offered relief: Douglas privately submitted to the State Department a draft of the promises that the First Chief would make if the United States recognized his government, including special protection of foreign lives and property, indemnity for foreign losses, no confiscation to resolve 'the agrarian question', a general amnesty, and respect for religion. In May a high State Department official and the Secretary of Interior promoted a variant counter-revolutionary plan, rigged around Eduardo Iturbide for president; the resulting government, if recognized by the United States, would receive a loan through Speyer of as much as $500 million. But preoccupied then with the *Lusitania* crisis, Wilson decided to press for revolutionary reconciliation. On 2 June he offered support to the 'man or group of men . . . who can . . . ignore, if they cannot unite, the warring factions of the country . . .

and set up a government at Mexico . . . with whom the program of the revolution will be a business and not merely a platform'.[21]

Wilson's offer arrived just as its chances for success sank. During May Villa had reorganized his forces and re-engaged Obregón's – now reinforced by Diéguez and Murguía – in a long, complex battle around León. Recalling Ángeles from the north-east, abandoning Monterrey to local Carrancistas, and cutting the siege of Tampico so thin that it crumbled before Treviño's defences, Villa concentrated 35,000 men against Obregón's 30,000. The decisive combat began on 1 June. By 3 June the Villistas had almost won again; Obregón was wounded, and his replacement, Hill, had only nominal command over Castro, Diéguez and Murguía. But short of ammunition the Villistas broke down tactically, and on 5 June they retreated north again.

On 9 June Villa accepted Wilson's call for reconciliation and proposed immediate discussions with Carranza. But the Carrancistas now had better reasons than ever for continuing to fight. They had some 100,000 men in arms against 40,000 Villistas and 20,000 Zapatistas. Local *oficinas de bienes intervenidos* and *comisiones reguladoras* supported their garrisons. González and Coss were building a new Eastern Army Corps in Puebla to recapture Mexico City. Four more chiefs became divisional generals – Castro, Diéguez, Hill and Murguía. The revenue for an offensive flowed heavily, not only from the oil districts and Veracruz but also from the Henequén Commission, which Alvarado had turned into a regular reservoir of dollars; within a month Alvarado became the seventh divisional general. On 11 June, urging Villistas and Zapatistas to reunify under his authority, Carranza published as his programme of government the promises that he had offered in April to the State Department, and declared his expectation of recognition.

On 18 June Wilson warned Carranza that the United States might soon intervene to save Mexico from herself, but he granted that if Carranza would make 'a genuine effort to unite all parties and groups', then the United States would 'seriously consider' recognizing him.[22] On 21 June Carranza replied that if the United States would remain neutral, 'the Constitutionalist cause will subdue the opposition'.[23] On 27 June the US Department of Justice subdued his main opposition in its jurisdiction, jailing Orozco and Huerta in El Paso. The news must have sharpened the bitterness of Don Porfirio's last days: on 2 July he died in

[21] Arthur S. Link, *Wilson: the struggle for neutrality, 1914–1915* (Princeton, 1960), 476–7.
[22] Haley, *Revolution and intervention*, 164.   [23] Link, *Wilson: the struggle*, 480.

Paris. (Orozco escaped from jail, but was killed by Texas police on 30 August. Huerta, released to house arrest in El Paso, died of cirrhosis of the liver on 13 January 1916.)

Meanwhile, a new opposition for the Carrancistas to subdue had erupted in Oaxaca. On 3 June, under the influence of local conservatives, the state government had declared its independence. But in early July Carranza confidently assigned an old subordinate of his brother's, Jesús A. Castro, to restore Carrancista authority there. More important, *villismo* collapsed as a potential ruling force. Its currency hardly circulated through the north. The practice of special levies decayed into forays of plunder. Many officers and batches of troops deserted; those forces that remained barely held Treviño in Monterrey, and could not stop Obregón, freshly munitioned and reinforced from Veracruz, from moving Cesáreo Castro, Murguía and 20,000 troops north towards Aguascalientes. There 10,000 Villistas mounted resistance. Combat began on 6 July. On 10 July Obregón's forces broke the Villista lines, and the Villistas retreated north yet again. Ángeles left the country to lobby in Washington. Meanwhile González had moved his 10,000-man Eastern Army on Mexico City, from which the Convention fled for the last time on 9 July, and he occupied the capital on 11 July. Local Carrancistas took San Luis Potosí and Murguía took Zacatecas. In a daring stab at recovery a Villista force still in the west bolted across the Bajío and attacked Obregón's supply lines with Veracruz. But on 17 July González evacuated Mexico City to defend the lines. On 2 August having with Coss and his forces repulsed the Villistas, he reoccupied the capital definitively. And Coss became the eighth divisional general.

As *carrancismo* expanded militarily, it became more interesting to big business. Because the Carrancistas now drew regular revenue from exports, they no longer had to levy special taxes; indeed they brought relief from Villa's levies. Their paper pesos increased inflation: from November 1914 to May 1915 the value of the Carrancista peso fell from $0.20 to $0.09 (see table 3). But because the European war and the civil war proscribed productive investment, inflation provided welcome alternatives in commodity speculation. In June the finance ministry made another issue to increase the supply to 215 million pesos, then in July announced that since much of the paper in circulation was counterfeit, it would soon issue a completely new currency of 250 million pesos – in effect soliciting speculation.

Some political connections developed with small businesses. The key was local military control. Because particular Carrancista chiefs commanded the railways, *oficinas de bienes intervenidos* and *comisiones reguladoras*, they positively obliged planters, ranchers, manufacturers and merchants in their districts to accept deals with them – or their kin, friends, and staff. Given inflation and two years of bad harvests, the highly profitable grain trade underpinned most of these partnerships. That summer the rains were poor again, promising another bad harvest, higher profits, and a consolidation of the new deals.

The Carrancistas also tightened their patronage of organized labour. Here too the key was local military control. The war itself, frequently shifting the command over the railways, had already ruptured the UCMGF and UMM. Now military favours for loyal service and threats of punishment for *villismo* paralysed them. Under military vigilance Mining Union locals in the north-east barely survived. Military tolerance of previous agreements kept the port unions moving freight. Similarly, with a couple of decrees raising wages, Aguilar kept the Orizaba textile workers in the mills. And Carrancista subsidies fostered Casas del Obrero, most of them docile, in 30 or so provincial cities and towns. In Mexico City, however, where under the Convention unions had grown freely, González could not maintain control. The electrical workers' SME had developed its own leadership and strength, and in May it had won its first strike. On 12 August, despite González, it began another, which, with help from comrades in Tampico, Pachuca, and the mines of El Oro in Mexico State, it carried on for eight days and won.

Wilson tried again to mediate among the contending armies. On 11 August in Washington a Pan-American Conference of delegates from the United States, the 'ABC' countries, Bolivia, Guatemala, and Uruguay called for 'all prominent civil and military authorities in Mexico' to arrange another revolutionary convention to devise a provisional government.[24] The Villista generals and Villa accepted at once, as did the Zapatistas. But none of the Carrancista generals would discuss the invitation; all referred the Pan-Americans to the First Chief. On 10 September Carranza formally answered, refusing to discuss anything but recognition of his government.

On 4 September the Villistas had lost Saltillo, their last foothold in the north-east. On 19 September they began evacuating Torreón, retreating to their old base in Chihuahua. On 26 September the last of them left the town, and on 28 September Murguía occupied it. In the same weeks

24 *Ibid.*, 493.

Carrancista forces moving up from Acapulco drove the Zapatistas back to their old base in Morelos.

Nearly a year of regular warfare among the revolutionaries had ended in Carrancista victory. And on 9 October the Pan-Americans concluded that 'the Carranza party is the only party possessing the essentials for recognition as the de facto government of Mexico . . .'.[25] On 19 October the United States recognized Carranza's government *de facto*, reducing the Villistas and Zapatistas to mere rebels.

OCTOBER 1915 – MAY 1917

In triumph Venustiano Carranza, the First Chief, defined *carrancismo*'s new task as 'the reconstruction of the Fatherland'. He meant more than restoring regular railway service and the value of the peso. His country having suffered a history that he now described as 'the disequilibrium of four centuries, three of oppression and one of internal struggles, . . . thirty years of tyranny, . . . the Revolution . . . and a horrible chaos . . ., a barracks coup and an assassination . . .', he meant the deliberate construction of a Mexican state.[26] After three years of civil war he had firmly in mind the form that the state should have. He did not recite theories about it, but he projected it clearly in the policies that he soon undertook – ignoring the Monroe Doctrine, raising taxes on foreign companies, establishing a central bank to manage Mexican finances and promote Mexican business, returning attached estates to the old landlords, institutionalizing the mediation of conflicts among business-men and between business and labour, and crushing disobedient peasants and workers. If these policies succeeded, a centralized state would keep national markets free of privilege, more benefits would go to all Mexicans, and in the consequent prosperity the old dreams of balance and order would come true.

Carrancista 'reconstruction' faced formidable obstacles, the worst being the power behind the Monroe Doctrine. The United States not only recognized Carranza's government on 19 October but also privately detailed its duties, including 'protection of foreign property and prevention of excessive taxation, . . . currency issue based on substantial guarantees', and 'early and equitable settlement' of foreign claims.[27] The

[25] *Ibid.*, 639.   [26] Fabela and Fabela, *Documentos históricos*, IV, 153–6.
[27] Canova to Lansing, 13 October 1915, United States National Archives (USNA), Record Group
59, 812.00/ 16546–1/2; Canova to Lansing, 16 October 1915, USNA 59, 812.00/ 16547–1/2;
Lansing, Memorandum to Arredondo, 19 October 1915, USNA 59, 812.00/ 16548–1/2.

domestic obstacles were several. An army of 100,000, which the government could not safely reduce immediately, took heavy doses of revenue. The few big Mexican companies had retrenched, and provincial businessmen, highly suspicious of local Carrancista commanders, conducted their affairs almost in secret. The Mexico City Casa del Obrero, which still had its Red Battalions in arms, had just declared its independence by announcing plans to form a national confederation of unions and affiliate it with 'the International'. Besides, the Villistas, Zapatistas, and exiles were still dangerous threats.

But Carranza had promising powers. At least he enjoyed recognition from the United States, which once more legalized imports of American arms and ammunition for his forces. On 10 November he received recognition from Germany too, and in December from Britain. Moreover he had flowing through his finance ministry the country's main currents of revenue – customs duties from almost all the major ports, mining and oil taxes, and henequén sales. By elaborate counterbalancing he dominated the eight divisional generals in charge of the army. The various offices of attached property he brought under a central Administración de Bienes Intervenidos. For advisers he had Douglas in Washington and several worldly and well-informed associates in Mexico: finance minister Cabrera, no financier but the country's shrewdest political analyst and sharpest polemicist; Alberto J. Pani, an engineer long connected with Mexico City contractors, trusted by Standard Oil, Director General of Constitutionalist railways since 1914, soon to be elected president of the national railways; Ignacio Bonillas, a MIT-trained engineer long connected with Sonora's mining and contracting companies, trusted by Southern Pacific, Constitutionalist minister of communications (railways) since 1913; and not least Fernando González Roa, counsel for Wells Fargo, the National Railways, the Yucatán railways, the Henequén Commission, and the department of agriculture, and senior partner in the law firm handling most foreign claims against Mexico. And he had the *renovadores* to organize support for eventual elections and serve in the regular government to follow.

He also had a sound strategy: discuss with the United States its concerns in Mexico, but delay resolutions until the war in Europe ended, when he could call on the Old World to redress the balance in the New; return estates to landlords who would deal with him; and reassure businessmen by keeping a firm grip on unions. The crucial manoeuvre would be a convention to write a new constitution, which would justify a short-term loan in New York, oblige landlords and businessmen to admit their stakes in the new state, and issue in the Carrancista domination of the regular government.

'Reconstruction' started strongly. At the First Chief's direction Douglas prepared for discussions of claims and a loan. In November and December a new Credit Regulatory Commission inspected the country's twenty-four chartered banks and closed fourteen of them, to prepare for a central bank. Unfortunately the peso fell to $0.04 (see table 3). But in January Cabrera went to Washington to consult with Douglas, then to New York to approach the House of Morgan.

Carrancista dissolution of the Villista threat seemed definitive. On 1 November Villa attacked Agua Prieta, hoping to raise a new war in Sonora and discredit the newly recognized government. But thanks to US permission, the First Chief had reinforcements from Torreón arrive via Eagle Pass, Texas, and Douglas, Arizona, in time to save the town. On 5 November Villa publicly denounced Carranza for having sold Mexico to the United States for recognition, and continued fighting south towards Hermosillo. But Carranza moved Diéguez from Jalisco up to Sonora, driving the Villistas back, and shifted Treviño from Monterrey to join Murguía in a campaign into Chihuahua. On 23 December Treviño occupied Chihuahua City and became the ninth divisional general. On 1 January, back in the Chihuahua mountains, Villa disbanded the remnants of his army into guerillas. On 14 January Carranza declared him an outlaw to be shot on sight.

The First Chief did not deny 'the agrarian question' that Villa and Zapata still represented. On 19 January 1916 he decreed the establishment of a National Agrarian Commission. This was not, however, to redistribute land, but to oversee and circumscribe local decisions on villages' claims. (For statistics on Carranza's land distribution, see table 4.)

Meanwhile the government checked a sudden burst of inflation-provoked challenges from organized labour. On 16 November the UCMGF and shop unions organized a strike on the Mexican Railway. On 30 November Carranza drafted all railway personnel. In November and December textile workers, bakers, typographers and the SME went on strike in Mexico City, as did miners in nearby El Oro, and on 2 January the city's Casa del Obrero and the SME took the lead in forming a new Federación de Sindicatos Obreros del Distrito Federal (FSODF),

Table 4. *Definitive distribution of land to villages under the degree of 6 January 1915 and Article 27 of the constitution of 1917, 1915–20*

Year	Villages	Heads of families	Hectares
1915	0	0	0
1916	1	182	1,246
1917	8	2,615	5,635
1918	57	15,071	68,309
1919	60	14,948	40,276
1920	64	15,566	64,333
TOTAL	190	48,382	179,799

Source: Eyler N. Simpson, *The Ejido. Mexico's way out* (Chapel Hill, 1937), table 17.
Note: The total area of Mexico was 198,720,100 hectares.

which declared a 'class struggle' for 'the socialization of the means of production'.[28] On 13 January Carranza ordered the Casa's Red Battalions mustered out. On 18 January González warned the FSODF that 'the government cannot sanction proletarian tyranny', and on 5 February stopped the Casa's subsidy.[29]

Carranza suffered sharp disappointments. Morgan spurned Cabrera's overture. And after the Mexican government cancelled a Standard Oil subsidiary's concession not registered under the 7 January 1915 oil decree, the oil companies and the State Department accused it of intending to nationalize oil. In February the companies began paying a regular monthly tribute to Manuel Peláez to police their Tampico–Tuxpan fields. And some connected with exiles in the United States, who with private help from inside the State Department rallied around Félix Díaz and secretly shipped him to Veracruz to raise a counter-revolution.

But new circumstances abroad improved the chances for a centralized consolidation. Adjusted to produce for the war in Europe, the American economy had already started to boom in 1915. On its strength, mining and manufacturing in Mexico began to recuperate in early 1916, providing new revenue. And the Carrancista government kept displaying power and competence. On 1 February it announced that González would command a 30,000-man campaign against the Zapatistas in

[28] Luis Araiza, *Historia del movimiento obrero mexicano* (4 vols. in one, Mexico, 1964–5), III, 115.
[29] *Ibid.*, III, 124.

Morelos. On 13 February it announced a commission to draft the new constitution. On 25 February, anticipating Felicista trouble, Carranza promoted Veracruz's Governor Aguilar to divisional general (the tenth). The same day he ordered Cabrera to prepare redemption of the various current pesos by a new issue of 500 million in paper impossible to counterfeit, *infalsificables*. The finance ministry directed governors to relinquish their *oficinas de bienes intervenidos* to its agents. On 5 March, capping an eight-month campaign, Jesús Castro's forces reoccupied Oaxaca City. Such progress favourably impressed the United States, and on 9 March the State Department swore in a regular ambassador to Mexico.

The Carrancista project failed, however, because the Carrancistas underestimated Villa's remaining power and audacity. On 9 March 1916 Villa led 500 guerillas across the border, attacked Columbus, New Mexico, killed seventeen Americans, and withdrew into the Chihuahua mountains. He intended to destroy the United States–Carranza connection, oblige Carranza's generals to overthrow him, and negotiate a new revolutionary coalition with them. This he did not accomplish. But his attack, outraging the American public in a year of US presidential elections, did cause a crisis in US–Mexican relations so serious that its impact altered the shape of 'reconstruction'.

On 15 March 1916 a US Army punitive expedition entered Chihuahua. Wilson had no plans for war with Mexico; his primary concern then was persuading Congress to increase US armed forces to counter Republican cries for a still greater increase for action in the war in Europe. The sinking of the *Sussex* on 24 March left all sober American politicians preoccupied with Europe. The expeditionary force numbered only 6,000 men (later reinforced to 10,000), and had orders only to disperse Villista bands near the border. But the United States took four months, until after the Republican and Democratic nominating conventions, to recover enough calm for deliberations to begin about the retreat of the force.

Through the crisis Carranza managed a masterly diplomacy in the defence of sovereignty and the preservation of peace. From the first he had Douglas's reports on Washington's limited aims. On 13 March, to bind the army into the government, he made Aguilar minister of foreign relations and Obregón minister of war. He let the expedition base itself in Chihuahua without military resistance; not until 12 April, because of a bloody pro-Villa riot in an important Chihuahua market town, did he demand that the expedition withdraw from Mexico. On 28 April negotiations between Wilson's envoys and his own, led by Obregón, began in Juárez. The Americans sought a Carrancista guarantee against another Mexican 'invasion of American territory' and, if Carrancista forces could not police the border, permission for US forces to act for them.[30] For a show of resolution Wilson placed an embargo on arms and ammunition shipments to the Mexican government. Obregón sought the expedition's unqualified and speedy withdrawal. For a show of power and determination to crush rebellion, Carranza had González storm Morelos. The border bandits raided into Texas, and Wilson called up the Texas, New Mexico and Arizona militia. On 11 May the envoys suspended negotiations. On 20 May Wilson won relief in the US Congress: the National Defense Act was passed, which allowed for middling increases in the army and the militia. Meanwhile Carranza had Douglas in Querétaro for consultation, and on 22 May he had Aguilar publish a long note to the State Department explaining that if the United States wanted order in Mexico, it would have to remove its troops from the country and reauthorize arms and ammunition shipments to the government. Aguilar also implied that the Mexican government would pay reparations for border raids.

On 10 June the Republicans nominated a moderate for president. On 12 June, to show Carrancista determination to restore constitutional order, Carranza announced countrywide municipal elections in September. On 16 June the Democrats nominated Woodrow Wilson. Relations between the two countries worsened anyway. Mexican-American rebels raided from Mexico into Texas, and on 18 June Wilson mobilized the entire US militia for service on the border. On 21 June an expeditionary patrol in Chihuahua provoked a skirmish with a Carrancista force and half its men were killed or captured. On 24 June Wilson threatened a major military intervention in Mexico. But Carranza ordered the release of the captured expeditionaries. By the end of the month Wilson had backed off. In early July he and Carranza accepted the renewal of negotiations in a Joint US–Mexico Commission to meet in the United States. But Carranza did not appoint his commissioners for another month, knowing that nothing substantial would happen in negotiations until after the US elections in November. The commissioners he then named were the Carrancistas most likely to make the American connections most advantageous to his government: Luis Cabrera, Alberto Pani, and Ignacio Bonillas.

---

[30] Arthur S. Link, *Wilson: confusions and crises, 1915–1916* (Princeton, 1960), 290.

But inside the country the First Chief lost much power. The key was the delivery of the war ministry to Obregón, who on 15 March also received Carranza's authorization to order payments directly from the treasury. Extraordinary corruption soon flourished throughout the army. The troop rolls expanded to 125,000. With or without Obregón's approval, generals practically appropriated railways, *oficinas de bienes intervenidos* and *comisiones reguladoras*. Independently, Treviño's command in Chihuahua became a model of graft, and González's campaign in Morelos a showcase of plundering.

Also debilitating was the spectacular failure of the government's monetary policy. On 4 April Carranza instituted the Monetary Commission, a rudimentary central bank, to issue the 500 million *infalsificables* in June. The news fuelled inflation, and as real wages plummeted again, organized labour became intensely combative. Already between 5 and 17 March a convention of delegates representing 100 or so unions in the Federal District and seven states, held by the FSODF and Veracruz anarchists in the port, had founded the Confederación de Trabajadores de la Región Mexicana, for 'class struggle' by 'direct action' for 'socialization of the means of production'.[31] In May the peso fell to $0.02. Defying war ministry regulations, the UCMGF and the main railway-shop unions organized a strike on the Constitutionalist railways for payment on a gold standard. The government repressed the movement, then granted the unions an eight-hour day, the first in any industry in Mexico. Simultaneously the FSODF carried out a general strike in Mexico City for gold-standard payment and at least on paper won its demands. In June the *infalsificable* appeared at $0.10, but currency speculation continued, at the expense of small debtors and workers, and on 31 July the FSODF called another general strike, which closed the city down for several days. The government repressed it, and a court-martial sent the leaders to prison. Strikes also hit mining districts and Tuxpan and Minatitlán oil installations.

In all this disappointment Carranza's only notable domestic success was against Félix Díaz. It took Díaz until July to get together with ex-Federal Army renegades in Veracruz, Oaxaca and Chiapas, and then, because of Jesús Castro's rule in the region, he could not raise an offensive. For such service Castro was made a divisional general, bringing the total to eleven.

As the crisis passed, the Carrancista 'reconstruction' resumed. On 15

[31] Rosendo Salazar and José G. Escobedo, *Las pugnas de la gleba, 1907–1922* (2 vols. in one, Mexico, 1923), I, 179.

August the government required foreign companies interested in natural resources to renounce their national rights. On 3 September it staged municipal elections, the first step towards centralized co-ordination of local chiefs. Although the Joint Commission began its sessions on 6 September and the Americans proposed to postpone discussions of the punitive expedition's withdrawal until Mexico provided 'formal assurance' of protection for foreign lives and property, on 14 September Carranza decreed that mining companies had to resume regular operations or lose title to their property.[32] The same day he announced elections on 22 October for a Constitutional Convention, and the following day he attached all banks and their metallic reserves, around $25 million in gold, to fund a central bank.

But because of the crisis, the substance of 'reconstruction' was regionalized. The crucial conflict in Mexico was now between the government, with a national project but little power, and probably twenty important generals, jealously divided among themselves – a few, mainly Aguilar and Cesáreo Castro, for Carranza; some freewheeling, principally Obregón and González; others in regional strongholds, like Calles in Sonora, Caballero in Tamaulipas, Diéguez in Jalisco, Jesús Castro in Oaxaca, or Alvarado in Yucatán, where he had organized a political machine, the Partido Socialista. Poor rains again that summer tightened the generals' grip on local affairs. And in this disarray the rebels resumed action. On 15–16 September Villa raided Chihuahua City for much military booty. Two weeks later the Zapatistas began raiding into the Federal District.

In October the First Chief and the generals defined their strategies for the new conflict. Carranza's was for the short run, to use his executive office to remove the reasons for his decline before the return to regular government. In his first direct approach to Germany he suggested to Berlin that if it helped to hasten Washington's withdrawal of the punitive expedition, he would provide facilities for U-boats in the Gulf. He waived tariffs on imports of food. And, the *infalsificable* having fallen to $0.03, he ordered payment of taxes and wages on a gold standard. The generals' strategy was, for the long run, not to challenge Carranza directly, but not to let him govern effectively either, and eventually to settle the succession to him among themselves. On 22 October Carranza's and the generals' placemen were elected to the Constitutional

[32] Robert F. Smith, *The United States and revolutionary nationalism in Mexico, 1916–1932* (Chicago, 1972), 57.

Convention. The next day González, Obregón and other generals met in Mexico City and formally founded the Partido Liberal Constitucionalista, a covering name for their personal political outfits. The PLC would, they announced, support Carranza for president. It would also provide him with a crippling opposition.

International circumstances in November 1916 fostered Mexico's political decentralization. As the stalemate on the Somme and Wilson's re-election brought the United States and Germany on to a collision course, both Washington and Berlin treated Carranza more cautiously. Neither now favoured a centralized Mexican government, for each expected that the other might eventually win its loyalty. To deny each other a significant ally, both countries encouraged the conflict between Carranza, the generals, and the rebels.

In November the First Chief made another overture to Berlin. He did not break neutrality, but bent it a long way, offering Germany close commercial and military co-operation. But the German foreign ministry rejected the 'suggestion'. Instead the German ambassador bought a surge of pro-Germanism among important generals, and the German secret services manoeuvred to support Villa and to plant saboteurs in Tampico. Once the German government on 9 January sealed its decision to resume unrestricted submarine warfare, foreign minister Zimmermann telegraphed the ambassador new instructions, which arrived on 19 January. The U-boats would go into unrestricted action on 1 February. If as expected the United States then declared war on Germany, the ambassador should propose a German–Mexican alliance to Carranza: 'joint pursuit of the war, joint conclusion of peace. Substantial financial support and an agreement on our part for Mexico to reconquer its former territories in Texas, New Mexico, and Arizona.'[33] But this was a formula for the destruction of the Mexican state.

On 24 November the Joint US–Mexican Commissioners signed a protocol unconditionally requiring the punitive expedition's withdrawal. The prior discussion, however, still implied that US forces could return to Mexico if the Mexican government did not protect foreign lives and property. Paying for the removal of even the implication of an American right to intervene again, Carranza abolished the infamous *infalsificables* (which had fallen to $0.005), decreed a return to gold and silver currency, and postponed for four months the requirement that

---

[33] Friedrich Katz, *The secret war in Mexico: Europe, the United States, and the Mexican Revolution* (Chicago, 1981), 354.

foreign companies renounce their national rights. Then his commissioners reported his refusal of the protocol. On 3 January the US commissioners recommended to Wilson a simple withdrawal, and Wilson ordered the expedition home. But Carranza gained no power. In January he had an envoy in New York ask Morgan for a short-term $10 million loan. Following the State Department's cues, Morgan would not consider the request. On 5 February, the day the last expeditionary troops returned to American soil, the Mexican government asked permission to import embargoed ammunition. The State Department refused to forward the request to Wilson. At the same time the new US military attaché in Mexico City warmly befriended war minister Obregón. Privately American agents began trying to restore contact with Villa, and tribute continued to flow to Peláez.

Meanwhile the generals rode higher and higher. War minister Obregón behaved like the head of an opposition, publicly lambasting the First Chief's *renovador* ministers and associates. The rebels stepped up their campaigns: on 27 November Villa raided Chihuahua City again, for much more military booty; in late December Villistas occupied Torreón for a week, forced a heavy loan, and took more booty. Villa shortly met his match, when Carranza returned Treviño to Monterrey and sent Murguía to Chihuahua. After a defeat by Murguía in early January, Villa drew his troops back into the Sierra Madre, but with the resources for a long guerilla war. In the Tampico–Tuxpan oil fields by mid-January, Peláez had a broad offensive underway. The Zapatistas recovered too. Spending their last silver to buy lots of arms and ammunition in the Carrancista black markets, they opened an offensive across Morelos and into Puebla. By mid-January they had driven González's forces out of their base and were organizing cadres and civilian administration. In early February they had Palafox start organizing local land commissions and a new regular military force.

As if in the eye of a hurricane, the Constitutional Convention opened in Querétaro on 20 November 1916. Most of the 200 or so deputies nominally represented districts in the populous states across central Mexico, from Jalisco to Veracruz, where various generals had had them elected. At least 80 per cent were bourgeois, and 75 per cent of these provincial petty bourgeois. Politically most had had considerable experience: 31 had served in the 26th Congress; probably another 150 had officiated in Maderista state governments, in the Constitutionalist bureaucracy in 1914–15, and on Constitutionalist military staffs.

Ideologically the great majority avowed a simple anti-clerical liberalism. A few of the most bookish professed a liberal reformism they called socialism. One was a serious syndicalist.

On 1 December 1916 the First Chief inaugurated the Convention, presented his draft for the new constitution, and instructed the deputies to terminate their proceedings by 31 January 1917. The only major changes he proposed to the 1857 constitution were to strengthen the presidency, weaken Congress and state governments, and authorize a central bank. In return he recommended a four-year presidential term and no re-election (no vice-presidency either), an independent judiciary, and guarantees for municipal autonomy.

Trusted Carrancistas ran the Convention's executive. But within a week they lost the leadership to a committee run by deputies who often consulted with Obregón and demanded social and economic reforms written into the constitution. On 11 December the committee began reporting revisions of Carranza's draft. The executive complained of a division between loyal 'Carrancista liberals' and upstart 'Obregonista Jacobins'.[34] Its opponents complained of a division between a rightist minority of old, Carrancista civilians and a leftist majority of young, popular soldiers. This was mostly oratory. Once the voting started, the deputies approved article after article with large majorities, some unanimously. Carranza won a stronger presidency and authorization for a central bank. The committee won its social and economic sections: Article 3 outlawed religious education; Article 27 vested in the Mexican nation the ownership of the country's natural resources, specified as Mexican all titles to land and water, and mandated the expropriation of large estates and their subdivision into small farms and communal landholdings; Article 123 limited a day's work to eight hours, guaranteed the right to unionize and to strike, and established compulsory arbitration; Article 130 regulated religious worship and prohibited priests from criticizing either the constitution or the government.

On 31 January 1917 the deputies signed the new constitution, and on 5 February Carranza promulgated it. The new president would enjoy much formal authority. But since he could not effectively impose it, his opposition would have vast scope for protest, denunciation, and agitation.

---

[34] *Diario de los debates del Congreso Constituyente, 1916–1917* (2 vols., Mexico, 1960), I, 641–82; E. Victor Niemeyer, Jr, *Revolution at Queretaro: the Mexican Constitutional Convention of 1916–1917* (Austin, Texas, 1974), 60–1, 220–2.

Already the international crisis had intensified. Responding to the German announcement on 1 February of its new U-boat policy, Wilson on 3 February had broken diplomatic relations with Berlin. The United States and Germany pulled ever harder against each other's influence in Mexico. American mining and oil companies protested vehemently against the new constitution, especially the 'confiscatory' Article 27.[35] On 8 February Zimmermann, the German foreign minister, advised his ambassador to Mexico to propose 'without delay' the German–Mexican alliance.[36] On 20 February the ambassador made the proposal to foreign minister Aguilar. Meanwhile the German secret services pumped funds to the generals and elaborated networks for sabotage around Tampico. On 1 March Wilson published Zimmermann's initial telegram on German–Mexican alliance, exciting a predictable American uproar. On 3 March the US ambassador to Mexico presented his credentials to Carranza, but shortly afterwards the State Department squashed a New York bank's proposal to lend the *de facto* government $20 million. It also secretly sanctioned ammunition shipments to Peláez. In mid-March German submarines sank three American ships in the North Atlantic. On 6 April the United States declared war on Germany.

Under so much pressure from both directions, Venustiano Carranza and the generals displayed consensus on two crucial questions. First, to avoid another American intervention, they stood together in favour of a foreign policy of neutrality in the war in Europe, a strategy of flirtation with both the United States and Germany. On 12 February Carranza named the pro-American Bonillas as ambassador to Washington, but the next day he publicly emphasized Mexico's neutrality. In the tense weeks following, he postponed the requirement that mining companies return to regular operations, announced that the forthcoming regular government would resume payments on the foreign debt, appointed the pro-American Pani minister of industry and commerce (in charge of oil), and denied to the United States that he even knew of a proposal for a German–Mexican alliance. After the United States declared war, he secretly declined Zimmermann's offer. On 24 April he again postponed the requirement that foreign companies renounce their national rights. But he gave haven to German spies and propagandists; wittingly he kept a Mexican agent for Germany as minister of communications.

[35] Haley, *Revolution and intervention*, 245; Smith, *United States and revolutionary nationalism*, 89, 91, 105–6. [36] Katz, *The secret war*, 363.

Secondly, Carranza and the generals together rigged a constitutional government. On 11 March the army supervised presidential and congressional elections. Of 213,000 votes for president, Carranza won 197,000 (González and Obregón shared the rest). All the congressional seats went to the PLC. On 1 April Carranza authorized provisional governors to hold elections for regular state governments. Almost immediately after the new Congress met on 15 April, the 200 or so deputies divided into 20 unconditional Carrancistas, 80 Obregonistas, and more than 100 'independents'.

On 1 May 1917 the new Mexican state formally appeared. The First Chief was sworn into office in Mexico City as the new president, to serve until 30 November 1920. And the new constitution went into effect. Meanwhile the real 'reconstruction' – the durable reconnection of foreign and domestic business with national and regional politics – continued.

MAY 1917 – OCTOBER 1918

Throughout 1917 the Mexican economy recovered. As the first world war stimulated the American economy, demand for Mexican exports increased. Standard Oil, Mexican Petroleum, and Águila raised oil production faster than ever. Mining companies did well too; their outputs of gold, silver, and copper reached nearly normal levels. Although the rains that summer were poor yet again, rich opportunities reopened in the north-west's irrigated agriculture, where Mexicali's cotton growers, Sonora's chickpea farmers, and Sinaloa's sugar planters became exporting tycoons. In Yucatán the Henequén Commission sharply reduced production, more than doubled the price, and took a record profit. And because of the exports, domestic markets rallied. Monterrey's Fundidora resumed a respectable production. Grain dealers did excellent business with their scant stocks.

The economic recovery offered increases in various kinds of political power: taxes, graft, contracts. But only the taxes flowed to the treasury, and they were not enough to allow Carranza to centralize the other kinds of power. The newly constituted government's revenue ran to 11 million pesos a month, more than previous governments had ever enjoyed. But current expenditures ran to 16.5 million pesos a month, of which 10 million went for the army. The deficit of 5.5 million was paid from the attached bank reserves, which at that rate would not last the year. The government needed a loan maybe just to survive, and certainly to consolidate itself. Otherwise the lion's share of graft and contracts would continue to accrue to whichever generals could command them, consolidating the decentralization of power.

President Carranza set out immediately to gain political and financial control. On 1 May he had war minister Obregón resign, and left his replacement, Jesús Castro, at the rank of undersecretary. On 8 May he asked Congress for legislation to found a central bank. In mid-May a Mexican banker in New York privately sounded Morgan on support. Morgan accommodatingly shunted him to Washington. In late May, at Carranza's invitation, a team of private American consultants arrived in Mexico City to advise the government on fiscal and financial reform. The resort to the United States disturbed Germany, and Zimmermann again secretly proposed an alliance to Carranza. But Carranza put him off.

Carranza continued catering to the old landlords by returning more and more estates to their owners. As one of Cowdray's managers in Mexico reported, 'A tendency to conservatism is observable now that the government is . . . not so dependent on the radical military element. Undoubtedly Carranza is doing his utmost to free himself from the extremists . . . You probably know that they have returned Don José Limantour's properties . . .'[37]

In June finance minister Cabrera announced Mexico's intention to ask American banks for a loan. He then left the ministry to take a seat in the Chamber of Deputies and defend the government's policy. From 12 July to 4 August Pani, the industry and commerce minister, led the country's highly suspicious merchants through a national convention that issued in ringing endorsements of the government and plans for a National Confederation of Chambers of Commerce. On 23 July Congress authorized the government to borrow 250 million pesos abroad, of which 100 million would establish a central bank. Privately Mexican envoys in New York persuaded Morgan to consider a five- or ten-year loan to repay defaults and an eventual refunding of the entire foreign debt. In early August, when the US ambassador reported the oil companies' extreme worries over Article 27, Carranza assured him that the new constitution did not provide for 'confiscation'.[38] Again Zimmermann secretly proposed German–Mexican alliance; again

[37] *Ibid.*, 293.
[38] United States Department of State, *Papers relating to the foreign relations of the United States, 1917* (Washington, DC, 1926), 1072.

Carranza put him off. On 20 August President Wilson announced that the State Department would morally approve American loans to Mexico, and on 31 August recognized Carranza's government *de jure*. On 1 September Carranza sent Cabrera to New York to start formal negotiations for a loan, and called Douglas to Mexico for a month of consultations. Two weeks later US Customs released the Mexican ammunition long embargoed on the border.

But all the palaver and activity yielded not a penny. In New York Cabrera found Morgan unwilling to lend anything unless Washington guaranteed it, and Washington, at war, would not guarantee anything unless Mexico committed itself against Germany. The State Department suggested that Mexico borrow from the US government. Carranza refused. Knowing his need to import specie and corn, the Department then tightened restrictions on American exports of gold, industrial equipment, and food to Mexico. In mid-October Cabrera attacked American oil companies for lobbying against a loan, and on 1 November he ended the New York negotiations.

Meanwhile the generals began to fortify themselves politically for the long run to 1920. Aguilar, now Carranza's son-in-law, left the foreign ministry to become governor of Veracruz. On leave from the army, Obregón made a quick fortune brokering Sonora's chickpea trade, and in mid-September set off on an obvious campaign across the United States, from Los Angeles to Washington, where he obliged Bonillas to introduce him to the Secretary of State. González, who made a fortune brokering Mexico City's grain trade, took charge of the September ammunition shipment to emerge as the country's main military figure. From their official posts in Mexico City, Hill and Treviño cultivated connections in the capital. Calles established his hold on Sonora and Diéguez, elected Jalisco's governor, extended his influence into the surrounding states. Murguía made himself the boss of Chihuahua. Coss was preparing to win the gubernatorial election in Coahuila. Caballero was doing the same in Tamaulipas. And Alvarado elaborated his rule over the entire south-east.

Moreover the economic recovery and the political divisions strengthened labour movements. The UCMGF and the UMM re-organized their old branches as independently as ever. Encouraged by the recent surge of IWW syndicalism in the United States, syndicalist organizers appeared in the mining districts, Torreón, and Tampico. Already in April oil workers in all the Tampico installations had been on strike. In May they had struck again in Minatitlán, in June staged a general strike in Tampico, and in October struck there again. From early September to mid-October textile workers in Puebla and Veracruz shut down several big mills. Most impressively, another labour convention took place in mid-October in Tampico. Delegates representing 29 organizations from the Federal District 'and 11 states reconstituted the CTRM as the Confederación General Obrera (CGO), declared 'class struggle' by 'direct action' for the 'communization of the means of production', and agreed to base the new CGO strategically in Torreón.[39]

Meanwhile the rebels had at least held their ground. In May Villistas had raided Ojinaga. In July they had raided in southern Chihuahua. Peláez had kept his control in the Tampico–Tuxpan oil fields. The Zapatistas in Morelos had started negotiating to co-operate with other rebel movements. And from June on, after floundering for a year, the Felicistas had been raiding in the Minatitlán oil fields.

With the exhaustion of the British army in Belgium in October and the Bolshevik revolution in Russia in November 1917, the first world war turned strategically into a race to the Western Front between American and German reinforcements. At the same time the terms of American–German conflict in Mexico changed again: whereas the United States, however, continued to oppose a Carrancista concentration of power, Berlin accepted Mexico's neutrality. In November, after his failure in New York, Cabrera went to Washington to request relaxation of the restrictions on American exports to Mexico. Carranza tried to ease agreement by setting up the claims commission that his American consultants had designed. But the State Department stalled so tellingly that Cabrera left Washington in mid-December. And another conspiracy, involving Standard Oil, a high official in the State Department, and the exiles around Iturbide, formed to overthrow the Mexican government. In contrast, German officials in Mexico now offered Carranza a 70 million peso loan to remain neutral for the duration of the war and to favour German trade and investment afterwards. But they could not get Berlin's confirmation.

Without American or German support Carranza had to raise new funds elsewhere, or the government would soon face grave financial difficulty. To pave the way for a domestic loan, he had Pani prepare a national convention of manufacturers. Meanwhile he had González plan an offensive to capture Morelos and its plantations, and he called Diéguez

---

[39] Salazar and Escobedo, *Las pugnas de la gleba*, I, 245.

from Jalisco and Murguía from Chihuahua for a major campaign to take the Tampico–Tuxpan oil fields. As a long shot he also arranged an approach to Cowdray, for the British collapse in Europe had made Águila acutely vulnerable to American challenges in Mexico.

All but one of these ventures proved disappointing. From 17 to 25 November 1917 the manufacturers met. But unlike the merchants they complained about the new constitution and resoundingly reaffirmed the privacy of their enterprises, which they would defend in a new National Confederation of Chambers of Industry. González's forces secured only the eastern third of Morelos, and the Diéguez–Murguía campaign actually lost ground. Diéguez moved into the oil fields, but Murguía had hardly left Chihuahua when the Villistas raided Ojinaga again, and he had to retreat to his weakened base. Thrashing around the north-east in December, Diéguez ruined the rigging of Coss's election in Coahuila, and provoked Coss to revolt. In Tamaulipas, where Diéguez disrupted Caballero's plans for election in February, a new Felicista band began its own rebellion, and the Pelaecistas strengthened their positions. Only the approach to Cowdray succeeded – a deal in mid-December over the Tehuantepec Railway Company (which Cowdray co-owned with the Mexican government) released $3 million in cash and $4.5 million in stock.

Sharp signs of new trouble soon appeared. On 1 January 1918 the PLC Obregonistas for the first time publicly rebuked the president, for interfering in state elections. On 12 January, because of renewed disturbances along the Texas border, the United States ordered its forces to pursue suspects into Mexico. On 14 January a military plot to overthrow Carranza was discovered, involving garrisons in Mexico City, Veracruz, and other important towns.

Carranza's search for support became increasingly improbable. To counteract the PLC, he encouraged the formation of a new Partido Nacional Cooperatista, starting with a national labour convention in Saltillo, to attract unions away from the CGO. While he went on returning attached properties and encouraged landlords to organize their peons as local militia, he had the National Agrarian Commission for the first time run steadily at least in low gear, in order to interest the villages in his government. Secretly he had Diéguez negotiate with Peláez. And he sent the undersecretary of finance to Washington to try again for relaxation of restrictions on American exports. The last two efforts quickly failed.

Carranza then took a major risk. On 18 February, under Article 27, he decreed a new tax for the oil industry, requiring as a first principle the registration of titles to all oil lands by 20 May, opening unregistered lands to denouncement, and taxing not only the lands but also the rents, royalties, and production on contracts dated before or since the new constitution had become valid. A few days later, as if in reward, Berlin approved a loan, but only five million pesos, and that buried in pesetas in an account in Madrid. The American oil companies not only protested against the tax law. In March they drew International Harvester and some other big companies into an unusually broad coalition to plot the overthrow of Carranza. This time they selected as their candidate to replace him a once notable agent of his, Alfredo Robles Domínguez, who eagerly accepted the duty. Meanwhile another general strike closed down Tampico. Violent American–Mexican confrontation increased along the Texas–Chihuahua border. On 2 April, the State Department charged that the tax law tended to violate vested American rights in Mexico. It warned that the United States might have 'to protect the property of its citizens . . . divested or injuriously affected . . .'.[40] Robles Domínguez started visiting the US Embassy and British Legation almost daily.

Carranza took one of his last chances for help abroad, sending an agent to deal with the Germans in Madrid. At home he barely had room for manoeuvre. The army claimed 65 per cent of the budget. The manufacturers again urged respect for private property, including that of Americans. By mid-April the uproar along the Texas–Chihuahua border sounded like the prologue to war, and Villa raided into southern Chihuahua. In Tamaulipas, having lost the last count in the gubernatorial election, Caballero revolted. Local feuds in Guerrero, Puebla, and Tlaxcala broke into revolts. The undersecretary of war himself had to assume command in Puebla.

Then Carranza's attempt to co-opt labour backfired. On 1 May delegates representing 115 working-class organizations in the Federal District and 16 states convened in Saltillo. Thanks to Carrancista preparations, more than a third of the organizations were docile Coahuila unions. But the Coahuilans lost control to the SME and the Tampico Casa del Obrero. The convention closed on 12 May with the formation of the Confederación Regional Obrera Mexicana (CROM), a shaky but politically independent coalition of trade unionists and syndicalists.

On 20 May Carranza extended the oil tax law's deadline for

---

[40] Smith, *United States and revolutionary nationalism*, 118.

registration of titles to 31 July, and Pani began discussions with American oil company lawyers about amending the law. The United States relented too, slightly. On 7 June Wilson expressed again the United States's desire for friendly relations with Mexico. Towards the end of the month the State Department decided on 'a most liberal embargo policy'.[41] Licences soon went out for several large shipments of commodities to Mexico, mainly corn.

But by late June the government was running on current revenue. Carranza's representative in Madrid had arranged nothing material with the Germans. The president could no longer have extracted even a prayer of support from Mexico's merchants or manufacturers. He stood no better with the UCMGF, the UMM, or the new CROM. The Villistas still posed a problem for Murguía in Chihuahua. Despite Diéguez's command in Monterrey there were three or four rebellions in Coahuila and Tamaulipas, and the Pelaecistas still patrolled the Tampico–Tuxpan oil fields. The Zapatistas still ruled most of Morelos, although without Palafox (dismissed in the reorientation of strategy towards negotiation). At least a dozen other rebel bands had recovered or sprouted new across the centre of the country. And the Felicistas had multiplied in Puebla, Oaxaca and Veracruz, where they stepped up their operations in the Minatitlán oil fields.

On 15 July 1918 the German army began its attack across the Marne. The drive would not only bring the first world war close to its end, but would also settle the still outstanding political question in Mexico. Congressional elections on 28 July returned a PLC Carrancista majority. And the rains that summer were good, for the first time in five years. But until the German drive had succeeded or failed, Mexican politicians remained in suspense. On 31 July Carranza extended the deadline for application of the oil tax for another two weeks.

Early in August the German failure finally became clear. On 14 August Carranza surrendered the tax law's first principle, cancelling the requirement of registration of titles, and instructed Pani to start negotiations with American oil company lawyers to frame Article 27 into a mutually acceptable organic law. But every politically informed person knew that the president no longer had a chance of regaining power over his rivals. In mid-September Obregón began liquidating his property for cash to enable him to go seriously into politics. Villa, stronger than he

41 *Ibid.*, 122.

had been in two years, raided again in southern Chihuahua. On 1 October Díaz published his praise of the Allies and called for a union of all 'patriots' to overthrow Carranza.[42] On 20 October his forces began their first major offensive in Veracurz, Puebla and Oaxaca.

NOVEMBER 1918 – JUNE 1920

On 11 November 1918 the first world war ended. The United States, the most powerful victor, enjoyed new freedoms around the world. In particular it enjoyed the freedom of exercising the only foreign pressure in Mexico. Without risking interference from other foreign powers, it could even revoke recognition of Carranza's government, unless, for example, Carranza agreed to negotiate on Article 27 of the constitution. This ended Mexico's chances for centralized government.

Economic conditions after the war confirmed a regionalized 'reconstruction' in Mexico. Although the American boom continued for another two years, American demands for Mexican products varied widely. The demand for precious metals and oil remained high, but the demand for copper dropped quickly and the demand for henequén crashed. The Spanish influenza pandemic, probably the most devastating blow to human life in Mexico in 350 years, also reduced production and trade. Hitting first in the north-east in early October 1918, its awful 'second wave' raged around the country until mid-January. In the army, of 125,000 men on the rolls, 25,270 fell ill with influenza, and 1,862 died. Altogether as many as five million Mexicans may have gone down with Spanish flue. A moderately low estimate of deaths ranges between 2.5 and 3 per cent of the population, around 400,000. And probably half the dead were aged between 20 and 40, so that in only four months 4 per cent of the most able-bodied Mexicans died. Through the economic trends and the pandemic the Gulf fared best, the north-east and north-west next, much better than the north and the west. And the last two regions, whatever their losses, fared better than the centre and the south, and much better than the south-east, which slid into a long depression.

National politics began to move in new directions. From November 1918 the country's most pressing conflicts became part of the struggle scheduled for resolution in the presidential election in July 1920. But although this was no longer a struggle for centralized power, it was much

---

[42] Liceaga, *Félix Díaz*, 489–504.

more than a provincial struggle for central office. It posed questions of historic consequence – whether or not in a deeply contentious Mexican society any provincial group could establish any rule in Mexico City, and if so, what kind of group and what kind of rule. It also posed the dangers of extensive violence again. Since neither Carranza nor any of his rivals had the power to control the succession, and since the PLC was no more than a name for nationally ambitious factions, the struggle would lead not to coalition but to a final test of strength, with each of the strongest factions struggling to impose itself on the others.

There were only two strategic bases for a politics of imposition, the north-west and the north-east. As soon as the war ended, Obregón started organizing his presidential campaign. Well regarded in California and Washington and one of the north-west's richest men, he retained as a civilian his national prestige as Mexico's top military hero. By January 1919 Calles had committed Sonora to him, and Hill in Mexico City built Obregonista support inside and outside the PLC. Meanwhile González started organizing his campaign. Well connected in Texas and the north-east and probably the country's richest general, he held active command in Mexico State, Morelos and Guerrero, and in December recaptured the rest of Morelos for his subordinates, most of them north-easterners, who leased the state's plantations for the 1919 harvest. In the north-east itself several of his kinsmen and old colleagues and subordinates promoted the Gonzalista cause. Treviño in Mexico City did likewise. Neither faction as yet asked organized labour for support – that field was too difficult and divided. The CROM had antagonized the UMM by encroaching on the railway shops, and in November, objecting to a CROM alliance with the American Federation of Labour against the IWW, the FSODF had seceded and founded a syndicalist Gran Cuerpo Central de Trabajadores in Mexico City.

Of the six other important generals, four remained neutral. They were Diéguez in Monterrey; Murguía, who resigned his Chihuahua command and retired to Mexico City; undersecretary of war Castro, who replaced Murguía in Chihuahua; and Alvarado, who left the declining Yucatán to publish a Mexico City newspaper obsessed with the presidential question.

Carranza did not name his candidate. Counting with certainty only on Aguilar and Cesáreo Castro, in Veracruz and Puebla, he had no reason to take so early a choice that would necessarily antagonize either Obregón and his allies or González and his, maybe both camps, and maybe all four neutrals. Thanks to oil and silver production, which steadily increased the government's revenue, he could delay confrontation. On 1 January 1919, he ordered a huge rise in army officers' pay and began a slow, quiet reduction of the troop rolls. On 15 January he publicly condemned presidential campaigns as premature and insisted on their postponement until the end of the year.

Meanwhile he pursued various alliances to strengthen his faction. In mid-November he had sent Pani as minister to France, hopefully to persuade the Paris Peace Conference to annul the Monroe Doctrine, or at least to revive the interest of British and French bankers in Mexico. He bowed to the American oil companies. On 14 November he had extended the exemption from denouncement to the end of the year. On 23 November the agreement that the company lawyers and Pani had drafted to give Article 27 organic form appeared as a president's bill to Congress. Most notably it exempted from its effects lands in which companies had invested for production before 1 May 1917. On 27 December Carranza extended the exemption from denouncement until Congress voted on the bill. (The pro-American trend impressed Cowdray, who three months later sold Águila to Royal Dutch Shell.) Domestically Carranza courted the Catholic hierarchs, proposing reforms of constitutional Articles 3 and 130 to restrain local anti-clerics, and inviting and receiving from Rome a prothonotary apostolic to reorganize the church in Mexico. He continued to return attached property to the landlords – among those favoured in March 1919 was the Terrazas family – and issued a flurry of decrees and circulars protecting their estates. In addition, he prepared local Carrancista candidates for the coming gubernatorial elections, the next in Sonora on 27 April.

Crucially Carranza also tried for an alliance in New York. Since October Morgan had been co-ordinating American, British, and French banks interested in the Mexican debt. In January Carranza's finance undersecretary joined their negotiations. On 23 February Morgan announced the formation of the International Committee of Bankers on Mexico, and a month later, to reassure the ICBM, Carranza allowed Limantour to return from France to visit Mexico. On 29 March his finance undersecretary returned with the Committee's offer: to refund the debt and issue new bonds for 'internal development' on the security of customs revenue under 'international administration'.[43] On 9 April

[43] Edgar Turlington, *Mexico and her foreign creditors* (New York, 1930), 275.

Carranza reappointed Cabrera as finance minister, to manage approval of the Article 27 bill and the ICBM offer in a special session of Congress opening on 1 May. He also acted to divide the Gonzalista campaign, dispatching Treviño on a lucrative tour of arms and ammunition plants in Europe.

But for all its promise the Carrancista faction soon suffered rude disappointments. In Paris in April the Council of Four recognized the Monroe Doctrine; Carranza rejected the invitation to Mexico to join the League of Nations. In Chihuahua Villa launched a wide offensive. González gained solid credit with landlords when his forces in Morelos ambushed and killed Zapata on 10 April. In the Sonora gubernatorial election, Carranza's candidate lost, and Calles's won – Adolfo de la Huerta. The special session of Congress would not approve the Article 27 bill or the ICBM offer.

Carranza called Diéguez from the north-east and Cesáreo Castro from Puebla to help Jesús Castro beat Villa down again. In mid-May he threatened force against unregistered new drilling in the oil fields. To divide the Obregonistas he appointed Calles as minister of industry and commerce (with responsibility for oil). To preoccupy González, he expanded his command to include Puebla, Tlaxcala and Oaxaca.

But Carranza's disappointments encouraged his opponents. On 1 June Obregón formally announced his presidential candidacy, and on 27 June he got his first formal endorsement, from Yucatán's Partido Socialista. Undersecretary of war Castro returned from Chihuahua to Mexico City and lent him private support through the war ministry. Despite his new duties, González too became bolder, publicly debating with Obregón how properly to declare a candidacy; and his north-eastern agents organized harder. In Chihuahua, Diéguez had scarcely fought his way into the state's capital when on 15 June Villistas raided Juárez and provoked a 24-hour US intervention. On 8 June the Nuevo León gubernatorial election went to a man whom Carranza had not approved (an old friend of Villarreal's). Carranza suspended the report of the electoral returns, and the state throbbed with agitation – for Obregón and González. In Tampico syndicalists led another general strike. Everywhere in the north-east, because Diéguez's removal had reduced its garrisons, the various rebels resumed frequent raids. On 6 June Murguía became commander in Monterrey, but quickly fell into feuds with local chiefs. On 25 June rebels raided Victoria. In the oil districts Peláez moved near Tampico.

During the summer Carranza made a few gains. Diéguez broke the Villista offensive and established command of Chihuahua. Cesáreo Castro controlled Torreón. González came to believe that he need not formally campaign for the presidency, that after many feints and parries the government and the army would save the succession for him. And a second season of good rains ensured relief from food shortages and imports before the election. But much more importantly the threat against unregistered oil drilling led to another confrontation with the United States. In late June the companies charged that the Mexican government had taken 'overt acts' to confiscate their property.[44] On 22 July the State Department warned Carranza that Washington might revoke recognition of his government. On 8 August the Senate set up a subcommittee chaired by its loudest interventionist, Albert B. Fall, 'to investigate Mexican affairs'.[45] On 19 August, from 60,000 US troops stationed along the border, the second punitive expedition entered Mexico for a week around Ojinaga.

Meanwhile Obregón made gains of his own. On 17 July, thanks to Hill, the PLC formally backed his candidacy. Undersecretary of war Castro planted sympathetic generals in strategic commands in the northern border towns. And Obregonista generals began private negotiations with the CROM's leaders. The Obregonistas wanted the CROM partly to stifle IWW agitation among Sonoran miners, mainly to promote Obregón's campaign elsewhere, not only in Mexico but also in the United States, with the AFL. The CROM's leaders wanted connections with Calles in the ministry of industry and commerce, to recover the organizing authority that they had been losing to the syndicalists. Soon afterward the FSODF left its syndicalist Cuerpo Central and joined the CROM. In the same weeks Governor de la Huerta of Sonora helped the UCMGF organize Sonora's Southern Pacific Railway workers.

On 8 September the Fall committee opened its 'investigation'. On 10–11 September its key witness, the president of the Board of Directors of Mexican Petroleum, testified for eight hours about Carrancista misrule.

Under this domestic and foreign pressure Carranza reached a private decision on his faction's candidate. Judging that connections in Washington mattered more than ever, he chose as his ambassador to the United

---

[44] Smith, *United States and revolutionary nationalism*, 154.
[45] United States Senate, Committee on Foreign Relations, *Investigation of Mexican affairs: preliminary report and hearings*, 66 Congress, 2nd session (2 vols., Washington, DC, 1920), I, 3.

States Douglas's political pupil, Ignacio Bonillas. In late September Carranza met Diéguez in Coahuila and won his commitment to the choice. On 2 October Bonillas joined them for talks that lasted a week.

Another confrontation with the United States emphasized the importance of Washington connections for Mexican politics. On 19 October the US vice-consul in Puebla disappeared, supposedly kidnapped by Pelaecista rebels. Washington resounded with cries for intervention in Mexico. On 26 October the vice-consul reappeared free, and Washington's cries subsided. On 1 November Carranza announced that now the presidential campaigns could start and that he backed Bonillas.

But in the next six weeks Obregón made his claim on the presidency irrevocable. On 27 October he had started a tour by rail down the west coast. By mid-December he had politicked through Sonora, Sinaloa, Nayarit, Colima, Jalisco, Michoacán, Guanajuato, Mexico State and Hidalgo, and for ten days in Mexico City. On 21 December his allies in CROM announced the formation of the Partido Laborista Mexicano.

González meanwhile reasserted himself. On 5 November he announced that he would soon declare his candidacy. Forces under his command in Puebla then provoked another confrontation with the United States, by arresting the USA vice-consul on 14 November, charging that he had colluded with his kidnappers to give his government a pretext to intervene in Mexican affairs. Washington resounded again with cries for intervention. While Douglas and Bonillas negotiated feverishly in Washington to calm the uproar, González induced Zapatista and Felicista chiefs to accept 'a patriotic amnesty', a truce with him.[46] On 27 November Gonzalistas in Mexico City announced the formation of a Gonzalista party, the Liga Democrática. On 28 November the Secretary of State told Bonillas that unless his government made 'a radical change in its attitude toward the United States', the American people would oblige their government to break relations with it, which would 'almost inevitably mean war'.[47] Back from Europe, Treviño appeared in Monterrey politicking for González. On 3 December Fall introduced a resolution in the Senate asking Wilson to sever diplomatic relations with Carranza's 'pretended government'.[48] On 4 December the vice-consul was released. On 8 December Wilson expressed his opposition to Fall's

---

[46] *El Universal*, 21 November, 30 November, 5 December, 6 December, 16 December, 24 December, 25 December 1919.   [47] Smith, *United States and revolutionary nationalism*, 162.

[48] *Congressional Record*, 66 Congress, 2nd session, LIX, Part 1 (1919–20), 73.

resolution, and the confrontation ended. On 10 December González formally accepted the Liga Democrática's presidential nomination.

Villa too launched a new campaign. On 2 November he had raided Saltillo, throwing the north-east deeper into division and agitation. In mid-December he raided the coal districts, on the road to Piedras Negras. Still feuding with the local chiefs, Murguía failed not only to drive the Villistas out of Coahuila but even to protect the Nuevo León and Tamaulipas railways from the local rebels.

It was clear in Washington and Mexico then that serious violence would erupt before the presidential election. The only question was who would act first – Carranza to crush Obregón, or Obregón to revolt. In either case, once the Carrancistas and Obregonistas joined battle, González could use his forces around the capital for a coup. Neither the Obregonistas nor the Gonzalistas took as menacing the most powerful bodies in favour of a revolt or a coup: American oil companies, the State Department and the US Senate.

In late December Carranza conferred with Aguilar, Diéguez, Murguía and others to prepare the repression. He also prepared Bonillas's campaign. On 13 January 1920, prompted by Douglas and Bonillas, the oil companies requested provisional drilling permits. On 17 January Carranza agreed to grant them. The following day the Partido Nacional Democrático, a group of Carrancista congressmen, governors, and generals, nominated Bonillas for president. In early February the foreign ministry initiated the preliminaries for negotiation of a treaty to establish a mixed claims commission. The reduction of the troop rolls continued.

Obregón expanded his organization in preparation for revolt. While he toured the Bajío and Michoacán again, the Partido Laborista formally pledged him its support. Several important northern politicians indicated their Obregonista sympathies, as did Alvarado. Obregonista agents secretly connected with Villarreal in Texas, the still rebellious Coss in Coahuila, and a major Felicista chief in Veracruz, who agreed to accept an 'amnesty' and await Obregón's instructions for new duty. On 1 February Calles resigned from the ministry of industry and commerce to take full part in the campaign. On 2 February the Obregonistas opened a national convention in Mexico City. On 4 February Obregón himself headed north to tour Aguascalientes and Zacatecas, then east to San Luis Potosí. On 15 February he arrived in Saltillo for two weeks of politicking.

González meanwhile developed his strength in Mexico City. On 31 December, declaring the pacification of the south complete, he took leave from the army. On 13 January, with a speech to the capital's wealthiest gentlemen, he started his formal bidding for allies. His agents multiplied in the north-east.

On 10 February Carranza dismissed Castro as undersecretary of war and appointed his own chief of staff to manage the army, by then 85,000 men. In mid-February Diéguez concluded a month-long inspection of his Chihuahua command. On 27 February, on special presidential orders, he appeared in Sonora for a three-week inspection of the army's forces there, continuing his tour through Sinaloa, Nayarit, Jalisco and Michoacán. The Villistas raided again in southern Chihuahua. Murguía conferred with Carranza in Mexico City and returned to Monterrey publicly opposed to Obregón. In Saltillo Obregón conferred with Calles and on 3 March began a tour of Coahuila, Nuevo León and Tamaulipas. In the Tampico–Tuxpan oil fields the Pelaecistas launched a wide offensive. Altogether these movements alarmed even peons: on 1 February the United States had removed a restriction on immigration from Mexico and by mid-March some 100,000 'vagrant Mexicans' had crossed the border to escape the approaching violence.[49]

In Morelos these movements had a different meaning – an opportunity for the Zapatistas to rise again for their land. In March Obregonista agents made secret contact with the surviving chiefs and won their promises of co-operation in return for promises of respect for their villages.

On 17 March Bonillas arrived in Nuevo Laredo and formally accepted his candidacy. On 21 March he arrived in Mexico City, where his welcoming parade clashed with an Obregonista demonstration. On 25 March Diéguez too arrived in the capital. On 28 March, after almost a year of lying low, Zapatistas resumed their raids in Morelos and the Federal District.

Public events in Washington seemed to favour Carranza. In January the US ambassador to Mexico, in town to help the Fall committee, had resigned. In mid-February Wilson had dismissed the Secretary of State, who had threatened revocation of recognition, and the Senate on 22 March confirmed Wilson's choice to replace him. The following day Wilson nominated a new 'progressive' ambassador to Mexico. But in fact the onslaught of US presidential politics augured ill for Carranza's plans. In March Democrats and Republicans began campaigning in earnest for

---

[49] J. T. Dickman, General Conditions along the Mexican Border, Weekly Report, No. 362, 20 March 1920, USNA 59, 812.00/ 22844.

their national nominating conventions in June and the elections in November. Both parties would benefit from the violent advent of a new government in Mexico, which would allow them to advocate recognition of it only if it complied with their demands on Article 27 and restored American rights, especially the rights of the oil companies.

On 30 March Carranza sprang the repression, expanding Diéguez's Chihuahua command to include Sonora, Sinaloa, Nayarit, Jalisco and Colima, instructing Diéguez to move heavy reinforcements at once into Sonora, and ordering the arrest of Obregón and the 'amnestied' Felicista chief on a military charge of conspiring to revolt. The attempt quickly failed. In Sonora de la Huerta and Calles denounced Diéguez's appointment, and on 3 April, on the pretext of a UCMGF strike against Southern Pacific, they seized the railways in the state, which blocked traffic along the west coast. Diéguez got to Guadalajara, but no further. On 4 April in Monterrey Obregón met privately with Alvarado, who left immediately for Nogales. Two days later Obregón appeared before a Mexico City court martial and denied the charges against him. On 9 April the Sonora legislature declared Sonoran independence from the federal government. On 10 April Calles took command of all armed forces in the state. On 12 April, under notice to reappear in court the next day, Obregón disappeared from Mexico City, and Hill too fled the city.

Calles sprang the revolt on 15 April, sending a Sonoran force to capture the main railway town in northern Sinaloa. The movement quickly expanded. From Nogales Alvarado raced to Washington and contracted Sherburne Hopkins for counsel to 'the Liberal Constitutionalist Revolution'. The Obregonistas in Sinaloa occupied Culiacán and besieged Mazatlán. The governors of Michoacán and Zacatecas revolted, as did commanders along the railways from Monterrey to Matamoros and Tampico, and in the Tampico–Tuxpan oil fields. Hiding in Morelos, Hill persuaded the Gonzalista commanders there that Obregón and González were secretly co-operating. Obregón himself reappeared in Guerrero, welcomed by the governor and the state commander. On 20 April in Chilpancingo the legislature endorsed Sonora's declaration of independence, Obregón published a Manifesto to the Nation and a Message to the People of the United States announcing his enlistment in Sonora's struggle for 'freedom of suffrage', and the Partido Laborista's executive committee called on Mexico's working class to revolt in the same cause.[50]

[50] Gamoy to State Department, 9 May 1920, USNA 59, 812.00/ 24119.

In response Carranza tried privately for an alliance with González. He proposed that if González halted his campaign for the presidency and offered the government his military services, Bonillas would withdraw his candidacy too, and Carranza and González would negotiate the choice of another civilian candidate. But González wanted more – if Bonillas withdrew his candidacy and Carranza requested González's services, González would halt his campaign and help suppress the revolt, but resume his candidacy 'at an opportune moment'.[51] Carranza refused.

On 22 April the Sonoran Obregonistas published the Plan de Agua Prieta in English.[52] The next day they published it in Spanish. Denouncing Carranza for violations of the constitution, Calles and other local officers and officials named the forces in revolt the Liberal Constitutionalist Army, appointed de la Huerta its interim Supreme Chief, promised that when Liberal Constitutionalists occupied Mexico City the present Congress would elect a provisional president to call general elections, and swore to guarantee 'all legal protection and enforcement of their legal rights to citizens and foreigners, and . . . especially favour the development of industry, trade, and all businesses'.[53] On 26 April the Chihuahua City and Ojinaga commanders revolted in favour of the Agua Prieta plan, and in western Mexico State and Morelos Gonzalista commanders publicly entered discussions with Obregón's agents.

On 27 April Carranza and González negotiated again. González agreed to withdraw his candidacy and help Carranza, if Carranza would replace Bonillas with González's nominee. But on 28 April Carranza refused his nominee and called Murguía to assume command around Mexico City.

In Washington the Republicans took full control of US policy towards Mexico. The Senate would not confirm Wilson's nomination of the new ambassador. The Fall committee shifted into high gear against Carranza: on 29 April it heard Hopkins's testimony that Carranza's government had been 'a ghastly failure', that Obregón would surely overthrow it, and that the new government would establish the right order for business.[54]

González sprang the coup on April 30, when he and Treviño fled the capital, formally denounced Carranza, and, without mentioning the Plan de Agua Prieta, called on the army to fight for 'revolutionary

---

[51] Hanna to State Department, 30 April 1920, *ibid.*, 812,00/ 23781.
[52] Clodoveo Valenzuela and Amado Chaverri Matamoros, *Sonora y Carranza* (Mexico, 1921), 274–5.
[53] *Ibid.*, 362.   [54] *The New York Times*, 30 April 1920.

principles'.[55] On 3 May the two generals occupied Puebla City and established the headquarters of the Liberal Revolutionary Army, in effect the Gonzalista forces of some 12,000 men in eastern Mexico State, Puebla and Tlaxcala. The coup destroyed the government. On 5 May Carranza postponed the election and, predicting a violent Obregonista–Gonzalista rivalry, called on the army and the people to support him until he could pass the presidency to a regularly elected successor. He ordered Murguía to secure an escape east, and on 7 May he, his Cabinet, Bonillas, the Supreme Court, and many congressmen, officials and their families entrained for Veracruz, where they hoped to reorganize the government under Aguilar's protection.

While the coup succeeded, the revolt expanded again. Villa, Peláez and various Felicista chiefs (although not Díaz himself) indicated their support. On 2 May Obregón, the formerly Gonzalista commanders in Morelos, and Zapatista chiefs – all now Liberal Constitutionalists – occupied Cuernavaca. On 3 May the Juárez commander revolted in favour of the Agua Prieta plan, and on 6 May the Saltillo and Veracruz commanders did likewise. On 7 May Cesáreo Castro surrendered his Torreón command to Liberal Constitutionalists.

As soon as Carranza left Mexico City, the rivalry between the revolt and the coup became explicit. On 7 May Treviño occupied the capital, and González appointed its authorities. The following day the rivalry became official. In Hermosillo, de la Huerta announced the formation of his Cabinet which included Calles as war minister and Alvarado as finance minister. In Mexico City, González also appointed his Cabinet, with himself as war minister. On 9 May, while Liberal Constitutionalists captured Nuevo Laredo, Obregón led 8,000 troops into the capital. The same day, again without mentioning the Plan de Agua Prieta, González asked Congress 'to resolve the present situation'.[56]

The revolt kept spreading. On 10 May Liberal Constitutionalists captured Mazatlán. On 11 May Diéguez's force in Guadalajara mutinied and arrested him, and the governors of Coahuila, Nuevo León, and Tamaulipas fled for the border; on Calles's orders Villarreal moved from El Paso to take command in Monterrey. The next day Coss took Piedras Negras, and the Tampico–Tuxpan Liberal Constitutionalist commander

[55] Partido Reconstrucción Nacional, *Recopilación de documentos y de algunas publicaciones de importancia* (Monterrey, 1923), 66–78.
[56] L. N. Ruvalcaba (ed.), *Campaña política del C. Alvaro Obregón, candidato a la presidencia de la República, 1920–24* (5 vols., Mexico, 1923), IV, 151.

and Peláez jointly occupied Tampico. Two days later Liberal Constitutionalists took the last border town, Matamoros.

On 12 May Obregón and González conferred at the war ministry.
They were in sufficient agreement not to fight each other. González
recognized de la Huerta's authority to convene Congress in order to elect
the provisional president. But he would not sign the Plan de Agua Prieta
or dissolve his Liberal Revolutionary Army until the provisional
president took office, and Treviño took command of both Obregonista
and Gonzalista forces pursuing Carranza. On 13 May, still in Hermosillo,
de la Huerta called Congress into a special session set for 24 May to elect
the provisional president. On 15 May González tried another manoeuvre, withdrawing his candidacy for the regular presidential election
and so freeing himself for the provisional office.

The news of the rivalry never reached Carranza. Hostile forces of
various stripes had blocked his convoy front and rear in Puebla. On 14
May Carranza, some close associates, and guards under Murguía headed
on horseback into the northern Puebla mountains, where on 21 May
Carranza was killed by local 'amnestied' Pelaecistas. Obregón and
González immediately denounced the crime and named a joint commis-
sion to investigate it. Treviño removed the captured Carrancistas –
Bonillas, Murguía, and a few others – to Mexico City's military prison.
On 22 May de la Huerta set the elections for the new Congress for 1
August and the presidency for 5 September.

By then the revolt had overwhelmed the coup. The oil companies,
which had withheld payment of taxes during the violence, agreed to pay
them to the Liberal Constitutionalists. On 24 May Congress voted for de
la Huerta over González by 224 to 28 votes. On 26 May Calles moved
into the war ministry. On 30 May de la Huerta arrived in the capital. On 1
June he was sworn into office as provisional president to serve until 30
November. On 2 June, after leading a big military parade through the
city, Obregón resigned his command, and a few days later resumed his
candidacy for the regular presidential election. On 5 June González
resigned his command and went home to Monterrey.

JUNE 1920 – DECEMBER 1920

In the final test the united north-westerners had defeated the divided
north-easterners and won responsibility for 'reconstruction'. But
because they did not have the strong ties that the north-easterners had

with the big national businesses in Mexico City and Monterrey, they did not have the respect and trust required for political establishment. They could not rule as tenured partners legitimately leading associates, but only as conquerors warily dealing with the very forces whose co-operation they needed most for the security of their regime.

Immediately, therefore, their paramount concern was to obtain US recognition as soon as possible. But the Fall committee had just submitted a forbidding report. With the State Department's approval, it recommended that the United States not recognize a government in Mexico without a treaty between the two countries exempting Americans from the application of certain articles of the Mexican constitution, principally Article 27. Under such a treaty, the committee recommended a large American loan to refund Mexico's debt and rehabilitate its railways. If Mexican authorities refused the treaty and applied the constitution to Americans as they did to others, the committee recommended that the United States send forces to Mexico to take charge of all lines of communication from Mexico City to the country's border and sea ports. On 12 June the Republican Convention nominated Harding for president. The party's platform on Mexico, which Fall had drafted, promised recognition when Americans in Mexico enjoyed 'sufficient guarantees' of respect for their lives and property.[57] On 6 July the Democratic Convention nominated Cox, whose party's Mexican platform promised recognition when the United States had 'ample proof' of Mexican respect for American lives and property.[58]

During the summer the north-westerners managed a remarkably orderly provisional government. De la Huerta sent a 'special ambassador' to Washington. On the attraction of rising regular revenue, thanks to the continued oil boom, he had Alvarado announce preparation of a financial programme to refund the foreign debt, then go to New York for private negotiations with Morgan. He admitted twenty-one new divisional generals and 13,000 new troops into the army. He appointed Treviño as minister of industry and commerce, to suffer the oil companies; a CROM leader governor of the Federal District, to check the capital's syndicalists, whom a new Partido Comunista had organized as the Federación Comunista del Proletariado Mexicano; and Villarreal as minister of agriculture, to devise an agrarian reform to pacify the Zapatistas. He kept Diéguez and Murguía in prison, but sent Bonillas

---

[57] *The New York Times*, 11 June 1920. [58] *Ibid.*, 3 July 1920.

and most of the other Carrancista civilians, along with Aguilar and
Cesáreo Castro, into exile. He settled a UCMGF–UMM strike on the
Mexican Railway and general strikes in Tampico and Veracruz. And he
drew Díaz into formal negotiations to end his rebellion. He even
achieved peace with Villa, who on 28 July accepted the government's
offer to retire with his men to a ranch in Durango.

Meanwhile Obregón, Hill, and Calles imposed north-western political
control on the country. They installed some champions of the revolt as
provisional and regular governors, others as state military commanders.
And they seized a gaping opportunity to retire González indefinitely. In
early July former subordinates of his, angry at the cancellation of their
claims to office and deals, tried to revolt in Coahuila and Nuevo León,
and failed completely. On 15 July González was arrested. The war
ministry court-martialled him on the same charge that Carranza had
brought against Obregón. On 20 July, after the court-martial remanded
the defendant to a civil court, Calles ordered his release: González
prudently retired to exile. On 1 August the congressional elections
yielded deputies and senators from the PLC, the Partido Nacional
Cooperatista, the Partido Laborista, and a new Partido Nacional
Agrarista (ex-Zapatistas), all for Obregón. The only show of enduring
opposition arose from the old *católicos*, who assembled the Partido
Nacional Republicano to nominate Robles Domínguez for president.

In mid-August de la Huerta had Alvarado launch a public campaign in
New York for recognition and a loan. On 26 August Alvarado made 'a
deep impression on the . . . financial, business, and professional men'
who heard him at the Bankers' Club.[59] In Mexico City the war ministry
announced its intention to stamp out entirely the lately organized
'Bolshevists', de la Huerta himself assuring *The New York Times* that
'Mexicans who look to the welfare of their country want foreigners in
Mexico for their investments . . .'[60]

The presidential election on 5 September went as planned, an orderly
landslide for Obregón. The campaign for recognition intensified. De la
Huerta praised Wilson as 'the greatest public man today', accused
Harding of 'imperialistic tendencies', deported a few foreign Communists, settled another UCMGF strike, and sent another Douglas pupil
as Confidential Agent to replace Alvarado in New York.[61] Obregón
declared: 'Our hope . . . is in economy and industry and friendship with

[59] *Ibid.*, 27 August 1920.   [60] *Ibid.*, 28 August, 31 August 1920.
[61] *Ibid.*, 9 September 1920.

our neighbors and foreign capitalists . . . First, we will take care of Mexico's foreign obligations.'[62] The respect Obregón held for American interests so impressed Mexican Petroleum that it leased 800,000 acres of Tamaulipas oil land.) In late September Wilson had a private envoy enter negotiations with Mexico's Confidential Agent for recognition. On 15 October, after consultations with the agent, Wilson's envoy, Obregón and Calles, de la Huerta stated that Mexico would not accept conditions for recognition but would pay 'all that it justly owes in conformity with . . . international law'.[63] On 26 October Mexico's agent formally asked the State Department for recognition, following which the United States and Mexico would exchange protocols recording Mexico's promises of claims and arbitration commissions and no retroaction on Article 27. The same day Mexico's Congress formally declared the victor in the presidential election, Obregón over Robles Domínguez, by 1,132,000 votes to 47,000. On 29 October the Secretary of State indicated that the United States and Mexico would shortly exchange protocols, following which Wilson would recognize the Mexican government.

On 2 November Harding beat Cox badly in the American elections. This ended the chance that the United States would soon recognize any Mexican government upholding the Mexican constitution. Still, the State Department expressed its desire to see Obregón 'auspiciously inaugurated', and the Speyer bank invited clients who held defaulted Mexican bonds to deposit them in anticipation of Mexico's resumption of payments on its foreign debt.[64] On 25 November the State Department proposed that Mexico name commissioners to negotiate a treaty eventually warranting US recognition of Obregón's government. The Justice Department broke pre-inaugural conspiracies among the new exiles on the border.

De la Huerta finished his provisional term in proper order. He ended a Coahuila coal miners' strike by having the government temporarily seize the mines, recall the workers with a pay rise, and transfer profits to the companies. He dispelled a Communist campaign for a national general strike. And on 20 November he staged the first official commemoration of Madero's insurrection ten years earlier, marking the triumph of 'the Mexican Revolution'.[65]

The 'revolution' had been in governance. There was nothing

---

[62] *Ibid.*, 10 September 1920.   [63] *Ibid.*, 16 October 1920.
[64] *Ibid.*, 18 November 1920.
[65] Bernardo J. Gastelum, *La revolución mexicana. Interpretación de su espíritu* (Mexico, 1966), 401.

historically definitive in its principal economic and social results: the same big companies existed as before, plus a few new ones, relying more heavily than ever on American markets and banks; a population reduced by war, emigration, and influenza from 15 million to around 14.7 million; a foreign debt of around 1,000 million pesos, plus more than 300 million pesos in overdue interest; a surplus in revenue amounting to 3 million pesos for the year; an army of almost 100,000 men claiming 62 per cent of the budget; national confederations of merchants and manufacturers; a national confederation of labour at odds with the country's railway unions and the new syndicalist movements; and a still largely landless peasantry still demanding its own lands.

On 1 December 1920, without US, British, or French recognition, Álvaro Obregón was sworn into the presidency. His Cabinet included Hill as minister of war, Calles as minister of the interior, de la Huerta as minister of finance, and Villarreal as minister of agriculture. Obregón also repaid the CROM, leaving its previously appointed leader in charge of the Federal District and granting its secretary-general the directorship of the federal arsenals.

Thus the struggle between the victors of 1914 resulted in a new regime. The central political institution was not a national leader or party but a regional faction, the north-western bourgeoisie, internationally unconsecrated, but indomitably entrenched in the highest levels of the state and ready to manage a flexible, regionalized 'reconstruction' through deals with factions from other classes. The new state itself would therefore serve as the nation's bourgeois party. Its function forecast its programme, a long series of reforms from above, to evade, divide, diminish, and restrain threats to Mexican sovereignty and capitalism from abroad and from below.

4

REVOLUTION AND RECONSTRUCTION
IN THE 1920s

The Mexican Revolution was initiated and directed for the most part by
the upper and middle classes of the Porfiriato. There were, however,
several revolutions within the Revolution. The revolutionary front line
was fluid and revolutionary groups were heterogeneous, with very
different, even contradictory, objectives. The mass of the people, upon
whom the profound changes of the period 1870–1910 had borne heavily,
had only a limited sense of what was at stake in the struggle for political
power. From 1913 the Sonorans, the north-west faction within the
Carrancista or Constitutionalist movement, sought national political
power, and in 1920 they finally seized it. The Sonoran hegemony proved
complete and long lasting. In effect it was an 'invasion' from the north.
The secular habits, the savage pragmatism and the violent struggle for
survival of the north-western frontier were totally alien to the Mexican
nation at large.[1]

An ex-minister of the period, Luis L. León, has given us a clear picture
of how these people of the north-west saw themselves and Mexico, and
the programme they wished to impose on the country.[2] He tells us that
between 1913 and 1920, the state of Sonora was for the Sonorans their
school and their laboratory, both as politicians and as men of business.
They described themselves as the Californians of Mexico, who wished to
transform their country into another California. Once they took on the
gigantic task of controlling national resources of water and land, they
were astonished to find that the centre and the south of the country were
quite different from their own far north-west. León tells us further that,

* Translated from the French by Mrs Elizabeth Edwards; translation revised by Lady Cynthia
  Postan and the Editor. The Editor wishes to thank Professor John Womack and Dr Alan Knight
  for their help in the final preparation of this chapter.
[1] See Hector Aguilar, *La frontera nómada. Sonora y le rev lución mexicana* (Mexico, 1977).
[2] Interviews with Luis L. León by Jean Meyer, Mexico, 1968 and 1973–4.

when they realized what kind of life was led by the peasants of traditional Mexico, they decided that the peasants were not men in the true sense of the term, as they kissed the hands of the great landowners and the priests, did not understand the logic of the marketplace and frittered away what money they had on alcohol and fireworks. The Sonorans had already had a similar experience in their own state with the Yaqui Indians, but this warrior tribe formed only a small minority (it was finally brought under control in 1926), while in the centre-south the majority of the population belonged to a world which the Sonorans did not understand and therefore condemned. Both the violence of the collision between state and church and the peasant insurrection (the Cristero rebellion, 1926–9) which followed were bound up with the profound difference between the men who were administering the state in order to modernize it and those, perhaps two-thirds of the population in 1920, who constituted traditional Mexico.

After a decade of civil war (1910–20) there emerged in Mexico between 1920 and 1930 a new capitalist state. In this respect conflict with foreign oil companies and the church as well as negotiations with organized labour, in particular the CROM (Confederación Regional Obrera Mexicana; Regional Confederation of Mexican Labour), were more significant than the traditional military insurrections of 1923, 1927 and 1929 or the election crises of 1928–9. Innovation was more economic than political, and it was in particular institutional and administrative. It is impossible to separate the main political innovation, the creation of the National Revolutionary party (PNR) in 1929, from the formation of a powerful state.

According to a classic definition, the state is the invitation extended by one group of men to others for the joint accomplishment of a common enterprise. In this case the invitation was not understood by the majority of Mexicans. How could a unified whole be assembled from so many heterogeneous pieces? It was the government which had the unity, that of *imperium* exercised by a small group. The abyss separating the two worlds caused the governors to be impatient and the governed to be resentful. Impatience led to violence, and resentment sometimes to revolt.

The state claimed to take care of all the economic, cultural and political deficiencies in the nation; the federal administration, despite its weakness, provided the country's spinal column. The state, however, although on the offensive, remained structurally weak, for it had to reckon with the strong men of the regions, the caciques or local political bosses, whose co-operation underpinned stability. These included Felipe Carrillo Puerto in Yucatán, Tomás Garrido Canabal, lord of Tabasco from 1920 to 1936, Saturnino Cedillo, *patron* of San Luis Potosí until 1937, Adalberto Tejeda, a power in Veracruz from 1920 to 1935, and many others who, without lasting quite so long, ruled in spite of the centre. Organized labour in the shape of the CROM tried to take over the state, starting with the ministry of industry and commerce headed by the secretary-general of the CROM, but it failed in the face of opposition from the army and other groups.

What emerged was a new form of enlightened despotism, a ruling conviction that the state knew what ought to be done and needed plenary powers to fulfil its mission; Mexicans had to obey. The state rejected the division of society into classes and would preside over the harmonious union of converging interests. The state had to accomplish everything in the name of everyone. It could not allow any criticism, any protest, any power apart from itself. Thus, it had to crush alike the Yaqui Indians, 'illegally' striking railways workers, 'red' workers who rejected the 'good' trade union, the Communist party when it ceased to collaborate (1929), and the Catholic peasants when they resorted to arms. Alongside the violence, and complementing it, the political charade of assemblies and elections concerned no more than a minority. However, the development of the political system and above all the foundation in 1929 of the PNR demonstrated that in a country in the process of modernization, political control has also to be modernized. 'A policy aimed to give to our nationality, once and for all, a firm foundation' was how President Calles defined his policy in 1926,[3] specifying that the construction of the state was a necessary condition for the creation of a nation.

During the presidency of Álvaro Obregón (1920–4) the most important problems were primarily political. These included relations with the United States; the re-establishment of the federal authority over a regionalism fortified by ten years of revolutionary crisis; and the presidential succession of 1924. Under the presidency of Plutarco Elías Calles (1924–8) and during the Maximato (1928–34, during which time Calles as *jefe máximo* continued to exercise real power without himself assuming the presidency), despite the events which surrounded first the

---

[3] Calles, 'The policies of Mexico to-day', *Foreign Affairs*, 1 (October 1926).

re-election and then the assassination of Obregón in 1928, priority was no longer given to political considerations but to economic and social questions, such as the general economic programme, oil, the war of the Cristeros and the impact of the world depression.

In 1920 the words 'revolution' and 'reconstruction' were synonymous. The desire for reconstruction was not a new one, but until 1920 there had been no peace, and without it nothing could be done. After 1920 there was peace of a sort. Interrupted by a military insurrection in December 1923, peace was brutally restored within weeks. From 1920 to 1924 the government had two preoccupations, first, to avoid American intervention and, to that end, to secure the long-desired diplomatic recognition; secondly, to resume payments on the foreign debt in order to regain international credit. These aims imposed prudence and moderation. José Vasconcelos could nevertheless light up the sky with his education policy, as we shall see. In 1924 Vasconcelos went into exile and his ministry was disbanded. Enthusiasm was then transferred to finance, industry and commerce. The year before the United States had recognized the Obregón régime; international credit had been restored and the hour was ripe for the great undertakings which had been planned between 1920 and 1924. Then came economic crisis, first in Mexico itself (1926) and then worldwide, which brought everything to a standstill. The time had come to retreat and to work out the new solutions which would be put into practice during the presidency of Lázaro Cárdenas (1934–40).

THE PRESIDENCY OF OBREGÓN, 1920–4

Álvaro Obregón, the son of a well-to-do Sonoran farmer, hardened by the struggle against nature and the Indian, a veteran of the revolutionary wars, was 40 when he came to power on 1 December 1920. Supported by the army and himself a soldier of genius, the conqueror of Pancho Villa, he was also a remarkable politician capable of allying himself with the labour unions and of rallying the Zapatista agrarian faction to his side. A socialist, a capitalist, a Jacobin, a spiritualist, a nationalist and an americanophile, he was not embarrassed by considerations of doctrine, even though he did preside over the establishment of an ideology – revolutionary nationalism. His main aims were national unity and national reconstruction, and he was to run the country like a big business.

Despite the postwar world depression, which produced a fall in the price of most primary products and an influx of Mexican workers expelled from the United States, the general economic situation in the early 1920s favoured Obregón. At that time Mexico produced a quarter of the world's oil, and oil along with other exports, chiefly mineral, guaranteed the prosperity of the state and the financing of the important social and economic projects characteristic of the period, including the achievements of the ministry of education under José Vasconcelos.

The generals who had determined the course of political life since 1913 were not career soldiers, but victorious revolutionaries, politicians on horseback, readily resorting to arms. Obregón, the prototype of the revolutionary general, understood better than anyone how to make use of the army (although this did not prevent him from having to face, in 1923, a formidable insurrection by his former comrades). The social base of the new system was formed by organized urban labour, which had been linked to the state since the pact of August 1919 concluded between Obregón and the CROM. Fortified by this alliance, the CROM aimed to control the whole labour movement and had in December 1919 organized a political agency, the Partido Laborista Mexicano. The second major pillar of the new regime were the *agraristas*, including the Agrarian Leagues and the Partido Nacional Agrarista of Antonio Díaz Soto y Gama, one of Zapata's secretaries. The common denominator of this triangular system – army, labour unions and *agraristas* – was nationalism. The president controlled it by the complicated ploy of calling on the unions and the rural militias to oppose the army and on the army to break strikes or to deal with the rural militias. The enrichment of the generals, union bosses and politicians, in short of the new governing class, was a feature of the system which also attracted the economic elite of the Porfiriato, without giving them any political power. Neither Obregón nor his successors tolerated the existence of any political party which might call into question the legitimacy of the regime. By force of circumstance, the Roman Catholic church filled the political void and played the part of a substitute opposition, which led, eventually, to the violent confrontation of 1926–9.

Obregón's paramount concern was US recognition. In defence of the interests of the oil companies and American citizens, the US State Department, however, demanded from the Mexican government that it should first take over the debt of the Díaz régime, that it should not apply to the oil companies the provisions of Article 27 of the constitution of

1917 which established the sovereignty of the state over land and subsoil deposits, and that there should be an indemnity for Americans whose interests had been damaged by the Revolution. No Mexican government could agree to such a capitulation. In the absence of sufficient goodwill or of adequate concessions in relation to the debt and the indemnities, Obregón soon gave up the attempt at reconciliation until 1923 when he desperately needed American help to meet a serious political crisis.

Until 1923 the government of Obregón was successful and the future of the Revolution seemed to be assured, despite the deaths of certain revolutionaries, some of them mysterious, like that of Banjamín Hill, the minister of war, who was poisoned, some violent, as in the case of Lucio Blanco, who was abducted in exile in the USA and assassinated. The 'Sonora triangle', Obregón, Adolfo de la Huerta (who had served as provisional president in 1920 and was now minister of finance), and Calles, minister of the interior, remained united; the system functioned well. In 1923 Obregón declared that his successor would be Calles, a man little known nationally and unpopular with many generals, but supported by the CROM and the *agraristas*. The malcontents had the wit to know how to alienate de la Huerta from Obregón and from Calles, in order to make him their candidate, and it was soon clear that the matter had to be settled by force of arms. Obregón, certain of the opposition of many of his comrades in arms, approached the United States to gain their support in the crisis. The Bucareli Street agreements in August 1923 sealed US–Mexican reconciliation at the price of weighty concessions favouring American interests. And it was at this juncture that Pancho Villa was murdered as a precautionary measure. The Revolution had devoured another of its children.

The military rebellion which broke out in December 1923 was of unexpected gravity, for two-thirds of the army were in active sympathy with the movement. Military operations remained frozen throughout December, however, while the fate of the rebellion was being played out in Washington, the issue being whether the State Department would support Obregón or the rebels. To gain the support of the United States, Obregón had to obtain from his Senate ratification of the Bucareli agreements. He obtained it by buying venal senators and terrorizing others with the assassination of their most outspoken member (Senator Field Jurado), as Martin Luis Guzmán related in his novel *La sombra del caudillo* (1929). President Coolidge immediately sent a fleet to blockade the Gulf against the rebels and to deliver the armaments Obregón's troops needed. War broke out on the following day, against rebels who were divided amongst themselves, soldier against civilian, general against general. Obregón took advantage of the situation and in the course of fifteen days and three battles conducted one of his finest campaigns. The rest was no more than a man-hunt: all the rebel leaders, 54 former Obregonistas, lifelong comrades, were shot. This great purge heralded others in 1927 and 1929 and finally brought about the subjugation of an army not yet professionalized which had lost its most important leaders,

The presidential succession crisis of 1923–4, which threw into relief the decisive role the United States still played in Mexican affairs, put an end to what remained of political liberalism in Mexico. Parliamentarians and judges of the Supreme Court were both brought to heel, and Calles won the pre-arranged elections before the eyes of an indifferent nation. Obregón's 'coup' had been successful, and he himself could look forward to returning to power in 1928. But the price had been high. It included the departure of José Vasconcelos from the ministry of education.

During the Obregón administration, Vasconcelos has a virtually free hand with state education. A member of that provincial middle class which had played an important part in the fall of Porfirio Díaz, and a Maderista from the beginning, he had spent long years of exile in the United States until recalled by the triumphant Sonorans in 1920 to take charge of the University of Mexico and, later, of state education.

Vasconcelos was, like all enthusiasts, both admired and detested, a great servant of the state and, though he himself denied it, a great politician. He was also a prodigious writer. According to Mariano Azuela, the story of his life is the best novel about the Mexican revolution. His qualities as a writer, his later flirtation with fascism (for reasons like Ezra Pound's) and his apparent recantation of his revolutionary past have caused his significance as a man of action to be forgotten. He is thought of as a man of letters, while his role as an organizer of an ideological programme upon which Mexican governments continue to depend until the present day is overlooked.

Educated as a lawyer, Vasconcelos was self-taught in cultural matters; he read a great deal (perhaps too much) from Plotinus to Lunacharski and from St Augustine to Tagore. For Mexican intellectuals he suddenly became their 'professor'. While Rector, he paid little attention to the university, though he saw to it that the ministry of education, suppressed by Carranza, was re-established. Then, as a minister, he travelled on horseback into the remotest country districts, debated in Congress, wrote for the newspapers and toured South America, for his brand of populist nationalism burgeoned into a dream of Spanish-American unity, of a 'cosmic race' which was to be born in America from the melting pot of all the ethnic groups.

He laboured to produce the new man, the twentieth-century Mexican, the future citizen of a state which had still not become a nation. This was why President Obregón supported this demonic individual who helped to legitimize his regime in the eyes of history. Obregón provided Vasconcelos with the financial means to do his work; to pay teachers better, build schools, open libraries and publish newspapers and books. Vasconcelos launched a gigantic scheme to implant literacy among children and adults, integrate the Indian into the embryonic nation, validate manual labour, and endow the country with technical training facilities. Even today Mexico has still not exhausted his inheritance.

Consistently with his ambition, Vasconcelos realized that the whole field of education needed attention, vertically and horizontally, from kindergarten to university, from evening classes to agricultural schools. The university interested him least, since it affected relatively few people. His utopian educational ideas could best be described as a form of cultural nationalism. They demanded, in the spirit of a religious crusade, the rapid and large-scale education of all Mexicans, young and old (illiteracy in 1921 was 72 per cent; in 1934 it was still 62 per cent). Teachers were regarded as 'missionaries' and were likened to the Franciscans in the sixteenth century. Books and libraries were essential to the fight, and the 'people's classics' were printed by the million to constitute a basic library in every school and village. Vasconcelos was fortunate in having the support of President Obregón; the budget of the ministry of education was raised from 15 million pesos in 1921 to 35 million in 1923.

Vasconcelos's programme was comprehensive: all the arts had to be mobilized to forge the nation and prevent it from becoming another Texas, another Puerto Rico. The Department of Fine Arts was given the responsibility of stimulating enthusiasm for painting, music and song, while cultural contacts were taken up with the rest of Spanish America. The Mexican school of mural painting emerged from this campaign. Vasconcelos provided painters with the materials to work with, gave them the walls of public buildings to cover and subjects (related to cultural nationalism) to illustrate, with the provocative demand: 'I wish the painting to be done as quickly as possible, over the widest possible area. Let it be a monumental and didactic art, at the opposite extreme from studio painting.' In 1923 the Manifesto of the Union of Workers, Technicians, Painters and Sculptors, signed by David Alfaro Siqueiros, Diego Rivera, José Clemente Orozco, Carlos Merida and others, made this declaration of populist optimism:

The popular art of Mexico is the most important and the healthiest of spiritual manifestations and its native tradition is the best of all traditions . . . We repudiate the so-called studio art and all the art-forms of ultra-intellectual coteries for their aristocratic elements and we extol the manifestations of monumental art as a public amenity. We proclaim that all forms of aesthetic expression which are foreign or contrary to popular feeling are bourgeois and should be eliminated, inasmuch as they contribute to the corruption of the taste of our race, which has already been almost completely corrupted in the towns.[4]

The departure of Vasconcelos in 1924 marked the end of this brief but brilliant phase during which intellectuals and artists had been harnessed to the service of the state under the auspices of the ministry of education. From then on two opposing points of view asserted themselves: on the one hand support for the regime, attended by a culture endowed with a certain social content; on the other, the cultural expression of a refusal to co-operate, accompanied by isolation or foreign exile. Thus, President Calles himself drew a distinction between 'intellectuals of good faith' and others.

Education in Mexico has not infrequently reflected the views of the minister in office: if Vasconcelos is invariably associated with the spiritual approach described above, Moisés Sáenz was the incarnation of the educational policy of Calles, which accorded great importance to rural schools, regarding them as the centre of the community and as a social substitute for the church. The emphasis was laid on instruction of a practical kind, as opposed to academic education. In the words of Sáenz, 'it is as important to rear chickens as to read poetry'.

Sáenz left Mexico at the beginning of the 1930s, after a difference with his successor, Narciso Bassols. He had just spent seven months in the village of Carapan, to observe the practical results of his rural school. His conclusions were published in a book, *México integro*, in which, disillusioned, he declared that the educational policy had been a failure. It

[4] José Clemente Orozco, *Autobiografía* (1945; Mexico, 1970), 57–63.

must be conceded that, after Vasconcelos, the share of the national budget allotted to education fell from 15 to 7 per cent and that there was, at least, a comparable decline in enthusiasm. Other educational utopian ideas were to arise during the 1930s, such as the emphasis on sex education and the socialist school; they were to incite considerable polemic, but none of them was to equal the utopia of Vasconcelos in its generosity or its compass.

The intellectuals and artists who had followed Vasconcelos no longer had their appointed place. A number of writers, Jorge Cuesta, José Gorostiza, Salvador Novo, Carlos Pellicer, Bernardo Ortiz de Montellano, Jaime Torres Bodet and Xavier Villaurrutia, together with the composer Carlos Chávez and the painters Agustín Lazo, Manuel Rodríguez Lozano and Rufino Tamayo, whose creative work was highly fashionable in the 1920s, formed a group around the review *Contemporáneos* (1928–31).[5] All, to a greater or lesser degree, bore the mark of Vasconcelos and all were savagely attacked as 'intellectuals of bad faith', 'traitors to the country', *descastados* (untouchables); they were, in fact, fighting the cultural nationalism of Calles, a caricature of that of Vasconcelos, demanding absolute freedom of expression and declaring that Mexico must open its doors to all cultures, particularly from Europe. They devoted a large part of their time to translating, with considerable expertise, the most important writers of the twentieth century. At no time has their influence been stronger than it is today, a fact which may be regarded as a posthumous triumph.

THE PRESIDENCY OF CALLES, 1924–8

The suppression of the de la Huertista rising in 1923–4 demonstrated that when a decision had been taken within the innermost councils of the government, it had to be acepted by the whole 'revolutionary family'; those who refused to submit to the rigours of this principle were crushed. Calles, who became president at the age of 47, was a shadowy figure. The bastard offspring of a powerful Sonoran landowning family, he had been a poor schoolteacher before the outbreak of the Revolution changed his life. He rose through the revolutionary army to become provisional governor of Sonora in 1917 and then minister of the interior under Obregón. Despite his radical reputation and socialist links, Calles was as

[5] Facsimile edition, Fondo de Cultura Económica, Mexico, 1981.

determined as Obregón to institute a programme of economic development on capitalist and nationalist lines. The state was to play an
important part and was in no sense opposed to landownership nor to
capital, whether domestic or foreign, provided that it served the national
interests. This form of nationalism led to a rupture not only with the
American oil companies but also with the railway unions as soon as they
opposed the reorganization of the network. Nationalism was the
essential factor in the conflict with the church. Although a nationalist
and a man of iron, Calles was also a realist and knew how to change
course when necessary, as he showed not only when facing the United
States, which he defied right to the edge of the precipice, but no further;
but also in his relations with the church, once the impossibility of
subduing the rebellious Cristeros became clear; and with the CROM, a
faithful ally whom he abandoned to his Obregonista enemies when it
became expedient to do so.

Among Calles's closest political allies were General Joaquín Amaro
and Luis N. Morones, the labour leader. Through Amaro, the minister of
war, Calles embarked upon the difficult task of domesticating the
praetorian guard and turning their officers into a professional officer
class. The attempt was halted by the campaign against the Cristeros
(1926–9) and the resistance of the Obregonista rebels, who were not
finally overcome until March 1929, eight months after Obregón himself
had been assassinated. The CROM, under the leadership of Morones,
minister of commerce, industry and labour, served as a counterbalance to
the army and to General Obregón. Morones, who had formerly played
the Obregonista card, became Calles's right hand and provided the
inspiration for a large part of his socio-economic policy.

Calles, put into the saddle by Obregón, was never strong enough to
shake off the burden of his sponsorship. Ex-president Obregón was
entrenched at the very heart of the political system as the senior and real
chief of the army. Calles was obliged to agree to the constitutional
reforms which made it possible for Obregón to be re-elected to the
presidency for a six-year term in July 1928, contrary to all revolutionary
tradition and at the risk of provoking a rebellion. (A rebellion was in fact
nipped in the bud in October 1927 and this provided an opportunity for
liquidating many of the remaining generals apart from Obregón.) Calles
made use of Morones against Obregón, but had to avoid an open breach.
There is no telling how these subtle manoeuvres would have ended if
Calles had not been relieved of both his powerful colleagues at the same

time. The assassination of Obregón on 17 July 1928, the day after his election, by the Catholic mystic José de León Toral enabled Calles to dismiss Morones, who was suspected by the Obregonistas of being implicated in the assassination.

The politics of the Calles administration were dominated, first, by a serious crisis over oil in the relations between Mexico and the United States; secondly, by the re-election crisis; and, thirdly, by a crisis in church–state relations. Mexico's rupture with the United States and growing domestic political difficulties coincided with a downturn in the economy. Everything and everyone then seemed to conspire against Calles, and this perhaps helps to explain the violence of his reactions against the most defenceless of his adversaries, the Catholic *campesinos*, hitherto mistakenly assumed not to be dangerous.

Conflict with the United States was inevitable from the moment when Calles refused to endorse the agreements negotiated by Obregón. In 1925, having secured the support of the bankers and chambers of commerce in the USA by resumption of payment of interest on the external debt, the Mexican government moved on to the offensive against the oil companies. The petroleum law drafted by Morones in December 1925 disregarded the Bucareli agreements of 1923 and adhered meticulously to the constitution. This could have led to expropriation, which Cárdenas was able to achieve in 1938. When the companies, supported by the American ambassador, Rockwell Sheffield, reacted violently, the attitude of Morones and Calles stiffened. In 1926 Mexico gave material help to the Nicaraguan insurgents against the American marines, and Augusto César Sandino received his general's stars from a Mexican general. Mexico thus appeared as the champion of the struggle against imperialism, and the anti-Mexican lobby in the United States pressed for military intervention, taking advantage of the emotions aroused by the conflict between church and state (see below).

The crisis was resolved in 1927–8, however, by a compromise skilfully negotiated by a new ambassador, Dwight Morrow, thanks to the good offices of the bankers of both countries. (Morrow himself was a partner in the firm of J. P. Morgan.) Without losing face, Calles made the desired concession: the oil law would not be retrospective. Henceforward there was no cloud in the relations between the two countries. As a result neither the Cristero insurgents, nor the conspirators against Obregón's re-election, nor the Obregonista rebels themselves could count on sympathy from the United States.

The dispute with the United States was complicated by the domestic crisis provoked by Obregón. There is no evidence of the existence of a pact between Obregón and Calles providing for them to serve alternate terms as president. From 1924, however, the Obregonistas were working to remove the constitutional barrier to re-election. They needed two years to attain their objective, as well as the personal intervention of Obregón in the congressional elections of 1926. After that, Obregón's intervention in politics became continuous and the struggle with Calles, although never overt, became permanent. Obregón did not agree with either Calles's oil policy or his religious policy. By the end of 1926 all the problems were interacting: constitutional reform and the presidential succession, the beginning of the Cristero war, a major railway strike (see below), insurrection by the Yaqui Indians of Sonora and the threat of American intervention. The general deterioration in Calles's position favoured Obregón. Soon three generals stood as possible candidates for the presidency in succession to Calles and, as in a Shakespearean tragedy, they were all three to die: Arnulfo Gómez and Francisco Serrano in 1927 at the time of the abortive putsch, and Obregón in July 1928, on the very day when, as president-elect, he was to meet Ambassador Morrow to try to put an end to the religious strife.

On church–state relations Calles took an extreme anti-clerical line. The people responded with violence, and the war of the Cristeros, known as the Cristiada, broke out. It was a terrible war of ordinary people rising against the state and its army, containing all the elements of both a revolutionary and of an anti-colonial war, though the government has since been depicted as representing the 'left' and the insurgents the 'counter-revolution'.

The anti-clericalism of the governing faction was a legacy of eighteenth-century rationalism and nineteenth-century liberalism, distorted by a political ignorance of Old Mexico, with its Indian/*mestizo* and Christian population. The constitution of 1917 gave the state the right to control the 'clerical profession', but Carranza and Obregón had been careful not to use it. The anti-clerical lobby, within both the military and the labour movement, re-appeared during the crisis of 1923–4. On the other side, the militants of the Catholic Action movement had been provoked, in February 1925, by the attempt of the CROM to create a schismatic church. The Catholics formed themselves into a fighting organization, the Liga, which returned blow for blow. In the heat of the dispute with the United States, the government, obsessed by the threat of a domestic battle-front, in fact created one – a self-fulfilling prophecy. Legislation was passed in 1926 to make infringements in religious matters criminal offences; the bishops replied with the suspension of church services from 31 July. In August, Calles berated the bishops who had come for an eleventh-hour interview: 'If you are not willing to submit, nothing but recourse to Congress or to arms remains for you.' Congress refused to examine the bishops' petition and a demand for reform signed by a large number of Catholics. There began a lengthy game of chess in which Rome and Washington, Obregón and the state bankers and, finally, Ambassador Morrow intervened. Negotiations dragged on for three years, while a war raged, a war which astonished the church as much as it did the state.

The first disturbances followed the suspension of church services and were spontaneous. Suppression only caused the movement to spread, for the country people (and Mexico was 75 per cent rural) no longer had any other means of protest. The Liga, which had gone underground, was now convinced of the futility of legal action and favoured a solution by force of arms; a general uprising was called for January 1927. In the five states of the west-centre, there was a large-scale insurrection, but the unarmed masses were machine-gunned by the army. Because their aims were fundamentally religious and therefore of permanent validity, the risings were resumed after the soldiers had gone. A state of war ensued which absorbed 45 per cent of the national budget. The severity of the repressive measures, the scorched-earth policy, the realignment of sections of the population, all served to inflame the revolt. The army could not cope with the problem, although it retained control of the towns and railways.

The Cristeros owed their name to the government, after their war-cry of 'Viva Cristo Rey; Long live Christ the King! Long live the Virgin of Guadalupe!' From a total of 20,000 in July 1927, numbers grew to 35,000 by March 1928 and were distributed over thirteen states. The great offensive launched against them by the government in 1928–9 was a failure. In June 1929 the movement was at its height, with 25,000 trained soldiers and 25,000 irregular guerillas. It was at this juncture that the state decided to reach a compromise with the church in order to rescue the rapidly deteriorating situation and, as we shall see, to avoid, in the autumn, the threatened alliance between the Cristeros and José Vasconcelos, a candidate for the presidency of the Republic.

Between 12 and 21 June the institutional conflict was settled in accordance with a plan drafted by Ambassador Morrow. The law of 1926 remained in force, but was not applied; the church resumed its services. When these *arreglos* (settlements) were announced, Mexican stocks rose on Wall Street, the bells rang out and the Cristeros went home. It proved, however, to be only a truce in the conflict between church and state.

THE MAXIMATO

Alvaro Obregón was assassinated on 17 July 1928, the day after his re-election. His 30 generals and his parliamentary bloc should have been able to overthrow Calles, who, with Morones, was suspected of having instigated the crime. Calles, however, knew how to temporize. Taking advantage of his rivals' differences, he entrusted the interim presidency for one year to Emilio Portes Gil, an important politician from Tamaulipas, who was a man of compromise and a follower at the same time of both Obregón and Calles. On 1 September 1928 Calles pronounced his celebrated 'political testament': with it the era of the *caudillos* came to an end and the era of the institutional state opened, beginning immediately with the foundation of the Partido Nacional Revolucionario (PNR), the forebear of the present PRI (Partido Revolucionario Institucional). This masterstroke left the Obregonistas unable to decide between an immediate putsch and an electoral campaign in 1929, as proposed by Calles. They lost several months before finally rebelling in March 1929, by which time it was too late. The praetorians Escobar and Manzo, who had dominated the political scene in July 1928, could not by then muster more than a third of the army to their side. Against them was the United States which provided Calles, by then minister of war, with the material support he needed to crush the revolt in a matter of weeks.

The election of 1929 was no mere formality, for the disappearance of Obregón encouraged those opposed to re-election and all those who were out of office. Faced with an unconvincing official candidate, Pascual Ortiz Rubio, who had been recalled from his ambassadorship in Rio de Janeiro, the still prestigious Vasconcelos tried to assume the mantle of Madero. His triumphal tour took on the glamour of a plebiscite and was so successful that the authorities resorted to all available means against him. The American secret service, whose agents were working for the election of Ortiz Rubio, reported: 'Vasconcelos probably has the largest number of followers, but it seems clear that he will be eliminated. He has the government machine against him, and also the fears of law-abiding and business people who are satisfied with a regime favouring the co-operation of capital and labor, and of the Church.'[6]

The government had been seriously alarmed by a possible combination of Cristero guns in the countryside and the popularity of Vasconcelos in the towns. In January 1929 there had been contact between these two forces. Ambassador Morrow, Portes Gil and Calles hastened to make their peace with the church, and there was then nothing for Vasconcelos to do but to comment: 'the news of the enforced surrender of the Cristeros sends a shiver down my spine. I see Morrow's hand in it. He has in this way deprived us of all grounds for the revolt which the vote-rigging would logically have provoked.'[7] The November elections were quite manifestly fraudulent and the unknown Ortiz Rubio won by a ratio of twenty to one. Vasconcelos escaped abroad, while the terror engulfed his followers.

After masterminding Portes Gil's presidency, Calles understood perfectly how to retain his mastery. He spent six years in the very same role as Obregón had played when he himself had been president, with the same difficulties but more power, for he saw to it that the presidents (three in six years) were reduced to underlings. Without reassuming the presidency himself, he made and unmade others and controlled all the ministries. He was rightly called the *jefe máximo* – hence the name given to this period, the Maximato.

Emilio Portes Gil, the transitional president, turned out in fact to be more difficult to manipulate than had been foreseen, and he adopted a style appropriate to his brief presidency, preferring compromise to repression and discussion to force. He has passed into history as being responsible for three positive decisions: the conclusion of the *arreglos* (settlements) of June 1929, which restored religious peace; the grant of autonomy to the University of Mexico, also in 1929; and the resumption of land distribution (see below), which set him in opposition to Calles. President Ortiz Rubio was dominated by the army, under General Calles, and cruelly derided by public opinion. The generals controlled the

[6] National Archives, Washington DC, Military Intelligence Division, 2657-G-605/210, 5 September 1929.   [7] José Vasconcelos, *Obras completas* (4 vols., Mexico, 1957–61), II, 162.

principal ministries and took their orders from the ex-president, without bothering to keep up appearances. Ortiz Rubio, victim of an attempt on his life at the beginning of his presidency and overwhelmed with insults, began to assert himself, timid though he was. General Amaro, for many years minister of war, encouraged him ('Go on, you are the president'). Calles got wind of a possible *coup*, took the initiative, forced Ortiz Rubio to resign on 3 September 1932 and instantly replaced him with General Abelardo Rodríguez, who was elected by acclamation in Congress. Rodríguez, the first millionaire president, who had made his fortune managing customs houses in California, was treated little better than Ortiz Rubio. He also, stimulated by the presidential office, tried to shake off the yoke of his patron, but he could not prevent his ministers from taking their orders from Calles before coming to the council chamber. He did, however, at least serve to the end of his term of office (in 1934).

Both Ortiz Rubio and Abelardo Rodríguez were burdened with an adverse economic situation since, for both national and international reasons, the mining industry was in disarray and agricultural production at its lowest ebb since 1900; moreover, after 1929 the safety-valve of emigration to the United States was no longer available. Even worse, between 1930 and 1934, the United States deported 400,000 Mexicans south across the Rio Grande. The financial collapse provoked by the world economic crisis entailed a 50 per cent devaluation, and the substitution of bank notes for coins of precious metal. But although the coinage disappeared, the public refused to accept notes. It was at this time that popular dissatisfaction with the authorities reached its height.

General Calles, whose political genius had founded the contemporary political system, was obliged to efface himself so that his works would endure. He had sworn, in his 'political testament' speech in 1928, that the time for strong men was past and that he no longer aspired to the presidency. He was not lying, for he never became president again, but it was from a position above the president that he governed the country for a further six years without violating the sacred principle of no re-election. The sole survivor of the heroes of the northern revolution, he reigned as the man of destiny in precarious isolation. A giant with feet of clay, however, his fall came suddenly, without major violence and amid general astonishment, within two years of the election of Lázaro Cárdenas to the presidency in July 1934. Calles had begun to institutionalize the revolution: it was for Cárdenas to complete the process.

ECONOMIC POLICY UNDER CALLES

Álvaro Obregón, like Porfirio Díaz, favoured 'much administration, little politics'; Plutarco Calles could have said 'much economic policy, no politics'. And the first aim of the economic policy of President Calles and his technical experts would seem to have been the liberation of the country from foreign economic domination. The project was part of a proudly nationalist programme of modernization aimed at systematically developing the productive forces of the country, while the structure of the state was being modified through a 'businesslike' re-organization of the federal government.[8] The state was thus transformed into an economic agency, as has been explained by Manuel Gómez Morín, one of the prime activists of this period:[9]

In recent years, the government has been the only source of capital. The old banks have turned to this source in order to re-establish themselves. The Banco de México and the Banco de Crédito Agrícola are its products, and for any enterprise which is planned, there is an inevitable tendency to think in terms of obtaining sufficient capital from the state. The banks, because of their lack of capital or because of the primitive way in which they operate . . . cannot constitute themselves as a direct source of capital . . . The foreign banks, as well as foreign companies, only develop those business activities which interest them, when it is in their interests to develop them, and in whatever ways may suit them, which do not always coincide with the best interests of Mexico. In this way, the state, if it wants to stimulate the economy, sees itself obliged to take the tremendous strain of subsidizing vast business enterprises in critical periods: the exploitation of natural resources remains outside the economic control of Mexico, and a whole range of useful or necessary enterprises are not undertaken, or are undertaken on terms which are far from satisfactory . . . There is not a single Mexican company which could seriously exploit our mineral resources. There is not a single Mexican company which could develop the technical ability to exploit our forestry resources. In short, there are no Mexican companies capable of making use of our natural wealth. With our present banking resources, with current credit procedure, it is impossible to think in terms of developing useful initiatives for the exploitation of our resources. There are no funds with which to start new enterprises or to give impetus to those which

[8] The expression comes from Manuel Gómez Morín, 1922.
[9] Memorandum of Manuel Gómez Morín, cited in Jean Meyer, *Historia de la Revolución mexicana*, XI (Mexico, 1977), 286.

already exist . . . And despite the nationalism which our laws proclaim, we are losing control day by day of our economy and, with it, all hope that we may one day fully control it. If Mexico wishes to create a national economy, its first step must be to seek the necessary instruments to carry out its purpose, that is, to obtain capital which may require the development of that economy. But we must not commit the same mistake as the previous generation. It is not a case of putting Mexico on the market. It is not a case of attracting capital to Mexico indiscriminately. We must obtain capital, but obtain it in accordance with prior planning, obtain it for our own development and not in order to be dispossessed, obtain it, in short, subject to our control and applied to our needs. Instead of foreign companies coming to Mexico to work when, where, and in whatever way may be convenient to them, with no other obligations than to political and administrative laws which, anyway, are always weak, ineffectual and prejudicial, we should try to create our own enterprises upon foundations which are both reasonable and secure, and in accordance with our plans and our purposes, and we should then seek to capitalize them abroad or within our own country. In this way, the capital which we may obtain will be financially subject to the aspirations and policies of Mexico and will be a servant rather than a master of the Mexican economy. To re-establish the confidence of foreign investors in Mexico is a difficult task, but it is not impossible. Its fulfilment requires, naturally, peace and security within the nation, but above all, it requires prudence and technical skills . . . One cannot talk of the domestic capital market, because such a market has never existed . . . But the potential for an internal market exists . . . And it is not absurd to consider that a concerted and intelligent effort could, within a short period of time, encourage new habits and activate local capital totalling between three hundred and five hundred million pesos, which is paralyzed and hidden not so much because of the political and economic situation, but because of the lack of financial methods which might make effective use of it.

It was a programme of classical liberalism – a balanced budget, the restoration of foreign confidence in Mexico's ability to pay its debts and a stable currency. Alberto Pani, minister of finance under Obregón and Calles (1923–7), reduced the salaries of civil servants, abolished departments in every ministry and imposed various other draconian economies. He instituted income tax and mounted other fiscal projects, the effects of which were spread over several generations. The result was that, by 1925, budgetary receipts considerably exceeded expenditure. At the end of 1925 Pani succeeded in renegotiating the foreign debt on better terms. In exchange, the state restored the nationalized railways (Ferrocarriles Mexicanos) to the private sector. With the economy thriving in the early 1920s, thanks mainly to oil exports, interest payments were resumed on the debt. In the same year Pani was able to carry out an ancient project, as ancient as independent Mexico, that of a central bank, the Banco de México, with an initial capital of 50 million pesos. Other banking institutions such as the Comisión Nacional Bancaria were set up, and new financial legislation was passed. In 1926 the Banco de Crédito Agrícola was founded, but plans for banks of Popular Credit, a Bank of Social Security (Banco de Seguridad Social) and a Workers' Bank (Banco Obrero) were frozen by economic recession.

Financial and banking activity was linked with the major public works. In 1925, since there was reasonable hope of obtaining the necessary credits, the Comisión Nacional de Caminos (National Highways Commission) launched a four-year programme to build 10,000 kilometres of roads. At the same time the modern road network was planned. The South Pacific railway, Nogales (Arizona) to Guadalajara, was completed in 1927 with the construction of the Tepic to Guadalajara section.

To open up new lands to modern methods of agriculture, major irrigation works were started. Dams and canals accounted for 6.5 per cent of the national budget between 1925 and 1928. Investment was concentrated in the north and the north-west.

In the mining, oil and electricity sectors, it was not a question of substituting domestic investment for that of foreign companies, but of bringing pressure on the latter to work in the interest of the country. The basic law of December 1925 with its regulating amendment of March 1926 made formal provision for the future recovery of national sovereignty over oil and the development of a petro-chemical industry. However, this initiative provoked such a serious row with the United States that, as we have seen, the Mexican government had to beat a retreat.

The Porfiriato and the first ten years of the Revolution had bequeathed a predominantly capitalist economy unevenly developed between regions: in the lead were the north-west and the north-east, the Federal District and the Gulf. Industry was concentrated in Mexico City and Monterrey and in the corridor linking Puebla with Veracruz, regions which had been relatively little affected by revolutionary violence. The oil boom reached its peak in 1922, after which production steadily declined. In the main centres industrial production had in 1920 just regained the level of 1910. In short, the period from 1910 to 1920 did not witness either the collapse of production or the paralysis of the economy.[10] Production recovered very rapidly but within an economy characterized by geographical and sectoral inequalities, a feature aggravated by the Revolution as well as by the links with the American economy. Despite recession in various sectors, it becomes clear from an overall view that the period from 1920 to 1940 was the second period of expansion (the first having occurred between 1880 and 1910), with a turning-point around 1925 signalling the beginning of a mini-recession, followed by depression. The international situation of Mexico did not change; on the contrary it was marked by greater foreign penetration. Between 1910 and 1929 British and American investment grew. Of the 4,600 million pesos of foreign capital invested in Mexico in 1929, 3,000 million was American and 900 million British. During the world depression, foreign holdings diminished in absolute terms, but the American percentage share increased. External trade continued to develop in the direction of reinforcing ties with the United States. In 1930, as in 1900, foreign trade represented 20 per cent of the gross national product (GNP); but during the period 1900–30 imports from the United States rose from 50 to 70 per cent of total Mexican imports, while exports to the United States were maintained at 70–80 per cent of total exports.

In spite of the postwar world depression, which witnessed a fall in the price of most primary products, the period from 1920 to 1925 was a golden age for Mexico because of its oil and other mineral exports. After a succession of favourable years, however, exports began to fall in 1926–7, and by degrees all, or almost all, sectors of the economy were affected. The Banco de México was obliged to be content with survival, standing impotently by as the recession spread. The public works programme had to be abandoned, and of the 20,000 kilometres of highway projected, fewer than 5,000 were completed. The railways were bankrupt and the state, which had restored them to private ownership, was obliged to take them back under its own control. A financial and banking crisis followed the economic crisis; both the national budget and the balance of payments were in deficit. The government made a desperate effort to honour its international commitments, but in August 1928 it had to resign itself again to suspending interest payments on the foreign debt. The treasury was empty; civil servants and the armed forces were paid in

[10] See John Womack Jr, 'The Mexican economy during the revolution, 1910–1920; historiography and analysis', *Marxist Perspectives*, 1/4 (1978), 80–123. Also see Chapter 3 of this volume.

Table 1. *Mexican exports, 1903–27 (millions of pesos)*

	Gold and silver	Petroleum and derivatives	Other minerals	Remaining exports				Total exports
				Total	Agricultural goods	Livestock products	Manufactures and other goods	
1903–4	103.4	—	29.4	77.5	60.5	10.9	6.1	210.3
1904–5	93.9	—	36.4	78.2	59.1	10.5	8.6	208.5
1905–6	157.1	—	35.6	78.4	62.9	11.7	3.8	271.1
1906–7	123.7	—	36.5	87.8	71.8	11.2	4.8	248.0
1907–8	124.9	—	33.5	84.3	70.2	9.6	4.5	242.7
1908–9	113.1	—	31.2	86.8	67.9	13.9	5.0	231.1
1909–10	119.0	—	37.5	103.5	77.7	20.1	5.7	260.0
1910–11	143.0	—	37.0	113.8	91.3	16.8	5.7	293.8
1911–12	139.5	—	46.7	111.8	83.6	19.9	8.3	298.0
1912–13	130.9	—	58.8	110.7	85.9	19.8	5.0	300.4
1920	134.0	516.8	77.2	127.1	105.4	6.5	15.2	855.1
1921	89.8	576.3	22.9	67.8	60.7	2.3	4.8	756.8
1922	109.9	412.0	46.1	75.6	67.1	4.4	4.1	643.6
1923	116.7	270.2	98.1	83.5	74.3	4.4	4.8	568.5
1924	122.2	293.3	94.8	104.4	96.1	5.0	3.3	614.7
1925	135.7	292.1	119.9	134.8	120.9	9.8	4.1	682.5
1926	137.5	227.6	159.7	167.0	147.6	14.2	5.2	691.8
1927	87.0	133.4	218.7	188.3	161.4	19.4	7.5	627.4

Source: Joseph E. Sterrett and Joseph S. Davis, *The fiscal and economic condition of Mexico.* Report submitted to the International Committee of Bankers on Mexico (1928), 110.

Table 2. *Value of exports, 1909–10 and 1926 (millions of pesos)*

Products	1909–10	1926	Percentage change
Minerals and petroleum	156.5	524.8	+ 336
Agriculture	77.7	147.6	+ 190
Cattle and livestock products	20.1	14.2	− 30
Manufactures and other goods	5.7	5.2	− 8
Total	260.0	691.8	+ 265

Source: Table 1.

arrears, and then only out of funds advanced by the American and British banks.[11] There was a considerable drop in Mexico's gold reserves. In May 1926 the banks had reserves of 110 million pesos, compared with 135 million in 1925. By the end of 1926 the reserves had fallen to 88 million and one year later to 73 million pesos.[12]

The main cause of the financial crisis and the collapse in confidence was a combination of unpropitious circumstances acting on the structure of the Mexican economy. Mexico relied heavily on foreign trade to finance its internal development. When the balance of trade ceased to be positive, in other words when exports ceased to pay for imports – consumer goods for the governing and middle classes, machinery, minerals and metals, vehicles, chemical products, and cereals from the United States following the fall in domestic production of essential foodstuffs (see below) – the whole economy was affected.

The structure of Mexico's foreign trade had not been altered by the Revolution. On the contrary its traditional features became even more entrenched. Mexico was more than ever a country producing and exporting raw materials (see tables 1 and 2). Whereas in 1910 60 per cent of exports had come from minerals and hydrocarbons, by 1926 this figure was 76 per cent. Although agricultural exports had undeniably increased, they were overtaken by the rising exports of oil and minerals. The fall in the figure for cattle reflected the break-up between 1913 and 1920 of the

[11] See G. Butler Sherwell, *Mexico's capacity to pay. A general analysis of the present international economic position of Mexico* (Washington, DC, 1929), 70, and J. E. Sterrett and J. S. Davis, *The fiscal and economic condition of Mexico*. Report submitted to the International Committee of Bankers on Mexico (1928), 124.   [12] *Estadística Nacional*, January 1928.

Table 3. *Mexico's oil industry, 1911–27*

	Production of crude petroleum (millions of barrels)	Export of crude petroleum and derivatives (millions of barrels)	Unitary value of production (pesos per barrel)	Value of production (millions of pesos)	Taxes on production and sale (millions of pesos)
1911	12.6	0.9	0.20	2.5	—
1912	16.6	7.7	0.25	4.1	0.5
1913	25.7	21.3	0.30	7.7	0.8
1914	26.2	23.4	0.30	7.9	1.2
1915	32.9	24.8	0.40	13.2	2.0
1916	40.5	27.3	0.55	22.3	3.1
1917	55.3	46.0	0.85	47.0	7.1
1918	63.8	51.8	1.40	89.7	11.5
1919	87.1	75.6	1.83	159.0	16.7
1920	157.1	145.5	2.00	314.1	45.5
1921	193.4	172.3	1.89	365.9	62.7
1922	182.3	180.9	1.93	351.7	86.0
1923	149.6	135.6	1.91	285.9	60.5
1924	139.7	129.7	1.95	272.1	54.6
1925	115.5	96.5	2.59	299.3	42.1
1926	90.4	80.7	2.49	225.1	34.8
1927	64.1	48.3	2.46	157.5	19.0

Source: Sterrett and Davis, *The fiscal and economic condition of Mexico*, 197.

system by which livestock was leased to farmers. Even fewer manufactured goods were exported. In 1922 64 per cent of imports came from the United States and by 1926 the figure had risen to 70 per cent. Again, in 1922 up to 80 per cent of all Mexico's exports went to the United States, but in 1926 only 71 per cent went there as a result of zinc being exported to Belgium and Germany.[13] The general tendency thus remained one of heavy dependence on the United States and the mining industry, a combination which gave the Mexican economy a certain fragility. The trend was visible after 1926, and the depression of 1929 confirmed the evidence.

Oil was the first product to cause problems. In 1921 Mexico was second in world production and oil represented 76 per cent of her exports. From 1921 to 1927 production and exports fell by 72 per cent, which included a drop of no less than 42 per cent in one year, 1926–7. There were several reasons, technical, economic and political, for this contraction, which continued to accelerate. Foreign companies had ruthlessly exploited the wells to the full extent of their capacity, sometimes actually destroying them by flooding with salt water.[14] The new borings were less profitable and the companies, angered by Morones's policy towards them, transferred their investments to Venezuela, which by 1927 actually surpassed Mexico in output (see tables 3 and 4).

At the end of 1924 the capital invested in the oil industry was estimated at 800 million pesos, of which 57.5 per cent was American, 26.2 per cent English, 11.4 per cent Dutch and only 3 per cent Mexican. In 1926 certain companies were still making 100 per cent net profit on the sale of crude oil. In 1924 there had been six refineries in Mexico capable of refining 800,000 barrels a day, but in 1927 output had fallen by 40 per cent. By March 1928 only two refineries were operating, and in 1927 almost all the light oil was sent to the refinery instead of being exported. Duties on petroleum, which in 1921 had represented one-third of the national revenue, about 85 million pesos, had fallen by 1927 to one-eighth, about 19 million, and in the same year the companies withdrew their bank deposits, thus bringing about the *de facto* devaluation of the peso.[15]

For a time the export of non-ferrous metals (zinc, copper and lead),

---

[13] *Estadística Nacional*, 15 July 1927, p. 5.
[14] Sterrett and Davis, *The fiscal and economic condition of Mexico*, 200.
[15] Merill Rippy, *Oil and the Mexican Revolution* (Muncie, Indiana, 1972), 166–7; Sterrett and Davis, *The fiscal and economic condition of Mexico*, 200–1.

Table 4. *World production of petroleum, 1910–27 (millions of barrels)*

	United States	Mexico	Russia	Persia	Dutch colonies	Venezuela	Colombia
1910	209.6	3.6	70.3	—	11.0	—	—
1911	220.4	12.6	66.2	—	12.2	—	—
1912	222.9	16.6	68.0	—	10.8	—	—
1913	248.4	25.7	62.8	1.9	11.2	—	—
1914	265.8	26.2	67.0	2.9	11.4	—	—
1915	281.1	32.9	68.5	3.6	11.9	—	—
1916	300.8	40.5	65.8	4.5	12.5	—	—
1917	335.3	55.3	63.1	7.1	13.2	0.1	—
1918	355.9	63.8	27.2	8.6	12.8	0.3	—
1919	378.4	87.1	31.8	10.1	15.5	0.4	—
1920	442.9	157.1	25.4	12.2	17.5	0.5	–
1921	472.2	193.4	29.0	16.7	17.0	1.4	—
1922	557.5	182.3	35.7	22.2	17.1	2.2	0.3
1923	732.4	149.6	39.1	25.2	19.9	4.2	0.4
1924	713.9	139.7	45.4	32.4	20.5	9.0	0.4
1925	763.7	115.5	52.4	35.0	21.4	19.7	1.0
1926	770.9	90.4	64.3	35.8	21.2	37.2	6.4
1927	903.8	64.1	72.4	36.8	21.4	64.4	14.6

Source: Sterrett and Davis, *The fiscal and economic condition of Mexico*, 198.

which had increased tenfold between 1921 and 1927, together with agricultural exports, enabled the country to withstand the strain. However, in 1926 exports of silver collapsed as a result of the drop in price on the world market; China and India, the principal purchasers, suspended their dealings. Exports of zinc, lead, copper and agricultural products were not enough by themselves to avert financial difficulties. Capital took flight to the United States, foreign investment declined and the deficit on the balance of payments reached 50 million pesos in 1926.[16]

This was the beginning of the economic crisis of the late 1920s, accompanied by unemployment, bitter strikes and emigration to the United States. At the same time the Cristero war ravaged the countryside and proved a heavy drain on the budget: in 1927 33 centavos out of every peso in the budget was spent on the army. Manuel Gómez Morín and Alberto Pani left office: considerations of politics and war once again prevailed over economic policy. Finally, in 1929 the two sectors not

---

[16] *Estadística Nacional*, February 1929, pp. 74–6, and Rippy, *Oil and the Mexican Revolution*, 124–5.

previously affected, zinc, lead and copper, and agriculture, were struck by the full force of the world depression. Agricultural exports, which between 1921 and 1927 had risen from 60 to 161 million pesos, dropped to 92 million in 1928 and 52 million in 1930.[17] Output in the mining sector lost half its value between 1929 and 1932.

ORGANIZED LABOUR AND THE STATE UNDER CALLES

One of the essential features of economic policy during the Calles administration was the attempt to reconcile class interests through the mediation of the state. The man identified with this initiative was Luis N. Morones, secretary-general of the principal labour organization, the CROM, who had been a colleague but subsequently became an enemy of Obregón, after the breakdown in their relations in 1923-4. Morones became Calles's right-hand man and was his powerful minister of industry, commerce and labour (1924-8), more powerful, for example, than the minister of the interior (Gobernación). To reconcile capital and labour under the aegis of the state, Morones undertook an enormous legislative and administrative task, in the execution of which he did not hesitate to eliminate 'irresponsible elements' and 'provocateurs' in the labour movement. As an American observer wrote in 1927:

The prime objective of the labor unions, which have secured for this purpose the cooperation of the great employers' organizations, is to create a structure for Mexican industry which will increase the numbers of the working class, provide it with better work and a higher standard of living and, finally, bring about the economic independence of the country.[18]

Morones started from the principle that there was nothing which could not be negotiated if both employers and workers showed 'responsibility' and 'moderation'. In speaking he made regular use of the words 'conciliation', 'co-operation' and 'co-ordination'. Every strike had to be official, agreed to by the union, which had to consult its national executive committee. The minister decided on the legality of the strike, and an illegal strike was doomed to failure. This was advantageous to the employers, who were, theoretically, protected from wildcat strikes on condition that they respected the law, which favoured the workers. In this legislation special attention was paid to problems raised by accidents

[17] National Archives, Washington DC, Military Intelligence Division, 2525-G-11/9, 24 May 1932.
[18] W. English Walling, *The Mexican question* (New York, 1927), quoted in Enrique Krauze, *Historia de la revolución mexicana*, x (Mexico, 1977), 25.

and illness; standards of safety were imposed, together with provisions for retirement and minimum wages.

In 1926–7 the reforms of Morones passed an important test with distinction. The textile industry had been in recession for years. Although it was the country's leading industry, it was technologically out of date and paralysed by constant disputes; in 1922 textile strikes represented 71 per cent of the total number of strikes. Morones came to grips with the problem and brought together the representatives of employers and workers in order to resolve the labour problems and to make a start with modernizing the industry. The result of this meeting was a collective contract (*contrato ley*) for the entire textile industry, the adoption of a wage-scale, and the introduction of arbitration at all levels by means of mixed commissions.

Complementing this strategy was a system of protection designed to encourage the creation of national industries, which doubled the fiscal advantages granted to industrialists. A publicity campaign urged Mexicans 'to consume the products of their own country'. Lawyers drafted legislation for nationalizing the electrical industry (*código nacional eléctrico*) and the oil industry, and prepared for the reform of the constitution to enable nationalization of mines, commerce, credit, Communications and the sources of energy. As a result of the economic and political crisis of the late 1920s, however, these measures remained a dead letter for many years.

This policy provoked strife with the oil producers and the State Department, as we have seen, but relations with foreign – chiefly American – bankers and manufacturers were good. Between 1924 and 1928, Ford, Siemens, Colgate, Palmolive, British-American Tobacco and International Match had all established themselves in Mexico. Certainly the degree of industrialization remained modest, for the combination of international and national circumstances was not very favourable; moreover, the majority of managers, technicians and ideologues considered that agriculture and mining products constituted the true riches of the country. From this aspect, Morones was a solitary visionary who heralded the developments of the 1940s. It is too simple to regard Morones as a traitor to the working class, who sold himself to capitalist interests. Morones, like Calles, was one of the great builders of the Mexican state, in which the labour movement played a decisive part.

It is inevitable that any discussion of the workers should concentrate on the CROM. However, the CROM represented only one element within the labour movement, and trade unionism represented only one aspect of the workers' daily life. From 1910 to 1918 the relationship of workers with the state went through successive phases of hostility, indifference, or collaboration; the hopes of the workers fluctuated according to shifts in the relationship. In 1918 Morones, a former electrician, made his famous address at the time of the foundation of the CROM under state patronage; from that point for the next ten years the CROM remained the embodiment of political realism and the sharing of responsibility with the state. In the words of Rosendo Salazar, an old union militant:

The state as an intermediary is the creation of the Mexican Revolution and implies neither the dictatorship of the proletariat nor that of the capitalist state. It excludes all foreign ideology from its sphere and promotes understanding between employers, workers and government. Labour adjusts its demands in accordance with the law and the state gives it protection against abuses by the employers.[19]

The organized labour movement thus became one component in the governmental machine, a situation which led to opportunism and corruption, but also gave much greater influence than the figures would suggest. Workers and artisans, numbering less than 600,000, carried more weight than 4 million peasants; 100,000 union members were instrumental in making the CROM a partner to be respected, because through its Labour party it sent deputies and senators to the Congress and even succeeded in gaining control of the government in several states.

It is difficult to give precise figures, for those which are available are not reliable. The CROM claimed to have 2 million members in 1928, but recognized that the actual membership was much lower and that half of these were peasants. The only reliable figure, that of members who paid dues, amounted to 15,000. In the absence of better information, it may be agreed that the CROM had mustered 100,000 workers, artisans, office workers, small traders and, in theory, 50,000 agricultural labourers. Catholic unions claimed 40,000; 30,000 more may be attributed to the railway workers, who had been weakened by the divisions resulting from the foundation of the CROM; and 20,000 to the CGT (Confederación General del Trabajo). Certainly the Communists, the sworn enemies of the CROM, did not succeed in gaining the confidence of 'the great masses of the workers and of the semi-proletarian peasants'.[20]

The peak of CROM influence was reached between 1924 and 1928

[19] Quoted in Jean Meyer, *La Révolution mexicaine* (Paris, 1973), 102.
[20] See, for example, *Correspondence Internationale*, 25 (20 February 1927), 327.

when its secretary-general Morones was the most important minister in the Cabinet of Calles. It took advantage of the situation in a positive way to improve the position of workers, and in a negative way to fight the other trade unions by all possible means. The religious conflict was exploited in order to eliminate the Catholic unions, and strikes were used to try to break rivals, such as the unions of oil workers, electricians, railway employees and textile workers, who had, all told, more members than the CROM. The CROM demanded that the workers should unite in a single confederation and respect the new laws (which were favourable to them). Strikes of unions not affiliated with the CROM were almost invariably designated as illegal. The economic crisis of 1926 caused strikes to multiply in all sectors, and not infrequently Morones switched from mediation to repression which sometimes caused further strikes.

For ten years the attitude of the CROM was decisive, whether in the promotion or termination of a strike. It launched, supported or revived movements in order to conquer new positions, destroy its enemies or establish a union monopoly. The advances made by the CROM were parallel with those of the government of Calles: when the latter undertook the reorganization of the railways, the CROM seized its opportunity and tried to take the place of the independent unions. In the oil dispute, the CROM went into battle against the companies. All this explains the often bloody character of a struggle which frequently brought workers into conflict with other workers.

The struggle was a bloody one because the independent forces, whether 'red' or 'white', did not lack strength; they were to be found in the textile industry, the railways, certain mines and in the bakeries. When, after Obregón was assassinated in 1928, the CROM suffered a rapid erosion of its power, the independent unions had the chance for revenge: the CROM was stripped of much of its strength, although it retained a considerable capacity for resistance. Between 1928 and 1937 the trade union movement was more deeply divided than ever. It was not until the Cárdenas administration that the CTM (Confederation of Mexican Workers) was founded and gained the dominant position.

All strikes were by nature political and inseparable from inter-party and parliamentary struggles, from conflicts over the presidential succession and from local and national disputes. The railway workers, in particular, had an old tradition of union independence and militancy which went back to the Porfiriato and had been consolidated during the civil war years when they were, by force of circumstances, in the front line. War was above all a matter of the railways. In 1920 the interim president, Adolfo de la Huerta, had facilitated the formation of a Confederation of Railway Workers' Union, then the biggest union in the country. In 1921 it opposed the government of Obregón and had great difficulty in obtaining recognition. When in the same year the Confederation had recourse to a strike, the government defined this decision as *rebelión abierta* (open revolt) and President Obregón sent the army to occupy workshops, stations and trains. The CROM pulled out of the dispute, while de la Huerta, playing the part of overall mediator, strengthened his position with the railway workers. In December 1923, therefore, the de la Huertista rebellion met with some support within the Confederation (as also from other unions, such as certain affiliates of the CGT, which opposed the CROM and the government).

A logical consequence of the defeat of de la Huerta was a purge of railway workers, a purge directed by the CROM, which took the opportunity to try to dominate a sector hitherto closed to it. This manoeuvre, together with the reorganization of the railways which reduced personnel, provoked a series of disputes in 1926 which led to the great railway strike of 1926–7. President Calles reacted in the same way as in 1921, when he was at the ministry of interior: he sent in the troops, one hundred soldiers into each workshop, and backed up Morones, who recognized new unions as so many weapons in the war against the Railway Confederation. In December 1926, when the strike had spread to all regions, the railwaymen did not perhaps fully realize the dangerous position of the government. In fact the dispute with the United States over petroleum and diplomatic issues was at its height and there was some talk of 'sending in the Marines' and of setting the oil wells on fire. In addition, the Yaqui war was raging, and in a matter of days the Cristeros would be in revolt.

The railway strike, which was very bitter, lasted for three months. Soldiers rode on locomotives driven by strike-breakers; it was never known how many trains had been derailed or how many railway workers and saboteurs had been shot. Gradually, during April and May 1927, the agitation lost its momentum and fizzled out in the course of the summer. The victory of government and CROM was a very costly one for workers and railways alike.

Other strikes, even though many and also bitter, paled by comparison with the 1926–7 railway strike. From 1920 to 1926 the textile industry was in a continuous state of unrest, aggravated by disputes between unions. There again the influence of the CROM was overpowering: in order to gain control of the entire national workers' movement, it was obliged, on the strength of its political allegiance, to destroy the unions unwilling to come into line. And each time the opportunity arose, it did so. In the textile sector it engaged in armed combat with the 'reds' and the 'free' unions in the capital city, the state of Mexico, Puebla and Veracruz. After the Textile Convention, there were many fewer strikes because of the agreements drawn up between the employers, the unions and the state. Then came the economic crisis, which weakened the position of the workers, threatened by the piling up of stocks and the slowing down of production.

In all sectors the trend was the same: strikes in 1921, followed by a period of relative quiet; strikes between 1924 and 1926 characterized by divisions within the unions; less numerous but often desperate strikes in subsequent years, under the shadow of economic crisis when factories and mines were closing down. What was the result of so much sound and fury? The hard-won victory of the CROM was to have no future, for in 1928–9 it was removed from governmental power, and it never again became the single organization for the Mexican workers that it would have liked to be.

The 1920s were especially characterized by the reorganization and modernization of existing industries. The process was, however, generally accompanied by a reduction in the numbers of workers, particularly in the mines, on the railways and in the textile industry, a fact which explains the often desperate nature of the workers' resistance. From 1925 onwards the CROM co-operated in the task of modernization and left resistance to its enemies, the 'reds'. Those workers fortunate enough to keep their jobs or to find other employment probably imagined that their lot would improve as a result of the new legislation and of the policy of Morones. Then the slump in Mexico and the world depression brought about the closure of many factories. The CROM and the government tried, without much success, to settle or re-settle unemployed workers in country areas. It was a curious attempt to turn back into peasants workers who had only just emerged from the peasantry in a country which was far from having resolved its own agrarian question. It demonstrates the extent to which Mexico was still, in 1930, a rural country.

AGRARIAN REFORM, AGRICULTURE AND THE PEASANTS

There has probably been some exaggeration of the agrarian contribution to the collapse of the Porfiriato. Similarly in the history of the Revolution the importance of agrarian reform has probably been overestimated. In the course of the civil war decisive legal measures were taken, in an improvised fashion and under pressure of necessity, against large-scale private landownership, as illustrated by the decree of January 1915 and Article 27 of the constitution of 1917. The application of a modified version of the principles embodied in the 1915 decree and Article 27 of the constitution, however, were only put into effect in 1934, and then only in a slow and confused way, with the publication of the Agrarian Code. In accordance with the constitution and the enabling code, land belonged to the nation which, through the state, could recognize it as legitimate private property or expropriate it and concede it either to communities defined by the term *ejido* or to individual smallholders. The concession was inalienable and could not be let, sold or inherited.

Somewhat timidly and halfheartedly, Carranza had already distributed 200,000 hectares before Obregón paid off the Zapatistas and other hard-core guerilla forces, along with his own soldiers, by ratifying the seizures made during the civil war, especially in the Zapatista zone (Morelos and Guerrero). In the course of four years Obregón distributed more than one million hectares, with the political aim of buying peace. President Calles at first followed this initiative, then slowed the process. Like Obregón, he would have preferred to contain agrarian reform within a political framework and to complete it quickly, in order to pass on to modernization and productivity – colonization, irrigation and large-scale capitalist agriculture – which interested him more than distribution.

Because of the Revolution, the colonizing movement begun under the Porfiriato, a pioneering assault on the dry, irrigable lands of Sonora and the tropical forests of Veracruz, Tabasco, Campeche, and so on, had to be halted. It was re-launched by Obregón and Calles with the support of the state (Law on Colonization of 5 April 1926). However, the world depression interfered with this project for massive public works, as we have seen: agricultural exports collapsed; 400,000 Mexicans returned from the United States; and the government was forced to revise economic strategy, thus playing into the hands of the agrarian lobby. Despite Calles's declaration in 1929 that 'Agrarianism such as we have understood and applied it has been a failure',[21] he was obliged to agree to a resumption of the distribution of land. Under Portes Gil in 1929–30, 1,700,000 hectares of land were distributed. During the period from 1915

---

[21] Meyer, *Révolution mexicaine*, 244–5.

to 1933 a total of 7,600,000 hectares was distributed. And in less than two years (1933–4) Abelardo Rodríguez handed out a further 2,500,000 hectares.

The balance sheet of agrarian reform in 1934, on the eve of Cárdenas's great distribution of 18 million hectares, reveals three features. First, the concessions were limited: ten million hectares, perhaps 10 per cent of the cultivated land, had gone to 10 per cent of the peasantry. (*Peones acasillados*, agricultural workers housed on the haciendas, did not benefit from agrarian reform until 1934.) The institutional result was a total of perhaps 4,000 *ejidos*. Secondly, the concessions were concentrated in a small number of districts. And thirdly, these districts were confined to the Old Mexico of the high central plateau and to its southern and southeastern tropical escarpment (Morelos, Veracruz, Hidalgo). In most cases the central core of the hacienda was respected and the *ejido* plots of land were allocated under separate titles, in small lots of from four to ten hectares. According to local conditions prevailing in each state, the reforms, administered by the authorities, were sometimes executed with vigour, sometimes evaded and sometimes postponed until a later time. Hence there emerged a wide variety of situations and a certain lack of control over the operations, which resulted in corruption and in extortion from the peasants, including those who benefited from the distribution.

Local politics complicated the agrarian problem, because it allowed caciques to control a substantial clientèle and at the same time manipulate landowners. Within the *ejido* the administrative committee arranged and rearranged the distribution of the plots of land to its own advantage, a fact which explains the violence of the struggle for power and the large number of murders perpetrated in the *ejidos*. Paul Friedrich has studied the massacres which lasted for more than 25 years in the region of Naranja (Michoacán), and Luis González has recorded one episode which he describes as 'murderous insanity' at San José de Gracia.[22] The *ejido* of Auchén even acquired the name of the '*ejido* of the widows', since all the men were dead except for one who had become the owner and exploited the whole *ejido*.

Not only did agrarian reform create divisions among the *ejidatarios* themselves, it also divided the peasantry into the 10 per cent who had received a plot of land and those who had received nothing. The tactic of

---

[22] Paul Friedrich, *Agrarian revolt in a Mexican village* (Englewood Cliffs, NJ, 1970); Luis González y González, *Pueblo en vilo; microhistoria de San José de Gracia* (3rd edn, Mexico, 1979), 186, 195.

dividing the peasants into hostile and irreconcilable factions guaranteed that the government controlled the land as well as the electoral loyalty of its owners. From its beginning the agrarian policy had been a weapon brandished alike against the landowners, who were threatened with expropriation, and against the beneficiaries, who were afraid of being ejected from the *ejidos*. Guns were handed out regardless of the risk of non-recovery, as in Veracruz in 1932, to the militias of the *ejidos* called 'social defence forces', so that they could serve as an instrument of repression against the other peasants and as a means of blackmail against the landowners large and small.

The traditional hacendado was hard hit by the threefold ordeal of wars in 1913–17 and 1926–9, economic crisis after 1929 and agrarian reform itself. Henceforth the rural conflict set the landless peasant against his landed neighbour, either traditional small private proprietor or *ejidatario*, and the small proprietor or the *comunero* (member of an Indian community) against the *ejidatario*. The agrarian programme was short-sighted, for mutual antagonisms were endlessly multiplied by the collapse of the established society and by the reform. There were other human elements involved, too – the tenant farmer, the sharecropper, the agricultural labourer, the migrant stockbreeder. Conflicts of class, race and culture raged, and the religious dispute certainly did not help to pacify popular feeling.

Different regional groups representing the provinces against the capital, the periphery against the centre and the north against the south all exploited the peasants, who had helped bring about the fall of Don Porfirio and who in some districts had succeeded by a brief show of force in recovering part of their lands from the great estates. The revolutionaries in power had never had a true agrarian programme; they had had an agricultural programme, which was not the same thing. They never attacked the principle of the hacienda, but were merely in favour of small and medium-sized properties. Between 1915 and 1928 only 10 per cent of the haciendas had been appropriated and, paradoxically, half of these had been small. In fact, the areas invaded by the peasants themselves were of much greater importance. The peasants were granted the temporary satisfaction of seizing and consolidating their power; they were then made use of to dismantle the large private estates in the interests of a capitalist agriculture. The peasants were to be both the instruments and the victims of a Mexican version of the primitive accumulation of capital.

Peasants obtained more than was included in the revolutionary programme, but their success was limited. The politician took the place of the hacendado and the peasant found himself in the same relationship to the government as he had formerly been to his employer, except that the government was to be feared in a different way. 'Nothing has been done to liberate the peasant from the politician', wrote Marjorie Clark in ' her *Organized labor in Mexico* (1934).

> If he wants to escape repression he must take care to belong to whichever is strongest in his region. He is promised land, money, implements if he behaves well; he is threatened with losing the land which he has already received, with seeing his harvests destroyed and his flock slaughtered if he fails to respond to the demands of the group in power. A tyranny equal to that of the *caciques* (bosses) under the régime of Porfirio Díaz has been established.[23]

It is not difficult to see why agrarian reform failed to arouse the enthusiasm of the peasants. The agrarian organizations were dominated by the bureaucracy; they never became genuine peasant bodies. Some peasants, preferring to stay outside them, refused the plots of land to which they were entitled. Such refusals have been attributed to fear, of the great landowner and his 'white guard' or of the priests who opposed the scheme and who sometimes, against the order of the bishops, declared it a mortal sin to accept an ejidal plot of land. Fear certainly played a part, but there was also the peasants' own conception of property and the proper means of acquiring it. All dreamed of becoming landowners, but not by just any method. Luis González has explained that there were only two honourable ways of becoming a landowner – by purchase or by inheritance. Hundreds of thousands of peasants left for the United States in the 1920s, working hard to save eight out of every ten dollars in order one day to buy a plot of land in their native village. A gift always compromises the recipient, and when it was offered by a traditionally mistrusted government, it was difficult to accept. It was definitely unacceptable between 1926 and 1929 when the state and the church were at war. During these terrible years the Cristeros often made the *agraristas* (at least those who had received plots of land) pay dearly, with their blood, for their connection with the state.

Obregón and Calles dreamed of creating a substantial class of dynamic smallholders and owners of medium-sized estates, on the model of the Californian 'farmer'. Such a class already existed in their native northwest – Obregón himself was a perfect representative – and it had

---

[23] Marjorie Clark, *Organized labor in Mexico* (Chapel Hill, NC, 1934), 161–2.

Table 5. *Agricultural
production per capita
(1900 = 100)*

Regions	1907	1929
Centre	112	69
South	145	98
North	60	318

Source: Clarke Reynolds, *The Mexican
economy: twentieth century structure and
growth* (New Haven, 1970), 105.

benefited from such economic activities of government as agricultural
credit, irrigation works and new roads. It seems that while the
government parcelled out bits of land on the plateau and in the south-
east, it poured money into the north-west. The distribution of land was
for the mass of the Mexican Indians and *mestizos* of Old Mexico, but
capital investments were for the owners of medium-sized and large
estates in other regions. In the northern areas favoured by the Sonorans,
there was scarcely an *ejido* to be found in 1934, but there were highways
and an irrigation programme representing one-quarter of public
investment between 1925 and 1935. In the words of Obregón: 'Fair
distribution of land to the proletariat is a first essential of the
revolutionary programme, but the foundations of the agricultural life of
the country must not be undermined.'[24]

From 1907 to 1929 the output of maize and black beans, the staple
foodstuffs of the people, fell by 40 and 31 per cent respectively, while the
population increased by 9 per cent. (Although as a result of war, famine,
epidemics and emigration Mexico had no more inhabitants in 1920 than
it had in 1910, the population grew from under 15 million to 16 million
between 1920 and 1930 and to 17 or 18 million – the data are inexact – in
1934.) Conditions in some regions were much graver than the overall
figures suggest. The central region, homeland of 45 per cent of the rural
population in 1930, witnessed a drop of 31 per cent in its total agricultural
production from 1913 to 1929. Table 5 demonstrates the disparities in
agricultural production per capita between 1907 and 1929. Total
production of maize, which had been 3.5 million tonnes in 1910 and 2.9

[24] In Luis González y González, *Los presidentes de México ante la nación* (Mexico, 1966), III, 423.

million tonnes in 1920, had fallen to 2.2 million in 1926 and only 1.5 million in 1929, because of the elimination of the corn-growing haciendas and the proliferation of small, poor producers.[25] Production of beans had grown steadily to over 200,000 tons in 1926, but then declined to under 100,000 tons by 1929.[26] In contrast, the export of foodstuffs expanded throughout the period 1920–7. For example, exports of coffee rose from 10,500 tons (9.3 million pesos) in 1920 to 26,100 tons (28.9 million pesos) in 1927; exports of bananas from 700 tons (0.3 million pesos) to 5,700 tons (8 million pesos); exports of tomatoes from 9,200 tons (0.7 million pesos) to 57,400 tons (19.6 million pesos); and exports of other fresh vegetables from 800 tons (0.2 million pesos) to 14,800 tons (5.5 million pesos).[27]

According to the founder of the Banco Nacional de Crédito Agrícola (1925), Manuel Gómez Morín, and also to President Calles, agrarian credit was to bring the peasantry on to the second stage of agrarian reform: production was to follow distribution. Unfortunately the initial capital was insufficient and the bank was not able to resist the practice of 'preferential loans', that is credit available for important personages, generals or politicians, the new *latifundistas*. In 1926 the major recipient of 'preferential' credit was General Obregón himself. In these circumstances the money did not reach those who really needed it, and it was a miracle that the bank survived until 1930, the year of financial disaster and plunder by the politicians.

The utopia of the Sonorans was an agriculturally prosperous Mexico, based on hard-driving and hard-working farmers served by a sound infrastructure of irrigation, roads, technology and bank loans. There was no serious thought of industrializing the country – Calles had said 'Our heavy industry is agriculture' – but only of giving an industrial finish to agricultural products for export. Mexico was to become a kind of agricultural United States: this principle was essential to the new economic policy, and the involvement first of General Obregón, then of General Calles, in large-scale agricultural undertakings in the north-west of the country is most significant. The northern regions did increase their production and obtained excellent results; their share of the national exports grew, despite all such obstacles as American competition and boycott, inexperience and shortage of credit.

[25] E. N. Simpson, *The ejido. Mexico's way out* (Chapel Hill, NC, 1937), 175, 214.
[26] *Estadística Nacional*, March 1929, p. 95, May 1929, p. 76, and Simpson, *The ejido*, 175, 214.
[27] Sterrett and Davis, *The fiscal and economic condition of Mexico*, 152.

CONCLUSION

In 1920, after ten years of revolution and civil war, a group of men from the Mexican north-west undertook an historic enterprise: nothing less than the transformation of the mosaic which was Mexico into a modern nation-state. During the 1920s Mexico's warring groups were eliminated by fire and sword. Not only was the army brought under control, but the leading revolutionary generals and *caudillos* disappeared, the regional military political bosses were pulled into line, and a kind of centralism triumphed. Saturnino Cedillo, in San Luis Potosí, was in the 1930s the only surviving old-style cacique. At the same time the workers were allowed a corporate existence, the church was put in its place and education given a national character. The problem of power and its orderly transmission in a more or less fragmented society, where parliamentary democracy could not function, was to some extent solved by the creation in 1929 of the PNR. Fifty years later its successor, the PRI, was still in power, providing an example of political stability unique in Latin America.

Under Obregón and Calles, economic as well as political power was once more concentrated in the hands of the president and his ministers and technical advisers. Absolute priority was given to the building of a modern economy, both national and capitalist. The role of the state was paramount: it assumed responsibility for the creation of the financial institutions and for the infrastructure projects which were beyond the means of Mexican private enterprise. There was an identity of interest between the state and the private sector. Indeed in this phase of state building and national capitalist development, there was a basic understanding between the 'revolutionary family', industrialists, bankers and business men, the CROM, capitalist rural interests, and even foreign capitalists. The oil companies, the anarchists and the Communist party were the only groups who refused to co-operate.

The ambitions of the men from Sonora, however, foundered on the twin rocks of economic dependence and economic recession. Mexico's capitalist development was financed in part by foreign investment and, above all, by exports. Since the 1870s the Mexican economy had been successfully integrated into the international economy through its mineral and agricultural exports. The Revolution had not changed the fundamental structure of the Mexican economy. And until 1926 exports financed economic growth. But seven lean years followed, and as the purchasing power of Mexican exports collapsed, the structural weakness of the Mexican economy was laid bare. The limits of that economic nationalism which had been asserted since 1917 had been reached. Obregón, Calles, Gómez Morín, Pani and Morones in the end were unable to perform the nationalist miracle of growth and independence.

5

THE RISE AND FALL OF CARDENISMO, *c.* 1930 – *c.* 1946

After the outbreak of Revolution in 1910, Mexico experienced a decade of armed upheaval followed by a decade of political and economic reconstruction. The revolutionary campaign destroyed the old regime of Porfirio Díaz, liquidated the Porfirian army, and brought to power a coalition that was heterogeneous yet strongly influenced by forces from the north and broadly committed to a project of state-building and capitalist development. If, in regard to these broad *ends,* the revolutionary leadership pursued Porfirian precedents, the *means* they employed were markedly different, as was the socio-political milieu in which they operated. It is true that Mexico's economy had not been revolutionized by the Revolution. The old pattern of export-led capitalist growth – *desarrollo hacia afuera* – had not fundamentally changed. The economic nationalist leanings of the regime, expressed in the Constitution of 1917, led to wrangles with the United States, but there was no complete rupture, and U.S. direct investment in Mexico was higher in 1929 than it had been in 1910. Furthermore, despite the decline in petroleum production after 1921, the economy recovered and grew, at least until 1927. In contrast, Mexico's social and political life was dramatically changed by the Revolution, albeit in an often unplanned and unforeseen manner. The armed mobilization of 1910–20 gave way to new forms of institutional mobilization: peasant leagues, trade unions and a mass of political parties, left and right, great and small. The result was not a decorous liberal politics, such as Francisco Madero had advocated in 1910; but neither was it a closed, personalist, autocratic system of the kind Díaz had maintained to the end. The political nation had expanded to become perhaps the largest in Latin America; a form of mass politics – restless, sometimes radical, often violent and corrupt – was gestating. Such a politics defies neat generalization. It embraced local *caciques* and regional *caudillos* (many, but not all, of them of new, revolutionary provenance);

radical agrarianism, as in Morelos, and conservative landlordism, as in Chiapas; revolutionary anti-clericalism and Catholic social action (not to mention Catholic conservative clericalism); an aggressive, ambitious praetorianism and an emergent civilian technocracy.

A major concern of the central government, especially during the presidency of Plutarco Elías Calles (1924–8), was the control and co-optation of these jostling, fissiparous factions. To this end, Calles warred with the Church, on the battlefield and in the schoolroom; he cut down and professionalized the bloated army; he cultivated organized labour, notably the official Confederación Regional Obrera Mexicana (CROM) led by Luis N. Morones; and he tolerated – sometimes tactically encouraged – peasant mobilization. Although state control over civil society thus increased – given the quasi-anarchy of 1910–20, it could hardly deteriorate – the state built by the leaders from Sonora (1920–34) was not an authoritarian leviathan. The rumbustious civil society of the 1920s defied such control. The Cristeros fought Calles to a bloody stalemate; local *caciques* and *caudillos* contested the expansion of state power; and the army rebelled twice. Regional elites, such as the powerful Yucateco planter class, resisted the reforms of self-styled Callistas. Organized workers and peasants often elected to ally with the state, but they usually did so conditionally and tactically, and there were many examples of popular dissidence.

This was a political panorama very different from that of the Porfiriato, with its personalist, centralized control, its narrow *camarilla* politics and outright denial of mass political participation. Under Díaz popular dissidence and protest occurred, but they were usually swiftly put down; they did not achieve institutional form and they certainly did not colonize the Porfirian state itself. What is more, by the 1920s the demands and rhetoric of popular movements – and of *políticos* who sought to capitalize on them – displayed a new radicalism, a new self-confidence. The Revolution had sapped old social certitudes and the deference which accompanied them. The CROM, the dominant official labour confederation, was not simply a cipher of the Callista state: it forced employers to reckon with labour as never before. Independent *sindicatos,* such as the railwaymen and oil-workers, stood further to the left, resisted the embrace of the CROM and relied on their own industrial muscle. Equally, the peasantry, which still constituted the bulk of the population, displayed a different temper compared with pre-revolutionary days. They, after all, had been the shock-troops of the revolution. It is true that the official agrarian reform came only slowly and gradually: by 1930, a mere 9 per cent of Mexico's land – by value – had been transferred to *ejidal* (communal) farms. But such figures are misleading and could arguably underestimate the scale of land distribution; certainly they fail to convey the changes in social relations and *mentalité* which the Revolution ushered in. Landlords retained the bulk of their land, but they did so on different terms, at greater cost. Their resident peons might – on the whole – remain docile; but neighbouring villagers, entitled to petition for land, presented a constant, enervating threat. Landlords thus had to contend with an increasingly organized peasantry and a state which, in its regional and national manifestations, was by no means as congenial or as reliable as its Porfirian predecessor. Some landlords had already gone bust during the upheaval of 1910–20; many now had to contend with heavier taxes, uncertain markets and higher labour costs. The landlord class yearned for the belle époque of the Porfiriato and lamented the rise of troublesome *agraristas* and the rabble-rousing parvenu politicians who abetted them. Some landlords prudently shifted their capital into urban industry and commerce, accelerating the demise of the traditional land-hungry, labour-intensive hacienda. The landlord class (which, of course, varied from region to region) was not eliminated by the armed revolution, but it was severely weakened – in some states, like Morelos, grievously so. Thus, well before the radical surgery of the 1930s, the hacienda system was displaying the symptoms of a progressive debilitating anaemia, and its prospective legatees were already gathering around the sickbed.

Meanwhile, although the extreme nationwide violence of 1910–20 had abated, local and regional violence remained endemic. The massive peasant mobilization engendered by the Cristero revolt of 1926–9 racked centre-west Mexico. In the localities, landlord fought with villager, *agrarista* with Cristero. *Caciques* battled for power; communities, for land or corporate independence. The Sonoran ship of state bobbed on the waves of an agitated society. At times – we may suggest with the benefit of hindsight – Mexico threatened to go the way of Colombia after 1949: that is, towards endemic, self-sustaining, factionalized conflict on the lines of the *Violencia*. That it did not was in some measure due to the statecraft of the victorious faction: of Venustiano Carranza, Alvaro Obregón and, above all, Calles, who never lost sight of the need for national integration and reconstruction. More importantly, Mexico's endemic violence was the outcome of – not the surrogate for – a genuine social revolution. It was not simply the aimless, stultifying violence of entrenched factions, nor the violence recurrently perpetrated by the

Porfirian old regime. And it was accompanied by a range of phenomena, important by-products of revolution: enhanced social and spatial mobility; migration, both national and international; the rise of new entrepreneurial groups and families; expanded educational programmes; *indigenismo* and 'revolutionary' art.

At the close of the 1920s, therefore, the Revolution had already changed Mexican society and politics in important ways. Yet the outcome of the Revolution remained unclear. Its course was still being run, and there were very different views as to where that course should lead. Classes, factions and regions contested with each other; the state's control of civil society grew, but even with Calles' sponsorship of the new official party, the Partido Nacional Revolucionario (PNR) in 1929, that control remained patchy and sometimes tenuous. The broad revolutionary ends of state-building and capitalist development were being advanced, but slowly and in the face of repeated challenges. And there were major disagreements – even among the ruling elite – as to the best means to be adopted.

For a time, during the favorable fiscal and economic conjuncture of 1924–6, the new Calles administration seemed imbued with a certain confidence. Banking reform and public works testified to the state's burgeoning powers. Seeking to implement the constitutional controls which had been placed upon the Church and the petroleum industry, Calles boldly challenged both the Catholics and the gringos. Soon, however, he faced the Cristiada uprising, conflict with the United States and a deteriorating economic situation. The Callista project began to falter; and the President shifted to the right. The assassination of former president (1920–4) and president-elect Alvaro Obregón in July 1928 added political crisis to economic recession, which, in Mexico, antedated the world slump of 1929. Calles now responded with ingenuity and statesmanship. He declined to prolong his own term of office, preferring to exercise power from the wings. Thus, three successive presidents – Emilio Portes Gil, Pascual Ortiz Rubio and Abelardo Rodríguez – governed during the following *sexenio,* with Calles, the *jefe máximo,* acting as the power behind the throne; hence the conventional title of this transitional period, the *maximato.*

The *maximato* was transitional in two senses. First, it witnessed a distinct shift from personalist to institutional rule. Having proclaimed the end of *caudillo* politics, Calles convened an assembly of a new official revolutionary party, the PNR, early in 1929. In the course of that hectic year an Obregonista military revolt was crushed; the Cristero rebellion was brought to a negotiated conclusion; and Ortiz Rubio, the lacklustre PNR candidate, overwhelmed the liberal, anti-reelectionist opposition of José Vasconcelos in the November presidential election. We can, then, date the unbroken hegemony of the official party back to 1929.

Nonetheless, the political institutionalization of the *maximato* was accompanied by growing social conflict and ideological polarization. Herein lay the genesis of Cardenismo, the political movement associated with President Lázaro Cárdenas (1934–40). Like all 'great men', Cárdenas was a product of his times: he lent his name to a period which – Mexican presidential supremacy notwithstanding – moulded him more than he moulded it. It is, however, valid to see the history of Mexico in the 1930s as the story of the rise and rule of Cardenismo: a radical, nationalist project which fundamentally affected Mexican society, and which represented the last, great reforming phase of the Mexican Revolution. The 1940s no less surely witnessed the decline of Cardenismo: the attenuation of its policies, the elimination of its political cadres, the rise of new leaders committed to an alternative project.

No historian questions the importance of Cardenismo, but many disagree as to its character. Traditionally, Cardenismo has been seen by both supporters and opponents of revolutionary orthodoxy as the culmination of the social revolution. Alternatively, Cardenismo has been depicted as a dramatic, radical interlude within the revolutionary process, for some a quasi-Bolshevist deviation. Recent scholarship has once again stressed continuities, though of a different kind: those of state-building, corporatism and capitalist development. Here, Cardenismo fits snugly within the revolution – the revolution, however, as a vehicle not of national redemption and popular radicalism but of statism and capital accumulation.

Any evaluation of Cardenismo must transcend the Cárdenas presidency. Its history is not the history of one man or even of one *sexenio*. Its origins derived from two broad socio-economic trends that intersected with two more specific political crises. In terms of ideology, personnel and class alignments, Cardenismo did indeed hark back to the Revolution of 1910. But it was also prompted by the experience of the depression and the social conflicts and ideological reassessments the depression provoked. If the first was an autochthonous influence, the second bears comparison with the wider Latin American experience. Cardenismo also sprang from successive political crises: that associated with the assassination of Obregón in 1928, which led to the formation of the PNR; and, more important, the battle for control of party and government which culminated in the struggle between Calles, the *jefe máximo,* and Cárdenas, the President, in 1935–6.

This struggle must be seen in terms of its immediate political background: the creation of the official party, the PNR, in 1929; the defeat of the rebellious Obregonista military in the same year; and the manipulation, humiliation and eventual ouster of the effete president Ortiz Rubio in 1932. This sequence of events demonstrated both the gradual solidification of the national regime and the pervasive personal power of Calles, whose control of the succeeding president, Abelardo Rodríguez (1932–4), was less blatant but no less real. Calles' achievement – the maintenance of personal power behind and despite the formal institutionalization of politics he had himself pioneered – was more precarious than many realized. It had earned him numerous and cordial political enemies; and it meant that any incoming president (especially the proud and obstinate Cárdenas, who had witnessed the destruction of Ortiz Rubio at close quarters) would be acutely aware of the dilemma he faced in his relations with the *jefe máximo:* to defer or to defy?

Enemies and critics of Calles and Callismo were the more numerous as a result of the impact of the Depression. Its effect in Mexico was cumulative rather than instantaneous, and it was less serious and protracted than in monoculture economies like those of Chile or Cuba. The country had already suffered falling export prices, deflation and economic contraction since 1926. Between 1929 and 1932 foreign trade fell by around two-thirds; the capacity to import halved; unemployment rose, swollen by the repatriation of some three hundred thousand migrants from the United States. Within the great 'commodity lottery' of the depression, however, Mexico was relatively fortunate. Gold, silver and petroleum, which together made up three-quarters of Mexico's exports, did not suffer so extreme a fall in demand and price as other raw materials; furthermore, employment in the export sector was small (a mere 3 per cent of the non-rural labour force generated two-thirds of Mexico's export earnings), hence the impact on wages, employment and living standards was less marked than in labour-intensive agrarian export economies like Brazil's. Meanwhile, Mexico's large subsistence agricultural sector recovered from the poor harvests of 1929–30 (the climate proved benignly counter-cyclical), while manufacturing industry – catering to domestic demand – was less severely affected than extractive industry and proved capable of benefiting from the country's incapacity to import. A process of import substitution industrialization was thus stimulated by the depression.

Between 1929 and 1932, therefore, Mexican gross domestic product (GDP) may have fallen some 16 per cent. The effect of this recession on the mass of the people is hard to evaluate. Real wages certainly fell (again, the trend may be discerned as early as 1927) and some historians identify a phase of 'frequent but fragmented mobilization' – characterized by strikes, land seizures and hunger marches – coinciding with the economic slump. It is clearer that popular militancy, following the familiar pattern, became more marked as the economy revived, which it did with some rapidity, thanks in part to the reflationary Keynesian policies pursued by Alberto Pani as Secretary of the Treasury (1932–3). Pani boosted the money supply (31 per cent in 1932, 15 per cent in 1933), and sacrificed the peso in the interests of growth. Exports, employment and real wages all revived. By 1934, GDP was back to 1929 levels, the peso was stabilized, and the economic outlook was encouraging. Cárdenas thus came to power as the effects of the depression receded, even though its political impact remained. For many, the *maximato* (1928–34) had meant hard times, and now the presidential succession offered a political *apertura* through which pent-up popular grievances might be channeled.

The political elite's response to the depression was mixed, producing polarization within the nascent PNR. For Calles and his supporters – the 'veterans' – recent events in no way invalidated the existing model of capitalist development based on private enterprise, exports, foreign investment, tight control of labour and a generally 'passive' state. Rather, the model should be refined, not least by curtailing anomalies like *ejidal* agriculture. In 1930 Calles pronounced the agrarian reform a failure: the *ejido* encouraged sloth; the future lay with private, capitalist farming. Efforts were made to bring the reform to a swift conclusion and *ejidal* grants became less frequent after the 1929 peak. Calles was also alarmed by labour agitation: capital needed security if it was to pull the country out of recession, and strikes should be severely discouraged. Calles continued to harp on the old anti-clerical theme, the leitmotiv of 1920s politics, and on the role of education as a means of revolutionary transformation. Minds, not means of production, were the appropriate objects of Sonoran social engineering. The anti-clerical issue was revived and the new Minister of Education, Narciso Bassols, gave fresh stimulus to the policy of laicization (1931). Three years later, in his celebrated Grito de Guadala-

jara, Calles called for a 'psychological' revolution, a 'new spiritual conquest' to win the hearts and minds of youth for the Revolution. Calles and
his 'veterans' clung to the norms and nostrums of the 1920s and, amid the
political and social flux of the early 1930s, seemed increasingly a force for
conservatism, admired by the right. Fascist examples were indeed uppermost in Calles' mind, and he cited Italy and Germany (as well as the Soviet
Union) as cases of successful political education.

Calles appreciated that a new generation, for which the heroics of 1910
were myth or history, and which was increasingly disillusioned with the
Sonoran-style revolution, was reaching political maturity. It rejected the
ideology of the 1920s – anti-clerical, economically liberal, socially
conservative – and advocated radical socio-economic change. It participated in the global shift from cosmopolitan laisser-faire to nationalist
dirigisme. If, like Calles, it drew on foreign models, it was the New Deal or
the economic planning of the Soviet Union (misconstrued, no doubt)
which carried weight. Even while Calles and the Callistas still ruled, new
men and ideas could not be ignored. After 1930 reformist and interventionist policies were tentatively introduced. A Federal Labour Law (1931)
offered concessions with regard to hours, holidays and collective bargaining, in return for closer state regulation of industrial relations. Seen as
dangerously radical by the right, it was castigated by the left as fascist,
while the more percipient saw that minimum wages could boost internal
demand to the advantage of industry. In 1934 an autonomous Agrarian
Department was established and a new Agrarian Code for the first time
allowed hacienda peons to petition for land grants. The Code also extended guarantees to private farms, this ambivalence reflecting profound
divisions within the PNR. From the 1933 party congress emerged a Six
Year Plan which, for all its lack of policy detail, embodied elements of the
new philosophy demanded by the rising generation of technocrats, *políticos*
and intellectuals. Implicitly critical of the Sonoran model, the plan
stressed the role of the interventionist state and the need for Mexican
resources to be developed by Mexicans; it promised labour minimum
wages and collective-bargaining rights; and it underlined the paramount
importance of the agrarian question, which required radical solutions
including the division of the great estates.

On the eve of the Cárdenas presidency, therefore, the ideological climate was fast changing. But the new ideas coexisted with the old political
cadres, who inhibited radical démarches in practice while tolerating rhetorical radicalism which left the substance of their power intact. Nor did

the Cárdenas candidacy appear to challenge their position. In choosing Lázaro Cárdenas as the official candidate for the 1934 election the PNR inclined left; but, so the old guard consoled themselves, thereby the better to control the left. Cárdenas had proved himself a radical – within orthodox, institutional terms – while governor of Michoacán (1928–32); but in most respects he was a model político whose career had taken him through the ranks of the revolutionary army (where he first served under Calles), through major commands in the 1920s, to the presidency of the party and the Ministry of Defence. A loyal lieutenant – though not an intimate crony – of Calles, he was a key general in the politico-military hierarchy. He had helped crush *cuartelazos* and had seen to the disarming of the *agraristas* in Veracruz in 1932. If he was not Calles' first choice, he was safe: in part, because he lacked a local base (his successor in Michoacán had dismantled what Cardenista machine there was) and in part because he seemed loyal – even dull and obtuse (a reputation reinforced by his austere, honest and puritanical personal life). Although the institutional left within the PNR backed his candidacy, his record did not inspire support among labour or the independent left; the Communists ran a rival candidate, declaring themselves to be 'with neither Calles nor Cárdenas; with the Cardenista masses'.

Once chosen as party candidate, however, Cárdenas began to display a wayward heterodoxy. His 1934 electoral campaign outdid all previous campaigns (save, perhaps, Madero's in 1909–10) in its scope and activity. Travelling some eighteen thousand miles, visiting towns, factories and villages, Cárdenas set a peripatetic style which was to be continued in office, taking him repeatedly into the provinces (over a year of the *sexenio* was spent outside Mexico City), sometimes to remote communities and 'well-nigh inaccessible places' which, to the consternation of the presidential entourage, had to be reached on horseback or even, it was said, by swimming ashore from the presidential ship.[1] The election campaign and the subsequent itineraries gave the president first-hand knowledge of conditions and, it is plausibly argued, served to radicalize him. Coupled with his reformist, especially *agrarista,* rhetoric, these trips raised popular expectations and demands; and they brought home to remote communities the realities of presidential power. No doubt Calles and the conservatives reasoned that this initial bravura would burn itself out; that once

---

[1] Rees, Mexico City, 19 December 1939, FO (Foreign Office) 371/24217, A359, Public Records Office, London.

Cárdenas was ensconced in the presidential palace, the old song would still apply and:

> 'el que vive en esta casa / es el señor presidente
> pero el señor que aquí manda / vive en la casa de enfrente'.[2]

After the rousing electoral campaign the election itself was a dull affair, quite unlike the battles of 1929 or 1940, and the new president, overwhelmingly elected, took power in December 1934 'in the greatest possible calm'.[3] Stability and continuity also seemed served by the composition of the new cabinet, which included Callistas in key positions, outweighing Cárdenas' partisans. Calles' hopes of a continued *maximato* were reflected in a disgruntled public opinion, which saw Cárdenas as another puppet, and in Cárdenas' own fears that he would go the way of Ortiz Rubio. As Cárdenas became acquainted with the apparatus of power, diehard Callistas like Tabasco's governor, Tomás Garrido Canabal – whose anti-clerical excesses now gathered pace – were at pains to embarrass and weaken the new executive.

Callista control was not, however, all it seemed; maybe it never had been. In the provinces, the Callismo of many local *caciques* was necessarily provisional. So long as a Callista allegiance shored up local power, they were for Calles, but a national crisis could induce a rash of defections. This happened in 1935–6. Nationally, where politics were more volatile, Callismo was on the wane. Callistas still controlled key ministries, army commands and labour unions, but a new generation was jostling at the door, nudging aside the 'veteran' generation which had been born in the 1880s and which had won power during the armed revolution. (It should, though, be noted that the newcomers' advancement also required tactical alliances with veterans - Saturnino Cedillo, Juan Andreu Almazán, Cándido Aguilar – who were strong respectively in San Luis, Nuevo León and Veracruz and who were ready to renege on Calles.) This new generation implied a change of character and political emphasis. Its members tended to be more urban and educated, and less conspicuously northern than their predecessors; and, like any rising generation, they fastened on the failings of their forebears (their sins of commission: anti-clericalism, militarism, graft; their sins of omission: agrarian and labour reform), stressing instead

---

[2] Loosely translated as 'the house you see before you / is the president's abode / but the man who calls the tune / lives in the house across the road'; Luis González, *Historia de la revolución mexicana, 1934–1940: Los días del presidente Cárdenas* (Mexico, 1981), p. 44.

[3] Farquhar, Mexico City, 6 December 1934, FO 371/18705, A706.

the new policies outlined in the Six Year Plan. All this they were free to do, being less bound by the prior commitments of middle age and established careers. The old revolutionaries had fulfilled their 'historic mission', Cárdenas later declared; it was time for a new generation to come forward, 'so that the masses can benefit from different political perspectives, produced by men who are fresh'.[4]

Intra-elite struggles were all the more significant because they coincided with demands and pressures evident in the country at large, which the incoming administration had at once to confront. Rival elites manipulated the masses, but the masses could, to an extent, manipulate the rival elites too. Thus, any president who bucked the control of the *jefe máximo*, and who sought mass support in opposition to Callista conservatism, had to move left towards the increasingly militant unions and restless peasantry. For now, as the economy revived, strikes proliferated. Official figures, which show a prodigious increase (13 strikes in 1933; 202 in 1934; 642 in 1935), are significant but misleading: they reflect a shift in government policy as more strikes were recognized as legal. Though figures of de facto strikes are hard to obtain, the impressionistic evidence is overwhelming as stoppages affecting the railways (long a focus of labour militancy), the mines and smelters, the oil camps and textile factories. The year 1934 witnessed an unprecedented spate of strikes in these and other, less crucial sectors. Sixty were pending in Mexico City alone as Cárdenas took power in December; and the early months of 1935 witnessed major strikes against the Aguila Oil Co., on the trams and railways, and on commercial haciendas, as well as attempted general strikes in Puebla and Veracruz. Cárdenas, it has been said, inherited a 'syndical explosion'.[5] Grievances were basically economic (some strikers sought to claw back what they had lost in the pay cuts of recent years), but they were aired with a new-found militancy. A high proportion of strikes was classified as sympathetic: the electricians of Tampico, striking in support of the workers' claim against the Huasteca Oil Co., received support as far afield as San Luis Potosí, Guanajuato, Yucatán, Michoacań, and Jalisco.

This state of affairs reflected both the radicalization of national politics and the growing sophistication of working-class organization. Since its heyday in the 1920s, the CROM had suffered a hemorrhage of support. In 1929 Fidel Velázquez and the *cinco lobitos* split away, taking with them

---

[4] González, *Los días del presidente Cárdenas*, p. 57.
[5] Alicia Hernández Chávez, *Historia de la revolución mexicana Periodo 1934–1940: La mecánica cardenista* (Mexico, 1979), p. 140.

thirty-seven unions, including the bulk of the capital's organized labour; they were followed by the electricians and railwaymen – traditionally well organized and militant – who formed the Cámara de Trabajo. In 1933 the CROM divided again as Vicente Lombardo Toledano's radical wing broke with the Morones leadership. The CROM – politically weakened since Obregón's assassination – found its numbers much reduced and its monopoly of labour representation within the PNR and on labour arbitration boards lost beyond recall. Meanwhile, the dissidents – Velásquez's Federación Sindical del Distrito Federal (FSTDF), the Lombardista CROM, and other anti-CROM groups, including the electricians – came together in October 1933 in the Confederación General de Obreros y Campesinos de México (CGOCM) which espoused a form of more militant, nationalist syndicalism. The Communists, too, driven into clandestinity after 1929, formed a new labour front, the Confederación Sindical Unitaria de México, (CSUM), which recruited with success among teachers and rural workers (notably in the Laguna and Michoacán), in the capital, and in the conservative bastion of Nuevo León. The diatribes of Calles and the CROM against communism were not entirely paranoid; by 1935 the party line was impelling the CSUM and the Partido Comunista Mexicano (PCM) towards a common front with progressive forces, which would include Lombardo's CGOCM and, eventually, Cárdenas' administration.

Meanwhile, the spectre of *agrarismo* revived. After the great upheaval of 1910–15, agrarian protest had ebbed or been channeled into the official and often manipulative reform, which peaked in 1929. The CROM had swollen its paper strength with *campesinos,* and *agraristas* had been recruited to fight the Cristeros. Old agrarian trouble spots, such as Zapata's Morelos, Cedillo's Valle del Maíz, had experienced the sedative of controlled reform; others – the Laguna, Michoacán – the concerted repression, physical and ideological, of governors, generals, landlords and not a few clerics. By the 1930s, however, the dammed streams of *agrarismo* again swelled and threatened to burst their banks. Already, some state governors had given a lead: Adalberto Tejeda in Veracruz, Portes Gil in Tamaulipas, Cárdenas himself in Michoacán. Although this was often for their own political advantage, it still required mobilization, which in turn offered experience and opportunity. But local mobilization was precarious and – in both Veracruz and Michoacán – it soon collapsed. The election and the new presidency, however, raised agrarian expectations – and revived landlords' fears. The anonymous struggle going on in much of the countryside now became vocal, noticeable and directly relevant to the struggle for national power. The early thirties witnessed sporadic land seizures, recurrent rural strikes and renewed agitation, local and national, for land distribution. The Rodríguez administration was pushed reluctantly towards reform; that of Cárdenas enthusiastically embraced it.

The radicalization of the regime was closely bound up with the struggle for power which dominated 1934–6 and in which Calles' conduct was no less important than that of Cárdenas. Known as a clerophobe, hostile to *agrarismo* and labour agitation, Calles proved unable to adjust to the changing climate of politics. When obsequious *políticos* came to pay court at Cuernavaca, Calles expounded on the industrial subversion jeopardizing the economy, and although reserving kind words for Cárdenas, he lambasted Lombardo and the radical labour leaders, denouncing such 'bastard interests' and hinting that a repeat of the presidential ouster of 1930 was on the cards. These 'patriotic declarations', as the Callista press called them, were promptly and widely published. As the confrontation built up, Calles drew attention to Cárdenas' weaknesses, denounced the 'Communist tendencies' he discerned at work and pointed to the wholesome example set by the fascist states of Europe.[6] Given both his character and the political pressures acting upon him, Cárdenas could not but respond; he would be no Ortiz Rubio. Anti-Callista leaders – radicals like Tejeda, opportunists like Almazán – were keen for the *jefe máximo* to get his come-uppance. So, too, were public opinion and organized labour. On the left, the threat of a renewed *maximato*, of repression, even a drift towards fascism, engendered an urge for solidarity, which complemented the official line now emanating from Moscow. Mexico in 1934–5 was fertile soil for popular frontism.

As Cárdenas and his allies moved to the attack, they faced a still formidable opponent. Calles might graciously proclaim his retirement from politics (as he did in June 1935, following the furor of the Cuernavaca interview) and he might roguishly confess his preference for golf over politics as he did in December, returning from the United States. Yet his continued ambition and antipathy to the new regime's course could not be disguised, and powerful groups were pushing him towards confrontation. Business feared the militancy of labour and looked to Calles for reassurance, while the urban middle class resented the rash of strikes disrupting city life. Plenty of Callista *políticos* survived in the Congress,

---

[6] John W. F. Dulles, *Yesterday in Mexico: A Chronicle of the Revolution, 1919–1936* (Austin, Tex., 1961), pp. 636–9; González, *Los días del presidente Cárdenas*, p. 78.

party, CROM and state governments, their political futures mortgaged to that of the *jefe máximo*. The army, too, had its restless elements, while the United States had misgivings about the drift of policy and hoped – maybe worked – for accommodation rather than confrontation between the two. Experienced *políticos*, like the Callista Juan de Dios Bojórquez, now Secretary of Gobernación, similarly advised compromise, arguing that confrontation could lead to civil war and shatter the precious political stability achieved by the Sonorans. As this scenario suggests, elements of bluff entered political calculations. Calles could destabilize the new administration, but at great risk to his life's work. Cárdenas, if he rejected compromise, would have to call on the support of the left, which implied new, radical commitments.

As it was, Cárdenas called Calles' bluff. He checked out the loyalty of key *políticos* and generals and, in the wake of the Cuernavaca interview, sacked several Callista cabinet ministers, promoting his own men including some anti-Callista veterans (in this crisis, the support of such figures as Cedillo, Almazán and Portes Gil was crucial). As the great electors were seen to shift, the Callista bloc in Congress crumbled. The PNR now experienced a gentle purge; obstreperous state governors, like the notorious Garrido Canabal of Tabasco, were ousted; and local *caciques* readily changed their colours. The army was a tougher proposition, but here Cárdenas was helped by his long years of service in and solicitude for the military, as well as by the loyalty of Manuel Avila Camacho who, as Subsecretary of War, had assiduously promoted the Cardenista cause. Army commands were shuffled, safe men were seeded throughout the country and the police were similarly renovated. This political house-cleaning, well under way by mid-1935, enabled Cárdenas to achieve a stalemate; next year, the President could go on the offensive, confident of victory. In the meantime, one consequence of this battle was the rapid turnover of generals and *políticos*. By 1938, of the 350 generals Cárdenas had inherited, 91 had been removed. Casualties now included old allies like Saturnino Cedillo, state boss of San Luis, and Joaquín Amaro, the chief architect of the professional post-revolutionary army. Even as it entered its radical, institutional phase, the Revolution retained a Darwinian character.

The struggle within the elite affected the temper of national politics to an unusual degree. Cárdenas, for example, set out to rein in the extreme anti-clericalism which had been the hallmark – and probably the most hated feature – of Callismo. After the brief truce between Church and state in 1929, official anti-clericalism revived in 1931; when Cárdenas took office, Garrido's anti-clerical excesses continued unabated, while some seven thousand Cristeros were still active in a hopeless cause in the north and west. Cárdenas played a careful hand. Though he had treated the Cristeros more decently than most army commanders, he was tarred with the anti-clerical brush. He still rehearsed the old theme of clerical oppression; and his educational policy, with its stress on socialist education, was calculated to inflame Catholic sensibilities. But political wisdom conspired with personal moderation in dictating a degree of détente. The anti-clerical issue conveniently distanced the new regime from the old; Calles continued to plant anti-clerical barbs, but Cárdenas was more circumspect; and Garrido, importing his red-shirt thugs from Tabasco to Mexico City (where he briefly served as Minister of Agriculture), incurred both Catholic protests and presidential displeasure, which led to his fall. Catholics, it was said, were heard crying, 'Viva Cárdenas' in the streets of the capital. Thereafter, the stricter anti-clerical regulations (limiting the number of priests and churches, and the dissemination of religious literature) were progressively relaxed, to the delight of the faithful and to the relief of the devout U.S. ambassador Josephus Daniels. Socialist education, the President was at pains to point out, combated fanaticism, not religion *per se*; he was even seen to hug a priest in public. While a few *enragés* continued to pen their anti-clerical tracts and vandalize churches, they were a dwindling minority. By the time they were written, Graham Greene's famous jeremiads were already out of date.

The counterpoint to this cessation of hostilities between Church and state was mounting class conflict. The President's cultivation of mass support and pugnacious rhetoric appeared to encourage this, but the Cárdenas government responded to demands as much as it initiated them. The break-up of the CROM heralded a more militant working-class politics, involving competitive recruitment by rival unions and *políticos*. The unions rallied behind Cárdenas, demonstrating against Calles' anti-labour declarations, and fighting street battles with Callista and conservative opponents (like the fascist Gold-shirts). And if the urban working class was in the forefront of such semi-official mobilization, the peasantry did not remain inert. Again, spontaneous movements meshed with the intra-elite struggle to help form a new radical coalition. Nationally, *agrarista* organizations, like the Confederación de Campesinos Mexicanos (CCM), had backed Cárdenas for the presidency. Locally, embattled *agraristas*, like those of Chiapas facing a hostile governor, now found they could look to a sympathetic 'centre', which could, in turn, mobilize *agraristas* against

Callismo. As the pace of agrarian reform quickened, revolutionary 'veterans' soon figured as victims: Calles and his family; the Riva Palacio brothers, bosses of Mexico state, who faced expropriation and expulsion from the official party; governors Villareal of Tamaulipas and Osornio of Querétaro, undermined by *agrarista* opposition; Manuel Pérez Treviño, *cacique* of Coahuila and Cárdenas' right-wing rival for the presidential candidacy in 1934, who suffered with others from the great Laguna *reparto* of 1936. Official *agrarismo* was already a proven weapon when it was deployed, perhaps most blatantly, in the ouster of Cedillo in 1938.

By then, the national schism had been long resolved. Cárdenas' deft combination of tactical alliance and popular mobilization had toppled the *maximato* and brought the era of Sonoran rule to an end. Following a six-month absence in the United States, Calles had returned – to a chorus of condemnation – late in 1935. As the polemics and street violence resumed, the administration took advantage of a terrorist attack on a Veracruz train to crack down. Police swooped on the leading Callistas: Morones, Luis León, and Calles himself, who was found in bed at his ranch near the capital, recovering from influenza and reading *Mein Kampf*. Still immersed in Hitler's rant – the story went – he was bundled onto a plane for the United States. By the spring of 1936, therefore, Cárdenas had rid himself of Calles' tutelage, affirmed his presidential power, and demonstrated an unexpected combination of steel and acumen. All this had been achieved without significant violence. Institutional conflict was pushing the *ultima ratio* of force into the background, at least at the upper level of politics, where 'sordid killing, as a way of enforcing the official will . . . well-nigh disappeared' during the *sexenio*.[7] In the process, popular demands and mobilization had necessarily been stimulated, the administration 'charting a course with an unknown destination', which would only become clear as the radical reforms of 1936–8 unfolded.[8]

Agrarian reform was the regime's key policy in 1936–7. It served both as a political weapon to cut down opponents and as an instrument to promote national integration and economic development. But its instrumentality – stressed by recent scholarship – should not be exaggerated. Reform was also a response to popular demands, often sustained in the face of official

---

[7] Frank L. Kluckhohn, *The Mexican Challenge* (New York, 1939), p. 3. At local level the decline of political violence was slower and more patchy.

[8] Nora Hamilton, *The Limits of State Autonomy: Post-revolutionary Mexico* (Princeton, 1982), pp. 144–5.

opposition in states where *agrarismo* was politically suspect: Sonora, Chiapas, Veracruz. None of this was new, but the agrarian reform was now carried farther and faster, in pursuit of grander national objectives. Where Calles had pronounced the reform finished, Cárdenas – backed by the vocal *agrarista* lobby – saw it as a means to transform rural society, and with it the nation. With his provincial Michoacano background, Cárdenas entertained a genuine sympathy for the *campesino,* a taste for the rustic life and a certain puritanical antipathy to the city (which made him the butt of cosmopolitan wits). Unlike his Sonoran predecessors, he conceived of the *ejido* not as a temporary way station on the road to agrarian capitalism nor as a mere political palliative, but as the key institution which would regenerate the countryside, liberate the *campesino* from exploitation and, given appropriate back-up, promote the development of the nation. In this respect, the new device of the collective *ejido,* which for the first time made feasible the wholesale expropriation of large capitalist farms, was to be crucial. Finally, the *ejido* would be the political training-ground of an educated, class-conscious peasantry. At the height of the *agrarista* campaign, no bounds were set to the *ejido's* potential: 'If the *ejido* is nurtured, as has been so far planned', Cárdenas declared, 'it is possible that the *ejidatarios* may be able to absorb all the land which today remains outside their jurisdiction'.[9]

Such a project might be termed Utopian, naive and populist, but it certainly cannot be seen as a strategy for industrial development, favouring capital accumulation. Nor, of course, was it seen in those terms at the time; on the contrary, it incurred the hostility of landlords and bourgeoisie alike.

This *agrarista* ascendancy – brief and anomalous within the history of the Revolution – must be seen within the contemporary context. The old project of export-led growth (with agriculture an important source of foreign exchange) had palpably failed, leaving once dynamic, commercial regions like Yucatán and the Laguna depressed and undercultivated. The social tensions first released by the Revolution, and subsequently compounded by the economic slump and the Calles–Cárdenas conflict, demanded resolution. A new generation, impressed with foreign, *dirigiste* examples and concerned to distance itself from its politically bankrupt predecessor, now sought power. This generation was more urban and less plebeian in origin than the revolutionary veterans, but it hailed from

[9] González, *Los días del presidente Cárdenas,* p. 114.

central rather than northern Mexico — hence, it showed greater sympathy to peasant interests — and it was convinced of the need for radical measures. Thus, while other Latin American regimes responded to the pressures of the 1930s through political reform, proletarian mobilization and economic nationalism, the Mexican government was unique in adding to these responses a sweeping agrarian reform — proof of the *agrarista* tradition which lay at the heart of the popular revolution and which now infused official thinking. *Agrarismo,* once equated by many with Bolshevism, was now politically respectable — even politically required. The jargon of *agrarismo* permeated political discourse; it inspired art, literature and cinema (not always to great aesthetic effect); it won both devotees and time-servers — not least within the burgeoning agrarian bureaucracy and among local *caciques.* Such sudden, superficial conversions did not, of course, augur well for the longevity or purity of the *agrarista* campaign.

Meanwhile, the achievements were impressive. By 1940, Cárdenas had distributed some 18 million hectares of land to some 800,000 recipients; *ejidos* now held 47 per cent of cultivated land, compared with 15 per cent in 1930; the *ejidal* population had more than doubled (from 668,000 to 1.6 million), and the landless population had fallen from 2.5 million to 1.9 million. As government revenue swelled with economic recovery, resources were channeled into agriculture. Compared with others, this administration 'worked miracles' in the provision of agricultural credit, which took a massive 9.5 per cent of total expenditures in 1936, the new National Bank of Ejidal Credit receiving the lion's share.[10] Additional resources went to irrigation, roads and rural electrification although these infrastructural investments probably benefited private agriculture more than the reform sector. Meanwhile, the *campesinos,* like the urban workers, were urged to organize, and their organizations — numerous, disparate, but growing in size and militancy — were increasingly linked to the state apparatus. In 1933, the CCM had backed the Cárdenas candidacy; two years later, Portes Gil assumed the task of forming a central peasant confederation, under the aegis of the PNR; thus, the nucleus of the future Confederación Nacional Campesina (CNC) (1938) was created.

The Cardenista agrarian reform, however, was not conducted in gradual, bureaucratic style, as reforms before and (usually) since have been.

---

[10] James W. Wilkie, *The Mexican Revolution: Federal Expenditure and Social Change Since 1910* (Berkeley, 1970), pp. 136–40.

Rather, it was launched with 'terrific fervour' and punctuated with dramatic presidential initiatives.[11] In regions of long-standing agrarian conflict the climate changed overnight; beleaguered *agraristas* suddenly found the weight of the 'centre' behind them. A classic case was the Laguna. A major centre of agrarian conflict and rebellion during the revolution, the region had known 'constant peasant agitation' during the 1920s, despite the hostile political climate.[12] Though the bulk of the Laguna workers were proletarians, wholly or partly employed on the cotton estates, they were by no means immune to the appeal of land reform, especially given high seasonal unemployment. Thus, classic 'proletarian' demands – for better pay and hours – coexisted with repeated petitions for land grants. The bad conditions (such that 'no self-respecting urang-outang would tolerate')[13] were exacerbated by the slump in cotton production in 1931–2. As the Communist Dionisio Encina took the lead organizing the peons, landlords responded with their habitual methods: violence, strike-breaking and company unions. They also thought it prudent to initiate a cosmetic reform, and two small land grants were made late in 1934, but the next year, labour troubles multiplied, and in May 1936 a general strike was called. As in the case of the later railway and oil expropriations, the government now stepped in to settle the dispute in radical fashion; labour disputes thus led to major restructuring of property relations. In October 1936, Cárdenas personally intervened and decreed a sweeping reform whereby three-quarters of the valuable irrigated land and a quarter of the non-irrigated were turned over to some thirty thousand *campesinos*, grouped in three hundred *ejidos*. Among the victims were several foreign companies and at least five revolutionary generals: 'The Revolution gave me the land', one observed philosophically, 'and the Revolution is taking it away'.[14]

The Laguna expropriation was unprecedented in scope and character. The 1936 expropriation law was invoked for the first time, and large commercial estates were handed over, in bulk, to their employees – to peons, not villagers. This novel expropriation demanded a novel approach. The regime opposed the fragmentation of large, productive units, and the beneficiaries followed official guidance in voting four to one in favour of collective *ejidos* rather than individual plots. Each collective would share

---

[11] R. H. K. Marett, *An Eye-witness of Mexico* (London, 1939), p. 142.

[12] Clarence Senior, *Land Reform and Democracy* (Gainesville, Fla., 1958), p. 52.

[13] Pegram, in Murray, Mexico City, 21 April 1936, FO 371/19792, A3895.

[14] González, *Los días del presidente Cárdenas*, p. 103.

land, machinery and credit and would be run by elected committees; the harvest would be shared among workers in proportion to their inputs of labour ('from each according to his labour': this was, at best, socialism; not, as critics alleged, communism). The Ejidal Bank would supply credit, technical advice and general supervision; the *ejido* itself would provide a range of educational, medical and recreational services. The performance of the Laguna collectives – key items of the Cardenista project – merits analysis, which must logically extend beyond 1940. Initially, landlords and businessmen confidently predicted failure: 'Give them two years and they'll crawl back on their hands and knees begging to be put back to work for their old employers'.[15] This did not happen. Cotton production (which was 70 per cent *ejidal* in 1940 compared with 1 per cent in 1930) rose immediately after expropriation, stabilized in the late 1930s, fell with the onset of the war and then boomed after 1941. Other crops, such as wheat, displayed an even more rapid increase. Collective farming thus proved capable of delivering the goods, in a material sense. Productivity, it is true, was reckoned to be lower on the collectives than on private farms; but the latter, representing the better irrigated land which landlords had conserved, enjoyed higher levels of capital investment. Indeed, here, as elsewhere in Mexico and Latin America, one major effect of the agrarian reform was to stimulate more efficient farming in the private sector. Meanwhile, with the active support of the Ejidal Bank, the standard of living of the Laguna *campesinos* rose, both absolutely and relatively, at least until 1939. Rural minimum wages, equal to the national average in 1934–5, were a third higher in 1939. There was, too, a perceptible increase in consumer spending, in literacy (hence a 'tremendous increase' in newspaper circulation) and in levels of health: on this, observers, both sympathetic and critical, agreed. And such quantifiable improvements were not all. With literacy and self-management the *campesinos* were thought to display new skills, responsibility and dignity. 'Before we lived like beasts. Now, at least, we are men and as we increase the crop, we earn more', one traveller was told.[16] Enhanced material and physical security went together: political unrest subsided and it was no longer de rigueur to carry pistols in the Laguna.

Nevertheless, the success of the experiment depended on favourable circumstances, on demand for cotton (which dipped in 1939–41 and

[15] Senior, *Land Reform and Democracy*, p. 97.
[16] Dutton, Torreón, 4 January 1939, FO 371/22780, A1015; Fernando Benítez, *Lázaro Cárdenas y la revolución mexicana, Vol. 3: El cardenismo* (Mexico, 1978), p. 66.

again in 1945–7); on adequate supplies of water (which even the new Lázaro Cárdenas dam, completed in 1946, could not guarantee); and, above all, on political back-up. Although Cárdenas was alert to the Laguna's problems, and the Ejidal Bank was generous, 1941 saw a new administration and an immediate change in priorities. The Ejidal Bank now imposed a more rigorous 'economic' policy, 'non-economic' projects were stringently cut back, credit was allocated more parsimoniously and the bank and its creditors had to resort to private sources, such as the Anderson Clayton Co. Parcellized *ejidos* now began to replace collectives, and within the collectives a payment system geared to incentives was introduced. The Central Union, the combative *ejidatarios'* association, found itself both losing control of economic resources (such as the machinery centres, which were transferred to the Ejidal Bank in 1942) and facing direct political competition as the government cut back its funds, alleged Communist influence (which had certainly grown during the early 1940s) and promoted the rival CNC. *Campesino* unity, which Cárdenas had tirelessly advocated and actively fostered, was shattered. The old leadership of the 1930s lost ground, and the Laguna became a site of factional squabbles. Thus was lost the best defence against bureaucratic sclerosis and corruption – which, already incipient in the thirties, reached grand proportions in the following decade.

In these new circumstances, the defects of the experiment were cruelly exposed. Like many Cardenista reforms, it was the result of hasty improvization; it needed time and solicitude to succeed. The original *reparto*, like others of the time, had been accomplished in six weeks, retaining the original 'crazy quilt' pattern of cultivation. It had left the landlords in control of the choice land and, above all, it had distributed the available land among too many recipients – including many non-resident migrants. These defects, of course, contained their virtues – speed, continuity of production, generosity of allocation – and, given will and time, might have been corrected. But after 1940 the will was lacking, and as population grew, the Laguna *ejidos* could no longer support the families crowded upon them. Here, as elsewhere, collectives underwent marked stratification between full *ejidatarios* and de facto proletarians. This the market encouraged and the government allowed. Egalitarian alternatives – involving the movement of population and drastic official intervention – were mooted; some argued that instead of 'distributing land among men' according to the classic *reparto* principle, the regime should 'distribute men among land', that is, 'place, in each unit of production, the number of men necessary to carry out that production without destroying the unity [of the enterprise]'.[17] Though entirely rational, such a solution would scarcely have been popular – as, indeed, the advocates' slogan 'haciendas without hacendados' tends to confirm. Cardenismo was not Stalinism. If reform was to be swift, ample and popular, defects were inevitable, which only later administrations could correct. This they chose not to do.

In terms of origins, scope, speed and outcome, the Laguna reform set precedents which were followed elsewhere: in the Mexicali Valley, where the Colorado Land Co. was expropriated in favour of *ejidadarios,* individual and collective, of smallholders and colonists; in Sonora, where the Yaqui and Mayo Indians won partial restitution of their lands; in Michoacán, where the properties of the Cusi family – progressive, socially conscious Italian entrepreneurs – were handed over, intact, to some two thousand *campesinos* grouped in nine *ejidos.* The south, too, long the preserve of the plantocracy, now experienced sweeping collectivist reform. Most dramatic – and least successful – was the great Yucatán reform, which closely followed the Laguna precedent. Because the *henequen* industry had declined steadily since the First World War boom, the opportunity cost of the reform was low and the demands of social justice all the more compelling. Moreover, reform offered a lever whereby the central government could insert itself into the traditionally intraverted politics of the southeast. Thus, in August 1937, the President arrived in the peninsula along with a boatload of generals, engineers, bureaucrats, journalists and curious foreigners. Eighty per cent of the *henequen* estates were at once given over to thirty-four thousand Maya peons, grouped in more than two hundred *ejidos:* it was the 'largest single episode of agrarian reform ever carried out in Mexico'. Yucatán would join the Laguna as a 'showpiece' of the collective *ejido.*[18] But the problems inherent in this precipitate reform were also soon apparent. Old productive networks were broken up, leaving some *ejidos* without access to the vital rasping machinery, many possessing *henequen* plants that were either too old or too young. Recipients, it was said, included many non-peasants, and the familiar complaints of graft and bureaucratic oppression were soon aired. But the chief problem – more acute in Yucatán than in the Laguna or even neighbouring Chiapas – was the state of the external market. Yucatán, which had cornered 88 per cent

---

[17] Iván Restrepo and Salomón Eckstein, *La agricultura colectiva en México: La experiencia de La Laguna* (Mexico, 1975), p. 35.

[18] See G. M. Joseph, *Revolution from Without: Yucatán, Mexico and the United States, 1880–1924* (Cambridge, 1982), pp. 288–9.

of world sisal trade in 1915, enjoyed only 39 per cent in 1933 and 17 per cent in 1949. From the outset, the socialization of a dependent, declining industry offered a poor showpiece for collectivization.

Even when demand remained buoyant – as it did for coffee – the internal obstacles to successful collectivization were formidable. The last major reform of the Cárdenas years was directed against the Chiapas planters, who had also beaten off peasant and proletarian challenges since the revolution and who, faced with the resurgent *agrarismo* of the thirties, redeployed their old weapons: pre-emptive division of properties, use of *prestanombres*, cosmetic reform, the co-option or elimination of opponents. Even as the reform got under way in 1939, the planters sought to use their processing and marketing facilities to bankrupt the new *ejidos*. Although an extension of the reform to include processing plants helped avert this threat, the change of administration in 1940 had an immediately unfavourable effect. The reform was halted; the large collectives were broken up; the Ejidal Bank and its allied *caciques* came to exercise a corrupt control over the reform sector: 'The Bank became a bureaucratic hacendado, the *ejidatario* a peon of the Bank'.[19] In the 1940 election the *ejidatarios* were reckoned to be the only local supporters of the official candidate. Thus, institutions developed during a phase of genuine peasant mobilization (*c.* 1930–40) soon began to serve as instruments to control – even to 'demobilize' – that same peasantry. When the post-war boom got under way (Chiapas' coffee production grew by two-thirds between 1945 and 1950) it was private agriculture – now basking in a newly benign climate – which benefited.

These spectacular, if problematic, reforms were paralleled by many lesser examples, some following the new, collective pattern (Atencingo, Zacatepec, El Mante), some cleaving to the old principle of individual usufruct. Over time, the first often gave way to the second, and by the 1940s, demands for the individual parcellization of communal lands had become strident and, in places, the source of violent conflict. Furthermore, even where the collective mode survived (as in the Laguna, Chiapas, Atencingo) it tended to produce internal stratification between full beneficiaries on the one hand and whole or semi-proletarians on the other. The result of brief, forced growth, the Cardenista collectives soon wilted in the uncongenial climate of the 1940s. Conventional *ejidos* survived more dog-

---

[19] Thomas Louis Benjamin, 'Passages to Leviathan: Chiapas and the Mexican State, 1891–1947', unpublished Ph.D. dissertation, Michigan State University, 1981, pp. 247–50.

gedly. They were often the fruits of long-standing agrarian struggles, and the Cardenista *dotación* was the culmination of years of petitioning, politicking and armed protest. Sometimes, as recent scholarship stresses, reform served the interests of opportunistic local elites or was imposed, alien and resented, from above; but even initially reluctant *ejidatarios* showed no desire to revert to peon status. Whatever the motives, the result was a massive transfer of resources that profoundly changed the socio-political map of Mexico. In the short term, it not only enhanced peasant living standards and peasant self-esteem but also shifted the political balance, conferring on peasant organizations a brief moment of conditional power. Conditional because the regime ensured that peasant mobilization was closely tied to the official party; brief because by the 1940s this tie, far from strengthening peasant organization and militancy, now served to bind the peasants to a political structure whose character was fast changing. The demise of the Cardenista project thus involved 'a demobilisation of class solidarity and independent struggle, rather than a disbanding of formal organizations'.[20] The Cardenista organizations lived on, but serving new ends.

Agrarian reform and peasant mobilization were inextricably bound up with the educational policy of the Cárdenas years, and with the commitment to 'socialist' education. Here, however, the administration displayed more continuity. The Sonorans, boosting the educational budget from 4 per cent to 14 per cent of government spending (1921–31), building six thousand rural schools and casting the *maestro* as the carrier of national, secular values, had shown more active commitment in this area than in that of agrarian reform. In education, therefore, the 'active state' was already in being. But with the 1930s came new initiatives which, antedating the Cárdenas presidency, were signalled by the appointment of Narciso Bassols to the Ministry of Education (1931). Young, high-powered and impatient, Bassols was the first Marxist to hold ministerial office. He rescued the ministry from a period of drift (1928–31) and began a phase of aggressive reform, seen by some as the state's response to the Cristiada. Under the guise of 'socialist' education, Bassols promoted the laicization of education through the enforcement of Article 3 of the Constitution: Catholic schools which failed to comply with lay principles were fined and sometimes closed, and Catholic hostility was compounded by Bassols' bold commitment to Mexico's first systematic sex-education programme.

[20] Ibid., p. 251.

These were not individual whims. Behind Bassols stood a phalanx of progressive groups, evidence of the changing ideological climate of the early 1930s. Teachers' associations now advocated a 'frankly collectivist' syllabus,[21] the largest (and not the most radical) teaching union calling for the socialization of primary and secondary education. Similar currents agitated the National University. More broadly, socialist realism became culturally fashionable. And the Six Year Plan included a deliberately ambiguous but significant commitment to education based on 'the socialist doctrine sustained by the Mexican Revolution'. More practically, the plan envisaged a 1 per cent annual increase in the educational budget, which would rise from 15 per cent to 20 per cent of total spending between 1934 and 1940. Finally, Congress bowed to the PNR's recommendation and approved a form of socialist state education that would combat prejudice and fanaticism (read 'clericalism') and instil a 'rational, exact concept of the Universe˘ and of social life'.[22] The commitment to 'socialist' education was therefore inherited by the Cárdenas administration.

'Socialism', of course, meant all things to all men. It had dignified the *étatiste* social Darwinism of Sonorans like Salvador Alvarado; the rampant anti-clericalism of Garrido; the pseudo-radicalism of the CROM. The educational debates of the 1930s revealed (one careful student has calculated) thirty-three different interpretations.[23] Even more than agrarian reform, education was susceptible to rhetorical camouflage. Callistas who by 1930 had turned their back on agrarian reform could still put on a show in the educational arena, the ideal place for displays of middle-aged radicalism. With fascist examples in mind, they hoped to capture the mind of youth and perhaps to divert attention from the miseries of recession. Thus, in his Grito de Guadalajara, Calles could sound like a young radical and an old Jesuit at the same time.

For many, 'socialism' was simply a new label for anti-clericalism, the old staple of Sonoran policy. 'Socialism' and 'rationalism' were used interchangeably. Others took the semantic shift seriously. Bassols stressed the practical role of education, which would stimulate a collectivist ethic; teachers would not only teach but would also 'modify systems of production, distribution and consumption', stimulating economic activity to the

---

[21] David L. Raby, *Educación y revolución social en México, 1921–1940* (Mexico, 1974), p. 39.

[22] Ibid., pp. 40–1.

[23] Victoria Lerner, *Historia de la revolución mexicana Periodo 1934–1940: La educación socialista* (Mexico, 1979), p. 83.

advantage of the poor.[24] Others went further, making education the central plank in a broad platform of radical reform. It would, the Secretary of Education asserted, combat capitalist and individualist values and inculcate, especially in youth, 'the revolutionary spirit, with a view to their fighting against the capitalist regime'.[25] Contemporary literature and rhetoric suggest that 'many teachers believed it was possible to overthrow capitalism solely by means of education'; a method which had the merit of being peaceful and exhortatory rather than violent.[26] Art and poetry – of a suitably committed kind – would work to the same end.

It was an old Mexican dream, entertained by nineteenth-century liberals and twentieth-century revolutionaries alike: education to change the social world. As the educational radicals of the 1930s harped on the familiar themes of Catholic obscurantism, and the liberating alliance of literacy, hygiene, temperance and productivity, so old, even positivistic, emphases reappeared in 'socialist' guise. Indeed, some socialist radicals boasted of their Comtean pedigree. 'Socialism' thus absorbed many of the developmental obsessions of an earlier generation (the most urgent necessity, an educational bureaucrat argued in 1932, was to 'teach the people to produce more'; Bassols' 'socialism' has been seen as a surrogate ideology of modernization).[27] It also embodied the traditional quest for cultural cohesion and national integration. Such continuities helped to explain the facile conversion to 'socialist' education even of those on the official right. But there were genuine radicals, too, who saw education as a means to subvert, not to sustain, old ways. The Soviet model again exerted influence. To old revolutionaries like Luis G. Monzón it offered the only alternative to a bankrupt capitalism. Soviet methods were imported – unsystematically and largely unsuccessfully – and Marxist texts circulated, even in the Colegio Militar. Although on the face of it, this mimetism accorded with the regime's stress on class consciousness and struggle, the Soviet example was more logically invoked by proponents of development and productivity. The Soviets were seen less as carriers of class war than successful exponents of large-scale modern industrialization: more Fordist than Ford. This appeal depended on the economic circumstances of the time and the radicalization they encouraged, both of which

[24] John A. Britton, *Educación y radicalismo en México. I: Los años de Bassols (1931–1934)* (Mexico, 1976), p. 52.
[25] Farquhar, Mexico City, 24 January 1935, FO 371/18705, A1338.
[26] Raby, *Educación y revolución social*, p. 60.
[27] Ibid., p. 38; Britton, *Los años de Bassols*, p. 17.

had direct impact on education. The resurgent left brandished its educational proposals; a more militant teaching profession (many though by no means all of them, on the left, and a significant minority of them Communist activists) pressed their political, pedagogical and syndical interests. Teachers had been hard hit by the recession and consequent government cuts, and Bassols, for all his radicalism, had been a parsimonious paymaster. Although teachers' numbers swelled through the 1930s, unemployment persisted; teachers' groups often figured in the forefront of local politics (they mounted the only serious challenge to Cedillo in his San Luis fief); and teachers' unions aligned with others out of material interest as well as ideological solidarity.

These factors assisted the official commitment to socialist education, which owed little to popular demand. Fifty thousand marched in the streets of Mexico City to applaud the new programme (October 1934) but the demonstration was one of the last flings of the CROM apparatus. Generally (but particularly in the countryside, for which the reform was especially destined) the popular response was tepid or downright hostile. If, as has been suggested, socialist education was a key device 'to recover the lost sympathy and support of the masses',[28] it was a failure; in fact, however, it was less opportunist populism than grand, somewhat naive social engineering. To a greater extent than the agrarian reform, socialist education came as a revolution from above, and often as an unwanted, blasphemous imposition.

Educational projects proliferated: the important programme for rural schools was greatly extended along with ancillary schemes – the Cultural Missions, the Escuela Normal Rural, the special army schools (a project close to the President's heart) and the 'Article 123' (company) schools. Special efforts were made – again, building on Sonoran precedent – to reach the Indian population, which, defined in terms of those who spoke an Indian language, constituted perhaps one-seventh of Mexico's total population. In this the President, the grandson of a Tarascan Indian, who had made much of the Indian question during his 1934 campaign, lent his personal energy and authority. But the emphases now shifted. *Indigenismo* figured less as an autonomous policy, geared to national integration, than as part of the broad Cardenista offensive against poverty, and inequality. Although the Department of Indian Affairs ran special educational and research programmes (in Chiapas, these were of grand

[28] Arturo Anguiano, *El estado y la política obrera del cardenismo* (Mexico, 1975), p. 45.

proportions), its budget was too small to bear the full burden of *indigenista* policy. Instead, the regime sought to subsume the Indian to the mass of workers and peasants, stressing class over ethnicity: 'the programme of the emancipation of the Indian is, in essence, that of the emancipation of the proleteriat of any country', although particular historical and cultural traits might have to be taken into account.[29] The aim – optimistic if not downright Utopian – was to achieve social and economic emancipation without destroying the fundamentals of Indian culture. The chief impact of government on the Indian was less through specifically *indigenista* programmes than through more general measures that affected Indians as *campesinos:* the rural education programme, and above all the agrarian reform in Yucatán, Chiapas and the Yaqui region (where Cárdenas was well remembered long after). *Indigenismo* itself achieved only limited, often transient, effects. One permanent consequence, however, was the growth of federal power as the Indian question became the preserve of national government, and could even be used to prise open hostile local *cacicazgos*. Even under Cárdenas it became clear that the federalization of the Indian question often meant the substitution of local *patrones* – landlord, *cacique*, priest, labour contractor – by new, bureaucratic bosses, agents of *indigenista* or agrarian programmes, some of them Indians themselves. After 1940 these trends accelerated. The Cardenista hope of achieving integration with equality and cultural survival was bound to fail; the Indians were integrated, but as proletarians and peasants, official clients and (occasionally) official *caciques*.

At the other end of the spectrum, higher education now faced the challenge of 'socialism', which exposed the position of the universities (especially the traditionally conservative, elitist and, since 1929, formally autonomous National University) as bastions of middle-class privilege. Like others in the educational field, this conflict antedated the Cárdenas presidency. In 1933 there had been a polemic between University factions, in which Lombardo Toledano – opposed by Antonio Caso – argued that the university align itself with the new, materialist ideology. Despite student fights and strikes, the liberals retained a precarious control; but, in response, the government cut the university's grant by half. Provincial universities, too, fearful of ideological browbeating, demanded similar autonomous status and at Guadalajara the state governor evicted the defiant university authorities from the premises by force. Many on the left

[29] González, *Los días del presidente Cárdenas*, p. 120.

applauded such humbling of the academic high-and-mighty (Cárdenas himself was said to entertain a healthy dislike of *hombres cultos,* which was often reciprocated).

Meanwhile, the political alarums of 1935 echoed through the halls of academe. In September 1935 a leftist faction of staff and students launched an internal coup and aligned the National University with official, 'socialist' policy. The government could now regularize its relations with the university, reaffirming its autonomy and restoring its subsidy; the university, in return, undertook some new, seemingly radical, initiatives (workers' legal services, 'relevant' social research) which probably represented outward conformity rather than genuine conversion. In addition, the regime created new higher education institutions more to its liking. Some of these, like the National Polytechnic Institute, survived and prospered; others, like the Workers' University, proved ephemeral.

Much more important were efforts and conflicts in the sphere of rural education. Here lay the chief innovation of the Cárdenas years; not in the formal content or organizational structure of education (for which there were ample precedents) but rather in the social and political context within which rural education was undertaken. The administration's commitment was unequivocal. Although the ambitious targets of the Six Year Plan could not be met, between 1935 and 1940 educational expenditure hovered at 12 per cent to 14 per cent of total government spending – levels unattained before or since. In real terms, this doubled Callista spending. Thus, the growth in rural schools, notable under Bassols, continued, and these schools were expected to do much more than inculcate basic literacy and numeracy. The teacher, Cárdenas explained, had a social, revolutionary role, 'the rural teacher is the guide of peasant and child, and must be concerned for the improvement of the village. The teacher must help the peasant in the struggle for land and the worker in his quest for the wages fixed by law'.[30] Nor was this empty rhetoric; just as teachers can impart literacy only where a demand for literacy exists, so teachers can engage in social engineering only when the appropriate parts lie to hand, as they did in Mexico in the 1930s. The *maestro rural* could fulfill his alotted function not because the peasants were an inert, malleable mass, but rather because he responded to actual – or, sometimes, realized latent – demands, especially in the field of agrarian reform. In the classic case of the Laguna collectives rural teachers played a key role in a set of

---

[30] Lerner, *La educación socialista,* pp. 114–5.

integrated reforms – educational, agrarian, technical, medical. In other cases, the *maestro* was pitched into existing local conflicts and his work necessarily became highly political, contentious and risky. *Maestros* were applauded (or condemned) for agrarian agitation in Chiapas, Michoacán, Jalisco, Colima, Sinaloa and elsewhere. They helped organize the Mixtec pueblos of Oaxaca, demanding 'Tierra y libertad' and a school in every village; in Mexico state they were held responsible for inciting land invasions; in Michoacán they were to be found explaining agrarian legislation, drawing up petitions and pursuing them through the relevant agencies. Critics alleged that hitherto tranquil Arcadias were disrupted by rabble-rousing socialist *maestros;* radicals, though putting the point differently, often liked to think the same. True, *maestros* sometimes stimulated a latent *agrarismo,* occasionally helping to foist *agrarismo* on reluctant communities; but there were also cases where teachers were won over to the agrarian cause by the *campesinos* themselves. Those who 'went to the people' like naive *Narodniki* got short shrift. Conversely, those who succeeded did so not by virtue of shrill agitation, but because they supplied practical help and, by their very presence, living proof of the regime's commitment. They engaged in agriculture, introducing new crops and methods; they placed their literate skills at the community's benefit; and above all, they facilitated that supra-communal organization which has often proved the key to success for peasant movements.

For this they paid a price. There is no surer proof of the real impact of the *maestro rural* than the record of violence which spans the 1930s. This must be seen in terms of the stark polarization which the socialist education programme provoked. If initially some on the left were critical, pointing out that it was illusory to attempt a transition to socialism by means of the superstructural machinery of education, most came round. This was especially the case with the Communists, who soon relinquished this position, which accorded well enough with the Comintern's 'third period', and espoused the programme as eagerly as they did popular frontism. At most a sixth of Mexico's teachers were Communists, but this activist minority was enough to feed the suspicions and assist the propaganda of critics. These were numerous, strenuous and often violent. The growing organization and militancy of the left were paralleled on the Catholic and conservative right – among the hierarchy, the Catholic student movement and lay associations such as the National Union of Parents. Socialist and sex education were their chief targets. Catholic students protested, struck and rioted. Parents voted with their children's feet and absenteeism grew, in both city and countryside; the private (Catholic) schools of San Luis, protected by Cedillo, bulged at the seams. To the extent that 'socialism' meant 'anti-clericalism', and anti-clerical excesses continued under 'socialist' auspices, this Catholic reaction was defensive, even legitimate. But in general the anti-clerical thrust was weakening, and Catholic opposition now focussed on wider issues, like medical services and mixed and sex education, which was denounced as a Communist plot, bringing pornography into the classroom. The Catholic press was appalled that country children – familiar enough with rutting pigs – should be shown pictures of flowers' sex organs.

Catholics also took a stand against *agrarismo* both in the abstract, by defending private property rights, and specifically, by aligning with landlords against *agraristas*. Priests were said to inveigh against the reform and incite mobs to violence (Contepec, Michoacán); they said mass for thugs who had murdered a teacher (Huiscolo, Zacatecas). Clerical influence was blamed for recurrent attacks in the Colotlán region of Jalisco, where in one year forty schools were allegedly put to the torch. Such allegations, of course, were sometimes exaggerated. Furthermore, like the teacher, the priest, was not a free agent. He figured in local conflicts not of his own making. Plenty of rural violence occurred without clerical intromission; it was 'spontaneous' or derived from the incitement of landlords, *caciques*, even state governors. The victims – *maestros* like López Huitrón of San Andrés Tuxtla, murdered in 1939, or the twenty-five *maestros* murdered in Michoacán up to 1943 – stand as a reminder that although the powers of the central government was expanding, they were still limited and liable to falter; they could not guarantee the safety, let alone the success, of their forward agents in hostile territory.

Thus, *maestros* often faced a lonely, dangerous task. Many were ill-prepared, certainly for the 'socialism' (sometimes even for the tuition) they were meant to impart; one critic sneered at them for being former 'motor lorry assistants, breadsellers off the streets, [and] overseers from coffee plantations'.[31] They were ill-paid and, save in cases of integrated reform like the Laguna, they usually lacked local, institutional allies. They often faced popular indifference and hostility. Their syndical organizations were plagued with conflict. With the expansion of education in the early 1930s, large-scale unionization became feasible; the pay-cuts of those years providing the teachers with plenty of grievances. They repeatedly

[31] Murray, Mexico City, 31 October 1935, FO 371/18707, A9693.

demanded better wages (which, in part, they got) and the federalization of education, which would concentrate decision-making with the sympathetic central government at the expense of capricious, state administrations. Although in this field, as in others, federalization accelerated through the decade, it was not wholly achieved. Meanwhile, the Ministry of Education pressed for the formation of a single teachers' union in the face of serious internal divisions (as many as 60 per cent of teachers were said to be Catholics and, despite purges and recruitment drives, the profession was never thoroughly radicalized). Since the left, too, was split between Communists and Lombardistas, unity proved chimerical and internal conflict endemic, to the detriment of morale.

There were permanent gains in the race between population growth and educational provision: literacy rates improved and the school's nationalist, integrating role was enhanced. As a system of socialist proselytization and social engineering, however, the project failed. No matter how congenial or appropriate in zones of *agrarismo* and class conflict, socialist education could not revolutionize capitalist society as a whole. Like many Cardenista reforms, it proved a fair-weather phenomenon, dependent on the briefly benign official climate. Even before Cárdenas left office, the climate began to change. By 1938 financial stringency and renewed opposition (now mobilized against the proposed 'regulation' of Article 3) forced a retreat. The *reglamento* ended as a compromise, the more radical textbooks were withdrawn, the Cultural Missions wound up; private education revived and ambitious educational projects, like those of the Laguna, were phased out. Cárdenas' last New Year message (January 1940) was decidedly conciliatory, as were the speeches of the official presidential candidate, Avila Camacho. And once the latter came to power, these changes gathered pace. 'Socialism' remained, for a time, the official line; but then – given the almost infinite flexibility of the term – it became synonymous with social conciliation and class equilibrium. The discourse of the Sonorans was revived. Educational socialism, like much of the Cardenista project, proved to be an interlude, not a millennium.

The battle against Calles in 1935 had involved a spate of strikes and a significant mobilization of the labour movement. Both continued after the fall of *jefe máximo*: 1935–6 were years when, unusually, Mexican strike action exceeded that in the United States; and 1937 (a year of growing inflation) saw a peak, at least in terms of official strikes. During this period, strikes affected all of Mexico's basic industries – mines, oil companies, railways, textile factories – as well as government services, and commercial agriculture. As in the Laguna, labour protest against foreign companies could presage government intervention and expropriation, in accordance with the doctrine boldly proclaimed in February 1936 by the President on his celebrated trip to the free-enterprise citadel of Monterrey, then hit by strikes and a lockout: if entrepreneurs could not avert industrial paralysis, the state would step in. Labour disputes thus afforded a lever against foreign enclaves. Meanwhile, union organization progressed, culminating in the formation of the new *central,* the Confederación de Trabajadores de México (CTM); and the militancy of labour contributed to the upward trend of real wages. This would not have happened without official backing, which, first evident during the political crisis of 1935, was maintained thereafter, albeit neither uniformly nor uncritically. The administration certainly adopted an interventionist approach to labour relations ('the government', Cárdenas declared at Monterrey, 'is arbiter and regulator of social problems'); arbitration became systematic (though not automatic) and generally favoured the workers' side. There were, however, cases of major strikes being opposed (notably that of the railwaymen in May 1936), and, especially after 1938, the government bent its efforts to pre-empt strikes, in the interests of the economy. Nonetheless, it would be wrong to seize upon these cases and assert the paramountcy of production and class conciliation, hence the continuity of a manipulative *política de masas,* as between Calles and Cárdenas. Intervention, arbitration and *política de masas* meant different things at different times. And under Cárdenas, especially before 1938, they involved active support for unions against business, encouragement as much as mollification of industrial conflict, and radical new departures in the field of workers' control. Again, therefore, Cardenista 'populism' differs in important respects from some of its presumed political kin.

The regime never lost sight of economic realities. It combated what it saw as irresponsible syndicalism (e.g., on the part of the oil-workers). It appreciated that raising wages would deepen the domestic market to the advantage of some sectors of industry. Yet this Keynesian approach cannot be seen as the raison d'être of Cardenista labour policy. A few enlightened businessmen and bankers shared this appreciation, but private enterprise – above all, the nucleus of the national bourgeoisie based at Monterrey – was overwhelmingly hostile and consistently critical of Cardenismo. Nor did this change after 1938. In 1940 business spokesmen were still denouncing the government's 'fantastic policy of unilateral betterment in compliance with promises made to the proletariat'. The new excess profits tax was an example of 'Hitlerite totalitarianism'.[32] If Cárdenas saved the Mexican bourgeoisie from revolution or collapse (which seems doubtful), the bourgeoisie did not show much gratitude.

It is also true that Cardenista labour policy, like Cardenista *agrarismo,* involved an educative or tutelary aspect; a facet of the *estado papá.* The President looked to the gradual maturation of the working class as an organized, unified, responsible entity; organized, so that its numbers would count; unified, so that its strength was not dissipated in fratricidal struggles; and responsible, so that it would not place excessive demands upon an underdeveloped economy recently emerged from recession (for, if it did, the workers themselves would be the main sufferers). From the 1934 election campaign to the 1940 farewell address, therefore, Cárdenas' constant theme was, like Lenin's, 'organize'. Organization required the active support of the state, but it would be wrong to see this as cynical manipulation, evidence of unbroken continuity from Calles and the CROM to Miguel Alemán and the *charrazos* of the 1940s. Nowadays labelled an ardent *étatiste,* Cárdenas in fact conceived of organized economic blocs and classes as the bases of politics. Thus, the surest guarantee of the continuation of his radical project was a powerful, organized working class. The formation of the CTM, the experiments in workers' control and socialist education, and the constant exhortation all served a distant, optimistic vision: a workers' democracy embodying the Cardenista virtues of hard work, egalitarianism, sobriety, responsibility and patriotism. This, roughly, was Cárdenas' long-term 'socialist' goal.

A degree of state tutelage was necessary because the creation of a united labour confederation was a formidable task, unlikely to occur spontaneously. The decline of the CROM had left labour militant but fragmented. But the coincidence of the campaign against Calles with rapid economic recovery afforded an opportunity for regrouping. The National Committee for the Defence of the Proletariat, marshalled by Lombardo against Calles and the CROM, served as nucleus for the emergent CTM, which, at its foundation in February 1936, rallied several key industrial unions prominent in the recent strikes (railwaymen, miners and metal-workers, electricians, printers and tram-workers) as well as the old anti-CROM confederations, Lombardo's CGOCM and the Communist CSUM. Claiming 3,594

[32] Rees, Mexico City, 3 January 1940, FO 371/24217, A547; Hamilton, *Limits of State Autonomy,* p. 192.

affiliates and 946,000 members, the CTM dwarfed both the rump anarcho-syndicalist Confederación General de Trabajadores (CGT) and the CROM, although the latter survived (some of its affiliates as company unions) and could still contest CTM hegemony, occasionally by violence, in certain regions and industries (e.g., textiles). Two additional barriers to CTM hegemony were erected by the state: the civil servants' union, the Federación de Sindicatos de Trabajadores en el Servicio del Estado (FSTSE), was prevented from affiliating (the whole question of civil servants' union rights was the subject of intense debate, culminating in special legislation); and, more important, the peasantry was preserved from the CTM embrace, notwithstanding the significant recruitment which had already taken place, chiefly in regions of commercial farming. Peasant organization remained the prerogative of the PNR. Though some residual CTM influence remained in the countryside, the leadership could not challenge the official ruling.

The ideology of the CTM mutated rapidly. During the struggle against Calles its constituent parts had stressed their independence from parties or factions. This commitment – radical, nationalist, autonomous – was carried over into the new CTM, which began life with lusty cries redolent of revolutionary syndicalism. But just as Calles had quietened the CROM, whose infantile noises had been similar, so Cárdenas won over the CTM. In this he was helped by the presence within the CTM of ex-CROMistas like Fidel Velázquez and the *cinco lobitos,* schooled in the Mexico City labour politics of the 1920s. As the CTM gained official subsidies, premises, and places on the arbitration boards, its leaders came to see the virtues of collaboration. For this, three reasons were adduced; the need to defeat the remnants of Callismo, to mount a united front against imperialism (soon to be identified with the Anglo-American oil companies), and to construct a popular front against fascism both international and, some said, domestic ('creole fascism', in Lombardo's phrase).

Indeed Lombardo Toledano now emerged as a pivotal figure in the politics of the period, second only to Cárdenas himself. Born of a once rich but ruined business family, Lombardo had progressed from the philosophical idealism of the Ateneo de la Juventud to Marxism (though he never joined the PCM). By the early 1930s he was a leading figure in the Mexico City intelligentsia – '*the* Mexican Marxist'[33] – active in labour and university politics; and with his secession from the CROM and creation of the

---

[33] Enrique Krauze, *Caudillos culturales en la revolución mexicana* (Mexico, 1976), p. 328.

CGOCM, he laid the foundation for his subsequent leadership of the CTM. Articulate, autocratic and narcissistic, Lombardo lacked an institutional base, regional or syndical. His power depended on the CTM bureaucracy, and government support (hence, in the 1940s, his ideological contortions to retain both). Having tactically backed Cárdenas in 1935, he now sought to cement the alliance, stressing first an old theme – the national responsibility of the working class – and second, a new one – the threat of fascism. In this context, Communist policy was crucial. Driven into clandestinity in 1929, the Communists remained active in local agrarian struggles as well as key unions, such as the railwaymen, printers and teachers. Although they had opposed Cárdenas' presidential candidacy, they were drawn into the anti-Calles coalition, and backed the CTM; and, providentially, 1935 saw a Comintern volte-face which legitimized – required – full collaboration with progressive, anti-fascist forces. The Mexican delegation returned from the Seventh Comintern Congress pledged to popular frontism, and thus to support for the PNR, the Six Year Plan and the Cárdenas government, now deemed to be a nationalist–reformist regime, quite different from its Callista predecessor. The CSUM therefore merged with the CTM and workers were enjoined to participate in elections. In 1937 the PCM and CTM joined in a common electoral front, in the following year the Communists supported the CTM's assumption of a central role in the new, official corporate party, the PRM. CTM collaboration had proceeded to the extent that CTMistas now held political office at local and national level, including thirty seats in the Chamber.

Within so large a conglomerate, divisions were inevitable. Lombardo and his lieutenants had no love for the Communists. Historical and ideological differences were compounded by their rival institutional bases: the Lombardistas depended on numerous small unions and federations, especially in the capital, and their lack of industrial muscle made collaboration with government attractive; the Communists' strength lay in the big industrial unions – railwaymen, printers, electricians – who leaned towards apolitical syndicalism. Each side battled for control of individual unions, such as the teachers', and of the CTM itself, where the Lombardistas relied on their superior numbers – even if they were paper numbers, dispersed among a legion of affiliates – to offset the Communists' industrial clout. In April 1937 a major schism opened up and the Communists, finding themselves frozen out of key jobs, quit the CTM, taking with them between a half and one-quarter of the membership, including such major unions as the railwaymen and electricians. Cardenista hopes of a united workers' front, apparently dashed, were resurrected as the Comintern came to the rescue. Earl Browder hurried down from the United States, Moscow exerted pressure, and after two months the errant Communists returned to the CTM fold. Some would not go to Canossa: the traditionally independent miners and railwaymen stayed out. But the bulk of the Communists complied, returning to a CTM yet further in fief to Lombardo; they agreed, furthermore, to support PNR candidates in internal party elections and to mute their already temperate criticism of the regime. It was the first of several 'necessary sacrifices' which the PCM, wedded to popular frontism and prodded by Moscow, was to make between 1935 and 1946, and which were to be instrumental in the assembly and maintenance of the Cardenista coalition.

Cárdenas' encouragement of working-class organization under the aegis of the state involved two key cases – railways and oil – in which wholly or partly foreign-owned enterprises, racked by labour disputes, were expropriated and fundamentally reorganized. In a manner analogous to the Laguna collectivization, therefore, labour disputes led to government intervention and experiments in new forms of economic organization (and, in the case of oil, to a major international wrangle). Interpretations differ: were these bold, generous and radical démarches, perhaps indicative of a residual syndicalism in official thinking? Or were they further examples of Realpolitik masked as radicalism, whereby a Machiavellian regime, flaunting its nationalism, off-loaded stricken industries upon workers who had then to subject themselves to the harsh discipline of the market?

The two industries were not directly comparable. While oil production showed a modest increase during the 1930s, the railways were in a parlous state: under-capitalised, over-manned, hit by road competition (which the government's vigorous road-building programme exacerbated) and heavily indebted to foreign bondholders. Indeed, there was a general recognition that some radical reorganization, possibly involving nationalization, was necessary. The traditionally militant railwaymen, organized in 1933 in the new Sindicato de Trabajadores Ferrocarrileros de la Républica (STFRM), strenuously resisted job losses, with which they were all too familiar (10,000 jobs had been shed in 1930–1). Strikes were called in 1935 and again in May 1936, when, to the disgust of the work force, the government refused to recognize a national strike in support of a new collective contract. The railwaymen's demands were met, but the basic economic problems remained. A year later the administration resolved to tackle than, Laguna-style, by means of a dramatic structural reform. In June

1937 the railways were nationalized, the bonded debt being consolidated with the national debt. After a year of direct government management and prolonged negotiations with the union, the enterprise was placed under workers' control on 1 May 1938. This was not a unique case. Other enterprises – mines, foundries, factories – had been turned over to the work force when labour disputes proved insurmountable, as Cárdenas had promised they would. But the railways, which still carried 95 per cent of Mexico's freight, were by far the most important instance.

The initial expropriation, exhibiting patriotism and political *machismo*, was welcomed even by right-wing middle-class groups more accustomed to carp at Cardenista policy. After all, José Yves Limantour, doyen of the Científicos, had begun the nationalization process thirty years before; and in creating a state-owned railway system, Mexico was doing nothing that had not already been done in several Latin American countries. Better this than socialist education or the confiscation of Mexican private assets via the agrarian reform. Even the foreign bondholders were glad to be relieved of a wasting asset. One group with misgivings was the railwaymen themselves. Although sympathetic to nationalization in the abstract (for some, like their militant leader, Juan Gutiérrez, it was a step towards a socialized economy), they feared that a sudden switch to federal employment would jeopardize their union rights and recently won contract. Thus, the union's decision to undertake the management of the railways was strongly influenced by the desire to preserve hard-won gains, even though, during the long union–government talks of 1937–8 it was made clear that the workers' control would operate under stringent financial conditions (including a government veto on increases in freight charges) and that a workers' administration would be no soft option.

Assuming control on these terms, the union grappled manfully with massive problems. It overhauled the administration, repaired old track and rolling stock, cut costs and met its initial financial obligations; even the U.S. commercial attaché was favourably impressed. However, starved of capital investment and operating at levels of demand and price the union could not influence, the railways soon ran into deficit. In addition, the new administration, in its anomalous role as both trade union and employer, faced major problems over pay differentials and work discipline. A series of crashes indicated the severity of these problems, which the administration frankly admitted; it also gave the conservative press (which, however sympathetic to nationalization, disliked workers' control) ample ammunition to snipe at this exercise in irresponsible, 'unpatriotic' behaviour. In his final year, Cárdenas devoted close attention to the railway question, and in accord with the prevailing trend towards 'moderation', both the payroll and the union's autonomy were cut back, leaving the railway administration 'a simple appendix of the state apparatus'.[34] These measures foreshadowed the complete termination of workers' control and imposition of full state management under Avila Camacho. The railway workers, now 'thoroughly disillusioned', figured prominently in the Almazanista opposition of 1940.[35]

Compared to the railways, the oil industry was wholly (98 per cent) foreign-owned; smaller (it employed some 14,000 to the railway's 47,000); and profitable. Since the peak production of 1921 (193 million barrels) output had declined to 33 million in 1932, reviving to 47 million in 1937, thanks partly to the big Poza Rica strike. By then, the industry had undergone a major intraversion since the halcyon days of export boom. It now played a major role in the domestic economy (nearly half the 1937 production was domestically consumed) and it logically figured in government development strategy. The Six Year Plan envisaged the creation of a state oil company, Petróleos Mexicanos (PEMEX) and the exploitation of new fields, which the oil companies – more interested in the Venezuelan bonanza – seemed reluctant to undertake. Such moderately *dirigiste* intentions were entirely consonant with post-revolutionary policy, which had generated successive confrontations – and compromises – between the government and the oil companies. The most recent, culminating in the Calles–Morrow accord of 1928, effectively preserved the companies' position; but by 1934, with the challenge of the Six Year Plan and PEMEX, this showed signs of breaking down. Cárdenas himself took a typically tough line. As military commander in the Huasteca (1925–8) he had gained first-hand experience of the oil industry, its enclave character, its penchant for bribery and *pistolerismo*. He had disdained the offer of a 'beautiful Packard sedan' made by a company as 'proof of its high esteem and respect'; ten years later he showed the same resistance to graft, which the oil companies and their friends, conditioned to Callista political mores, found incredible. The new President, they complained, was 'curiously naive in these matters and did not appreciate business convention as understood in Mexico'.[36]

[34] González, *Los días del presidente Cárdenas*, p. 289.
[35] Davidson, Mexico City, 15 August 1940, FO 371/24217, 3818.
[36] William Cameron Townsend, *Lázaro Cárdenas, Mexican Democrat* (Ann Arbor, Mich., 1952), pp. 43–51; Murray, Mexico CIty, 15 July 1935, FO 371/18707, A6865.

Cárdenas, therefore, had no love for the oil companies. He made clear his intention of making them conform to national needs as laid down in the Six Year Plan, and he later undertook to raise royalties. But none of this heralded expropriation. Foreign investment – in oil and other sectors – still figured in government plans; expropriation per se was not sought. The foreign-owned mines (collectively more important than the oil industry) were never considered ripe for nationalization despite some pressure from the miners' union; foreign investment in the electricity and other industries was actively encouraged. Thus, while Cardenista policy towards foreign investment in general was pragmatic, oil was something of a special case. It was a 'sacred symbol' of national identity and independence; conversely, the oil companies represented a perverse, parasitic imperialism. So the eventual expropriation was less a typical example of consistent economic nationalist policy than a spectacular exception, brought about by the intransigence of the companies (some of whom persisted in 'conceiving of Mexico as . . . a colonial government to which you simply dictated orders').[37] Furthermore, it transpired after years of mounting industrial conflict in which the struggle between capital and labour constituted a crucial autonomous factor, making for unforeseen results.

Like the railwaymen, the oil-workers had a reputation for independence and militancy, which was enhanced with the foundation of the unified Sindicato de Trabajadores Petroleros de la Républica Mexicana (STPRM) in August 1935. In the recurrent strikes of 1934–35 the companies faced demands they considered 'preposterous'; in November 1936 they were threatened with strike action if a new national collective contract was not conceded. The worker's claims – running to 240 clauses – included rapid Mexicanization of the work force, the replacement of 'confidential' (non-union) employees by union members in all but a handful of posts, greatly improved wages and social benefits, and a forty-hour week. According to the companies such demands threatened both managerial prerogatives and economic viability; they costed the claim at 500 per cent of the current wage bill (the union preferred 130 per cent, which it maintained was justified by profit levels; throughout the dispute, figures were traded like blows in a prize fight). The companies' counter-proposals served only to reveal the huge gulf between the parties, which lavish company propaganda (denouncing the greed of the oil-workers – the 'spoiled darlings' of

---

[37] The attitude of Sir Henry Deterding, of Royal Dutch Shell, described by the managing director of Shell's Mexican subsidiary, El Aguila, in Murray, Mexico City, 17 September 1935, FO 371/ 18708, 8586.

Mexican industry) did nothing to narrow. After protracted talks failed, the workers struck (May 1937), alleging an 'economic conflict' before the Federal Arbitration Board.[38] Arbitration was clearly favoured by both the CTM and the government, which exerted pressure to achieve a settlement and avert further economic disruption (the notion that the government incited the dispute in order to justify a planned expropriation is unconvincing). By August, a massive federal commission had reported, recommending a modest increase on the companies' offer, and similarly modifying the 'social' demands; but it also lambasted the companies for their monopolistic, enclave status, their record of political meddling, their devious bookkeeping, tax privileges and excessive profits. The initial labour dispute thus opened up much wider economic questions.

The companies remained intransigent, impugning the report's accuracy and refusing to increase their offer. When the Arbitration Board accepted 'almost in their entirety' the commission's recommendations, the companies took the case to the Supreme Court; and when the latter found against them, they again ignored the finding. Meanwhile, they propagandized and lobbied in both Mexico and the United States. They had, however, painted themselves into a corner. Confident of their essential economic role – and thus convinced that both union and government would have to compromise as in 1923 and 1928 – the companies held out to the last, rejecting a financially feasible settlement (the difference in cash terms was not so great), fearful of the impact this might have in other oil-producing nations. Initially a labour dispute, the conflict now centred on grand questions of prestige and principle. For by early 1938, the government also faced limited options: a humiliating surrender, a temporary take-over of the companies' properties, or outright expropriation. Although the third alternative was the final outcome, it was not the government's persistent aim, as the companies alleged in the face of official denials. Nationalization of this basic resource was, for some, a long-term objective, but there is no evidence that 1938 was pre-selected as the *annus mirabilis*. On the contrary, official pragmatism was evident in the grant of new oil leases in 1937, and in the discussions held, after expropriation, with a view to possible foreign investment in the oil industry. What is more, the cabinet was divided during the critical early weeks of 1938, and few doubted the risks – economic, financial, political – which expropria-

---

[38] See Joe C. Ashby, *Organized Labor and the Mexican Revolution Under Lázaro Cárdenas* (Chapel Hill, N.C., 1963), pp. 197–212.

tion would involve. But even these risks could not justify a humiliating climb-down. 'We would burn the oil-fields to the ground', as Cárdenas put it, 'rather than sacrifice our honour'.[39] When, at the last, it became clear that their bluff was being called, the companies sought a compromise. It was now too late. The government was resolved, the public mood exalted. On 18 March 1938, Cárdenas broadcast to the nation, rehearsing the sins of the companies and announcing their outright expropriation. Workers were already moving in to take physical control of the plants. As one declared, barring the entry of British employees to the Minatitlán refinery: 'The ambition of the foreigner is at an end'.[40]

In terms of political drama and presidential prestige, the oil expropriation was the high point of the Cárdenas years. The companies were 'stunned'.[41] From the bishops to the students of the National University, Mexicans rallied to the national cause, endorsing the president's patriotic stance and admiring, probably for the first time, his personal *machismo*. Massive demonstrations were held: perhaps a quarter of a million paraded through the streets of the capital carrying mock coffins inscribed with the names of the fallen giants: Standard, Huasteca, Aguila. Government bonds, issued to cover the future indemnity, were snapped up in a spirit of patriotic euphoria, and women of all classes stood in line to donate cash, jewellery, sewing machines, even wedding rings. Never before, or after, did the nation display such solidarity. Briefly, the popular frontism of the CTM seemed to encompass the entire population. In this congenial atmosphere, the PNR gathered for its third national assembly and turned itself into the new, corporately structured Partido de la Revolución Mexicana (PRM).

Popular euphoria could not pump oil, but it helped: the oil-workers – armchair experts collaborating with veteran drillers – displayed great energy and ingenuity in taking control of an under-capitalized industry. A twenty-eight-year-old found himself in charge of the Aguila Company's prize Poza Rica field. As the distant precedent of 1914 suggested, Mexicans were entirely capable of running the industry. The companies who, like the Laguna landlords, predicted that their departure would signal chaos, were proved wrong. However, the companies had more power than the landlords to realize their prediction. As the American and British governments made their official protests – the Americans circumspectly,

[39] Ibid., p. 180.
[40] Marett, *An Eye-witness of Mexico*, p. 227, where the author stresses the spontaneity of the comment.
[41] Ashby, *Organized Labor*, p. 237.

the British rudely – the companies at once went on the attack, shipping funds out of Mexico, boycotting Mexican sales, pressuring third parties to enforce the boycott and refusing to sell equipment. Coinciding with other economic troubles (inflation, growing government deficit, falling trade surplus), this action had serious consequences. Business confidence wavered, credit dried up and – with the United States temporarily suspending its purchases of Mexican silver – the peso slipped. For once, it was said, even the phlegmatic President had a sleepless night. Regarding the oil industry itself, export sales halved and production fell by about a third. The outbreak of the Second World War compounded the industry's problems and by the end of 1939 it was running a marked deficit. Again, therefore, a Cardenista economic reform was conducted under extreme conditions. Parallels with the railways became evident. The oil workers – traditionally syndicalist and confident of the industry's viability – favoured a workers' administration although they, too, were leery about assuming 'federal' status. However, the government would not relinquish control of so valuable an asset, and PEMEX was constituted on the basis of joint government–union collaboration. This gave local sections of the union considerable power and autonomy, while the government retained ultimate control of policy and finance. The union leaders – the meat in the sandwich – faced a recurrent dilemma: traitors to their country if they obstructed the running of this new national asset, they were traitors to their class if they scrupulously followed government direction. And there were ample grounds for conflict: over the size of the payroll, the organization of the union, promotion policy and managerial prerogatives. In this, the expropriation settled nothing and exacerbated a good deal. The industry was potentially healthy, but the boycott and war invalidated previously optimistic prognoses. Furthermore, as the labour force grew (from some 15,000 to 20,000) and wages rose, so the industry's wage bill shot up (around 89 per cent by late 1939). With PEMEX now in deficit, the government faced a difficult problem. Cárdenas and the CTM called for reorganization and cut-backs. Work discipline, it was said, had suffered; the workers had arrogated to themselves excessive rights, to the detriment of management; payrolls were too long, wages too high, perks too generous. Indeed, with expropriation, the fundamental status of the industry had changed, invalidating the 1937 award; like the railwaymen, the oil-workers were now enjoined to tighten their belts in the national and – the CTM stressed – their own class interest. For their part, the workers blamed inherited problems and poor management, and they argued for more, not less, workers' autonomy. By 1940, strikes were occurring and a rift opened between the union leadership and the more militant sections. As with the railways, Cárdenas spent much of his last year grappling with the reorganization of this newly nationalized enterprise (he was often to be found working in the old Aguila Co. offices). He backed the management's retrenchment plan, urging wage and job cuts, greater effort and discipline – in all of which he was faithfully seconded by the CTM. There was a modest improvement in PEMEX's trading position in 1940, but basic problems remained, raising hopes in some quarters that the properties might be returned to their previous owners. The next administration, which faced a serious strike threat in 1943, prevaricated; the showdown between government and union was postponed until the aftermath of the war.

With the oil expropriation, the diplomatic furor and economic repercussions it provoked, and the onset of the war, foreign relations for the first time assumed central importance for the regime, Hitherto its foreign policy – if conducted with unusual moral fervour and consistency – followed familiar 'revolutionary' traditions: respect for national sovereignty, non-intervention, self-determination. These principles were vigorously sustained in the League of Nations and in successive Pan-American conferences, where Mexican spokesmen advocated the peaceful settlement of international disputes and, in even-handed fashion, denounced aggression, be it American support for Somoza's coup; the Italian invasion of Abyssinia; Japanese imperialism in China; the Anschluss and Nazi attack on Poland; and – to the chagrin of the PCM – the Soviet campaign against Finland, which, given the geopolitical parallels, excited genuine condemnation. But it was the Spanish Civil War which drew greatest attention, official and popular. At the outset Cárdenas acceded to a Republican request for arms, and supplies continued – at a modest rate – as the war went on. Official condemnation of the Nationalists was seconded by the CTM; and, as the Republican cause failed, Mexico became a haven for Spanish refugees (ultimately some thirty thousand), who included a clutch of distinguished intellectuals as well as the Basque football team, both of whom left their mark on their host country.[42] Like the coincidental arrival in Mexico of Leon

---

[42] The Casa de Espanā, composed of refugee intellectuals, later metamorphosed into the illustrious Colegio de México; the Basque footballers helped convert Mexico from the 'rough, graceless style' originally imparted by the English to one more attuned to the 'Mexican personality': González, *Los días del presidente Cárdenas*, pp. 229–35, 276.

Trotsky (another example of Cárdenas' even-handedness), the war impinged directly on domestic politics. Given the obvious parallels, it was not surprising that Mexican opinion polarized, and that right-wing, Catholic and fascist groups endorsed Franco. Some, indeed, hoped wistfully for a Mexican Generalísimo; they condemned the government's support for atheistic communism, and they deplored the arrival in Mexico of its defeated agents. In 1938 jubilant posters proclaimed Cárdenas vanquished at Teruel. The Spanish Civil War thus helped define domestic alignments during the approach to the 1940 election.

Meanwhile, with the oil expropriation, Mexican relations with the United States – always the cardinal point of the diplomatic compass – deteriorated. Hitherto they had seemed to prosper, the Calles–Morrow détente being reinforced by the supposed (though easily exaggerated) congruence between Cardenismo and the New Deal, by Roosevelt's Good Neighbor Policy, and by the happy choice of Josephus Daniels as American ambassador. If during the Calles–Cárdenas struggle American sympathies, both private and official, had been divided, and American influence had been exerted in favour of compromise, it was clear that the United States would have no truck with rebellion – which decision, of course, favoured the legal incumbent. Daniels gave staunch support to the regime in defiance of State Department and American Catholic opinion, and his puritan progressivism and boyish enthusiasm endeared him to Cárdenas as much as they appalled European career diplomats. With the formulation of the Good Neighbor Policy, Mexican and American delegates to successive Pan-American conferences found themselves in unusual accord.

Domestic developments soon began to chill this warmer relationship. The expropriation of American landholdings elicited stern protests; and if the railway nationalization relieved more headaches than it caused, that of the oil industry was immediately contested. The U.S. government backed the companies' boycott, demanded an indemnity (if not the return of the properties), halted talks on a commercial treaty, and suspended silver purchases. Britain's response – less efficacious and more offensive – provoked a diplomatic rupture. American official opinion was divided, rival economic interests (silver miners, manufacturers whose Mexican investments had recently grown, and exporters who now looked to oust the Germans from Mexican markets) favouring conciliation over confrontation. Roosevelt, encouraged by Daniels, was prepared to ignore the hawkish advice of the oil companies, State Department and financial press. He conceded Mexico's right to expropriate, ruled out the use of force and tried to mitigate the damage done to U.S.–Mexican relations. Silver purchases were resumed and talks began on the question of companies' indemnity (the principle of which the Mexican government did not contest). The companies, however, busy lobbying in Europe and the United States, held out for the full restitution of their properties, which, as the boycott bit and the fortunes of Mexico's oil industry and economy sank, they anticipated with unswerving confidence.

Crucial in the formulation of U.S. policy were perceptions of the growing Axis threat. These – already evident in the cultivation of Pan-Americanism – now dominated policy, as the Cárdenas government had anticipated. Furthermore, the boycott obliged Mexico to conclude sales agreements with the Axis powers, which (although they were neither economically favourable nor ideologically congenial to Mexico, nor even strategically vital to the Axis) exacerbated U.S. fears of German political and economic penetration of Mexico. As the spectre of Nazi fifth columnism grew apace, the U.S. government decided that détente with Mexico was as essential as it had been twenty-five years before. Even the hawkish Secretary of State, Cordell Hull, grew impatient with the oil companies' intransigence and eager for a settlement, even at their expense. Intransigence appeared all the more anomalous as the Sinclair Co. broke ranks and reached a unilateral settlement (May 1940) and as other outstanding U.S.–Mexican differences were resolved under the pressure of war. In November 1941 a general settlement of American property losses arising from the Revolution was concluded; in return, the United States agreed to increase silver purchases, to furnish credit in support of the peso and to begin talks on a commercial treaty. Finally, in April 1942, the oil companies settled for compensation of $23.8 million – 4 per cent of their original claim.

The U.S.–Mexican détente covered wider issues and had a notable impact on domestic politics. As war approached, the United States tightened its relations with Latin America and, at successive Pan-American conferences (Panama, 1939; Havana, 1940), concluded agreements pledging hemispheric security and warning off belligerent powers from the New World. Brazil and Mexico emerged as the key actors in this hemispheric alignment and during 1940–1, as American fears of Japan were quickened and finally justified, Mexico came to figure as the political and strategic pivot of American policy in the continent. Cárdenas' staunch anti-fascism now afforded grounds for a rapprochement with the United States which his successor would further develop and which, in turn, favoured the moderation of the 'Cardenista project' in the years after 1938. The President was forthright in his condemnation of Nazi aggression and his support for the democracies; he promised full cooperation against any Axis attack on the American continent, and to underwrite this commitment, he authorized U.S.–Mexican military talks. German propaganda in Mexico was curbed. In addition, a reorganization of the armed services was begun; military expenditure, which had dropped to a post-revolutionary low of 15.8 per cent of total spending in 1939, jumped to 19.7 per cent in 1940. A new Military Service Law established a year's service for all eighteen-year-olds which, it was hoped, would not only prepare Mexicans 'to cooperate in the defence of our Continent' (Ezequiel Padilla's words), but also inculcate 'a disciplined education which would benefit the youth of our country in all works of life' (Avila Camacho's).[43] Symptomatic of the times, and of the new priority of national over class rhetoric, the rural school (now under threat) was supplanted by that other, classic instrument of national integration, the barracks.

Here, however, official action outran public opinion. The CTM, foghorn of the official left, blared its support for the democratic crusade against fascism, anticipating eventual Mexican participation, which would combine ideological correctness with economic advantage. But Lombardista belligerence cooled with the onset of the phony war, and the CTM line echoed that of the PCM: the war was an imperialist 'war for markets', and Mexico should remain strictly neutral. Yet later in 1940 the CTM veered back to its pro-war, anti-fascist line, which more comfortably fitted its domestic stance, and by early 1941 Lombardo was pledging 'all . . . material and moral help' against fascism and hoping for American participation.[44] With the Nazi attack on the Soviet Union, the PCM joined the patriotic democratic front, whose membership was completed thanks to Pearl Harbor. If the left, official and Communist, first leaned, then lurched, to the Allied side, the right naturally, dissented. Conservative and fascist groups, such as Acción Nacional and the Unión Nacional Sinarquista (UNS), inclined to the Axis cause and criticized military collaboration with the United States, at least at the outset. In this, they espoused a popular cause. For most Mexicans the war was an irrelevant conflict in remote lands, and very few people took a real interest in its progress. There was little incentive to fight, and the new

---

[43] Ibid., p. 308; *Hoy*, 20 September 1940.
[44] Blanca Torres Ramírez, *Historia de la revolución mexicana Periodo 1940–1952: México en la segunda guerra mundial* (Mexico, 1979), pp. 66–7.

military service raised memories of the hated *leva* (the pressgang of Porfirian and revolutionary times) and provoked violent protest when implemented after 1941. To the extent that popular sympathies were engaged in the war, they inclined towards Germany: an international victim in 1918, some felt; the 'antithesis of Communism' for others; or the fount of anti-Semitism, then on the rise in Mexico.[45] If Mexico was to be committed to the Allied cause, it would require active government encouragement.

As foreign affairs absorbed growing attention, domestic politics underwent important realignments. Amid the euphoria of the oil expropriation, a staple Cardenista objective was achieved: the restructuring of the official party (now the PRM) along corporate lines. This, Cárdenas hoped, would guarantee the continuation of reform and overcome the factionalism which still gnawed at the vitals of the PNR, especially as the left (Francisco Múgica, Gonzalo Vázquez Vela, Ernesto Soto Reyes) feuded with the 'centre', unofficially captained by that great fixer and survivor, Portes Gil. The latter, installed as party president for his help in the ouster of Calles (July 1935) set out to 'purify' the PNR (that is, to eliminate the vestiges of Callismo) and to broaden its appeal by extensive use of film, radio, newspapers and conferences. State committees were urged to recruit and involve working-class members; the PNR (not the CTM) undertook the national organization of the peasantry. Like some medieval inquisitor, however, Portes Gil fell foul of his own 'purification' campaign and was replaced by the radical Cardenista Barba González (August 1936). Meanwhile, the process of party organization and sectoral integration went on: with the union of the PNR, CTM, CCM and PCM in an electoral pact (February 1937); with the genesis, a year later, of the PRM, which grouped the military, the workers (CTM), the peasants (initially represented by the CCM, soon to be supplanted by the all-encompassing CNC), and the 'popular' sector, a catch-all of cooperatives, officials and unorganized (largely middle-class) elements, which would not achieve formal corporate existence until 1943. Again, this new mass organization combined a tutelary aspect with a long-term commitment to radical change: the party would undertake 'the preparation of the people for the creation of a workers' democracy and to achieve a socialist regime'.[46]

---

[45] González, *Los días del presidente Cárdenas*, p. 256; Davidson, Mexico City, 4 January 1940, FO 371/ 24217, A813.
[46] González, *Los días del presidente Cárdenas*, p. 183.

Ironically, the creation of the PRM, pledged to these grand objectives, came just when the regime began to falter; when, under the joint pressure of internal and external forces, the President chose to consolidate, to avoid further radical commitments and to prepare for a peaceful, democratic and politically congenial succession. The year 1938, which began in patriotic exaltation, ended with the radicals in retreat; if there was a Cardenista Thermidor – when the forward march of the revolution was halted and reversed – it came in 1938, not 1940. Of course, leftist critics see Cardenismo as a protracted Thermidor; while for loyal partisans there was no retreat, only tactical withdrawals. But the evidence such partisans cite as proof of sustained radicalism after 1938 (continued socialist education, excess profits tax, legislation covering the electricity industry) hardly compares with the sweeping reforms of earlier years. If there was not a full-scale retreat, there was certainly a 'notable change of direction',[47] which, however, was the product of circumstances rather than autonomous decision. There was a dramatic decline in presidential power in 1938–40, the result of new political pressures, the ending of the sexenio and Cárdenas' unprecedented refusal to cultivate a successor. Squabbles within the PRM, and the final electoral debacle of 1940, revealed this erosion of power, which in turn undermined the entire Cardenista coalition, with the CTM chiefly affected. As in the early 1930s, the ideological climate brusquely changed; by 1940, conservatives were confidently reporting that 'the great majority of thinking people . . . are now sick of socialism'; and that 'the trend over the next few years will be to the right'.[48]

Both the war and internal pressures encouraged caution and consolidation. Foremost among these pressures was the state of the economy. Cárdenas had inherited an economy recovering from the depression in which manufacturing industry and certain exports (e.g., silver) were buoyant. Even without radical changes in the tax structure, government income rose (almost twofold between 1932 and 1936). But so, too, did government expenditure: modestly in 1934–5, when the battle with Calles enjoyed priority, rapidly after 1936 as the major reforms got under way. Thus, expenditure rose, in real terms, from 265 million pesos (1934) to 406 million (1936), 504 million (1938), and 604 million (1940), with 'social' and 'economic' spending in the van. Exports, however, peaked in

[47] Ibid., p. 272; cf. Tzvi Medin, *Ideología y praxis política de Lázaro Cárdenas* (Mexico, 1972), pp. 204–6.
[48] Davidson, Mexico City, 4 January 1940, FO 371/24217, A813.

1937, and the government ran budget deficits that grew from 5.5 per cent of income in 1936 to 15.1 per cent in 1938. By then, deficit financing had become an effective tool whereby the government – possessed of political will and powers of monetary intervention that were alike unprecedented – countered the effects of renewed recession, transmitted from the United States in 1937–8. Compared with a decade before, Mexico was now better placed to withstand such external shocks.

But the inflationary pressures thus engendered were now aggravated by the rising costs of both imports and domestic foodstuffs. *Ejidal* inefficiency was readily, but usually wrongly, blamed for the cost of food. In fact, though agricultural production was hit by the upheaval of the agrarian reform and the landlords' consequent reluctance to invest, total output of maize in 1935–9 was about the same as it had been ten years before; given both a larger population and cultivated area, these (official) figures suggest a 17 per cent drop in per capita consumption and a 6 per cent fall in yields per hectare. It is very probable, however, that these figures (which are contradicted by alternative evidence) under-estimate both peasant production and peasant consumption, which were, of course, more decentralized and elusive than previous hacienda equivalents.[49] All the same, if the *ejidatarios* ate better, the supply of food to the cities was constricted and prices began to edge up. Like Germany, Mexico had had recent experience of hyper-inflation and opinion was sensitive to this ominous – albeit modest – rise in prices. Adverse comment was heard as early as 1936; even Lombardo admitted there were problems. Between 1934 and 1940 the retail price index rose 38 per cent, but between 1936 and 1938 – the years of dramatic social reform – it jumped 26 per cent, with foodstuffs worst affected. However, apocalyptic analyses positing a sustained fall in real wages through the depression, the inflationary later 1930s and the yet more inflationary 1940s, are unconvincing. Under Cárdenas the minimum wage outstripped inflation, and the aggregate purchasing power of wages rose, to the advantage of the domestic market. The chief beneficiaries were the *ejidatarios*, organized labour and workers – like the *gente decente* employed by General Motors – who took advantage of the changing occupational structure as agricultural jobs gave way to industrial. Rural proletarians (especially those employed by haciendas facing expropriation) did less

[49] E. Alanis Patiño and E. Vargas Torres, 'Observaciones sobre algunas estadísticas agrícolas', *Trimestre Económico* 12 (1945–6): 578–615.

well, while it was the urban middle class – Cárdenas' loudest critics – who were relatively worst hit by inflation.

Nevertheless, inflation jeopardized recent working-class gains, and thus working-class support for the regime. It also deterred private investment and encouraged capital flight. The government's response was contradictory – further evidence, perhaps, of the structural constraints under which Cardenismo operated. A serious attempt was made to regulate food prices: as the hostile reaction of private enterprise suggested, this was no mere palliative, and during the last quarter of 1938 the general price index fell modestly (4 per cent), the index for foodstuffs significantly (8 per cent). In pursuit of more fundamental solutions, the government raised tariffs (December 1937) and, following the 1938 devaluation, imposed new export taxes and cut capital projects (per capita spending on public works fell 38 per cent between 1937 and 1938; road-building was 'practically halted'). Workers in the public sector – such as railways and oil – had to tighten their belts. With government agricultural credit also falling, *ejidatarios* went short or, like the Laguneros, looked to private sources. And after the heady days of 1936–7, the pace of agrarian reform slowed – some said out of deference to U.S. interests. Certainly the government entertained hopes of an American loan and the U.S. government, although favouring a broader 'programme of economic assistance', was not entirely averse. But the oil expropriation ruled out any deal.[50]

As economic problems built up, the administration lost momentum and political opposition mounted. On the one hand, as the Cardenista coalition fissured, erstwhile supporters (chiefly working-class groups) defected; on the other, conservative and Catholic opponents, in retreat since the fall of Calles if not the defeat of the Cristiada, made a decisive recovery. Although official strike figures fell after 1937 (reflecting official reluctance to recognize strikes as legal), de facto industrial action grew, with major strikes by bakers, teachers, electricians, miners and sugar, textile and tram workers, as well as conflicts on the railways and in the oil industry. By 1940 there was ample evidence of working-class support for the opposition presidential candidate; even the May Day rally in Mexico City was marred by anti-government catcalls. Nor did business love the regime any the more for its new-found moderation. Price regulation and tax increases were denounced; attacks on militant unions became more vociferous, and as the export of capital weakened the economy, so the

[50] Hamilton, *Limits of State Autonomy*, p. 224.

political opposition reorganized and acquired fresh funding. Following the regime's example, business itself now displayed greater corporate organization, as did the conservative and fascist opposition. The year 1937 saw the birth of the Unión Nacional Sinarquista (UNS), a mass-based Catholic integralist movement (it rejected the concept of 'party'), which roundly rejected the Revolution, liberalism, socialism, class struggle and gringo materialism, offering instead the values of religion, family, private property, hierarchy and social solidarity. Possibly helped by business subsidies but primarily dependent on genuine peasant support, especially in the old Cristero regions of west–central Mexico, the Sinarquistas fast grew in numbers (they claimed half a million by 1943), mounting massive revivalist rallies in the towns of the Bajío. Initially sharing a similar ideology, but recruiting urban-middle-class support along more conventional lines, was Acción Nacional, founded in 1939 under the leadership of Manuel Gómez Morín, with the support of lay Catholics and the financial backing of the Monterrey bourgeoisie.

The 'secular' right was less numerous but just as strident.[51] As 1940 approached, a crop of lesser parties sprouted, some clinging to individual revolutionary veterans who, as they aged, grew rich, and fell to lamenting the revolution's decline, became converts to conservatism or downright fascism (Marcelo Caraveo, Ramón F. Iturbe, Cedillo, Joaquín Amaro). Some, like Jorge Prieto Laurens' Partido Social Demócrata (PSD), appealed to the anti-Cardenista middle class, tapping the liberal tradition which had manifested itself in 1929; but most, with their denunciations of communism, the influx of Spanish subversives and the pervasive influence of the Jews, revealed how a large slice of the middle class had been pushed to the far right by the political polarization of the 1930s. The shift was typified by José Vasconcelos, paragon of the anti-reelectionist opposition in 1929, who now flirted with fascism in the pages of *Timón*, arguing that the Axis would win the war, that Hitler constituted an Hegelian world-historical figure (it took one to know one) and that Mexico would have to conform to such historicist imperatives and submit to authoritarian rule. Both anti-communism and anti-Semitism were now the vogue. Bernardino Mena Brito regaled fellow-veterans with exposés of the role of 'universal Jewry', which the Sinarquistas also propagated. The Partido Revolucionario Anti-Comunista (PRAC), founded in 1938 by the old FNR boss and landlord Manuel Pérez Treviño, proclaimed in its title its

---

[51] Hugh G. Campbell, *La derecha radical en México, 1929–1949* (Mexico, 1976), p. 47 ff.

raison d'être. Many organizations like this were set up in 1938–40; feeble, fly-by-night, often dependent on the whims and ambition of an ageing *caudillo*. But they indicated a real shift in the ideological climate: a resurgence of the right (a shrinking liberal right, and a growing aggressive, authoritarian right, attuned to foreign examples); a new nostalgia for the Porfiriato, evident in the cinemas's loving evocation of *ranchero* life; and a corresponding loss of political initiative by the left.

The right increasingly aped the methods of the left. It formed mass organizations or even filched those of its opponents (as Almazán did with the dissident unions in 1940), thus participating in the gradual institutionalization and 'massification' of politics which characterized the 1930s. Even in regions of Sinarquista activity, the politics of the later thirties were relatively peaceful compared to the gross violence of the Cristiada; the more so since the Catholic hierarchy strove to contain the movement's radical fanatics. In this, the leader of Partido Acción Nacional (PAN) – the smart, articulate intellectual Gómez Morín, the right's answer to Lombardo – was more typical and effective than old veterans like Amaro, whose bloody record and autodidact mentality disqualified him from the presidential office he coveted. Amaro may have itched to take power by *cuartelazo*, but the times were no longer propitious; Almazán talked rebellion in 1940, but went no further. One veteran, however, clung to the old ways, unable to fathom the new. For years Saturnino Cedillo had run the state of San Luis Potosí more as a grand 'village patriarch' than the machine politician who was fast becoming the norm.[52] He counted on the support of his agrarian colonists (who had fought for him in the Revolution and Cristero wars), on the sympathy of the Catholics, whom he protected, and on a network of petty municipal *caciques*. Sponsor of an extensive personal and popular agrarian reform, Cedillo now tolerated landlords and businessmen who sought refuge from Cardenista radicalism. His relations with the labour movement were generally hostile, and as Minister of Agriculture (which Cárdenas had made him by way of reward after Cedillo had backed him against Calles) he dispensed patronage, promoted colonization over collectivization and earned the hatred of radicals like Múgica. In San Luis, where his power endured, independent unions gathered strength with the support of the CTM, which took advantage of strikes at the Atlas and Asarco plants to weaken Cedillo's local control, alleging that he was a friend of international fascism (doubtful) and an enemy of organized labour (true). In 1937, the PNR joined the game, contesting Cedillo's control of congressional elections, and his removal from the Ministry of Agriculture was contrived, according to the Cedillistas, by Múgica, Lombardo and the left. By late 1937, Cedillo was sulking in San Luis, thinking rebellious thoughts, encouraged by ambitious advisers and by the palpable growth of conservative discontent.

The conversion of general discontent into effective opposition was not easy, especially since Cedillo's ideas were primitive and his potential allies so disparate. Although he planned a political, possibly presidential, campaign, he also anticipated and probably relished the prospect of armed revolt. Overtures to prospective allies, however, were largely unsuccessful: Monterrey business chipped in some cash; the oil companies were approached but no deal was struck (the notion that Cedillo's revolt was not only financed but also concocted by the oil companies is ubiquitous but false); and prominent conservatives like General Almazán, who commanded in the north-east, or Román Yocupicio, the governor of Sonora, preferred political obstructionism to outright rebellion. Cedillo had to rely on his local resources, notably his fifteen thousand agrarian veterans. But here, too, he was thrown on to the defensive. Apprised of Cedillo's intentions, the government shuffled military commands, encouraged CTM recruitment in San Luis, and, most dramatically, launched a major agrarian reform which, by distributing up to a million hectares of Potosino land, created a rival *agrarista* clientele in Cedillo's back yard. The Cedillo *cacicazgo,* it was clear, was going the way of Garrido's in Tabasco or Saturnino Osornio's in Querétaro. But Cárdenas offered his old ally an honourable exit by appointing him military commander in Michoacán. Through the spring of 1938, Cedillo debated, planned and negotiated. Ultimately he refused to leave San Luis, and Cárdenas, fearful lest this defiance prove contagious, came to get him. In another dramatic presidential initiative, Cárdenas arrived in San Luis (May 1938), addressed the populace and called on Cedillo to retire. Instead, Cedillo rebelled; or, as a supporter put it, 'No se levantó, lo levantaron' ('He didn't rebel, they made him'). It was a half-hearted affair, more a display of pique than a serious *pronunciamiento*. Indeed, Cedillo humanely advised most of his followers to stay at home, preferring to take to the hills in the hope of some favourable *apertura* in 1940 (exactly as he had done in 1915). But by 1938 times had changed. There were only the merest echoes of sympathetic revolts in Jalisco, Puebla and Oaxaca; even in San Luis itself the

Cedillistas were split, and many rallied to Cárdenas, who remained in the state, travelling, propagandizing and revealing to all the hollowness of Cedillo's pretentions. Of those who rebelled, many were amnestied; a few, including Cedillo himself, were hunted down and killed. Cárdenas, it was said, genuinely mourned.

Thus ended the last old-style military rebellion of the long revolutionary cycle. Even as Cedillo was being pursued through the hills of San Luis, the conservative opposition was marshalling its forces to contest the 1940 election in peaceful fashion. The government, alarmed by Cedillo's revolt and the deteriotating economic situation, set out to conciliate. Reform was curtailed and rhetoric softened. On his extensive 1939 tour through Almazán's territory in the north, Cárdenas was at pains to deny the 'Communist' taint; at Saltillo he praised north-eastern business, which formed 'a constituent part of the respectable, vibrant forces of the country' (terms which contrasted with the reproof delivered three years earlier at Monterrey). By now, this denial of 'Communism' and stress on constitutional consensus was standard fare.[53] Congress was busy watering down the socialist education programme; the CTM showed its concern for national unity and social equilibrium by pressing unions to avoid strikes (many of which were pending), while denying that it sought the abolition of property or the dictatorship of the proletariat. That such denials were felt necessary was comment enough on conservative scare-mongering. But there was sound logic behind Cardenista conciliation – which the right, in a sense, accepted. Instead of compromising and deploying its ample resources within the capacious arena of official politics, the right preferred to remain outside, grouped in a congeries of conservative and fascist-like parties, hopeful that continued radicalism would lead to the complete collapse of Cardenismo, from which the right would benefit hugely and permanently. Accordingly, the right 'prefer[red] to see [an] acceleration of [the] radical programme, on the grounds that some reaction would be all the more likely under the new administration'.[54] Indeed, were Cárdenas to impose a radical successor espousing a radical programme, a conservative coup, possibly linking army and Sinarquistas, could not be ruled out. In such a climate – ignored by armchair critics – conciliation had a definite logic.

[53] Ariel José Contreras, *México 1940: industrialización y crisis política: Estado y sociedad civil en las elecciones presidenciales* (Mexico, 1977), pp. 154–5; Luis Medina, *Historia de la revolución mexicana Período 1940–1952: Del Cardenismo al Avilacamachismo* (Mexico, 1978), p. 93.

[54] Davidson, Mexico City, 9 January 1940, FO 371/24217, A1301.

It was in this climate that the succession question was broached in the summer of 1938. Rival groups inside and outside the PRM began to shape up, aware that the 1940 election would be politically crucial. Here was a chance to halt Cardenismo (already a decelerating vehicle) in its tracks; to install a moderate or downright conservative regime; or, alternatively, to continue the pace of reform. Cárdenas' own role, often debated, was important but not decisive. His personal power was waning and he was unable to stop speculation about the succession. Even had he wanted, he alone could not determine the outcome; neither could the PRM, which, if it constituted a leviathan, was a gross, uncoordinated beast lacking a directing brain commensurate with its corporate bulk. Internally divided, the party could not guarantee a smooth succession; indeed, the emergent heir-apparent, Avila Camacho, built his nomination campaign on parallel organizations outside the party, and the PRM endorsed his candidacy once it was a fait accompli. Conflict was aggravated by Cárdenas' political self-abnegation. He ruled out his own re-election and advocated a genuinely free choice within the PRM. The succession would be determined by the new mass organizations established during the 1930s. However bold or enlightened, this novel refusal of an outgoing president to pick – or at least to influence strongly – the succession constituted an invitation to factionalism, a self-mutilation of presidential power and a death sentence for the official left. The latter, backing Cárdenas' close friend and adviser Francisco Múgica, were disappointed not to receive presidential backing. Their centre-right rivals, supporting Secretary of Defence Avila Camacho, stole a march on them by defying presidential wishes and getting their campaign under way in 1938, after which the left was on the defensive. Furthermore, Avila Camacho had prepared the ground well. A member of a powerful political family from Puebla, a shrewd ally of Cárdenas through the 1930s, he was – despite his general's pips – more career politician than *caudillo*. Yet as Secretary of Defence (and Defence was still the presidential anteroom that Gobernación would later become), he had won the ample, if not overwhelming, support of the military – a crucial consideration in view of current fears of *cuartelazo*, which, for the last time, seriously affected the succession question. He also counted on the majority of the state governors, who had been lined up by his adroit campaign manager, the governor of Veracruz, Miguel Alemán; and with them came many local *caciques* who, in order to maintain their fiefs in the face of burgeoning federal power, converted an opportunistic Cardenismo into an opportunistic Avilacamachismo. Congress, especially the Senate, became a nest of Avilacamachistas.

The organized sectors of the party, discerning the drift of events and directed by their leaders, soon acquiesced. The CNC, left by Cárdenas to reach its own decision, fell prey to lesser manipulators and its overwhelming vote for Avila Camacho was at once denounced by the Mugiquistas as a travesty of peasant opinion, evidence that the CNC had rapidly become a mere 'ghost' controlled by unrepresentative bureaucrats.[55] More important, the CTM declared for Avila Camacho, its leaders arguing a now familiar case: that unity was vital, that in the face of fascist threats, internal and external, 1940 was a time for consolidation, not advance (the PCM, rebuffing Mugiquista overtures, took the same line). The CTM sublimated its radicalism by compiling a massive second Six Year Plan which envisaged further economic *dirigisme,* workers' participation in decision-making, and a form of 'functional' democracy. Reviled by the right as both communist and fascist, the plan displayed a naive faith in paper proposals and in the CTM's ability to realize them. As for the candidate whom the CTM thus hoped to bind, Avila Camacho obligingly endorsed the proposals. In the event, the final PRM programme was a predictably moderate document.

Favoured by circumstances, Avila Camacho could garner the support of both centre and left. He also pitched an appeal to the right: as candidate and president-elect he cultivated the 'moderate' rhetoric of the time, echoing Cárdenas' denials of Communism and contriving to align himself – PCM support for his candidacy notwithstanding – with the growing anti-communist sentiment. Workers were warned against militancy and advised to protect existing gains; small property-owners were reassured; Monterrey's businessmen were praised as those 'who dream and plan for the prosperity and greatness of Mexico'.[56] Regarding education (still a live issue), Avila Camacho was again for moderation and conciliation, rejecting doctrinaire theory and advocating respect for family, religion and national culture; it was noted that he was 'cordially welcomed' in the old Cristero heartland of Los Altos.[57] And in September 1940, now elected, he ringingly declared his faith: 'Yo soy creyente'. Throughout, his campaign rhetoric – stressing liberty, democracy (now often counterposed to Communism) and, above

---

[55] Contreras, *Mexico 1940,* pp. 55–6.
[56] Ibid., pp. 155–6.
[57] Rees, Mexico City, 9 February 1940, FO 371/24217, A1654.

all, *unity* – contrasted with the pugnacious radicalism of Cárdenas six years before. It soon became clear that Avila Camacho was 'little by little denying the continuity with Cardenismo expressed in the Six Year Plan'.[58] Nevertheless the CTM, the first begetter of that plan, continued to back the candidate and even to echo his soporific sophisms.

Avila Camacho thus offered all things to all men, cultivating CTMistas and Cristeros, workers and capitalists; here – rather than with Cárdenas six years before – was a thoroughly populist appeal in which differences of creed and class were submerged in a glutinous national unity. The circumstances of 1940 were propitious and the strategy worked, to an extent. The Monterrey bourgeoisie hedged their bets in the classic fashion of big business: responding positively to Avila Camacho's overtures, they established some purchase within the official party; but they also sponsored its main Catholic rival, the PAN (and perhaps the UNS too). The PAN agonized whether to back the opposition or – as their Monterrey paymasters probably preferred – to take the more prudent line of abstention. Finally, the party resolved to support the opposition 'in a very conditional form', which represented the worst of both worlds. The Sinarquista leaders, too, trimmed their sails, spurned Almazán and, coaxed by Alemán, urged abstention: further evidence of the growing division between them and their radical rank and file, which the ouster of the populist leader Salvador Abascal in 1941 accentuated.

The hesitations of the PAN and UNS further divided an already divided opposition. The plethora of conservative parties, groups and would-be candidates attested to the breadth of anti-government sentiment but also made co-operation against the common enemy difficult. The PAN and UNS – the intellectual brain and popular muscle of the Catholic right – were manipulated and marginalized. Other groups served the personalist interests of ageing *caudillos:* the Frente Constitucional Democrático Mexicano (FCDM) supported the perennially opportunist and optimistic General Rafael Sánchez Tapia; the PRAC, captained by old Callista bosses like Manuel Pérez Treviño, backed Amaro, but when Amaro's candidacy floundered (his image as a violent throwback to a former praetorian age did not help, and was enhanced by the belligerent manifesto with which he opened his campaign), the PRAC peevishly refused to switch its support to the main contender, Almazán.[59] For it was Almazán, backed by a

[58] Medina, *Del Cardenismo al Avilacamachismo,* pp. 92–3.
[59] Ibid., pp. 100–5; Virginia Prewett, *Reportage on Mexico* (New York, 1941), pp. 184–8.

diverse coalition, who now emerged as the chief challenge to Avila
Camacho. Politically experienced, rich (he was reckoned to be worth $5
million), and smarter than Amaro (he had dispayed 'an impressive talent
for hoax and skulduggery' during his chequered revolutionary career, and
was 'too astute' to back Cedillo in 1938), Almazán had extensive interests
in Nuevo León, where his military command was based and where he
enjoyed warm relations with the Monterrey group.[60] Denied the chance to
channel his known ambitions through the PRM – as Cárdenas hoped he
would – Almazán benefited from the errors and failings of his fellow-
oppositionists; and, denied the full support of organized right-wing
groups (PRAC, PAN, UNS), he depended more on large, diffuse
constituencies – Catholics, the middle class, smallholders – which were
only loosely integrated into the Almazanista party, the Partido Revolucionario de Unificación Nacional (PRUN). If it was organizationally
weak, Almazanismo was potentially powerful, especially because the candidate exercised a broader appeal than a spurred and booted *caudillo* like
Amaro. He mobilized middle-class liberals, who relived the constitutional
protest of 1929; peasants, disenchanted with the chicanery of the CNC
and the slow pace or downright corruption of the agrarian reform; junior
army officers (their commanders were sewn up by the PRM); and many
working-class groups – notably the big industrial unions, the railwaymen
and oil-workers, who resisted Lombardista log-rolling and Cardenista coercion, as well as the electricians and tram-workers, sections of the miners
and the fissiparous teachers' union, the *sindicatos* of Guadalajara and the
sugar-workers of Los Mochis, recent victims of a CTM-engineered internal
coup. The capacious bosom of Almazanismo embraced the Trotskyist
Partido Revolucionario Obrero Campesino (PROC), led by Diego Rivera,
whose illicit liaison with the right was the logical result of the PCM's
scarcely more licit liaison with the centre.

   Almazanismo thus constituted a cave of Adullam in which gathered all
groups hostile to official manipulation and critical of a regime which, in
their candidate's words, 'far from realizing the promises of the Revolution
has disorganized the economy . . . and brought dearth and poverty to the
people'.[61] Almazán pitched his appeal at this level: broad, eclectic, critical
of the regime but neither too specific nor too radical in its proposed
alternatives. He harped on economic failure, official corruption, and nox-

[60] John Womack, Jr., *Zapata and the Mexican Revolution* (New York, 1969), p. 80; Davidson, Mexico
   City, 9 January 1940, FO 371/24217, A1301.
[61] González, *Los días del presidente Cárdenas*, p. 227.

ious foreign influence, Nazi or Communist; he lambasted the left (notably Lombardo) and resorted to an alternative populism, concluding speeches with cries of 'Viva la Virgen de Guadalupe' and 'Mueran los Gachupines' (these Gachupines being no longer the spurred Spaniards of the colony but the hated Republican refugees). Given Avila Camacho's own stress on national values and repudiation of communism, there was a distinct sameness about the candidates' rhetoric; Luis González exaggerates only slightly when he observes that 'Almazán could have been the candidate of the PRM and Avila Camacho of the PRUN'.[62]

Cárdenas hoped for an open debate and free election. He would not impose a successor on party or country. 'If the people want Almazán', he told a colleague, 'they shall have him'.[63] This approach, if characteristic, was novel and risky. The President himself might remain unperturbed as Almazán's candidacy – backed by monster rallies unseen since the days of Madero – began to boom; he might even concede, on election night, that the opposition had won and Almazán should take office. But others, seeing their positions and policies jeopardized, displayed less democratic equanimity; *la révolution en danger* justified tough measures. The CTM swung into action, pressuring constituent unions, mounting demonstrations, physically attacking opposition headquarters, engineering internal coups in recalcitrant organizations (such as the CGT and STFRM). Almazanistas complained of sackings and beatings; trains and meetings were attacked, sometimes with fatal consequences. The administration also delayed legislation on female suffrage, rightly apprehensive that the women's vote would go to the opposition. A dirty campaign culminated in a dirty election (July 1940), conducted under electoral rules that were an invitation to rigging and violence. Throughout the country, PRM and PRUN factions fought for control of polling booths, the CTM seizing many by force. Ballot boxes were stolen, there were numerous injuries (and thirty fatalities in the capital alone) and widespread complaints of official abuse. At Monterrey, the capital of Almazán's fief, post-office workers and even prisoners were reported as being dragooned into voting for the official ticket, which triumphed by 53,000 votes to 13,000 (the PRUN claimed to have polled 63,000). All this was fresh evidence, the press commented, of the 'democratic incapacity' of the Mexican people. Cárdenas possibly agreed. But if force and fraud were evident, so, too, was

[62] Ibid., p. 259.
[63] According to Luis Montes de Oca, in a memorandum of E. D. Ruiz, 5 August 1940, FO 371/24217, A3818.

widespread participation. Towns like Tampico recorded the biggest turn-out ever.[64]

The final result gave Avila Camacho 2.26 million votes to Almazán's 129,000. The PRUN claimed 2.5 million, and its claim did not lack foundation. Certainly Almazán carried the major cities, where official control was more difficult and CTM mobilization proved indifferent; but, here as elsewhere in Latin America, the *voto cabreste* went the way of the government, thus justifying the Secretary of the Interior's reassuring election-night report to the President: 'The peasants' vote had . . . turned the election result in favour of Avila Camacho'.[65] Like Madero in 1910, Almazán retired to the United States, crying foul and breathing defiance. The parallel was noted: the Almazanista martyr General Zarzosa, killed when police attempted his arrest, was cast as the Aquiles Serdán of 1940. But the parallel did not hold. Times had changed and Almazán was too shrewd – also too 'fat, sick and rich' – to chance rebellion.[66] The United States (as Alemán confirmed on a flying visit) would lend Almazán no aid or comfort. And Almazán's coalition, though broad, was too disparate to present a concerted challenge (Lombardo feared the military, but Avila Camacho and his backers had done their homework, and Cárdenas took the precaution of switching key commands and paying a personal visit to the Almazanista north; by now, Lombardo's fears of militarism and fascism were acquiring a certain theatrical contrivance). In a *país organizado,* rebellion had to be a professional business, not a Quixotic re-run of 1910; the regime of the PRM was not the regime of Porfirio. Above all, political discontent did not imply revolutionary commitment. Many on the right (above all, the Monterrey group) were content to give the regime a bloody nose, which would encourage caution in future. Equally, the industrial unions, by flirting with Almazán, no more committed themselves to revolution than to conservative populism, although they did set themselves up as targets for the incoming administration, which did not forget their defection. Therefore, 1940 was less a revolution *manqué* than a requiem for Cardenismo: it revealed that hopes of a democratic succession were illusory; that electoral endorsement of the regime had to be manufactured; and that the Cardenista reforms, while creating certain loyal clien-

---

[64] González, *Los días del presidente Cárdenas,* pp. 302–3; *El Universal,* 8 July 1940; Rees, Mexico City, 12 July 1940, FO 371/24217, A2619, and enclosures.
[65] Medin *Ideología y praxis política,* p. 222.
[66] Rees, Mexico City, 9 February 1940, FO 371/24217, A1654.

teles (some loyal from conviction, some by virtue of co-option) had also raised up formidable opponents who now looked to take the offensive.

Avila Camacho ran for office stressing conciliation and national unity, rejecting communism and class struggle.[67] So he continued after 1940, the rhetoric reinforced by the electoral trauma of that year, by Mexico's growing involvement in the war and by the economic and military dependence on the United States which the war encouraged. Systematically, the *presidente caballero* appealed for unity in order to produce, export and industrialize, and to resist fascism, inflation and communism. In the process, much of the dissident right of 1940 was incorporated into official politics (if it did not colonize the PRM, it nevertheless conformed to the rules of the game, as did the PAN and even the UNS leaders). The left, meanwhile, found itself acting more as instrument – or victim – than as maker of policy. It was unable or unwilling to halt the rightward drift which the rhetoric of consensus concealed: the decline of agrarian reform, the curtailment of workers' control, renewed stress on private enterprise and commercial agriculture, the dynamic growth of private and foreign investment (and of profits at the expense of wages), accommodation with the Church and the elimination of socialist education.

Détente with the United States was already under way as Avila Camacho took power. The events of 1941–2, which brought both the United States and Mexico into the war, served to accelerate this trend. In the wake of Pearl Harbor, Mexico broke relations with the Axis powers, extended special rights to the U.S. Navy and from January 1942 collaborated in a Joint Defense Commission. Mexico's chief contribution was still economic: the 'battle for production', which the President announced in his 1942 New Year message. In May of that year, the sinking of Mexican ships by 'totalitarian' (German) submarines in the Gulf provoked protests and – when these were ignored – a statement to the effect that a 'state of war' existed between Mexico and the Axis. By this novel diplomatic concept (no formal declaration of war was issued) the government implied that the war was a defensive struggle, thrust upon a reluctant people. During 1942–3, defence of the continent, especially the west coast, dominated Mexican and U.S. strategic thinking. Military co-operation soon began, but it encountered serious obstacles, monuments to the two countries'

---

[67] Davidson, Mexico City, 9 January 1940, FO 371/24217, A1301; Prewett, *Reportage on Mexico*, pp. 191, 221.

historically antagonistic, unequal relationship. On the Mexican side, reorganization and modernization of the armed forces were high priorities. By 1942, national military service and civil defence were instituted, the Supreme Defence Council was set up, and Cárdenas – already commanding in the crucial Pacific zone – was appointed Minister of Defence (a measure which calmed nationalist fears that collaboration was proceeding too far and too fast, and which further reinforced both the left's commitment to the war and its confidence in the future). During the long, ticklish talks concerning American military rights in Mexico (radar surveillance, landing rights, naval patrols, chains of command) the ex-president proved an obdurate negotiator. Meanwhile, the United States furnished credit for the modernization of Mexico's armed forces, and during 1940–3 the secular decline in military expenditure was briefly reversed. The new *matériel* was put on display at the annual military parade of 16 September 1942 in the hope that it would quicken the enthusiasm of the pacific masses and, more certainly, of the recipient generals, whose itch to participate in the war grew as re-equipment proceeded and the fortunes of war changed. For by early 1943, with the battles of Stalingrad and (more important) Midway won, Mexico's defensive posture lost its rationale. The ancient fear of a Japanese descent on Baja California and points south was finally laid to rest. Now the question of active participation arose, encouraged by generals who wanted to fight, by politicians who sought a place at the post-war peace conference, and by the United States, which saw Mexican participation as advantageous in respect of the rest of Latin America and of future Mexican–American relations. Accordingly, an air force squadron – the famous no. 201 – was selected, trained and sent to the Pacific front, where it arrived for combat in spring 1945.

This was an important and – from the government's point of view a successful – symbolic action, although it involved only forty-eight air crews, all of them professionals. More delicate was the question of national conscription, which revealed the gulf between official commitment to the war and popular indifference or hostility. Conscripts were not sent to the front, but this fact did not overcome the old antipathy to military service, and the problem was compounded by the drafting into the U.S. Army of Mexican citizens resident north of the border. (Condoned by government agreement, this practice resulted in the recruitment of some 15,000 Mexicans, 10 per cent of whom became casualties.) Within Mexico military service provoked wide-spread, sometimes violent, protest in which the old anti-revolutionary Catholic cause blended with a new, genuine grievance

(Cárdenas' presence at the Ministry of Defence encouraged this amalgam). Telegraph lines were cut, army trucks and barracks attacked, to cries of 'death to Cárdenas and conscription', 'Long live Sinarquismo', and 'Long live the Virgin of Guadalupe'. In the biggest incident, three hundred rebels fought with the army in Puebla. But with official assurances that conscription would not involve service outside Mexico, the protest ebbed; the UNS – already weakened by internal divisions and by its moderate leaders' desire for accommodation with the regime – lost its last, best cause and went into decline. In 1944 it was dissolved by government decree.

Violent protest was only the most extreme example of the gap separating official and popular attitudes to the war. Mexico's participation had been endorsed by the left (CTM, PCM) and, surprisingly and significantly, by the Catholic hierarchy, by most of the right-wing press, by the PAN and other conservative groups. Something of the bipartisan nationalism of 1938 was thus revived. Yet, as polls revealed, even party members and officials were divided over the issue; the man in the street did not share the belligerence of the regime unless he happened to be a committed leftist. As *El Tiempo* neatly summarized the situation, it was the *pueblo no organizado* who were least belligerent and most suspicious.[68] Like previous official causes – anti-clericalism, socialist education – belligerence was foisted upon a skeptical population by an organized minority. Facing such indifference, and fearful of fifth-column activity (none of which occurred), the government resorted to controls and exhortation. Constitutional guarantees were lifted, internal surveillance was increased, the executive was voted extraordinary powers. In general, these were used with sufficient moderation to deflect criticism. The administration also mounted a sustained propaganda campaign designed to win popular support: the war thus offered superb terrain on which to build the national consensus to which the regime was committed and to which the United States now also contributed – not, as in 1938, as the external enemy but as a fellow-democracy and military ally. Leading *políticos* joined in a chorus of patriotic union which, beginning with the solemn burial of a victim of the torpedoed tanker *Potrero de Llano,* culminated in the military parade of 16 September 1943, which six ex-presidents reviewed, Cárdenas standing shoulder-to-shoulder with Calles and, of course, Avila Camacho. The press, curbed by law but positively encouraged by a generous supply of

[68] Torres, *México en la segunda guerra mundial*, pp. 85–6.

American newsprint, readily collaborated; street posters and cinemas (the latter also favoured by American largesse) rammed home the message of patriotism, hemispheric unity and productive effort. Propaganda, both Mexican and American, drenched the population, 'diluting anti-Americanism and encouraging, first, conformity and, second, adherence to the Allied cause'.[69] The penetration of American mores – the *pochismo* which Vasconcelos had been denouncing for years and which had grown with the roads, tourism and manufacturing of the 1930s – thus accelerated during the war, in Mexico as in Europe. Coke, Garbo, Palmolive and Protestantism seemed ubiquitous; and Protestants (by no means the most effective agents of *pochismo*) began to experience a fierce Catholic backlash.

The specific impact of wartime propaganda is hard to evaluate, easy to exaggerate. Economic collaboration was more effective in changing Mexican ways and linking the destinies of the two neighbours. The trends may be statistically summarized: in 1937–8 a third of Mexico's trade was with Europe; by 1946 this had fallen to 5 per cent (of imports) and 2 per cent (of exports); the United States took 90 per cent of Mexican exports in 1940 and supplied 90 per cent of imports in 1944. Furthermore, Mexico's foreign trade had grown appreciably: exports from 6.9 million pesos (1939–41 average, in 1960 pesos) to 9.1 million (1943–5), 1.1 million of which derived from migrants' remittances; imports grew from 6.1 million to 9.1 million. In the process, Mexico passed from a surplus on visible trade in 1942–3 to a modest deficit in 1944 (1.6 million pesos) and yet larger deficits in 1945 (2.8 million) and 1948 (5.4 million), as U.S. controls were relaxed and imports flooded in. With increased trade came increased U.S. investment, especially in manufacturing industry. The transition from an economy based on the export of primary goods to one in which a sizeable manufacturing industry catered to domestic demand was accelerated during the war, though with the consequence of enhanced U.S. participation and an unprecedented degree of external dependency (for once the term is entirely appropriate).

In the economic as in the military field Mexico and the United States did not establish their new intimacy easily. Industrialization was now the key item of government policy, stressed by Avila Camacho, Lombardo and others as a means to enlarge the social product, escape agrarian backwardness and mitigate – if not escape – the vicissitudes of the trade cycle. Cooperation with the United States offered a fast route to industrialization,

[69] Ibid., p. 104.

but if it was to confer the desired economic autonomy it had to be co-operation on the right terms. The oil companies' attempt to exploit war-time collaboration and PEMEX's shortage of funds in order to reclaim their properties was resisted, even if foreign credit was thereby restricted. For similar reasons, negotiations for a bilateral trade treaty (a long-term Mexican objective) proved arduous, although they were ultimately success-ful. Throughout, Mexico sought to protect domestic industry while nego-tiating a lowering of American tariffs, access to American credit, and easier import of capital goods and certain raw materials (which were in short supply and subject to American wartime controls). The United States sought short-term, guaranteed access to key Mexican resources (minerals, oil and, no less, manpower) and perhaps the long-term subordi-nation of the Mexican to the American economy. A general commercial treaty concluded in December 1942 was supplemented by a range of specific agreements, covering particular products; between 1943 and 1945 the Mexican–American Commission for Economic Cooperation channeled U.S. credit into a variety of projects: steel, paper, dams, hydro-electric power, cement and chemicals. Thus, the earlier plans for co-operation favoured by Cárdenas and Roosevelt but shelved in 1938 came to fruition. The provision of credit, however, was of limited duration and quantity: by 1946 the United States had switched its priorities to Europe, asserting the obligation of private institutions to meet Mexico's requirements.

The Second World War, like the First, produced a dramatic turn in the recurrent ebb and flow of Mexican migration to the United States (it also had the less publicized effect of sucking Guatemalan migrants into south-ern Mexico, with dire consequences for local labour). Some ten years after the hordes of migrants had headed south, they began to return north again – at the rate of some 6,000 a month by the summer of 1942. They came from all parts of Mexico and embraced a wide range of trades and backgrounds; most were young and unmarried, while many were em-ployed, skilled, even educationally qualified. Both governments sought to control this spontaneous tide: the American, in order to guarantee suffi-cient labour for a voracious war economy; the Mexican, to avert labour shortages at home and abuses of migrant workers abroad, which the half-hearted efforts of the American authorities could not prevent. By 1942, numbers and terms of employment had been fixed by governmental agree-ment. But so great was the demand for jobs that when official labour recruitment began in Mexico, the offices were besieged by supplicants; in March 1944, 3,000 gathered in Mexico City's national stadium for precious *bracero* permits. A year later the official programme covered more than 120,000 workers, whose remittances constituted 13 per cent of total foreign exchange earnings. Illegal migration, however, was running at the same rate (and with it recurrent deportations which, as American demand began to drop after 1944, were running at 7,000 a month). During 1945–6 the official quota was progressively cut; *braceros* joined the deportees being herded south, where they joined the jams at the border or lodged in the shanty-towns of San Diego and the Imperial Valley. For many, the return south proved temporary because a renewed boom soon pulled migrants – legal and illegal – back to the fields and factories of the north.

Economic collaboration with the United States thus favoured the Avilacamachista project of industrialization, social conciliation and national consensus. These, in turn, demanded of the President an ostensibly even-handed approach to the distribution of power and determination of policy. He had to appear a 'trimmer', not a 'partisan'.[70] The initial cabinet neatly balanced left and right; in Congress the leftist Chamber countered the conservative Senate. But just as Cárdenas was pushed left, so his successor was moved by circumstances as well as inclination to the right. In the field of education there was a retreat from 'socialism', first in spirit, then in name. Under the new minister Vejar Vázquez (1941–3), the so-called *escuela de amor* (which had nothing to do with Bassols' sex education) officially replaced the socialist schools; education now served to endorse the anodyne slogans of the regime, and Communist *maestros* were weeded out. Conservative and Catholic groups, delighted at this development, also welcomed the warmer relations between Church and State. The official right, in the shape of the President's brother Maximino, also controlled the Ministry of Communications, where the incumbent fostered his own presidential ambitions, feuded with Lombardo and other surviving radicals, and (it was said) entertained grand plans for the emasculation of the CTM. In the states, too, gubernatorial elections brought a shift to the right (by 1945 only eight out of thirty-one governors were reckoned to be Cardenistas); in Congress, debates, votes and appointments revealed a degree of conservative self-confidence and aggression not seen since the days of the *maximato*. The official right – with Maximino Avila Camacho and Abelardo Rodríguez prominent – now constructed a new rhetoric, allied to the administration's line in its concern for unity, democracy, and

[70] Bateman, Mexico City, 14 February 1944, FO 371/38312, AN798.

the defeat of fascism, but also stridently anti-communist, critical of the CTM and designed to depict Cardenismo in the same crude red colours. Indeed, there were underhanded attempts to embarrass Cárdenas himself, and a dirty press campaign against Lombardo. Leftists even found the hand of the executive working against them, in murky circumstances.[71] The left was not powerless in the face of such provocation: the President had to make them concessions (for example, throwing the Secretary of Economy to the CTM wolves in 1944); and it had its own repertoire of dirty tricks (such as, the contrived court-martial of Macías Valenzuela, the ex-governor of Sinaloa). The National University, too, was the scene of a careful political balancing act. The tight embrace of national consensus, to which most political actors had surrendered, made outright ideological pugilism difficult; the result was dirty in-fighting in which the executive, with its control of the courts, electoral machinery and parastatal agencies, was at a decisive advantage over mass organizations like the CTM. Both the climate, and the modus operandi of politics were changing.

Despite judicious displays of presidential balance, the trend – revealed in the 1943 congressional elections – was inexorably right. In part this responded to the President's desire to build up a solid, centre-right clientele in the legislature. A convenient instrument was at hand: the Confederación Nacional de Organizaciones Populares (CNOP), hitherto a diffuse conglomerate, which now became the institutional representative of the political class in particular, and of the middle class in general (a class increasingly flattered by official rhetoric). It also proved a loyal creature of the executive and a counter-weight to both the official left (chiefly the CTM) and also the middle-class opposition which had upset PRM calculations in 1940. This became clear in the 1943 congressional elections, conducted in indecent haste and with the usual fixing. The CNOP was rewarded with 56 of the 144 PRM candidacies (the CTM got 21) and the extra-official extremes were shut out. Both the Communists and Bassols' Liga de Acción Política were denied seats; the PCM stoically accepting another reverse in the name of wartime consensus, protested less shrilly than Bassols. The PAN, running a clutch of middle-class candidates on a conservative Christian Democratic ticket (leftist allegations of fascism were now rather dated), was also disappointed. Indeed, the radical right found its popular appeal fast diminishing as the regime itself 'moderated' and the provocations of Cardenismo faded into the past.

[71] Medina, *Del cardenismo al avilacamachismo*, pp. 163–72, 222–4.

The official left was also changing. In 1943 the Cardenista stalwart Graciano Sánchez quit the CNC leadership in favour of Gabriel Leyva Velázquez, son of a revolutionary martyr but a dedicated Avilacamachista and an implacable enemy of the Communists. The CTM bent its efforts to curb strikes and sustain economic production (arguably it made a virtue of necessity: the government had powers to compel if collaboration was not forthcoming); and in June 1942 it joined with rival confederations in the Pacto Obrero, which abjured strikes and provided for rapid arbitration of disputes. In return, the government established a social security law which became operative – albeit in controversial fashion – in 1943. By now Lombardo had, with typical rhetorical flourish, quit the leadership of the CTM and was busy rallying to the Allied cause the Confederación de Trabajadores de América Latina (CTAL), of which he had been president since its birth in 1938. His influence endured, though less tenaciously than he himself imagined; and it was used to bolster his successor, Velázquez, against the attacks of Communists and dissident Lombardistas. The official left thus tolerated the growing conservative presence in government, and the frequent barbs of the resurgent right. Unity remained the watchword.

With the left quiescent and his own authority enhanced, Avila Camacho could pursue his chosen policy of industrialization via co-operation with the United States. Industrialization had, of course, been espoused by Lucas Alamán in the aftermath of independence, by Porfirio Díaz, by Calles and by Cárdenas; it had prospered during the 1930s despite the Cárdenas reforms, but the unique circumstances of the war seemed unusually propitious. The social truce and Pacto Obrero conferred industrial tranquillity while the United States, newly complaisant of Mexico's needs, provided both a market and, with qualifications, a source of capital goods and investment. The promises made to private enterprise in 1940 were honoured in continued rhetorical reassurance and numerous practical measures: the elimination of the superprofit tax, the development of Nacional Financiera as a major source of industrial finance, the maintenance of a regressive fiscal system, generous tax concessions and tariff protection, and a Supreme Court hostile to labour. Between 1940 and 1946 manufacturing output grew 43 per cent in constant pesos (59 per cent if construction is included: Mexico City especially enjoyed a prodigious building boom). Food, textiles, chemicals and metals were prominent. Manufacturing investment quintupled, and manufacturers' profits were bountiful, reaching 18 per cent on invested capital in 1941–2. Thus, the ratio of returns to labour and capital shifted from 52:48 in 1939 to 39:61 in 1946. In 1942 the Monterrey group expressed their confidence that the President 'would not follow the labour policies of his predecessor'; which confidence (as arbitration rulings showed) was not misplaced.[72] The PAN's assumption of the role of a loyal Christian Democratic opposition was, then, not entirely due to its enthusiasm for the Allied cause.

As the *sexenio* drew to a close, however, the economic climate worsened. Inflation grew, generating enhanced profits (1945–6 were boom years for industry) but also bringing renewed labour unrest, which could less easily be checked by patriotic appeals. The surge of American imports helped the supply of capital goods, but it also jeopardized the balance of payments and Mexico's infant industries. The industrial bourgeoisie – now organized to an unprecedented degree - exhibited two responses. Representatives of the nascent manufacturing industry, grouped in the Confederación Nacional de la Industria de Transformación (CNIT), favoured corporate agreements with labour, mixed arbitration of labour disputes, a degree of state intervention in industrial relations, tariff protection, and close regulation of foreign investment. On this basis, the CNIT could reach agreement with the CTM (March 1945) reaffirming in vague terms the old wartime alliance for production. But the senior business organizations – especially the Confederación Patronal de la República Mexicana (COPARMEX), which the Monterrey group dominated – disapproved of the liaison with labour (they had never espoused the Pacto Obrero), favoured tougher laws to deter strikes, and adhered to traditional laisser-faire notions of the role of government. Business emerged from the war politically and economically stronger but also divided, and with a major sector advocating policies of red-blooded, free-enterprise conservatism.

Labour chafed at the restraints placed upon it – by government and unions alike – at a time of mounting inflation. By 1942 the U.S. connection, compounded by domestic factors (population growth, government deficits, and poor harvests in 1943–5) began to generate inflation rates far higher than those which had caused concern in the later 1930s. The cost-of-living index (1939=100) rose to 121 in 1942, 198 in 1944 and 265 in 1946, with food and basic consumer goods making the running (while the retail price index rose by two and two-thirds between 1940 and 1946, the price of maize tripled, that of beans and meat quadrupled). Moreover, official counter-measures were less effective than in 1938–9. Attempts to

[72] Ibid., p. 300.

limit the money supply, avert speculation and hoarding, and curtail price rises began in 1941; their failure was evident in the accelerating inflation and the booming black market, and in the further controls, measures and penalties which proliferated after Mexico's entry into the war. Private enterprise, earning handsome profits, cavilled at the constraints, whereas the CTM called for tougher measures to curb inflation and/or raise wages. The squeeze on wages was acute; between 1940 and 1946 prices almost tripled but the minimum wage barely doubled; 1946–7 marked a historic low for real wages, which had fallen by as much as a quarter in industry, and more in other sectors. Popular hardship contrasted with the conspicuous consumption of the wartime nouveaux riches – 'the privileged classes whose one idea was to get rich quick before the war ended'.[73] Both the president and his heir-apparent had to take note. By 1942–3 the reasoned complaints of the CTM were seconded by Sinarquistas, by demonstrators on the streets, and by increased – often wildcat – strikes. Buses were burned in Monterrey as a protest against fare increases; by 1944 food lines and hunger marches had become familiar. Even the new social security system, introduced to appease labour, had the opposite effect, the deduction of contributions from slim wage-packets generating a series of riots, the most serious in Mexico City in July 1944. Strikes, both official and unofficial, increased during 1943–4, as did pre-emptive wage rises designed to buy off the industrially powerful. Members of the big unions were therefore better protected against inflation than most rural or white-collar workers, the hardships of whom were compounded by wartime shortages (e.g., oil and rubber) and cuts in urban services (transport, electricity). Some – to the detriment of public ethics – sought compensation in the *mordida*, the back-hander.[74]

Labour, too, began to question the purpose of the 'social truce', which now seemed chiefly a means of boosting profits at the expense of wages. In facing renewed militancy, the government found an ally in Lombardo, whose commitment to consensus had evolved from a tactic into an article of faith. Because the much flourished fascist menace was fading, Lombardo now argued for a national alliance of workers and bourgeoisie against foreign imperialism. The CTM–CNIT agreement of March 1945 seemed to foreshadow this, but the CNIT did not speak for all Mexican business. The Monterrey group had no time for pacts and no taste for

[73] Cheetham, Mexico City, 10 January 1944, FO 371/38312, AN293.
[74] Ibid.; Lesley Byrd Simpson, *Many Mexicos*, 4th ed. (Berkeley, 1971), pp. 342–4.

labour militancy. It crossed swords with the CTM in a major dispute at the Cristalería Monterrey (summer 1946), during which the city was briefly paralysed and a general strike narrowly averted. Presidential intervention calmed but could not settle a conflict that remained unresolved as Avila Camacho left office, bequeathing his successor a legacy of high inflation, falling real wages and renewed industrial conflict.

In agriculture, as in industry, the administration claimed to stand on the middle ground, guaranteeing *ejidal* and private property alike. In practice, however, the *ejido,* the central item of the Cardenista project, was relegated to a secondary role and its internal workings changed. The new emphasis was in part a reaction against Cardenismo; in part a response to Sinarquismo and Almazanismo; and in part a recognition of the need to boost agricultural production, for both consumption and export (a need reinforced by the dearth and inflation of the war). More private land was protected and the new concessions to private farmers embodied in the Agrarian Code of 1942 also figured as incentives in the administration's plans for coastal colonization: the 'march to the sea'. The guarantees against expropriation offered to small proprietors by Cárdenas were extended, and private landowners benefited disproportionately from the administration's major investments in irrigation, from available public credit and from inflation. Although the distribution of land did not cease, it slowed to one-third the rate of the Cárdenas years. The land was now of inferior quality (some recipients declined to accept it), and the administrative delays lengthened. The days of grand presidential initiatives, of drastic dismemberments of ancient latifundia, were over. Landlords appreciated they could now count on the neutrality if not the positive support of the central government – historically the crucial agent in determining the pace of reform. Litigation again became prolonged, expensive and corrupt, as the old stratagems of the *maximato* were revived: *prestanombres,* pseudo-division of estates, white guards and violence. The restoration of the agrarian *amparo* (a key weapon of landlord legal defence) was considered, and finally implemented under the next administration. As the CNC moved towards boss rule and co-optation, *ejidatarios* increasingly provided the loyal clienteles of president or governor, and private landlords organized themselves to an unprecedented degree.

Ejidatarios now faced mounting insecurity which reinforced such clientalistic dependence: shortages of credit, political sniping (the collective *ejidos* were favourite targets), even the outright loss of *ejidal* land, especially in zones where land values were boosted by tourism (e.g., Guerrero) or urbanization. The relative, though not the absolute, size of the *ejidal* sector began gradually to decline. Internal structures changed as the government encouraged the parcellization of collectives (a policy for which there was general demand and broad political support from the UNS to the PCM). The collective form was retained where it was deemed economic (that is, profitable: some collective *ejidos* were highly productive and made a contribution to exports); but it was now subject to the imperatives of a global market, of an administration keen to promote exports and of an increasingly corrupt officialdom. Sugar co-operatives had to obey rules favouring the private *ingenios;* in Yucatán the demands of war production justified the *hacendados'* recovery of their rasping machines (as one landlord put it, robbing *ejidatarios* was no crime as *ejidatarios* were themselves *ladrones*). Internal stratification accelerated as *ejidal caciques* gained control and the *ejidatarios* polarized into a relatively affluent elite and a semi-proletarian majority, whose numbers were swollen by rapid population growth.

Campesino resistance to these changes was inhibited by the wartime social truce, by the landlords' political recovery and by the flaccidity of the CNC. *Bracerismo* and internal migration, too, offered palliatives. Hence land seizures, notable in 1941–2, declined thereafter. Protest continued in areas of traditional militancy: the Laguna, and Morelos, where Rubén Jaramillo's guerrillas became active after 1943, demanding continued reform and guarantees for existing *ejidos*. But these struggles went against the political grain. The stress laid by the president himself and the new technocrats of the 1940s on productivity and profit, the assumption that private farming was superior to the *ejido* – and for that matter, industry to agriculture – indicated a profound ideological shift since the 1930s. And their objectives seemed to be attained. During the *sexenio* agricultural output grew some 3.5 per cent a year in real terms (about the same rate as industry), with gains accruing from higher productivity rather than expanded cultivation; exports, too, rose even faster. Private and *ejidal* farmers alike contributed to this growth: the former including both 'neo-latifundista' agrarian capitalists and *rancheros* who reaped the benefit of secure tenure, mounting demand and better road links. No longer a social and economic project in its own right, the linch-pin of Cardenista policy, the *ejido* was fast becoming a productive adjunct of the booming urban, industrial economy, and the *ejidatarios* the most docile clients of the official party.

Avila Camacho's presidency ended amid inflation, *ejidal* decline, industrial boom, and unprecedented dependence on the United States. The left, not least Lombardo Toledano, entertained hopes of a major recovery in its fortunes. The right for its part including the burgeoning industrial bourgeoisie, looked askance at growing labour militancy and sought to contain the unions and the left, thus guaranteeing continued industrial advance and ensuring that Avilacamachismo would prove not a hiatus between bouts of radicalism, but a bridge linking the dangerous Cardenismo of the past to the secure conservatism of the future. For both sides it seemed there was all to play for; and the outcome of their conflict in 1946–9 would determine Mexico's future for over a generation.

The presidential succession – which quickened ambitions as early as 1942 – focused on two aspirants: Miguel Alemán, ex-governor of Veracruz, Avila Camacho's campaign manager in 1940 and then Secretary of Gobernación (which ministry now began to take on its role as the nursery of presidents); and Ezequiel Padilla, an old Callista, Mexican ambassador to the United States and major architect of the new Mexican-American detente. Both were civilians; the wartime professionalization of the army had delivered the *coup de grâce* to *caudillismo*. Leftist candidates – Javier Rojo Gómez, Miguel Henríquez Guzmán – played brief, inglorious roles, before it was made clear that Avila Camacho favoured Alemán, that Cárdenas and most state governors acceded to the presidential choice and that the left had better bow to the inevitable, which it did, with Lombardo supplying the appropriate sophisms. By autumn 1945 the CTM, CNC, CNOP and even the PCM had endorsed Alemán, and Padilla was obliged to play the part of an independent candidate, backed by a makeshift party.

In retrospect, the left's endorsement appears a costly error. Perhaps resistance was futile since the CTM leaders, scarcely popular, wielded power by following the rules of the game, not by bucking them. But contemporary estimations of Alemán differed from those of posterity. He was the candidate of the centre, Padilla, the candidate of the right; and, like Avila Camacho, he preached a bland populism; he also promised some democratization of the party. To private enterprise he offered reassurance and an end to wartime controls, but he also affirmed the state's concern for the working class and responsibility for the problems of dearth and inflation. Although his reassurances covered foreign investment, Alemán was seen as the nationalist candidate who would resist the economic hegemony of the United States (even the Americans took this view). Misconceived though this was, it was music to the ears of Lombardo, who was persuaded by the outgoing President to postpone plans for the launch of a new Lombardista party of the left until the election was over. Alemán's presumed nationalism gave the left's ultimately bitter liaison with him an initial ideological savour.

Although Alemán was assured of victory, it was felt necessary to impart greater democratic legitimacy to the electoral process and to avert a repeat of 1940. A new electoral law required stricter national organization of parties and closer federal supervision of elections: this inhibited the kind of decentralized chaos and conflict seen in 1940, and enhanced both official control of the opposition and the President's role as the Great Elector. The official party, conforming to the new order, underwent its final metamorphosis from PRM to the Partido Revolucionario Institucional (PRI): a change more cosmetic than real, in which the promise of internal democratization chiefly involved a demotion of the power of the CTM. Under this new dispensation the 1946 elections were almost free of violent incident despite the usual abuses and opposition complaints. Neither Padilla nor the fragmented, independent left, nor the right – the PAN and the Sinarquista successor party, Fuerza Popular – could mount a challenge comparable to Almazán's six years before. Alemán with 78 per cent of the vote won the presidency by a huge margin.

Thus mandated, the new President had less need than his predecessor to trim. His cabinet was packed with young men – most, like the President himself, too young to be revolutionary veterans. Four industrialists now figured, evidence of the new bourgeois power within the bosom of the party, and only two ministers were military. With the continued elimination of Cardenista governors (sometimes by constitutional strong-arming) it became clear that power had shifted to a new, technocratic generation for whom the revolution was less a personal experience than a convenient myth. Their rise paralleled the rise of the CNOP, which, as the CTM declined, assumed the political direction of the party, supplied the *políticos* of the day (much as the army had in the past) and served as a firm basis for presidential power. It paralleled, too, the growth of graft on a grand scale. It was now – rather than in the 1920s or 1930s – that the regime acquired its distinctive contemporary characteristics: presidential preeminence, the political monopoly of the official party, the deft manipulation of mass organizations, the dilution of class and ideological differences in the solvent of nationalism.

The ideas and mechanisms of Cardenismo were now put to new purposes. Alemán's succession came at a time when U.S. influence – economic, political, cultural–was pervasive and unprecedented, above all because of the new purchase it acquired in domestic circles. In the past, revolutionary Mexico had had to contend with White House liberals who were vaguely sympathetic if sometimes meddlesome (Wilson, FDR); or conservative pragmatists (Taft, Coolidge) whose antipathy was tempered by businesslike caution. Now, Mexico faced the America of Truman, the Truman Doctrine, 'containment' and National Security Council resolution 248; ideology and geopolitics underpinned systematic policies of intervention, pressure and co-option. Already, under Roosevelt, the United States had shown itself eager to sustain the close military co-operation of the war into peace time; and at the 1945 Chapultepec Conference, it pressed its obsessive case for an open, free-trading system–thus, for continued American hegemony in Latin America. Alemán, seen as a prickly nationalist, was at pains to reassure the United States, promising continued economic collaboration, and pandering to the new prejudices of the Cold War. In this, he set the tone of the *sexenio,* when anti-communism, incorporated into traditional, nationalist discourse and presented in terms of the new polarization of democracy and communism, became a staple of Mexican politics, 'elevated to the rank of an official doctrine'.[75] The revolutionary tradition ruled out the cruder forms of McCarthyism; but it also provided the best ideological defence against communism, which, like fascism in previous years, could be depicted as a dangerous alien import. Thus, in Mexico as in Europe, the democratic crusade against fascism transmuted imperceptibly into the democratic crusade against communism and, as in the early 1930s, the ideological temper of politics rapidly changed, leaving the left weakened and defensive, the right in brazen possession of a new, democratically justified, nationalist cause. Alemán's anti-communism was soon echoed by the party president, by leaders like Fernando Amilpa, the CTM veteran and crony of Fidel Velázquez, and by business mouthpieces like the Confederación Patronal de la República Mexicana (COPARMEX), which alleged the subversive role of Communist cells in the big industrial unions. Anti-communism was particularly effective at a time when Lombardo was cobbling together his new party of the left, when the major unions were displaying renewed militancy, and when, of course, the climate of international politics was rapidly, propitiously freez-

[75] Luis Medina, *Historia de la revolución mexicana Periodo 1940–1952: Civilismo y modernización del autoritarismo* (Mexico, 1979), p. 110.

ing. The most decisive achievement of the Alemán administration was thus a negative one: its isolation and emasculation of the left, and its concerted campaign against organized labour.

Lombardo, having obligingly deferred the launch of his new party, now sought the continuation of the old Lombardista project – a broad, nationalist, anti-imperialist alliance of progressive groups – outside, but not in opposition to, the official party. But the PRI did not appreciate this comradely rivalry; nor were the Communists entirely sympathetic. Eventually founded in June 1948, the Partido Popular (PP) grouped disaffected members of the official left (Lombardo, Bassols, Rivera) and certain worker and peasant groups behind a moderate, nationalist programme. But, as state elections revealed in 1949, the PRI would have no truck with the PP and Lombardo (whose own presidential candidacy was to flounder in 1952) was now widely depicted as a fellow-traveller or downright instrument of Stalin, 'bought by Moscow gold'. The CTM, which initially gave Lombardo tepid support in return for his co-operation against the independent unions, now came out in opposition, casting similar aspersions, which wholly accorded with their present, systematic, anti-communist line.

Times had changed since 1933, when Lombardo had successfully launched his breakaway CGOCM, and the fast-maturing official party was now keen and able to stifle such challenges. Crucial to the outcome was the regime's confrontation with organized labour. The prolonged wartime collaboration and inflation had left a legacy of division, dissent and accumulated demands, on which Lombardo hoped to capitalize. In particular, the major industrial unions (foremost among them the STFRM) resented continued CTM docility, and by 1947 were ready to challenge its leaders – who, in turn, could count on the support of a host of minor unions and federations. The old division of 1937 thus resurfaced, aggravated by wartime trends and now posed in terms of 'purification' (i.e., change and militancy) against *continuismo*. The government, dedicated to industrialization, could not accommodate union militancy; and the erosion of Lombardo's influence ruled out his familiar arbitral role, ensuring that the confrontation with organized labour would be all the sharper. The indecisive skirmishing of 1938–46 thus gave way to the outright conflict of 1947–9.

The challenge to the CTM leaders was parried by the usual methods of electoral manipulation; the CTM thus opted for *continuismo*, *charrismo*, and generally uncritical support of a government of the right, which was justified in terms of nationalism and moderation ('no to extremism; rejection of the left and imperialism alike'). Those militants who stayed with the CTM (including some self-sacrificing Communists) lost all power. The vestigial remnants of syndicalism and socialism were swept away. The tactic of the general strike was repudiated and the old CTM slogan – 'for a classless society' – was replaced by nationalist flummery: 'for the emancipation of Mexico'.[76] In response, the railwaymen led a secession from the CTM which involved electricians, tram-workers and lesser unions (March 1947). Their new organization, the Confederación Unica de Trabajadores (CUT), was soon backed by the other, major dissidents, the oil-workers and miners, with whom a solidarity pact was concluded, forming a Mexican triple alliance openly defiant of the CTM and its 'tattered banner of anti-communism'. Fragmentation of the CTM went further, with internal dissent, expulsions and in 1948 the creation of a rival *central,* the Alianza Obrera Campesina Mexicana (AOCM), in which peasant elements, especially the *ejidatarios* of the Laguna, were prominent. Opposed and probably outnumbered by these rivals, the CTM faced its biggest test since 1937; and now neither Lombardo nor Moscow, nor even the regime (which wanted victories rather than compromises) would urge conciliation.

The key to the conflict lay with the main independent unions, the oil-workers and railwaymen. The former had struck in the first month of the *sexenio* (it was the culmination of sporadic wartime conflict in the industry). The government declared the strike illegal, deployed troops and imposed an arbitrated settlement. Divided in its response, the union accepted the new agreement, under which PEMEX was able to stabilize the payroll and increase managerial control (both objectives which the administration, keen to boost production and secure American credit, fully endorsed). In the subsequent battle for power within the union, the government bent its efforts to ensure a victory for collaboration and *charrismo.* It also looked to a similar rationalization of the railways, which had been the subject of a major inquiry in 1948. Again the union was split, and the government intervened on behalf of the fervently anti-communist faction of Jesús Díaz de León (*el charro*). His main rival was gaoled following plausible charges of corruption; independent union branches were seized; Communists were systematically removed. With the union's independence broken and the *charro* faction installed in power, the government could proceed to reorganize the railways, under threat of mass

[76] Ibid., p. 132.

sackings and wage cuts. But the new union leadership faced the classic dilemma of the official labour bureaucracy (with which Fidel Velázquez was to live for over a generation): although Díaz de León's 'moralization' campaign won him some genuine support, he was ultimately a creature of the government; but both he and the government had to maintain a semblance of workers' representation and co-operation. Coercion alone could not run the railways. *Charrazo* was therefore followed by negotiation and a new collective contract (1949), which combined cost-cutting with judicious job protection. Thus, even *charrismo* could be seen to deliver some of the goods; and to many it seemed preferable to a perilous, quixotic militancy. As one labour leader put it in 1947: 'better a bad collective contract (bad in that it curtails our rights) but which is at least honoured, than a good one which remains a dead letter'.[77] In this lay the secret of the CTM's success in the decades to come. To put it differently, Alemán's counter-revolution – the defeat of those radical, syndical and Cardenista elements which resisted the Alemanista project – had to be a good deal more subtle and moderate than those later implemented elsewhere in Latin America, following a comparable rationale but requiring outright military repression.

With the independence of the STFRM broken, the cause of the other industrial unions – miners, oil-workers, electricians – wilted. They had greeted the *charrazo* with protests but no strikes. Only the miners and the divided oil-workers affiliated to the new Lombardista central federation, the Unión General de Obreros y Campesinos de México (UGOCM); and the latter, like its political cousin the PP, soon proved a vulnerable target of government hostility. It was denied recognition; strikes it espoused were declared illegal; its affiliates suffered internal intervention and coup; its peasant members were subjected to the various persuasions of the CNC and the *ejidal* bureaucracy. The oil-workers' union, once it was securely in the hands of the *charro* faction, returned to the CTM fold (1951), setting a precedent other affiliates would follow. CTM control was thus reasserted, at a price. With the independent left emasculated, and the radical right either disappearing or fast mutating into a loyal Christian Democratic opposition, the peace of the PRI prevailed. The regime could pursue its chosen model of industrial development and capital accumulation without fear of major social mobilization. Nationally, 1949 revealed 'a panorama

---

[77] Hernández Abrego, of the oil-workers' unions, quoted in Rosalía Pérez Linares, 'El charrismo sindical en la decada de los setenta. El sindicato petrolero', in *Historia y crónicas de la clase obrera en México* (Mexico, 1981), p. 172.

totally distinct from that . . . of 1946'; locally, too, the late 1940s saw
the crystallization of 'a political structure and pattern of political behaviour that has continued to this day.'[78] If the revolution experienced a
decisive Thermidor, it was then. The Cardenista experiment, increasingly
controlled after 1938, was now terminally halted, by new men who,
ingeniously, found new uses for the old laboratory equipment. Or, changing the metaphor, the civilians and *técnicos* of the Alemán *sexenio,* imbued
with a modernizing, Cold War ideology, and a get-rich-quick ethic, quar-
ried the rubble of Cardenismo and utilized the material – the corporate
party, the mass institutions, the powerful executive, the tamed army and
subordinated peasantry – to build a new Mexico. The material was
Cardenista, but the ground-plan was their own. It was build to last.

[78] Ibid., p. 94; Benjamin, 'Passages to Leviathan', p. 268.

6

MEXICO SINCE 1946: DYNAMICS OF
AN AUTHORITARIAN REGIME

Mexico stands out as a paragon of political stability within contemporary Latin America. There have been no successful military coups since the nineteenth century and hardly any serious attempts since the Revolution of 1910–20. Presidential successions have become genteel negotiations within the semi-official party, the Partido Revolucionario Institucional (PRI), which has dominated the electoral arena for more than half a century. Civilians have gained control of the ruling apparatus. Consensus appears to prevail on most policy questions, and the Constitution of 1917 – forged in the heat of armed conflict – has continued to provide the regime an aura of legitimacy. Claiming a revolutionary heritage and wielding a practical monopoly over the instruments of power, the Mexican state has appeared to function smoothly, steadily and (in its own way) efficiently. The consequent achievement of stability has thus come to be hailed as the political component of the post-war 'Mexican miracle'.

Indeed, the perception of Mexico's political stability has imbued much of the scholarly literature on contemporary Mexico with a tacit presumption of continuity, a sense almost of timelessness. There tends to be an unspoken assumption that nothing much has changed in Mexican politics since the late 1930s, much more attention being given to the workings of the system and the mechanisms of authority than to historical events or discrete occurrences; most existing literature reveals a general, abstract quality. This may illustrate one of the implicit biases of what has come to be called 'systems analysis' in political science: preoccupation with the maintenance of the political system rather than with patterns of transformation. Viewed in this perspective, post-war Mexico often looks flat and one-dimensional.

In an effort to redress this imbalance this chapter will consider the experience and socio-economic context of political change in Mexico since

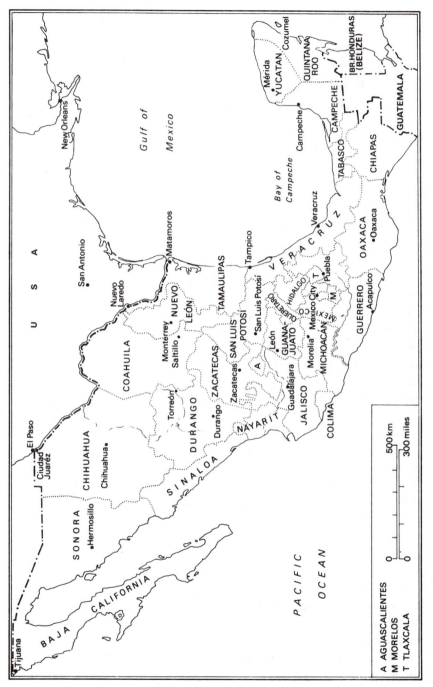

Contemporary Mexico

the Second World War. In these years three separate historical phases can be identified: first, a period of definition and consolidation of the contemporary system, from the mid-1940s to the late 1950s; second, an era of domination and hegemony, from the late 1950s to perhaps the early 1970s; and third, a time of system stress and declining power, from the mid-1970s to the late 1980s. Since precise dates are difficult to fix, such a periodization provides only a general guideline for the analysis of political change, which, it should be stressed, is itself a very amorphous concept. At one end of the spectrum, it can refer to an alteration of political regime, as from democracy to authoritarianism. At the other end, it can refer to the kind of self-regulating adjustments which often help perpetuate a regime. Here, however, attention will be focussed on an intermediate level, on qualitative and quantitative transformations *of* and *within* the authoritarian regime which Mexico has maintained throughout the contemporary era. For this, it is necessary to assess the system's ability to satisfy the preconditions for stability – political balance, economic growth and rapprochement with the United States. These preconditions depend, in turn, on a number of salient factors: (1) the composition of the ruling coalition; (2) the coherence of the ruling coalition; (3) the power and legitimacy of the ruling coalition; (4) the policy orientations; and (5) the actions, responses and reactions of the system's constituent groups.

POSTWAR ECONOMY, SOCIETY AND POLITICS: AN OVERVIEW

The accomplishment of political stability is all the more remarkable in light of the dynamic transformations that have taken place in Mexican society. Over the past century the Mexican economy has undergone two fundamental transitions, one based on the export of primary products and the other characterized by import substitution industrialization (ISI). The first phase followed the consolidation of political power under Porfirio Díaz (1876–1911). A liberal in economic matters, Díaz opened the country to foreign investment and strengthened Mexico's commercial links to the outside world. Stimulated by the construction of a railway system, the volume of foreign trade increased nine times between 1877 and 1910. As well as silver and gold, Mexico began to export such industrial minerals as copper and zinc, mainly from the north; goods produced from cattle- and sheepherding, also from the north; sugar, from the centre-south; and fibre, especially *henequen* from Yucatán. Oil production started just after 1900, and by the 1920s Mexico was one of the world's leading sources of petroleum. Like many other Latin American countries, Mexico pursued the classical strategy of 'comparative advantage', exporting raw materials and importing manufactured goods. The United States became the nation's leading source of investment and trade, and by 1910, at the centennial celebration of national independence, it seemed to many observers that Mexico was heading for prolonged prosperity. However, that year witnessed the outbreak of the Revolution, which took a massive human and economic toll, and then, just as an economic recovery was starting to pick up in the 1920s, the world depression struck. Investment stopped and commerce plummeted. In 1930, Mexico's gross domestic product (GDP) fell to 12.5 per cent below its 1925 level. The Mexican economy followed that of the United States, and the 1930s proved to be an arduous decade.

Mexican leaders now took a new tack. Instead of relying on international trade, which made the country vulnerable to economic trends elsewhere (especially in the United States), they began to favour industrialization. Instead of importing finished goods from abroad, Mexico proceeded to manufacture its own products for domestic consumption. The state, moreover, assumed an active role in the economy. President Lázaro Cárdenas (1934–40) expropriated foreign-owned oil companies in 1938 and placed them under the control of Petróleos Mexicanos (PEMEX), a state-run enterprise which would eventually become one of the most important institutions in the country. The Second World War provided substantial impetus for Mexico's nascent industrial development by cutting back the flow of imports from the United States. The government took advantage of these conditions by implementing a variety of protectionist measures. Import quotas and tariffs kept foreign competition within acceptable bounds, and the devaluation of the peso in 1948–49 (and later in 1954) discouraged Mexican consumers from purchasing imported goods. (The exchange rate soared from 4.85 pesos per U.S. dollar to 12.50.) The result was to stimulate local manufacturing and to create a new cadre of prominent industrialists.

By some standards Mexico's import substitution policies met with resounding success. Between 1940 and 1960 the GDP grew from 21.7 billion pesos to 74.3 billion pesos (in constant 1950 prices, thus adjusting for inflation), an average annual increase of 6.4 per cent. During the 1960s Mexico managed to sustain this level of growth, achieving – despite one of the most rapidly swelling populations in the world – a solid per capita growth rate of 3.3 per cent per year. By the late 1970s

Table 2.1. *The structure of production: 1960 and 1979*
(percentage of gross domestic product)

	1960	1979
Agriculture	16.2	9.0
Industry:		
manufacturing	19.3	24.9
mining	4.2	5.2
construction	4.8	6.6
utilities	0.8	1.8
(subtotal, industry)	(29.1)	(38.5)
Services and other:		
transport and communication	2.7	3.6
commerce	28.6	26.7
housing and other	24.1	22.3
Size of GDP (billions of 1970 dollars)	16.2	51.2

Source: *Statistical Abstract of Latin American 21* (Los Angeles: UCLA Latin American Center, 1983).

manufacturing represented nearly one-quarter of the GDP and, as shown in Table 2.1, the industrial sector as a whole accounted for 38.5 per cent of national output. It was this performance that came to be known as the 'Mexican miracle', an exemplary combination of economic progress and political stability in an area of the developing world.

Yet Mexico encountered limits in the process of import substitution industrialization. Protectionist policies helped local industry to displace foreign competition from the consumer market, and by 1950 only 7 per cent of the final value of non-durable *consumer goods* was imported from abroad. Mexico also made some headway with regard to *intermediate goods* such as fuel and fabric. But there was conspicuously less progress in the *capital goods* sector (technology and heavy machinery) which from 1950 to 1969 declined from 74 per cent to 51 per cent of the total, remaining thereafter in this general range. As a consequence, Mexico's industrial expansion continued to call for substantial amounts of imports – which could only be paid for by exports. Despite the quest for self-sufficiency, Mexico continued to rely on international trade.

A second weakness derived from a long-term shortage of capital. Industrialization is expensive. Some local entrepreneurs, as in the city of

Monterrey, managed to finance a fair share of industrial development. The Mexican state likewise assumed a *dirigiste* role, extending credit through such lending institutions as the Nacional Financiera (NAFINSA) and creating an impressive array of government-run companies. Foreign capital provided yet another source of funds. By 1970 direct foreign investment amounted to nearly $3 billion, 80 per cent of which came from the United States. In contrast to previous eras, when mining, communications and transport were the dominant activities for foreigners, nearly three-quarters (73.8 per cent) of this investment was in the manufacturing sector, mostly in critical industries: chemicals, petrochemicals, rubber, machinery and industrial equipment. Yet another solution was to obtain funding from the international credit market. During the 1960s Mexico cautiously began to borrow capital abroad, and by 1970 the country had a cumulative debt (both public and private) of about $3.2 billion. Subsequent governments were more extravagant, and by the mid-1970s the figure was close to $17 billion. The impact of this burden would depend on Mexico's capacity to repay. As the debt continued to mount – passing $80 billion by 1982 and topping $100 billion by 1987 – the costs would become painfully clear.

A third, and paradoxical, consequence of Mexico's ISI strategy was widespread unemployment. The nation's industrial sector was more capital-intensive than labour-intensive; increases in production tended to come from investments in machines and technology rather than from hiring more workers. (The agricultural sector, by contrast, has been more labour-intensive, with about 40 per cent of the work force producing about 10 per cent of the GDP.) As a result of this tendency Mexico experienced a remarkable rate of joblessness: by the mid-1970s open unemployment was around 10 per cent but under-employment may have been as high as 40 per cent, creating a functional unemployment rate equivalent to around 20 per cent. By the mid-1980s between nine hundred thousand and one million young people were entering the labour force each year in search of jobs.

Partly for these reasons, the policies of ISI led to the increasingly uneven distribution of national income. As revealed in Table 2.2, the percentage share of income going to the poorest 20 per cent of Mexican households dropped from 5.0 per cent in 1958 to only 2.9 per cent in 1977. The proportional income of the highest stratum also decreased; for the top 10 per cent it declined from nearly 50 per cent to just over 40 per cent. The biggest relative gain was made by the so-called fourth quintile,

Table 2.2. *Patterns of income distribution: 1958 and*
1977 (percentage shares for household groups)

	1958	1977
Lowest 20 per cent	5.0	2.9
Second quintile	7.2	7.0
Third quintile	10.0	12.0
Fourth quintile	14.9	20.4
Highest 20 per cent	62.9	57.7
(Top 10 per cent)	(49.3)	(40.6)

Sources: Ifigenia M. de Navarrete, 'La distribución del ingreso en México: tendencias y perspectivas', in *El perfil de México en 1980* I (Mexico, 1970), p. 37; and World Bank, *World Development Report 1987* (New York, 1987), p. 253.

whose share of income went from 14.9 per cent in 1958 to 20.4 per cent in 1977, and by those in the 11–20 per cent bracket (the ninth decile). These figures clearly illustrate the economic conquests of the Mexican middle class as well as demonstrating a fact evident throughout the developing world: ISI tends to exacerbate, rather than alleviate, inequalities of income distribution.

A final result of Mexico's import substitution strategy was that the nation's industrial sector came to be inefficient and, by international standards, uncompetitive. Assured of domestic markets and protected from foreign challenges, manufacturers kept costs down – and profits up – by making only minimal investments in plant renewal and modernization. Hardly any national firms made significant budgetary allocations to research and development. Reliance on imported technology tended to elevate production costs and to ensure built-in obsolescence. Consequently the Mexican private sector became highly dependent on its near monopoly of the domestic market and on protection by the state. The socio-economic costs inherent in ISI began to take their toll in the early 1970s. Production declined and conflict mounted. National leaders attempted to forge a new consensus around a vision of 'shared development' (in contrast to 'stabilizing development'), but their entreaties were in vain. Mexico seemed to be heading for trouble.

Then the country struck oil. As the international price of petroleum continued to climb, Mexico discovered massive new reserves and quickly regained its status as a major producer. This not only enhanced the country's international position but also provided state authorities with a huge windfall of foreign exchange, enabling the government to embark on a large-scale program of public spending designed to alleviate the shortcomings of ISI development. The petroleum bonanza thus temporarily postponed any thoughts of implementing structural change in the economy. However, when the oil boom collapsed in the early 1980s, the government sought to confront the deepening crisis by adopting a policy designed to 'liberalize' the national economy and to promote the exportation of manufactured goods. This would require the abandonment of long-standing assumptions, the rearrangement of relations between the state and the private sector, and the renovation of the nation's industrial plant. The challenges were formidable.

Mexico's economic transformation since the 1940s greatly affected – and was affected by – changes in its agricultural sector. Official policies for the most part kept agricultural prices artificially low, and the consequently modest cost of food to urban consumers amounted to a large-scale transfer of resources from the countryside to the city, this subsidy playing an essential part in maintaining social peace there. At times agricultural exports earned significant amounts of foreign exchange, and these profits helped provide capital for industrial development.

From the mid-1930s to the mid-1960s, Mexico achieved a remarkably well-balanced pattern of overall growth. As industrialization took place via import substitution, agricultural production was steadily increasing at an average annual rate of 4.4 per cent. By the early 1960s Mexico was exporting basic grains (including wheat) as well as 'luxury' crops (such as avocados and tomatoes). To the degree there was a 'Mexican miracle', some analysts have said, it may have taken place in the agricultural sector. Within ten years this situation suffered a drastic reversal. By 1975 Mexico was importing 10 per cent of the grain it consumed; by 1979 it was importing 36 per cent of its grains, and in 1983 it imported roughly half the grain it needed. Food became a scarcity for some, and malnutrition may have come to afflict nearly forty million Mexicans. This not only revealed a national crisis in agriculture. It also meant that Mexico had to divert capital which could be used for other purposes, such as job-producing investments.

Mexican agriculture lost its internal balance. Growth continued in the commercialized sectors, especially in high-value crops (fruits and vegetables) and livestock feeds (sorghum and forage for poultry and pigs; beef cattle are grass-fed in Mexico). Government policies sustained relatively high levels of production for export, mainly to the United States, and for consumption in the cities, mainly by the middle class. This emphasis was reinforced by the entry of large-scale agribusiness – transnational corporations which acquired major interests in the agricultural arena, particularly in the animal-feed industry. Small farmers and peasants did not, however, share in the benefits. From the 1960s onward Mexican governments permitted the real prices of staple goods (especially corn) to undergo long-term decline, a policy which favoured working-class consumers in the short run but discouraged agricultural output in the long run. Credit went to large-scale operators and agribusiness took control of large parcels of land. By the mid-1980s approximately four million Mexican peasants had no land. From time to time their frustration boiled over and bands of *campesinos* seized and occupied lands for their own use.

These developments have produced considerable controversy over the legacy of agrarian reform in Mexico and, in particular, of the collective *ejidos*. Production on the *ejidos* has not grown as rapidly as on large-scale private farms (whose per-acre output increased by 147 per cent between 1950 and 1970, compared to 113 per cent for the *ejidos*). This has prompted some observers to conclude that agrarian reform and collective ownership have reduced agricultural productivity and exacerbated economic difficulties. But other factors have also been at work: *ejidos* generally had lower-quality land and less access to credit and technology; they also tended to concentrate less on luxury crops for export than on staple foodstuffs for the domestic market. In what may be a revealing comparison, *ejido* productivity increased more rapidly than that of small-scale farmers (113 per cent to 73 per cent for 1950–70). The problem may lie not in *ejidos* themselves but in their resources and incentives.

Economic growth and industrial development in the post-war period exerted a profound impact on Mexico's social structure. One of the most conspicuous features of this change, both cause and effect of the country's economic transformation, was a secular trend towards urbanization. As land and jobs in the countryside grew scare, peasants left their villages in search of sustenance or work in the cities. Sometimes they would move alone, sometimes as family units; sometimes whole villages would set out on a hegira. As often as not they would find their way into the slums or, more commonly, they would establish entire communities on the outskirts of the country's major cities. Some of these shanty-towns would become mini-cities in their own right. In 1900 only 9.2 per cent of the Mexican population lived in cities (defined as communities with 20,000 inhabitants or more). By 1940 the figure had climbed to 18 per cent, and by 1970 it stood around 35 per cent. In the meantime Mexico City became one of the largest metropolises on earth, its population in the late 1980s being estimated at between 14 and 16 million. Contrary to widespread assumption, Mexico was no longer a rural society of sedentary *campesinos*. The proportion of the economically active population engaged in agriculture had fallen from approximately 70 per cent at the beginning of the century to 40 per cent. Concurrently, the percentage of workers employed in industry rose steadily, from roughly 10 per cent in 1900 to 30 per cent in 1980.

Notwithstanding questionable statistics and scholarly disputes over the precise meaning of 'class', it is evident that economic transformation had a major impact on Mexico's social structure. The census of 1960 suggests that Mexico's 'upper' class had remained very small, about half of 1 per cent of the population, and that it had shifted its social location from the countryside to the city – as traditional *hacendados* gave way to bankers and industrialists. The 'middle' class had grown to approximately 17 per cent of the total, with urban and rural components becoming nearly equal in magnitude. (By the mid-1980s the middle class represented as much as 25 or 30 per cent of the total population.) In fact, the distinction between upper- and middle-class occupational strata is extremely tenuous because many people in middle-class jobs had upper-class incomes (and vice versa), and it might well be preferable to combine the two into a single social class: the non-manual class, consisting of those who do not work with their hands. In all events, one fundamental point comes through: relatively speaking, the middle class has been a privileged class, people with middle-class incomes falling into the upper third of the country's income distribution.[1] The 'lower' class consists of those who perform manual labour. This stratum appears to have declined from over 90 per cent in 1900 to around 82 per cent in 1960 and, perhaps, to 65–75 per cent by 1980. But this should not obscure the constant increase in absolute size as a result of population expansion. The lower class has also become increasingly industrialized and, within limits, proletarianized.

Population growth sharply accelerated from the 1940s. From the late

---

[1] See Arturo González Cosío, 'Clases y estratos sociales', in Julio Durán Ochoa et al., *México: cincuenta años de revolución*, vol. 2: *La vida social* (Mexico, 1961), p. 55. For a subsequent discussion and some alternative estimates, see James W. Wilkie and Paul D. Wilkens, 'Quantifying the Class Structure of Mexico, 1895–1970', in *Statistical Abstract of Latin America*, vol. 21 (Los Angeles, 1983).

colonial period until the 1930s the Mexican population grew at a relatively modest rate, partly because of periodic devastation – once during the wars of independence (1810–21) and again during the Mexican Revolution (1910–20). Thereafter the population started a steady climb, from 20 million in 1940 to 36 million in 1960 and 70 million in 1980. By the late 1960s, Mexico had one of the highest population growth rates in the world, around 3.6 per cent per year. Since then, partly in response to governmental policies, the growth rate has subsided, hovering around 2.5 per cent in the mid–1980s. Nonetheless a basic fact persisted: nearly half the nation's population was under the age of sixteen. One of the political ramifications of this demographic growth has been a weakening of links to the past. Of the 70 million Mexicans alive in 1980 only 13.3 per cent were aged fifteen or over in 1950 and could have direct memories from that period. Nearly half the 1980 population (45 per cent) had still not reached the age of fifteen – so their adulthood lay in the future. Demography discouraged the maintenance of inter-generational continuity.

These social and demographic developments manifested important regional variations. Although Mexico City exercised political dominance, it was somewhat less commanding than the capital cities of some other major Latin American nations. The vast majority of Mexicans – at least three-quarters – lived in some other part of the nation, and the socioeconomic contours of daily life provided each region with a distinct flavour. The central zone of the country was in itself richly varied. Although some of its cities (Toluca, Puebla, Querétaro) fell within the cultural and political orbit of Mexico City, parts of the central zone maintained strong regionalist traditions. Guadalajara, the nation's second largest city, with 3.6 million inhabitants by the 1980s, had a conservative and Catholic tone; paradoxically, as the home of mariachi music and tequila, it was also a nationalist symbol. Veracruz, a languid port on the Caribbean, had the dubious historical distinction of having been the launching point for various foreign invasions from the arrival of Hernán Cortes to the incursion of U.S. marines. Neither Guadalajara nor Veracruz possessed an industrial elite which might challenge Mexico City's business giants, and both cities collaborated with social forces in the capital.

The south had been much less privileged and less developed. The states of Oaxaca and Chiapas maintained relatively large indigenous populations, often living in traditional subsistence communities on the margins of national society. The south played precious little part in the rush toward industrialization, and as a result it remained rural and impoverished.

Tourism gave a boost to Guerrero and Quintana Roo through such lavish international resorts as Acapulco and Ixtapa and Cozumel, and Yucatán recovered from the collapse of the international market for *henequen*. Parts of southern Mexico, as well as the Gulf, became centers for the petroleum boom. But for the most part, southern states received relatively modest attention (and funding) from the national government, and – perhaps as a result – they nourished opposition parties, radical politics and secessionist movements.

The north stood at the other end of the economic spectrum. A cradle of private entrepreneurship, the city of Monterrey became the nation's second largest industrial center and third largest metropolis (with more than 2.2 million residents). The driving force behind this development was provided by two families, the Garza and the Sada clans, who started with a brewery around the turn of the century and eventually built a huge conglomerate which included steel, glass, chemicals and finance. The northern states of Sonora and Chihuahua witnessed the pre-eminence of wealthy conservative farmers and ranchers while the border regions, with such thriving cities as Ciudad Juárez and a refurbished Tijuana, came to benefit from economic links with the United States. In general the north was prosperous, conservative, pro-American – and distant from Mexico City. However, all sectors of Mexican society – not only in the north – came to feel the impact of American popular culture. Through movies, television, language and the marketplace, Mexico underwent a steady and accelerating process of 'Americanization' – a trend which gave added urgency to the protection of national identity.

The complexity of Mexico's political system has long defied straightforward classification. In the optimistic spirit of the 1950s some analysts depicted the regime as a one-party structure in the process of modernization and democratization. With the disenchantment of the 1970s, most observers stressed the 'authoritarian' qualities of the regime, but even this characterization would be subject to qualification. Mexico has had a pragmatic and *moderate* authoritarian regime, not the zealously repressive kind that emerged in the Southern Cone during the 1960s and 1970s; an *inclusionary* system, given to co-optation and incorporation rather than exclusion or annihilation; an *institutional* system, not a personalistic instrument; and a *civilian* leadership, not a military government. Whatever else might be said, the Mexican regime has confronted and apparently resolved one of the most intractable problems for non-democratic systems, the issue of elite renewal and executive succession. It is an authoritarian system, but one with many differences.

Political power resides at the top. Mexican presidents rule for non-renewable six-year terms, during which time they command supreme authority: they possess the final word on all major policy questions, they control vast amounts of patronage, and, given the importance of the state, they have enduring influence on the path of national development. But once their terms are up, they are out. The constitutional prohibition on re-election (a legacy of the Mexican Revolution) has become a sacrosanct principle of politics – in part, one suspects, because it signifies the regular renovation of opportunities for public office. For these reasons the para-mount event in Mexican politics has been the presidential succession. Selection of the president is the pre-eminent decision in national life, the process which sets and controls the sexennial rhythm of public and politi-cal activity. The precise mechanisms behind the succession have been withheld from public view, but it appears that they have undergone some meaningful change. Two assertions seem to be beyond dispute: first, the outgoing president plays a central (usually dominant) role in the selection of his successor; and second, the unveiling (or *destapamiento*) of the president-to-be prompts an immediate and virtually unanimous declara-tion of support from members of the political establishment. Competition comes to an end with the *destape*.

Elections have been regularly dominated by the Partido Revolucionario Institucional (PRI). Opposition parties have been fragmented and weak, although their potential has grown over time. Until the late 1970s a handful of political parties – principally the Partido de Acción Nacional (PAN), the Partido Popular Socialista (PPS), and the Partido Auténtico de la Revolución Mexicana (PARM) – provided the regime with loyal parlia-mentary dissent. With low-to-minuscule electoral support, their leaders accepted seats in the Congress, criticized occasional decisions (but never the system itself), made frequent deals with the PRI and, by their mere existence, strengthened the government's claim to popular support and legitimate authority. In the 1970s less collaborationist parties appeared – on both the left and the right – but in the mid-1980s they did not yet pose a serious electoral threat to the regime on a national scale. Outside the party structure there were terrorist movements, both urban and rural, to which the government offered no quarter. Crackdowns and anti-guerrilla campaigns by army and police units crushed armed rebellions ruthlessly. The regime took political prisoners, a fact authorities often denied, and there were moments of outright repression. Activists and agitators mysteriously disappeared from time to time.

One of the most pervasive aspects of popular feeling was apathy. Voter turn-out in presidential elections ranged from 43 per cent to 76 per cent, though the ballot was obligatory, and as a whole the Mexican people tended to perceive their government as distant, elitist and self-serving. A sizeable share of the populace, perhaps as much as one-third, was under-fed, underschooled, underclothed, and so marginal to the political process that it came to represent, in Pablo González Casanova's phrase, an 'internal colony'. Although indicative of potential discord, apathy and marginalization did not necessarily constitute dangers for the regime since they often permitted it freedom of action; if the Mexican political system exhibited authoritarian features, it possessed flexibility too. Top-heavy as it was, the PRI was organized around three distinct sectors: one for peasants, one for workers and one, quixotically called 'the popular sector', for almost everyone else. The structure provided at least token representation for broad strata of Mexican society and helps explain the passive acceptance, if not enthusiastic endorsement, the regime enjoyed among the mass of the population. A steady rotation of political personnel meant that new people, some with new ideas, were able to gain access to high office. When signs of discontent appeared, Mexico's rulers usually co-opted mass leaders by providing them with public positions, further broadening the base of support for the system. And every decade or so the system underwent a period of self-examination that often led to some kind of reform. The results were normally less than dramatic, but they affirmed the system's basic code, which one close observer succinctly summarized: two carrots, even three or four, but then a stick if necessary.

The Mexican power structure in this period can perhaps best be viewed as an interlocking series of alliances or pacts – *acuerdos,* in the expressive Spanish term. In the broadest sense, the country's ruling coalition contained three separate segments: the state, the local private sector and the foreign sector (transnational banks and corporations and their governments). Relationships between these partners were sometimes uneasy and tense, and it was not uncommon for two to join together against a third. Yet beneath these struggles there existed a deep-seated consensus, a set of understandings which kept the power structure intact: (1) Mexico would pursue a capitalist path to economic growth, a premise requiring that (2) the popular masses would be kept under control, which meant that (3) the state must play a dominant role in this arrangement, while (4) the state and entrepreneurs could still compete for relative superiority. In such a 'mixed economy' the state assumed multiple tasks: it protected the capitalist system, it established the rules for development and it took part as the largest single entrepreneur.

The state was led by a political elite which contained in turn, three identifiable groups. One consisted of *técnicos,* a highly trained corps of bureaucrats whose main resource was technical expertise; they played critical roles in policy planning, especially in the economy. The second group was the *políticos,* seasoned politicians who made their way up through the PRI hierarchy and whose institutional base came from electoral posts (in town councils, state assemblies, state governorships and the national Congress). Rivalry between *políticos* and *técnicos* was a recurrent theme in Mexican politics from the 1950s, and it very much affected the balance of power within the national elite.[2] A third group, often unnoticed by observers, consisted of the professional army. The Mexican military maintained a low profile in the period after the Second World War, but it consistently performed a number of crucial duties – hunting down guerrillas, supervising tense elections, repressing vocal opponents and generally upholding law and order. In effect, the army operated as a 'silent partner' within the political class and its collaboration was essential.

Mexico's political regime relied on popular support from three main social-class groups. Particularly prominent was the middle class, the relatively privileged and largely urbanized stratum which received many of the benefits of economic growth. Special symbolic significance was given to the rural masses, especially the peasantry, although its share of material rewards was disproportionately small. Equally, the maintenance of the regime depended upon the urban workers, whose unions collaborated under the centralized leadership of the Confederación de Trabajadores de México (CTM). Each group was a separate unit within the PRI, which simultaneously provided an institutional outlet for the expression of sectoral interests and kept them under control. For this purpose it was especially important to keep workers and peasants apart from each other, thereby preventing the formation of a lower-class coalition that could threaten the system as a whole. As former president Miguel Alemán once recalled, in the late 1930s and early 1940s 'there was an effort to merge the peasant organizations with those of the workers. . . . With that',

[2] See Peter H. Smith, 'Leadership and Change: Intellectuals and Technocrats in Mexico', in Roderic A. Camp (ed.), *Mexico's Political Stability: The Next Five Years* (Boulder, Colo. 1986), pp. 101–17, esp. 102–4.

insisted Alemán, 'the political stability of Mexico would have disappeared. Who would have appeased this group? . . . Would we have been able to preserve stability in such a situation'?[3] To forestall this outcome Mexico instead constructed a corporate state, and the PRI and its sectors constituted its fundamental pillars of support.

Over time it became apparent that Mexico's political stability depended upon three major conditions. First, there was the maintenance of an *equilibrium* among the constituent groups. Although there might be inequalities, it proved essential to retain the notion of access for all and supremacy for none. Legitimacy rested on the acceptance and participation of sectoral leaders, and this entailed the belief – or the myth – that redress of particular grievances and advancement of general interests would always be possible; the watchword of this system was 'balance'. The second condition was the continuing *distribution* of material rewards – made possible, in turn, by long-run patterns of economic growth. These benefits could take a variety of forms, usually under the sponsorship of the state (subsidies, price controls, wage agreements), permitting the regime to retain support from its heterodox and contradictory social-class constituencies. This kind of populist coalition required a steady stream of pay-offs, the state's ability to deliver depending upon the performance of the national economy. The Mexican regime therefore needed economic growth: the post-war 'economic miracle' and the maintenance of political stability possessed a symbiotic and dialectical relationship to each other.

The third broad condition for stability was the cultivation of a mutually acceptable relationship with the United States, a kind of *bilateral détente*. While upholding the sacrosanct notions of national sovereignty and self-determination, the Mexican regime assiduously sought to avoid direct confrontations with its neighbour to the north. Relations with the United States were a constant preoccupation of policy-makers, whose memories included not only the humiliating wars of the nineteenth century but also the military interventions of the early twentieth century and virulent hostility toward the oil nationalization of 1938. Keeping the lion at political bay while cultivating productive economic connections proved to be a precarious exercise that often took the form of legalistic evasion and practical ambiguity.

In the period from the 1940s Mexico's relations with the United States exhibited three enduring features. First, asymmetry: the United States was bigger, stronger and richer than Mexico, and had been ever since the early nineteenth century. There could be no bargaining here between equals: the United States would always have a much larger influence on Mexico than Mexico would have on the United States. Second, conflict: despite some common outlooks and goals, there could be disagreement on specific issues. What was good for Mexico was not always good for the United States and vice versa (or, more precisely, what was good for certain interests in Mexico might not be good for certain interests in the United States). The task of Mexican authorities was to represent national interests without incurring an excessively negative response from the United States. Third, diplomatic limitations: government-to-government negotiations lacked the capacity to resolve all key bilateral issues in a definitive manner. This was partly due to the nature of important issues at stake, such as labour migration, which responded mainly to socio-economic stimuli and stoutly resisted official regulation. It also reflected diversity and contradictions in policy-making, multitudinous agencies taking part in the U.S. policy process, whereas in Mexico presidential will tended to prevail.[4]

For the most part, Mexican leaders from the mid-1940s to the mid-1980s managed to fulfill these three conditions. They nurtured the idea of balance among constituent groups; they supported the drive towards economic growth; and they maintained an appropriately ambiguous – but essentially supportive – relationship with the United States. The result of these efforts proved to be as remarkable as it was rare: a stable political regime under the aegis of civilian leaders.

1946–58

At the end of the Second World War, Mexico was on exceptionally good terms with the United States. In 1941, as the conflict approached, President Franklin Delano Roosevelt had urged the petroleum companies to accept a negotiated settlement to the 1938 nationalization. In 1942, after Germany torpedoed two oil tankers bound for the United States, Mexico declared war on the Axis, and that same year the government signed accords with Washington on trade, opening American markets to Mexican goods, and on migrant labour, providing for Mexican *braceros* to work on American railroads and farms and later in other sectors. The tone of these

---

[4] On these and other matters, see Peter H. Smith, 'U.S.–Mexican Relations: The 1980s and Beyond', *Journal of Interamerican Studies and World Affairs* 27, no. 1 (February 1985): 91–101; and Josefina Zoraida Vazquez and Lorenzo Meyer, *The United States and Mexico* (Chicago, 1986), passim.

agreements stressed harmony and collaboration. Indeed, some influential Mexicans believed that they heralded the beginning of a 'special relationship' between the two countries. Wartime conditions had also encouraged industrial development. There appeared a nascent business class, nurtured and protected by the state, along with the outlines of a modern middle class (accounting for perhaps 15 per cent of the population as a whole at the time). Yet much of Mexican society retained its traditional rural and immobile character; with some 2 million residents, Mexico City was far from the megalopolis it would later become.

Within this setting, the inauguration of Miguel Alemán in 1946 marked a decisive change in Mexico's politics. Only forty-six years old, a civilian, he was the first post-revolutionary president not to have played a conspicuous role in the armed conflict of 1910–20; educated as a lawyer, he represented a generation of ambitious *universitarios;* articulate in Spanish (and fluent in English), he brought a new combination of skills into the nation's executive office. He had, however, diligently worked his way up through the system, entering the Senate in 1934, becoming governor of Veracruz in 1936, and directing the presidential campaign of Manuel Avila Camacho in 1939–40. For his efforts Alemán was rewarded with the Ministry of the Interior (Gobernación), a post where he showed both toughness and skill.

By late 1944 there were numerous credible contenders for the succession. Five were civilians: Javier Rojo Gómez, regent (appointed head) of the Federal District; Marte R. Gómez, Secretary of Agriculture; Dr. Gustavo Baz, Secretary of Health; Ezequiel Padilla, Secretary of Foreign Relations; and Alemán himself. Four were from the military: Miguel Henríquez Guzmán, Enrique Calderón, Jesús Agustín Castro and Francisco Castillo Nájera. Early speculation tended to favor Gómez and Padilla, both seasoned and prominent *políticos,* but Alemán employed his portfolio to build up a personal following – especially among the state governors and also among key leaders of worker and peasant organizations. The groundwork had been well prepared when in May 1945, Alemán resigned from the cabinet. The Workers' Federation of Veracruz publicly supported its favourite son. The national leadership of the CTM met in special session and backed Alemán. Other groups, from the middle class to the Communists, then joined the bandwagon. Meanwhile Avila Camacho extolled the virtues of military professionalism in a speech to the Higher War College. (His meaning was not lost on the assembled officers: get ready for a civilian president). Rojo Gómez and Henríquez Guzmán withdrew from the race, and early in 1946 a pliant congress of the ruling party, which changed its name from the Partido de la Revolución Mexicana (PRM) to the Partido Revolucionario Institucional (PRI), nominated Alemán unanimously. A campaign nonetheless ensued. Two of the disgruntled generals, García Castro and Calderón, headed tickets for short-lived parties while Ezequiel Padilla, who had guided foreign policy through the Second World War and gained great favour in the United States, launched an independent candidacy with the creation of the conservative Partido Demócrata Mexicano (PDM). Energetic but quixotic, Padilla may have suffered from his pro-American label. In all events, the outcome of the election was clear: 78 per cent for Alemán, 19.3 per cent for Padilla, only token returns for García Castro and Calderón. There were neither protests nor violence, and Alemán took office in December 1946 amid tranquillity.

The country's new leader had a clear national project. Alemán was determined to continue and extend the process of import substitution industrialization that had started during the war. To achieve this goal he would forge an alliance between the state and private capital, both national and foreign. As he explained in a speech to the CTM:

Private enterprise should have complete freedom and be able to count on support from the state, so long as it acts on behalf of the general interest. Property ownership should preferably be in the hands of Mexican citizens, in accord with the lines already established by our legislation; but foreign capital that comes to unite its destiny with that of Mexico will be able to freely enjoy its legitimate profits.

'The role of the state', he went on to say,

is to guarantee for workers the right to organize, to reach collective contracts and to defend themselves as necessary through fair and legal means, not through procedures outside the law. At the same time, the state should guarantee the rights of businessmen to open centers of production and to multiply the country's industries, confident that their investments will be safe from the vagaries of injustice.[5]

His vision called for a conciliation of classes, not the promotion of struggle, with the state as ultimate arbiter.

To implement this strategy the Alemán administration poured considerable state investment into public works. Large-scale dams on the Colorado River, the lower Rio Grande and the Papaloapán River controlled flooding, increased arable land acreage and generated much-needed electric

[5] Quoted in Luis Medina, *Historia de la Revolución Mexicana*, vol. 20: *1940–1952: Civilismo y modernización del autoritarismo* (Mexico, 1979), pp. 37–8.

power. Roads, highways and an international airport in Mexico City strengthened communications and transportation networks. A new campus for the National University not only boasted major architectural and artistic achievements but also bespoke the government's commitment to the formation of highly educated cadres of public servants and private entrepreneurs. At the same time as he opened the doors to foreign enterprise, Alemán sought to strengthen Mexico's own business class through a variety of protectionist measures. Import quotas and tariffs kept competition within acceptable bounds, and the devaluation of 1948, from 4.85 pesos per dollar to 8.65 pesos per dollar, discouraged Mexican consumers from purchasing imported goods (and raised the cost of living). Thus began the 'Mexican miracle'.

The agricultural component of this strategy promoted a programme of modernization that quickly came to be known as 'the green revolution'. Concentrating on the improvement of crop yields and productivity, the programme employed a variety of instruments: the development and use of new plant varieties, many resulting from the efforts of an Office of Special Studies established in 1943 in the Secretariat of Agriculture with the support of the Rockefeller Foundation; government restrictions on the costs of inputs (such as energy, seeds and fertilizers); and state-sponsored subsidies for credit and commercialization. But the most conspicuous contribution, especially during the Alemán era, was the extension of irrigation, the Secretariat of Water Resources, established in 1946, playing a central role in the development of infrastructure. The green revolution emphasized productivity and profit, not land distribution. Much of the government's investment, especially irrigation, was directed towards the large haciendas and ranches of the north rather than towards the peasant states of the center and the south. And, as if in defiance of land reform itself, the Alemán group supported a constitutional amendment raising the allowable size of 'small properties' to 100 hectares. As a result there was an improvement in efficiency and productivity: corn yields increased from 300 to 1300 kilos per hectare; wheat, from 750 to 3200 kilos per hectare.[6] However, these policies also deepened fissures within the Mexican countryside. Alemán and his successors clearly favored the large-scale, mechanized, commercialized producers of the north who sold their goods either in Mexico City or in the United States; small-scale and traditional

---

[6] 'Wheat, not corn, was the principal protagonist of the green revolution, above all during the early years', Gustavo Esteva has argued in *La batalla en el México rural* (Mexico, 1980), p. 21.

farmers of the center and south were mostly left behind. The green revolution not only exacerbated these differences but also tended to fragment the array of interests in the rural sector. As a consequences, the major agrarian organization, the Confederación Nacional Campesina (CNC), came to represent a multiplicity of often conflicting groups: small farmers (*ejidatarios*), landless wage-labourers (*jornaleros*) and commercial owners (so-called *pequeños proprietarios*). The social effects of the green revolution – plus the tenacity of rural bosses, the *caciques* – thus lie behind the continuing weakness of the post-war peasant movement and the CNC.

Alemán's political record was mixed. Allegiance to the Allies in the Second World War had stirred hopes for democratization, and in 1945 Avila Camacho took a step in this direction by proposing to centralize and reform the system of electoral practice which had long favoured local bosses and *caciques*. The CTM predictably expressed disapproval, but the legislature nonetheless endorsed the plan after a timely intervention by a young deputy from Puebla named Gustavo Díaz Ordaz. Within the PRM/ PRI party, leaders agreed to base nominations on internal elections while attempting to avoid internecine conflict by respecting 'the principle of majority rights within each of the sectors'.[7] It was not self-evident what this would mean, except that the national state was taking over from regional *caciques* in the name of democratization. Indeed, the Alemán administration gave a consistency and shape to the Mexican political system which would endure for many years. As it developed, the overall project revealed several interrelated features: the imposition of a single ruling group; the elimination of the left from the official coalition; the state domination of the labour movement; and the cultivation and co-optation of sectoral leaders.

The insistence on homogeneity was most apparent in Alemán's cabinet. Almost to a man, the new ministers resembled the President himself: they were young (average age: forty-four), articulate and highly educated. Most important, they had close personal ties to the President (around 20 per cent of Alemán's own law-school class would reach high positions in national politics). This was not a coalition government, a tactfully constructed consensus of rival factions, as under Avila Camacho. This was Alemán's personal instrument. In keeping with this outlook, Alemán ousted governors who represented other groups – most conspicuously Marcelino García Barragán, the Cardenista (and later Henriquista) governor of

---

[7] Medina, *Historia*, p. 79.

Jalisco, and the Emilio Portes Gil supporter J. Jesús González Gallo in the state of Tamaulipas.

The isolation and exclusion of the left coincided with the Cold War era. It began in 1946 with the proclamation of stringent registration requirements for political parties, which made it impossible for the Communists to maintain their legal status, and it picked up in 1947 when Teófilo Borunda, secretary-general of the PRI, announced that the party would steer a middle course 'neither extreme left nor extreme right'. Rodolfo Sánchez Taboada, the party president, issued a ringing denunciation of Marxist influence:

We declare with firmness and clarity that we are not Communists and we will not be Communists; that we love above all else liberty and we do not accept any imperialism; that we affirm our belief in and our commitment to democracy, and that we are ready to fight at the side of the people, including against those who, with pretentious displays of verbal gymnastics, tend to expound ideas which do not accord with Mexican realities.[8]

Anti-communism thus became identified with anti-imperialism and, at bottom, with the affirmation of Mexican nationalism.

Perhaps the most important development in the containment of the left was the decision by Vicente Lombardo Toledano, intellectual leader of the Mexican labour movement and a former secretary-general of the CTM, to create a new political party. Its platform was twofold: to promote industrialization, thus creating the material base for social progress; and to foster anti-imperialism, thus defending national sovereignty from the post-war hegemony of the United States. At Avila Camacho's request Lombardo Toledano had agreed to postpone plans for the new party until after the succession of 1946. Attention then shifted to the CTM, where a radical contingent sought to challenge the dominant Fidel Velázquez faction in a battle over the secretary-generalship in 1947. Lombardo attempted to mediate the dispute, the Velázquez group artfully agreeing to support the formation of a new party in exchange for Lombardo's backing. In the face of such manoeuvres the radical unionists, led by railway leader Luis Gómez Z., founded a dissident anti-CTM organization, the Confederación Unica de Trabajadores (CUT). The Velázquez group consequently won a resounding victory within the CTM, installing Fernando Amilpa as secretary-general while formally agreeing to contribute to the creation of a new party for the masses.

[8] *Excélsior*, 1 September 1947.

This was hardly Amilpa's intent. An enthusiastic supporter of Alemán, he was eager to consolidate labour's position within the PRI and to expunge it of communist elements. On one occasion he sought to expel Lombardo Toledano from the CTM; on another, he withdrew his union from the Confederación de Trabajadores de América Latina (CTAL), which Lombardo had created in 1938. By the time Lombardo finally founded his new Partido Popular, in 1948, he had become almost entirely isolated from the CTM, which he once headed. The left had gained its party but lost its position within the constellation of ruling forces. From now on it would have to work from the outside.

In addition to excluding the left, the Alemanista regime sought to gain direct control of the mainstream labour movement. The tensions of the mid-1940s led to a profound division within the organized working class, pro-government forces claiming about 500,000 members and the dissidents having around 330,000. While many in the rank and file accepted the injunctions of Alemán and the CTM leaders to reject radical views as alien and unpatriotic, this was challenged by unions in the public sector, especially in nationalized industries, whose workers tended to identify national sovereignty with an anti-imperialist opposition to foreign investment. There was a minor revolt in 1946 among oil workers, which was quickly snuffed out after soldiers took command of PEMEX installations.

A larger crisis came in 1948 when railway-workers protested against real-wage cuts deriving from devaluation of the peso. Dissident labor leader Luis Gómez Z. had just turned over the secretary-generalship of the union to Jesús Diaz de León, an opportunistic operator nicknamed *el charro* because of his devotion to rodeo-type fiestas of the Mexican cowboy (*charro*). The government immediately began to support Díaz de León in his struggle against the popular Gómez, who insisted both on compiling a report about the impact of the devaluation and on presenting it to the board of his newly founded CUT, not to the railway union. An angry Díaz de León responded by accusing Gómez of fraud, a charge the government surprisingly – and inappropriately – agreed to investigate. In exchange for the President's backing Díaz de León accepted a new contract granting management the right to fire as many as two thousand workers whose jobs had formerly been secure. This established a pattern since known by the opprobrious epithet of *charrismo:* docile labour leadership would sell out the interests of its membership and receive, in return, political backing (and financial benefits) from the state and/or management. Labour would thus be controlled through the co-optation of its leadership, and the consequent arrangements would permit and facilitate the pursuit of capitalist growth via industrialization.

Independent unionists continued to search for a new vehicle, and in mid-1949 dissident mining and petroleum leaders joined with Lombardo Toledano to form the Unión General de Obreros y Campesinos de México (UGOCM). The government responded with hostility – refusing to recognize a strike against Ford Motors, negating UGOCM registration on a technicality and supporting a breakaway group within the union. Some miners withdrew from the UGOCM and in 1951 the oil-workers decided to return to the CTM. The UGOCM continued in existence but without posing a significant challenge. The political lesson was clear: with the emasculation of the UGOCM, Lombardo Toledano and the Partido Popular would not have any institutional base. At the same time, the government placed constrictions on the CTM, supporting the formation in 1952 of the Confederación Regional de Obreros y Campesinos (CROC), a nationwide labour organization within the PRI, as a counter-weight. By this divide-and-rule tactic, the Mexican state once again demonstrated its determination to maintain tight control over organized labour.

Alemán and his collaborators also sought to discipline the PRI. After tentative experiments with internal primaries, the President turned against the idea after the midterm congressional elections of 1949, and sent congress a law to prohibit parties from holding their own public elections. In 1950, Sánchez Taboada managed to gain re-election as PRI president against some opposition from old-time *políticos,* but he surrendered his commitment to primaries (candidates would henceforth be selected by party assemblies) and agreed to changes in the leadership structure. The party's dinosaurs returned to the fold, the Young Turks lost their advantage and PRI negotiations went back behind closed doors.

As a result, speculation about the 1952 succession was muted. Asked what to do about the transition in June 1951, Alemán uttered a classic response: 'Just wait'.[9] Perhaps because there was no obvious front-runner within the cabinet, some observers began to gossip about a constitutional amendment which would either permit Alemán's re-election or extend his term (an idea Lázaro Cárdenas strenuously opposed). Others focussed on the able Secretary of the Treasury, Ramón Beteta, but he suffered the

---

[9] Daniel Cosío Villegas, *La sucesión presidencial* (Mexico, 1975), p. 112.

political misfortune of having an American wife. Others discussed Fernando Casas Alemán, the regent of the Federal District, who was the President's cousin and said to be his favorite despite having a reputation for corruption.

It was in this context that Miguel Henríquez Guzmán, the career military officer and pre-candidate in 1946, decided to launch his own campaign. He garnered early support from three principal elements: Cardenistas, including members of the Cárdenas family, opposed to the conservative policies of the 1940s; alienated factions of the elite who resented their exclusion from power; and dissident leaders of the popular movement. Leaders of the Henriquista movement included such prominent figures as Antonio Espinosa de los Monteros, Mexican ambassador to Washington; Pedro Martínez Tornell, ex-Secretary of Public Works; Ernesto Soto Reyes, former leader of the Senate; Wenceslao Labra, ex-governor of the state of Mexico; and, among other military officers, the ubiquitous Marcelino García Barragán. This was not, at first, an opposition movement. Henriquista strategists sought to work within the system, not against it. They wanted to stop the candidacy of Casas Alemán, to have the PRI give serious consideration to Henríquez Guzmán, to incorporate democratic practices in the nominating procedure and to halt the excessive corruption taking place under Alemán. The ideological standard of the movement was vacuous and brief; 'not to depart to the slightest degree from the ideals of the Mexican Revolution', and, of course, to uphold the Constitution of 1917.[10] A change of leaders, not of national purpose, would be sufficient to rectify the course of public life. The iconoclastic ex-general eventually adopted some tacitly radical positions, such as support for small rural producers and independent labour unions, but he took care not to develop their implications.

Predictably enough, the docile PRI expressed adamant opposition to the upstart Henriquistas and attempted to throw them out of the party. Seeing no alternative, the dissidents created a new vehicle – the Federación de Partidos del Pueblo (FPP) – in March 1951, well in advance of the PRI's nominating convention. Henríquez Guzmán began waging an intense campaign, gaining support among such disparate constituencies as idealistic students, pro-democratic elements of the middle class, independent *campesino* groups and disenchanted workers. It is said that Alemán took this challenge seriously enough to dispatch an emissary to Cárdenas

[10] *Excélsior*, 30 July 1951.

in order to explain the dangers it posed to the system – including the possibility of a military coup.[11]

Early in October the word came down that the establishment's choice would be Adolfo Ruiz Cortines, the fifty-five-year-old Secretary of Gobernación from the state of Veracruz. Colorless but honest, he was clearly a compromise candidate, someone who might be able to heal the rifts within the country's political class. The machinery promptly went to work. Fidel Velázquez had already announced that labour would support the PRI instead of the Communists or, more pointedly, Lombardo Toledano's Partido Popular. 'The Mexican proletariat has today taken the most transcendental decision of its life', he intoned before the crowd on May Day: 'to identify itself definitively with the Revolution, with the fatherland, and to discard as incompatible all alien doctrines and ideologies'.[12] Or in translation: Marxists need not apply. At the same time, Sánchez Taboada offered Catholics a place within the PRI in order to weaken conservative support for Efraín González Luna of the PAN. The ruling elite spared no effort to create a ground-swell of public acceptance for Ruiz Cortines.

In the end they could claim success: official results of the 1952 election gave 74.3 per cent of the vote to Ruiz Cortines, 15.9 per cent to Henríquez Guzmán, 7.8 per cent to González Luna and 1.9 per cent to Lombardo Toledano. This was, however, the highest opposition vote recognized since 1929, and it proved to be the last of the open campaigns. Some Henriquistas protested against the result, a few went to prison, some pursued dreams of a military coup and some found their way back into the regime (the most spectacular case of co-optation being García Barragán, who eventually became Secretary of Defence in 1964–70). In 1954 the FPP dissolved and Henriquismo disappeared. After that, as Daniel Cosío Villegas has written, 'the true era of the *tapado* begins'.[13]

Despite his modest political credentials, Ruiz Cortines managed to maintain the PRI's subordination to the President. An opening statement at a party assembly in early 1953 identified its guiding lights: 'The people is its guide, the Constitution is its slogan, and Adolfo Ruiz Cortines is its standard-bearer'. And in keeping with rhetorical imperative, party leaders dedicated themselves to historical tradition and personalistic solidarity:

[11] Cosío Villegas, *La sucesión*, p. 131.
[12] Ibid., p. 115.
[13] Ibid., p. 139.

'the PRI will follow the revolutionary path shown by President Ruiz Cortines', who might have been surprised by this characterization of his political performance.[14] Notwithstanding such support, the new President faced several challenges. Perhaps the most pervasive problem was the unpopularity of the ruling elite, the widespread disenchantment with the greed of Alemán and his collaborators. The necessary response was simple but formidable: to strengthen and restore the political legitimacy of the regime – but without imposing any major change in policy. Ruiz Cortines went about this task in several ways. One was to stress the austerity of his own personal example, to promote the image of a hard-working and solid civil servant. Another was to distance himself and his team from the Alemán group, quietly punishing selected members of the previous administration (including Agustín García López, the former Secretary of Transportation, who lost millions in speculative ventures).[15] A third measure was to grant political rights to women, thus invoking the time-honored notion of the female as moral guardian while also broadening the government's popular base. Finally, the president announced impressive-sounding reforms in laws on corruption and public responsibility; although never strictly applied during his *sexenio,* these had a temporarily cathartic effect.

The Ruiz Cortines administration faced a second major challenge in the rising cost of living. The purchasing power of the mass of the population had been declining for several years, partly because of Alemán's economic strategy, and more recently because of international inflation resulting from the Korean War. To attack this problem – and to emphasize his administration's anti-corruption drive – Ruiz Cortines promoted a measure which would impose strict fines on monopolies and on the hoarding of goods. As the new President declared soon after taking office, 'One of the most basic objectives of my government will be to find adequate legal means to prevent an increase in the cost of living'.[16] One of his first economic measures was to lower the retail price of corn and beans, the government declaring its solidarity with the workers and the dispossessed. This stance appeared to jeopardize the close alliance between the state and private capital forged by Alemán. Cautious at first, business leaders refrained from opposing pro-consumer measures, but as time went on they

[14] *El Nacional,* 7 February 1953.
[15] Peter H. Smith, *Labyrinths of Power: Political Recruitment in Twentieth-Century Mexico* (Princeton, 1979), pp. 273–4.
[16] *Excélsior,* 24 December 1953.

expressed serious misgivings about any alteration of the basic economic model. Spokesmen for the Confederación de Cámaras Nacionales de Comercio (CONCANACO) insisted that government intervention would distort the marketplace and create inefficient monopolies. In other words, the state should sustain and protect the market but not participate directly in it.[17] In 1953, the business sector resorted to its ultimate weapon: reduced investment and capital flight. The result was a slow-down in economic growth and a consequent threat to the viability of the overall import substitution strategy. Here was an obvious challenge: in effect, the capitalists went on strike.

It was not long before the government caved in. By early 1954 the Ruiz Cortines administration began to favour the business sector with incentives and resources for increased production, including tax relief and easy credit. In mid-April the government took a decisive step by devaluing the peso from 8.65 per dollar to 12.50 (where it would remain for many years). As in 1948, the idea was to provide across-the-board protection for local industrialists and to entice them to reinvest in Mexico. By the end of the year production had picked up and growth resumed. The recovery of the U.S. economy from the high-inflation years of the Korean War further improved the general outlook. Mexico was back on the road to its miracle.

Confirmation of the business–government alliance made it all the more necessary for the state to assert its control over organized labour. Perhaps sensing the change in policy, prominent labour leaders came out in support of the April 1954 devaluation and pledged that the working class would make the necessary sacrifice. When Ruiz Cortines offered public employees a modest 10 per cent compensatory rise, exhorting the private sector to do the same, Fidel Velázquez proclaimed 'the strongest support' from the working class. However, UGOCM rivals and grass-roots spokesmen denounced the increase as insufficient, and the ever-alert Velázquez quickly persuaded the CTM to demand a 24 per cent increase – or threaten a general strike in mid-July. Into this breach stepped Adolfo López Mateos, the dashing young Secretary of Labour, who proceeded to head off a potential crisis through persuasion and negotiation. Some stoppages occurred, most notably in textiles and the movies, but López Mateos managed to avoid large-scale confrontations. The average raise came out to

[17] Olga Pellicer de Brody and José Luis Reyna, *Historia de la Revolución Mexicana*, vol. 22: 1952–1960: *El afianzamiento de la estabilidad política* (Mexico, 1978), p. 25.

be around 20 per cent: somewhat less than labour wanted and far less than labour's loss in purchasing power, but enough to silence criticism and keep Velázquez in charge. Once again, the velvet glove was shown to sheathe an iron fist. In order to institutionalize this outcome the Ruiz Cortines administration backed the formation in 1955 of the Bloque de Unidad Obrera (BUO), an umbrella organization designed to centralize the labour movement under Velázquez and his cronies. The impetus for the Bloque came mainly from the CTM, although it was supported by· numerous other unions, including the CTM's arch-rival, CROC. Notwithstanding governmental benevolence, however, the BUO never became a major force in itself; as Luis Araiza has observed, it was 'a giant blindman without any guide' (*'un gigante ciego sin lazarillo'*).[18] Industrial relations were generally subdued in the mid-1950s, workers winning minor victories in the electrical and textile industries. Turmoil beset the teachers' union from 1956 to 1958, when independent leadership under Othón Salázar Ramírez provoked resistance among the rank and file in Mexico City. A demonstration in August 1958 was repressed by the police, but the government later permitted one of Salázar Ramírez' allies to win a union election. Coercion and co-operation appeared to work.

This relative tranquility on the labour scene was disturbed by the railway strikes of 1958–9. The railway-workers' union, the Sindicato de Trabajadores Ferrocarrileros de la República (STFRM), had a long tradition of radical nationalism, and their strategic location in the country's transportation network gave them considerable leverage. Under the forceful leadership of Luis Gómez Z. and Valentín Campa, founders of the dissident CUT, they had energetically protested the devaluation of 1948; and ever since the imposition of Díaz de León in the *charrazo* the workers had steadily lost ground. Between 1952 and 1957 their real wages declined by -0.3 per cent a year – while the electricians, for instance, steadily improved their lot.[19] In February 1958 anti-*charro* forces within the STFRM sought an open confrontation by demanding an increase in wages. Union leaders eventually agreed to create a committee to study the real-wage problem. The report, issued in May, estimated a 40 per cent loss in purchasing power since 1948 and recommended an immediate wage increase of 350 pesos a month (around U.S.\$28). Díaz de León instead called for a raise of 200 pesos, and the management ostentatiously under-

---

[18] Luis Araiza, *Historia del movimiento obrero mexicano* (Mexico, 1965), p. 281.
[19] Kevin Jay Middlebrook, 'The Political Economy of Mexican Organized Labor', unpublished Ph.D. dissertation, Harvard University, 1982.

took to study this proposal during a sixty-day period – and, conveniently, to render its decisions after the presidential elections of July 1958.

Resistance consolidated behind Demetrio Vallejo, a rank-and-file dissident who had served on the wage–price commission. As head of a new general action committee he declared a series of 'escalating stoppages' (*paros escalonados*), starting with a two-hour stoppage and gradually working up to an eight-hour stoppage and then a general strike. The Ruiz Cortines government responded by jettisoning one of the *charro* leaders, installing another and decreeing a wage increase of 215 pesos in July. But co-optation failed to work this time: in August union members voiced their protest by electing the obstreperous Vallejo to head the STFRM. Within months Vallejo began threatening strikes over further demands, including calculation of the 215-peso increase on the basis of a six-day (not seven-day) work week. After achieving satisfaction from Ferrocarriles Nacionales, the most important line, he brought these same concerns before three other companies in March 1959, just before the Holy Week vacation. The pro-establishment BUO denounced Vallejo's audacity, while labour dissidents – some teachers, telephone operators, oil-workers – rallied behind the STFRM. A frightened government declared the strike to be illegal, the army commandeered the railroads, the police imprisoned Vallejo and thousands of his followers. Within weeks the strike was broken and the leadership replaced. Vallejo finally came to trial in 1963 and, convicted of conspiracy and sabotage under the law of 'social dissolution', he went back to jail for sixteen years.

The railway strikes proved to be a momentous episode. As José Luis Reyna and Olga Pellicer observed, 'this was the first important proletarian social movement that, for a moment, put the political system into a crisis. . . . It [was], without doubt, the most important movement to occur since 1935.'[20] But if it posed a challenge to the system, it also conveyed a sobering lesson: there would be little tolerance of independent unionism. As it showed in the case of Vallejo, the Mexican state demanded obsequious compliance from the leaders of organized labour.

So, too, in regard to the peasants, although there was not much provocation from this quarter. Mexican agriculture underwent a major transformation in the 1940s, as rising international prices encouraged production for export and capital investment (especially in irrigation) led to increasing yields on medium- and large-scale commercial farms. Although most

---

[20] Pellicer and Reyna, *Historia* 22:157.

campesinos did not share these benefits, the leaders of the peasant federation, the CNC, offered unwavering allegiance to the system. When Secretary of Agriculture Gilberto Flores Muñoz unveiled a plan for increased food production which favored large-scale proprietors at the expense of medium- and small-scale farmers, the secretary-general of the CNC expressed his support for the project in disarming style. 'Given this example of unquestionable and positive activity, peasants affiliated to the CNC have only to fulfill once again their patriotic duty'.[21]

Peasants mounted some successful local movements in Nayarit and other places, and the UGOCM made some sporadic attempts to mobilize *campesinos* in the north. The sharpest challenges occurred in 1958, when land invasions in Sinaloa spread to Sonora, Colima and Baja California, Flores Muñoz assuaging some of the agitation with modest schemes for land distribution. By far his most inventive response was the expropriation 'for the public interest' of a latifundio in Sonora leased to the U.S.-owned Cananea Cattle Company: billed as a nationalistic and populistic measure, the decision included a provision to repay the owners for the land's commercial value in hard cash. The proprietors were content, the UGOCM leaders went to jail, the peasants returned to work and the system survived intact. This was not an untypical solution.

Throughout their *sexenios* both Alemán and Ruiz Cortines cultivated close relations with the United States to the end of establishing a 'special relationship'. This entailed a low profile in the international arena and general support for the United States. The main exception to this rule came in 1954, as Washington prepared to launch a move to overthrow the reformist government of Jacobo Arbenz in Guatemala – partly because of the spectre of international communism, partly because land-reform measures threatened the interests of the United Fruit Company. At an inter-American conference in Caracas, the U.S. Secretary of State, John Foster Dulles, sought a condemnation of the Arbenz regime. Invoking the principle of non-intervention, Mexico joined with only two other nations – beleaguered Guatemala and Peronist Argentina – in opposing the U.S. proposal. When the CIA-sponsored movement overthrew the Arbenz regime in June 1954, Mexico's leftist and nationalist groups protested, but in vain. The Mexican government's stance was most revealing: having upheld the principle of non-intervention, it thereafter remained silent.

---

[21] *El Nacional*, 26 January 1953.

The episode thus revealed the limits of, as well as the capacity for, independent action by Mexico.

1958–70

The suppression of the railway strikes in 1958–9 inaugurated a period of relative political tranquility in Mexico. Continuation of the economic 'miracle' provided the material foundation for consensus and co-optation, and the ruling elite displayed a clear capacity for both coercion and persuasion. The state directed economic growth through a delicate alliance with private capital, domestic and foreign. There was effective political co-operation at the top between *politicos, técnicos* and military officers. The verticalist organization of workers and peasants secured a popular base for the regime, while prospering urban middle classes – inchoate, opportunistic and politically volatile – offered substantial support for a system that served them well. There would be protests and disturbances, but throughout this period the state exercised a generally impressive degree of hegemony.

The presidential succession of 1958 both symbolized and strengthened the centralization of authority. All the leading candidates came from the cabinet: Angel Carvajal, the Secretary of Gobernación; Ernesto P. Uruchurtu, regent of the Federal District; Antonio Carrillo Flores, Secretary of the Treasury and a consummate bureaucrat; Ignacio Morones Prieto, Secretary of Health, a *político* of long-standing prominence; Gilberto Flores Muñoz, the Secretary of Agriculture and political boss from the rural state of Nayarit; and Adolfo López Mateos, the accomplished Secretary of Labour. Virtually every major faction within the system had a pre-candidate: Carrillo Flores was seen as an Alemanista, Flores Muñoz as a Cardenista; labour and the peasantry, *políticos* and *técnicos,* all had their representatives. It would seem that López Mateos won because of his performance in containing the labour movement, because of his ties to Ruiz Cortines (whose campaign he had managed in 1952) and because of his acceptability to both Cardenistas and Alemanistas. The selection process was discreetly dominated by Ruiz Cortines: as Alfonso Corona del Rosal would later say, the outgoing president 'selects his successor, supports him, and sets him on his course'[22] – and by this time there would be no visible internal opposition. Energetic and charming, López Mateos ran a whirlwind campaign, obtaining endorse-

[22] *Excélsior,* 14 September 1975.

ments from the PPS and the PARM as well as from the PRI; even opposition parties joined the juggernaut. Token resistance came only from the *panista* candidacy of Luis H. Alvarez. With women voting in their first presidential election, 7.5 million people went to the polls in July 1958, and more than 90 per cent cast their ballots for López Mateos. The PRI and its machinery looked invincible.

Once in office López Mateos startled some observers, especially the Eisenhower administration in the United States, by declaring himself to be 'on the extreme left within the Constitution'. The statement was shrewd and significant. It pre-empted any move on the radical wing of the PRI and isolated the anti-establishment left, specifically the PPS and other Marxists who were presumed to be 'outside' the Constitution. It signalled an ideological solidarity with Zapata, Villa and other major figures of the Revolution, and it asserted Mexico's sovereignty from the United States, still in the grip of the Cold War. Moreover, it reaffirmed the incontestable fact of presidential power.

In keeping with this stance, López Mateos increased the role of the state in the national economy. The government gained control of the electric-power sector by buying out the American and Foreign Power Company, and it also purchased controlling shares in the motion-picture industry from long-resident U.S. millionaire William Jenkins. Government spending as a ratio of GNP rose from 10.4 per cent under Ruiz Cortines to 11.4 per cent. López Mateos also took an outspoken stand on land reform. In order to consolidate loyalty among the peasantry, he ordered the distribution of approximately 11.4 million hectares of land to more than 300,000 *campesinos,* an activist record that placed him second only to Cárdenas.[23] In 1963 he raised the basic price for staple commodities, later likening the measure to 'a minimum wage for workers in the countryside'.[24] Credit and basic services were harder to provide, but the political message was clear: at least symbolically, the government was siding with the masses.

The President adopted a similarly populist posture toward labour, proposing in 1961 a measure to institute profit-sharing between workers and proprietors. In belated fulfilment of a key clause in the Constitution of 1917 (with which López Mateos so closely identified himself), the new law seemed to represent a major victory for labour. However, the amount of profit to be shared was so small as to be acceptable to employers, and

[23] In actual practice, however, only 3.2 million hectares were distributed: Esteva, *Batalla,* pp. 230–1.
[24] Esteva, *Batalla,* p. 85.

the final law – adopted in 1963 – was never strictly enforced. Labour had achieved only a paper triumph, and business had successfully defended its own interests. Yet, by proposing the legislation without consulting business leaders, the politicians displayed their willingness and ability to take autonomous action. And the state acquired yet another weapon with which it could, in the future, threaten or challenge private capital.

Despite these populist gestures (and perhaps in deliberate combination with them) López Mateos continued to engage in selective crackdowns and repression. In 1959 David Alfaro Siqueiros, the internationally renowned painter, was put in jail (and not released until 1964). In 1963, as we have seen, Demetrio Vallejo was convicted of sedition and jailed for sixteen years. Peasant leaders fared no better, the most infamous case bring that of Rubén Jaramillo, an old Zapatista from Morelos who had brought his guerrilla band down from the hills in order to accept an amnesty and truce from López Mateos himself. When presidential blandishments failed to result in land for his people, Jaramillo ordered the occupation of fields owned by prominent politicians. Fruitless negotiations followed, and as a stalemate developed, Jaramillo and his family were found dead in the spring of 1962. No one doubted that orders for the murder had come from Mexico City.

The López Mateos administration continued to support the business sector and to court foreign capital. Investment was high and Mexico began raising capital abroad, especially in the New York bond market. The government managed to control inflation so strictly that López Mateos could retain the fixed exchange rate of 12.50 pesos to the dollar; there was no devaluation during this *sexenio*. Nor were there any statutory limits on profit remittances, allowing foreign investors to repatriate their earnings at a predictable (and favourable) rate of exchange, a factor which greatly encouraged foreign investment. The economy continued its path of high growth.

López Mateos attempted to establish diplomatic independence from the United States as Washington's relations with Cuba deteriorated and the Eisenhower administration began to pressure the Mexicans for support. López Mateos sought to walk a thin line: Mexico wanted to sustain the principles of non-intervention and self-determination, but it also wanted to avoid direct confrontation with the United States. Throughout 1960, therefore, Mexican representatives attempted to achieve these goals by upholding non-intervention without defending either communism or the Soviet Union. At the same time Mexico did not come out in favour of the

United States because this would have meant accepting the leadership of the Organization of American States (OAS), which (at Washington's insistence) had turned its back on Cuba and urged Mexico to follow suit: this itself would have compromised Mexico's own sovereignty. In the midst of these delicate negotiations López Mateos invited Cuban president Osvaldo Dorticós for a state visit in June 1960. The ceremonies led to a ritual identification of the Cuban Revolution of 1959 with the Mexican Revolution of 1910. A Mexican legislator condemned U.S. actions against Cuba, especially the closing of the sugar market. U.S. officials expressed their disapproval. The situation was tense but ambiguous.

After the Bay of Pigs invasion, and especially after Fidel Castro's profession of Marxist-Leninism, the Mexican government began to view the issue as an East–West problem, but they still rejected the idea of intervention. The Bay of Pigs fiasco prompted anti-U.S. demonstrations, Mexican spokesmen condemning the U.S. action as a violation of self-determination and maintaining that the problem should be discussed within the United Nations (where Cuba would get substantial support) and not in the OAS (where the U.S. would easily prevail). This position changed in 1962. Early in the year Mexican foreign minister Manuel Tello stated that 'there is an incompatibility between belonging to the OAS and to a Marxist-Leninist profession', but he simultaneously rejected the idea of expelling Cuba since the OAS charter made no provision for such a possibility.[25] Then came the missile crisis of October. Subjected to an extraordinary barrage of pressures, López Mateos finally came out in public support of the U.S. blockade of Cuba and instructed his representative at the OAS to vote in favour of a resolution demanding the withdrawal of the missiles. Mexico still imposed a face-saving condition – the vote was not to be used as justification for another invasion of Cuba. But even this stance had its limits: Mexican authorities systematically put passengers to Cuba on a black list, confiscated political material and maintained a silent blockade in disguise. Once again, the limits of autonomy became apparent.

The overall emphasis in foreign policy was on moderation and pragmatism. López Mateos held personal meetings with three successive U.S. presidents – Eisenhower, Kennedy and Johnson – and in 1964 he succeeded in regaining Mexican sovereignty over the Chamizal, a disputed section of land which had become part of U.S. territory after the Rio Grande changed its course. U.S. and Mexican leaders continued to pro-

[25] Vázquez and Meyer, *United States*, p. 178.

mote an atmosphere of harmony, and Washington even came to accept some measure of independence for Mexican foreign policy. Although direct U.S. investment in Mexico increased from $922 million in 1959 to nearly $1.3 billion in 1964, there was not much governmental aid, even under the Alliance for Progress. On the other hand, no restrictions were imposed on Mexico's access to international capital markets. Even under a self-declared leftist, Mexico's bilateral connection to the United States retained the appearance of a 'special relationship'.

In 1963, López Mateos promulgated an electoral reform that guaranteed a minimum number of five seats in the Chamber of Deputies to any party winning more than 2.5 per cent of the total vote (with an additional seat for each 0.5 per cent of the vote, up to a maximum of twenty). This way opposition parties could obtain representation in the national legislature without actually winning any electoral races. The point was to co-opt the challengers – the PPS, the PARM, and above all the PAN – and to create a loyal opposition. This would strengthen the legitimacy of the regime, especially in the aftermath of the repression of 1958–9 and in the light of the Cuban Revolution, further isolating the anti-establishment left and defining the Mexican regime as representative of a national consensus. López Mateos thereby finished out his term with a characteristic flourish.

The presidential succession of 1964 went smoothly. As usual, top contenders all came from the cabinet: Javier Barros Sierra of public works, Donato Miranda Fonseca of *presidencia,* Antonio Ortiz Mena of the treasury and Gustavo Díaz Ordaz from Gobernación. There were rumors that López Mateos favoured Miranda Fonseca, his erstwhile companion in Vasconcelos' movement of 1929 and a seasoned politician from Guerrero, but he ultimately settled on Díaz Ordaz – the competent but unglamorous ex-legislator from the state of Puebla. His selection appeared to confirm a tradition that, everything else being equal, the Secretary of Gobernación would become the next president (as had happened with Alemán and Ruiz Cortines). A mestizo by origin, much darker in appearance and less handsome than his predecessors, Díaz Ordaz instantly became the butt of savage jokes, including perhaps the most sardonic line of all: 'Anyone can become president'.

Once in office, Díaz Ordaz ruled with an iron hand. Without hesitation he dismissed office-holders with either too much political power, in which case they threatened him, or with too little political power, in which case they embarrassed him. In August 1965 he dismissed Amador Hernández, the head of the CNC, after an armed clash broke out between rival peasant groups. In late 1966, Díaz Ordaz fired Ernesto Uruchurtu, long-time mayor of Mexico City (and erstwhile presidential pre-candidate), after the much-criticized bull-dozing of a squatter settlement. He ousted Enrique Ceniceros from the governorship of Durango for failing to suppress a popular protest against foreign mining companies, and Ignacio Chávez from the rectorship of UNAM, the National University, for failing to crush a student strike. Unlike López Mateos, who managed to blend coercion with an artful dose of co-optation, Díaz Ordaz tended to rely on force and discipline alone.

Perhaps the most telling instance of this concerned the internal organization of the PRI. In 1964 the party presidency passed to Carlos Madrazo, forty-nine-year-old ex-governor of Tabasco and the first civilian in nearly twenty years to lead the PRI (thus marking yet another retreat by the military from the public eye). Himself a controversial figure, Madrazo sought to reinvigorate the party through the series of reforms, the most important being a plan for primary elections at the local level. Old-line *políticos* resisted, just as they had in the late 1940s, and Díaz Ordaz eventually decided to throw his weight behind the anti-democratic forces. Madrazo lost his post in 1966 and, in what many see as a suspicious airplane crash, lost his life in 1969. So ended the impulse for reform. Reinforced, if not rejuvenated, the traditional machinery asserted its dominance. The PAN was allowed to capture a municipality near Monterrey in Nuevo León in 1965, but the PRI reimposed its own mayor in 1969. In Sonora the PAN took Hermosillo in 1967, but Mexico City insisted on the triumph of the official candidate for governor. A year later hotly contested elections in Baja California were annulled because of 'irregularities' and the PRI claimed total victory. In 1969 the Díaz Ordaz government refused to accept what many thought was a PAN victory in the race for governor of Yucatán, dispatching the army to assure law and order (and a PRI victory).

Díaz Ordaz continued the policy of cultivating close links to the United States, although there was some tension in 1965 when Mexico – along with four other Latin American countries – refused to support the U.S. occupation of the Dominican Republic. Late in 1969, too, Díaz Ordaz protested when the Nixon administration's Operation Intercept, a blunt instrument against narcotics, led to the interruption of social and commercial traffic in the border area. But both sides saw these as fairly minor incidents, and the U.S.–Mexican relationship was generally smooth.

Perhaps more than any government since Alemán, the Díaz Ordaz team established intimate working connections with the nation's private sector. This alliance was clearly manifested in the question of tax reform, the government proposing to close two of the most egregious loopholes in Mexico's income-tax code: one permitting the fragmentation of total income into separate categories (so lower rates would apply on each); another allowing for the anonymous ownership of stocks and bonds (*al portador*). The President appeared at first to support the measure but soon withdrew the key provisions. As Secretary of the Treasury Antonio Ortiz Mena explained, tax reform should come from consultation not by fiat:

> In the process of the tax reform initiated but not concluded . . . we gave top priority to acquiescence of the different sectors of the population, because little can be done in any system without a general conviction of the various sectors as to the necessity of the measures and the justice and timeliness of their implementation. . . . The income tax law . . . was made listening to the viewpoints of the affected sectors.[26]

In other words, the government would not incur the opposition of the private sector. The law that finally passed resulted in a highly regressive tax: revenue from labour income as a proportion of total governmental receipts from the individual income tax went up from 58.1 per cent in 1960 to 77.9 per cent in 1966.

To help domestic industry the government imposed an additional 6 per cent increase in tariffs in 1965, and broadened the effect of quotas by creating about a thousand new import categories per year, so that by the end of the *sexenio* the total number was nearly 13,000. In Clark Reynolds' memorable phrase, the state and local entrepreneurs happily formed an 'alliance for profits'.[27]

Such overtures to business required Díaz Ordaz to reassert governmental control over organized labour. The ties between labour and the state had never fully recovered from the traumas of 1958–9, and the Bloque de Unidad Obrera – Ruiz Cortines' attempt to centralize and consolidate those links – had become little more than a phantom. Hence, early in 1966 the Díaz Ordaz regime supervised the formation of the Congreso del Trabajo (CT) as a new vehicle that would ratify the supremacy of Fidel Velázquez and reaffirm close state–labour linkages. The CT granted lead-

[26] Leopoldo Solís, *Economic Policy Reform in Mexico: A Case Study for Developing Countries* (New York, 1981), pp. 24–5.
[27] See Reynolds, *The Mexican Economy: Twentieth-Century Structure and Growth* (New Haven, 1970), esp. pp. 185–90.

ing roles to Velázquez's CTM and to the government-workers' union, the Federación de Sindicatos Trabajadores en el Servicio del Estado (FSTSE), thereby developing strong links with both the worker and the popular sectors of the PRI. The traditional structures continued to reign supreme.

Cultivation of the urban sectors, including labor, was undertaken at the expense of the countryside. The Díaz Ordaz government never once raised the minimum price for the purchase of basic grains from the level established by López Mateos in 1963, and reduced the relative share of agricultural credit from 15 per cent of the total in 1960 to only 9 per cent in 1970. In 1966 the administration initiated a program of agrarian warehouses, the so-called *graneros del pueblo,* ostensibly designed to assure the poorest farmers and *ejidatarios* a timely and effective support price for basic commodities (especially corn, beans and wheat). But the network of storage facilities suffered from hasty construction, poor location and incompetent administration; by 1971 only 15 per cent of the *graneros* were in use. Peasants erupted in isolated protest against their mistreatment – in land seizures, hunger marches, occasional outbursts of violence – but the voice of the *campesino* fell on deaf ears.

It was the middle classes, not the poor, that staged the most visible disturbances. Near the end of 1964 medical interns in Mexico City went on strike, initially over the withholding of their traditional Christmas bonus (the *aguinaldo*) and eventually over workplace conditions. Early in 1965, Díaz Ordaz, only months into his presidency, met with the strikers and their moderate supporters and issued a decree addressing some but not all of the demands. When a dissident faction of young doctors launched another strike in April 1965, the government took a tough stance and the interns went back on the job. And when they proclaimed yet another strike, this time in August, the regime responded with brute force. Riot police took possession of the Veinte de Noviembre hospital in Mexico City, prominent sympathizers were jailed, and after Díaz Ordaz had issued a stern warning in his state-of-the-nation address of 1 September, more than two hundred strikers were fired. The rest returned to work.

By contrast, the student movement of 1968 shook the system to its foundations. There had been a long and venerable tradition of student activism in Mexico, with disturbances customarily put down either by limited force (as in Guerrero, Morelia and Sonora) or by the dismissal of the rector (as at UNAM in 1966). In such instances authorities and students recognized and accepted rules of the game, a set of boundaries and codes that neither side would transgress. This time would be different.

The tortuous path of events commenced in July 1968, when police broke up a series of demonstrations by pro-Castro student groups. On 26 July (the anniversary of the Cuban Revolution) a loose federation of student organizations from the Polytechnic Institute, the agriculture school at Chapingo and the UNAM issued a set of demands: indemnization for families of students injured or killed in the disturbances, release of those in jail, abolition of the anti-subversion law on 'social dissolution', and elimination of special shock-troop police squads. Otherwise, the youths announced, there would be a general student strike. The authorities answered with a lock-out, closing all university-related institutions in the Federal District. Police forces shelled the San Ildefonso preparatory school (in what came to be known as the *bazukazo*) and stormed the premises. Another squadron invaded the Instituto Nacional de Bellas Artes and arrested seventy-three student demonstrators. In a major speech on 1 August Díaz Ordaz offered 'an outstretched hand', but by this time the students were beyond reconciliation.

Popular mobilization set the stage for confrontation. With remarkable boldness UNAM rector Javier Barros Sierra led a public march of 80,000 to mourn police invasions of the campuses in violation of longstanding traditions of university autonomy. A 13 August demonstration drew about 150,000 participants, and on 27 August, in an event of unprecedented magnitude, approximately 300,000 protestors took part in a march from Chapultepec Park down the Paseo de la Reforma to the central square or *zócalo*. In the meantime students organized a Comisión Nacional de Huelga (CNH) to coordinate actions and to promote the demands first set forth in July. Tension mounted. With Mexico about to host the Olympic Games in October, Díaz Ordaz used his address of 1 September to accuse the protestors of anti-patriotic conspiracy. The CNH proposed a dialogue but nothing happened. On 10 September an ever-pliant Senate authorized the President to call out the armed forces 'in defense of the internal and external security of Mexico'.[28]

Matters came to a head on 2 October, when students and supporters came together for another round of speeches and proclamations in the open plaza of the Tlatelolco apartment complex in downtown Mexico City. Without advance warning, white-gloved security agents waved in security forces that opened fire on the helpless crowd. At least two thousand demonstrators were placed under arrest. An official report admitted that

---

[28] Evelyn P. Stevens, *Protest and Response in Mexico* (Cambridge, 1974), p. 228.

forty-nine people were killed; a *New York Times* correspondent placed the death toll at more like two hundred, with hundreds of others wounded. It was a brutal massacre, since remembered as Mexico's contemporary *noche triste* ('sad night'), a primitive occasion when the system inexplicably chose to devour its own young. Schools reopened and the CNH dissolved, but Tlatelolco cast a long shadow over Mexican society and politics. Some high-level officials resigned in disgust. A wary public speculated about who bore primary responsibility – Luis Echeverría, the Secretary of Gobernación; Alfonso Corona del Rosal, regent of the Federal District; Marcelino García Barragán, the Secretary of Defence; or the President himself. Beneath the palpable anguish there lurked unsettling questions: Was this the product of Mexico's miracle? Was it the price of political stability? What kind of nation was Mexico?

While many engaged in painful soul-searching, others turned to violence. Terrorist groups began to appear in the cities, the most prominent being the September 23rd League, and rebellious peasants took to the hills. The best-known agrarian revolutionary of this era was Lucio Cabañas, who began forming a guerilla movement in the mountains of Guerrero in 1968; he and his band subsequently won considerable renown, at one point kidnapping the state governor, but he would meet his death at the hands of the military in 1974. Violence only begat more violence.

The Tlatelolco massacre had a more enduring effect in engendering the progressive alienation of the intelligentsia from the regime. For decades after the Revolution the nation's intellectuals had tended to collaborate with state authorities. The promotion of education was a primary goal of revolutionary leaders, and universities developed into crucial training grounds for national leaders. Artists and writers dedicated themselves to the articulation and elaboration of a political ideology which came to form the basis of a national consensus, a set of assumptions which endowed the state with the legacy of the Revolution itself. In tacit recognition of this service the Mexican government constantly cultivated contact with intellectual figures and supported their endeavours, frequently enticing them into semi-honorific public offices. The state and the intelligentsia both needed and supported each other. Tlatelolco shattered this long-standing pact. Such leading writers as Octavio Paz and Carlos Fuentes strongly denounced the repression – the memory of which inspired a whole genre of Tlatelolco literature – and essayists began to question the basic legiti-

macy of a regime that would wage such brutal war on its youth.[29] The
increasingly radicalized universities became hotbeds of opposition. The
relationship between students and the state, historically enriching for
both, degenerated into mutual resentment and open hostility. Tlatelolco
would by no means spell the end of the regime; but it opened a delicate
fissure in the edifice of state.

The close of the Díaz Ordaz *sexenio* also brought an end to the postwar
era of the Mexican economic miracle, the epoch of *desarrollo estabilizador*
marked by continuous economic growth, price stability and balance-of-
payments stability. Under the skilful orchestration of Antonio Ortiz
Mena, Secretary of the Treasury under both López Mateos and Díaz Ordaz,
and Rodrigo Gómez, long-time director of the central bank, economic
policy employed a variety of fiscal and monetary instruments: tax incentives to favour reinvestment, public-sector spending and foreign borrowing, and control of credit and the money supply. Interest rates were
pegged at attractive levels (above prevailing U.S. rates) to encourage
domestic savings and foreign investment. By conventional standards Mexico's post-war industrialization policies had been a resounding success:
during the decade of the 1960s Mexico sustained high levels of growth,
around 7 per cent a year, and – with one of the most rapidly swelling
populations in the world – achieved a solid per capita average growth rate
of 3.3 per cent. Inflation was negligible, around 3.5 per cent a year, and
the peso maintained its rate of 12.50 per dollar.

Yet the strategy of 'stabilizing development' was beginning to reveal its
weaknesses. If the hard-money policy had become a symbol for the stability and strength of the political regime, it also imposed economic burdens, not the least of which was to discourage exports because Mexico's
rate of inflation was generally higher than in the United States. (In fact the
peso became overvalued by the mid-1960s, after a burst of high-growth
inflation in 1964, but this was largely camouflaged by U.S. inflation
resulting from Vietnam.) Gradually, the effects of overvaluation showed
up in the trade deficit, which increased from $367 million in 1965 to
$946 million by 1970. During this period Mexico accordingly began to
borrow capital abroad, and by 1970 the country had a cumulative debt
(both public and private) of about $4.2 billion. Unemployment (and

---

[29] See Dolly J. Young, 'Mexican Literary Reactions to Tlatelolco 1968', *Latin American Research Review*
20, no. 2 (1985): 71–85.

under-employment) continued at high levels.[30] And by the mid-1960s the depletion of agriculture had started to require the large-scale importation of foodstuffs.[31] Even as the performance of Mexico's political economy approached its zenith, there were signs of trouble on the horizon. The party was far from over, but the lights were beginning to dim.

1970–90

Mexico's political system had demonstrated extraordinary effectiveness in resolving the crises and challenges that beset the country through the 1960s. A variety of state-directed programs – subsidies, price controls, wage agreements – provided the mass of the population with sufficient tangible benefits to prevent any serious radical challenge to the system as a whole. Such policies may not have complied with orthodox economic doctrine, but they met a crucial political goal; labour and the peasantry both continued to be essential pillars of the system. Discontent appeared mainly among the middle classes, among doctors and students, and although Tlatelolco had bequeathed a painful legacy, the regime had shown the resilience to overcome even this episode.

Mexico continued to experience rapid social change in the 1970s. Although rates of growth declined, the population increased from fewer than 50 million in 1970 to 70 million in 1980 and nearly 80 million by 1985. Almost a million new people entered the labour force every year, posing enormous pressure for the creation of jobs. As a result, Mexicans were on the move: migrants set out constantly in search of work, either going to the cities or crossing the border into the United States (where they would be declared 'illegal aliens', the *bracero* agreement having expired in 1964). Alarmists and politicians in the United States rabidly denounced what they viewed as a 'silent invasion,' proclaiming that there were 8 to 12 million 'illegals' in the United States. Although detailed research revealed that most 'undocumented workers' returned to Mexico and that the accumulated stock may have been in the range of 1.5 to 3.5 million, this did not prevent the surge of anti-Mexican nativism.[32]

---

[30] See Clark W. Reynolds, 'Why Mexico's "Stabilizing Development" Was Actually Destabilizing (With Some Implications for the Future)', *World Development* 6, nos. 7–8 (July-August 1978): 1005–18.

[31] Esteva clearly sees 1965 as the turning-point: *Batalla*, pp. 17, 71.

[32] Kenneth Hill, 'Illegal Aliens: An Assessment', in Daniel B. Levine, Kenneth Hill, and Robert Warren (eds.), *Immigration Statistics: A Story of Neglect* (Washington, D.C., 1985), pp. 225–50.

Population growth and social mobility also propelled the expansion of Mexico City, which swelled to a megalopolis with 14 to 16 million inhabitants by the mid-1980s. About half of this growth came from internal migration (indeed, about half the country's migrants headed for the capital). By official estimates there were at least 5 million poor people in Mexico City and its environs, as in Netzahuálcoyotl, a burgeoning community outside the Federal District that began as a squatter settlement in the 1960s and claimed more than 2 million residents by the 1980s. Notwithstanding this spread of poverty, the middle classes increased in magnitude and prominence, embracing perhaps one-third of the nation's population by the early 1980s. Unequal distribution of the benefits from 'stabilizing development' also enriched an upper layer, a wealthy and well-connected cadre that may have accounted for another 1 or 2 per cent of the total. The expansion of these middle- and upper-class sectors became clearly evident in consumption patterns: weekend shopping trips to Los Angeles and Houston became a matter of course, while the number of registered automobiles increased from 1.2 million in 1970 to 4.3 million by 1980. (It would seem, at times, as though each and every one of them was jammed into a single intersection in downtown Mexico City.)

This period also witnessed the development of the Mexican north, which became increasingly distant – economically, politically and culturally – from the center of the nation. By 1980 there were over 3.4 million residents in such border towns as Tijuana, Ciudad Juárez and Matamoros. The cities of Chihuahua, Torreón, Tampico and Monterrey continued to grow in importance and size. As many as 250,000 people worked in special 'in-bond' factories (*maquiladoras*) that produced goods for export to the United States (the number would fluctuate according to demand in the United States). Always fiercely independent, many *norteños* would come to see themselves as having little in common with the *chilangos* of Mexico City. Such perceptions would sometimes stimulate opposition to the regime and the PRI. In fact, this may have reflected an even more fundamental process – the appearance (however skeletal the form) of 'civil society' in Mexico. Independent citizens' organizations emerged in a variety of fields, no longer necessarily seeking tutelage or support from the state. Professionals, businessmen, academics and others came to adopt a somewhat more independent and less pliant attitude toward the regime; from outward impressions it seemed that political culture was becoming more activist and participatory, less passive and submissive.[33] It was also taking new forms, especially through the expression of growing concern about the authenticity of the electoral process. Further evidence, ominous to some, lay in the partial re-emergence of the Catholic Church as a public social force. For decades there had prevailed a tacit *modus vivendi,* a silent agreement for the Church and state to leave each other alone – so long as priests would refrain from politics. This began to change. In 1983, for instance, the Church managed to block a move to legalize abortion, and in 1986 an archbishop spoke out against electoral fraud. Conversations throughout informed circles often prompted intense speculation about the mysterious power of Opus Dei.

As the breach between the government and intellectuals widened, an independent press began to appear. Julio Scherer García, the displaced editor of the prominent newspaper *Excélsior,* took many of his top writers and created a weekly news magazine, *Proceso.* A new daily, *Unomásuno,* challenged *Excélsior's* position as the foremost paper in Mexico City. In 1984 it was followed by *La Jornada,* led by some of the most prominent young intellectuals in the country. Reviews like *Nexos,* modeled after *The New York Review of Books,* provided still other outlets. In effect, radical critics of the regime found new means of expression. They would still be dependent upon official toleration, and they would pay heavy prices for transgressions. (Journalists became common targets of attack, and some – like the well-known Manuel Buendía – were even murdered.) Dissidents were mostly confined to the Mexico City print media; television remained firmly in pro-establishment hands, while radio occupied a kind of middle ground. But the bounds of permissibility had nonetheless been stretched – and the range of possibilities increased.

In 1970 Luis Echeverría became Mexico's fifth post-war president. He appeared to be the embodiment of Mexico's political elite; born in Mexico City in 1922, he had studied at UNAM, taken a degree in law and taught courses there as well. He married into a prominent political family from the state of Jalisco, promptly entering the PRI and, more importantly, joining the *camarilla* of party president Rodolfo Sánchez Taboada. After the *cacique's* death Echeverria became *oficial mayor* of the PRI, and acquired prominence through his work during the López Mateos campaign; in 1958

---

[33] Solid evidence for this point simply does not exist; for a recent review of the literature, see Ann L. Craig and Wayne A. Cornelius, 'Political Culture in Mexico: Continuities and Revisionist Interpretations', in Gabriel A. Almond and Sidney Verba (eds.), *The Civic Culture Revisited* (Boston, 1980), pp. 325–93.

he landed the crucial position of Subsecretary of Gobernación under Díaz Ordaz. When in 1964 Díaz Ordaz assumed the presidency, Echeverría received the post of secretary. Six years later Echeverria repeated the move that Alemán, Ruiz Cortines, and Díaz Ordaz all had made before, from Gobernación to the presidency.

Throughout his career, Echeverría had labored intensively behind the scenes. He was the first constitutional president since the end of the Mexican Revolution who had never held a single elective position. He had become, over the years, a master of bureaucratic manoeuvring. Only one event – the massacre of students in 1968 – had brought him into the limelight, and though many held him responsible for that wanton display of naked force, his role was not at all clear. In spite, or possibly because, of that episode he managed to edge out several strong rivals for the presidency, including Alfonso Corona del Rosal, the head of the Federal District; Juan Gil Preciado, the Secretary of Agriculture; Emilio Martínez Manautou, Secretary of the Presidency; and Antonio Ortiz Mena, the Secretary of the Treasury widely regarded as the architect of Mexico's economic miracle. An austere, ambitious man, balding, bespectacled, non-smoking, teetotalling and trim, Luis Echeverría was the consummate expression of Mexico's new breed: the bureaucrat-turned-president.

Reflecting his experience in Gobernación, Echeverría moved quickly to strengthen and consolidate his own political power. From the outset, he strove to isolate and dismantle some rival *camarillas*, pointedly failing to give a cabinet appointment to one of his leading pre-presidential rivals, Alfonso Corona del Rosal. In June 1971, a bloody assault on students by paramilitary thugs gave him an opportunity to expel Alfonso Martínez Domínguez, then head of the Federal District. Echeverría ousted no fewer than five state governors from office (in Guerrero, Nuevo León, Puebla, Hidalgo, Sonora) and he made frequent changes in his cabinet: by November 1976 only six out of the seventeen secretaries still occupied their original positions. Echeverría cultivated his own political base from a cadre of young men, mostly in their early thirties, to whom he gave top-level, sensitive posts: Francisco Javier Alejo, Juan José Bremer, Ignacio Ovalle, Fausto Zapata, figureheads for what came to be known, with derision at the end, as a 'youthocracy' (*efebrocracia*). Here was a new generation, defined by both outlook and age, nurtured and brought to power by the President, a group who would presumably remain in his debt for many years to come. It also bespoke his desire, perhaps in the wake of Tlatelolco, to re-establish links with the country's intelligentsia.

Once in office, Echeverría revealed the power of his personality. Impatient and energetic, he took to his work with passion to re-establish official legitimacy in the aftermath of Tlatelolco, attempting to create a means for dialogue, a so-called *apertura democrática* in which he would himself play the central role (rather than impose an institutional reform). Exhorting his countrymen to labour with 'creative anguish' and apparently hoping to become a latter-day Cárdenas, he went everywhere, saw everyone, gave speeches, made pronouncements, talked and talked some more; as Daniel Cosío Villegas wryly observed, talking seemed to be a 'physiological necessity' for the new president. Echeverría's style of rule was neither institutionalized nor bureaucratized. It was extremely, urgently and intensively personal, and his style and rhetoric took on a highly populist tinge.[34]

As the United States accepted its defeat in Vietnam and moved toward détente with the Soviet Union, Echeverría sought to take advantage of the opportunity by establishing Mexico as a leader of the Third World countries, with himself as major spokesman. He was frequently critical of the United States, and traveled widely, reaching China in 1973. He exchanged visits with Salvador Allende, welcoming hundreds of Chilean exiles after the coup of 1973 (including Allende's widow) and eventually withdrawing recognition of the military junta. At the United Nations, he promoted a Charter of Economic Rights and Obligations and, in 1975, he instructed the Mexican ambassador to support an anti-Israeli denunciation of Zionism as a form of 'racism' (thus precipitating a tourist boycott by Jewish leaders in the United States; the next time around, Mexico would quietly abstain). Greatly over-estimating his prestige, Echeverría also presented himself as a candidate for the secretary-generalship of the UN near the conclusion of his presidential term.

On the domestic front, economic down-turns posed an immediate challenge for the government. Echeverría's initial reaction was to adjust and modify longstanding policies rather than to undertake any major innovations. To counter deficits his treasury secretary tried to hold down government spending, but the resulting decline in public investment led to sharp recessions in 1971–2 (with growth rates under 4 per cent). An opportunity to revise foreign-exchange policy came in August 1971, when President Nixon took the dramatic steps of imposing a 10 per cent tax on imports (including those on Mexico, thus bringing an end to the idea of a

[34] Daniel Cosío Villegas, *El estilo personal de gobernar* (Mexico, 1975), p. 31.

'special relationship' between the two countries) and taking the dollar off the gold standard to float on the international market. Some of Echeverría's advisers argued that this would be the time to float or devalue the peso as well, rather than keep it pegged to the dollar. But Secretary of the Treasury Hugo Margáin voiced quick disapproval: devaluation, he remarked, 'is a word that does not exist in my dictionary'.[35]

Echeverría also took a cautious approach toward the long-standing issue of tax policy. By late 1972 his economic advisers had put together a tax bill based on the one that Díaz Ordaz had scuttled in 1964–5, a proposal that would face the problems of fragmented income and anonymous holdings. Impressed by the logic of the proposal, the President instructed his finance minister to explain the bill to private-sector representatives. Margáin hosted two meetings at his private residence with leading industrialists from CONCAMIN and CANACINTRA, bankers and merchants. The businessmen offered strenuous objections, but according to one top adviser, the treasury secretary (and ex-ambassador to the United States) 'showed all his diplomatic skill in overlooking the carping tone' of his guests and countered their every argument. Without a word of explanation, however, the government suddenly dropped the whole plan.[36] Apparently the Ortiz Mena dictum of the 1960s still held true: tax reform cannot be achieved against the wishes of the private sector.

At the same time, Echeverría was preparing to cast aside the old formulas of 'stabilizing development' in favor of what he would come to call *desarrollo compartido* or 'shared development'. The year 1973 marked the final end of the financial boom of the late 1950s and 1960s. As inflation mounted, Echeverría appointed a new treasury minister, José López Portillo, who immediately began to take decisive steps. Price hikes in energy (gas and electricity) were followed by a wage and salary increase in September 1973, together with price controls on basic consumer products. As businessmen complained about these measures – and quietly threatened capital flight – Echeverría responded in tones of exasperation and anger. In his state-of-the-nation address in 1973 the President complained about idle industrial capacity and attacked criticism of the government as 'a lie that only benefits the interest of reactionary groups'. A year later he departed from his prepared text to launch a diatribe against speculators, the *'little rich ones'* who 'are despised by the people, by their own sons, because they are not strengthening the fatherland for their sons'.[37] The pact between the state and the private sector was suffering from strain.

As Echeverría's strategy for 'shared development' took shape, it came to stress the importance of distribution as well as production: for ethical and social reasons, it was held, the masses would need to share significantly in the benefits of growth. To achieve this goal and impose the necessary policies, the state would be a strong and autonomous force; private capital could play a constructive role, but profit would be less important than social equity. Whereas 'stabilizing development' relied on a close alliance between the state and the private sector, the political logic of the 'shared development' model called for a populist coalition of workers and peasants under the tutelage of a powerful state.

Desarrollo compartido placed special emphasis on the agrarian sector and on the long-suffering *campesinos*. The institutional cornerstone of this orientation would be Compañía Nacional de Subsistencias Populares (CONASUPO), an established organization with three major objectives: to regulate the market for basic commodities, to increase income for poor farmers and to ensure the availability of basic goods to low-income consumers. These goals could be contradictory, of course, and from Alemán to Díaz Ordaz, CONASUPO and its predecessors tended to protect the interests of urban consumers at the expense of rural producers. As one Echeverría official flatly observed, 'the traditional role of CONASUPO . . . has been to protect consumers. The government's economic policy was to keep prices stable, especially in urban areas, keeping salaries low and stimulating industry. That is why DICONSA [the chain of retail stores] has grown so greatly in urban areas and why corn was bought in the areas of highest production with little thought to the protection of producers'.[38]

Under Echeverría this was to change. In 1970, Mexico had to import more than 760,000 tons of corn, a symbolic and economic set-back that apparently stunned the President. He placed CONASUPO under the directorship of Jorge de la Vega Domínguez, an able and experienced political administrator, whose staff worked for nearly two years on a diagnosis of the country's agrarian problem. Presenting their results in mid-1972, the research team argued that previous agriculture policies had placed too much stress on the modern, mechanized commercial sector

---

[37] Quoted in ibid., pp. 81–2.
[38] Merrilee Serrill Grindle, *Bureaucrats, Politicians, and Peasants in Mexico: A Case Study in Public Policy* (Berkeley and Los Angeles, 1977), p. 75.

(mainly in the north). The key to self-sufficiency and income redistribution lay in the traditional corn-producing sector (mainly in the centre and south). A crucial obstacle was not just market forces but the role of middlemen, often powerful *caciques* who dominated villages or regions with the approval and support of superior authorities. According to the team, the answer to this lay in a programme of 'integrated' development, one that would by-pass the power of local *caciques* and reach directly to the peasants. The state should therefore intervene to help the poor, CONASUPO offering an integrated package of services (fair prices for inputs, reasonable price supports for harvests, adequate credit and storage facilities, assistance with marketing and advice for reinvestment).

The integrated programme for rural development soon became national policy and one of Echeverría's highest personal priorities. By the end of his *sexenio,* agriculture accounted for 20 per cent of the federal budget, by far the highest figure since the 1940s (when Miguel Alemán was pouring funds into large-scale irrigation projects). As its own budget quintupled, CONASUPO grew into a massive agency with as many as 15,000 employees (including subsidiary companies). Its purchasing agents focussed their attention on low-income *campesinos;* retail stores mushroomed in the countryside as well as in the cities, the total number increasing from around 1,500 in 1970 to 2,700 in 1976. But the agrarian programme could claim only limited success. The challenge, of course, was enormous. The resistance of unenthusiastic bureaucrats in rival organizations, such as the Secretariat of Agriculture, was considerable. And the tenacity of the *caciques* proved to be ferocious. In the end, the much-touted plan for integrated development fell victim to bureaucratic inertia and to the politics of presidential succession, already under way by late 1974.

The commitment to 'shared development' also entailed a rapprochement with organized labour. In the first few years Echeverría and Secretary of Labour Porfirio Muñoz Ledo tried to curtail the power of CTM boss Fidel Velázquez and even flirted with the idea of ousting him from his position. One government tactic was to grant tacit encouragement to an insurgent 'independent' worker movement, which became especially strong among auto-workers, railway-workers, and electricians – in the most modern and mechanized sectors, where traditional patron–client ties were weaker. In this vein, Echeverría extended legal recognition to the Unidad Obrera Independiente (UOI), an organization that explicitly defied the CTM. However, when inflation began to accelerate in 1973, Echeverría came to recognize his need for Velázquez's control of rank-and-file demands for compensatory wage increases. The President thus made amends, Velázquez continuing his prolonged supremacy as the state threw its weight behind his leadership and the independent movement withered away (by 1978 it accounted for merely 7 per cent of Labour Congress membership).[39] Labour was back in safe hands.

Echeverría nonetheless continued to pursue an activist, growth-oriented economic policy. In keeping with his nationalistic and *tercermundista* pronouncements, Mexico passed new laws in 1973 to regulate – but by no means eliminate – the actions of foreign enterprise, especially the multinational corporations. The role of the state, already large, expanded sharply; total government revenue rose from around 8 per cent of the gross domestic product in 1970 to roughly 12.5 per cent in 1975. Public spending poured into housing, schooling and other development programmes. Agriculture credit increased. The nation doubled its capacity to produce crude oil, electricity, and iron and steel. As a result, Echeverría proudly pointed out, the GDP grew at an annual average rate of 5.6 per cent. Nonetheless, this expansion of state activity brought Echeverría into constant conflict with the domestic private sector, caught in a squeeze between multinational corporations and the Mexican state. Only the strongest local firms could survive, and the government bought out many of the weaker ones (the number of state-owned corporations swelled remarkably, from 86 to 740 during Echeverría's regime). Between 1970 and 1976 the money supply grew about 18 per cent a year, compared to previous rates around 12 per cent, and the federal deficit increased sixfold. This contributed to an inflationary spiral – prices rose by about 22 per cent a year – which, in turn, priced Mexican goods out of international markets. As a result, the deficit in the balance of payments tripled between 1973 and 1975 – thus placing great, ultimately overbearing pressure on the value of the peso.

As the *sexenio* wore on there were signs that the still young Echeverría intended to broaden and perpetuate his influence. Five of his cabinet secretaries left office in order to assume state governorships, and a sixth started running for another just after the conclusion of the presidential term. Several members of the sub-cabinet became governors of states as well. Most observers noted that these politicians, Echeverrista to a man, would be solidly ensconced in state capitals well after the President stepped down. It was in this context that Echeverría broke all precedent by publicly calling attention to the forthcoming presidential succession.

[39] See Middlebrook, 'Political Economy', p. 316.

'It is useful', he stated in late 1974, 'for public opinion to analyze and evaluate men in relation to the presidential succession, and it is good for it to be that way. . . . I should think that public opinion will start to define its preferences sometime in the latter part of next year; but in the meantime, everyone should be the object of study, observation, and judgement. That is democratically healthy.'[40] He returned to the subject on subsequent occasions, and in April 1975, Leandro Rovirosa Wade, the Secretary of Hydraulic Resources, startled the press by announcing the names of plausible contenders. The move was so novel that it could only have been prompted by Echeverría, perhaps to demonstrate his own control of the selection process.

Thus revealed before 'public opinion', the so-called *tapados* were seven: Mario Moya Palencia, forty-two, Echeverría's successor at Gobernación and for that reason widely regarded as the front-runner; Hugo Cervantes del Río, forty-nine, Secretary of the Presidency; José López Portillo, fifty-four, Secretary of the Treasury and a boyhood friend of the President; Porfirio Muñoz Ledo, forty-one, Secretary of Labour and a well-known intellectual; Carlos Gálvez Betancourt, fifty-four, director of the Social-Security Institute; Augusto Gómez Villanueva, forty-four, Secretary of Agrarian Reform; and Luis Enrique Bracamontes, fifty-one, Secretary of Public Works. 'Any one of them is excellent', concluded Rovirosa Wade. 'Each one has managed admirably to perform the tasks with which President Echeverría has entrusted him'.[41]

At the time of this announcement, Jesús Reyes Heroles, president of the PRI, proclaimed the party's intention to draft a 'basic plan of government' for the 1976–82 administration. The idea would be to forge a platform, a series of policy commitments by the government. With Echeverría's evident approval, Reyes Heroles revealed that the plan would be ready by late September and submitted to the party leadership for ratification. The candidate would be selected in October, presumably as the person most capable of carrying out the plan. The slogan went forth: 'First the programme, then the man'! It seemed, to some, that Echeverría had found a novel way to tie the hands of his successor. On the morning of 22 September, right on schedule, Reyes Heroles was chairing a meeting about the 'basic plan' when he received a call from the presidential residence. He returned to the session, disconcerted and surprised, and hurried

[40] Andrés Montemayor H., *Los pridestinados* (Monterrey, 1975), p. 8.
[41] *Hispano Americano*, 21 April 1975.

out to Los Pinos for a brief visit at midday. In the afternoon, three of the presidential hopefuls – Moya Palencia, Cervantes del Río and Gálvez Betancourt – were together with Echeverría at a ceremonial lunch. When interrupted by an aide, Moya Palencia reportedly turned pale and left the table. The choice was López Portillo. Meanwhile, Fidel Velázquez was publicly proclaiming labour's support for the Secretary of the Treasury, and others were rapidly joining the ranks. For some the *destapamiento* was a surprise, for others it was a shock. A leader of the CNC was asked if the peasant sector would add its backing: "To whom?" he enquired. Shown a copy of the afternoon paper, with López Portillo's name in the headline, he merely nodded and said: 'Of course'. Velázquez and other party leaders went to the treasury building to offer their congratulations, and early in the evening a crestfallen Moya Palencia came to express his own capitulation: 'José López Portillo is the best man the Mexican Revolution has. Let us believe in him'.[42]

Even as they climbed upon the bandwagon, people in the political world mused over the choice of López Portillo. Although a lifelong friend of the President, he had never been able to curry the favor of labour or the peasant sector in the course of his relatively brief public career. In mid-November, Echeverría himself offered a clue when he made the remarkable declaration – breaking all precedent again – that López Portillo won out 'because he was the one with the fewest political attachments, the one who had not reached any secret or discreet agreement, the one who dedicated himself to the service of the country without engaging in cheap politics (*política barata*)'.[43] The denunciation of *política barata* was widely interpreted as a rebuke to Moya Palencia, generally regarded as the *tapado* with the widest political support. But López Portillo's greatest asset was also his greatest liability: he did not have a team of his own. From Echeverría's point of view, this might be the easiest person to control from behind the scenes.

In the following months Echeverría held the spotlight while López Portillo, true to form, remained in the shadows. The July 1976 election was itself a desultory affair, partly because an internal schism had prevented the PAN from fielding any candidate at all. This made the campaign a race between López Portillo and abstentionism, and if it is true that 69 per cent of the eligible population went to the polls, with 94 per cent casting ballots in favor of the PRI candidate, this would have to go

---

[42] *Excélsior*, 23 September 1975.
[43] Ibid., 13 November 1975.

down as a triumph for López Portillo, who had shown himself to be easy-going and friendly – *simpático.*

But a sense of malaise began to spread. Early in July a rebellion had erupted within the staff of *Excélsior,* then Mexico City's leading newspaper, owned collectively as a co-operative venture. The insurgents resorted to numerous illegal tactics, but governmental authorities – from Echeverría on down – refused to take any action. The uprising succeeded, the direc-torship changed hands, and what had become a proud and critical voice was now stilled. (The departed staff would go on to found the magazine *Proceso.*) And when it was reported that Echeverría had become a major shareholder in a new newspaper group controlling thirty-seven dailies, the implications became ominous. On 11 August an unidentified terrorist organization, possibly the leftist September 23rd League, attacked a car that was carrying Margarita López Portillo, a sister of the President-elect. She was unhurt but one of her bodyguards was killed, three others were wounded and the leader of the gang was shot to death. Viewed in isola-tion, the incident was unsettling enough, but the unanswered questions were deeply disturbing: Who was really behind the attack? What if López Portillo had been the real target? How could this happen in broad daylight in Mexico City?

There followed a crushing blow. On 31 August, after months of official denial, the government devalued the peso for the first time since 1954. The drain on the country's foreign reserves had reached intolerable limits, there had been large-scale capital flight since the previous April, and exports remained overpriced. As a result the government finally decided to 'float' the peso, letting it find its new level – which the Bank of Mexico pegged at 19.90 on 12 September, a 37 per cent drop in value from the long-standing rate of 12.50. As if this were not enough, the government refloated the peso a second time, on 26 October, and the exchange rate quickly jumped to 26.50 to the dollar. Within two months, the interna-tional value of the peso had been cut in half. For those who viewed the currency's position as a sign of strength and stability, a manifestation of the 'Mexican miracle' and a hallmark of national pride, this was bitter medicine indeed.

Rumours started to intensify. Somewhat cryptically, Echeverría de-nounced 'insidious attacks' against Mexico in his final state-of-the-nation address,[44] and gossip spread throughout the capital. There would be an

----

[44] Ibid., 2 September 1976.

assault on Echeverría's wife. There would be an attempt on López Portillo's wife. Someone would try to murder Hermenegildo Cuenca Díaz, Echeverría's Secretary of Defence. A local boss in Jalisco had put out a contract on the life of the redoubtable Marcelino García Barragán. But the chief rumour, the one that captured the popular imagination, was the most implausible of all: there would be a military coup. The first time around, the coup was to occur on 16 September, the anniversary of Mexico's independence. After that, attention focussed on another date: 20 November, the anniversary of the Revolution, only ten days before the end of Echeverría's term. On 29 November a series of explosions took place in the capital, causing extensive damage but provoking no outward challenge to the regime.

Especially during November, events in the north created further tension and exacerbated popular gullibility. Around the middle of the month peasant groups seized extensions of land in Sonora, Sinaloa and Durango. The actions reflected long-standing grievances, and agrarian resentment had been smouldering for years; what was novel about these confrontations was the timing, only days before the end of a regime. On 20 November Echeverría, not about to give up power till the final minute, suddenly expropriated nearly 100,000 hectares of rich privately owned land in Sonora for collective *ejidos*. Outraged by this action, land-owners protested, and in Sinaloa some 28,000 announced a stoppage in the fields. In a demonstration of solidarity, businessmen and merchants in Puebla, Chihuahua and Nuevo León joined in brief work stoppages. Encouraged by the outcome in Sonora, peasants invaded other lands in Durango and Jalisco.

At the inauguration López Portillo delivered an eloquent call for collaboration instead of conflict, and then he instaled his new team. One source of cabinet leaders came from the president's own political background, people with whom he had worked in the course of his career – *técnicos* in charge of economic policy, men such as Rodolfo Moctezuma Cid, Carlos Tello, and the youthful Andrés Oteyza. López Portillo also drew on personal friends (Antonio Farell Cubillas at IMSS, Pedro Ojeda Paullada in labour, Jorge Díaz Serrano at PEMEX) and family relations (sister Margarita, for example, became a departmental director within Gobernación), the administration eventually coming under withering criticism for nepotism. In all these ways, López Portillo managed to construct a *camarilla* that had as its common denominator personal loyalty to himself.

To extend and strengthen popular support for the regime, López Portillo adopted a time-tested strategy: electoral reform. The legacy of Tlatelolco still cast a pall over the nation's politics, especially among the young, and the tumult of the Echeverría years had created a widespread sense of apprehension. Electoral abstention caused considerable concern, and it became apparent that the system would have to open up in order to provide orderly channels for the opposition, especially since the the PPS and the PARM had long lost their relevance and followings. Moreover new parties were starting to appear, at least one on the right (the Partido Demócrata Mexicano, founded 1971) but most on the left: the Partido Socialista de los Trabajadores, or PST (1973); the Unidad de Izquierda Comunista or UIC (1973); the Movimiento de Acción y Unidad Socialista, or MAUS (1973); the Partido Mexicano de los Trabajadores (1974); the Partido Popular Mexicano, or PPM (1975); the Partido Socialista Revolucionario, or PSR (1976); and the Partido Revolucionario de los Trabajadores, or PRT (1976).

In response to these developments the reform measure of December 1977 contained three basic elements: first, a liberalization of the procedures for party registration (which could now be achieved either by getting 1.5 per cent of total vote in any national election or by enrolling 65,000 members); secondly, an expansion of the Chamber of Deputies to four hundred members, with three hundred elected by simple majority in single-member districts and one hundred by proportional representation (in other words, these seats were reserved for opposition parties); and, finally, extension of access to mass media for opposition parties and opposition candidates. Initially, the left appeared to benefit most. Under the new registration laws the Partido Comunista Mexicano was in 1979 able to take part in its first election since 1946, and in 1981 the PCM joined with several other leftist parties to form the Partido Socialista Unificado de México (PSUM). Not all radical parties joined this coalition, which would soon be rent by internal divisions, but the mere prospect of a unified electoral left signified a profound change in the tenor and tone of national politics.

It was, however, the economy, more than the political opposition, that posed the most crucial challenge. By the mid-1970s import substitution industrialization had lost much of its dynamism, unemployment was rampant, and inflation was starting to rise. Echeverría seemed only to aggravate social tension through his incendiary rhetoric, his permissive stance toward land seizures in the countryside, and his continuing conflict with the entrepreneurial sector. As José López Portillo assumed the presidency in December 1976, many Mexicans were anticipating difficult times. Then the country struck oil.

Here, it seemed, was the solution to Mexico's problems. For decades after the expropriation of foreign-owned companies in 1938, Mexico had kept a low profile in the international world of petroleum. PEMEX functioned efficiently enough, producing steady supplies of oil at very low prices for the nation's growing but relatively modest needs. Exports were negligible and imports occasionally significant. By 1976 successive oil discoveries had raised Mexico's proven oil reserves to approximately 6.3 billion barrels, suggesting that PEMEX would be able to satisfy domestic requirements for the foreseeable future. Talk of bonanza began. Announcements of new discoveries, especially in the south, doubled and redoubled official estimates of Mexican oil reserves. By September 1979, López Portillo could confirm that the country's oil and natural gas deposits contained the energy equivalent of 45.8 billion barrels of 'proven' reserves, 45 billion barrels of 'probable' reserves and 110 billion barrels of 'potential' reserves – a grand total of 200 billion barrels in all. (According to these estimates, Mexico possessed about 5 per cent of world proven reserves of crude oil and 3 per cent of world proven reserves of natural gas.)

The oil discoveries prompted intense debate within Mexican political circles. What was to be done with the deposits? The left, led by students and intellectuals, called for limitations on petroleum production that would preserve the nation's patrimony, avert over-dependence on buyers and prevent the social dislocations – inflation, frustration and inequality – seen in such countries as Iran. The right, mainly industrialists, clamoured for a rapid-development policy in order to pay off the national debt, acquire reserves of foreign exchange and ward off potential commercial threats from alternative energy sources. After some hesitation the López Portillo administration took an intermediate course, seeking to satisfy domestic needs and to export 1.25 million barrels per day (bpd). The aim was to stimulate growth, promote employment and pay for imports – without creating inflation or excessive dependence on oil sales. Under no circumstances, government officials vowed, would Mexico become beholden to its bounty.[45] Yet, to meet the need for foreign exchange, both to stimulate growth and to deal with the debt, the López Portillo administration pushed ahead with petroleum exports, increasing the daily ceiling to 1.50 million bpd. And as the international price of oil kept

---

[45] See Gabriel Székely, *La economía política del petróleo en México, 1976–1982* (Mexico, 1983).

rising, owing largely to the efforts of the Organization of Petroleum Exporting Countries (OPEC), so did Mexico's receipts. Oil earnings soared from $311 million in 1976 to nearly $14 billion by 1981, by that time accounting for nearly three-quarters of Mexican exports. At the same time, there was a relative decline in the role of non-oil exports, especially agricultural commodities. Almost in spite of itself, the Mexican economy was undergoing a process of 'petrolization'.

In a sense the strategy appeared to work. In real terms (that is, allowing for inflation) the GDP grew by the highest rates in recent memory: 8.2 per cent in 1978, 9.2 per cent in 1979, 8.3 per cent in 1980 and 8.1 per cent in 1981. This was an extraordinary achievement, especially during a period when the United States and the industrial world were floundering through stagflation and recession, and it seemed to justify the government's headlong pursuit of petroleum-led growth. This expansion resulted in the creation of all-important new jobs – nearly a million of them in the spectacular year of 1979 – and it also increased the magnitude of the economic role of the state.

The López Portillo government attempted to use this expanded influence to develop a new and coherent policy for the long-beleaguered agrarian sector. As Mexico continued to import basic grains and the dimensions of the country's agricultural crisis became apparent, López Portillo and his advisers designed and in 1980 launched the Mexican Food System programme (Sistema Alimentario Mexicano, or SAM). The goal was to achieve self-sufficiency in food production, thus eradicating malnutrition and asserting national autonomy with a single stroke. The strategy was to channel income from oil exports into the countryside for both the production and the consumption of basic grains – 'sowing the petroleum', as the catchy slogan stated. SAM was an ambitious and expensive plan, costing nearly $4 billion in 1980 alone. Exceptional weather yielded a bumper crop in 1981, and grain production was nearly 30 per cent higher than in the drought year of 1979. Officials claimed instant success for SAM. Others kept an eye on the weather, and greeted dry spells in 1982 and 1983 with a sense of deep foreboding.

Petroleum revenues also enhanced Mexico's position in the international arena as the OPEC-driven price shock of 1979 flaunted the apparent power of the oil-producing nations. Although Mexico never became a formal member of OPEC (preferring to have the ambiguous status of official observer), national leaders firmly believed that this economic leverage would provide the basis for a new assertiveness in foreign affairs. As López

Portillo himself liked to say: 'You can divide the countries of the world into two types, the ones that have oil and the ones that do not. We have oil'.[46] Having kept a low diplomatic profile for decades, Mexico was now ready to impose itself on the international scene. As though in reflection of this feeling, Mexico hosted a massive North–South dialogue in the glittering resort town of Cancún in October 1981.

This ebullience became particularly apparent in Mexico's stance toward the evolving crisis in Central America. While the United States was denouncing Soviet and Cuban influence in the isthmus, Mexican officials tended to see political conflicts within the region as the logical response to historic conditions of repression and inequity. In the hope of encouraging negotiated settlements, the López Portillo regime showed public sympathy with revolutionary causes. The Mexican government broke relations with the Somoza regime in Nicaragua well before the insurgent victory in mid-1979, and then proceeded to lend unequivocal support to the Sandinista government. In 1980, Mexico (together with Venezuela) began offering petroleum to Nicaragua on generous concessionary terms. The following year Mexico joined with France to issue a call for recognition of the Salvadoran Democratic Revolutionary Front (FDR–FMLN) as a 'legitimate political force'. This involvement of an extra-continental power in hemispheric affairs violated a long-standing tenet of regional diplomacy, one that the United States had sought to enforce ever since the declaration of the Monroe Doctrine in 1823, and the Reagan administration looked on with sullen disapproval.

In a February 1982 speech in Managua, López Portillo publicly offered Mexico's help to unravel what he called 'three knots that tie up the search for peace' in the region – the internal conflict in El Salvador, distrust between the United States and Nicaragua and hostility between the United States and Cuba. He reiterated the call for a negotiated settlement in El Salvador, proposed a non-aggression treaty between the United States and Nicaragua, and urged further dialogue between the American government and the Castro regime. All by itself, Mexico was thus proposing to assume a major leadership role in regional affairs. Predictably enough, the U.S. response to this initiative was at best lukewarm; a few discussions took place and then withered away.

López Portillo's high-growth economic strategy incurred important

---

[46] Quoted in George W. Grayson, 'Mexico's Opportunity: The Oil Boom,' *Foreign Policy* 29 (Winter 1977–8): 65–89, esp. 65.

costs, one principal drawback being the balance of trade. Although the value of exports increased dramatically, the quantity of imports grew even more. The result was a staggering commercial deficit: $2.1 billion in 1978, $3.6 billion in 1979, $3.2 billion in 1980 and again in 1981. Economic expansion required importation, especially of intermediate and capital goods, and Mexico continued to purchase more than it sold. Such deficits were formerly off-set by two special links with the United States – the tourist trade and border transactions (including exports from *maquiladoras*). But by 1981 tourism yielded almost no surplus at all, as high-income Mexicans spent lavish amounts of money abroad (the over-valued peso made foreign travel cheap), and border industries suffered from the recession in the United States. In 1981 Mexico's overall balance of payments ran up a deficit of $11.7 billion dollars, an enormous sum by any standard – even for a country rich in oil.

Meanwhile, the government itself went into debt. To implement its high-growth approach the López Portillo administration undertook high-cost initiatives that increased the economic participation of the state. In relative terms, the government's deficit went from around 7 per cent of GDP in the 1970s, a level sustained during much of the decade, to 14 percent in 1981 and 18 percent in 1982. The deficit and the balance of payments left only one option: to borrow funds from abroad. Mexico's private businesses and state agencies searched for capital in the international money market. And foreign bankers, apparently bedazzled by the oil discoveries, hastened forward with massive loans. The national debt continued its inexorable climb, from around $30 billion in 1977–8 through $48 billion in 1980 to more than $80 billion by 1982. About three-quarters of this debt belonged to the public sector. Inflation acceler-ated too. Almost alone among developing nations, Mexico had success-fully resisted inflation through the 1960s, keeping annual rates around 5 per cent or less. In the mid-1970s price increases moved up around 20 per cent, still reasonable by international standards, but then they jumped to 30–40 per cent under the high-growth strategies of the López Portillo administration. By 1982 the rate was nearly 100 per cent. This inflation-ary pattern reduced the purchasing power of the workers and, especially because it came so suddenly, threatened to bring on social tension. 'The bottom had to fall out', said an economist at one of Mexico's biggest banks. 'Nobody expected it so fast.'[47]

[47] *Boston Globe*, 3 October 1982.

It appears that the López Portillo administration committed two major errors in economic policy. One was to place too much confidence in petroleum exports. The extraction and commercialization of Mexico's oil reserves required large-scale investments, so a considerable share of petro-dollar earnings were plowed back into the oil industry. As the energy sector expanded, therefore, the rest of the economy languished. Moreover, the urgent need to create new jobs tempted López Portillo to push for high rates of growth. In addition, the 'no re-election' clause may have lured him into short-run strategies that would achieve tangible results during the course of his non-renewable presidential term. At any rate, Mexico began to spend its petroleum earnings before they were safely in hand. Mexico thus became extraordinarily dependent on its energy exports, which made the country vulnerable to changes in the international price of oil. In mid-1981 a world-wide glut led to sharp drop in prices. Mexico attempted to resist this trend, and internal policy disputes led to the abrupt dismissal of Jorge Díaz Serrano from the directorship of PEMEX. López Portillo eventually had to settle for a price reduction, however, and this brought a significant drop in export earnings. Because of overambitious policies, Mexico fell victim to forces beyond its control.

The second mistake was continued overvaluation of the peso. By 1980 and 1981 the constant drain on dollar reserves (because of trade deficits and capital flight) was exerting pressure for devaluation of the peso. Such a step would reduce imports, increase exports and stem the flight of capital – because dollars would cost more pesos than before. But López Portillo and his advisers did not go along with this, partly because the economy was booming anyway and partly because interest rates were rising on the foreign debt (which required repayment in hard currency). The effect was to build up even more pressure for devaluation and to encourage even more capital flight.

A further important miscalculation concerned the ethics of public life. For various reasons Mexican society had long tolerated the idea of self-enrichment through the possession of political office – what is often called corruption. One practical consequence of this tradition, if not a motive for it, was to permit people of modest background to pursue politics as a full-time career; another was to encourage them to accept the prospect of early exit from high office, thus permitting the turn-over – and the extension of patronage – that helped stabilize the system. But even in Mexico the practice had its limits. And according to wide-spread rumour, López Portillo and his friends transgressed those time-honored boundaries by helping themselves to excessive amounts of the public treasury and in too flagrant a fashion. The President constructed an ostentatious palatial residence for himself and his family on the outskirts of Mexico City, while government officials were reliably reported to lose hundreds of thousands of dollars at gaming tables 'without blinking an eye'. The direct result was to cast the López Portillo presidency under an unprecedented light of general opprobrium. An indirect result was to raise questions about the conduct and legitimacy of the entire political elite.

The political dimensions of an impending crisis began to appear in September 1981, when López Portillo revealed his choice for the presidential succession. Prominent pre-candidates included Pedro Ojeda Paullada, the tough and experienced Secretary of Labour; Jorge de la Vega Domínguez, a versatile politician (and ex-CONASUPO director) in charge of the Ministry of Commerce; Miguel de la Madrid Hurtado, a skilled technocrat and Secretary of Budget and Planning; Javier García Paniagua, the son of ex-defence minister Marcelino García Barragán and the president of the PRI; and, mainly because of his post at Gobernación, the old-time *político* Enrique Olivares Santana. Although it was anticipated that the *destape* would come in October, after the North–South meeting in Cancún, it took place at the traditional time in late September.

The selection was Miguel de la Madrid, a close personal friend (and one-time student) of López Portillo's who had played a prominent part in the formulation of economic policy. Though Budget and Planning had never produced any presidents before, de la Madrid showed every sign of the intellectual and bureaucratic capacity required by the presidency (including a graduate degree from Harvard). He had only one major drawback: a technocrat par excellence, he had never held elective office and had weak connections with the PRI. This made it all the more significant when the president of the party, Garcia Paniagua, lost his job after openly expressing unhappiness over the selection.

The scale of Mexico's economic difficulties became apparent in February 1982, when the López Portillo administration decided to float the peso on the international market – as Echeverría had done in 1976 – and it promptly plummeted from 26 per dollar to around 45 per dollar. Inflation continued its upwards climb. In March the Secretary of Finance resigned. In August the government decreed another devaluation, the peso falling further, to 75–80 per dollar. As a result, Mexico announced that, given its shortage of foreign exchange, it might not be able to meet its debt obligations. The 'Mexican crisis' had suddenly acquired extraordinary importance for the international financial community, requiring its leading representatives – most notably Paul Volcker of the U.S. Federal Reserve – rapidly to assemble an emergency relief plan in order to avoid the incalculable consequences of an outright default by a major debtor nation.[48] In the meantime, López Portillo complained about capital flight, decried the existence of speculation against the peso, and denounced the 'vultures' seeking ill-gotten gains.

In his annual message on 1 September 1982, López Portillo stunned his audience by declaring state expropriation of privately owned banks (foreign-owned banks were exempted). At the same time the government imposed controls on the foreign-exchange rate, set promptly at 70 pesos per dollar for commercial purposes and 50 per dollar for preferential transactions. The left applauded the nationalization, López Portillo predictably claiming his place in history. And though the measure was widely criticized, it did represent a plausible (if unworkable) set of options for the Mexican state. By nationalizing the banks – and, perhaps more importantly, by setting up exchange controls – López Portillo ruptured the time-honored partnership between the state, the private sector and foreign investors.[49] With control over 70 per cent of investment the state could now attempt to go it alone, and in so doing it could consolidate its tenuous alliance with workers and peasants. Thus, López Portillo sought to resurrect and fortify the 'populist' political alternative for Mexico, a model designed to link a mass following with elite leadership through the mediation and guidance of a dynamic and powerful state. In this endeavour the President could count on the collaboration of both traditional *políticos* and nationalistic *técnicos*. In a style reminiscent of Cárdenas, López Portillo added a conspicuous flourish to the final signature for his six-year term in office.[50]

De la Madrid had won the election of 4 July with nearly 75 per cent of the vote, but, as custom demanded, he kept silent until his own inauguration on 1 December. When his opportunity finally came, he roundly criticized 'financial populism' and called for the 'moral renovation' of society and government. The bank expropriation itself was 'irreversible',

[48] See Joseph Kraft, *The Mexican Rescue* (New York, 1984).
[49] It would be noted, later on, that nationalization meant that the state would assume both the debts and the losses of companies owned by the banks, but this objective reality had little to do with subjective perception of private investors and foreign lenders. They continued to denounce the measure.
[50] For an insider's description of these events, see Carlos Tello, *La nacionalización de la banca* (Mexico, 1984).

he conceded, but his administration would take the true road to recovery. 'The first months of the government will be arduous and difficult', he warned. 'The situation requires it. The austerity is obligatory'.[51]

De la Madrid appointed a cabinet full of proficient technocrats like himself, retaining Jesús Silva Herzog as Secretary of Finance and reinstating Miguel Mancera (who had opposed the exchange controls) as head of the central bank. Moving with remarkable speed, the new President accepted the conditions of the International Monetary Funds (IMF) for renegotiation of the debt, including a provision that the budget deficit be gradually reduced from nearly 18 per cent of GDP in 1982 to 3.5 per cent in 1985. He lifted price controls on 2,500 consumer items and provided pricing flexibility on 2,000 more, and he floated the peso yet again so that its free-market value fell to around 150 per dollar. With such measures de la Madrid attempted to restore Mexico's credit with the international community and, in so doing, to repair the relationship between the state and the foreign sector.

The President also took steps to revive and reassure the local business community. In sharp contrast to López Portillo's heated denunciation of profit-seeking 'vultures', de la Madrid used his inaugural address to express praise for 'responsible and patriotic entrepreneurs – who form a majority'. Although the bank nationalization could not be reversed, he intimated that the private sector would still have an important role in the economy. 'To rationalize is not to state-ize (*estatizar)'*, de la Madrid insisted. 'We shall not state-ize society'. True to his word, in January 1983 the President sent a bill to Congress that would authorize the sale of 34 per cent ownership in the newly nationalized banks to private investors. In February he announced a plan for extending financial credit to 'productive' enterprises. Later in the year, the government began paying compensation (in ten-year bonds) to former owners of the banks.

De la Madrid was clearly trying to restore Mexico's long-standing ruling alliance: the three-way coalition between the state, the private sector and the foreign sector which had been initially forged by Alemán and had guided the nation on its post-war path to economic growth. The strategy was to consolidate power at the uppermost reaches of the social order, in other words, and to utilize this strength as a means of shaping and implementing policy. From the start, either by necessity or by choice, the de la Madrid administration moved in a conservative direction. This orien-

[51] The full text of de la Madrid's inaugural speech appears in *Unomásuno*, 2 December 1982.

tation posed complications for the country's political class. De la Madrid drew almost his entire cabinet from the ranks of *técnicos,* sophisticated experts whose bureaucratic and technical capacity seemed to provide ideal credentials for executing an austerity program. *Políticos,* the old-time politicians and party bosses, were most conspicuous by their exclusion from the new administration; there was some muttering and grumbling within the PRI, but no outright rebellion. Signals from the military were also unclear, but de la Madrid showered the armed services with lavish praise in his inaugural address, and it was widely thought that the President would go to considerable lengths to preserve intact the silent partnership between civilian rulers and military leaders.

De la Madrid's economic strategy imposed a large cost, and the burden of payment fell on one key social sector: the working class. Throughout 1983 inflation was running at between 70 and 90 per cent, but labour had to settle for wage increases in the region of 25 per cent. The removal of price ceilings and public subsidies raised the cost of basic necessities. In July 1983, for example, the government announced a 40 per cent hike in the price of corn tortillas and a 100 per cent increase in the price of bread. Economists estimated that the real purchasing power of the working class was declining at the rate of 15 to 20 per cent a year.

Urban labour therefore presented a grave political problem. A mid-1983 round of salary negotiations resulted in stalemate and confrontation. Workers in some thousand companies threatened to strike, a prospect averted in most cases only by the postponement of discussions (rather than the settlement of issues). For a while the struggle came out in the open: on behalf of labour Fidel Velázquez called for a wage–price freeze, and in exasperation de la Madrid denounced the idea as 'demagogic'. Conciliation followed, but it was clear that the relationship between labour and the government was under strain.

The food-price increases represented a deliberate attempt to stimulate agricultural development but did not herald the articulation of any large-scale agrarian program. De la Madrid abandoned SAM, along with other 'statist' elements of the López Portillo regime, and in late 1983 replaced it with a modest food-production program. In mid-1985 he followed up with a so-called national programme of integral rural development, which envisaged little more than inflationary adjustments in the guaranteed minimum price for basic commodities (corn, beans, wheat) and some infrastructural investments in rain-fed areas. The emphasis was on enhancing production, not distribution, through market forces and price incentives. The administration cut back the role of CONASUPO and relied instead on the interaction of supply and demand. Agrarian reform, once the centerpiece of revolution, appeared to have lost its place on the national agenda.

In short, de la Madrid's attempt to re-establish and consolidate the ruling coalition ran the risk of alienating the system's social bases of support, especially the urban working class. The peasantry kept silent and would probably stay under control, but doubts remained over the reaction of the middle class, which had became the most vocal and potentially the most volatile of the regime's constituencies. Perhaps in recognition of this, and in a general effort to shore up his support, de la Madrid continued to insist on 'moral renovation' in a campaign widely interpreted as an attack on López Portillo and his collaborators. In late 1983, after months of public rumors, the de la Madrid government went after one of the former president's most prominent associates, bringing charges against Jorge Díaz Serrano, the former head of PEMEX and a senator from Sonora, for alleged participation in a multimillion-dollar fraud. It was later learned that the ex-president's sister Alicia López Portillo was the target of a parallel investigation, but this was soon brought to a halt. A separate indictment led to the eventual extradition from the United States of Arturo Durazo Moreno, nicknamed *el negro,* the former chief of the Mexico City police and close friend of the ex-president. Such accusations bore no precedent in recent history, and they underscored de la Madrid's determination to free his own administration as far as he could from identification with the López Portillo government.

Corruption thus became a major public issue, and complicated Mexico's relationship with the United States, especially with respect to the growing traffic in narcotics. Collaboration between Mexico and the United States had in fact been rather smooth until February 1985, when a U.S. drug enforcement agent, Enrique Camarena, disappeared and was later found murdered – only a year after the State Department had singled out Mexico's anti-narcotics campaign for special praise. After the Camarena affair officials in Washington began to protest that about one-third of U.S. imports of marijuana and heroin came from Mexico and that perhaps 30 per cent of the imported cocaine passed through that country. But it was Mexico's apparent inability to solve the Camarena case, plus a subsequent murder, that led to allegations about corruption and cover-up – most notably, but not exclusively, in a series of unprecedented Senate subcommittee hearings chaired by arch-conservative Republican Jesse Helms in May 1986.

The de la Madrid administration angrily denied accusations of complicity with drug-runners and, indeed, the evidence appeared to support its contentions. Thousands of Mexican policemen and about 25,000 military troops were assigned to the anti-narcotics campaign; hundreds were wounded or killed. Some individual office-holders no doubt collaborated with such powerful narcotics lords as Rafael Caro Quintana, but the political establishment had every reason to oppose the traffic in drugs. The consolidation of narcotics kingdoms threatened to create empires within the empire and fostered a type of corruption which proved counter-productive for political authority. Drug-trade patronage lay outside the control of the regime (in contrast, for instance, to the petroleum bonanza of the late 1970s) and, in a time of declining governmental resources, it posed an unwelcome challenge.

The question of migration to the United States came to a head with passage of what came to be called the Simpson–Rodino Bill, which President Ronald Reagan signed into law in November 1986. Hailed as a major revision of United States immigration policy, the law had two major provisions: economic sanctions against employers who knowingly hired illegal aliens, and an amnesty for undocumented workers who could prove continuous residence in the United States from January 1982. The U.S. Congress also envisioned a 50 per cent increase in the size of the border patrol (which would require a separate budgetary allocation). Implementation of the law did not lead to massive deportations from the United States, as Mexican alarmists had frequently predicted; nor did it result in massive applications for amnesty, as U.S. officials had nervously foreseen. It seemed likely that the law would encourage employer discrimination against workers of Mexican origin or ethnic appearance, but even that was not self-evident. There was a reasonable chance that Simpson–Rodino would not work. Employer sanctions had met with little success when tried before, as in the state of California. There were simply too many loopholes for effective enforcement. In this case, illegal immigration could be expected to resume its mid-1980s pace, with perhaps a million crossings a year but (since most go back to Mexico) an additional *net* immigration of between 300,000 and 500,000 per year. The total number of undocumented Mexicans in the United States would thus increase from around 3 million to 4 or 5 million by the early 1990s.

Partly because of economic pressure from the United States and partly because of his own political reasons, de la Madrid took a cautious approach to foreign policy. In early 1983 Mexico abandoned high-profile diplomacy and joined together with Colombia, Panama and Venezuela – the so-called Contadora group – in order to explore the possibilities for regional mediation of the conflict in Central America. In support of this general strategy Peru, Brazil, Uruguay and Argentina declared their support for the Contadora enterprise. The Reagan administration, on the other hand, continued to show a notable lack of enthusiasm, and it was obvious to all that Contadora could not succeed without strong U.S. backing. Whatever the final result, Mexico's role in the Contadora group marked a substantial change from both the ebullience of the López Portillo years and, even more dramatically, from the diplomatic cautiousness of the 1950s.

Overall results from de la Madrid's domestic and international policies seemed inconclusive by the halfway mark of his *sexenio,* 1985 proving to be a particularly difficult year. First, it became apparent that the government's economic 'adjustment' plan was meeting with indifferent success. Productivity was picking up but at a modest pace. Labour and the middle classes lost additional real purchasing power as the annual inflation rate continued at around 60 per cent. The total foreign debt was up to $96 billion (from the 1982 level of $82 billion); debt service for the year amounted to $13 billion, but the balance of payments was just over half that, around $7–8 billion. Investment was low and capital flight persisted at around $5 billion. The public deficit for 1985 was around 8 per cent of GDP, not the 4 per cent agreed with the IMF, which was on the brink of holding up payments on fresh loans.

Then came two external shocks. One was a natural catastrophe. At 7:19 A.M., 19 September 1985, Mexico City suffered an enormous earthquake measuring 8.1 on the Richter scale, and the following evening the city was hit by another which measured 7.3. The damage was greatest in the old downtown area, where tumbling buildings took the lives of at least 7,000 persons and maybe as many as 20,000. Well over 100,000 were injured or homeless, as the world looked on in horror and dismay. The citizens of Mexico City responded with generosity and courage, giving instant aid and shelter to the *damnificados* in a spontaneous outpouring which prompted some observers to take note of the emergence of 'civil society'. Direct economic damage was estimated to be at around $4 billion, a sum that debt-strapped Mexico could ill afford; according to one estimate this would amount to a negative impact on the 1985 GDP of minus 3.4 per cent. There was political fall-out too. Amid the rubble were signs of corruption in that some of the collapsed buildings had failed to comply with construction codes. Many Mexicans felt that the government had responded with too little too late, that de la Madrid had not been able to rise to the occasion. There was concern about the excessive centralization in Mexico City, and a wide-spread clamour for having the regent of the Federal District chosen by election rather than presidential appointment. Grass-roots mobilization continued and helped bring down a cabinet minister.

The second external shock was a precipitous decline in the international price of oil. Between December 1985 and July 1986 the average price for Mexico's export mix plunged from $23.70 per barrel to $8.90 per barrel, the resulting loss of income from oil sales amounting to approximately $8.2 billion dollars. This was equivalent to a drop of minus 6.4 per cent in the GDP for 1986. The costs of reliance on international market forces were again becoming clear. In this general context of economic malaise, de la Madrid and his advisers decided to adopt a dramatic shift in policy, undertaking long-term structural reform in terms that were characterized both at home and abroad as the 'liberalization' of the Mexican economy.

There were two major pillars to the programme. One was to reduce and recast the economic role of the state. From 1983 through 1985 the government had sought to reduce public spending – by as much as one-third – but now the de la Madrid administration sought to redesign the state's economic role, principally through a program of 'privatization' (or, as it was known in Mexico, *desincorporación*). Of the 1,115 publicly owned companies his government inherited in late 1982, de la Madrid managed by late 1986 to sell off 96 (including some major ownings in the hotel and automobile business), to merge 46 and to transfer 39 to state governments. The government also closed down some 279 inefficient plants, including a large steel mill near Monterrey. And in the strategic sectors designated for continued government control – petroleum, railroads, electricity, telecommunications – the government undertook a programme of 'industrial reconversion' to improve efficiency. The para-statal sector continued to be large, but the administration was making a decisive move to curtail it.

The second component of the new policy was commercial liberalization and an 'opening up' of the economy. This was most dramatically demonstrated by Mexico's accession to the General Agreement on Tariffs and

Trade (GATT) in September 1986, which meant a long-term commitment to the reduction of barriers to imports from abroad. This amounted to an almost complete abandonment of the post-war policies of ISI. Liberalization had two main corollaries. One was the phasing out of tariffs. In 1982, 100 per cent of Mexico's imports were controlled by the granting of licenses; by 1987, only 9 per cent remained under such a restrictive regime. In general this meant that the Mexican domestic market, long protected for local industrialists, would be opened up to producers in other countries – especially, of course, the United States. The second corollary was the promotion of exports, especially non-petroleum exports. A key element here was a controlled devaluation of the peso – at a rate higher than domestic inflation – to enhance the competitiveness of Mexican industry. (In early 1987 the exchange rate moved beyond 1,000 pesos per dollar; by midyear it was close to 1,400 pesos per dollar.) As a result of these and other measures, non-oil exports began to pick up. Exports of manufactures approached $1 billion per year. Government officials also reported that flight capital of the early 1980s was returning to the country, perhaps as much as $3 billion to $5 billion for 1986–7.

These policies of liberalization amounted to a radical shift in the historic direction of the Mexican economy. Some observers predicted that the de la Madrid administration, so embattled for so long, would go down as a watershed in Mexican history. But in the late 1980s there were at least two formidable obstacles for the Mexican economy: inflation and the foreign debt. Inflation which stood at 105 per cent for 1986 and which, by mid-1987, was running at an annual rate of 140 percent, had a corrosive effect on Mexican society, from its discouragement of investment (and exportation) to its ruinous effect on income distribution. Government officials saw no obvious way to deal with the problem, other than to continue the programme of commercial liberalization and press on with structural reforms. For many economists, inflation was the principal policy challenge of the late 1980s.

For the first half of his administration de la Madrid appeared to regard the foreign debt as a 'liquidity' problem, rather than a structural deficiency, and this emphasis on cash management influenced a series of negotiations with international creditors. In 1983–85 the government achieved a postponement of short-term payments and a reduction of costs ('spreads' above international interest rates went down from around 2.3 per cent to less than 1 per cent). But from 1986 onwards the government began to insist on a resumption of economic growth. Differences of opinion over how to achieve this goal led to the abrupt dismissal in June 1986 of Jesús Silva Herzog, the charismatic finance minister who was seen by many as the logical successor to de la Madrid. (It was not quite clear what the debate was about: rumours indicated that Silva Herzog wanted to propose either a unilateral moratorium on debt service and/or the imposition of a 'heterodox shock' like the *plan austral* in Argentina.) Between late 1986 and early 1987 Mexico managed to negotiate with its creditors a new package that called for fresh loans of $12 billion to help stimulate growth of 3 to 4 per cent. Repayments were to be made over a period of twenty years, and additional funds were to be made available if the international price of petroleum went below $9 per barrel. Even with these terms, the general question persisted: how could Mexico devise a viable strategy for economic growth in light of its debt obligations? By late 1987 the total debt was well over $100 billion. Could Mexico continue to make debt-service payments of $8 billion to $12 billion a year and still meet the needs of its people?

In addition to these economic problems, the de la Madrid government faced serious challenges on the political front. The President's declaration of a 'moral renovation' in his inaugural address had stimulated hopes that he would extend the 1977 reforms and insist on open elections with genuine possibilities for opposition victories. In 1982–3 the PAN was permitted to win significant municipal victories in the north – in Ciudad Juárez, Hermosillo, Durango, Chihuahua and San Luis Potosí – and the hopes for liberalization seemed justified. But then de la Madrid began to equivocate. In the south, the state legislature of Oaxaca voted in August 1983 to remove the moderately leftist mayor of the town of Juchitán, Leopoldo de Gyvés of the Coalición de Obreros, Campesinos, y Estudiantes del Istmo (COCEI). After a violent confrontation, the army ousted the COCEI group from city hall and installed the PRI candidate, who claimed victory in the November elections. Around this time it appeared that Mexico City had reached a compromise solution: it would permit the right to win local elections but not the left.

Yet even this supposition was shattered in 1985, when congressional by-elections and several key gubernatorial contests in the north began to draw considerable attention. The PAN fielded especially strong candidates in Sonora and Nuevo León, and the international media gathered to witness the struggle of the opposition. Whatever the actual results, the PRI and the regime proclaimed almost-total victory, sweeping the seven governorships and all but a handful of seats in the Chamber of Deputies.

The PRI took 65 per cent of the votes, granting 15.5 per cent to the PAN, 3.2 percent to PSUM, and scattering the rest among small parties. As a result of electoral procedures both the PAN and PSUM actually lost seats in the legislature, while insignificant micro-parties stood to benefit. Widespread accusations of fraud ensued as the PRI asserted its capacity to control the electoral process and subjected the opposition to divide-and-conquer tactics.

In 1986 there was more of the same. Elections included four gubernatorial contests, the most hotly contested occurring in the northern state of Chihuahua. As the race between PRI candidate Fernando Baeza Meléndez and the PAN's Francisco Barrios Terrazas neared its end, opposition leaders – from the PAN, the business sector and the Catholic Church – demanded the annulment of the elections, the *panista* mayor of the city of Chihuahua, Luis H. Alvarez, embarking on a protest hunger strike. The authorities responded with petulance, ousting left-wing *pesumista* poll-watchers from the registries in Chihuahua and Ciudad Juárez while the opposition responded by blockading state highways (including the bridge across the border to the United States). Election day proved to be peaceful, however, and the PRI claimed total triumph once again. According to the official count, Baeza defeated Barrios with 64.3 per cent of the vote; the PRI took all the other three races for governor, 106 out of the 109 mayorships and almost all the local deputyships. The political machinery was back to the *carro completo* ('full wagon'), but President de la Madrid lost a good deal of prestige. Either he had given the PRI hierarchy permission to rig the elections, in which case he had given up his campaign for reform, or he had been unable to impose his will on recalcitrant provincial bosses and local *caciques*. Moreover, there was a conspicuous absence of a clear-cut political strategy.

It was in this context that speculation began to mount about the presidential succession of 1987–8. As the time for decision approached, it appeared that this succession would differ from tradition in at least three ways. First, the institutional power of the presidency seemed less overwhelmingly dominant than before: it was still the paramount office in the land, but the travails of the 1970s and 1980s had tarnished its sense of omnipotence. So if de la Madrid had the final word in the selection of his successor, it appeared likely that he would have to listen more closely to other opinions – including that of Fidel Velázquez, the octogenarian labor boss who had managed to keep the unions in line during a period of sharply falling wage rates. Second, a dissident group of *priista* leaders –

including Cuauhtémoc Cárdenas, the son of Lázaro Cárdenas and former governor of Michoacán, and Porfirio Muñoz Ledo, former cabinet minister, erstwhile presidential aspirant and former head of the PRI itself – joined together to form the *corriente democrática* and to call for an opening of the process of presidential succession. Leaders of the *corriente* received brutal criticism within the PRI and the press because a development of this sort had not been seen for decades. Third, the international media would be paying unprecedented attention to the process of succession. The decision might take place behind closed doors, but the whole world would know about it.

Characteristically enough, rumours raced through political and intellectual circles. The removal of Silva Herzog from the cabinet – and the competition – sent shock waves through the political establishment. So did the subsequent designation of Jorge de la Vega Domínguez, the seasoned politician and ex-rival of the President, as leader of the PRI. Some observers said there were four major pretenders. Some said six. The business organization, COPARMEX, issued a remarkable report announcing six plausible candidates for the presidency.[52] But by an unspoken consensus, most attention focussed on three:

Manuel Bartlett Díaz, fifty-one, was the Secretary of Gobernación. The son of a former governor of the state of Tabasco, he had been active in the PRI since 1963 and was thought by many to have convinced de la Madrid of the need to resort to the electoral strategy of the *carro completo*.

Alfredo del Mazo González, forty-four, was the Secretary of Energy and Mines. A UNAM graduate in business administration with extensive overseas study, del Mazo had, like his father, been the governor of the state of Mexico (1981–6). A protegé of Fidel Velázquez, he had a close personal relationship with de la Madrid.

Carlos Salinas de Gortari, thirty-nine, the Secretary of Planning and Budget, had a formidable intellect. With advanced degrees in economics from UNAM and Harvard, Salinas started a career in public administration while in his mid-twenties. His father, a former cabinet minister and ambassador, was a senator in 1982–8. Salinas was widely regarded as a principal architect of the de la Madrid economic policy and an advocate of state activism.

All these pre-candidates had worked within the system, were relatively young, were cabinet ministers, and had close relations with the outgoing

[52] *Excélsior*, 15 May 1987.

president. But they also shared another characteristic, one that expressed a telling message about the evolution and status of the regime: they were sons of prominent politicians. The system, it appeared, was reproducing itself in the most literal sense. The separation of political from economic elites thus continued to persist, but it was no longer clear that careers in politics would provide Mexican society with a meaningful channel to upward mobility.

Excitement mounted in mid-August 1987 when the head of the PRI, Jorge de la Vega Domínguez, took the unprecedented step of announcing that there were indeed six candidates for the presidential nomination and that they would be invited to make public appearances (*comparaciencias*) before the party hierarchy. In addition to Bartlett, del Mazo and Salinas, the list included Ramón Aguirre Velázquez, the regent of the Federal District; Sergio García Ramírez, the Attorney General; and Miguel González Avelar, the Secretary of Education. In alphabetical order, the pre-candidates appeared before an assemblage of PRI notables at that most venerable of occasions, the political breakfast (*desayuno político*), where they gave formal presentations about their visions of the national future. The press and the political community hung closely on each gesture and word, looking for clues to the outcome. There had never been anything quite like this before: did it herald a new process of 'democratization' in the selection of the president, or was it merely a cosmetic change?

To most observers the selection of Carlos Salinas de Gortari meant that de la Madrid had retained control of the process of succession. (It also underscored the political weakness of organised labour.) Indeed, it was widely believed that de la Madrid had decided on Salinas well in advance of the *comparaciencias*. The presidential succession of 1988 thus far had complied with previous patterns. Then came the electoral campaign, which was normally an opportunity for acclamation of the official party nominee, but which became much more than that in 1988.

The first major development came with the formation of the Frente Democrático Nacional (FDN), a coalition of leftist parties with the *corriente democrática* in the spring of 1988. Moreover, the Frente decided to put forward a single candidate for the presidency, Cuauhtémoc Cárdenas. The Cárdenas candidacy immediately confronted the ruling establishment with a genuine electoral opposition. Constantly invoking his father's name, Cárdenas sought to rally workers and peasants under a common banner. He appealed to themes of nationalism, sovereignty, justice and reform – in short, to the time-honoured causes of the Mexican Revolution. Claiming that *técnicos* in the administration and *políticos* in the PRI had forsaken the needs of the people, Cárdenas proposed dramatic solutions to the country's economic crisis – including a suspension on petroleum exports and a unilateral moratorium on debt service. The Cardenista candidacy drew impressive crowds throughout the country, and it appeared to pose a plausible threat to the hegemony of the PRI. Meanwhile, the conservative PAN nominated as its candidate Manuel Clouthier, a prominent agribusinessman, former *priista* and firebrand orator. Clouthier developed as his main campaign theme freedom – for religious worship, for private enterprise and for political opposition. He looked for support from the private sector, from the middle classes and – conspicuously – from the newly emergent Catholic Church. Throughout the campaign, spokesmen for the FDN and the PAN joined together in the call for a free and open election in 1988. The opposition thus made the conduct of the election itself one of the primary issues of Mexican politics.

Salinas de Gortari, for his part, developed the theme of 'modernization'. Mexico, he said repeatedly, need not disinherit its national legacies; it must nurture and strengthen its traditions in a constructive fashion. Modernization of the economy would require effective control of inflation, improved productivity and the continuation of structural reform. Political modernization, he declared in an extensive statement on 'the challenge of democracy', must begin with a reform of the electoral code. There should be a stronger, more independent legislature, a better court system and a positive role for the media. He envisioned a strong (but loyal) opposition: 'We want strong and responsible political parties', Salinas proclaimed, in one of his major public statements, 'respectful of laws and institutions, that work in a democratic manner to expand their social bases'. He called for internal reforms of the PRI to include stronger ties to local constituencies, better procedures for selecting candidates and greater opportunities for young politicians. The speech consisted of generalities but nonetheless marked a sharp departure from the triumphal discourse of previous *priista* presidential candidates. 'This is a historic time', Salinas recognized. 'Everyone is clamoring for more democracy'.[53]

Tension mounted as the election approached. Two of Cárdenas' campaign aides were murdered. Many observers feared an outbreak of more generalized violence. However, the day of the election, 6 July, passed in relative tranquillity. Then Manuel Bartlett, still Secretary of Gobernación,

---

[53] Text of speech to the Comité Ejecutivo Nacional of the PRI (Puebla, July 1988).

announced that the government's computers had broken down for 'environmental reasons'. Opposition spokesmen and numerous observers accused the PRI of rigging the results. In claiming victory, Salinas de Gortari observed, remarkably: 'We are ending an era of what was practically one-party rule and entering a new political stage in the country with a majority party and very intense opposition from the competition'.[54] When the election commission finally declared Salinas to be the winner with a bare majority of the vote – 50.4 percent against 31.1 per cent for Cárdenas and 17.1 per cent for Clouthier – the Cardenistas immediately claimed fraud and staged some massive protest demonstrations. And the *panistas* called for a brief campaign of 'civic resistance'.

Thus, Salinas began his *sexenio* in a relatively weak position. He could not claim the traditionally overwhelming popular mandate of previous presidents. (Indeed, an absention rate of 48.4 per cent meant that Salinas won active approval from only about one-quarter of the adult population.) And in view of the disputed returns, he could not claim victory in a totally clean election. Moreover, even according to official figures, the Cardenista movement had established itself as a powerful electoral force in the nation. It remained to be seen whether it could transform itself into a durable, opposition political party. In the Chamber of Deputies, the PRI had 260 seats but the combined opposition had 240. Moreover, the opposition had won four seats in the Senate – including both seats for the Federal District, where Ifigenia Martínez and Porfirio Muñoz Ledo of the FDN claimed decisive triumphs. As the ruling establishment was soon to discover, this heralded a major transformation in the position of the legislature, until then a supine and subordinate instrument of the PRI and the presidency.

The new president faced his challenges with vigour and determination. Salinas accelerated the process of economic liberalization, privatizing public-sector companies (including telephones and banks) and initiating free-trade negotiations with the United States. In the political realm he ousted some entrenched union leaders, including the longtime boss of the oil-workers, streamlined the PRI, and permitted a *panista* candidate to win the governorship of Baja California. The president's supporters insisted that, by example and by deed, he was transforming the face of Mexican society and politics. Critics, noting his harsh treatment of rivals and especially of the Cardenistas, claimed that Salinas was promoting a strategy of "*perestroika* without *glasnost*," of economic restructuring without a genuine political opening. The Mexican people continued to demand the democratization of the post-war authoritarian political system.

[54] *Excélsior*, 8 July 1988.

BIBLIOGRAPHICAL ESSAYS

LIST OF ABBREVIATIONS

The following abbreviations have been used for works which occur repeatedly in the bibliographical essays:

AESC   *Annales: Économies, Sociétés, Civilisations*
CHLA   *Cambridge History of Latin America*
HAHR   *Hispanic American Historical Review*
HM   *Historia Mexicana*
JGSWGL   *Jahrbuch für Geschichte von Staat, Wirtschaft und Gesellschaft Lateinamerikas*
JLAS   *Journal of Latin American Studies*
LARR   *Latin American Research Review*

1. FROM INDEPENDENCE TO THE LIBERAL REPUBLIC, 1821–1867

Ernesto de la Torre Villar *et al.* (eds.), *Historia documental de México* (2 vols., Mexico, 1964) is an important documentary collection. F. Tena Ramírez (ed.), *Leyes fundamentales de México 1808–1973* (5th rev. edn, Mexico, 1973), reproduces all the constitutions and their drafs as well as the most important laws and decrees. For economic and social aspects of the period from around 1800 to 1852, L. Chávez Orozco (ed.), *Colección de documentos para la historia del comercio exterior de México*, in two series: series 1 in 7 vols. (Mexico, 1958–62); series 11 in 4 vols. (Mexico, 1965–67) should be consulted; it covers much more ground than the title indicates. Documentation on the Juárez era can be found in J. L. Tamayo (ed.), *Benito Juárez, documentos, discursos y correspondencia* (14 vols., Mexico, 1964–70), and Secretaría de la Presidencia (ed.), *La administración pública en la*

época de Juárez (3 vols., Mexico, 1973). For foreign relations, see
L. Díaz (ed.), *Versión francesa de México. Informes diplomáticos 1853–1867* (4
vols., Mexico, 1963–7), and L. Díaz (ed.), *Versión francesa de México 1851–
67. Informes económicos* (consular reports) (2 vols., Mexico, 1974).

There are a number of general works which include substantial
treatment of Mexican history in the period after independence. Most
notable among older works are Lucas Alamán, *Historia de México, 1808–
1849* (5 vols., Mexico, 2nd edn, 1942–8), vol. v, Vicente Riva Palacio
(ed.), *México a través de los siglos* (Mexico, 1889; facsimile edn, Mexico,
1958), Vols IV and V; Francisco de Paula de Arrangoiz, *México desde 1808
hasta 1867* (4 vols., Mexico, 1871–2; 2nd edn, 1974). More recently Luis
González y González (ed.), *Historia general de México* (4 vols., El Colegio
de México, Mexico, 1976), Vol. III (1821–1910), and Jan Bazant, *A concise
history of Mexico from Hidalgo to Cárdenas* (Cambridge, 1977), chapters 2
and 3, have provided valuable syntheses. Still useful is Justo Sierra,
Evolución política del pueblo mexicano, now available in English as *The
political evolution of the Mexican people* (Austin, Texas, 1970).

On particular aspects of the period, Charles A. Hale, *Mexican liberalism
in the age of Mora 1821–1853* (New Haven, 1968) is essential for the study of
ideas. J. Bazant, *Historia de la deuda exterior de México 1823–1946* (Mexico,
1968), replaces the older book by Edgar Turlington, *Mexico and her foreign
creditors* (New York, 1930). Michael P. Costeloe, *Church and state in
independent Mexico. A study of the patronage debate 1821–1857* (London,
1978), is an excellent study of church-state relations. R. W. Randall, *Real
del Monte, a British mining venture in Mexico* (Austin, Texas, 1972), is one of
the few books on mining. Robert A. Potash, *El Banco de Avío de México
1821–1846* (Mexico, 1959), is essential for the history of manufacturing
and government banking. For background on the Yucatán Caste War,
there are three well-researched articles by Howard F. Cline: 'The "Auro-
ra Yucateca" and the spirit of enterprise in Yucatán, 1821–1847',
HAHR, 27 (1947), 30–60; 'The sugar episode in Yucatán. 1825–1850',
Inter-American Economic Affairs, 1/4 (1948), 79–100; 'The Henequén
episode in Yucatán', *Inter-American Economic Affairs*, 2/2 (1948), 30–51.
See also Moisés González Navarro, *Raza y Tierra* (Mexico, 1970), and
N. Reed, *The Caste War of Yucatán* (Stanford, 1964). On agrarian
structures and the history of the hacienda, see Charles H. Harris III, *A
Mexican family empire. The latifundio of the Sánchez Navarros 1765–1867*
(Austin, Texas, 1975); J. Bazant, *Cinco haciendas mexicanas. Tres siglos de
vida rural en San Luis Potosí, 1600–1910* (Mexico, 1975), a summary of parts

of which was published in English in K. Duncan and I. Rutledge, *Land and labour in Latin America. Essays on the development of agrarian capitalism in the 19th & 20th centuries* (Cambridge, 1977); Herbert J. Nickel, *Soziale Morphologie der mexikanischen Hacienda* (Wiesbaden, 1978), one of the best hacienda studies so far published; David A. Brading, *Haciendas and ranchos in the Mexican Bajío* (Cambridge, 1978). Finally, on the difficult question of church wealth and its disposal, see M. P. Costeloe, *Church wealth in Mexico* (Cambridge, 1967), and J. Bazant, *Alienation of church wealth in Mexico. Social and economic aspects of the liberal revolution 1856–1875* (Cambridge, 1971; 2nd revised edn in Spanish, *Los bienes de la iglesia en México*, Mexico, 1977). Charles R. Berry, *The reform in Oaxaca, 1856–76. A micro-history of the liberal revolution* (Lincoln, Nebraska, 1981) is a detailed regional study of the question. There are two collections of essays on aspects of the economic and social history of Mexico in the nineteenth century edited by Ciro F. S. Cardoso: *Formación y Desarrollo de la Burguesía en México. Siglo XIX* (Mexico, 1978) and *México en el siglo XIX (1821–1910). Historia económica y de la estructura social* (Mexico, 1980).

For the period 1821–35, contemporary descriptions include J. Poinsett, *Notes on Mexico* (London, 1825) and H. G. Ward, *Mexico in 1827* (2 vols., London, 1828). Günther Kahle, *Militär und Staatsbildung in den Anfängen der Unabhängigkeit Mexikos* (Cologne, 1969), is a pioneer study of the formation of the Mexican army through the amalgamation of guerrilla fighters for independence and former royalist officers. Michael P. Costeloe, *La primera república federal de México 1824–1835* (Mexico, 1975), is a study of political parties, based on research in the press and pamphlets. Also worthy of note are R. Flores C., *Counterrevolution: the role of the Spaniards in the independence of Mexico 1804–1838* (Lincoln, Nebraska, 1974); H. D. Sims, *La expulsión de los españoles en México, 1821–1828* (Mexico, 1974), which contains valuable statistical information; and Brian R. Hamnett, *Revolución y contrarrevolución en México y el Perú* (Mexico, 1978), for the difficult first years of independent Mexico.

The Texas revolution and the Mexican war have naturally received a great deal of attention from U.S. and Mexican historians, contemporary and modern. See R. S. Ripley, *The war with Mexico* (2 vols., New York, 1849, reprinted 1970); R. Alcaraz, *et al.*, *The other side: or notes for the history of the war between Mexico and the United States* (trans. and ed. by A. C. Ramsey, New York, 1850), in which 15 prominent Mexicans describe the war; Carlos E. Castañeda (ed. and trans.), *The Mexican side of the Texan revolution 1836* (Washington, D.C., 1971) contains accounts by five chief Mexican participants, including Santa Anna; J. F. Ramírez, *Mexico during the war with the United States*, ed. by W. V. Scholes, trans. by E. B. Sherr (Columbia, Mo., 1950); G. M. Brack, *Mexico views Manifest Destiny 1821–1846, An essay on the origins of the Mexican War* (Albuquerque, N.M., 1975), a sympathetic account, well documented from Mexican newspapers and pamphlets; Charles H. Brown, *Agents of Manifest Destiny. The lives and times of the Filibusters* (Chapel Hill, N.C., 1980), a very useful study of these adventurers.

For the period after 1848 there are two studies of the later years of Santa Anna: F. Díaz D., *Caudillos y caciques* (Mexico, 1972) and M. González Navarro, *Anatomía del poder en México 1848–1853* (Mexico, 1977). On liberal politics, see W. V. Scholes, *Mexican politics during the Juárez Régime 1855–1872* (2nd edn, Columbia, Mo., 1969) and Richard N. Sinkin, *The Mexican Reform, 1855–1876. A study in liberal nation-building* (Austin, Texas, 1979); on French intervention, J. A. Dabbs, *The French Army in Mexico 1861–1867, a study in Military government* (The Hague, 1963); and on the empire, Alfred Jackson Hanna and Kathryn Abbey Hanna, *Napoleon III and Mexico. American triumph over monarchy* (Chapel Hill, N.C., 1971).

A number of political biographies are worthy of note: W. S. Robertson, *Iturbide of Mexico* (Durham, N.C., 1952) which is heavily based on archival materials (see also *Memoirs of Agustín de Iturbide* (Washington, D.C., 1971)); J. E. Rodríguez, O., *The emergence of Spanish America. Vicente Rocafuerte and Spanish Americanism 1808–1832* (Berkeley, 1975), a fine biography of an Ecuadorean liberal who took part in the struggle for the Mexican republic; Wildrid H. Callcott, *Santa Anna* (Norman, Oklahoma, 1936) and O. L. Jones Jr, *Santa Anna* (New York, 1968) which should be read together with A. F. Crawford (ed.), *The Eagle. The autobiography of Santa Anna* (Austin, Texas, 1967); Thomas E. Cotner, *The military and political career of José Joaquín de Herrera 1792–1854* (Austin, Texas, 1949); Frank A. Knapp, *The life of Sebastián Lerdo de Tejada 1823–1899* (Austin, Texas, 1951) and C. G. Blázquez, *Miguel Lerdo de Tejada* (Mexico, 1978); I. E. Cadenhead, Jr, *Benito Juárez* (New York, 1973), which to a considerable extent replaces the older and more voluminous biography by R. Roeder, *Juárez and his Mexico* (2 vols., New York, 1947); also by Cadenhead, *Jesús González Ortega and Mexican national politics* (Texas Christian University Press, 1972); finally, Joan Haslip, *The crown of Mexico, Maximilian and his Empress Carlota* (New York, 1971), a comprehensive biography, both personal and political, of the two tragic figures.

2. THE LIBERAL REPUBLIC AND THE PORFIRIATO, 1867–1910

In 1958 Daniel Cosío Villegas, one of Mexico's greatest historians whose special field was the history of Mexico from 1867 to 1910, stated that, quite apart from the period of the Restored Republic (1867–76), nearly 2,000 books and pamphlets had been written on the Porfirian period (1876–1910) alone. Yet, with a number of significant exceptions, the most important works on this period of Mexican history have appeared since the 1950s. The secondary literature on the period 1867–1910, and especially on the Porfiriato, is assessed in Daniel Cosío Villegas, 'El Porfiriato: su historiografía o arte histórico', in *Extremos de América* (Mexico, 1949), 113–82; John Womack, Jr, 'Mexican political historiography, 1959–1969', in *Investigaciones contemporáneas sobre historia de México* (Mexico and Austin, Texas, 1971); Enrique Florescano, *El poder y la lucha por el poder en la historiografía mexicana* (Mexico, 1980); and Thomas Benjamin and Marcial Ocasio-Meléndez, 'Organizing the memory of modern Mexico: Porfirian historiography in perspective, 1880s–1980s', *HAHR*, 64/2 (1984), 323–64. The most important, most comprehensive work on the whole period from 1867 to 1910 is the monumental *Historia moderna de México* (Mexico, 1958–72), a huge thirteen-volume collective work edited by Daniel Cosío Villegas. It was written in the 1950s and 1960s under Cosío's direction by a team of historians who collected every available piece of evidence in Mexican, American and European archives, and examined all aspects of life in Mexico, embracing political, economic and social as well as intellectual history.

The Restored Republic has on the whole provoked far less discussion, controversy and literature than the Díaz era that followed it. Most of the controversy on the earlier period has focused on Juárez the man, on the policies of his regime, and on the nature and basis of liberalism. See, for example, Jesús Reyes Heroles, *El liberalismo mexicano* (Mexico, 1957). And see *CHLA* III, bibliographical essay 10. On the question of whether the Juárez regime was basically different from that of Porfirio Díaz, three very different viewpoints have been expressed: Francisco Bulnes, *El verdadero Juárez y la verdad sobre la intervención y el imperio* (Paris, 1904);

Cosío Villegas (ed.), *Historia moderna*, vol. 1; and Laurens B. Perry, *Juárez and Díaz, machine politics in Mexico* (DeKalb, 1978). The presidency of Lerdo has produced no such controversies and there are no really sharp differences between the interpretations of Cosío Villegas and Frank A. Knapp, *The life of Sebastián Lerdo de Tejada, 1823–1899* (Austin, 1951).

Four contemporary or near-contemporary works are representative of the wide spectrum of opinion on the Porfiriato: Justo Sierra, *México y su evolución social* (Mexico, 1901), a multi-volume series of essays edited by Porfirio Díaz's best-known intellectual supporter, constitutes a self-portrait and self-justification of the Díaz regime; *El verdadero Díaz y la Revolución* (Mexico, 1920) by Francisco Bulnes, another of the Díaz regime's most influential intellectual supporters and its most critical and intelligent defender in the period during and after the Mexican Revolution; and John Kenneth Turner, *Barbarous Mexico* (2nd edn, 1910; reprint, Austin, Texas, 1969) and Carleton Beals, *Porfirio Díaz, dictator of Mexico* (New York, 1932), two works by Americans which constitute the strongest indictments of the Díaz regime. José C. Valadés, *El porfirismo: historia de un régimen* (3 vols., Mexico, 1941–7) was the first general assessment of the Díaz regime to utilize a large array of hitherto unavailable internal documents of the regime.

One of the most important points of dispute, closely linked to the economic development of Mexico from 1867 to 1910, is the discussion of the origins of Mexico's economic underdevelopment. Was it primarily the result of the laissez-faire economics of the Díaz regime? Or was Mexico's underdevelopment mainly due to the inheritance of the colonial period and to the ceaseless civil wars of the first 50 years after Mexico gained its independence? Was there a real alternative to what developed? What were the effects of foreign investment and penetration? Can Mexico's economy in that period be characterized as feudal, capitalist, dependent? What more general theories (imperialism, dependency, etc.) can be applied to the Mexican case? These are some of the issues that are dealt with in very different ways in Ciro Cardoso (ed.), *México en el siglo XIX. Historia económica y de la estructura social* (Mexico, 1980); John Coatsworth, *Growth against development: the economic impact of railroads in Porfirian Mexico* (DeKalb, 1980; Spanish editions: Mexico, 1976; 2nd edn, Mexico, 1984); Sergio de la Peña, *La formación del capitalismo en México* (Mexico, 1976); and Enrique Semo (ed.), *México bajo la dictadura porfiriana* (Mexico, 1983).

A second problem which has been the centre of controversy and discussion about the Díaz period could broadly be summarized as the agrarian question. This involves a very different set of problems. How important was the expropriation of the lands of free villages and what were the economic and social consequences of this development? What kind of labour conditions existed on Mexico's large haciendas? Was labour predominantly free or was peonage the dominant form of labour on the estates? Were the hacendados mainly feudal landlords thinking above all in terms of power or prestige or were they 'capitalists' seeking to maximize their profits and taking economically rational decisions? The terms of the discussion of the agrarian issue were set by two authors who wrote in the Porfirian period: Andrés Molina Enríquez, *Los grandes problemas nacionales* (Mexico, 1909) and Wistano Luis Orozco, *Legislación y jurisprudencia sobre terrenos baldíos* (2 vols., Mexico, 1895). From 1910 until today practically all writings on the agrarian issue have in one way or the other either confirmed, refuted or in some way dealt with the 'theories expounded by these two authors. Some of the very different points of view on the agrarian issue are expressed in Friedrich Katz, 'Labour conditions on haciendas in Porfirian Mexico. Some trends and tendencies', *HAHR*, 54/1 (1974), 1–47 and Katz (ed.), *La servidumbre agraria en México en la época porfiriana* (Mexico, 1977); Frank Tannenbaum, *The Mexican agrarian revolution* (Washington, DC, 1929); Arturo Warman, *Venimos a contradecir: Los campesinos de Morelos y el estado nacional* (Mexico, 1976), Eng. trans. *We come to object. The peasants of Morelos and the national state* (Baltimore, 1981).

A more recent subject of discussion has been the nature and the real power and effectiveness of the Mexican state which has been examined from differing viewpoints in John H. Coatsworth, 'Los orígenes del autoritarismo moderno en México', *Foro Internacional*, 16 (1975), 205–32, and Juan Felipe Leal, *La burguesía y el estado mexicano* (Mexico, 1972). The discussion about the nature of the state is closely linked to research about the ideology, above all positivism and social Darwinism, of Mexico's leaders during the Restored Republic and the Porfirian era; for example, Arnaldo Córdova, *La ideología de la Revolución Mexicana: la formación del nuevo régimen* (Mexico, 1973); William D. Raat, *El positivismo durante el Porfiriato: 1876–1910* (Mexico, 1975); and Leopoldo Zea, *Positivism in Mexico* (Austin, Texas, 1974).

An important corollary to the analysis of the power of the central state is an examination of the importance and influence of regional and local institutions. This problem has been examined in recent years not only by historians but also by anthropologists. See, for example, Paul Friedrich, *Agrarian revolt in a Mexican village* (Englewood Cliffs, NJ, 1970); Luis

González y González, *Pueblo en vilo: microhistoria de San José de Gracia* (Mexico, 1967), Eng. trans. *San José de Gracia: Mexican village in transition* (Austin, Texas, 1974); G. M. Joseph, *Revolution from without: Yucatán, Mexico and the United States, 1880–1924* (Cambridge, 1982); Mark Wasserman, *Capitalists, caciques, and revolution: elite and foreign enterprise in Chihuahua, 1854–1911* (Chapel Hill, 1984); John Womack, *Zapata and the Mexican Revolution* (New York, 1969); Héctor Aguilar Camín, *La frontera nómada: Sonora y la Revolución Mexicana* (Mexico, 1977).

These local studies are inextricably linked to attempts to analyse the different social classes that developed during the Porfirian period at the local, regional and national level. Apart from the peasantry, increasing attention has focused on the working class: see Rodney Anderson, *Outcasts in their own land: Mexican industrial workers, 1906–1911* (DeKalb, 1976); Ciro F. S. Cardoso, Francisco G. Hermosillo and Salvador Hernández, *La clase obrera en la historia de México, de la dictadura porfirista a los tiempos libertarios* (Mexico, 1980); John M. Hart, *Anarchism and the Mexican working class, 1860–1931* (Austin, Texas, 1978); Juan Felipe Leal and José Woldenberg, *La clase obrera en la historia de México: del estado liberal a los inicios de la dictadura porfirista* (Mexico, 1980); and David Walker, 'Porfirian labor politics: working class organizations in Mexico City and Porfirio Díaz, 1876–1902', *The Americas*, 37 (January 1981), 257–87. On intellectuals, see Jesús Silva Herzog, *El agrarismo mexicano y la reforma agraria* (Mexico, 1964) and James Cockcroft, *Intellectual precursors of the Mexican Revolution, 1900–1913* (Austin, Texas, 1968).

One field that has been the subject of long and varied discussion has been that of the relations of Mexico with other countries during the Porfirian era. For a long time, the only major archives available for this period were the American State Department files, and both Mexican and American historians concentrated on US–Mexican relations to the exclusion of other countries. This situation changed in the 1950s when Daniel Cosío Villegas was able to consult not only American but hitherto inaccessible Mexican records as well. As a result, he wrote a detailed analysis of Mexican–American relations between 1867 and 1910: *The United States versus Porfirio Díaz* (Lincoln, Nebraska, 1963). Unlike the 30-year limit of American archives, most European archives had a 50-year limit; works on the relations between Mexico and the major European powers in the Díaz period came out at a much later date. See Alfred Tischendorf, *Great Britain and Mexico in the era of Porfirio Díaz*

(Durham, NC, 1961); Friedrich Katz, *Deutschland, Diaz und die mexikanische Revolution: Die deutsche Politik in Mexiko 1870–1920* (Berlin, 1964).

3. THE MEXICAN REVOLUTION, 1910 – 1920

Printed sources, bibliography and historiography

The latest, most inclusive and best organized guide to the literature on the Mexican Revolution is W. D. Raat, *The Mexican Revolution. An annotated guide to recent scholarship* (Boston, 1982). Indispensable guides to official documents, pamphlets, newspapers, manifestos, and published correspondence are L. González y González (ed.), *Fuentes de la historia contemporánea de México: libros y folletos* (3 vols., Mexico, 1962–3) and S. R. Ross (ed.), *Fuentes de la historia contemporánea de México: periódicos y revistas* (4 vols., Mexico, 1965–76). The most important body of printed materials is I. Fabela and J. E. de Fabela (eds.), *Documentos históricos de la revolución mexicana* (27 vols. and index, Mexico, 1960–76). Useful reprints from the Mexican press appear in M. González Ramírez (ed.), *Fuentes para la historia de la revolución mexicana* (4 vols., Mexico, 1954–7).

Recent bibliographies and historiographic articles with analysis of the main currents in the literature on the Revolution include: D. M. Bailey, 'Revisionism and the recent historiography of the Mexican Revolution', *HAHR*, 58/1 (1978), 62–79; G. Bringas and D. Mascareño, *La prensa de los obreros mexicanos, 1870–1970. Hemerografía comentada* (Mexico, 1979); C. W. Reynolds, 'The economic historiography of twentieth-century Mexico', in *Investigaciones contemporáneas sobre historia de México. Memorias de la tercera reunión de historiadores mexicanos y norteamericanos* (Mexico and Austin, Texas, 1971), 339–57; J. D. Rutherford, *An annotated bibliography of the novels of the Mexican Revolution* (Troy, 1972); E. Suárez Gaona (ed.), *El movimiento obrero mexicano. Bibliografía* (Mexico, 1978); H. W. Tobler, 'Zur Historiographie der mexikanischen Revolution, 1910–1940', *JGSWGL*, 12 (1975), 286–331; J. Womack, Jr, 'Mexican political historiography, 1959–1969', in *Investigaciones contemporáneas*, 478–92, 'The historiography of Mexican labor', in *El trabajo y los trabajadores en la historia de México. Ponencias y comentarios presentados en la V reunión de historiadores mexicanos y norteamericanos* (Mexico and Tucson, 1979), 739–56, and 'The Mexican economy during the Revolution, 1910–1920: historiography and analysis', *Marxist Perspectives*, 1/4 (1978), 80–123.

General and interpretive

The fullest and still the best chronicle of the Mexican Revolution is J. C. Valadés, *Historia general de la revolución mexicana* (10 vols., Mexico, 1963–7), vols. I–VII.

Notable as old standards which are more or less in defence of the Revolution as a great popular victory are M. S. Alperovich, B. T. Rudenko and N. M. Lavrov, *La revolución mexicana: Cuatro estudios soviéticos* (Mexico, 1960); A. Brenner, *The wind that swept Mexico: the history of the Mexican Revolution* (Austin, Texas, 1971); M. González Ramírez, *La revolución social de México* (3 vols., Mexico, 1960–6); J. Silva Herzog, *Breve historia de la revolución mexicana* (2 vols., Mexico, 1960); F. Tannenbaum, *Peace by revolution: an interpretation of Mexico* (New York, 1933); E. Wolf, *Peasant wars of the twentieth century* (New York, 1969). ·

Notable as old standards more or less hostile to the Revolution are F. Bulnes, *El verdadero Díaz y la revolución* (Mexico, 1920); E. Gruening, *Mexico and its heritage* (New York, 1928); W. Thompson, *The people of Mexico: who they are and how they live* (New York, 1921); E. D. Trowbridge, *Mexico to-day and to-morrow* (New York, 1919); J. Vera Estañol, *Historia de la revolución mexicana: orígenes y resultados* (Mexico, 1957).

Among the new works, the most suggestive essays are Peter Calvert, 'The Mexican Revolution: theory or fact?' *JLAS*, 1/1 (1969), 51–68; Barry Carr, 'Las peculiaridades del norte mexicano, 1880–1927: ensayo de interpretacion', *HM*, 22/3 (1973), 320–46; François-X. Guerra, 'La révolution mexicaine: d'abord une révolution minière?' *AESC*, 36/5 (1981), 785–814; Jean A. Meyer, 'Periodización e ideología', in *Contemporary Mexico: Papers of the IV International Congress of Mexican History* (Los Angeles and Mexico, 1976), 711–22; Albert L. Michaels and Marvin D. Bernstein, 'The modernization of the old order: organization and periodization of twentieth-century Mexican history', in *Contemporary Mexico*, 687–710; and Enrique Semo, 'Las revoluciones en la historia de México', *Historia y Sociedad*, 2nd ser., 8 (1975), 49–61.

The main revisionist works are J. D. Cockcroft, *Mexico: class formation, capital accumulation, and the state* (New York, 1983); A. Córdova, *La ideología de la revolución mexicana. La formación del nuevo régimen* (Mexico, 1973); A. Gilly, *The Mexican Revolution* (London, 1983); N. M. Lavrov, *La revolución mexicana, 1910–1917* (Mexico, 1978); Jean Meyer, *La révolution mexicaine* (Paris, 1973); R. E. Ruiz, *The great rebellion. Mexico, 1905–1924* (New York, 1980).

Foreign relations, politics and war

The literature about these subjects is most abundant. One outstanding book treats them all three together: Friedrich Katz, *The secret war in Mexico. Europe, the United States, and the Mexican Revolution* (Chicago, 1981). The other notable studies in this category focus on specific or particular questions of state. The most significant such question is foreign relations. The literature on it is almost exclusively about Mexico's relations with the United States. Indispensable as a background is the work of Arthur S. Link, *Wilson: the new freedom* (Princeton, 1956), *Wilson: the struggle for neutrality, 1914–1915* (Princeton, 1960), *Wilson: confusions and crises, 1915–1916* (Princeton, 1960), and *Wilson: campaigns for progressivism and peace, 1916–1917* (Princeton, 1965).

The two most comprehensive treatments, from very different perspectives, are M. S. Alperovich and B. T. Rudenko, *La revolución mexicana de 1910–1917 y la política de los Estados Unidos* (Mexico, 1960) and P. E. Haley, *Revolution and intervention. The diplomacy of Taft and Wilson with Mexico, 1910–1917* (Cambridge, 1970). The view is at least as broad, but the chronological focus is closer, in P. Calvert, *The Mexican Revolution, 1910–1914. The diplomacy of the Anglo-American conflict* (Cambridge, 1968); M. T. Gilderhus, *Diplomacy and revolution: U.S.–Mexican relations under Wilson and Carranza* (Tucson, 1977); K. J. Grieb, *The United States and Huerta* (Lincoln, 1969); R. F. Smith, *The United States and revolutionary nationalism in Mexico, 1916–1932* (Chicago, 1972); and B. Ulloa, *La revolución intervenida. Relaciones diplomáticas entre México y Estados Unidos, 1910–1914* (Mexico, 1971).

The particular questions that caused the worst problems in Mexican–American relations were oil and Francisco Villa. On oil, see Lorenzo Meyer, *México y los Estados Unidos en el conflicto petrolero (1917–1942)* (Mexico, 1968), translated as *Mexico and the United States in the oil controversy 1917–1942* (Austin, Texas, 1977); Dennis J. O'Brien, 'Petróleo e intervención. Relaciones entre Estados Unidos y México, 1917–1918', *HM*, 27/1 (1977), 103–40; and Emily S. Rosenberg, 'Economic pressure in Anglo-American diplomacy in Mexico, 1917–1918', *Journal of Inter-American Studies and World Affairs*, 17/2 (1975), 123–52. On Villa, see Clarence C. Clendenen, *The United States and Pancho Villa. A study in unconventional diplomacy* (Ithaca, 1981); and Alberto Salinas Carranza, *La expedición punitiva* (2nd edn, Mexico, 1957). Less important but still considerable among Mexico's foreign problems during the Revolution are the topics studied by Larry D. Hill, *Emissaries to a revolution: Woodrow Wilson's executive agents in Mexico* (Baton Rouge, 1973); and W. Dirk Raat, *Revoltosos: Mexico's rebels in the United States, 1903–1923* (College Station, Texas, 1981).

On politics, which in this literature means the struggle to dominate and manage the federal government, the books and articles are most numerous. Particularly interesting are contemporary reports: H. Baerlein, *Mexico. The land of unrest* (2nd edn, Philadelphia, 1914); E. I. Bell, *The political shame of Mexico* (New York, 1914); J. L. De Becker, *De cómo vino Huerta, y cómo se fue. Apuntes para la historia de un régimen militar* (Mexico, 1914); R. Prida, *De la dictadura a la anarquía* (2nd edn, Mexico, 1958). Biased but nevertheless revealing are certain memoirs: A. Breceda, *México revolucionario, 1913–1917* (2 vols., Madrid, 1920 and Mexico, 1914); F. González Garza, *La revolución mexicana. Mi contribución político-literaria* (Mexico, 1936); F. F. Palavicini, *Los diputados* (2nd edn, Mexico, 1976), *Historia de la constitución de 1917* (2 vols., Mexico, 1938), and *Mi vida revolucionaria* (Mexico, 1937); A. J. Pani, *Apuntes autobiográficos* (2 vols., 2nd edn, Mexico, 1950), and *Mi contribución al nuevo régimen, 1910–1933* (Mexico, 1936).

The first professional histories of the initial and middle phases of revolutionary politics remain the best surveys, despite their mistakes, errors, and omissions: C. C. Cumberland, *Mexican Revolution. Genesis under Madero* (Austin, Texas, 1952), and *Mexican Revolution. The constitutionalist years* (Austin, Texas, 1972). The latest surveys of the political history of the period are B. Ulloa, *Historia de la revolución mexicana, período 1914–1917*, vol. IV, *La revolución escindida* (Mexico, 1979), vol. V, *La encrucijada de 1915* (Mexico, 1979), and vol. VI, *La constitución de 1917* (Mexico, 1983).

Political monographs typically have a biographical focus. The standard work on the Maderista government remains Stanley R. Ross, *Francisco I. Madero, apostle of Mexican democracy* (New York, 1955). On Madero's main military lieutenant and nemesis, see Michael C. Meyer, *Mexican rebel, Pascual Orozco and the Mexican Revolution, 1910–1915* (Lincoln, 1967). The most intriguing book about Madero's conservative opposition remains Luis Liceaga, *Félix Díaz* (Mexico, 1958). And the standard work on the general who overthrew Madero and provoked the Constitutionalist movement is Michael C. Meyer, *Huerta, a political portrait* (Lincoln, 1972). Manifestly partisan and faulty but still the most informative treatments of the Villista movement are Federico Cervantes, *Francisco Villa y la revolución* (Mexico, 1960), and *Felipe Ángeles en la revolución* (3rd edn, Mexico, 1964). On Carranza and *carrancismo*, see Álvaro Matute, *Historia de la revolución mexicana, período 1917–1924*, vol. VIII, *La carrera del caudillo* (Mexico, 1980); and Douglas W. Richmond, *Venustiano Carranza's nationalist struggle, 1893–1920* (Lincoln, 1984). Pablo González, Jr, compiled a useful hagiography of his father, *El centinela fiel del constitucionalismo* (Monterrey, 1971). On Carranza's other, more fortunate lieutenant, see Linda Hall, *Álvaro Obregón, power and revolution in Mexico, 1911–1920* (College Station, Texas, 1981).

The first monograph on a collective political exercise is Robert E. Quirk, *The Mexican Revolution, 1914–1915. The Convention of Aguascalientes* (Bloomington, 1960). It is still commendable. But preferable on the same topic is Luis F. Amaya C., *La soberana convención revolucionaria, 1914–1916* (Mexico, 1966). The most accurate account of the *congreso* that delivered the new constitution is E. Victor Niemeyer, Jr, *Revolution at Queretaro. The Mexican Constitutional Convention of 1916–1917* (Austin, Texas, 1974). For an instructive comparison of the two conclaves, see Richard Roman, *Ideología y clase en la revolución mexicana. La convención y el congreso constituyente* (Mexico, 1976).

On the army in politics, the most substantial and interesting study is Alicia Hernández Chávez, 'Militares y negocios en la revolución mexicana', *HM*, 35/3 (1985). Another considerable analysis of the military is Jean A. Meyer, 'Grandes compañías, ejércitos populares y ejército estatal en la revolución mexicana (1910–1930)', *Anuario de estudios americanos*, 31 (1974), 1005–30.

On the church, the best guide to the early years is Jean A. Meyer, 'Le catholicisme social au Mexique jusqu'en 1913', *Revue historique*, 260 (1978), 143–59. For the middle and later years, see, despite its principled bias, Antonio Rius Facius, *La juventud católica y la revolución mejicana, 1910–1925* (Mexico, 1963).

The only serious treatment of political ideas is James D. Cockcroft, *Intellectual precursors of the Mexican Revolution, 1900–1913* (Austin, Texas, 1968). The only substantial study of an institution is Marte R. Gómez, *Historia de la Comisión Nacional Agraria* (Mexico, 1975). And the only account of governments' budgetary policies and practices is in James W. Wilkie, *The Mexican Revolution, federal expenditures and social change since 1910* (Berkeley, Calif., 1967).

Politics in the provinces has provided the material for many contemporary reports and professional histories. Outstanding is H. Aguilar Camín, *La frontera nómada. Sonora y la revolución mexicana* (Mexico, 1977). Also useful on Sonora are Francisco Almada, *Historia de la revolución en el estado de Sonora* (Mexico, 1971), and Clodoveo Valenzuela and A. Chaverri Matamoros, *Sonora y Carranza* (Mexico, 1921). A lively and detailed narrative of the Magonista struggle on the California border during the Maderista insurrection is Lowell L. Blaisdell, *The desert revolution, Baja California, 1911* (Madison, 1962). The most useful treatments of Chihuahua are Francisco Almada, *Historia de la revolución en el estado de Chihuahua* (2 vols., Mexico, 1964–5), and William H. Beezley, *Insurgent governor, Abraham Gonzalez and the Mexican Revolution in Chihuahua* (Lincoln, 1973). The only commendable book on a northeastern state is Ildefonso Villarello Vélez, *Historia de la revolución mexicana en Coahuila* (Mexico, 1970).

Among the studies of politics in other regions of the country, the best are Romana Falcón, *Revolución y caciquismo: San Luis Potosí, 1910–1938* (Mexico, 1984); Alicia Hernández Chávez, 'La defensa de los finqueros en Chiapas, 1914–1920', *HM*, 28/3 (1979), 335–69; Ian Jacobs, *Ranchero revolt: the Mexican Revolution in Guerrero* (Austin, Texas, 1983); and Gilbert M. Joseph, *Revolution from without: Yucatán, Mexico and the United States, 1880–1924* (Cambridge, 1982). See also the essays in David A. Brading (ed.), *Caudillo and peasant in the Mexican Revolution* (Cambridge, 1980).

On war in Mexico between 1910 and 1920, the most important book is still J. Barragán, *Historia del ejército y de la revolución constitucionalista* (2 vols., Mexico, 1946). Also valuable is Miguel A. Sánchez Lamego, *Historia militar de la revolución constitucionalista* (4 vols., Mexico, 1956–7). On particular Constitutionalist and Carrancista campaigns, see the memoirs of Manuel W. González, *Con Carranza. Episodios de la revolución constitucionalista, 1913–1914* (Monterrey, 1933), and *Contra Villa. Relato de la campaña, 1914–1915* (Mexico, 1935); and Álvaro Obregón, *Ocho mil kilómetros en campaña* (3rd edn, Mexico, 1959). For details on Villista campaigns, see Alberto Calzadíaz Barrera, *Hechos reales de la revolución* (5 vols., Mexico, 1967–8).

Peasant and labour movements

References in the literature to *campesinos* and *obreros* are innumerable. In fact virtually all of the revolutionary, counter-revolutionary, independent, and neutralist movements in Mexico from 1910 to 1920 were of 'country people' and 'workers'. But movements by country people for country people, or by workers for workers, that is peasant or labour movements, were the exception, not the rule.

The surest and most suggestive guide to the agrarian history of these years, since there is still no book on the subject, is F. Katz, 'Peasants in the Mexican Revolution of 1910', in J. Spielberg and S. Whiteford (eds.), *Forging nations. A comparative view of rural ferment and revolt* (Lansing, 1976), 61–85.

Also considerable is Hans W. Tobler, 'Bauernerhebungen und Agrarreform in der mexikanischen Revolution', in Manfred Mols and Hans W. Tobler, *Mexiko, die institutionalisierte Revolution* (Cologne, 1976), 115–70. For indications of how little the distribution of agricultural and ranching property in 1910 changed until the 1920s, see Frank Tannenbaum, *The Mexican agrarian revolution* (Washington, 1929), a classic.

The most interesting monographs on peasant movements have properly had a provincial focus. On the north, see Friedrich Katz, 'Agrarian changes in northern Mexico in the period of Villista rule, 1913–1915', in *Contemporary Mexico*, 259–73. On the midwest, Michoacán, see Paul Friedrich, *Agrarian revolt in a Mexican village* (Englewood Cliffs, NJ, 1970). And on Mexico's mideast, see Raymond Th. J. Buve, 'Peasant movements, caudillos, and landreform [sic] during the revolution (1910–1917) in Tlaxcala, Mexico', *Boletín de estudios latinoamericanos y del Caribe*, 18 (1975), 112–52, and 'Movilización campesina y reforma agraria en los valles de Nativitas, Tlaxcala (1917–1923)', *El trabajo y los trabajadores*, 533–64. The south, in particular Morelos, was the home of Mexico's most famous, exceptional, and significant peasant movement, that of the Zapatistas. Among several articles and books about their struggle, the best are François Chevalier, 'Un facteur décisif de la révolution agraire au Mexique: Le soulèvement de Zapata, 1911–1919', *AESC*, 16/1 (1961), 66–82; Gildardo Magaña, *Emiliano Zapata y el agrarismo en México* (5 vols., 2nd edn, Mexico, 1951–2); Jesús Sotelo Inclán, *Raíz y razón de Zapata* (2nd edn, Mexico, 1970); and John Womack, Jr, *Zapata and the Mexican Revolution* (New York, 1968). For an important and illustrative comparison, see Ronald Waterbury, 'Non-revolutionary peasants: Oaxaca compared to Morelos in the Mexican Revolution', *Comparative Studies in Society and History*, 17/4 (1975), 410–42.

The first survey of labour movements during the revolutionary years is still useful: V. Lombardo Toledano, *La libertad sindical en México* (2nd edn, Mexico, 1974), as are two other old labour histories: M. R. Clark, *Organized labor in Mexico* (Chapel Hill, 1934), and A. López Aparicio, *El movimiento obrero en México: antecedentes, desarrollo y tendencias* (2nd edn, Mexico, 1952).

An important essay suggesting the lines of a major revision of this history is Marcela de Neymet, 'El movimiento obrero y la revolución mexicana', *Historia y Sociedad*, 1st ser., 9 (1967), 56–73. Two different revisionist labour histories are Barry Carr, *El movimiento obrero y la política en México, 1910–1929* (2 vols., Mexico, 1976), and Ramón E. Ruiz, *Labor and the ambivalent revolutionaries, Mexico, 1911–1923* (Baltimore, 1976). A recent notable survey is Sergio de la Peña, *La clase obrera en la historia de México*, vol. IV, *Trabajadores y sociedad en el siglo XX* (Mexico, 1984).

The particular problems in labour history that have attracted most attention are ideologies and putative or real national federations. On ideologies, see Barry Carr, 'Marxism and anarchism in the formation of the Mexican Communist party, 1910–19', *HAHR*, 63/2 (1983), 277–305; François-X. Guerra, 'De l'Espagne au Mexique: Le milieu anarchiste et la révolution mexicaine (1910–1915)', *Mélanges de la Casa de Velázquez*, 9 (1973), 653–87; and John M. Hart, *Anarchism and the Mexican working class, 1860–1931* (Austin, Texas, 1978). On the famous proto-federation of 1914–15 and its 'red battalions', see Barry Carr, 'The Casa del Obrero Mundial. Constitutionalism and the pact of February, 1915', *El trabajo y los trabajadores*, 603–32; John M. Hart, 'The urban working class and the Mexican Revolution. The case of the Casa del Obrero Mundial', *HAHR*, 58/1 (1978), 1–20; Alicia Hernández Chávez, 'Los Batallones Rojos y Obregón: un pacto inestable', unpublished manuscript, 1979; and Jean A. Meyer, 'Les Ouvriers dans la révolution mexicaine. Les Bataillons rouges', *AESC*, 25/1 (1970), 30–55. On the first serious federation, see Rocío Guadarrama, *Los sindicatos y la política en México: La CROM, 1918–1928* (Mexico, 1981); Pablo González Casanova, *La clase obrera en la historia de México*, vol. VI, *En el primer gobierno constitucional (1917–1920)* (Mexico, 1980); and Harry A. Levenstein, *Labor organizations in the United States and Mexico, a history of their relations* (Westport, Conn., 1971).

There are only two notable books on unions in a particular industry, which, as it happens, was the most strategic of all industries in the country. Neither is so much a study as a memoir: Servando A. Alzati, *Historia de la mexicanización de los Ferrocarriles Nacionales de México* (Mexico, 1946); and Marcelo N. Rodea, *Historia del movimiento obrero ferrocarrilero, 1890–1943* (Mexico, 1944). And there are only two notable treatments of unions in a particular place: S. Lief Adleson, 'La adolescencia del poder: la lucha de los obreros de Tampico para definir los derechos del trabajo, 1910–1920', *Historias*, 2 (October 1982), 85–101; and Francisco Ramírez Plancarte, *La ciudad de México durante la revolución constitucionalista* (2nd edn, Mexico, 1941).

Business, economy, and demography

For a comprehensive and annotated bibliography of most of the old and a large part of the new literature on these subjects, see J. Womack Jr's article in *Marxist Perspectives*, cited above. Though somewhat frustrating, D. G. López Rosado, *Historia y pensamiento económico de México* (6 vols., Mexico, 1968–74) is indispensable.

The history of business in Mexico, in any period, is timid, meagre and obscure. It is possible, however, to draw reasonable inferences and to find significant details in studies done for other purposes. On industries important during the Revolution, see Fred W. Powell, *The railroads of Mexico* (Boston, 1921); Marvin D. Bernstein, *The Mexican mining industry, 1890–1950: a study of the interaction of politics, economics, and technology* (Albany, 1964); Manuel G. Machado, Jr, *The North Mexican cattle industry, 1910–1975: ideology, conflict, and change* (College Station, Texas, 1980); Gonzalo Cámara Zavala, 'Historia de la industria henequenera hasta 1919', *Enciclopedia Yucatanense* (8 vols., Mexico, 1947), III, 657–725; and Enrique Aznar Mendoza, 'Historia de la industria henequenera desde 1919 hasta nuestros días', *Enciclopedia Yucatanense*, III, 727–87. On banking, the most useful treatments are Antonio Manero, *La revolución bancaria en Mexico, 1865–1955* (Mexico, 1957); Walter F. McCaleb, *Present and past banking in Mexico* (New York, 1920), and *The public finances of Mexico* (New York, 1921); and Edgar Turlington, *Mexico and her foreign creditors* (New York, 1930). On companies and entrepreneurs, see Benjamin T. Harrison, 'Chandler Anderson and business interests in Mexico: 1913–1920: when economic interests failed to alter U.S. foreign policy', *Inter-American Economic Affairs*, 33/3 (1979), 3–23; J. C. M. Oglesby, *Gringos from the far north: essays in the history of Canadian–Latin American relations, 1866–1968* (Toronto, 1976); and Julio Riquelme Inda, *Cuatro décadas de vida, 1917–1957* (Mexico, 1957).

The most suggestive books about the structure and operation of the economy during the Revolution remain C. L. Jones, *Mexico and its reconstruction* (New York, 1921), and W. Thompson, *Trading with Mexico* (New York, 1921). Among notable studies in economic history are Donald B. Keesing, 'Structural change early in development: Mexico's changing industrial and occupational structure from 1895 to 1950', *Journal of Economic History*, 29/4 (1969), 716–38; and Edwin W. Kemmerer, *Inflation and revolution: Mexico's experience of 1912–1917* (Princeton, NJ, 1940). See also Frédéric Mauro, 'Le développement économique de Monterrey, 1890–1960', *Caravelle: Cahiers du monde hispanique et luso-brésilien*, 2 (1964), 35–126; and Isidro Vizcaya Canales,

Los orígenes de la industrialización de Monterrey: Una historia económica y social desde la caída del segundo imperio hasta el fin de la revolución, 1867–1920 (Monterrey, 1969). The most important work on demography is Moisés González Navarro, *Población y sociedad en México (1900–1970)* (2 vols., Mexico, 1974). See also Robert G. Greer, 'The demographic impact of the Mexican Revolution, 1910–1921', unpublished manuscript 1966.

Culture and images

There is a large body of literature on the novel and the mural of the Revolution. But these figments are almost entirely post-revolutionary phenomena. Three novelists actually lived through the Revolution and wrote memorably about it: M. Azuela, *Obras completas* (3 vols., Mexico, 1958–60); M. L. Guzmán, *El águila y la serpiente* (Madrid, 1928), and *Memorias de Pancho Villa* (4 vols., Mexico, 1938–40); and J. Vasconcelos, *Ulíses criollo* (Mexico, 1935), and *La tormenta* (Mexico, 1936).

Another useful contemporary account is John Reed, *Insurgent Mexico* (New York, 1914). See also John D. Rutherford, *Mexican society during the Revolution: a literary approach* (Oxford, 1971), and Merle E. Simmons, *The Mexican corrido as a source of interpretive study of modern Mexico (1870–1950)* (Bloomington, 1957). The images are clearest in the great photographic collection: G. Casasola, *Historia gráfica de la revolución mexicana, 1900–1970* (10 vols., Mexico, 1973), vols. II–V. A highly significant study of the creation and absorption of images is A. de los Reyes, *Cine y sociedad en México, 1896–1930* (Mexico, 1981).

4. REVOLUTION AND RECONSTRUCTION IN THE 1920S

R. Potash, 'The historiography of Mexico since 1821', *HAHR*, 40/3 (1960) remains useful though now out of date. David M. Bailey, 'Revisionism and the recent historiography of the Mexican Revolution', *HAHR*, 58/1 (1978) is an excellent recent survey of the literature on the Revolution. See also Barry Carr, 'Recent regional studies of the Mexican Revolution', *LARR*, 15/1 (1980). The proceedings of the regular meetings of Mexican and US historians are invaluable for their surveys of recent research: from the Oaxtepec meeting in 1969, *Investigaciones contemporáneas sobre historia de México* (Mexico and Austin, Texas, 1971); from Santa Monica (1973), *Contemporary Mexico* (Los Angeles and

Mexico, 1976), from Pátzcuaro (1977), *El trabajo y los trabajadores en la historia de México* (Mexico and Tucson, 1979).

Among general works Jorge Vera Estañol, *Historia de la revolución mexicana: orígenes y resultados* (Mexico, 1957) remains useful if a little old-fashioned and dull. José C. Valadés, *Historia general de la revolución mexicana* (5 vols., Mexico, 1976) is much more than a general history: it is full of otherwise inaccessible material and brilliant insights. John W. F. Dulles, *Yesterday in Mexico: a chronicle of the Revolution 1919–36* (Austin, Texas, 1961) is a detailed narrative account of the period. Gustavo Casasola, *Historia gráfica de la revolución mexicana, 1900–1970*, (10 vols., Mexico, 1973) is an important collection of photographs. Recent syntheses include Adolfo Gilly, *La revolución interrumpida* (Mexico, 1972); Arnaldo Córdova, *La ideología de la revolución mexicana* (Mexico, 1973), the best Marxist interpretation; and Jean Meyer, *La Révolution mexicaine* (Paris, 1973).

The old classics by American authors, many of whom had close relations with Mexican leaders, are still indispensable, even though outdated: Charles Hackett, *The Mexican Revolution and the United States* (Boston, 1926); Frank Tannenbaum, *The Mexican agrarian revolution* (Washington, DC, 1929) and *Peace by revolution* (New York, 1933); Wilfrid Hardy Callcott, *Liberalism in Mexico, 1857–1929* (Stanford, 1931); E. N. Simpson, *The ejido, Mexico's way out* (Chapel Hill, NC, 1937); and Ernest Gruening, *Mexico and its heritage* (New York, 1928). Howard Cline, *The United States and Mexico* (Cambridge, Mass., 1953) represents the best of early US scholarship on the Mexican Revolution. See also Charles Cumberland, *Mexico: the struggle for modernity* (New York, 1968).

The best of Mexican revisionism can be found in Luis González y González (ed.), *Historia de la Revolución Mexicana*, (Mexico, 1977). Vols. x and xi on the Calles administration (1924–8) are by Enrique Krauze and Jean Meyer; vols. xii and xiii on the Maximato (1929–34) are by Lorenzo Meyer, Rafael Segovia, Alejandra Lajous and Beatriz Rojas. Peter Smith, *Labyrinths of power: political recruitment in 20th century Mexico* (Princeton, 1978), an important work by an American political scientist, illuminates the whole century and prepares a new theory of the Revolution, as apotheosis of the middle classes.

There are no good biographies of either Obregón or Calles. But on Obregón's early career, see Linda B. Hall, *Álvaro Obregón: power and revolution in Mexico, 1911–20* (College Station, Texas, 1981). Narciso Bassols Batalla, *El pensamiento político de Obregón* (Mexico, 1967) is useful, as are Jorge Prieto Laurens's memoirs, *50 años de política mexicana*

(Mexico, 1968) and Alberto J. Pani, *Mi contribución al nuevo régimen 1910–1933* (Mexico, 1936). José Vasconcelos is too important as a public figure and as a writer to be neglected. See his memoirs in *Obras completas* (4 vols., Mexico, 1957–61), and on one particular episode, John Skirrius, *Vasconcelos y la campaña presidencial de 1929* (Mexico, 1978). Francisco Javier Gaxiola, *El Presidente Rodríguez (1932–1934)* (Mexico, 1938) remains the best book on the last administration of the Maximato.

On Mexico's relations with the United States, Robert F. Smith, *The United States and revolutionary nationalism in Mexico 1919–1932* (Chicago, 1972) remains the best study for this period although it is somewhat weak on Mexican events. The Mexican point of view can be found in Luis G. Zorrilla, *Historia de las relaciones entre México y los Estados Unidos de América 1800–1958* (2 vols., Mexico, 1965) and in Lorenzo Meyer, *México y los Estados Unidos en el conflicto petrolero 1917–1942* (Mexico, 1968), Eng. trans. *Mexico and the United States in the oil controversy 1917–42* (Austin, Texas, 1977). George W. Grayson, *The politics of Mexican oil* (Pittsburgh, 1980) is the most recent contribution on this subject.

Regional and local politics have become an important new subject of research. On the political bosses of the south-eastern states see, for example, on Felipe Carrillo Puerto, Francisco Paoli and Enrique Montalvo, *El socialismo olvidado de Yucatán* (Mexico, 1977), and G. M. Joseph, 'The fragile revolution: cacique politics in Yucatán', *LARR*, 15/1 (1980) and *Revolution from without. Yucatán, Mexico and the United States 1880–1924* (Cambridge, 1982); on Garrido Canabal, Carlos Martínez Assad, *El laboratorio de la Revolución* (Mexico, 1979). David Brading (ed.), *Caudillo and peasant in the Mexican Revolution* (Cambridge, 1980) includes case studies on Chihuahua, Guerrero, San Luis Potosí, Michoacán, Veracruz, Tlaxcala and Yucatán.

The standard accounts of the Revolution were distorted by a failure to take seriously the Cristero movement. But see David Bailey, *Viva Cristo Rey. The Cristero rebellion and the Church–State conflict in Mexico* (Austin, Texas, 1974); Jean Meyer, *La Cristiada* (3 vols., Mexico, 1978) and *The Cristero Rebellion. The Mexican people between church and state 1926–1929* (Cambridge, 1976); and, breaking new ground in Mexican local history, Luis González y González, *Pueblo en vilo: microhistoria de San José de Gracia* (Mexico, 1967). Here the 1920s are represented as the true revolutionary years at least in the western and central states, but the revolution was regarded as a murderous apocalypse by the rural population.

Studies of labour in this period are scarce, but see *El trabajo y los tabajadores* mentioned above. Marjorie R. Clark, *Organized labor in Mexico*

(Chapel Hill, NC, 1934) remains the best work on the subject after half a century; Alfonso López Aparicio, *El movimiento obrero en México: antecedentes, desarrollo y tendencias* (Mexico, 1952) is a short but classic account. Excellent for the period to 1924 is Barry Carr, *El movimiento obrero y la política en México, 1910–29* (2 vols., Mexico, 1976). See also Ramón E. Ruiz, *Labor and the ambivalent revolutionaries, Mexico 1911–1923* (Baltimore, 1976).

The economic, social and political history of rural Mexico in this period has still for the most part to be written. Paul Taylor, *Arandas, a Spanish Mexican peasant community* (Berkeley, 1933) was a pioneer work and Nathan L. Whetten, *Rural Mexico* (Chicago, 1948) is excellent. See also Simpson, *The ejido,* and Tannenbaum, *The Mexican agrarian revolution* mentioned above. Marte R. Gómez, *La reforma agraria de México. Su crisis durante el período 1928–1934* (Mexico, 1964) is written by a political actor of the period. Paul Friedrich, *Agrarian revolt in a Mexican village* (Englewood Cliffs, NJ, 1970) is an important study of Michoacán during the 1920s. Important recent publications in this field include: Heather Fowler Salamini, *Agrarian radicalism in Veracruz, 1920–1938* (Lincoln, Nebraska, 1978); Frans J. Schryer, *The rancheros of the Pisaflores. The history of a peasant bourgeoisie in twentieth century Mexico* (Toronto, 1980); and Ann L. Craig, *The first agraristas. An oral history of a Mexican agrarian reform movement* (Berkeley, 1983).

5. THE RISE AND FALL OF CARDENISMO, c. 1930 – c. 1946

The best guide to Mexican history in the period is the multi-volume, multi-authored *Historia de la revolución mexicana* published by the Colegio de México, ten volumes of which cover the period 1928–52. The first two, written by Lorenzo Meyer, Rafael Segovia and Alejandra Lajous, entitled *Los inicios de la institucionalización* (Mexico, 1978) and *El conflicto social y los gobiernos del maximato* (Mexico, 1978), deal respectively with the political and social history of the Calles *maximato*. Four successive volumes cover the Cárdenas presidency: Luis González, *Los artífices del Cardenismo* (Mexico, 1979), sets the scene; the same author's *Los días del presidente Cárdenas* (Mexico, 1979) deftly captures both the key events and the President's character; Alicia Hernández Chávez, *La mecánica cardenista* (Mexico, 1979) offers acute analysis and original research; Victoria Lerner, *La educación socialista* (Mexico, 1979), deals with education policy in the 1930s. Historical research on the 1940s – a crucial but relatively little-studied decade – has been pioneered by Luis Medina, *Del cardenismo al avilacamachismo* (Mexico, 1978); Blanca Torres Ramírez, *México en la segunda guerra mundial* (Mexico, 1979); Luis Medina, *Civilismo y modernización del autoritarismo* (Mexico, 1979); and Blanca Torres Ramírez, *Hacia la utopía industrial* (Mexico, 1984).

The Colegio series, however, offers no broad interpretations of Cardenismo. These can be found in Fernando Benítez, *Lázaro Cárdenas y la revolución mexicana*, vol. 3: *El cardenismo* (Mexico, 1978), which is persuasively sympathetic; Tzvi Medin, *Ideología y praxis política de Lázaro Cárdenas* (Mexico, 1972), a sound, balanced analysis; Anatoli Shulgovski, *México en la encrucijada de su historia* (Mexico, 1968), an unusually good piece of Soviet historiography; and Nora Hamilton, *The Limits of State Autonomy: Post-Revolutionary Mexico* (Princeton, 1982), which places Cardenismo within an accessible theoretical context. Some sense of contrasting interpretations of Cardenismo is provided by: Octavio Lanni, *El estado capitalista en la época de Cárdenas* (Mexico, 1977); Arnaldo Córdova, *La política de masas del cardenismo* (Mexico, 1974); Romana Falcón, 'El surgimiento del agrarismo cardenista – Una revisión de las tesis populistas', *Historia Mexicana* 27, no. 3 (1978): 333–86; Liisa North and David Raby, 'The Dynamics of Revolution and Counter-revolution: Mexico Under Cárdenas, 1934–40', *Latin American Research Unit Studies* (Toronto), 2, no. 1 (October 1977). The place of Cardenismo within the broad revolutionary process is discussed by Donald Hodges and Ross Gandy, *Mexico 1910–1982: Reform or Revolution* (London, 1983); Juan Felipe Leal, 'The Mexican State, 1915–1973: A Historical Interpretation', *Latin American Perspectives* 2, no. 2 (1975): 48–63; and Alan Knight, 'The Mexican Revolution: Bourgeois, Nationalist, or Just a "Great Rebellion"?,' *Bulletin of Latin American Research* 4, no. 2 (1985): 1–37.

More personalist in approach are Nathaniel and Sylvia Weyl, *The Reconquest of Mexico: The Years of Lázaro Cárdenas* (London, 1939), and William Cameron Townsend, *Lázaro Cárdenas, Mexican Democrat* (Ann Arbor, Mich., 1952), both somewhat hagiographic; they can be contrasted with Victoriano Anguiano Equihua's critical *Lázaro Cárdenas, su feudo y la política nacional* (Mexico, 1951), which has in turn influenced Enrique Krauze, *General misionero, Lázaro Cárdenas* (Mexico, 1987). In contrast to these analytical and judgemental sources, John W. F. Dulles, *Yesterday in Mexico: A Chronicle of the Revolution, 1919–1936* (Austin, Tex., 1961), offers a straightforward, detailed narrative of the early 1930s.

On the crucial agrarian question, Eyler B. Simpson, *The Ejido, Mexico's Way Out* (Chapel Hill, N.C., 1937) is a compendious classic, but its analysis stops c. 1934; Nathan L. Whetten, *Rural Mexico* (Chicago, 1948), covers the whole period. Many excellent local studies shed light on the agrarian reform (as well as on local politics, *caciquismo,* and state–federal relations): Dudley Ankerson, *Agrarian Warlord, Saturnino Cedillo and the Mexican Revolution in San Luis Potosi* (De Kalb, Ill., 1984); Raymond Buve, 'State governors and peasant mobilisation in Tlaxcala', in D. A. Brading (ed.), *Caudillo and Peasant in the Mexican Revolution* (Cambridge, 1980); Ann L. Craig, *The First Agraristas: An Oral History of a Mexican Agrarian Reform Movement* (Berkeley, 1983), which deals with los Altos de Jalisco; Romana Falcón, *Revolución y caciquismo. San Luis Potosí, 1910–1938* (Mexico, 1984); Romana Falcón and Soledad García Morales, *La semilla en el surco, Adalberto Tejeda y el radicalismo en Veracruz, 1883–1960* (Mexico, 1986), whose subject has also been tackled by Heather Fowler Salamini, *Agrarian Radicalism in Veracruz, 1920–1938* (Lincoln, Neb., 1971); Paul Friedrich, *The Princes of Naranja: An Essay in Anthrohistorical Method* (Austin, Tex., 1986), which deepens and extends the author's earlier study of the radical Michoacan community of Naranja, *Agrarian Revolt in a Mexican Village* (Chicago, 1970). Geographically close but politically distant stands San José de Gracia, the subject of Luis González, *Pueblo en vilo: microhistoria de San José de Gracia* (Mexico, 1968; English trans., 1974), a classic study of a Michoacan community through the *longue durée* from the Conquest down to the 1960s. Less evocative but more analytical is Tomás Martínez Saldana and Leticia Gándara Mendoza, *Política y sociedad en México: el caso de los Altos de Jalisco* (Mexico, 1976), which ranges from the Revolution to the 1970s. David Ronfeldt, *Atencingo: The Politics of Agrarian Struggle in a Mexican Ejido* (Stanford, 1973) describes agrarian activism and politicking in Puebla during the same period; Frans J. Schryer, *The Rancheros of Pisaflores: The History of a Peasant Bourgeoisie in Twentieth-Century Mexico* (Toronto, 1980), is a perceptive study of highland Hidalgo; Arturo Warman, . . . *Y venimos a contradecir: los campesinos de Morelos y el estado* (Mexico, 1976; Eng. trans., 1980), and Guillermo de la Peña, *A Legacy of Promises: Agriculture, Politics and Ritual in the Morelos Highlands of Mexico* (Manchester, 1982), analyse the post-revolutionary experience of Zapata's fellow-Morelenses.

The important Laguna conflict and expropriation have been analysed in Clarence Senior, *Land Reform and Democracy* (Gainesville, Fla., 1958); Joe C. Ashby, *Organized Labor and the Mexican Revolution under Lázaro Cárdenas* (Chapel Hill, N.C., 1963); Iván Restrepo and Salomón Eckstein, *La agricultura colectiva en México: La experiencia de la Laguna* (Mexico, 1975); and Barry Carr, 'The Mexican Communist Party and Agrarian Mobilization in the Laguna, 1920–40: A Worker-Peasant Alliance', *Hispanic American Historical Review* 62, no. 3 (1987): 371–404. The rise and fall of collective *ejidos* outside the Laguna are recounted by Fernando Benítez, *Ki: El drama de un pueblo y de una planta* (Mexico, 1962), which deals with Yucatán; Susan Glantz, *El ejido colectivo de Nueva Italia* (Mexico, 1974), on Michoacán; and Ronfeldt, *Atencingo*. Moisés González Navarro, *La Confederación Nacional Campesina: un grupo de presión en la reforma agraria mexicana* (Mexico, 1968), tackles the official *campesino* movement.

Studies on the labour movement include Ashby, *Organized Labor;* Arturo Anguiano, *El estado y la política obrera del cardenismo* (Mexico, 1975), a leftist critique of Cardenismo; Victor Manuel Durand, *La ruptura de la nación: Historia del Movimiento Obrero Mexicano desde 1938 hasta 1952* (Mexico, 1986); and the valuable series edited by Pablo González Casanova, *La clase obrera en la historia de México,* the relevant volumes of which are: Arnaldo Córdova, *En una época de crisis (1928–1934)* (Mexico, 1980); Samuel León and Ignacio Marván, *En el cardenismo (1934–1940)* (Mexico, 1985); and Jorge Basurto, *Del avilacamachismo al alemanismo (1940–1952)* (Mexico, 1984).

The petroleum-workers' movement and the expropriation of 1938 are best covered by Lorenzo Meyer, *México y los Estados Unidos en el conflicto petrolero (1917–42)* (Mexico, 1968). E. David Cronon, *Josephus Daniels in Mexico* (Madison, Wis., 1960), analyses the important role of the U.S. ambassador, whose own memoirs appeared as *Shirt-Sleeve Diplomat* (Chapel Hill, N.C., 1947). General overviews of U.S.–Mexican relations are provided by Howard Cline, *The United States and Mexico* (New York, 1963), and Karl M. Schmitt, *Mexico and the United States, 1821–1973: Conflict and Co-existence* (New York, 1974); while Mexican economic nationalism – the nub of several U.S.–Mexican disputes in the inter-war period – is discussed by Alan Knight, 'The political economy of revolutionary Mexico, 1900–1940', in Christopher Abel and Colin M. Lewis (eds.), *Latin America: Economic Imperialism and the State* (London, 1985).

On the politics of the left during the period, see Manuel Márquez Fuentes and Octavio Rodríguez Araujo, *El partido comunista mexicano (en el período de la Internacional Comunista, 1919–1943)* (Mexico, 1973); Karl M. Schmitt, *Communism in Mexico, A Study in Political Frustration* (Austin, Tex., 1965); and Arturo Anguiano, Guadalupe Pacheco and Rogelio Viscaíno, *Cárdenas y la izquierda mexicana* (Mexico, 1975). The key figure of Vicente Lombardo Toledano is described by Robert Paul Millon, *Mexican Marxist – Vicente Lombardo Toledano* (Chapel Hill, N.C. 1966). For the development of the official party, first PNR then PRM, see the meticulous study of Luis Javier Garrido, *El partido de la Revolución institucionalizada: La formación del nuevo Estado en México (1928–1945)* (Mexico, 1986). Data on the political elite are analysed in Peter H. Smith, *Labyrinths of Power: Political Recruitment in Twentieth-Century Mexico* (Princeton, 1979).

Education has been well-researched by Lerner, *La educación socialista;* John A. Britton, *Educación y radicalismo en México,* 2 vols. (Mexico, 1976); Josefina Vázquez de Knauth, 'La educación socialista de los años treinta', *Historia Mexicana* 18, no. 3 (January–March, 1969): 408–23; and David L. Raby, *Educación y revolución social en México, 1921–1940* (Mexico, 1974).

On anti-clericalism, see the final section of Jean Meyer, *La Cristiada, I, La guerra de los cristeros* (Mexico, 1973); and, for an important case study, Carlos Martínez Assad, *El laboratorio de la revolución: El Tabasco garridista* (Mexico, 1979). The resurgent Catholic radical right of the 1930s has been researched by Jean Meyer, *El sinarquismo, un fascismo mexicano?* (Mexico, 1979); for older, more hostile analyses, see Whetten, *Rural Mexico,* chap. 20, and Mario Gill, *El sinarquismo: Su origen, su esencia, su misión* (Mexico, 1944). Hugh G. Campbell, *La derecha radical en México, 1929–49* (Mexico, 1976), analyses both the Catholic and the secular radical right. T. G. Powell, *Mexico and the Spanish Civil War* (Albuquerque, 1981), discusses the foreign-policy issue which most agitated domestic politics. These several currents fed into the contentious 1940 presidential election discussed by José Ariel Contreras, *Mexico 1940: industrialización y crisis política* (Mexico 1977), and Albert L. Michaels, 'The Crisis of Cardenismo', *Journal of Latin American Studies* 2 (May 1970): 51–79.

The broad patterns of government policy and budgeting during the 1930s and 1940s are charted in James W. Wilkie, *The Mexican Revolution: Federal Expenditure and Social Change since 1910* (Berkeley, 1970). Economic trends can be followed in Clark W. Reynolds, *The Mexican Economy: Twentieth-Century Structure and Growth* (New Haven, 1970), and Leopoldo Solís, *La realidad ecónomica mexicana: retrovisión y perspectivas* (Mexico, 1970). Trade is discussed by Timothy King, *Mexico: Industrialization and Trade Policies since 1940* (London, 1970); mining, by Marvin D. Bernstein, *The Mexican Mining Industry 1890–1950* (New York, 1964); agriculture, by Cynthia Hewitt de Alcántara, *La modernización de la agricultura mexicana, 1940–1970* (Mexico, 1978), and Steven E. Sanderson, *Agrarian Populism and the Mexican State: The Struggle for Land in Sonora* (Berkeley, 1981), both of which combine general analysis with case studies of the state of Sonora; on the process of import substitution stimulated by the depression, see Enrique Cardenas, 'The Great Depression and Industrialization: The case of Mexico', in Rosemary Thorp, (ed.), *Latin America in the*

1930s: The Role of the Periphery in World Crisis (London, 1984), pp. 222–41. Sanford A. Mosk, *Industrial Revolution in Mexico* (Berkeley, 1954) focusses on wartime industrialization.

Finally, foreign eye-witness accounts of the 1930s and early 1940s include: Graham Greene, *The Lawless Roads* (London, 1939), an anti-anticlerical tract; Frank L. Kluckhohn, *The Mexican Challenge* (New York, 1939), by a journalistic critic of Cardenista policy; R. H. K. Marett, *An Eye-witness of Mexico* (London, 1939), and Virginia Prewett, *Reportage on Mexico* (New York, 1941), which are rather more neutral; and Betty Kirk, *Covering the Mexican Front* (Norman, Okla., 1942), which emphasizes the Axis threat. Partisan and often unreliable as these are, they at least engage with current political and social issues. In contrast, the eye-witness accounts of the later 1940s and 1950s tend towards bland travelogues: proof that Mexico was seen no longer as a troublesome nest of banditry and Bolshevism, but rather as a safe haven of tourism and tequila.

6. MEXICO SINCE 1946: DYNAMICS OF AN AUTHORITARIAN REGIME

There is not yet an extensive historiographical literature on Mexico in the period after 1946 because of both its proximity to the present day and the absence of epic events. Nor is there a long-standing tradition of political or public memoirs, although this may now be in an incipient phase. For a general overview, see Michael C. Meyer and William L. Sherman, *The Course of Mexican History* 3d ed. (New York, 1987). Interpretive studies of Mexican politics include Daniel Levy and Gabriel Székely, *Mexico: Paradoxes of Stability and Change* (Boulder, Colo., 1983; rev. ed., 1987); Roberto Newell, G. and Luis Rubio F., *Mexico's Dilemma: The Political Origins of Economic Crisis* (Boulder, Colo., 1984); and Roderic A. Camp (ed.), *Mexico's Political Stability: The Next Five Years* (Boulder, Colo., 1986); Judith Gentleman (ed.), *Mexican Politics in Transition* (Boulder, Colo., 1987). Earlier analyses include José Luis Reyna and Richard S. Weinert (eds.), *Authoritarianism in Mexico* (Philadelphia, 1977), and Miguel Basáñez, *La lucha por la hegemonía en México, 1968–1980* (Mexico, 1981).

Standard works on the Mexican political system by North Americans include Robert E. Scott, *Mexican Government in Transition* (Urbana, Ill., 1958; 2d ed., 1964); Frank R. Brandenburg, *The Making of Modern Mexico* (Englewood Cliffs, N.J., 1964); L. Vincent Padgett, *The Mexican Political System* (Boston, 1966; rev. ed., 1976); and Kenneth F. Johnson, *Mexican Democracy: A Critical View* (Boston, 1971; 3d rev. ed., 1984). Studies of political economy include Raymond Vernon, *The Dilemma of Mexico's Development: The Roles of the Private and Public Sectors* (Cambridge, 1963), and Roger D. Hansen, *The Politics of Mexican Development* (Baltimore, 1971). A classic Mexican interpretation of the regime is Pablo González Casanova, *Democracy in Mexico* (New York, 1970). On the formation of political elites, see Peter H. Smith, *Labyrinths of Power: Political Recruitment in Twentieth-Century Mexico* (Princeton, 1979), and the many works of Roderic A. Camp, especially *Mexico's Leaders: Their Education and Recruitment* (Tucson, 1980). What little we know about the contemporary army is contained in David Ronfeldt (ed.), *The Modern Mexican Military: A Reassessment* (La Jolla, Calif., 1984). Essential research tools are provided in Roderic A. Camp, *Mexican Political Biographies, 1935–1975* (Tucson, 1976), and Presidencia de la República, *Diccionario biográfico del gobierno mexicano* (Mexico, 1984).

For speculation and analysis on the presidential succession, see Roderic A. Camp, 'Mexican Presidential Candidates: Changes and Portents for the Future', *Polity*, 16, no. 4 (1984), Daniel Cosío Villegas, *La sucesión presidencial* (Mexico, 1975), and Francisco José Paoli, *El cambio de presidente* (Mexico, 1981). On elections, see Arturo Alvarado (ed.), *Electoral Patterns and Perspectives in Mexico* (La Jolla, Calif., 1987), and essays by Kevin J. Middlebrook, Juan Molinar Horcasitas and Wayne A. Cornelius in Paul W. Drake and Eduardo Silva (eds.), *Elections and Democratization in Latin America, 1980–1985* (La Jolla, Calif., 1986). A broad analysis of political forces and prospects appears in Wayne A. Cornelius, Judith Gentleman and Peter H. Smith (eds.), *Mexico's Alternative Political Futures* (La Jolla, Calif., 1989).

Path-breaking work on the period from the Second World War to 1960 appears in a series of studies on the *Historia de la Revolución Mexicana* carried out by a team at El Colegio de México. These include, on 1940–52, Luis Medina, *Civilismo y modernización del autoritarismo* (Mexico, 1979), and on 1952–60, Olga Pellicer and José Luis Reyna, *El afianzamiento de la estabilidad política* (Mexico, 1978), and Olga Pellicer de Brody and Esteban L. Mancilla, *El entendimiento con los Estados Unidos y la gestación del desarrollo estabilizador* (Mexico, 1978). Other treatments of this period include James W. Wilkie, *The Mexican Revolution: Federal Expenditure and Social Change Since 1910* (Berkeley and Los Angeles, 1967). An illustrative case study from the López Mateos era can be found in Susan Kaufman Purcell, *The Mexican Profit-Sharing Decision: Politics in an Authoritarian Regime* (Berkeley and Los Angeles, 1975). On the López Portillo *sexenio*, see Gabriel Székeley, *La economía política del petróleo en México,*

1976–1982 (Mexico, 1983), and Carlos Tello, *La nacionalización de la banca* (Mexico, 1984). A unique source on the de la Madrid presidency is the annual publication of the Unidad de la Crónica Presidencial, Presidencia de la República, *Crónica del sexenio. Las razones y las obras: Gobierno de Miguel de la Madrid.* A compelling description of the 1982 crisis appears in Joseph Kraft, *The Mexican Rescue* (New York, 1984); for a broad perspective, see William R. Cline (ed.), *International Debt and the Stability of the World Economy* (Washington, D.C., 1983). An important recent contribution is Rosario Green, *La deuda externa de México de 1973 a 1988: de la abundancia a la escasez de crédito* (Mexico, 1989).

Important studies of economic policy include Clark W. Reynolds, *The Mexican Economy: Twentieth-Century Structure and Growth* (New Haven, 1970) and his well-known interpretive article 'Why Mexico's "Stabilizing Development" Was Actually Destabilizing (With Some Implications for the Future)', *World Development* 6, nos. 7–8 (July-August 1978): See also Leopoldo Solís, *Economic Policy Reform in Mexico: A Case Study for Developing Countries* (New York, 1981). On foreign investment, see Bernardo Sepúlveda and Antonio Chumacero, *La inversión extranjera en México* (Mexico, 1973); Gary Gereffi, *The Pharmaceutical Industry and Dependency in the Third World* (Princeton, 1983); Douglas C. Bennett and Kenneth E. Sharpe, *Transnational Corporation versus the State: The Political Economy of the Mexican Automobile Industry* (Princeton, 1985); and Harley Shaiken and Stephen Herzenberg, *Automobile and Global Production: Automobile Engine Production in Mexico, the United States, and Canada* (La Jolla, Calif., 1987). For broad treatments of Mexican agriculture, see Gustavo Esteva, *La batalla en el México rural* (Mexico, 1980), Paul Lamartine-Yates, *Mexico's Agricultural Dilemma* (Tucson, 1981), and Susan W. Sanderson, *Land Reform in Mexico: 1910–1980* (Orlando, Fla., 1984). Merilee Serrill Grindle provides an valuable analysis of Echeverría's 'integrated' development plan in *Bureaucrats, Politicians, and Peasants in Mexico: A Case Study in Public Policy* (Berkeley and Los Angeles, 1977). On the policies of the López Portillo administration, see Cassio Luiselli Fernández, *The Route to Food Self-Sufficiency in Mexico: Interactions with the U.S. Food System* (La Jolla, Calif., 1985), and Jonathan Fox, "The Political Dynamics of Reform: The Case of the Mexican Food System, 1980–1982," (unpublished Ph.D. dissertation, Massachusetts Institute of Technology, 1986). On the official *campesino* movement, see Moisés González Navarro, *La Confederación Nacional Campesina: un grupo de presión en la reforma agraria mexicana* (Mexico, 1968). On political attitudes in the countryside, see Carlos Salinas de Gortari, *Political Participation, Public Investment, and Support for the System:*

A Comparative Study of Rural Communities in Mexico (La Jolla, Calif., 1982). The political outlook and resources of migrant slum dwellers form the subject of Wayne A. Cornelius, *Politics and the Migrant Poor in Mexico City* (Stanford, 1975), and Susan Eckstein, *The Poverty of Revolution: The State and the Urban Poor in Mexico* (Princeton, 1977). Among the remarkably scarce studies of organized labour are Kevin Jay Middlebrook, 'The Political Economy of Mexican Organized Labor, 1940–1978,' (unpublished Ph.D. dissertation, Harvard University, 1982), and César Zarzueta and Ricardo de la Peña, *La estructura del Congreso del Trabajo. Estado, Trabajo y capital en Mexico: Un acercamiento al tema* (Mexico, 1984). A welcome addition to this field is Ian Roxborough, *Unions and Politics in Mexico: The Case of the Automobile Industry* (Cambridge, 1984).

Donald J. Mabry offers a sweeping historical interpretation of campus politics in *The Mexican University and the State: Student Conflicts, 1910–1971* (College Station, Tex., 1982). Daniel C. Levy analyses the contemporary scene in *University and Government in Mexico: Autonomy in an Authoritarian System* (New York, 1980). For compelling material on the student movement of 1968 and the Tlatelolco massacre, see Ramón Ramírez, *El movimiento estudiantil de México: julio-diciembre de 1968,* 2 vols. (Mexico, 1969), and Elena Poniatowska, *La noche de Tlatelolco* (Mexico, 1971).

Standard sources on Mexican foreign policy are the masterful studies by Mario Ojeda, *Alcances y límites de la política exterior de México* (Mexico, 1976), and *México: El surgimiento de una política exterior activa* (Mexico, 1986). On relations with the United States, see Joséfina Zoraida Vázquez and Lorenzo Meyer, *The United States and Mexico* (Chicago, 1986); Carlos Vásquez and Manuel García y Griego (eds.), *Mexican-U.S. Relations: Conflict and Convergence* (Los Angeles, 1983); Clark Reynolds and Carlos Tello (eds.), *U.S.-Mexican Relations: Social and Economic Aspects* (Stanford, 1983); and George W. Grayson, *The United States and Mexico: Patterns of Influence* (New York, 1984). A subsequent flurry of books around the time of the presidential succession of 1988 included Robert A. Pastor and Jorge Castañeda, *Limits to Friendship: The United States and Mexico* (New York, 1988); George W. Grayson (ed.), *Prospects for Mexico* (Washington, D.C., 1988); Susan Kaufman Purcell (ed.), *Mexico in Transition: Implications for U.S. Policy* (New York, 1988); and the report of the Bilateral Commission on the Future of United States–Mexican Relations, *The Challenge of Interdependence: Mexico and the United States* (Lanham, Md., 1988), an effort that also led to the publication of Rosario Green and Peter H. Smith (eds.), *Dimensions of United States–Mexican Relations,* 5 vols. (La Jolla, Calif., 1989).

INDEX

Index

429

ership of, 81; nationalization of, 383, 384; reserve and requirements, 147; *see also* central bank
Banque de Paris et des Pays-Bas, 143
Barcelonettes, 52, 78
Barclay and Company, 7–8
Barriso Terrazas, Francisco, 392
Barron and Forbes (trading house), 63
Barros Sierra, Javier, 356, 360
Bartlett Díaz, Manuel, 383, 394, 395–6
Bassols, Narciso, 209, 247, 266, 267, 269, 307, 308, 317; in Ministry of Education, 264–5
Baz, Dr. Gustavo, 338
Beteta, Ramón, 344–5
Blancarte, José M., 28
Blanco, Lucio, 148, 151, 152, 153, 159, 205
Bleichroeder (banking house), 78
Bloque de Unidad Obrera (BUO), 349, 350, 358
Bocoyna, 117
Bojórquez, Juan de Dios, 254
Bolivia, 165
Bolshevik revolution, 181
Bonillas, Ignacio, 167, 171, 180, 190, 197–8; ambassador to U.S., 177; presidential candidacy of, 191, 192, 194, 195, 196
border regions; social structure of, 332
border transactions, 380
Borunda, Teófile, 342
Bourbon dynasty, 4
bourbonists, 4, 5, 8
bourgeoisie, 52; and Cardenismo, 273–4; industrial, 310, 314; in Mexican Revolution, 128–9; north-western, 200
Bracamontes, Luis Enrique, 372
braceros, 307, 337
Brassetti, Manuel, 101–2
Bravo, General Nicolás, 2, 6, 7, 12, 27; death of, 31; presidency of, 19; vice-presidency of, 9–10
Brazil, 149, 150, 165, 286, 388
Bremer, Juan José, 366
British-American Tobacco (co.), 228
Bucareli Street agreements, 206, 212
budget: balanced, 219; for education, 264, 265, 269; for military, 183, 226
budget deficit, 27, 371
Buendía, Manuel, 365
Bünz, Karl, 123
bureaucracy, 52, 54, 84, 113, 153
business, 197, 253; and Cárdenas administration, 291–2; and Carranza administration, 166–7; conflict about, 129–30, 135, 136; and de la Madrid administration, 384; and Díaz Ordaz administration, 358; and

Echeverría administration, 368–9; and López Mateos administration, 354; and Mexican Revolution, 127, 128, 135, 142, 143–4, 159, 164–5, 200; post-World War II, 310; and Ruiz Cortines administration, 347–8; *see also* private sector
business class, 338, 340
Bustamente, Colonel Anastasio, 2, 11, 12, 13, 14, 16–17

Caballero, Luis, 146, 148, 152, 159, 171, 173, 180, 182; revolt by, 183
Cabañas, Lucio, 361
cabinet(s): of Alemán, 315, 341–2; of Alvarez, 31; of Avila Camacho, 307; of Cárdenas, 250; of Carranza, 160; of Comonfort, 32; of de la Huerta, 195; of de la Madrid, 384, 385; of Echevarría, 366, 371; of González, 72; of Juárez, 38; of López Portillo, 375; of Maximilian, 45, 46; of Obregón, 200; of Santa Anna, 28
Cabrera, Luis, 138, 159, 160, 171, 188; in Carranza government, 167, 168, 169, 170; and loans from U.S., 179–80, 181
caciques, 49, 203, 243, 254, 258; and agrarian reform, 234, 239, 263, 341, 370; Callismo of, 250; in Díaz regime, 66–7; *ejidal*, 313; and local autonomy, 88; in mass politics, 241, 242; replaced by Díaz, 82–3, 84; support of, for Avila Camacho, 296–7
Calderón, Enrique, 338, 339
California, 22, 387
Calles, Plutarco Elías, 148, 159, 173, 180, 186, 178, 189, 192, 198, 199, 216, 258, 265, 273, 274, 304; agrarian reform of, 238; in cabinet of de la Huerta, 195, 196; Cárdenas and, 246, 249–50, 253–6; economic policy under, 218–27; exiled, 256; in government of Obregón, 200, 206; ideology of, 247–8, 252; institutionalization of Revolution by, 217–18; land distribution by, 233, 236–7; organized labour and state under, 227–32; ouster of, 288; personal power of, 246; political testament of, 215; presidency of, 203–4, 207, 209, 210–15, 239, 240, 242, 243, 244–5, 309; and presidential campaign, 191; revolt by, 193, 194; struggle against, 272, 274, 275, 289
Calles–Morrow accord, 279, 285
Callismo, 244, 246, 250, 254, 256, 275, 288
Callistas, 248, 250, 253–4, 255; reforms of, 243, 266; suppression of, 256
Cámara de Trabajo, 252
Camarena, Enrique, 386
Campa, Valentín, 349
Campeche, 233

United States (*cont.*)
185, 290, 348; and expropriation of oil companies, 282–3; fears of annexation by, 113–14; granted rights of way, 40–1; hegemony of, in Latin America, 316; immigration policy of, 192, 363, 387; influence of, on Mexico, 316, *see also* U.S.–Mexico relations; investment of, in Mexican economy, 77–9, 221, 241; Mexican dependence on, 225, 302, 314; and Mexican politics, 192–3; and Mexican Revolution, 121, 128, 131, 132, 136–7, 148–9, 151, 157–8, 163, 165; Mexican territories acquired by, 18f, 29, 49; policy of, toward Mexico, 194; popular culture of, 332; presidential elections in, 192–3; and recognition of government(s) of Mexico, 68–9, 166–7, 168, 197–9, 204, 205–6; and regional diplomacy, 379; and revolutionary government, 140–1, 144, 146–7; support of, for Villa, 160–1, 162–3; and Vietnam War, 367; and war(s) with Mexico, 20–2, 26; and World War I, 185
unity: in government, 202; Obregón administration and, 204; as theme of Avila Camacho, 298, 302, 307–8, 309
universities, 361, 362; provincial, 268; *see also* National University
Unomásuno (newspaper), 365
upper classes, 36, 64, 105; in Díaz regime, 66–7, 87, 109, 110, 119; in Juárez's political strategy, 56; in Mexican Revolution, 125, 128; size of, 330
urban labour, 385; and Obregón administration, 205; in support of political regime, 335–6
urban sectors, 359
urban trades, 135–6
urbanization, 329–30
Uruchurtu, Ernesto P., 352, 357
Uruguay, 165, 388
U.S. Army, punitive expedition of, into Mexico, 170–1, 173, 174
U.S. Department of Justice, 163
U.S. Department of State, 169, 170, 171, 175, 177, 180, 181, 183, 184, 189, 191, 197, 285, 386
U.S. intervention in Mexico, 121–2, 131, 137–8, 148–9, 150, 166–7, 174, 177, 204, 213, 214, 316; fears of, 124; by military, 182, 188, 189, 231, 336
U.S.–Mexican border: conflict along, 183; mobilization of troops along, 123–4; and U.S.–Mexican relations, 68–9
U.S.–Mexico relations, 19–23, 51–2, 67–9, 71, 170, 184, 185, 203, 215, 241, 314; in Avila Camacho administration, 302–7; busi-

ness in, 220; in Calles administration, 211, 212–13; conflicts in, 189–90, 244; cooperation in industrialization in, 309–10; crises in, 170–1, 173, 174; in Díaz Ordaz administration, 357–8; in Díaz regime, 109; economic, 305–7, 324; features in, 336–7; in López Mateos administration, 354–6; military cooperation in, 302–3, 316, narcotics traffic in, 386–7; in Obregón government, 206–7; oil companies in, 205–6; oil expropriation and, 285–7; and political stability, 323, 336; post-World War II, 337–8, 351–2; and special reciprocity arrangement, 72–3; and 'special relationship', 338, 351–2, 356, 367–8; and trade, 380, 396
U.S. Navy, 302
U.S. Senate, 191, 194; Foreign Relations Committee, 137

Valenzuela, Macías, 308
Valle del Maíz, 252
Vallejo, Demetrio, 350, 354
Valladolid, 123
values, national, 297–8, 300
Vasconcelos, José, 245, 292, 305; education policy of, 204, 205, 206–9, 210; presidential candidacy of, 214, 215–16
Vázquez, Vejar, 307
Vázquez Gómez, Emilio, 134, 136
Vázquez Gómez, Francisco, 131, 134
Vázquez Vela, Gonzalo, 288
Vazquista uprising, 136
Velázquez, Fidel, 251–2, 275, 316, 319, 342, 346, 348, 349, 373, 385, 393; power of, 358–9, 370–1, 392
Venezuela, 225, 379, 388
Veracruz, 1, 21, 28, 40, 41, 77, 138, 182, 186, 195, 250, 331; agrarian reform in, 234, 235, 252, 257; anarchists in, 141, 172; colonization in, 233; Díaz revolt and, 185; Felicistas in, 184; French invasion of, 16, 43; industrial development in, 81; industrial workers in, 105; and Iturbide's rule, 5–6; Juárez in, 38, 39; rebellion in, 70, 123; strikes in, 112, 181, 198, 251; textile industry in, 13; unions in, 135, 141, 232; U.S. marines in, 149, 150, 151, 152, 154, 158, 159
Viadas, Lauro, 77
Victoria, 146; raids in, 188
Victoria, Guadalupe, 2, 6, 7, 9–10, 11
Victorio (Apache chief), 59
Viente de Noviembre hospital, 359
Vietnam War, 367
Villa, Francisco (Pancho), 123, 131, 168, 204, 353; formation of government by, 161; Ger-